THE SOCIAL CONSTRUCTION
OF DIFFERENCE AND INEQUALITY

THE SOCIAL CONSTRUCTION OF DIFFERENCE AND INEQUALITY
Race, Class, Gender, and Sexuality

Second Edition

Tracy E. Ore
Saint Cloud State University

Boston   Burr Ridge, IL   Dubuque, IA   Madison, WI   New York
San Francisco   St. Louis   Bangkok   Bogotá   Caracas   Kuala Lumpur
Lisbon   London   Madrid   Mexico City   Milan   Montreal   New Delhi
Santiago   Seoul   Singapore   Sydney   Taipei   Toronto

McGraw-Hill Higher Education 🐝

A Division of The **McGraw-Hill** *Companies*

THE SOCIAL CONSTRUCTION OF DIFFERENCE AND INEQUALITY:
RACE, CLASS, GENDER, AND SEXUALITY
Published by McGraw-Hill, a business unit of The McGraw-Hill Companies, Inc., 1221 Avenue of the Americas, New York, NY, 10020.

Some ancillaries, including electronic and print components, may not be available to customers outside the United States.

This book is printed on acid-free paper.

1 2 3 4 5 6 7 8 9 0 FGR/FGR 0 9 8 7 6 5 4 3 2

ISBN 0-7674-2928-1

Publisher: *Phillip A. Butcher*
Sponsoring editor: *Sally Constable*
Developmental editor: *Jill S. Gordon*
Senior marketing manager: *Daniel M. Loch*
Project manager: *Ruth Smith*
Lead production supervisor: *Lori Koetters*
Senior designer: *Jenny El-Shamy*
Supplement producer: *Nathan Perry*
Typeface: *10/12 Antiqua*
Compositor: *Carlisle Communications, Ltd.*
Printer: *Quebecor World Fairfield Inc.*

Library of Congress Cataloging-in-Publication Data

The social construction of difference and inequality : race, class, gender, and sexuality / [selected and edited by] Tracy E. Ore.—2nd ed.
   p. cm.
   ISBN 0-7674-2928-1 (softcover : alk. paper)
     1. Pluralism (Social sciences)—United States. 2. Equality—United States. 3. Minorities—United States—Social conditions. 4. Social classes—United States. 5. Women—United States—Social conditions. 6. Gays—United States—Social conditions. 7. Discrimination—United States. 8. United States—Social conditions—1980-9. United States—Race relations. 10. United States—Ethnic relations. I. Ore, Tracy E.
HN59.2 .S585 2003
305'.0973—dc21

2002069561

www.mhhe.com

*This book is dedicated to the memory of my brother Brian . . .
and to all others lost in the continuing crisis of AIDS.*

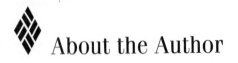

About the Author

Tracy E. Ore is an assistant professor of Sociology and Director of the Applied Sociology Program at Saint Cloud State University. She received her Ph.D. in sociology from the University of Michigan. Her teaching areas include race and ethnicity, social inequality, democracy and citizenship, and the ethics of sociological practice. She does research in the areas of technology and the scholarship of teaching and learning, race and ethnicity, oppression and inequality, and the development of effective teaching pedagogy. She serves as a consultant for multicultural education and curriculum to a variety of organizations and agencies and conducts workshops and trainings related to issues of inequality. She is an active member of the American Sociological Association, the Midwest Sociological Society, the Sociologists for Women in Society, and the Society for Applied Sociology.

Contents

Sex and Gender   99

Sexuality   136

PART II. MAINTAINING INEQUALITIES: SYSTEMS OF OPPRESSION AND PRIVILEGE   182

Examining what elements of social structure work to maintain systems of stratification based on constructions of difference.

Social Institutions   205

Family   205

PART III: EXPERIENCING DIFFERENCES AND INEQUALITY IN EVERYDAY LIFE   511

Examining the impact of constructions of difference and maintaining inequalities on members of society.

PART IV: RESISTANCE AND SOCIAL CHANGE   579

Examining how people working within individual and institutional contexts transform difference from a system of inequality to a system of liberation.

 Preface

Teaching about issues of inequality in a culture that focuses on individualism can be a very daunting task. Having been raised in such a culture, students in my classes often arrive with little knowledge of the systemic nature of inequality in society. While they may be aware of their own experiences of disadvantage (and perhaps privilege), they are generally not aware of how structural arrangements in society result in systems of difference and inequality. This book, which focuses on how race, class, gender, and sexuality are socially constructed as categories of difference and are maintained as systems of inequality, is an effort to help students move toward a more systemic understanding.

WHY ANOTHER RACE, CLASS, GENDER (AND SEXUALITY) READER?

With the plethora of readers on race, class, and gender currently on the market, one may wonder why another is needed. Indeed, some excellent anthologies are available that can be quite effective in demonstrating the impact of race, class, and gender inequality on the life chances of various individuals and groups in our society. However, very few of these texts thoroughly explain how such categories of difference are created, and even fewer demonstrate how social institutions work to maintain systems of inequality. The text here is structured in a way that examines how and why the categories of race, class, gender, and sexuality are socially constructed, maintained, and experienced.

This reader is divided into four parts. Each part begins with an introductory essay that offers a conceptual framework illustrating concepts and theories (which are highlighted by boldface type) useful for understanding the issues raised by the readings in that section. These essays are not merely introductions to the readings but rather provide material that will enable students to move beyond them. Part I provides a thorough discussion of what it means to think critically as well as an extensive overview of how and why categories of difference are socially constructed. Part II discusses in greater detail how categories of difference are transformed and maintained as systems of inequality by social institutions. Part III examines how categories of difference and systems of inequality impact the everyday experiences of individuals in our society. Finally, Part IV offers a useful look at perspectives on social change and provides examples of barriers and opportunities to transforming systems of oppression and privilege into a system of equal access to opportunity.

In each of these sections the readings and examples were selected to cover a variety of racial and ethnic groups as well as experiences of multiracial identity. In addition, issues of sexuality are incorporated throughout each of the parts of this reader. While a few anthologies have begun to incorporate readings that address inequality on the basis of sexuality, the majority do so only on a superficial level. With the current political and social debate regarding civil rights and sexuality, it is important that texts provide sufficient material to address this area of inequality. Overall, the readings represent a myriad of individuals with various perspectives and life experiences. Such diversity will aid students' ability to understand perspectives and experiences that differ from their own. Finally, the part introductions as well as many of the readings selected demonstrate the intersections of race, class, gender, and sexuality and stress the importance of viewing them as interlocking systems of oppression and privilege. By moving beyond traditional additive models of examining inequality, students will be better able to see how forms of inequality are interconnected.

A NOTE ON LANGUAGE

As discussed in Part II, language serves as a link between all of the different forms of culture in a society. Although language enables us to communicate with and understand one another, it also incorporates cultural values. Thus, the words we use to describe ourselves and others with regard to race, class, gender, and sexuality reflect not only our own values but those of the dominant ideology and popular discourse.

In discussing the experiences of different groups, issues of language can become particularly problematic. For example, as discussed in Part I, categories of race and ethnicity are socially constructed. In addition, the externally created labels for these categories are not always accepted by those viewed as belonging to a particular group. For example, those of Latin American descent may not accept the term *Hispanic*. Similarly, those who are indigenous to North America may not accept the term *American Indian*. However, there is rarely agreement among all members of a particular racial or ethnic group regarding the terminology with which they would like to be identified.

Recognizing the problems and limitations of language, I have attempted to be consistent in the terminology I have used in each of the part introductions. For example, I use the term *Latina/o* to refer to those of Latin American descent, even though not all people in this group may identify themselves in this way. I also use the terms *black* and *African American* interchangeably, as I do *American Indian* and *Native American*. In using such terms it is not my intention to homogenize divergent experiences. Rather, it is done in an effort to allow discussion of common experiences within groups as well as across groups. The terminology used by the authors of the readings was not altered, however. It is important that readers be mindful of the limitations of my language use as well as those of the other authors within this anthology.

◆ Changes to the Second Edition

With this second edition, I have continued to cover a variety of racial and ethnic groups and to incorporate sexuality throughout. In addition, I have maintained the focus on the intersections of race, class, gender and sexuality as interlocking systems of oppression. To keep the text current with regard to economic conditions, issues of gender and sexuality, the political and social discourse on race, as well as recent events in our country and world, I have changed 15 readings and added two others. These readings include an essay by Ibish Hussein on the political programs and policies that led to the constructing of Arabs and Arab-Americans as "other"; Melvin Oliver and Thomas Shapiro's article on "Race, Wealth, and Equality," which provides an overview of the historical forces that resulted in a wealth gap between whites and blacks; an article by Michael Kimmel that illustrates the connections between homophobia and the construction of masculinity; and a portion of Scott Coltrane's Work on Chicano families, particularly focusing on the role of men. As with the first edition, I selected readings that are engaging to students and that reflect a variety of experiences. I welcome any feedback that instructors and students may have on this edition.

INSTRUCTOR'S MANUAL

I have written an instructor's manual to accompany this text that contains questions for critical thinking and discussion for each reading, short-answer and essay questions, suggestions for classroom activities, and recommendations for films/videos. These items were compiled to help instructors further student comprehension of the issues addressed in this volume.

RACE/CLASS/GENDER/SEXUALITY SUPERSITE

This companion Website provides information about the book, including an overview, summaries of key features and what's new in the third edition, information about the authors, and Practice Test Questions.

Non-text-specific content on this site includes an annotated list of Weblinks to useful sites; a list of professional resources (e.g., professional journals); links to Websites offering Census 2000 information; a glossary;

flashcards; and a comprehensive list (annotated and listed by category) of films and videos in the areas of race, class, gender, ethnicity, and sexuality.
Visit the SuperSite by going to <u>www.mhhe.com/raceclassgender</u>

ACKNOWLEDGMENTS

The inception and completion of this project were made possible through the efforts of many people. Foremost among these, I would like to acknowledge the students at the University of Illinois and their efforts in lobbying for a class on multiculturalism and inequality that would incorporate students' doing service in the community. Without their perseverance and commitment, I would likely not have had the opportunity to teach a course that provided such a wonderful foundation for this book. As has been the case throughout my teaching career, my students are my best teachers. Thanks go to all of my students at the colleges and universities where I have taught. I continue to learn from each of them.

I also would like to acknowledge the work of a wonderful team of reviewers: Jodi Burmeister-May, St. Cloud State University; Denise M. Dalaimo, Mt. San Jacinto College; Sharon Elise, California State University at San Marcos; Kristin G. Esterberg, University of Massachusetts at Lowell; Susan A. Farrell, Kingsborough Community College; Lisa M. Frehill, New Mexico State University; Melinda Goldner, Union College; Kelley Hall, DePauw University; Melissa Herbert, Hamline University; Eleanor A. Hubbard, University of Colorado at Boulder; Melissa Latimer, West Virginia University; Betsy Lucal, Indiana University South Bend; Anne Roschelle, State University of New York at New Paltz; Steve Schacht, State University of New York at Plattsburgh; Susan Shaw, Oregon State University; and Brett Stockdill, California State Polytechnic University at Pomona. Their insights, comments, and suggestions served me greatly in clarifying the direction of this project. I value the contribution each of them made to its completion.

For the second edition, I would like to thank the following team of reviewers: Peter Meiksins, Cleveland State University; Jackie Hogan, Bradley University; Philip A. Broyles, Shippensburg University; Heather E. Dillaway, Michigan State University; Elizabeth J. Clifford, Towson University; Tom Gershick, Illinois State University; Susan A. Farrell, Kingsborough Community College; Kristin G. Esterberg, University of Massachusetts at Lowell; and Eleanor A. Hubbard, University of Colorado at Boulder.

The production of the first edition of this book and its adherence to schedule was due to the work of many people. Specifically, I would like to thank Jan Fisher, Kathryn Mikulic, and Dave Mason at Publication Services for their excellent copyediting and other support. At Mayfield Publishing I would like to thank Mary Johnson, April Wells-Hayes, Marty Granahan, and Jay Bauer. My deepest thanks go to Serina Beauparlant for believing in this project and for supporting me throughout. With her vision and perseverance, I couldn't have asked for a better editor.

The creation of the second edition is due to the work of Jill Gordon, Sally Constable, Amy Shaffer, Ruth Smith, Lori Koetters, Jenny El-Shamy, Nathan Perry, and Dan Loch at McGraw-Hill. I appreciate your patience, creative efforts, and attention to detail.

Completing this project was also made possible through the support and caring of a wonderful community of friends. My thanks go to Eileen Gebbie for reading earlier drafts of this work. I would also like to thank my allies on the Sociology 100 team at the University of Illinois. I could always count on them for unconditional support. Thanks also go to my fellow activists who help me to always keep one foot in reality so that I do not lose perspective. Special thanks go as well to Kristin Aukstik for her enduring patience and friendship. Finally, I would like to thank Karín Aguilar-San Juan for sharing her knowledge, insight, and support. Her consistent encouragement and companionship carries me through.

Tracy E. Ore

PART I

Constructing Differences

INTRODUCTION

In the United States, the Census Bureau attempts to conduct a complete accounting of all residents every 10 years. The data gathered by the Bureau is very important, because it serves to determine the distribution of federal dollars to support housing assistance, highway construction, employment services, schools, hospital services, programs for the elderly, and other funding targets. In the year 2000, persons filling out census forms were given a unique opportunity. For the first time ever, those with mixed racial heritage were permitted to select more than one racial category. As a result of new governmental policy, the category "multiracial" is now a reality in the United States.

Does this mean that people who are multiracial have never before existed in this country? Of course not. Even a superficial exploration of U.S. history will show that multiracial people have been present throughout. The recent news of DNA tests confirming that Thomas Jefferson was the father of at least one child by his slave Sally Hemings is but one example of how the history of slavery in the United States has contributed to the existence of people of multiracial descent. However, until recently government policies in the United States have not allowed for the recognition of a multiracial identity. Rather, they have enforced policies such as the rule of **hypo-descent**—one drop of black blood makes you black—to maintain distinct racial categories.

The preceding example clearly illustrates how the categories that we use to describe ourselves and those around us are the product of social rather than biological factors. Biologically, people who are multiracial certainly exist throughout the United States. Indeed, it is unlikely that anyone is "racially pure." Nevertheless, it is the social recognition, definition, and grouping of these factors that make them culturally significant in our daily interactions. Our reliance on such distinct categories is made clear when we ask someone whose race is not immediately discernible to us, "What are you?"

These culturally defined classifications are also significant in that they are structured as categories that are fundamentally *different* from one another. Thus, we expect people to be black or white, never in between. It is important to point out, however, that difference isn't necessarily a negative quality. On the contrary, the existence of categories of difference adds a great deal of richness to our lives. The presence of different cultural traditions, types of food, forms of music, and styles of dance serves to make society more interesting. It is not the differences that are the causes of inequality in our culture. Rather, it is the meanings and values applied to these differences that makes them harmful. For example, it is not that people of color are defined as different from whites in the United States but that whites are viewed as superior and as the cultural standard against which all others are judged that transforms categories of race *differences* into a system of racial *inequality*.

The readings in this text explore how categories of difference with regard to race/ethnicity, social class, sex/gender, and sexuality are constructed and then *transformed* into systems of inequality. We will investigate *what* creates these categories and *how* they are constructed, and consider some explanations about *why* these categories are created. It is important that we understand how the processes that construct these categories simultaneously create structures of **social stratification**—a system by which society ranks categories of people in a hierarchy—and how social stratification results in systems of inequality. The readings in this text will aid us in understanding the effects that categories of difference have on *all* members of our society and how this inequality can be addressed. By examining closely the processes that construct categories of difference, we will better understand how they impact our lives. Furthermore, by recognizing how systems of inequality are socially created, we can gain a greater understanding of how to transform such systems into ones of equality.

CRITICAL THINKING

A fundamental component in examining constructions of difference and systems of inequality is **critical thinking** about the social constructs on which systems of inequality rely. This requires us to examine how the social structure has affected our values, attitudes, and behaviors. The object of this text is not to negate your present belief system and provide you with a new one, but rather to provide the tools that will allow you to think critically about the attitudes and opinions you have been given. By thinking critically, we are better able to develop a belief system that we can claim as our own.

Many of us are unsure of what is meant by critical thinking. According to various scholars, critical thinking can involve logical reasoning, reflective judgment, exploring assumptions, creating and testing meanings, identifying contradictions in arguments, and determining the validity of empirical findings and generalized conclusions. For the purposes of this text, to think critically is to ask questions about what is assumed to be real, valued, and significant in our culture. Stephen Brookfield (1987) offers a useful framework for asking these questions. He sees critical thinking as having four primary elements.

First, we must *identify and challenge assumptions*. We should try to identify the assumptions that are at the foundation of the concepts, values, beliefs, and behaviors that we deem important in our society. Once we have identified these assumptions, we need to explore their accuracy and legitimacy, considering whether or not what we take for granted does indeed reflect the realities we experience. For example, a common assumption in the United States is that women are inherently more nurturing than men and that men are inherently more aggressive than women. When thinking critically, ask whether such assumptions reflect reality or if they shape what we observe in the behaviors of women and men. In other words, do we observe women indeed being more nurturing, or do we make note of only their nurturing behavior? In addition, we need to ask whether our expectations of women and men shape the ways in which they act. For example, do men behave in a more aggressive manner because that is what is expected of them? Through identifying and challenging assumptions, we become more aware of how uncritically examined assumptions shape our perceptions and our understanding of our environments.

Second, thinking critically involves *awareness of our place and time in our culture.* When asking questions about aspects of our culture, we need to be aware of our own **standpoint**—the position from which we are asking these questions. In other words, we need to be aware of our location at a particular intersection of culture and history; how that is influenced by our race/ethnicity, social class, sex/gender, sexuality, ability, age, and other factors; and how these in turn influence the questions we ask and the answers we accept. For example, a millionaire examining the strengths and weaknesses of the U.S. economic system would likely see different problems and solutions to these problems than would a working-class individual. Their respective class standpoints (as well as their race/ethnicity, sex/gender, sexuality, etc.) affect the ways in which they examine the world.

One's standpoint also influences what one sees as "normal" or "ordinary" behavior. This relates to the concept of **enculturation**—immersion in our own culture to the point where we assume that our way of life is "natural" or "normal." Because we are so enculturated into our own societal standards and practices, we often assume that they are the only options and, as a result, we are unaware of alternatives. Furthermore, we often view those who have other cultural standards or practices as behaving in a strange or unnatural manner. For example, people raised in a culture with strict religious teachings based on the idea of a supreme being may be so enculturated that they view those with different notions of religion (or none at all) as strange or odd. As a consequence of the depth of our enculturation we also often possess some level of **ethnocentrism**—the practice of judging another culture using the standards of one's own. Such judging is based on the assumption that one's own group is more important than or superior to other groups (Sumner, 1959). Thus we may judge those who possess different religious beliefs than ourselves not only as strange but as *wrong.* For example, many non-Muslim Americans, fueled by media stereotypes, view the practices of those that follow Islam as inappropriate, if not "un-American."

It is important to point out, however, that ethnocentrism is not in and of itself problematic. Every social system to some degree promotes its ideas and standards. Ethnocentrism becomes a problem when such ideas are used as a basis for treating people in an unequal manner. An alternative to ethnocentrism is **cultural relativism**—judging a culture by its own cultural rules and values. By being cultural relativists we can gain a better understanding of the real meaning of another culture's ideas and standards. In thinking critically it is important that we recognize the depth of our enculturation and how it is manifested in our ethnocentrism, so that we can become aware of our own standpoint and be better able to judge other cultures by their own values and ideas.

Third, when thinking critically we need to *search for alternative ways of thinking.* This means examining the assumptions that form the basis of our ideas and ways of behaving. For example, the United States is currently a society based on the notion of **civil rights**—a system based on majority rule. When we vote, the will of the "majority" becomes the will of all. This system is designed to bring *the greatest good for the greatest number.* In addition, there is a fundamental belief that if one is a "good" citizen, one *earns* rights within society, such as liberty. In a civil rights system some people inevitably do not benefit. Implicit in the statement "the greatest good for the greatest number" is the assumption that society cannot provide for everyone. To think critically about a civil rights system, we must imagine an alternative to this reality. For example, what might it be like to live in a society that operates under a **human rights** framework? Such a system recognizes each person as an individual and as valuable. It is based on the belief that everyone has inalienable rights to housing, food, education, and health care, and that society must provide these to those unable to provide for themselves. What structural changes are necessary to bring about such a society? Furthermore, if we were to create such a society, how might our own lives be transformed? Considering alternatives to current ways of thinking can provide us with new insights about widely accepted ideas.

Fourth, to think critically one must *develop a reflective analysis.* Such an analysis requires that we be skeptical, not in the sense that we don't believe anything we see but rather that we question rigid belief systems. For example, once we become aware that it is possible to have a society that operates under a human rights framework, we come to question those who claim that a system based on civil rights is the only way to operate. A reflective analysis requires that we challenge dominant ideas and popularly held notions regarding solutions to social problems.

Thinking critically frees us from personal, environmental, and institutional forces that prevent us from seeing new directions (Habermas, 1979). Furthermore, once we become critical thinkers, we are no longer passive recipients of knowledge and products of socialization. Rather, through practicing thoughtful scrutiny and continuously asking questions we become active participants and arrive at our own ideas and commitments. As a result, we ground our ideas on a solid and informed foundation, all the while realizing that we may still be wrong. When we face challenges to our ideas, we are better prepared to provide justification and evidence in their support. The readings in this text provide us with many essential tools for becoming discerning critical thinkers.

ESSENTIALISM AND SOCIAL CONSTRUCTION

As mentioned earlier, in the United States we have a system of stratification that is based on many categories of difference, including race/ethnicity, social class, sex/gender, and sexuality. We tend to view this system as fixed because of our assumptions that these categories are unchangeable. Such assumptions are often based on a belief of **essentialism**—the tenet that human behavior is "natural," predetermined by genetic, biological, or physiological mechanisms and thus not subject to change. Human behaviors that show some similarity are assumed to be expressions of an underlying human drive or tendency. In the United States, gender and sexuality are among the last realms to have their natural or biological status called into question. For most of us, essentialism informs the way we think about such things as gender and remains the **hegemonic** or culturally dominant belief in our culture. For example, many of us attribute great importance to what we perceive as biological differences between women and men and see them as central to the organization of human society. Essentialism guides the way we order our social world and determines what we value as well as what we devalue.

This text proceeds from a different perspective, however. As you read the selections in Part I, you will note that they all begin with the premise that categories such as race/ethnicity, social class, sex/gender, and sexuality are *socially constructed*. Peter Berger and Thomas Luckmann, on whose work this premise is based, state that "social order is not part of the 'nature of things,' and it cannot be derived from the 'laws of nature.' Social order exists *only* as a product of human activity" (1966, p. 52). **Social construction theory** suggests that what we see as "real" (in this case, cultural categories of difference and systems of inequality) is the result of human interaction. Through such interaction we create aspects of our culture, objectify them, internalize them, and then take these cultural products for granted. A suitable companion to critical thinking, social construction theory encourages us to ask new questions but does not imply a particular answer. Using a critical thinking framework based on the notion of social construction requires that we be committed to asking questions and challenging assumptions that impair our ability even to imagine these questions.

Adopting a framework based on social construction theory means understanding that we are not born with a sense of what it means to be male, female, or intersexual; with a disability or not; black, Latina/o, Asian, white, or Native American; gay, straight, asexual, or bisexual; or rich, working-class, poor, or middle-class. We learn about these categories through social interaction, and we are given meanings and values for these categories by our social institutions, peers, and families. What we learn depends on the culture in which we live as well as on our place within that culture. Further, how we are defined by our culture often determines how we experience our social world. As W. I. Thomas noted, if we "define situations as real, they are real in their consequences" (1966, p. 301). For example, when we define one group as inferior to another, this does not make that group inferior, yet it may result in their being experienced as inferior. To illustrate this, consider the vicious cycle that results from the assignment of substandard resources to people who are poor. For example, low-income housing is generally located in geographic areas that lack quality resources such as good public schools and access to adequate health care. Lacking such quality resources results in further social disadvantage, which can perpetuate the poverty of this group. Thus, although reality is initially *soft* as it is constructed, it can become *hard* in its effects. We will examine these effects throughout this text.

According to Berger and Luckmann, reality is socially constructed in three stages. In the first stage, **externalization,** we create cultural products through social interaction. These cultural products may be material artifacts, social institutions, or values or beliefs concerning a particular group. When these products are created, they become "external" to those who have produced them; they become products outside ourselves. For example, as Judith Lorber describes in Reading 9, "The Social Construction of Gender," the construction of gender identity starts at birth with placement within a sex category (male or female). Through dress and adornment, others become aware of the sex of the child and they treat the child according to the gendered expectations they have for that particular sex. Children then behave and respond differently because of the different treatment they receive. A situation defined as real thus becomes real in its consequences. Girls and boys are taught to act differently from each other and thus *do* act differently. As a result, boys and girls are seen as *being* different from each other.

A second example of externalization can be found in the first reading, "Racial Formations," by Michael Omi and Howard Winant. They note that the concept of race has varied over history and is subject to a great deal of debate. Using the term **racial formation,** they describe "the process by which social, economic, and political forces determine the content and importance of racial categories, and by which they shape racial meanings." The example cited at the beginning of this essay clearly illustrates the social forces involved in determining racial categories. The recognition of a multiracial identity involves more than individuals being identified as multiracial. Rather, interaction that takes place at the social, economic, and political levels serves to construct such categories of race.

The second stage, **objectivation,** occurs when the products created in the first stage appear to take on a reality of their own, becoming independent of those who created them. People lose awareness that they themselves are the authors of their social and cultural environment and of their interpretations of reality. They feel as if the products have an objective existence, and they become another part of reality to be taken for granted. For example, most of us take race categories for granted, employing an essentialist perspective that views race categories as the result of biological or genetic factors. However, as mentioned earlier, a variety of social, economic, and political forces are involved in the construction of race categories. When we forget our part in the social construction of race, or fail to recognize the social forces that operate to construct race categories and the meanings associated with them, these categories take on objective realities. The objective realities that many of us attribute to racial categories can be seen in the findings of the recent census conducted by the U.S. Census Bureau. Nationwide, 2.5 percent of respondents identified themselves as being of mixed race. The reasons for such a low response rate vary from lack of knowledge of the options to a strong identification with one race, regardless of one's multiracial heritage. These findings demonstrate that most respondents hold on to what they see as the objective reality of clear and mutually exclusive race categories.

In the final stage, **internalization,** we learn the supposedly "objective facts" about the cultural products that have been created. This occurs primarily through **socialization,** the process of social interaction in which one learns the ways of the society and one's specific **roles**—the sets of rules and expectations attached to a social position (or **status**) in that society. In this stage we make these "facts" part of our subjective consciousness. Because of the process of internalization, members of the same culture share an understanding of reality and rarely question the origins of their beliefs or the processes by which the beliefs arose. For example, as Gregory Mantsios discusses in Reading 6, "Media Magic: Making Class Invisible," the mass media serves as a very powerful tool for shaping the way we think. A significant part of our culture, mass media operates as a very important socialization mechanism. What we see presented in the mass media, as well as how it is presented, delivers important messages about who and what is or is not valued. Specifically, mass media helps us to internalize certain constructs about class in our society, perpetuating a variety of myths. Among these myths are that poverty is not a significant problem in this country, that those who are poor have only themselves to blame, that we are a middle-class society, and that blue-collar and union workers are to blame for declining economic security. As mass media presents us with these images, we develop a particular view of the class structure in our country. In addition, we internalize beliefs about members of a specific class (e.g., the poor are lazy) as if they were objective facts. The role of the media in maintaining constructions of difference and the resulting systems of inequality will be explored in Part II of this text.

It is important to note here that viewing cultural products as being produced in stages does not imply that the creation of reality occurs in a neat and overt progression. In some cases, the process of externalization in the creation of a social category is clear, as shown in Jonathan Katz's discussion in "The Invention of Heterosexuality" (Reading 13) of the creation of a "heterosexual identity." However, the construction of reality is not always such a clear process. Thinking in terms of a cultural product as produced in stages, though, provides a general understanding of how the knowledge that guides our behavior is established and how it becomes a part of culture and common sense. In addition, it is important to be aware that while categories of difference are being constructed and subsequently transformed into systems of inequality, such systems of inequality are often being *maintained* by the same social forces and practices. To clearly understand how categories of difference become systems of inequality, we begin by examining the processes that construct them. The social factors that serve to maintain these constructs and their corresponding systems of inequality will be examined in detail in Part II.

WHAT CONSTRUCTS CATEGORIES OF DIFFERENCE?

The readings in this text explore how the categories of race, class, gender, and sexuality are socially constructed and transformed into systems of inequality. The preceding in-depth explanation of social construction theory was intended to give us an understanding of *how* these categories are socially constructed. To thoroughly comprehend this process, however, it is important to understand what social factors are at work in creating these categories.

Simply put, categories of difference are the result of human activity guided by the values of our culture. When parents teach their child how to behave like a "lady" or act like a "gentleman," when one child labels another a "sissy" or a "fag," or when a girl decides to stop playing "rough" to avoid being labeled a "tomboy"—each is engaged in the process of creating categories of difference. We take these everyday actions for granted, but they play a fundamental role in how we view the world. The kinds of categories we create, as well as the meanings we give to them, are guided by our cultural values regarding who or what is important.

This process of creating these categories occurs in a variety of contexts that we encounter every day. Perhaps the most significant of these is the **institutional context**. An **institution** is the set of rules and relationships that govern the social activities in which we participate to meet our basic needs. The major social institutions that we will examine are:

The family: responsible for reproducing and socializing and protecting the young, regulating sexual behavior, and providing emotional comfort and support for its members.

Education: responsible for teaching members of society the knowledge, skills, and values considered most important for the survival of the individual as well as society.

The economy: creates, controls, and distributes the human and material resources of a society.

The state: possesses the legal power to regulate the behavior of members of that society, as well as the relationship of that society to others.

The media: responsible for supplying members of society with information, for reinforcing the policies of other institutions, and for socializing members of society with regard to appropriate ways of behaving and accepted cultural values.

From the policies and practices of each of these institutions, influenced by our cultural values, categories of difference are created. Thus, when parents teach their child how to behave like a "lady" or act like a "gentleman," they create categories of difference within the institutional context of the family.

Another context in which we create categories of difference is the **interpersonal context**—our daily interactions with others. In these interactions we rely on common guidelines for behavior (**norms**) to define situations and create these categories. For example, when an individual, operating on stereotypes based on race and ethnicity, labels another a "foreigner," she or he is relying on what are assumed images of what is an "American." As a result, she or he creates categories of difference within an interpersonal context.

Finally, we create categories of difference in **internal contexts** by internalizing the values and beliefs established in institutional and interpersonal contexts. When a girl decides to stop playing "rough" to avoid being labeled a "tomboy," she is internalizing the ideas of what it means to be a girl that were taught to her by her family as well as her peers.

CONSTRUCTING RACE AND ETHNICITY

The institution of the state, which determines how the census should be taken and how individuals should be counted, plays an integral role in defining race categories in an institutional context. **Race** denotes a group of people who perceive themselves *and are perceived by others* as possessing distinctive hereditary traits. **Ethnicity** denotes a group of people who perceive themselves *and are perceived by others* as sharing cultural traits such as language, religion, family customs, and food preferences. As Omi and Winant illustrate in "Racial Formations," what is important about the construction of race categories is not necessarily our perception of our own race but the recognition by social institutions of our membership in that race category. Furthermore, racial and ethnic categories are significant in that they are constructed in a hierarchy from "superior" to "inferior." Karen Brodkin Sacks explains in "How Jews Became White" (Reading 4) that Jewish people, as well as some other immigrants to the United States in the late 19th century, were once seen as belonging to an inferior race. The institutions of the economy and the state, as well as others, played an integral role in constructing them as inferior and in later "reconstructing" them as white and no longer an inferior race. Further, as Ibish illustrates in "They Are Absolutely Obsessed with Us" (Reading 3), the institutions of the state and the media have constructed Arabs as "other" and "the enemy." Both authors illustrate that such processes of construction are tied to economic and political changes in the United States.

Racial categories are also constructed in interpersonal contexts. As Waters discusses in "Optional Ethnicities" (Reading 2), many of us, but particularly whites, will ask someone whose race or ethnicity is not immediately apparent, "What are you?" We do not, however, generally ask such a question of those whom we perceive to be white. Thus, in our efforts to define others we not only attempt to construct distinct racial categories but we also create white as an "unmarked" category and as a standard against which all others are judged.

Finally, race is constructed in internal contexts, where we reinforce those categories and the meanings associated with them within ourselves. This process is particularly evident when a person of color who is light-skinned attempts or desires to "pass" as a white person. Through internalizing the idea that to be other than white is to be less valued, they participate in constructing race categories as well as the meanings associated with them.

CONSTRUCTING SOCIAL CLASS

The categories of social class are also constructed within institutional contexts. Although we may view social class as a result of how much **income** (wages and salaries from earnings and investments) and **wealth** (the total amount of valuable goods) a person possesses, it is in fact more than this. What class we belong to is determined not just by how much money we have or the material possessions we own but also by the institutions of our society, including state policies and the structuring of the economy. For example, definitions of poverty created by the government affect the access some members of our society have to certain important resources. The "Thrifty Food Plan"—the least costly of four nutritionally adequate plans designed by the Department of Agriculture, based on their 1955 Household Food Consumption Survey—demonstrates how the establishment of the **poverty line**—an annual income level below which a person or family was defined as poor and therefore entitled to certain benefits—creates who is seen as poor. The poverty line is problematic, however, in the way it is determined because it relies on material standards of the 1950s rather than contemporary standards. As a result, while the government determined in 2000 that the poverty line for a family of four was $17,603, a more accurate calculation, employing contemporary standards, would have been $30,000. The more accurate figure would result in doubling the number of individuals defined as poor. As institutions establish definitions and measures, they determine a person's access to resources (i.e., the ability of people living in poverty to receive government aid). In this way, constructions of class provide the foundation for a system of inequitably distributed resources. The impact of such a system will be discussed in greater detail later in this text.

In addition to establishing who is poor, social institutions also function to establish who is wealthy, as illustrated by Melvin Oliver and Thomas Shapiro in "Race, Wealth, and Equality" (Reading 5). Furthermore, as Holly Sklar,

Chuck Collins, and Betsy Leondar-Wright discuss in Reading 7, the state, influenced by the economy, creates a social class stratification system that is increasingly divided by a "wealth gap." Finally, the values that we place on members of social classes are further influenced by social institutions such as the media, as explained by Gregory Mantsios in "Media Magic: Making Class Invisible." According to Mantsios those who control the media (i.e., the upper class) can use this institution to create class divisions as well as define our attitudes about members of different social classes. All of these articles clearly illustrate that the rules, practices, and policies of social institutions serve to construct categories of class differences and establish a system of class inequality.

Categories of social class are also constructed in interpersonal contexts. We define who is rich, poor, middle-class, and so forth, in our interactions with others. In addition, we attach meanings to each of these categories. For example, if we see a well-dressed, "clean-cut" individual driving an expensive car, we not only may judge this individual as belonging to the upper class but we may also admire her or him and the class position we assume she or he has achieved. On the other hand, if we observe people purchasing groceries with food stamps and then taking the bus, we not only judge them as poor but are also likely to think less of them as a result of their presumed class. In each of these instances, we rely on **stereotypes**—rigid, oversimplified, often exaggerated beliefs that are applied both to an entire category of people and to each individual in it. As a result of stereotypes we treat individuals according to the values we attribute to these classes.

It is likely that the individuals in the preceding examples would be aware of the assumptions made about them on the basis of their social class. Mantsios illustrates that such stereotypes about class dominate our media. As these individuals internalize these messages, they impact their sense of self-worth. In addition, these individuals aid in creating categories of class and the meanings associated with them.

CONSTRUCTING SEX AND GENDER

Categories of sex and gender are also socially constructed in institutional contexts. This claim may, at first glance, seem quite strange. Whether or not a person is female or male is generally seen as a biological condition. However, as Judith Lorber in "The Social Construction of Gender" and Anne Fausto-Sterling in "The Five Sexes" (Reading 10) discuss, the categories of male and female are not always sufficient to describe the variety of sexes that exist in reality. As Fausto-Sterling points out, individuals born **intersexual**—the physical manifestation of genital/genetic/endocrinological differentiation that is viewed as different from the norm—may constitute as much as 4 percent of live births. However, these infants are placed in a program of hormonal and surgical management almost immediately after birth so that they can become "normal" males or females in society. Thus, the institutions of science and medicine and advances in physiology and surgical technology aid in constructing a reality in which there are only two sexes.

What is significant about **sex**—the genetic (and sometimes scientific) determination of male and female—is the corresponding expectations that we place on people occupying these categories with regard to **gender**—the socially defined roles expected of males and females. As Lorber and others clearly explain, gender constructs are created and justified by a variety of institutions, including the family, the state, and the economy. Thus, gender constructs are transformed into a **gender system** in which men and masculinity are at the top of the hierarchy and women and femininity are at the bottom. Our ideas about gender therefore influence the way people are sorted into social positions. For example, our expectations of women to be feminine and our corresponding assumptions about their ability to handle certain kinds of strenuous or stressful work contribute to the underrepresentation of women as CEOs and heads of governing bodies. Similarly, our expectations that males be masculine and our corresponding assumption that they are less able to be nurturing contribute to their being less likely to pursue careers as nurses or elementary school teachers, for example. Because such a gendered division of labor is established in a society that is based on **patriarchy**—a form of social organization in which males dominate females—what results is not only a gendered division of labor but an occupational hierarchy in which the work of men is valued over that of women.

Further examples of how we construct categories of difference are found in interpersonal contexts. We construct these categories by acting out the two polar sex categories and fulfilling the corresponding gendered expectations that have been constructed by the social institutions of the family, education, and others. As West and Zimmerman (1987) note, we do gender through our attempts to define others and through our expectations that others display appropriate gender identity. Similar to the ways in which we view race, we are often frustrated with ambiguities of sex and gender. If the sex/gender of another individual does not fit our expectations of opposite sex categories with corresponding gendered behavior, we often seek to define the person, again asking, "What are you?" In so doing we aid in the process of constructing a sex/gender system that allows for only two sexes and requires gender categories to be distinct and polar opposites.

Finally, gender is also created in internal contexts. As Michael Kimmel illustrates in "Masculinity as Homophobia" (Reading 12), males often insecure with their "manhood" will often act as "bullies" to prove their manhood, not only to others but to themselves. As this reading illustrates, feelings of **alienation**—a sense of not belonging to the culture or the community (as in the case with males fearing they will be labeled "sissy" if they do not "act like men")—as well as feelings of **self-alienation**—hatred for one's own position and oneself—also play a significant role in how we create these categories within ourselves. As a result, we often perpetuate the ways in which these categories are constructed in other contexts.

CONSTRUCTING SEXUALITY

Categories of sexuality are also constructed within institutional contexts. Claims that sexuality is constructed may at first appear as strange as claims of sex being a social construct. Just as we generally recognize only two categories of sex, we often recognize sexuality as existing in only two opposing categories: gay and straight. Furthermore, we tend to see these categories as polar opposites, with each fundamentally different from the other. However, as Jonathan Katz notes in "The Invention of Heterosexuality," current notions of sexuality are but one way of imagining the social relations of the sexes. Like all of the previously discussed categories, sexuality is, in fact, a very complex yet culturally defined construct. **Sexuality** can involve attraction on a physical, emotional, and social level as well as fantasies, sexual behaviors, and self-identity (Klein, 1978). However, just as we may be required to distill our variations in racial and ethnic heritage into one of a few categories, we are often required to place all of the varying aspects of our sexuality into one of two categories. Thus, a complex part of who we are becomes socially defined within rigid and limiting constructs.

As Katz illustrates through his exploration of changes in the institutions of the economy and of work, religion, and science and medicine, social institutions influence the ways in which we construct categories of sexuality. Again, what is significant about categories of sexuality is that they are transformed into systems of inequality, where one form of sexuality is valued and viewed as more appropriate than others. For example, in the United States the policies and practices of the federal government recognize some forms of sexuality and not others (as in the Defense of Marriage Act, which allows states to exclude same-sex couples from the right to marry). Such recognition, or the lack thereof, serves to grant access to resources to heterosexuals but to deny them to lesbians and gays, thus creating systems of inequality.

We also create different sexuality categories in interpersonal contexts. Susan Bordo describes in "Pills and Power Tools" (Reading 14) how our language often relfects the expectations that men will sexually perform. As Kate Bornstein notes in "Naming All the Parts" (Reading 16), constructions of sexuality are culturally linked to constructions of gender. Each of these readings illustrates not only how constructions of difference in institutional contexts are reflected in interpersonal interactions, but also how the social construction of one category of difference is generally dependent on the social construction of another. The interrelatedness of various constructions of difference will be addressed later.

We also create categories of sexuality in internal contexts. Again, this is generally done in response to the ways sexuality is defined in the larger society. As Paula Rust illustrates in "Sexual Identity and Bisexual Identities" (Reading 15), our descriptions of sexuality divisions and our own membership in them are determined by the "sexual landscape" of the culture and what are viewed as appropriate or available categories. As we define ourselves, we perpetuate the ways in which these categories are created in other contexts.

In summary, the construction of categories of difference occurs within a variety of contexts. The readings in Part I illustrate this process. In addition, they demonstrate how the meanings we attach to these categories result in structures of inequality.

WHY CATEGORIES OF DIFFERENCE?

Often the most difficult aspect of understanding the construction of categories of difference is not the how or what but the *why*. We have difficulty understanding why such categories are created and transformed into systems of inequality. Many explanations regarding why categories of difference and their corresponding hierarchies are constructed have been offered from a variety of perspectives.

The readings in Part I offer a variety of explanations. For example, Omi and Winant in "Racial Formations" discuss some of the reasons European explorers created separate categories for the people who were indigenous to the lands that they "discovered." They explain that when the European explorers came upon people who looked different from them, their assumptions about the origin of the human species were called into question. As a result, religious debates regarding creation and whether or not God created a single species of humanity led to questions about whether or not the natives of the New World could be "saved" as well as about how they should be treated. By deeming the European settlers as children of God and indigenous people "other," the European settlers not only were able to maintain their world view but were also able to justify systems of mistreatment, including slavery, coercive labor, and extermination.

Social theorists also offer explanations regarding why elements of social structure work to create systems of stratification. For example, Kingsley Davis and Wilbert Moore (1945) assert, in what has come to be known as the **Davis-Moore thesis,** that social stratification is a universal pattern because it has beneficial consequences for the operation of society. This is the case, they reason, because societal inequality has important functions for social organization. They note that society is a complex system of many occupational positions, each of which has a particular importance. Some jobs, they argue, are easy to do (with a little instruction) and can be performed by just about anyone. Others are far more challenging and can only be accomplished by certain people who possess certain scarce talents. Functionally speaking, according to Davis and Moore, the latter positions of high day-to-day responsibility are the most important.

Other social theorists argue, however, that such a perspective is too conservative and fails to point out the inequality and exploitation of such systems of stratification. Thus, they argue that social stratification is a system by which some people gain advantages at the expense of others. Karl Marx (1959), for example, contended that systems of class stratification involve inequality and exploitation and are created so that capitalists can maximize their profits. He went on to say that the economy has primary importance as the social institution with the greatest influence on the rest of society. Other institutions also create systems of stratification but do so, in general, to support the operation of the economy.

Still other theorists, such as Marilyn Frye (1983), argue that the social construction of difference is initiated with the purpose of discrimination and **oppression**—a relationship in which the dominant group benefits from the *systematic* abuse, exploitation, and injustice directed at a subordinate group. Thus, the construction of difference is not arbitrary but systematically created and transformed into systems of inequality in an effort to advantage some at the expense of others. The roles of domination and subordination in the construction of difference and the maintenance of inequality will be addressed in greater detail in Part II.

CATEGORIES OF DIFFERENCE WITHIN A MATRIX OF DOMINATION

Candace West and Sarah Fenstermaker (1995) note that, although gender, race, and class (and sexuality) involve very different attributes and effects, they are comparable devices for creating social inequality. Up to this point in our discussion we have looked at the construction of each category of difference—race/ethnicity, social class, sex/gender, and sexuality—distinctly, yet the similarities in the processes of construction serve to provide a foundation for understanding how their subsequent systems of oppression interconnect. To fully understand the process of transforming difference into inequality, it is necessary to recognize the interrelationships between these systems.

What we have discussed as distinct categories of difference and systems of inequality are, according to hooks (1989), systems of oppression that interconnect in an overarching structure of domination. She argues that oppression based on race, class, gender, and sexuality is part of an interlocking politics of domination which is "a belief in domination, and a belief in the notions of superior and inferior, which are components of all of those systems" (p. 175). Patricia Hill Collins (1991) refers to this interlocking system as a **matrix of domination.** This model provides the framework for our efforts in this text in seeking to understand how categories of difference are transformed into systems of inequality and maintained as systems of oppression. Such a framework will allow us to move beyond simply describing the similarities and differences between various systems of oppression and will help us to focus on how they interconnect. We will thereby be better able to see how each system of oppression relies on the others. The ways in which these systems of oppression rely on each other to maintain inequality will be discussed in detail in Part II.

The matrix of domination also provides a framework that permits us to avoid additive analyses of systems of oppression (e.g., a black woman being viewed as doubly oppressed as a white woman). Such analyses are problematic in that they suggest that oppression can be quantified. Attempts to do this would result in our placing ourselves in competition with one another, arguing over who is more oppressed and which form of oppression is the worst. Such debates generally divide us and prevent us from working toward equality. Viewing oppression and inequality in the form of a matrix of domination enables us to see commonalities in the sources of inequality and thus provides a clearer perspective on how these inequalities should be addressed.

Viewing constructions of difference and corresponding systems of inequality as interconnected also helps us to see how all groups experience both privilege and oppression in one socially constructed system. Each of us has had a life experience that is unique, and each of us has likely experienced both oppression and privilege. As Collins (1991) notes, a person may occupy the position of oppressor, oppressed, or both. The matrix of domination permits us to understand how we all experience both oppression and privilege.

Just as categories of difference are constructed in a variety of contexts, so too is the matrix of domination. To thoroughly understand the process of social construction, as well as to understand the matrix of domination, it is important to understand what is constructed, what does the constructing, how these constructs are created, and how their corresponding systems of inequality intersect. As you read the selections in Part I, note the explanations provided by each of the authors and be aware of your reactions to them. These readings will provide you with a framework to better understand contemporary constructions of race/ethnicity, social class, sex/gender, and sexuality in the United States. In addition, by understanding the process of social construction we can be more optimistic in working toward positive social change. If we recognize the processes by which systems of inequality are constructed as interlocking systems of oppression, we can gain a greater understanding of how to deconstruct these systems while constructing systems of equality.

A FINAL COMMENT

As stated earlier, this text will help us begin the process of understanding contemporary constructions of race/ethnicity, social class, sex/gender, and sexuality in the United States. A fundamental component to examining these constructs is to think critically. In addition, it is important to employ **empathy**—the ability to identify with the thoughts and experiences of another, even though you have not shared them. Thus it is important to remain aware of your own **standpoint**—your location in society, and how that is impacted by your race/ethnicity, social class, sex/gender, sexuality, ability, age, and other personal qualities. As you read about experiences that you have not had or are challenged by perspectives offered by the authors, try not to shut yourself off to what they have to say. Rather, use this challenge as an opportunity to better understand your own ideas. As the process of critical thinking indicates, becoming aware of alternative experiences and perspectives can result in a greater understanding of why we think what we do. Finally, you may find that you come away from this text with more questions than you had upon entering. If so, see this as a positive outcome, for it is not only a sign of success in learning to think critically, but also an indication that the process of critical thinking will continue beyond this text.

REFERENCES

Berger, Peter L., and Thomas Luckmann. 1966. *The Social Construction of Reality: A Treatise in the Sociology of Knowledge*. New York: Doubleday.

Brookfield, Stephen D. 1987. *Developing Critical Thinkers: Challenging Adults to Explore Alternative Ways of Thinking and Acting*. San Francisco: Jossey-Bass.

Collins, Patricia Hill. 1991. *Black Feminist Thought: Knowledge, Consciousness, and the Politics of Empowerment*. New York: Routledge.

Davis, Kingsley, and Wilbert Moore. 1945. Some Principles of Stratification. *American Sociological Review*, 10(2): 242–49.

Frye, Marilyn. 1983. *The Politics of Reality: Essays in Feminist Theory*. Trumansburg, NY: Crossing Press.

Habermas, Jurgen. 1979. *Communication and the Evolution of Society*. Translated by Thomas McCarthy. Boston: Beacon Press.

hooks, bell. 1989. *Talking Back: Thinking Feminist, Thinking Black*. Boston: South End Press.

Klein, Fritz. 1978. *The Bisexual Option*. New York: Arbor House.

Marx, Karl. 1959 (orig. 1859). "A Contribution to the Critique of Political Economy." In Karl Marx and Friedrich Engels, *Marx and Engels: Basic Writings on Politics and Philosophy*, edited by Lewis S. Feurer, 42–46. Garden City, NY: Anchor Books.

Sapir, Edward. 1949. *Selected Writings of Edward Sapir in Language, Culture, and Personality*, edited by David G. Mandelbaum. Berkeley: University of California Press.

Sumner, William Graham. 1959 (orig. 1906). *Folkways*. New York: Dover.

Thomas, W. I. 1966 (orig. 1931). "The Relation of Research to the Social Process," In *W. I. Thomas on Social Organization and Personality*, edited by Morris Janowitz, 289–305. Chicago: University of Chicago Press.

West, Candace, and Don H. Zimmerman. 1987. "Doing Gender." *Gender & Society*, 1(2): 125–51.

West, Candace, and Sarah Fenstermaker. 1995. "Doing Difference." *Gender & Society*, 9(1) (February): 8–37.

RACE AND ETHNICITY

1

RACIAL FORMATIONS

MICHAEL OMI • HOWARD WINANT

In 1982–83, Susie Guillory Phipps unsuccessfully sued the Louisiana Bureau of Vital Records to change her racial classification from black to white. The descendant of an eighteenth-century white planter and a black slave, Phipps was designated "black" in her birth certificate in accordance with a 1970 state law which declared anyone with at least one-thirty-second "Negro blood" to be black. The legal battle raised intriguing questions about the concept of race, its meaning in contemporary society, and its use (and abuse) in public policy. Assistant Attorney General Ron Davis defended the law by pointing out that some type of racial classification was necessary to comply with federal record-keeping requirements and to facilitate programs for the prevention of genetic diseases. Phipps's attorney, Brian Begue, argued that the assignment of racial categories on birth certificates was unconstitutional and that the one-thirty-second designation was inaccurate. He called on a retired Tulane University professor who cited research indicating that most whites have one-twentieth "Negro" ancestry. In the end, Phipps lost. The court upheld a state law which quantified racial identity, and in so doing affirmed the legality of assigning individuals to specific racial groupings.[1]

The Phipps case illustrates the continuing dilemma of defining race and establishing its meaning in institutional life. Today, to assert that variations in human physiognomy are racially based is to enter a constant and intense debate. *Scientific* interpretations of race have not been alone in sparking heated controversy; *religious* perspectives have done so as well.[2] Most centrally, of course, race has been a matter of *political* contention. This has been particularly true in the United States, where the concept of race has varied enormously over time without ever leaving the center stage of US history.

Omni, Michael & Winant, Howard. "Racial Formations," from *Racial Formations in the United States: From the 1960s to the 1980s.* London: Routledge, 1986. With permission from the publisher.

WHAT IS RACE?

Race consciousness, and its articulation in theories of race, is largely a modern phenomenon. When European explorers in the New World "discovered" people who looked different than themselves, these "natives" challenged then existing conceptions of the origins of the human species, and raised disturbing questions as to whether *all* could be considered in the same "family of man."[3] Religious debates flared over the attempt to reconcile the Bible with the existence of "racially distinct" people. Arguments took place over creation itself, as theories of polygenesis questioned whether God had made only one species of humanity ("monogenesis"). Europeans wondered if the natives of the New World were indeed human beings with redeemable souls. At stake were not only the prospects for conversion, but the types of treatment to be accorded them. The expropriation of property, the denial of political rights, the introduction of slavery and other forms of coercive labor, as well as outright extermination, all presupposed a worldview which distinguished Europeans— children of God, human beings, etc.—from "others." Such a worldview was needed to explain why some should be "free" and others enslaved, why some had rights to land and property while others did not. Race, and the interpretation of racial differences, was a central factor in that worldview.

In the colonial epoch science was no less a field of controversy than religion in attempts to comprehend the concept of race and its meaning. Spurred on by the classificatory scheme of living organisms devised by Linnaeus in *Systema Naturae,* many scholars in the eighteenth and nineteenth centuries dedicated themselves to the identification and ranking of variations in humankind. Race was thought of as a *biological* concept, yet its precise definition was the subject of debates which, as we have noted, continue to rage today. Despite efforts ranging from Dr. Samuel Morton's studies of cranial capacity[4] to contemporary attempts to base racial classification on shared gene pools,[5] the concept of race has defied biological definition. . . .

Attempts to discern the *scientific meaning* of race continue to the present day. Although most physical anthropologists and biologists have abandoned the quest for a scientific basis to determine racial categories, controversies have recently flared in the area of genetics and educational psychology. For instance, an essay by Arthur Jensen which argued that hereditary factors shape intelligence not only revived the "nature or nurture" controversy, but raised highly volatile questions about racial equality itself.[6] Clearly the attempt to establish a *biological* basis of race has not been swept into the dustbin of history, but is being resurrected in various scientific arenas. All such attempts seek to remove the concept of race from fundamental social, political, or economic determination. They suggest instead that the truth of race lies in the terrain of innate characteristics, of which skin color and other physical attributes provide only the most obvious, and in some respects most superficial, indicators.

RACE AS A SOCIAL CONCEPT

The social sciences have come to reject biologistic notions of race in favor of an approach which regards race as a *social* concept. Beginning in the eighteenth century, this trend has been slow and uneven, but its direction clear. In the nineteenth century Max Weber discounted biological explanations for racial conflict and instead highlighted the social and political factors which engendered such conflict.[7] The work of pioneering cultural anthropologist Franz Boas was crucial in refuting the scientific racism of the early twentieth century by rejecting the connection between race and culture, and the assumption of a continuum of "higher" and "lower" cultural groups. Within the contemporary social science literature, race is assumed to be a variable which is shaped by broader societal forces.

Race is indeed a pre-eminently *sociohistorical* concept. Racial categories and the meaning of race are given concrete expression by the specific social relations and historical context in which they are embedded. Racial meanings have varied tremendously over time and between different societies.

In the United States, the black/white color line has historically been rigidly defined and enforced. White is seen as a "pure" category. Any racial intermixture makes one "nonwhite." In the movie *Raintree County*, Elizabeth Taylor describes the worst of fates to befall whites as "havin' a little Negra blood in ya'—just one little teeny drop and a person's all Negra."[8] This thinking flows from what Marvin Harris has characterized as the principle of *hypo-descent:*

> By what ingenious computation is the genetic tracery of a million years of evolution unraveled and each man [sic] assigned his proper social box? In the United States, the mechanism employed is the rule of hypo-descent. This descent rule requires Americans to believe that anyone who is known to have had a Negro ancestor is a Negro. We admit nothing in between. . . . "Hypo-descent" means affiliation with the subordinate rather than the superordinate group in order to avoid the ambiguity of intermediate identity. . . . The rule of hypo-descent is, therefore, an invention, which we in the United States have made in order to keep biological facts from intruding into our collective racist fantasies.[9]

The Susie Guillory Phipps case merely represents the contemporary expression of this racial logic.

By contrast, a striking feature of race relations in the lowland areas of Latin America since the abolition of slavery has been the relative absence of sharply defined racial groupings. No such rigid descent rule characterizes racial identity in many Latin American societies. Brazil, for example, has historically had less rigid conceptions of race, and thus a variety of "intermediate" racial categories exist. Indeed, as Harris notes, "One of the most striking consequences of the Brazilian system of racial identification is that parents and children and even brothers and sisters are frequently accepted as representatives of quite opposite racial types."[10] Such a possibility is incomprehensible within the logic of racial categories in the US.

To suggest another example: the notion of "passing" takes on new meaning if we compare various American cultures' means of assigning racial identity. In the United States, individuals who are actually "black" by the logic of hypo-descent have attempted to skirt the discriminatory barriers imposed by law and custom by attempting to "pass" for white.[11] Ironically, these same individuals would not be able to pass for "black" in many Latin American societies.

Consideration of the term "black" illustrates the diversity of racial meanings which can be found among different societies and historically within a given society. In contemporary British politics the term "black" is used to refer to all nonwhites. Interestingly this designation has not arisen through the racist discourse of groups such as the National Front. Rather, in political and cultural movements, Asian as well as Afro-Caribbean youth are adopting the term as an expression of self-identity.[12] The wide-ranging meanings of "black" illustrate the manner in which racial categories are shaped politically.[13]

The meaning of race is defined and contested throughout society, in both collective action and personal practice. In the process, racial categories themselves are formed, transformed, destroyed, and re-formed. We use the term *racial formation* to refer to the process by which social, economic, and political forces determine the content and importance of racial categories, and by which they are in turn shaped by racial meanings. Crucial to this formulation is the treatment of race as a *central axis* of social relations which cannot be subsumed under or reduced to some broader category or conception.

RACIAL IDEOLOGY AND RACIAL IDENTITY

The seemingly obvious "natural" and "common sense" qualities which the existing racial order exhibits themselves testify to the effectiveness of the racial formation process in constructing racial meanings and racial identities.

One of the first things we notice about people when we meet them (along with their sex) is their race. We utilize race to provide clues about *who* a person is. This fact is made painfully obvious when we encounter someone whom we cannot conveniently racially categorize—someone who is, for example, racially "mixed" or of an ethnic/racial group with which we are not familiar. Such an encounter becomes a source of discomfort and momentarily a crisis of racial meaning. Without a racial identity, one is in danger of having no identity.

Our compass for navigating race relations depends on preconceived notions of what each specific racial group looks like. Comments such as, "Funny, you don't look black," betray an underlying image of what black should be. We also become disoriented when people do not act "black," "Latino," or indeed "white." The content of such stereotypes reveals a series of unsubstantiated beliefs about who these groups are and what "they" are like.[14]

In US society, then, a kind of "racial etiquette" exists, a set of interpretative codes and racial meanings which operate in the interactions of daily life. Rules shaped by our perception of race in a comprehensively racial society determine the "presentation of self,"[15] distinctions of status, and appropriate modes of conduct. "Etiquette" is not mere universal adherence to the dominant group's rules, but a more dynamic combination of these rules with the values and beliefs of subordinated groupings. This racial "subjection" is quintessentially ideological. Everybody learns some combination, some version, of the rules of racial classification, and of their own racial identity, often without obvious teaching or conscious inculcation. Race becomes "common sense"—a way of comprehending, explaining, and acting in the world.

Racial beliefs operate as an "amateur biology," a way of explaining the variations in "human nature."[16] Differences in skin color and other obvious physical characteristics supposedly provide visible clues to differences lurking underneath. Temperament, sexuality, intelligence, athletic ability, aesthetic preferences and so on are presumed to be fixed and discernible from the palpable mark of race. Such diverse questions as our confidence and trust in others (for example, clerks or salespeople, media figures, neighbors), our sexual preferences and romantic images, our tastes in music, films, dance, or sports, and our very ways of talking, walking, eating, and dreaming are ineluctably shaped by notions of race. Skin color "differences" are thought to explain perceived differences in intellectual, physical, and artistic temperaments, and to justify distinct treatment of racially identified individuals and groups.

The continuing persistence of racial ideology suggests that these racial myths and stereotypes cannot be exposed as such in the popular imagination. They are, we think, too essential, too integral, to the maintenance of the US social order. Of course, particular meanings, stereotypes, and myths can change, but the presence of a *system* of racial meanings and stereotypes, of racial ideology, seems to be a permanent feature of US culture.

Film and television, for example, have been notorious in disseminating images of racial minorities which establish for audiences what people from these groups look like, how they behave, and "who they are."[17] The power of the media lies not only in their ability to reflect the dominant racial ideology, but in their capacity to shape that ideology in the first place. D. W. Griffith's epic *Birth of a Nation*, a sympathetic treatment of the rise of the Ku Klux Klan during Reconstruction, helped to generate, consolidate, and "nationalize" images of blacks which had been more disparate (more regionally specific, for example) prior to the film's appearance.[18] In US television, the necessity to define characters in the briefest and most condensed manner has led to the perpetuation of racial caricatures, as racial stereotypes serve as shorthand for scriptwriters, directors and actors, in commercials, etc. Television's tendency to address the "lowest common denominator" in order to render programs "familiar" to an enormous and diverse audience leads it regularly to assign and reassign racial characteristics to particular groups, both minority and majority.

These and innumerable other examples show that we tend to view race as something fixed and immutable—something rooted in "nature." Thus we mask the historical construction of racial categories, the shifting meaning of race, and the crucial role of politics and ideology in shaping race relations. Races do not emerge full-blown. They are the results of diverse historical practices and are continually subject to challenge over their definition and meaning.

RACIALIZATION: THE HISTORICAL DEVELOPMENT OF RACE

In the United States, the racial category of "black" evolved with the consolidation of racial slavery. By the end of the seventeenth century, Africans whose specific identity was Ibo, Yoruba, Fulani, etc., were rendered "black" by an ideology of exploitation based on racial logic—the establishment and maintenance of a "color line." This of course did not occur overnight. A period of indentured servitude which was not rooted in racial logic preceded the consolidation of racial slavery. With slavery, however, a racially based understanding of society was set in motion which resulted in the shaping of a specific *racial* identity not only for the slaves but for the European settlers as well. Winthrop Jordan has observed: "From the initially common term *Christian*, at mid-century there was a marked shift toward the terms *English* and *free*. After about 1680, taking the colonies as a whole, a new term of self-identification appeared—*white*."[19]

We employ the term *racialization* to signify the extension of racial meaning to a previously racially unclassified relationship, social practice, or group. Racialization is an ideological process, a historically specific one. Racial ideology is constructed from pre-existing conceptual (or, if one prefers, "discursive") elements and emerges from the struggles of competing political projects and ideas seeking to articulate similar elements differently. An account of racialization processes that avoids the pitfalls of US ethnic history[20] remains to be written.

Particularly during the nineteenth century, the category of "white" was subject to challenges brought about by the influx of diverse groups who were not of the same Anglo-Saxon stock as the founding immigrants. In the nineteenth century, political and ideological struggles emerged over the classification of Southern Europeans, the Irish, and Jews, among other "non-white" categories.[21] Nativism was only effectively curbed by the institutionalization of a racial order that drew the color line *around*, rather than *within*, Europe.

By stopping short of racializing immigrants from Europe after the Civil War, and by subsequently allowing their assimilation, the American racial order was reconsolidated in the wake of the tremendous challenge placed before it by the abolition of racial slavery[22] With the end of Reconstruction in 1877, an effective program for limiting the emergent class struggles of the later nineteenth century was forged: the definition of the working class *in racial terms*—as "white." This was not accomplished by any legislative decree or capitalist maneuvering to divide the working class, but rather by white workers themselves. Many of them were recent immigrants, who organized on racial lines as much as on traditionally defined class lines.[23] The Irish on the West Coast, for example, engaged in vicious anti-Chinese race-baiting and committed many pogrom-type assaults on Chinese in the course of consolidating the trade union movement in California.

Thus the very political organization of the working class was in important ways a racial project. The legacy of racial conflicts and arrangements shaped the definition of interests and in turn led to the consolidation of institutional patterns (e.g., segregated unions, dual labor markets, exclusionary legislation) which perpetuated the color line *within* the working class. Selig Perlman, whose study of the development of the labor movement is fairly sympathetic to this process, notes that:

> The political issue after 1877 was racial, not financial, and the weapon was not merely the ballot, but also "direct action"— violence. The anti-Chinese agitation in California, culminating as it did in the Exclusion Law passed by Congress in 1882, was doubtless the most important single factor in the history of American labor, for without it the entire country might have been overrun by Mongolian [sic] labor and *the labor movement might have become a conflict of races instead of one of classes.*[24]

More recent economic transformations in the US have also altered interpretations of racial identities and meanings. The automation of southern agriculture and the augmented labor demand of the postwar boom transformed blacks from a largely rural, impoverished labor force to a largely urban, working-class group by 1970.[25] When boom became bust and liberal welfare statism moved rightwards, the majority of blacks came to be seen, increasingly, as part of the "underclass," as state "dependents." Thus the particularly deleterious effects on blacks of global and national economic shifts (generally rising unemployment rates, changes in the employment structure away from reliance on labor intensive work, etc.) were explained once again in the late 1970s and 1980s (as they had been in the 1940s and mid-1960s) as the result of defective black cultural norms, of familial disorganization, etc.[26] In this way new racial attributions, new racial myths, are affixed to "blacks."[27] Similar changes in racial identity are presently affecting Asians and Latinos, as such economic forces as increasing Third World impoverishment and indebtedness fuel immigration and high interest rates, Japanese competition spurs resentments, and US jobs seem to fly away to Korea and Singapore.[28] . . .

Once we understand that race overflows the boundaries of skin color, superexploitation, social stratification, discrimination and prejudice, cultural domination and cultural resistance, state policy (or of any other particular social relationship we list), once we recognize the racial dimension present to some degree in every identity, institution, and social practice in the United States—once we have done this, it becomes possible to speak of *racial formation*. This recognition is hard-won; there is a continuous temptation to think of race as an *essence*, as something fixed, concrete and objective, as (for example) one of the categories just enumerated. And there is also an opposite temptation: to see it as a mere illusion, which an ideal social order would eliminate.

In our view it is crucial to break with these habits of thought. The effort must be made to understand race as *an unstable and "decentered" complex of social meanings constantly being transformed by political struggle.* . . .

NOTES

1. *San Francisco Chronicle,* 14 September 1982, 19 May 1983. Ironically, the 1970 Louisiana law was enacted to supersede an old Jim Crow statute which relied on the idea of "common report" in determining an infant's race. Following Phipps's unsuccessful attempt to change her classification and have the law declared unconstitutional, a legislative effort arose which culminated in the repeal of the law. See *San Francisco Chronicle,* 23 June 1983.

2. The Mormon church, for example, has been heavily criticized for its doctrine of black inferiority.

3. Thomas F. Gossett notes:

   Race theory . . . had up until fairly modern times no firm hold on European thought. On the other hand, race theory and race prejudice were by no means unknown at the time when the English colonists came to North America. Undoubtedly, the age of exploration led many to speculate on race differences at a period when neither Europeans nor Englishmen were prepared to make allowances for vast cultural diversities. Even though race theories had not then secured wide acceptance or even sophisticated formulation, the first contacts of the Spanish with the Indians in the Americas can now be recognized as the beginning of a struggle between conceptions of the nature of primitive peoples which has not yet been wholly settled. (Thomas F. Gossett, *Race: The History of an Idea in America* (New York: Schocken Books, 1965), p. 16.)

   Winthrop Jordan provides a detailed account of early European colonialists' attitudes about color and race in *White Over Black: American Attitudes Toward the Negro, 1550–1812* (New York: Norton, 1977 [1968]), pp. 3–43.

4. Pro-slavery physician Samuel George Morton (1799–1851) compiled a collection of 800 crania from all parts of the world which formed the sample for his studies of race. Assuming that the larger the size of the cranium translated into greater intelligence, Morton established a relationship between race and skull capacity. Gossett reports that:

   In 1849, one of his studies included the following results: The English skulls in his collection proved to be the largest, with an average cranial capacity of 96 cubic inches. The Americans and Germans were rather poor seconds, both with cranial capacities of 90 cubic inches. At the bottom of the list were the Negroes with 83 cubic inches, the Chinese with 82, and the Indians with 79. (Ibid., p. 74.)

On Morton's methods, see Stephen J. Gould, "The Finagle Factor," *Human Nature* (July 1978).

5. Definitions of race founded upon a common pool of genes have not held up when confronted by scientific research which suggests that the differences *within* a given human population are greater than those *between* populations. See L. L. Cavalli-Sforza, "The Genetics of Human Populations," *Scientific American* (September 1974), pp. 81–9.

6. Arthur Jensen, "How Much Can We Boost IQ and Scholastic Achievement?" *Harvard Educational Review*, vol. 39 (1969), pp. 1–123.

7. Ernst Moritz Manasse, "Max Weber on Race," *Social Research*, vol. 14 (1947), pp. 191–221.

8. Quoted in Edward D. C. Campbell, Jr., *The Celluloid South: Hollywood and the Southern Myth* (Knoxville: University of Tennessee Press, 1981), pp. 168–70.

9. Marvin Harris, *Patterns of Race in the Americas* (New York: Norton, 1964), p. 56.

10. Ibid., p. 57.

11. After James Meredith had been admitted as the first black student at the University of Mississippi, Harry S. Murphy announced that he, and not Meredith, was the first black student to attend "Ole Miss." Murphy described himself as black but was able to pass for white and spent nine months at the institution without attracting any notice (ibid., p. 56).

12. A. Sivanandan, "From Resistance to Rebellion: Asian and Afro-Caribbean Struggles in Britain," *Race and Class*, vol. 23, nos. 2–3 (Autumn–Winter 1981).

13. Consider the contradictions in racial status which abound in the country with the most rigidly defined racial categories—South Africa. There a race classification agency is employed to adjudicate claims for upgrading of official racial identity. This is particularly necessary for the "coloured" category. The apartheid system considers Chinese as "Asians" while the Japanese are accorded the status of "honorary whites." This logic nearly detaches race from any grounding in skin color and other physical attributes and nakedly exposes race as a juridical category subject to economic, social, and political influences. (We are indebted to Steve Talbot for clarification of some of these points.)

14. Gordon W. Allport, *The Nature of Prejudice* (Garden City, New York: Doubleday, 1958), pp. 184–200.

15. We wish to use this phrase loosely, without committing ourselves to a particular position on such social psychological approaches as symbolic interactionism, which are outside the scope of this study. An interesting study on this subject is S. M. Lyman and W. A. Douglass, "Ethnicity: Strategies of Individual and Collective Impression Management," *Social Research*, vol. 40, no. 2 (1973).

16. Michael Billig, "Patterns of Racism: Interviews with National Front Members," *Race and Class*, vol. 20, no. 2 (Autumn 1978), pp. 161–79.

17. "Miss San Antonio USA Lisa Fernandez and other Hispanics auditioning for a role in a television soap opera did not fit the Hollywood image of real Mexicans and had to darken their faces before filming." Model Aurora Garza said that their faces were bronzed with powder because they looked too white. "I'm a real Mexican [Garza said] and very dark anyway. I'm even darker right now because I have

a tan. But they kept wanting me to make my face darker and darker" (*San Francisco Chronicle,* 21 September 1984). A similar dilemma faces Asian American actors who feel that Asian character lead roles inevitably go to white actors who make themselves up to be Asian. Scores of Charlie Chan films, for example, have been made with white leads (the last one was the 1981 *Charlie Chan and the Curse of the Dragon Queen*). Roland Winters, who played in six Chan features, was asked by playwright Frank Chin to explain the logic of casting a white man in the role of Charlie Chan: "The only thing I can think of is, if you want to cast a homosexual in a show, and you get a homosexual, it'll be awful. It won't be funny . . . and maybe there's something there . . ." (Frank Chin, "Confessions of the Chinatown Cowboy," *Bulletin of Concerned Asian Scholars*, vol. 4, no. 3 (Fall 1972)).

18. Melanie Martindale-Sikes, "Nationalizing 'Nigger' Imagery Through 'Birth of a Nation'," paper prepared for the 73rd Annual Meeting of the American Sociological Association, 4–8 September 1978 in San Francisco.
19. Winthrop D. Jordan, op. cit., p. 95; emphasis added.
20. Historical focus has been placed either on particular racially defined groups or on immigration and the "incorporation" of ethnic groups. In the former case the characteristic ethnicity theory pitfalls and apologetics such as functionalism and cultural pluralism may be avoided, but only by sacrificing much of the focus on race. In the latter case, race is considered a manifestation of ethnicity.
21. The degree of antipathy for these groups should not be minimized. A northern commentator observed in the 1850s: "An Irish Catholic seldom attempts to rise to a higher condition than that in which he is placed, while the Negro often makes the attempt with success." Quoted in Gossett, op. cit., p. 288.
22. This analysis, as will perhaps be obvious, is essentially DuBoisian. Its main source will be found in the monumental (and still largely unappreciated) *Black Reconstruction in the United States 1860–1880* (New York: Atheneum, 1977 [1035]).
23. Alexander Saxton argues that:

    North Americans of European background have experienced three great racial confrontations: with the Indian, with the African, and with the Oriental. Central to each transaction has been a totally one-sided preponderance of power, exerted for the exploitation of nonwhites by the dominant white society. In each case (but especially in the two that began with systems of enforced labor), white workingmen have played a crucial, yet ambivalent role. They have been both exploited and exploiters. On the one hand, thrown into competition with nonwhites as enslaved or "cheap" labor, they suffered economically; on the other hand, being white, they benefited by that very exploitation which was compelling the nonwhites to work for low wages or for nothing. Ideologically they were drawn in opposite directions. *Racial identification cut at right angles to class consciousness.* (Alexander Saxton, *The Indispensable Enemy: Labor and the Anti-Chinese Movement in California* (Berkeley and Los Angeles: University of California Press, 1971), p. 1, emphasis added.)
24. Selig Perlman, *The History of Trade Unionism in the United States* (New York: Augustus Kelley, 1950), p. 52; emphasis added.
25. Whether Southern blacks were "peasants" or rural workers is unimportant in this context. Some time during the 1960s blacks attained a higher degree of urbanization than whites. Before World War II most blacks had been rural dwellers and nearly 80 percent lived in the South.

26. See George Gilder, *Wealth and Poverty* (New York: Basic Books, 1981); Charles Murray, *Losing Ground* (New York: Basic Books, 1984).
27. A brilliant study of the racialization process in Britain, focused on the rise of "mugging" as a popular fear in the 1970s, is Stuart Hall et al., *Policing the Crisis* (London: Macmillan, 1978).
28. The case of Vincent Chin, a Chinese American man beaten to death in 1982 by a laid-off Detroit auto worker and his stepson who mistook him for Japanese and blamed him for the loss of their jobs, has been widely publicized in Asian American communities. On immigration conflicts and pressures, see Michael Omi, "New Wave Dread: Immigration and Intra-Third World Conflict," *Socialist Review,* no. 60 (November–December 1981).

2

OPTIONAL ETHNICITIES
For Whites Only?

MARY C. WATERS

ETHNIC IDENTITY FOR WHITES IN THE 1990s

What does it mean to talk about ethnicity as an option for an individual? To argue that an individual has some degree of choice in their ethnic identity flies in the face of the common sense notion of ethnicity many of us believe in—that one's ethnic identity is a fixed characteristic, reflective of blood ties and given at birth. However, social scientists who study ethnicity have long concluded that while ethnicity is based in a *belief* in a common ancestry, ethnicity is primarily a *social* phenomenon, not a biological one (Alba 1985, 1990; Barth 1969; Weber [1921] 1968, p. 389). The belief that members of an ethnic group have that they share a common ancestry may not be a fact. There is a great deal of change in ethnic identities across generations through intermarriage, changing allegiances, and changing social categories. There is also a much larger amount of change in the identities of individuals over their life than is commonly believed. While most people are aware of the phenomenon known as "passing"—people raised as one race who change at some point

Waters, Mary C., "Optional Ethnicities: For Whites Only?" from Pedraza, Sylvia & Ruben G. Rumbaut (eds.), *Origins and Destinies.* Belmont, CA: Wadsworth Publishing Company, 1996. Reprinted with permission of Wadsworth, a division of Thomson Learning.

and claim a different race as their identity—there are similar life course changes in ethnicity that happen all the time and are not given the same degree of attention as "racial passing."

White Americans of European ancestry can be described as having a great deal of choice in terms of their ethnic identities. The two major types of options White Americans can exercise are (1) the option of whether to claim any specific ancestry, or to just be "White" or American (Lieberson [1985] called these people "unhyphenated Whites"), and (2) the choice of which of their European ancestries to choose to include in their description of their own identities. In both cases, the option of choosing how to present yourself on surveys and in everyday social interactions exists for Whites because of social changes and societal conditions that have created a great deal of social mobility, immigrant assimilation, and political and economic power for Whites in the United States. Specifically, the option of being able to not claim any ethnic identity exists for Whites of European background in the United States because they are the majority group—in terms of holding political and social power, as well as being a numerical majority. The option of choosing among different ethnicities in their family backgrounds exists because the degree of discrimination and social distance attached to specific European backgrounds has diminished over time.

The Ethnic Miracle

When European immigration to the United States was sharply curtailed in the late 1920s, a process was set in motion whereby the European ethnic groups already in the United States were for all intents and purposes cut off from any new arrivals. As a result, the composition of the ethnic groups began to age generationally. The proportion of each ethnic group made up of immigrants or the first generation began to gradually decline, and the proportion made up of the children, grandchildren, and eventually great-grandchildren began to increase. Consequently, by 1990 most European-origin ethnic groups in the United States were composed of a very small number of immigrants, and a very large proportion of people whose link to their ethnic origins in Europe was increasingly remote.

This generational change was accompanied by unprecedented social and economic changes. The very success of the assimilation process these groups experienced makes it difficult to imagine how much the question of the immigrants' eventual assimilation was an open one at the turn of the century. At the peak of immigration from southern and central Europe there was widespread discrimination and hostility against the newcomers by established Americans. Italians, Poles, Greeks, and Jews were called derogatory names, attacked by nativist mobs, and derided in the press. Intermarriage across ethnic lines was very uncommon—castelike in the words of some sociologists (Pagnini and Morgan 1990). The immigrants and their children were residentially segregated, occupationally specialized, and generally poor.

After several generations in the United States, the situation has changed a great deal. The success and social mobility of the grandchildren and great-grandchildren of that massive wave of immigrants from Europe has been called "The Ethnic Miracle" (Greeley 1976). These Whites have moved away from the inner-city ethnic ghettos to White middle-class suburban homes. They are doctors, lawyers, entertainers, academics, governors, and Supreme Court justices. But contrary to what some social science theorists and some politicians predicted or hoped for, these middle-class Americans have not completely given up ethnic identity. Instead, they have maintained some connection with their immigrant ancestors' identities—becoming Irish American doctors, Italian American Supreme Court justices, and Greek American presidential candidates. In the tradition of cultural pluralism, successful middle-class Americans in the late twentieth century maintain some degree of identity with their ethnic backgrounds. They have remained "hyphenated Americans." So while social mobility and declining discrimination have created the option of not identifying with any European ancestry, most White Americans continue to report some ethnic background.

With the growth in intermarriage among people of European ethnic origins, increasingly these people are of mixed ethnic ancestry. This gives them the option of which ethnicity to identify with. The U.S. census has asked a question on ethnic ancestry in the 1980 and 1990 censuses. In 1980, 52 percent of the American public responded with a single ethnic ancestry, 31 percent gave multiple ethnic origins (up to three were coded, but some individuals wrote in more than three), and only 6 percent said they were American only, while the remaining 11 percent gave no response. In 1990 about 90 percent of the population gave some response to the ancestry question, with only 5 percent giving American as a response and only 1.4 percent reporting an uncodeable response such as "don't know" (McKenney and Cresce 1992; U.S. Bureau of the Census 1992).

Several researchers have examined the pattern of responses of people to the census ancestry question. These analyses have shown a pattern of flux and inconsistency in ethnic ancestry reporting. For instance, Lieberson and Waters (1986, 1988, p. 93) have found that parents simplify children's ancestries when reporting them to the census. For instance, among the offspring in situations where one parent reports a specific single White ethnic origin and the other parent reports a different single White origin, about 40 percent of the children are not described as the logical combination of the parents' ancestries. For example, only about 60 percent of the children of English-German marriages are labeled as English-German or German-English. About 15 percent of the children of these parents are simplified to just English, and another 15 percent are reported as just German. The remainder of the children are either not given an ancestry or are described as American (Lieberson and Waters 1986, 1993).

In addition to these intergenerational changes, researchers have found changes in reporting ancestry that occur at the time of marriage or upon leaving home. At the ages of eighteen to twenty-two, when many young Americans leave home for the first time, the number of people reporting a single as opposed to a multiple ancestry goes up. Thus while parents simplify children's ancestries when they leave home, children themselves tend to report less complexity in their ancestries when they leave their parents' homes and begin reporting their ancestries themselves (Lieberson and Waters 1986, 1988; Waters 1990).

These individual changes are reflected in variability over time in the aggregate numbers of groups determined by the census and surveys. Fairly (1991) compared the consistency of the overall counts of different ancestry groups in the 1979 Current Population Survey, the 1980 census, and the 1986 National Content Test (a pretest for the 1990 census). He found much less consistency in the numbers for northern European ancestry groups whose immigration peaks were early in the nineteenth century—the English, Dutch, Germans, and other northern European groups. In other words each of these different surveys and the census yielded a different estimate of the number of people having this ancestry. The 1990 census also showed a great deal of flux and inconsistency in some ancestry groups. The number of people reporting English as an ancestry went down considerably from 1980, while the number reporting German ancestry went up. The number of Cajuns grew dramatically. This has led officials at the Census Bureau to assume that the examples used in the instructions strongly influence the responses people give. (Cajun was one of the examples of an ancestry given in 1990 but not in 1980, and German was the first example given. English was an example in the 1980 instructions, but not in 1990.)

All of these studies point to the socially variable nature of ethnic identity—and the lack of equivalence between ethnic ancestry and identity. If merely adding a category to the instructions to the question increases the number of people claiming that ancestry, what does that mean about the level of importance of that identity for people answering the census? Clearly identity and ancestry for Whites in the United States, who increasingly are from mixed backgrounds, involve some change and choice.

Symbolic Ethnicities for White Americans

What do these ethnic identities mean to people and why do they cling to them rather than just abandoning the tie and calling themselves American? My own field research with suburban Whites in California and Pennsylvania found that later-generation descendants of European origin maintain what are called "symbolic ethnicities." Symbolic ethnicity is a term coined by Herbert Gans (1979) to refer to ethnicity that is individualistic in nature and without real social cost for the individual. These symbolic identifications are essentially leisure time activities, rooted in nuclear family traditions and reinforced by the voluntary enjoyable aspects of being ethnic (Waters 1990). Richard Alba (1990) also found later-generation Whites in Albany, New York, who chose to keep a tie with an ethnic identity because of the enjoyable and voluntary aspects to those identities, along with the feelings of specialness they entailed. An example of symbolic ethnicity is individuals who identify as Irish, for example, on occasions such as Saint Patrick's Day, on family holidays, or for vacations. They do not usually belong to Irish American organizations, live in Irish neighborhoods, work in Irish jobs, or marry other Irish people. The symbolic meaning of being Irish American can be constructed by individuals from mass media images, family traditions, or other intermittent social activities. In other words, for later-generation White ethnics, ethnicity is not something that influences their lives unless they want it to. In the world of work and school and neighborhood, individuals do not have to admit to being ethnic unless they choose to. And for an increasing number of European-origin individuals whose parents and grandparents have intermarried, the ethnicity they claim is largely a matter of personal choice as they sort through all of the possible combinations of groups in their genealogies.

Individuals can choose those aspects of being Italian, for instance, that appeal to them, and discard those that do not. Or a person whose father is Italian, and mother part Polish and part French, might choose among the three ethnicities and present herself as a Polish American. With just a little probing, many people will describe a variety of ancestries in their family background, but do not consider these ancestries to be a salient part of their own identities. Thus the 1990 census ancestry question, which estimated that 30 percent of the population is of mixed ancestry, most surely underestimates the degree of mixing among the population. My research, and the research of Richard Alba (1990), shows that many people have already sorted through what they know of their ethnic ancestries and simplified their responses before they ever answer a census or survey question (Waters 1990).

But note that this freedom to include or exclude ancestries in your identification to yourself and others would not be the same for those defined racially in our society. They are constrained to identify with the part of their ancestry that has been socially defined as the "essential" part. African Americans, for example, have been highly socially constrained to identify as Blacks, without other options available to them, even when they know that their forebears included many people of American Indian or European background. Up until the mid-twentieth century, many state governments had specific laws defining one as Black if as little as one-thirty-second of one's ancestors were defined as Black (Davis 1991; Dominguez 1986; Spickard 1989). Even now when the one-drop rule has been dropped from our legal codes, there are still strong societal pressures on African Americans to identify in a particular way. Certain ancestries take precedence over others in the societal rules on descent and ancestry reckoning. If one believes one is part English and part German and identifies in a survey as German, one is not in danger of being accused of trying to "pass" as non-English and of being "redefined" English by the interviewer. But if one were part African and part German, one's self-identification as German would be highly suspect and probably not accepted if one "looked" Black according to the prevailing social norms.

This is reflected in the ways the census collects race and ethnic identity. While the ethnic ancestry question used in 1980 and 1990 is given to all Americans in the sample regardless of race and allows multiple responses that combine races, the primary source of information on people defined racially in the United States is the census race question or the Hispanic question. Both of these questions require a person to make a choice about an identity. Individuals are not allowed to respond that they are both Black and White, or Japanese and Asian Indian on the race question even if they know that is their background. In fact, people who disobey the instructions to the census race question and check off two races are assigned to the first checked race in the list by the Census Bureau.

In responding to the ancestry question, the comparative latitude that White respondents have does not mean that Whites pick and choose ethnicities out of thin air. For the most part people choose an identity that corresponds with some element of their family tree. However, there are many anecdotal instances of people adopting ethnicities when they marry or move to a strongly identified neighborhood or community. For instance Micaela di Leonardo (1984) reported instances of non-Italian women who married into Italian American families and "became Italian." Karen Leonard (1992) describes a community of Mexican American women who married Punjabi immigrants in California. Some of the Punjabi immigrants and their descendants were said to have "become Mexican" when they joined their wives' kin group and social worlds. Alternatively she describes the community acknowledging that Mexican women made the best curry, as they adapted to life with Indian-origin men.

But what do these identities mean to individuals? Surely an identity that is optional in a number of ways—not legally defined on a passport or birth certificate, not socially consequential in terms of societal discrimination in terms of housing or job access, and not economically limiting in terms of blocking opportunities for social mobility—cannot be the same as an identity that results from and is nurtured by societal exclusion and rejection. The choice to have a symbolic ethnicity is an attractive and widespread one despite its lack of demonstrable content, because having a symbolic ethnicity combines individuality with feelings of community. People reported to me that they liked having an ethnic identity because it gave them a uniqueness and a feeling of being special. They often contrasted their own specialness by virtue of their ethnic identities with "bland" Americanness. Being ethnic makes people feel unique and special and not just "vanilla" as one of my respondents put it.

Because "American" is largely understood by Americans to be a political identity and allegiance and not an ethnic one, the idea of being "American" does not give people the same sense of belonging that their hyphenated American identity does. When I asked people about their dual identities— American and Irish or Italian or whatever—they usually responded in a way that showed how they conceived of the relationship between the two identities. Being an American was their primary identity; but it was so primary that they rarely, if ever, thought about it—most commonly only when they left the country. Being Irish American, on the other hand, was a way they had of differentiating themselves from others whom they interacted with from day to day—in many cases from spouses or in-laws. Certain of their traits—being emotional, having a sense of humor, talking with their hands—were understood as stemming from their ethnicity. Yet when asked about their identity as Americans, that identity was both removed from their day-to-day consciousness and understood in terms of loyalty and patriotism. Although they may not think they behave or think in a certain way because they are American, being American is something they are both proud of and committed to.

Symbolic ethnicity is the best of all worlds for these respondents. These White ethnics can claim to be unique and special, while simultaneously finding the community and conformity with others that they also crave. But that "community" is of a type that will not interfere with a person's individuality. It is not as if these people belong to ethnic voluntary organizations or gather as a group in churches or neighborhoods or union halls. They work and reside within the mainstream of American middle-class life, yet they retain the interesting benefits—the "specialness"—of ethnic allegiance, without any of its drawbacks.

It has been suggested by several researchers that this positive value attached to ethnic ancestry, which became popular in the ethnic revival of the 1970s, is the result of assimilation having proceeded to an advanced stage for descendants of White Europeans (Alba 1985; Crispino 1980; Steinberg 1981). Ironically, people celebrate and embrace their ethnic backgrounds precisely because assimilation has proceeded to the point where such identification does not have that much influence on their day-to-day life. Rather than choosing the "least ethnic" and most bland ethnicities, Whites desire the "most ethnic" ones, like the once-stigmatized "Italian," because it is perceived as bringing the most psychic benefits. For instance, when an Italian father is married to an English or a Scottish or a German mother, the likelihood is that the child will be reported to the census with the father's Italian ancestry, rather than the northern European ancestries, which would have been predicted to have a higher social status. Italian is a good ancestry to have, people told me, because they have good food and a warm family life. This change in the social meaning of being Italian American is quite dramatic, given that Italians were subject to discrimination, exclusion, and extreme negative stereotyping in the early part of the twentieth century.

RACE RELATIONS AND SYMBOLIC ETHNICITY

However much symbolic ethnicity is without cost for the individual, there is a cost associated with symbolic ethnicity for the society. That is because symbolic ethnicities of the type described here are confined to White Americans of European origin. Black Americans, Hispanic Americans, Asian Americans, and American Indians do not have the option of a symbolic ethnicity at present in the United States. For all of the ways in which ethnicity does not matter for White Americans, it does matter for non-Whites. Who your ancestors are does affect your choice of spouse, where you live, what job you have, who your friends are, and what your chances are for success in American society, if those ancestors happen not to be from Europe. The reality is that White ethnics have a lot more choice and room to maneuver than they themselves think they do. The situation is very different for members of racial minorities, whose lives are strongly influenced by their race or national origin regardless of how much they may choose not to identify themselves in terms of their ancestries.

When White Americans learn the stories of how their grandparents and great-grandparents triumphed in the United States over adversity, they are usually told in terms of their individual efforts and triumphs. The important role of labor unions and other organized political and economic actors in their social and economic successes is left out of the story in favor of a generational story of individual Americans rising up against communitarian, Old World intolerance and New World resistance. As a result, the "individualized" voluntary, cultural view of ethnicity for Whites is what is remembered.

One important implication of these identities is that they tend to be very individualistic. There is a tendency to view valuing diversity in a pluralist environment as equating all groups. The symbolic ethnic tends to think that all groups are equal; everyone has a background that is their right to celebrate and pass on to their children. This leads to the conclusion that all identities are equal and all identities in some sense are interchangeable—"I'm Italian American, you're Polish American. I'm Irish American, you're African American." The important thing is to treat people as individuals and all equally. However, this assumption ignores the very big difference between an individualistic symbolic ethnic identity and a socially enforced and imposed racial identity. When White Americans equate their own symbolic ethnicities with the socially enforced identities of non-White Americans, they obscure the fact that the experiences of Whites and non-Whites have been qualitatively different in the United States and that the current identities of individuals partly reflect that unequal history.

In the next section I describe how relations between Black and White students on college campuses reflect some of these asymmetries in the understanding of what a racial or ethnic identity means. While I focus on Black and White students in the following discussion, you should be aware that the myriad other groups in the United States—Mexican Americans, American Indians, Japanese Americans—all have some degree of social and individual influences on their identities, which reflect the group's social and economic history and present circumstance.

Relations on College Campuses

Both Black and White students face the task of developing their race and ethnic identities. Sociologists and psychologists note that at the time people leave home and begin to live independently from their parents, often ages eighteen to twenty-two, they report a heightened sense of racial and ethnic identity as they sort through how much of their beliefs and behaviors are idiosyncratic to their families and how much are shared with other people. It is not until one comes in close contact with many people who are different from oneself that individuals realize the ways in which their backgrounds may influence their individual personality. This involves coming into contact with people who are different in terms of their ethnicity, class, religion, region, and race. For White students, the ethnicity they claim is more often than not a symbolic one—with all of the voluntary, enjoyable, and intermittent characteristics I have described above.

Black students at the university are also developing identities through interactions with others who are different from them. Their identity development is more complicated than that of Whites because of the added element of racial discrimination and racism, along with the "ethnic" developments of finding others who share their background. Thus Black students have the positive attraction of being around other Black students who share some cultural elements, as well as the need to band together with other students in a reactive and oppositional way in the face of racist incidents on campus.

Colleges and universities across the country have been increasing diversity among their student bodies in the last few decades. This had led in many cases to strained relations among students from different racial and ethnic backgrounds. The 1980s and 1990s produced a great number of racial incidents and high racial tensions on campuses. While there were a number of racial incidents that were due to bigotry, unlawful behavior, and violent or vicious attacks, much of what happens among students on campuses involves a low level of tension and awkwardness in social interactions.

Many Black students experience racism personally for the first time on campus. The upper-middle-class students from White suburbs were often isolated enough that their presence was not threatening to racists in their high schools. Also, their class background was known by their residence and this may have prevented attacks being directed at them. Often Black students at the university who begin talking with other students and recognizing racial slights will remember incidents that happened to them earlier that they might not have thought were related to race.

Black college students across the country experience a sizeable number of incidents that are clearly the result of racism. Many of the most blatant ones that occur between students are the result of drinking. Sometimes late at night, drunken groups of White students coming home from parties will yell slurs at single Black students on the street. The other types of incidents that happen include being singled out for special treatment by employees, such as being followed when shopping at the campus bookstore, or going to the art museum with your class and the guard stops you and asks for your I.D. Others involve impersonal encounters on the street—being called a nigger by a truck driver while crossing the street, or seeing old ladies clutch their pocketbooks and shake in terror as you pass them on the street. For the most part these incidents are not specific to the university environment; they are the types of incidents middle-class Blacks face everyday throughout American society, and they have been documented by sociologists (Feagin 1991).

In such a climate, however, with students experiencing these types of incidents and talking with each other about them, Black students do experience a tension and a feeling of being singled out. It is unfair that this is part of their college experience and not that of White students. Dealing with incidents like this, or the ever-present threat of such incidents, is an ongoing developmental task for Black students that takes energy, attention, and strength of character. It should be clearly understood that this is an asymmetry in the "college experience" for Black and White students. It is one of the unfair aspects of life that results from living in a society with ongoing racial prejudice and discrimination. It is also very understandable that it makes some students angry at the unfairness of it all, even if there is no one to blame specifically. It is also very troubling because, while most Whites do not create these incidents, some do, and it is never clear until you know someone well whether they are the type of person who could do something like this. So one of the reactions of Black students to these incidents is to band together.

In some sense then, as Blauner (1992) has argued, you can see Black students coming together on campus as both an "ethnic" pull of wanting to be together to share common experiences and community, and a "racial" push of banding together defensively because of perceived rejection and tension from Whites. In this way the ethnic identities of Black students are in some sense similar to, say, Korean students wanting to be together to share experiences. And it is an ethnicity that is generally much stronger than, say, Italian Americans. But for Koreans who come together there is generally a definition of themselves as "different from" Whites. For Blacks reacting to exclusion, there is a tendency for the coming together to involve both being "different from" but also "opposed to" Whites.

The anthropologist John Ogbu (1990) has documented the tendency of minorities in a variety of societies around the world, who have experienced severe blocked mobility for long periods of time, to develop such oppositional identities. An important component of having such an identity is to describe others of your group who do not join in the group solidarity as devaluing and denying their very core identity. This is why it is not common for successful Asians to be accused by others of "acting White" in the United States, but it is quite common for such a term to be used by Blacks and Latinos. The oppositional component of a Black identity also explains how Black people can question whether others are acting "Black enough." On campus, it explains some of the intense pressures felt by Black students who do not make their racial identity central and who choose to hang out primarily with non-Blacks. This pressure from the group, which is partly defining itself by not being White, is exacerbated by the fact that race is a physical marker in American society. No one immediately notices the Jewish students sitting together in the dining hall, or the one Jewish student sitting surrounded by non-Jews, or the Texan sitting with the Californians, but everyone notices the Black student who is or is not at the "Black table" in the cafeteria.

Institutional Responses

Our society asks a lot of young people. We ask young people to do something that no one else does as successfully on such a wide scale—that is to live together with people from very different backgrounds, to respect one another, to appreciate one another, and to enjoy and learn from one another. The successes that occur every day in this endeavor are many, and they are too often overlooked. However, the problems and tensions are also real, and they will not vanish on their own. We tend to see pluralism working in the United States in much the same way some people expect capitalism to work. If you put together people with various interests and abilities and resources, the "invisible hand" of capitalism is supposed to make all the parts work together in an economy for the common good.

There is much to be said for such a model—the invisible hand of the market can solve complicated problems of production and distribution better than any "visible hand" of a state plan. However, we have learned that unequal power relations among the actors in the capitalist marketplace, as well as "externalities" that the market cannot account for, such as long-term pollution, or collusion between corporations, or the exploitation of child labor, means that state regulation is often needed. Pluralism and the relations between groups are very similar. There is a lot to be said for the idea that bringing people who belong to different ethnic or racial groups together in institutions with no interference will have good consequences. Students from different backgrounds will make friends if they share a dorm room or corridor, and there is no need for the institution to do any more than provide the locale. But like capitalism, the invisible hand of pluralism does not do well when power relations and externalities are ignored. When you bring together individuals from groups that are differentially valued in the wider society and provide no guidance, there will be problems. In these cases the "invisible hand" of pluralist relations does not work, and tensions and disagreements can arise without any particular individual or group of individuals being "to blame." On college campuses in the 1990s some of the tensions between students are of this sort. They arise from honest misunderstandings, lack of a common background, and very different experiences of what race and ethnicity mean to the individual.

The implications of symbolic ethnicities for thinking about race relations are subtle but consequential. If your understanding or your own ethnicity and its relationship to society and politics is one of individual choice, it becomes harder to understand the need for programs like affirmative action, which recognize the ongoing need for group struggle and group recognition, in order to bring about social change. It also is hard for a White college student to understand the need that minority students feel to band together against discrimination. It also is easy, on the individual level, to expect everyone else to be able to turn their ethnicity on and off at will, the way you are able to, without understanding that ongoing discrimination and societal attention to minority status makes that impossible for individuals from minority groups to do. The paradox of symbolic ethnicity is that it depends upon the ultimate goal of a pluralist society, and at the same time makes it more difficult to achieve that ultimate goal. It is dependent upon the concept that all ethnicities mean the same thing, that enjoying the traditions of one's heritage is an option available to a group or an individual, but that such a heritage should not have any social costs associated with it.

There are many societal issues and involuntary ascriptions associated with non-White identities. The developments necessary for this to change are not individual but societal in nature. Social mobility and declining racial and ethnic sensitivity are closely associated. The legacy and the present reality of discrimination on the basis of race or ethnicity must be overcome before the ideal of the pluralist society, where all heritages are treated equally and are equally available for individuals to choose or discard at will, is realized.

REFERENCES

Alba, Richard D. 1985. *Italian Americans: Into the Twilight of Ethnicity.* Edgewood Cliffs, NJ: Prentice-Hall.

———. 1990. *Ethnic Identity: The Transformation of White America.* New Haven, CT: Yale University Press.

Barth, Frederik. 1969. *Ethnic Groups and Boundaries.* Boston: Little, Brown.

Blauner, Robert. 1992. "Talking Past Each Other: Black and White Languages of Race." *American Prospect* (Summer):55–64

Crispino, James. 1980. *The Assimilation of Ethnic Groups: The Italian Case.* Staten Island, NY: Center for Migration Studies.

di Leonardo, Micaela. 1984. *The Varieties of Ethnic Experience: Kinship, Class and Gender Among Italian Americans.* Ithaca, NY: Cornell University Press.

Dominguez, Virginia. 1986. *White by Definition: Social Classification in Creole Louisiana.* New Brunswick, NJ: Rutgers University Press.

Fairly, Reynolds. 1991. "The New Census Questions about Ancestry: What Did It Tell Us?" *Demography* 28:411–29.

Feagin, Joe R. 1991. "The Continuing Significance of Race: Antiblack Discrimination in Public Places." *American Sociological Review* 56:101–117.

Gans, Herbert. 1979. "Symbolic Ethnicity: The Future of Ethnic Groups and Cultures in America." *Ethnic and Racial Studies* 2:1–20.

Greeley, Andrew M. 1976. "The Ethnic Miracle." *Public Interest* 45 (Fall):20–36.

Leonard, Karen. 1992. *Making Ethnic Choices: California's Punjabi Mexican Americans.* Philadelphia: Temple University Press.

Lieberson, Stanley. 1985. "Unhyphenated Whites in the United States." *Ethnic and Racial Studies* 8:159–80.

Lieberson, Stanley, and Mary Waters, 1986. "Ethnic Groups in Flux: The Changing Ethnic Responses of American Whites." *Annals of the American Academy of Political and Social Science* 487:79–91.

———. 1988. *From Many Strands: Ethnic and Racial Groups in Contemporary America.* New York: Russell Sage.

———. 1993. "The Ethnic Responses of Whites: What Causes Their Instability, Simplification, and Inconsistency?" *Social Forces* 72(2):421–50.

McKenney, Nampeo R., and Arthur R. Cresce. 1992. "Measurement of Ethnicity in the United States: Experiences of the U.S. Census Bureau." Paper presented at the Joint Canada–United States Conference on the Measurement of Ethnicity, Ottawa, Canada, April 1–3.

Spickard, Paul R. 1989. *Mixed Blood.* Madison: University of Wisconsin Press.

Steinberg, Stephen. 1981. *The Ethnic Myth: Race, Ethnicity, and Class in America.* Boston: Beacon Press.

U.S. Bureau of the Census. 1992. *Census of Population and Housing, 1990: Detailed Ancestry Groups for States.* Supplementary Reports CP-S-1-2. Washington, D.C.: U.S. Government Printing Office.

Waters, Mary C. 1990. *Ethnic Options: Choosing Identities in America.* Berkeley and Los Angeles: University of California Press.

Weber, Max. 1921. *Economy and Society: An Outline of Interpretive Sociology,* edited by Guenther Roth and Claus Wittich, translated by Ephraim Fischoff. New York: Bedminster Press.

3

"THEY ARE ABSOLUTELY OBSESSED WITH US"
Anti-Arab Bias in American Discourse and Policy

HUSSEIN IBISH

The persistent negative stereotyping of Arabs in American popular culture has been so often lamented that when discussing this subject one becomes, ironically, hostage to the oxymoron of a cliché which has had no cultural impact. The key industries of American mass culture, Hollywood and television, for decades have been bastions of anti-Arab stereotyping, and have consistently resisted positive or realistic representations of Arabs and

From: Stokes, Curtis; Theresa Melendez; and Genice Rhodes-Reed (eds.). 2001. *Race in 21st Century America.* East Lansing, MI: Michigan State University Press.

Arab Americans. Negative representations in popular culture reinforce, and are reinforced by, biased and at times hostile journalism in the mainstream news media, academic polemics that urge a confrontational and aggressive approach to the U.S. role in the Middle East, and government programs and policies that are informed by anti-Arab bias and at times even involve the acting out of stereotypes received from popular culture. The result is a self-perpetuating vicious cycle of negativity about Arabs, Arab Americans, and Muslims, who have been all-too-successfully represented and accepted as "the enemy" in contemporary American culture. Thus, even as these stereotypes are increasingly critiqued and demystified by cultural observers, they retain their ubiquity and resulting negative impact on American relations with the Arab peoples and the circumstances for Arab Americans and Arabs living in the United States.

The positioning of the Arab as the "other" of contemporary American society ought, at the outset, to be viewed as an example, albeit a particularly egregious one, of what can be regarded as the universal political function of distinguishing self from other. Politically, the process of "othering" creates the boundaries that define group identity and allow for collective action. Definition of the self in terms of the other is a fundamental prerequisite of ideology, without which rationalization for collective social action is virtually impossible. Whether identified in class terms (i.e., the bourgeoisie), in religious terms (i.e., Jews or Muslims), or in ethnic terms, the other against which the collectivity is defined is a ubiquitous feature of political thought and action. As Ali A. Mazrui puts it, "The 'us' versus 'them' tendency is, in the political arena, almost universal."[1] This process is not arbitrary, and when we see it at work it is answering a specific sociopolitical demand. In American national ideology the other has variously consisted of savage Indians, tyrannical English, corrupt Mexicans, treacherous Confederates, decadent Spaniards, baby-killing Germans, fiendish Japanese, the Evil Empire of World Communism, and now the Green Menace of radical Islam. The need for a demonic common enemy has been most strikingly satisfied when "national interest" has required an ideological and emotional rationale, as in the examples cited previously. The ideological demand, and concomitant public appetite, for a vilified national enemy makes the task of the propagandist under such circumstances one of the simplest social functions—one can hardly fail to engender the requisite loathing to satisfy the ideological demand, no matter how crude, preposterous, or incompetent the defamatory representation of the enemy is. Hence, stereotyping is also strongly linked to "bad art," since it provides a most convenient shortcut for the lazy and unimaginative cultural worker in search of villains. . . .

The phenomenon of anti-Arab representation in American culture, the othering of the Arab American and the Arab world, especially popular culture, is undoubtedly overdetermined: it would be virtually impossible to single out a discrete locus for these negative representations, and any attempt to do so is bound to be an exercise in oversimplification. There are, however, a number of important factors in the equation that demand investigation and acknowledgment. As has been demonstrated at length by Edward Said and Michael Suleiman, among others, contemporary bias against Arabs in the United States draws heavily on a longstanding Western antipathy for its Islamic rival.[2] Orientalism and its antecedents laid the groundwork and set in place most of the basic stereotypes that inform our current anti-Arab prejudices. As Michael Suleiman has pointed out, this generalized inheritance from Western culture has combined with several more specifically American ideas to create especially favorable conditions for the positive reception of anti-Arab stereotypes in the American psyche. These particular American tendencies, as Suleiman demonstrates, include "a greater emphasis on the Bible as a literal representation of what happened in the Middle East" in ancient times, the identification of the contemporary Arab people with those peoples of the biblical Middle East who are cast as villains or the enemies of God and the Hebrews, and an identification of many of the Puritan founders of early American society with the ancient Israelites.[3] In this century, Zionists have astutely reversed this identification, casting themselves in the role of the pioneers battling a hostile natural environment and hostile indigenous savages to bring bounty and civilization to a barren land. Thus the Arab in general, and the Palestinian in particular, becomes identified with the Native American. For example, during the 1991 Gulf War, Iraqi-held territory was routinely referred to as "Indian country" by American military personnel.[4] Interestingly, the celebrated Palestinian poet Mahmoud Darwish has also embraced this identification between Arabs, especially Palestinians, and Native Americans, but from the perspective of colonial victim rather than colonial hero. Such specifically American orientations have promoted the development of a particularly negative image of the Arab in the United States during the twentieth century.

As our model of the othering process anticipates, the emergence of this exceptionally negative image has been clearly linked to political developments during the past fifty years, in particular the tension between competing American ambitions for dominance in the Middle East and Arab ambitions for greater independence from Western influence, as well as the problem of Zionism and colonialism in Palestine. As the power of Britain and France waned in the years following the Second World War, the colonial baton in the Middle East was gradually passed from these old imperial powers to the United States. American interest in controlling the oil resources of the Persian Gulf has never been a secret or the subject of any sustained denial. This interest has repeatedly placed United States foreign policy at odds with political movements that express the aspirations of millions of Arabs, such as Arab nationalism or, more recently, revolutionary Islamism. Since the early part of this century, Arab nationalism has emphasized a break with Western powers and influence, a greater Arab unity and independence, and, of course, control of the natural resources of the Middle East, above all, oil. This anti-colonial orientation of Arab nationalism was, both in general and at specific moments of crisis, incompatible with the neocolonial role the United States aspired to play in the Arab world, especially the Persian Gulf region and Iran. Thus the United States repeatedly found itself at odds with Arab nationalist movements and regimes, and some of the leading "villains" in the American worldview of past decades include prominent secular Arab nationalist leaders such as Gamal Abdel Nasser, Yassir Arafat, Muammar Qaddafi, and Saddam Hussein. More recently, the rise of revolutionary Islamist movements, as secular Arab nationalism is increasingly regarded as both a proven failure and an inauthentic mimicry of Western political movements, has created a new set of enemies in the American worldview. Islamism in the Arab world received a significant boost from the Iranian revolution and the successful "jihad" against the Soviet Union in Afghanistan, which suggested that both neocolonial superpowers could be successfully ousted from Muslim lands. The status and influence of Islamist movements continue to develop in many parts of the Arab world and, much as Arab nationalism had before it, sets itself against Western influence, both cultural and political, in the Middle East. Islamists, including Ayatollah Khomeini, the leaders of Hamas and Hizbullah, and Osama Bin Laden, have emerged in recent years as the quintessential international villains in the American perspective.

A second major factor in the development of the heightened form of anti-Arab prejudice in contemporary American thought is the Zionist movement and its highly successful propaganda campaign to cast Arabs in general and Palestinians in particular as the villains in the Arab-Israeli conflict. Against the cultural and political background described previously, and operating for decades without significant challenge or critique, the Zionist movement portrayed Arab resistance to the establishment of an ethnically cleansed colonial settler-state in Palestine as a function of Arab fanaticism, intolerance, and anti-Semitism (a theme I shall investigate further). Pro-Israeli propaganda ("hasbara"), particularly emanating from Hollywood and certain forms of extremely biased journalism, has played a major role in casting the Arab in his or her most insidious stereotype—that of the terrorist. This is without question the dominant and most damaging, not to mention unwarranted, image of the Arab in contemporary American culture. It is so pervasive that Arabs are easily and arbitrarily blamed by irresponsible journalists and politicians for events that they have had nothing to do with, such as the bombing of the Federal Building in Oklahoma City or the crash of TWA Flight 800. Ironically, although it has been clearly established that Arabs were not involved in these events, the effect has not been to expose the fallacy at the heart of the stereotypes that gave rise to the error, but rather to reinforce an irrational and semi-conscious identification between Arabs and terrorism. The two remain as firmly linked in the cultural landscape as ever and expressions of surprise that Arabs were not responsible for such acts in effect reiterated the stereotypes that produced the rushes to judgment. Thus the Arab remains the quintessential "terrorist" and, in cultural terms, continues to bear a measure of guilt for these events, since these tragedies look like the kind of things for which Arabs are believed to be typically responsible. So insidious are the processes reinforcing these associations that papers such as this one, which attempt to debunk the stereotypes, may ironically have the subtle effect of further solidifying the association between Arabs and terrorism. The "I am not a terrorist" discourse so prevalent among Arab Americans in this sense falls into a trap not unlike that set in the proverbial "candidate's nightmare" question, "when are you going to stop beating your wife?," a question for which there can be no constructive answer. Until we develop an alternative discourse, however, Arab Americans are going to remain in what may well be the self-defeating position I am taking here, of calling attention to the stereotypes by analyzing and objecting to them.

These associations are most damagingly propagated by a widespread but particularly insidious form of "journalism" which makes a fetish out of an alleged connection between Islam, traditional Arab culture, and terrorism, and which is calculated to spread fear and hatred of Arabs and Islam. The worst work of this kind has been done by Steven Emerson, who has argued that almost all major Arab and Muslim organizations in the United States are fronts for or supporters of "terrorist groups." His 1994 television documentary, *Jihad in America,* which was widely broadcast by PBS, advanced the dubious and unsubstantiated thesis that there was an extensive fund-raising network in the United States for "Middle Eastern terrorists." Consisting of little more than innuendo, guilt by association, and unsubstantiated allegations, *Jihad in America* has come to be regarded by many professional journalists as an embarrassing piece of fear-mongering, akin in tone and substance to Red-baiting screeds of the McCarthy era. Yet the atmosphere in the immediate aftermath of the World Trade Center bombing was such that "Jihad in America" won the prestigious Polk Award for Excellence in Journalism. In retrospect, respected journalists like Robert Freidman have accused Emerson of attempting to "create mass hysteria against American Arabs."[5] Emerson has been quick to point the finger at Arabs for any number of tragedies and disasters, publicly blaming Arabs for the bombing of the Federal Building in Oklahoma City and for the crash of TWA Flight 800. Emerson, then a CBS News consultant, told the nation that the 1995 Oklahoma City bombing exhibited "a Middle Eastern trait," insofar as it "was done with the intent to inflict as many casualties as possible."[6] In spite of his penchant for false accusation and wild statements, such as his 1994 claim that the aim of pro-Palestinian Muslims in the United States was the "mass murder of all Jews, Christians, and moderate Muslims," and his well-documented links with Israeli intelligence operatives and right-wing ideologues, Emerson is still called upon as a "terrorism expert" by some of the major American media.[7] Emerson's work is merely the most egregious example of this kind of Arab-bashing, which is by no means unusual in contemporary American journalism.

As Emerson's work has become increasingly discredited, much of the anti-Arab tone and substance of his work has been taken up by one of his former employers, Daniel Pipes, director of the Philadelphia-based pro-Israel

Middle East Forum. Like Emerson, Pipes was quick to blame Arabs and Muslims for the bombing of the Oklahoma City Federal Building. Pipes told *USA Today* on the day after the bombing that "the West is under attack. . . . People need to understand that this is just the beginning. The fundamentalists are on the upsurge, and they make it very clear that they are targeting us. They are absolutely obsessed with us."[8] In the *New York Post,* Pipes dismissed the very identity of the Palestinian people by arguing that three of the most prominent Palestinians, Yassir Arafat, Edward Said, and George Antonius, were never Palestinians at all, and that they had "decided at various points in the 20th century—the 1920s, 1950s, 1970s—to become Palestinians." Far from a national identity, Pipes concludes, "Being Palestinian, in other words, is a good career move."[9] In the *Los Angeles Times,* Pipes claimed that most American Muslim organizations "aspire to make the United States a Muslim country, perhaps along the Iranian or Sudanese models." Echoing Emerson's dark conspiracy theories from *Jihad in America,* Pipes warns that "Some of this ilk even talk about overthrowing the U.S. government and replacing it with an Islamic one. Although it sounds bizarre, this attitude attracts serious and widespread support among Muslims, some of whom debate whether peaceful means are sufficient or whether violence is a necessary option."[10] Pipes also claims that the overwhelming majority of Muslims harbor intense anti-Jewish beliefs. In the right-wing magazine *Commentary,* for example, Pipes alleged that "At huge conventions closed to the press and public, in speeches and publications that tend to be couched in the historic Muslim languages rather than in English, nearly every Muslim organization in the United States—emphatically including those that carefully maintain a proper demeanor for public, English-language consumption—spews forth a blatant and vicious anti-Semitism, a barrage of bias, calumny, and conspiracy mongering of a sort that has otherwise all but disappeared from American discourse."[11] Ironically, Pipes, whose stock in trade is conspiracy theories about fabricated Palestinian identities and Islamic plots to overthrow the U.S. government, is the author of a book on the political functioning of conspiracy theories: *Conspiracy: How the Paranoid Style Flourishes, and Where It Comes From.*

Such shoddy journalism has its academic corollaries, too numerous to list, but certainly the most influential of these is Samuel Huntington's *The Clash of Civilizations and the Remaking of World Order.* Huntington, who is widely regarded as one of the most distinguished and influential political scientists in the United States, argues that an unavoidable conflict is emerging between the West and the Islamic world, among other foes. Huntington's arguments about the uniquely violent and conflict-oriented nature of Muslims and Islamic societies are "demonstrated" by social pseudoscience, including charts purporting to quantify the "Militarism of Muslim and Christian Countries" and "Ethnopolitical" and "Ethnic" conflicts. From this he concludes that "Muslims have problems living peaceably with their neighbors."[12] Huntington states simply that "Muslim bellicosity and violence are late–twentieth century facts which neither Muslims nor non-Muslims can deny," and that "quantitative evidence from every disinterested source conclusively demonstrates its validity."[13] Huntington's thesis of a "clash of civilizations" has proved highly influential in academic, journalistic, and governmental circles, and, although it has been widely criticized, it has clearly left its mark on contemporary American worldviews about Arabs, Arab Americans, and the Middle East.

The United States government itself has actively adopted and promoted anti-Arab sentiments through foreign policies that are biased and hostile to the interests of millions of Arab people, through domestic repression of organized Arab American political activity, and by enacting stereotypical representations in government activities. The double standards that inform the U.S. government's approach to the question of Palestine, which can be best characterized as a total and unwavering commitment to the interests of the Israeli state and a systematic rejection of Palestinian human and national rights, play a major role in the vicious cycle of self-reinforcing negative representations of Arabs in American culture and American policies that reflect an anti-Arab bias. These double standards are expressed through the massive financial, diplomatic, and military support for Israel from the United States, which appear to be entirely unrelated to Israeli compliance with international norms of conduct. Perhaps most galling to Arabs are the double standards revealed in the steadfast American diplomatic support for Israeli human rights violations. One particularly shocking example of this was the role of the Clinton administration in blocking criticism of Israel at the United Nations over the 1996 Qana massacre, in which the Israeli military bombed a U.N. observer camp in southern Lebanon, killing more than one hundred Lebanese civilians. Another astonishing instance was the 9 February 1999 U.N. General Assembly vote convening a conference on the enforcement of the Geneva Convention in the Israeli-occupied territories, which was opposed by only the United States and Israel. Such actions reflect and promote a prejudice that devalues the rights, including the most basic human rights, and interests of Arabs, and champions the rights, interests, and ambitions of others, most notably Israelis. The news media, guided to a great degree by the government on foreign policy matters and informed by the same cultural background as policy-making officials, repeat these prejudices and communicate them to the public. Double standards wherein some peoples' rights are important while others' are less so, some peoples' suffering is interesting while others' is not, and some people are properly the subjects of history while others are its objects, typify Western journalism on the Middle East. One of the most striking features of U.S. news reporting on events in Palestine, for example, is that it is almost always the Israeli actors who are subjectified, whatever their role. So, for example, when Israelis are victims of Palestinian violence, emphasis is on the suffering of the victims and their families, but when an Israeli such as Baruch Goldstein massacres Palestinians in a mosque, the focus is on the Israeli subject, on what type of twisted thinking could have driven an Israeli army reservist, an American doctor from Crown Heights no less, to do such a thing. In almost all incidents of violence in Palestine, to Western news reports the Palestinians, whether victims or perpetrators, remain a nameless, faceless mass. The bias is even more stark in reporting on Arab-Israeli violence in Lebanon, where the death of each Israeli soldier is accorded great significance, while the deaths of Lebanese civilians are noted in passing, if at all.[14] One of the most respected and accomplished Western correspondents in the Middle East, Robert Fisk of the British newspaper the *Independent,* explained to a recent gathering at the Center for Policy Analysis on Palestine in Washington, D.C., that he declines to use the term "terrorism" or "terrorist" in covering violence in Palestine and Lebanon because he believes that in this context the term has lost its meaning and is now simply an ethnic pejorative against Arabs, to whom it is exclusively attached. Discriminatory policies, slanted official rhetoric, and biased reportage thus become mutually reinforcing.

Certainly double standards that indicate a disregard for the rights of Arabs are apparent in the attitude both the government and the media of the United States have taken toward Iraq in the 1990s. Journalists have enthusiastically joined with government officials in demonizing Iraq, the Iraqi people, and above all President Saddam Hussein, in the buildup to the 1991 Gulf War and since. To recall only one small example of this disturbing phenomenon, the well-known news magazine *The New Republic* featured a cover in September 1990 sporting a photograph of Saddam Hussein that had been altered to make the Iraqi leader's moustache look more like Adolph Hitler's and that, in a bad pun, was prominently titled "Furor in the Gulf."[15] The Iraqi invasion of Kuwait (which was disapproved of by a great many Arabs and Arab Americans) notwithstanding, the implacable hostility of the United States toward Iraq has been extraordinary. In particular, the genocidal effects of the U.S.-enforced sanctions against Iraq, which have killed well over a million Iraqis, mostly children, have reinforced the impression among both Arabs and Americans that Arab people in general are seen by the U.S. government to be the enemies of this country. The chillingly bland observation by Secretary of State Madeleine Albright that the deaths of over 500,000 Iraqi children have been "worth it" for U.S. foreign policy aims clearly suggests to Americans and Middle Easterners alike that the lives of Arabs, including Arab children, are not particularly valued in the eyes of the United States government.[16] The news media has generally either ignored or downplayed the fact that, according to the United Nations, more than a million individuals have died needlessly over the past seven years in Iraq, and coverage of what many people regard as a humanitarian catastrophe at least, if not an outright genocide, has been amazingly thin. Arabs, in both the United States and the Middle East, are convinced that there are few other ethnic groups whose needless suffering on such a massive scale would be tolerated and ignored, let alone deliberately inflicted. Again one is hard pressed not to see a connection between the dehumanizing representations of Arabs in American popular culture and the casual manner in which American policy dispenses with Arab rights and Arab lives.

Moreover, President Clinton's protestations that his 1998 bombing attacks against Iraq, Afghanistan, and Sudan were not reflective of an anti-Islamic or anti-Arab animus or a generalized conflict between the United States and the Arab World in fact served only to reinforce this very impression. After all, why would one feel the need to specifically deny that these attacks were aimed at targets whose principal characteristics are that they are Arab or Muslim, if this were not a reasonable conclusion, likely to be widespread? Attacks on a manifestly innocent pharmaceutical factory in Sudan and on training camps in Afghanistan for guerrillas who fight Indian rule in Kashmir would appear to have had no logical relevance to the as-yet-unsolved embassy bombings in Kenya and Tanzania, for which the attacks were supposed to be retaliation. Yet, as symbolic targets, they make sense in the context of such recurring themes of the "green menace" as global cabals of Islamist radicals, regionwide terrorist networks that cut across all ideological lines, and the fear of chemical, biological, and nuclear terrorism, which invokes the specter of Saddam Hussein. These themes, familiar to anyone who has been to the movies lately, draw together all Middle Easterners and Muslims who would oppose U.S. policies in the Middle East into one undifferentiated terrorist mass, so that any target in the Muslim world potentially becomes a "legitimate" focus of aggression or vengeance. Indeed, the destabilizing, militarily meaningless, and politically counterproductive cruise missile attacks against Sudan and Afghanistan in 1998 make sense only in terms of a hysterical discourse that in effect brands all Arabs and Muslims as terrorists and therefore function precisely as attacks on Arabs and Islam in general. Official American denials only serve to reinforce this effect, both in the United States and in the Middle East. A similar effect generated by the news media can be seen in the recent spate of implausible news stories suggesting that Abu Nidal, who had been reportedly on his deathbed in Egypt, and Osama Bin Laden, who has been living in caves in Afghanistan for years, had been brought to Baghdad by Saddam Hussein in order to form a new "terrorism international."[17] This silly tale was based on effacing all ideological and other obvious differences between these individuals, whose only connection is that they have been branded Arab arch-terrorists by the government and media, again creating the impression of an undifferentiated terrorist mass.

Arab Americans, particularly those engaged in organized political activity, have encountered official political repression and discrimination that is often informed by anti-Arab bias or stereotypes and that, in turn, reinforce those stereotypes. Arabs, Muslims, and those traveling to and from the Middle East are routinely singled out for often abusive special security measures by airline security and customs officials, based on mandatory government profiling systems. While the specific content of these profiles is secret, the discriminatory nature and disparate impact of such profiling has been well documented by Arab American civil rights organizations such as the American-Arab Anti-Discrimination Committee (ADC).[18] Though the discriminatory nature of the profiling system strongly indicates that it is based in large measure on racist stereotypes of Arabs and Muslims, the Federal Aviation Administration (FAA) has been unable to document a single instance where an individual who posed a danger to airport or airplane security has been apprehended or identified through the profiling system. Such pointless but abusive and discriminatory profiling is a clear example of a government policy that has a mutually reinforcing relationship with popular stereotypes and negative representations of Arab people. The CEO of Northwest Airlines forcefully made this point when he addressed the National Convention of the American-Arab Anti-Discrimination Committee in June of 1996. In response to complaints that airport profiling had led to discrimination against Arab and Arab American travelers, he candidly stated that even if airline agents were given directives not to discriminate on the basis of ethnicity, their behavior would still be affected by what they saw about Arabs in films and on television.

Since the passage of the 1996 Anti-Terrorism and Immigration Acts, the Immigration and Naturalization Service (INS) has begun using secret evidence in politically charged deportation cases. As a result at least twenty-five individuals, all politically active Arabs and Muslims, are currently incarcerated without charge on the basis of secret evidence, which they are unable to challenge or even evaluate. Most of these individuals have resided peacefully in the United States for a number of years, and many have spouses and children who are U.S. citizens. Some have satisfied an immigration judge that they would face certain persecution if returned to their home country. Yet almost all of them remain detained because an INS prosecutor has presented a judge with secret, and therefore unchallenged and untested, evidence alleging that the individual is a "terrorist" or has some "terrorist" affiliation. James Woolsey, former director of the CIA, told a senate judiciary subcommittee on 8 October 1998 that "The INS' procedure in these sorts of cases— uncannily reminiscent of Franz Kafka's *The Trial*—is to collect rumors and unfounded allegations, not investigate them, submit them in camera [i.e., secretly] to the immigration judge, and then demand that the individual in question be held a threat to national security if he does not succeed in refuting the charges of which he is unaware." Woolsey, who is defending six Iraqi men being held on the basis of secret evidence, added that a clear anti-Arab racist bias was present in some of the secret evidence the government had submitted against his clients which was later released, stating that "In ex parte testimony, belatedly declassified, more than one interrogator explicitly expressed bias (e.g., Arabs 'lie an awful lot,' 'there is no guilt in the Arab world') to the immigration court."[19] In an August 1998 letter to Attorney General Janet Reno and INS Commissioner Doris Meissner, Senators Spencer Abraham (R-Mich.) and Edward Kennedy (D-Mass.), the chair and ranking member of the senate subcommittee on immigration, expressed "grave concerns" about the use of secret evidence. "Some believe that recent actions create the appearance that the INS may be using secret evidence only in cases against Arab immigrants," wrote the senators. "This is especially disturbing since many of these cases appear to be based not on any actions of the immigrants, but rather on their purported associations," they added. . . .

The U.S. government has also employed stereotypical negative representations of Arabs in its law enforcement and military operations. Among the most notorious of these incidents was the 1980 "Abscam" scandal, in which the FBI had an Italian-American agent posing as a stereotypical Arab "oil-sheikh" bribe several members of Congress, whose corruption was captured on videotape. As former U.S. Senator James Abourezk recalls in his memoirs, "After the scandal broke in the press, FBI Director William Webster was asked why the agent had been dressed as an Arab. He responded that it was necessary to choose some ethnic group that the public would believe was capable of bribing congressmen. And yet, no Arab or Arab American had ever been accused of bribing an American politician. There had been, of course, lots of publicity about Koreans, Wasps, Jews, and members of other ethnic groups convicted of bribery, but not about Arabs. Why Webster, ordinarily a respected public servant, felt it was necessary to use any ethnic group is a mystery, but his choice was solid evidence of the bottoming out of the image of Arabs in the United States." Abourezk goes on to state flatly that the "use of a phony Arab figure in Abscam was the direct result of the seven-year escalation, following the oil embargo, of anti-Arab racism that was projected by the media and cheered on by the Israeli lobby."[20] Dismay over "Abscam" and the unabashed endorsement by the FBI of some of the most malicious anti-Arab stereotypes in the operation led directly to the founding of the American-Arab Anti-Discrimination Committee (ADC), the largest Arab American political and civil rights organization in the United States.

Almost twenty years after "Abscam," the government continues to enact, and thereby reinforce, negative stereotypes of Arabs. In the middle of March 1999, The Marine Warfighting Lab conducted another in its ongoing series of "Urban Warrior" exercises at Monterey and Oakland, California. The exercise involved simulations of urban warfare, with several mock foreign locations created for different scenarios. Among the most troubling aspects of the exercise was the simulation of "ethnic groups" by trainees from the Defense Language Institute in the mock urban settings. These actors portrayed stereotypical "Arabs" and "Koreans" in urban crowd situations, taunting the Marines, serving as distractions in the hunts for the "terrorists" in their midst, and begging for help in staged disasters. In this case, the U.S. military apparently found it useful to promote stereotypes and anticipate the ethnicity of enemies and bystanders in future missions for its training exercises. Such exercises are likely to reinforce negative impressions of the ethnic groups and notions of who are "the enemy," while adding nothing essential to training for urban conflict. Just as in "Abscam," the stereotypes used in the Urban Warrior exercises are not only offensive but utterly gratuitous.

The government and news media are, if anything, outdone in defamation of Arabs by the entertainment industry. The shameful history of Hollywood and U.S. television programs in projecting negative stereotypes of Arabs and Muslims (which are often wrongly treated as identical sets by the entertainment industry and, consequently, the public) has been more than adequately catalogued in the work of scholars such as Jack Shaheen, Edward Said, Michael Suleiman, and Yahya Kamalipour. These critics have charted the development of dominant entertainment industry stereotypes of Arabs from the romantic image of the barbaric and hyper-sexualized desert bedouin of the silent film era to the more unambiguous corrupt oil sheikhs and anti-Western, anti-Semitic fanatics of more recent decades. The ubiquity of negative images and the consistency of the anti-Arab stereotypes that are deployed has often been noted. As Jay Stone asked, "When was the last time you saw an Arab character in a movie who was anything but one of the three B's (billionaire, bomber, belly dancer)?"[21] Yet at present the dominant and most damaging stereotype is that of the crazed Arab/Muslim terrorist, which has become a staple of the action film genre, among others. Most observers agree that the 1960 film, *Exodus,* a shamelessly distorted account of the founding of the State of Israel, was a turning point in Hollywood's treatment of Arabs as a demonic and thoroughly evil people who typically commit unspeakable acts against the innocent. The image of the Arab as quintessential terrorist competed with the more dominant image of the corrupt and boorish oil sheikh in Hollywood movies during the 1970s.

By the 1980s, the image of the terrorist, increasingly cast as a hysterical Islamic militant, superseded all other stereotypes as the dominant Hollywood characterization of the Arab. This was the villain of choice in countless low-budget action films of the 1980s, many produced by Canon Films of the Israeli Golan and Globus production company. Films such as *Wanted Dead or Alive* (1987), *Iron Eagle* (1986), *Delta Force* (1986), and many others did their best to promote the ugliest stereotypes of the cruel but cowardly Arab terrorist as the essential and fundamental enemy of the West and Israel specifically, and decency and humanity in general. In the main these films were, however, characterized also by a distinctly low-budget, low-brow quality that partially helped to offset their defamatory content. The 1990s saw a mainstreaming of these images into higher budget, higher profile films, a process that culminated in the 20th Century Fox blockbuster *True Lies* (1994), a high-budget, high-profile vehicle for Arnold Schwarzenegger. While *True Lies* clearly indicates the arrival of the Arab-demonizing action flick at the top of the Hollywood pyramid, the film retains the cartoonish and preposterous qualities of its low-budget precursors.

The same cannot be said of 20th Century Fox's latest Arab-bashing film, *The Siege* (1998). Compared to most of the earlier action films featuring crazed Arab terrorists, including *True Lies,* which never asked to be taken seriously, *The Siege* is a complicated and relatively sophisticated film. It presents itself as a serious intervention in a major public policy and political debate about how the United States should respond to a potential "terrorist threat." Indeed, and in yet another instance of the symbiotic and self-reinforcing relationship between discriminatory policies and defamatory representations, the inspiration for *The Siege* was one of the most troubling government documents to be uncovered in recent years—a Justice Department contingency plan for the mass arrest of thousands of Arabs in the United States, their detention in concentration camps in Florida and Louisiana, and their possible deportation.[22] *The Siege* depicts a savage terrorist campaign by Arab Americans in New York City, and the government's response of rounding up all young Arab males in detention camps. . . .

Of all the stereotypes propagated through films such as these and other forms of entertainment, as well as through biased journalism and discriminatory policies, none could be more unfair, distressing, or damaging than that of the Arab as anti-Jewish anti-Semite. This stereotype places on the Arab a double burden of anti-Semitism, whereby the Arab is perceived as a Semite through the lens of traditional European anti-Semitic stereotypes, and at the same time is identified as the arch-Jewish anti-Semite. Arabs are bearing the burden, therefore, not only of being the target of stereotypical Western anti-Semitic images, but also of the historical responsibility for a culture of ethnic and religious anti-Semitism which belongs, in fact, to European, not Arab, civilization. Thus the Arab becomes both the target and the supposed source of the worst forms of Western anti-Semitism.

Many of the images used to defame Arabs, especially in the past fifty years, draw on stock images of the Western anti-Semitic canon. As Jack Shaheen has pointed out, "Resembling the hook-nosed screen Arab wearing burnooses and thobes, screen Jews [in Nazi-inspired German films] also dress differently than the films' protagonists, wearing yarmulkes and black robes. They too appear as unkempt money-grubbing caricatures who seek world domination, who worship a different God, who kill innocents, and who lust after blond virgins."[23] The caricature of Semitic racial characteristics that typifies traditional Western anti-Jewish imagery has been largely transferred to the Arab as overt anti-Jewish anti-Semitism has fallen out of fashion. The similarities between the image of the wealthy, filthy, greedy, vulgar oil sheikh and anti-Jewish imagery are obvious. Yet the parallel also applies to most of the other negative images of Arabs in Western culture today, including the crazed religious fanatic who worships a cruel and alien God. The rise of anti-Arab stereotypes in the United States in recent decades in many ways represents the continued thriving of traditional Western anti-Semitism, in a new guise.

All the more ironic then that one of the most pervasive stereotypes of Arabs is that of the Arab racist, particularly the anti–Jewish anti–Semite. This theme is a standard feature of the defamatory films, television programs, and journalism misrepresenting the Arab-Israeli conflict. The main idea is that opposition to Israel is driven not by concern for Palestinian human and national rights or the injustices of colonialism, but by a hatred toward or dislike of Jews that is supposedly characteristic of Arabic culture and/or Islam. This is often accompanied with rubbish about three thousand years of warfare or an age-old conflict in Palestine, when, of course, the Zionist movement itself is barely one hundred years old. In this way, the passionate Arab opposition to the Zionist movement can be neatly explained without allowing that the establishment of the Israeli state came at another people's expense. Some of the most extreme apologists for Israel in the press and in Congress have taken to insisting that the anger and resentment Palestinians living under Israeli occupation feel toward their oppressors comes not from the experience of having been ethnically cleansed or living under colonial rule and foreign military occupation, without rights or citizenship, but is produced instead by a calculated campaign of indoctrination of hatred in Palestinian schools and media. Resistance to colonialism, resentment of oppression, and struggling for one's human rights thereby become the product of miseducation, indoctrination, and a deep-seated cultural and religious antipathy toward Jews.

While it is true that some elements of Western anti-Semitic discourse have begun to creep into the rhetoric of those living under Israeli occupation, such ideas are still clearly marginal and alien to Arab cultural precepts. There is no foundation for these intolerant attitudes in Arab culture or Islam, and their influence is likely to remain marginal at best, even though they might correspond to the ideological needs of those resisting Israeli occupation.

The characterization of the Arab-Israeli conflict as being driven by traditions of Arab intolerance and anti-Jewish hatred is an attempt to rob Arabs of the right to object to colonialism and oppression, lest they be labeled "anti-Semitic." It is an attempt to shift the primary burden for centuries of religious and ideological anti-Semitism in the West, which has no corollary in Arab tradition, and which culminated in the Holocaust, onto the Arab peoples. The historical record, however, is clear. Even more disturbingly, this discourse threatens to rob Arabs of the heritage of an extraordinary tradition of tolerance and coexistence. The only appropriate response is to reject this stereotype more vigorously than any other, and reclaim and extend this legacy of tolerance and coexistence as robustly as we can. Certainly this is a response that is suggested by the model of identification with which we began. Perhaps the seeds of an alternative discourse on Arab Americans lie in such a gesture, which dispenses with the self-defeating "I am not a terrorist" motif and allows for a far more constructive dialogue. Let the next discussion begin with this.

NOTES

1. Ali A. Mazrui, *Cultural Forces in World Politics* (London: James Curry, 1990), 13.
2. See, for example, Edward Said, *Orientalism* (New York: Vintage Books, 1978).
3. Michael Suleiman, *The Arabs in the Mind of America* (Brattleboro, Vt.: Amana Books, 1988), 7–12.
4. "Apocalypse Near," *Newsweek,* 1 April 1991, p. 14.

5. John Sugg, "Steven Emerson's Crusade," *Extra,* January/February 1999, pp. 17–20.
6. *CBS News,* 19 April 1995.
7. Sugg, "Crusade," 17–20.
8. "Bomb an 'Act of Evil,' " *USA Today,* 20 April 1995, p. A1.
9. Daniel Pipes, "Perjurious Palestinians," *New York Post,* 8 September 1999, p. 31.
10. Daniel Pipes, "It Matters What Kind of Islam Prevails," *Los Angeles Times,* 22 July 1999, p. B9.
11. Daniel Pipes, "America's Muslims against America's Jews," *Commentary* 107, no. 5 (1999): 31.
12. Samuel Huntington, *The Clash of Civilizations and the Remaking of World Order* (New York: Simon and Schuster, 1996), 256–58.
13. Ibid, 258.
14. Hussein Ibish, "Retaliating in Advance," *Extra* 12, no. 5 (1999): 24–25.
15. "Aw, Shucks," *New Republic* 204, no. 20 (1991): 11.
16. Denis H. Halliday and Jennifer E. Horan, "A New Policy Need for Iraq," *Boston Globe,* 22 March 1999, p. 19.
17. See, for example, "Officials: Bin Laden 'Missing'; Muslim Militant Could be in Iraq," *Arizona Republic,* 14 February 1999, p. A8; "Saddam's New Weapon: Terror; Courting Bin Laden and Nidal," *New York Post,* 1 February 1999, p. 2.
18. *Hate Crimes and Discrimination against Arab-Americans, 1996–97* (Washington, D.C.: American-Arab Anti-Discrimination Committee, 1997).
19. "Prepared Statement of R. James Woolsey before the Senate Judiciary Committee Technology Terrorism and Government Information Subcommittee," Federal News Service Transcript, 8 October 1998.
20. James G. Abourezk, *Advise and Dissent* (Chicago: Lawrence Hill Books, 1989), 253.
21. Jack Shaheen, *Arab and Muslim Stereotyping in American Popular Culture* (Washington, D.C.: Center for Muslim-Christian Understanding, 1997), 12.
22. *Hate Crimes and Discrimination Against Arab-Americans, 1990–91* (Washington, D.C.: American-Arab Anti-Discrimination Committee, 1991).
23. Shaheen, *Arab and Muslim Stereotyping,* 15.

4

HOW JEWS BECAME WHITE

KAREN BRODKIN SACKS

The American nation was founded and developed by the Nordic race, but if a few more million members of the Alpine, Mediterranean and Semitic races are poured among us, the result must inevitably be a hybrid race of people as worthless and futile as the good-for-nothing mongrels of Central America and Southeastern Europe.
— KENNETH ROBERTS, QTD. IN CARLSON AND COLBURN 1972:312

It is clear that Kenneth Roberts did not think of my ancestors as white like him. The late nineteenth and early decades of the twentieth centuries saw a steady stream of warnings by scientists, policymakers, and the popular press that "mongrelization" of the Nordic or Anglo-Saxon race—the real Americans—by inferior European races (as well as inferior non-European ones) was destroying the fabric of the nation. I continue to be surprised to read that America did not always regard its immigrant European workers as white, that they thought people from different nations were biologically different. My parents, who are first-generation U.S.-born Eastern European Jews, are not surprised. They expect anti-Semitism to be a part of the fabric of daily life, much as I expect racism to be part of it. They came of age in a Jewish world in the 1920s and 1930s at the peak of anti-Semitism in the United States (Gerber 1986). They are proud of their upward mobility and think of themselves as pulling themselves up by their own bootstraps. I grew up during the 1950s in the Euroethnic New York suburb of Valley Stream where Jews were simply one kind of white folks and where ethnicity meant little more to my generation than food and family heritage. Part of my familized ethnic heritage was the belief that Jews were smart and that our success was the result of our own efforts and abilities, reinforced by a culture that valued sticking together, hard work, education, and deferred gratification. Today, this belief in a Jewish version of Horatio Alger has become an entry point for racism by some mainstream Jewish organizations against African Americans especially, and for their opposition to affirmative action for people of color (Gordon 1964; Sowell 1981; Steinberg 1989: chap. 3).

Sacks, Karen Brodkin. "How Jews Became White." From Gregory, Steven & Roger Sanjek (eds.) *Race,* New Brunswick, NJ: Rutgers University Press, 1994, pp. 78–102. Reprinted by permission of the publisher.

It is certainly true that the United States has a history of anti-Semitism and of beliefs that Jews were members of an inferior race. But Jews were hardly alone. American anti-Semitism was part of a broader pattern of late-nineteenth-century racism against all southern and eastern European immigrants, as well as against Asian immigrants. These views justified all sorts of discriminatory treatment including closing the doors to immigration from Europe and Asia in the 1920s.[1] This picture changed radically after World War II. Suddenly the same folks who promoted nativism and xenophobia were eager to believe that the Euro-origin people whom they had deported, reviled as members of inferior races, and prevented from immigrating only a few years earlier were now model middle-class white suburban citizens.

It was not an educational epiphany that made those in power change their hearts, their minds, and our race. Instead, it was the biggest and best affirmative action program in the history of our nation, and it was for Euromales. There are similarities and differences in the ways each of the European immigrant groups became "whitened." I want to tell the story in a way that links anti-Semitism to other varieties of anti-European racism, because this foregrounds what Jews shared with other Euroimmigrants and shows changing notions of whiteness to be part of America's larger system of institutional racism.

EURORACES

The U.S. "discovery" that Europe had inferior and superior races came in response to the great waves of immigration from southern and eastern Europe in the late nineteenth century. Before that time, European immigrants—including Jews—had been largely assimilated into the white population. The twenty-three million European immigrants who came to work in U.S. cities after 1880 were too many and too concentrated to disperse and blend. Instead, they piled up in the country's most dilapidated urban areas, where they built new kinds of working-class ethnic communities. Since immigrants and their children made up more than 70 percent of the population of most of the country's largest cites, urban America came to take on a distinctly immigrant flavor. The golden age of industrialization in the United States was also the golden age of class struggle between the captains of the new industrial empires and the masses of manual workers whose labor made them rich. As the majority of mining and manufacturing workers, immigrants were visibly major players in these struggles (Higham 1955:226; Steinberg 1989:36).[2]

The Red Scare of 1919 clearly linked anti-immigrant to anti-working-class sentiment—to the extent that the Seattle general strike of native-born workers was blamed on foreign agitators. The Red Scare was fueled by economic depression, a massive post-war strike wave, the Russian revolution, and a new wave of postwar immigration. . . .

Not surprisingly, the belief in European races took root most deeply among the wealthy U.S.-born Protestant elite, who feared a hostile and seemingly unassimilable working class. By the end of the nineteenth century, Senator Henry Cabot Lodge pressed Congress to cut off immigration to the Untied States; Teddy Roosevelt raised the alarm of "race suicide" and took Anglo-Saxon women to task for allowing "native" stock to be outbred by inferior immigrants. In the twentieth century, these fears gained a great deal of social legitimacy thanks to the efforts of an influential network of aristocrats and scientists who developed theories of eugenics—breeding for a "better" humanity—and scientific racism. Key to these efforts was Madison Grant's influential *Passing of the Great Race* in which he shared his discovery that there were three or four major European races ranging from the superior Nordics of northwestern Europe to the inferior southern and eastern races of Alpines, Mediterraneans, and, worst of all, Jews, who seem to be everywhere in his native New York City. Grant's nightmare was race mixing among Europeans. For him, "the cross between any of the three European races and a Jew is a Jew" (qtd. in Higham 1955:156). He didn't have good things to say about Alpine or Mediterranean "races" either. For Grant, race and class were interwoven: the upper class was racially pure Nordic, and the lower classes came from the lower races.

Far from being on the fringe, Grant's views resonated with those of the nonimmigrant middle class. A *New York Times* reporter wrote of his visit to the Lower East Side:

> This neighborhood, peopled almost entirely by the people who claim to have been driven from Poland and Russia, is the eyesore of New York and perhaps the filthiest place on the western continent. It is impossible for a Christian to live there because he will be driven out, either by blows or the dirt and stench. Cleanliness is an unknown quantity to these people. They cannot be lifted up to a higher plane because they do not want to be. If the cholera should ever get among these people, they would scatter its germs as a sower does grain (qtd. in Schoener 1967:58).[3]

Such views were well within the mainstream of the early-twentieth-century scientific community. Grant and eugenicist Charles B. Davenport organized the Galton Society in 1918 in order to foster research and to otherwise promote eugenics and immigration restriction.[4] . . .

By the 1920s, scientific racism sanctified the notion that real Americans were white and real whites came from northwest Europe. Racism animated laws excluding and expelling Chinese in 1882, and then closing the door to immigration by virtually all Asians and most Europeans in 1924 (Saxton 1971, 1990). Northwestern European ancestry as a requisite for whiteness was set in legal concrete when the Supreme Court denied Bhagat Singh Thind the right to become a naturalized citizen under a 1790 federal law that allowed whites the right to become naturalized citizens. Thind argued that East Indians were the real Aryans and Caucasians, and therefore white. The Court countered that the United States only wanted blond Aryans and Caucasians, "that the blond Scandinavian and the brown Hindu have a common ancestor in the dim reaches of antiquity, but the average man knows perfectly well that there are unmistakable and profound differences between them today" (Takaki 1989:298–299). A narrowly defined white, Christian race was also built into the 1705 Virginia "Act concerning servants and slaves." This statute stated "that no Negroes, mulattos and Indians or other infidels or jews, Moors, Mahometans or other infidels shall, at any time, purchase any Christian servant, nor any other except of their own complexion" (Martyn 1979:111).[5]

The 1930 census added its voice, distinguishing not only immigrant from "native" whites, but also native whites of native white parentage, and native whites of immigrant (or mixed) parentage. In distinguishing immigrant (southern and eastern Europeans) from "native" (northwestern Europeans), the census reflected the racial distinctions of the eugenicist-inspired intelligence tests.[6]

Racism and anti-immigrant sentiment in general and anti-Semitism in particular flourished in higher education. Jews were the first of the Euroimmigrant groups to enter colleges in significant numbers, so it wasn't surprising that they faced the brunt of discrimination there.[7] The Protestant elite complained that Jews were unwashed, uncouth, unrefined, loud, and pushy. Harvard University President A. Lawrence Lowell, who was also a vice president of the Immigration Restriction League, was openly opposed to Jews at Harvard. The Seven Sisters schools had a reputation for "flagrant discrimination." . . .

My parents' conclusion is that Jewish success, like their own, was the result of hard work and of placing a high value on education. They went to Brooklyn College during the Depression. My mother worked days and started school at night, and my father went during the day. Both their families encouraged them. More accurately, their families expected this effort from them. Everyone they knew was in the same boat, and their world was made up of Jews who advanced as they did. The picture of New York—where most Jews lived—seems to back them up. In 1920, Jews made up 80 percent of the students at New York's City College, 90 percent of Hunter College, and before World War I, 40 percent of private Columbia University. By 1934, Jews made up almost 24 percent of all law students nationally, and 56 percent of those in New York City. Still, more Jews became public school teachers, like my parents and their friends, than doctors or lawyers (Steinberg 1989:137, 227). Steinberg has debunked the myth that Jews advanced because of the cultural value placed on education. This is not to say that Jews did not advance. They did. "Jewish success in America was a matter of historical timing. . . . [T]here was a fortuitous match between the experience and skills of

Jewish immigrants, on the one hand, and the manpower needs and opportunity structures, on the other" (1989:103). Jews were the only ones among the southern and eastern European immigrants who came from urban, commercial, craft, and manufacturing backgrounds, not least of which was garment manufacturing. They entered the United States in New York, center of the nation's booming garment industry, soon came to dominate its skilled (male) and "unskilled" (female) jobs, and found it an industry amenable to low-capital entrepreneurship. As a result, Jews were the first of the new European immigrants to create a middle class of small businesspersons early in the twentieth century. Jewish educational advances followed this business success and depended upon it, rather than creating it (see also Bodnar 1985 for a similar argument about mobility).

In the early twentieth century, Jewish college students entered a contested terrain in which the elite social mission was under challenge by a newer professional training mission. Pressure for change had begun to transform the curriculum and reorient college from a gentleman's bastion to a training ground for the middle-class professionals needed by an industrial economy. "The curriculum was overhauled to prepare students for careers in business, engineering, scientific farming, and the arts, and a variety of new professions such as accounting and pharmacy that were making their appearance in American colleges for the first time" (Steinberg 1989:229). Occupational training was precisely what drew Jews to college. In a setting where disparagement of intellectual pursuits and the gentleman's C were badges of distinction, it was not hard for Jews to excel.

How we interpret Jewish social mobility in this milieu depends on whom we compare Jews to. Compared with other immigrants, Jews were upwardly mobile. But compared with that of nonimmigrant whites, their mobility was very limited and circumscribed. Anti-immigrant racist and anti-Semitic barriers kept the Jewish middle class confined to a small number of occupations. Jews were excluded from mainstream corporate management and corporately employed professions, except in the garment and movie industries, which they built. Jews were almost totally excluded from university faculties (and the few that made it had powerful patrons). Jews were concentrated in small businesses, and in professions where they served a largely Jewish clientele (Davis 1990:146 n. 25; Silberman 1985:88–117; Sklare 1971:63–67). . . .

My parents' generation believed that Jews overcame anti-Semitic barriers because Jews are special. My belief is that the Jews who were upwardly mobile were special among Jews (and were also well placed to write the story). My generation might well counter our parents' story of pulling themselves up by their own bootstraps with, "But think what you might have been without the racism and with some affirmative action!" And that is precisely what the postwar boom, the decline of systematic, public anti-immigrant racism and anti-Semitism, and governmental affirmative action extended to white males.

EUROETHNICS INTO WHITES

By the time I was an adolescent, Jews were just as white as the next white person. Until I was eight, I was a Jew in a world of Jews. Everyone on Avenue Z in Sheepshead Bay was Jewish. I spent my days playing and going to school on three blocks of Avenue Z, and visiting my grandparents in the nearby Jewish neighborhoods of Brighton Beach and Coney Island. There were plenty of Italians in my neighborhood, but they lived around the corner. They were a kind of Jew, but on the margins of my social horizons. Portuguese were even more distant, at the end of the bus ride, at Sheepshead Bay. . . . We left that world in 1949 when we moved to Valley Stream, Long Island, which was Protestant, Republican, and even had farms until Irish, Italian, and Jewish ex-urbanites like us gave it a more suburban and Democratic flavor. Neither religion nor ethnicity separated us at school or in the neighborhood. Except temporarily. In elementary school years, I remember a fair number of dirt-bomb (a good suburban weapon) wars on the block. Periodically one of the Catholic boys would accuse me or my brother of killing his God, to which we would reply, "Did not" and start lobbing dirt-bombs. Sometimes he would get his friends from Catholic school, and I would get mine from public school kids on the block, some of whom were Catholic. Hostilities lasted no more than a couple of hours and punctuated an otherwise friendly relationship. They ended by junior high years, when other things became more important. Jews, Catholics, and Protestants, Italians, Irish, Poles, and "English" (I don't remember hearing WASP as a kid) were mixed up on the block and in school. We thought of ourselves as middle class and very enlightened because our ethnic backgrounds seemed so irrelevant to high school culture. We didn't see race (we thought), and racism was not part of our peer consciousness, nor were the immigrant or working-class histories of our families.

Like most chicken and egg problems, it's hard to know which came first. Did Jews and other Euroethnics become white because they became middle class? That is, did money whiten? Or did being incorporated in an expanded version of whiteness open up the economic doors to a middle-class status? Clearly, both tendencies were at work. Some of the changes set in motion during the war against fascism led to a more inclusive version of whiteness. Anti-Semitism and anti-European racism lost respectability. The 1940 census no longer distinguished native whites of native parentage from those, like my parents, of immigrant parentage, so that Euroimmigrants and their children were more securely white by submersion in an expanded notion of whiteness. (This census also changed the race of Mexicans to white [U.S. Bureau of the Census, 1940:4].) Theories of nurture and culture replaced theories of nature and biology. Instead of dirty and dangerous races who would destroy U.S. democracy, immigrants became ethnic groups whose children had successfully assimilated into the mainstream and risen to the middle class. In this new myth, Euroethnic suburbs like mine became the measure of U.S. democracy's victory over racism. Jewish mobility became a new Horatio Alger story.

In time and with hard work, every ethnic group would get a piece of the pie, and the United States would be a nation with equal opportunity for all its people to become part of a prosperous middle-class majority. And it seemed that Euroethnic immigrants and their children were delighted to join middle America.[8]

This is not to say that anti-Semitism disappeared after World War II, only that it fell from fashion and was driven underground. . . .

Although changing views on who was white made it easier for Euroethnics to become middle class, it was also the case that economic prosperity played a very powerful role in the whitening process. Economic mobility of Jews and other Euroethnics rested ultimately on U.S. postwar economic prosperity with its enormously expanded need for professional, technical, and managerial labor, and on government assistance in providing it. The United States emerged from the war with the strongest economy in the world. . . . The postwar period was a historic moment for real class mobility and for the affluence we have erroneously come to believe was the U.S. norm. It was a time when the old white and the newly white masses became middle class.

The GI Bill of Rights, as the 1944 Serviceman's Readjustment Act was known, was arguably the most massive affirmative action program in U.S. history. It was created to develop needed labor-force skills, and to provide those who had them with a life-style that reflected their value to the economy. The GI benefits ultimately extended to sixteen million GIs (veterans of the Korean War as well) included priority in jobs—that is, preferential hiring, but no one objected to it then; financial support during the job search; small loans for starting up businesses; and, most important, low-interest home loans and educational benefits, which included tuition and living expenses (Brown 1946; Hurd 1946; Mosch 1975; *Postwar Jobs for Veterans* 1945; Willenz 1983). This legislation was rightly regarded as one of the most revolutionary postwar programs. I call it affirmative action because it was aimed at and disproportionately helped male, Euro-origin GIs. . . .

EDUCATION AND OCCUPATION

It is important to remember that prior to the war, a college degree was still very much a "mark of the upper class" (Willenz 1983:165). Colleges were largely finishing schools for Protestant elites. Before the postwar boom, schools could not begin to accommodate the American masses. Even in New York City before the 1930s, neither the public schools nor City College had room for more than a tiny fraction of potential immigrant students.

Not so after the war. The almost eight million GIs who took advantage of their educational benefits under the GI bill caused "the greatest wave of college building in American history" (Nash et al. 1986:885). White male GIs were able to take advantage of their educational benefits for college and technical training, so they were particularly well positioned to seize the opportunities provided by the new demands for professional, managerial, and technical labor. "It has been well documented that the GI educational benefits transformed American higher education and raised the educational level of that generation and generations to come. With many provisions for assistance in upgrading their educational attainments veterans pulled ahead of nonveterans in earning capacity. In the long run it was the nonveterans who had fewer opportunities" (Willenz 1983:165).[9] . . .

Even more significantly, the postwar boom transformed the U.S. class structure—or at least its status structure—so that the middle class expanded to encompass most of the population. Before the war, most Jews, like most other Americans, were working class. Already upwardly mobile before the war relative to other immigrants, Jews floated high on this rising economic tide, and most of them entered the middle class. Still, even the high tide missed some Jews. As late as 1973, some 15 percent of New York's Jews were poor or near poor, and in the 1960s, almost 25 percent of employed Jewish men remained manual workers (Steinberg 1989:89–90).

Educational and occupational GI benefits really constituted affirmative action programs for white males because they were decidedly not extended to African Americans or to women of any race. White male privilege was shaped against the backdrop of wartime racism and postwar sexism. During and after the war, there was an upsurge in white racist violence against black servicemen in public schools, and in the KKK, which spread to California and New York (Dalfiume 1969:133–134). The number of lynchings rose during the war, and in 1943 there were antiblack race riots in several large northern cities. Although there was a wartime labor shortage, black people were discriminated against in access to well-paid defense industry jobs and in housing. In 1946 there were white riots against African Americans across the South, and in Chicago and Philadelphia as well. Gains made as a result of the wartime Civil Rights movement, especially employment in defense-related industries, were lost with peacetime conversion as black workers were the first fired, often in violation of seniority (Wynn 1976:114, 116). White women were also laid off, ostensibly to make jobs for demobilized servicemen, and in the long run women lost most of the gains they had made in wartime (Kessler-Harris 1982). We now know that women did not leave the labor force in any significant numbers but instead were forced to find inferior jobs, largely nonunion, parttime, and clerical.

Theoretically available to all veterans, in practice women and black veterans did not get anywhere near their share of GI benefits. Because women's units were not treated as part of the military, women in them were not considered veterans and were ineligible for Veterans' Administration (VA) benefits (Willenz 1983:168). The barriers that almost completely shut African-American GIs out of their benefits were more complex. In Wynn's portrait (1976:115), black GIs anticipated starting new lives, just like their white counterparts. Over 43 percent hoped to return to school and most expected to relocate, to find better jobs in new lines of work. The exodus from the South toward the North and far West was particularly large. So it wasn't a question of any lack of ambition on the part of African-American GIs.

Rather, the military, the Veterans' Administration, the U.S. Employment Service, and the Federal Housing Administration (FHA) effectively denied African-American GIs access to their benefits and to the new educational, occupational, and residential opportunities. Black GIs who served in the thoroughly segregated armed forces during World War II served under white officers, usually southerners (Binkin and Eitelberg 1982: Dalfiume 1969; Foner 1974; Johnson 1967; Nalty and MacGregor 1981). African-American soldiers were disproportionately given dishonorable discharges, which denied them veterans' rights under the GI Bill. Thus between August and November 1946, 21 percent of white soldiers and 39 percent of black soldiers were dishonorably discharged. Those who did get an honorable discharge then faced the Veterans' Administration and the U.S. Employment Service. The latter, which was responsible for job placements, employed very few African Americans, especially in the South. This meant that black veterans did not receive much employment information, and that the offers they did receive were for low-paid and menial jobs. "In one survey of 50 cities, the movement of blacks into peacetime employment was found to be lagging far behind that of white veterans: in Arkansas 95 percent of the placements made by the USES for Afro-Americans were in service or unskilled jobs" (Nalty and MacGregor 1981:218, and see 60–61). African Americans were also less likely than whites, regardless of GI status, to gain new jobs commensurate with their wartime jobs, and they suffered more heavily. For example, in San Francisco by 1948, Black Americans "had dropped back halfway to their pre-war employment status" (Wynn 1976:114, 116).[10]

Black GIs faced discrimination in the educational system as well. Despite the end of restrictions on Jews and other Euroethnics, African Americans were not welcome in white colleges. Black colleges were overcrowded, and the combination of segregation and prejudice made for few alternatives. About twenty thousand black veterans attended college by 1947, most in black colleges, but almost as many, fifteen thousand, could not gain entry. Predictably, the disproportionately few African Americans who did gain access to their educational benefits were able, like their white counterparts, to become doctors and engineers, and to enter the black middle class (Walker 1970).

SUBURBANIZATION

In 1949, ensconced at Valley Stream, I watched potato farms turn into Levittown and into Idlewild (later Kennedy) Airport. This was a major spectator sport in our first years on suburban Long Island. A typical weekend would bring various aunts, uncles, and cousins out from the city. After a huge meal we would pile in the car—itself a novelty—to look at the bulldozed acres and comment on the matchbox construction. During the week, my mother and I would look at the houses going up within walking distance.

Bill Levitt built a basic 900–1,000-square-foot, somewhat expandable house for a lower-middle-class and working-class market on Long Island, and later in Pennsylvania and New Jersey (Gans 1967). Levittown started out as two thousand units of rental housing at sixty dollars a month, designed to meet the low-income housing needs of returning war vets, many of whom, like my Aunt Evie and Uncle Julie, were living in quonset huts. By May 1947, Levitt and Sons had acquired enough land in Hempstead Township on Long Island to build four thousand houses, and by the next February, he'd built six thousand units and named the development after himself. After 1948, federal financing for the construction of rental housing tightened, and Levitt switched to building houses for sale. By 1951 Levittown was a development of some fifteen thousand families. . . .

At the beginning of World War II, about 33 percent of all U.S. families owned their houses. That percentage doubled in twenty years. Most Levit-towners looked just like my family. They came from New York City or Long Island; about 17 percent were military, from nearby Mitchell Field; Levittown was their first house; and almost everyone was married. The 1947 inhabitants were over 75 percent white collar, but by 1950 more blue-collar families moved in, so that by 1951, "barely half" of the new residents were white collar, and by 1960 their occupational profile was somewhat more working class than for Nassau County as a whole. By this time too, almost one-third of Levittown's people were either foreign-born or, like my parents, first-generation U.S. born (Dobriner 1963:91, 100).

The FHA was key to buyers and builders alike. Thanks to it, suburbia was open to more than GIs. People like us would never have been in the market for houses without FHA and VA low-down-payment, low-interest, long-term loans to young buyers.[11] . . .

The FHA believed in racial segregation. Throughout its history, it pub-licly and actively promoted restrictive covenants. Before the war, these for-bade sale to Jews and Catholics as well as to African Americans. The deed to my house in Detroit had such a covenant, which theoretically prevented it from being sold to Jews or African Americans. Even after the Supreme Court ended legal enforcement of restrictive covenants in 1948, the FHA continued to encourage builders to write them against African Americans. FHA under-writing manuals openly insisted on racially homogeneous neighborhoods, and their loans were made only in white neighborhoods. I bought my Detroit house in 1972 from Jews who were leaving a largely African-American neighborhood. By that time, after the 1968 Fair Housing Act, restrictive covenants were a dead letter (although blockbusting by realtors was rapidly replacing it).

With the federal government behind them, virtually all developers re-fused to sell to African Americans. Palo Alto and Levittown, like most sub-urbs as late as 1960, were virtually all white. Out of 15,741 houses and 65,276 people, averaging 4.2 people per house, only 220 Levittowners, or 52 house-holds, were "nonwhite." In 1958 Levitt announced publicly at a press confer-ence to open his New Jersey development that he would not sell to black buyers. This caused a furor, since the state of New Jersey (but not the U.S. government) prohibited discrimination in federally subsidized housing. Levitt was sued and fought it, although he was ultimately persuaded by township ministers to integrate. . . .

The result of these policies was that African Americans were totally shut out of the suburban boom. An article in *Harper's* described the housing avail-able to black GIs. "On his way to the base each morning, Sergeant Smith passes an attractive air-conditioned, FHA-financed housing project. It was built for service families. Its rents are little more than the Smiths pay for their shack. And there are half-a-dozen vacancies, but none for Negroes" (qtd. in Foner 1974:195).

Where my family felt the seductive pull of suburbia, Marshall Berman's experienced the brutal push of urban renewal. In the Bronx in the 1950s, Robert Moses's Cross-Bronx Expressway erased "a dozen solid, settled, densely populated neighborhoods like our own; . . . something like 60,000 working- and lower-middle-class people, mostly Jews, but with many Ital-ians, Irish and Blacks thrown in, would be thrown out of their homes. . . . For ten years, through the late 1950s and early 1960s, the center of the Bronx was pounded and blasted and smashed" (1982:292).

Urban renewal made postwar cities into bad places to live. At a physical level, urban renewal reshaped them, and federal programs brought private developers and public officials together to create downtown central business districts where there had formerly been a mix of manufacturing, commerce, and working-class neighborhoods. Manufacturing was scattered to the pe-ripheries of the city, which were ringed and bisected by a national system of highways. Some working-class neighborhoods were bulldozed, but others remained (Greer 1965; Hartman 1975; Squires 1989). In Los Angeles, as in New York's Bronx, the postwar period saw massive freeway construction right through the heart of old working-class neighborhoods. In East Los An-geles and Santa Monica, Chicano and African-American communities were divided in half or blasted to smithereens by the highways bringing Ange-lenos to the new white suburbs, or to make way for civic monuments like Dodger Stadium (Pardo 1990; Social and Public Arts Resource Center 1990:80, 1883:12–13).

Urban renewal was the other side of the process by which Jewish and other working-class Euroimmigrants became middle class. It was the push to suburbia's seductive pull. The fortunate white survivors of urban renewal headed disproportionately for suburbia, where they could partake of pros-perity and the good life. . . .

The record is very clear that instead of seizing the opportunity to end in-stitutionalized racism, the federal government did its best to shut and double seal the post-war window of opportunity in African Americans' faces. It consistently refused to combat segregation in the social institutions that were key for upward mobility: education, housing, and employment. Moreover, federal programs that were themselves designed to assist demobilized GIs and young families systematically discriminated against African Americans. Such programs reinforced white/nonwhite racial distinctions even as intrawhite racialization was falling out of fashion. This other side of the coin, that white men of northwestern or southeastern European ancestry were treated equally in theory and in practice with regard to the benefits they received, was part of the larger postwar whitening of Jews and other eastern and southern Europeans.

The myth that Jews pulled themselves up by their own bootstraps ignores the fact that it took federal programs to create the conditions whereby the abilities of Jews and other European immigrants could be recognized and rewarded rather than denigrated and denied. The GI Bill and FHA and VA mortgages were forms of affirmative action that allowed male Jews and other Euro-American men to become suburban homeowners and to get the training that allowed them—but not women vets or war workers—to become professionals, technicians, salesmen, and managers in a growing economy. Jews' and other white ethnics' upward mobility was the result of programs that allowed us to float on a rising economic tide. To African Americans, the government offered the cement boots of segregation, redlining, urban renewal, and discrimination.

Those racially skewed gains have been passed across the generations, so that racial inequality seems to maintain itself "naturally," even after legal segregation ended. Today, in a shrinking economy where downward mobility is the norm, the children and grandchildren of the postwar beneficiaries of the economic boom have some precious advantages. For example, having parents who own their own homes or who have decent retirement benefits can make a real difference in young people's ability to take on huge college loans or to come up with a down payment for a house. Even this simple inheritance helps perpetuate the gap between whites and nonwhites. Sure Jews needed ability, but ability was not enough to make it. The same applies even more in today's long recession.

NOTES

This is a revised and expanded version of a paper published in *Jewish Currents* in June 1992 and delivered at the 1992 meetings of the American Anthropological Association in the session *Blacks and Jews, 1992: Reaching across the Cultural Boundaries* organized by Angela Gilliam. I would like to thank Emily Abel, Katya Gibel Azoulay, Edna Bonacich, Angela Gilliam, Isabelle Gunning, Valerie Matsumoto, Regina Morantz-Sanchez, Roger Sanjek, Rabbi Chaim Seidler-Feller, Janet Silverstein, and Eloise Klein Healy's writing group for uncovering wonderful sources and for critical readings along the way.
  1. Indeed, Boasian and Du Boisian anthropology developed in active political opposition to this nativism; on Du Bois, see Harrison and Nonini 1992.

2. On immigrants as part of the industrial work force, see Steinberg 1989:36.
3. I thank Roger Sanjek for providing me with this source.
4. It was intended, as Davenport wrote to the president of the American Museum of Natural History, Henry Fairfield Osborne, as "an anthropological society . . . with a central governing body, self-elected and self-perpetuating, and very limited in members, and also confined to native Americans who are anthropologically, socially and politically sound, no Bolsheviki need apply" (Barkan 1991:67–68).
5. I thank Valerie Matsumoto for telling me about the Thind case and Katya Gibel Azoulay for providing this information to me on the Virginia statute.
6. "The distinction between white and colored" has been "the only racial classification which has been carried through all the 15 censuses," "Colored" consisted of "Negroes" and "other races": Mexican, Indian, Chinese, Japanese, Filipino, Hindu, Korean, Hawaiian, Malay, Siamese, and Samoan. (U.S. Bureau of the Census, 1930:25, 26).
7. For why Jews entered colleges earlier than other immigrants, and for a challenge to views that attribute it to Jewish culture, see Steinberg 1989.
8. Indeed, Jewish social scientists were prominent in creating this ideology of the United States as a meritocracy. Most prominent of course was Nathan Glazer, but among them also were Charles Silberman and Marshall Sklare.
9. The belief was widespread that "the GI Bill . . . helped millions of families move into the middle class" (Nash et al. 1986:885). A study that compares mobility among veterans and nonveterans provides a kind of confirmation. In an unnamed small city in Illinois, Havighurst and his colleagues (1951) found no significant difference between veterans and nonveterans, but this was because apparently very few veterans used any of their GI benefits.
10. African Americans and Japanese Americans were the main target of wartime racism (see Murray 1992). By contrast, there were virtually no anti-German American or anti-Italian American policies in World War II (see Takaki 1989:357–406).
11. See Eichler 1982:5 for homeowning percentages; Jackson (1985:205) found an increase in families living in owner-occupied buildings, rising from 44 percent in 1934 to 63 percent in 1972; see Monkkonen 1988 on scarcity of mortgages; and Gelfand 1975, esp. chap. 6, on federal programs.

REFERENCES

Binkin, Martin, and Mark J. Eitelberg. 1982. *Blacks and the Military.* Washington, D.C.: Brookings.

Bodnar, John. 1985. *The Transplanted: A History of Immigrants in Urban America.* Bloomington: Indiana University Press.

Brody, David. 1980. *Workers in Industrial America: Essays of the Twentieth Century Struggle.* New York: Oxford University Press.

Brown, Francis J. 1946. *Educational Opportunities for Veterans.* Washington, D.C.: Public Affairs Press, American Council on Public Affairs.

Carlson, Lewis H., and George A. Colburn. 1972. *In Their Place: White America Defines Her Minorities, 1850–1950.* New York: Wiley.

Dalfiume, Richard M. 1969. *Desegregation of the U.S. Armed Forces: Fighting on Two Fronts, 1939–1953.* Columbia: University of Missouri Press.

Davis, Mike. 1990. *City of Quartz.* London: Verso.

Dobriner, William M. 1963. *Class in Suburbia*. Englewood Cliffs, N.J.: Prentice-Hall.

Eichler, Ned. 1982. *The Merchant Builders*. Cambridge, Mass.: MIT Press.

Fields, Barbara Jeanne. 1990. Slavery, Race, and Ideology in the United States of America. *New Left Review* 181:95–118.

Foner, Jack. 1974. *Blacks and the Military in American History: A New Perspective*. New York: Praeger.

Gans, Herbert. 1962. *The Urban Villagers*. New York: Free Press.

———. 1967. *The Levittowners*. New York: Pantheon.

Gordon, Milton. 1964. *Assimilation in American Life*. New York: Oxford University Press.

Hartman, Chester. 1975. *Housing and Social Policy*. Englewood Cliffs, N.J.: Prentice-Hall.

Higham, John. 1955. *Strangers in the Land*. New Brunswick, N.J.: Rutgers University Press.

Hurd, Charles. 1946. *The Veterans' Program: A Complete Guide to Its Benefits, Rights, and Options*. New York: McGraw-Hill.

Jackson, Kenneth T. 1985. *Crabgrass Frontier: The Suburbanization of the United States*. New York: Oxford University Press.

Johnson, Jesse J. 1967. *Ebony Brass: An Autobiography of Negro Frustration amid Aspiration*. New York: Frederick.

Karabel, Jerome. 1984. Status-Group Struggle, Organizational Interests, and the Limits of Institutional Autonomy. *Theory and Society* 13:1–40.

Kessler-Harris, Alice. 1982. *Out to Work: A History of Wage-Earning Women in the United States*. New York: Oxford University Press.

Martyn, Byron Curti. 1979. Racism in the U.S.: A History of Anti-Miscegenation Legislation and Litigation. Ph.D. diss., University of Southern California.

Mosch, Theodore R. 1975. *The GI Bill: A Breakthrough in Educational and Social Policy in the United States*. Hicksville, N.Y.: Exposition.

Nalty, Bernard C., and Morris J. MacGregor, eds. 1981. *Blacks in the Military: Essential Documents*. Wilmington, Del.: Scholarly Resources.

Nash, Gary B., Julie Roy Jeffrey, John R. Howe, Allen F. Davis, Peter J. Frederick, and Allen M. Winkler. 1986. *The American People: Creating a Nation and a Society*. New York: Harper and Row.

Pardo, Mary. 1990. Mexican-American Women Grassroots Community Activists: "Mothers of East Los Angeles." *Frontiers* 11:1–7.

Postwar Jobs for Veterans. 1945. *Annals of the American Academy of Political and Social Science* 238 (March).

Saxton, Alexander. 1971. *The Indispensible Enemy*. Berkeley and Los Angeles: University of California Press.

———. 1990. *The Rise and Fall of the White Republic*. London: Verso.

Silberman, Charles. 1985. *A Certain People: American Jews and Their Lives Today*. New York: Summit.

Sklare, Marshall. 1971. *America's Jews*. New York: Random House.

Sowell, Thomas. 1981. *Ethnic America: A History*. New York: Basic.

Steinberg, Stephen. 1989. *The Ethnic Myth: Race, Ethnicity, and Class in America*. 2d ed. Boston: Beacon.

Synott, Marcia Graham. 1986. Anti-Semitism and American Universities: Did Quotas Follow the Jews? In *Anti-Semitism in American History*, ed. David A. Gerber. Urbana: University of Illinois Press, 233–274.

Takaki, Ronald. 1989. *Strangers from a Different Shore*. Boston: Little, Brown.

Tobin, Gary A., ed. 1987. *Divided Neighborhoods: Changing Patterns of Racial Segregation*. Beverly Hills: Sage.

U.S. Bureau of the Census. 1930. *Fifteenth Census of the United States*. Vol. 2. Washington, D.C.: U.S. Government Printing Office.

———. 1940. *Sixteenth Census of the United States*. Vol. 2. Washington, D.C.: U.S. Government Printing Office.

Walker, Olive. 1970. The Windsor Hills School Story. *Integrated Education: Race and Schools* 8(3):4–9.

Willenz, June A. 1983. *Women Veterans: America's Forgotten Heroines*. New York: Continuum.

Wynn, Neil A. 1976. *The Afro-American and the Second World War*. London: Elek.

SOCIAL CLASS

5

RACE, WEALTH, AND EQUALITY

MELVIN L. OLIVER • THOMAS M. SHAPIRO

INTRODUCTION

Over a hundred years after the end of slavery, more than thirty years after the passage of major civil rights legislation, and following a concerted but prematurely curtailed War on Poverty, we harvest today a mixed legacy of racial progress. We celebrate the advancement of many blacks to middle-class status. In sharp contrast to previous history, school desegregation has enhanced educational access for blacks since the late fifties. Educational attainment, particularly the earning of the baccalaureate, has enabled substantial numbers of people in the black community to take advantage of white-collar

From: Oliver, Melvin L. & Thomas M. Shapiro. 1995. *Black Wealth/White Wealth: A New Perspective on Racial Inequality*. New York: Routledge, pp. 11–32.

occupations in the private sector and government employment. An official end to "de jure" housing segregation has even opened the door to neighborhoods and suburban residences previously off-limits to black residents. Nonetheless, many blacks have fallen by the wayside in their march toward economic equality. A growing number have not been able to take advantage of the opportunities now open to some. They suffer from educational deficiencies that make finding a foothold in an emerging technological economy near to impossible. Unable to move from deteriorated inner-city and older suburban communities, they entrust their children to school systems that are rarely able to provide them with the educational foundation they need to take the first steps up a racially skewed economic ladder. Trapped in communities of despair, they face increasing economic and social isolation from both their middle-class counterparts and white Americans.

The stratified nature of racial inequality highlights the importance of social class background as a factor in the continuing divergence in the economic fortunes of blacks and whites. The argument for class, most eloquently and influentially stated by William Julius Wilson in his 1978 book[1] *The Declining Significance of Race,* suggests that the racial barriers of the past are less important than present-day social class attributes in determining the economic life chances of black Americans. Education, in particular, is the key attribute in whether blacks will achieve economic success relative to white Americans. Discrimination and racism, while still actively practiced in many spheres, have marginally less effect on black Americans' economic attainment than whether or not blacks have the skills and education necessary to fit in a changing economy. In this view, race assumes importance only as the lingering product of an oppressive past. As Wilson observes, this time in his *Truly Disadvantaged,* racism and its most harmful injuries occurred in the past, and they are today experienced mainly by those on the bottom of the economic ladder, as "the accumulation of disadvantages . . . passed from generation to generation."[2]

We believe that a focus on wealth reveals a crucial dimension of the seeming paradox of continued racial inequality in American society. Looking at wealth helps solve the riddle of seeming black progress alongside economic deterioration. Black wealth has grown, for example, at the same time that it has fallen further behind that of whites. Wealth reveals an array of insights into black and white inequality that challenge our conception of racial and social justice in America. The continuation of persistent and vast wealth discrepancies among blacks and whites with similar achievements and credentials presents another daunting social policy dilemma. At stake here is a disturbing break in the link between achievement and rewards. If educational attainment is the panacea for racial inequality, then this break carries distressing implications for the future of democracy and social equality in America.

Disparities in wealth between blacks and whites are not the product of haphazard events, inborn traits, isolated incidents or solely contemporary individual accomplishments. Rather, wealth inequality has been structured over many generations through the same systemic barriers that have hampered blacks throughout their history in American society: slavery, Jim Crow, so-called de jure discrimination, and institutionalized racism. How these factors have affected the ability of blacks to accumulate wealth, however, has often been ignored or incompletely sketched. By briefly recalling three scenarios in American history that produced structured inequalities, we illustrate the significance of these barriers and their role in creating the wealth gap between blacks and whites.

RECONSTRUCTION

From Slavery to Freedom without a Material Base

> *Reconstruction was a bargain between the North and South to this effect: "We've liberated them from the land—and delivered them to the bosses."*
> —JAMES BALDWIN, "A TALK TO TEACHERS"

> *"De slaves spected a heap from freedom dey didn't get. . . . Dey promised us a mule an' forty acres o' lan'."*
> —ERIC FONER, *RECONSTRUCTION*

> *The tragedy of Reconstruction is the failure of the black masses to acquire land, since without the economic security provided by land ownership the freedmen were soon deprived of the political and civil rights which they had won.*
> —CLAUDE OUBRE, *FORTY ACRES AND A MULE*

The close of the Civil War transformed four million former slaves from chattel to freedmen. Emerging from a legacy of two and a half centuries of legalized oppression, the new freedmen entered Southern society with little or no material assets. With the North's military victory over the South freshly on the minds of Republican legislators and white abolitionists, there were rumblings in the air of how the former plantations and the property of Confederate soldiers and sympathizers would be confiscated and divided among the new freedmen to form the basis of their new status in society. The slave's often-cited demand of "forty acres and a mule" fueled great anticipation of a new beginning based on land ownership and a transfer of skills developed under slavery into the new economy of the South. Whereas slave muscle and skills had cleared the wilderness and made the land productive and profitable for plantation owners, the new vision saw the freedmen's hard work and skill generating income and resources for the former slaves themselves. W. E. B. Du Bois, in his *Black Reconstruction in America,* called this prospect America's chance to be a modern democracy.

Initially it appeared that massive land redistribution from the Confederates to the freedmen would indeed become a reality. Optimism greeted Sherman's March through the South, and especially his Order 15, which confiscated plantations and redistributed them to black soldiers. Such wartime actions were eventually rescinded and some soldiers who had already started to cultivate the land and build new lives were forced to give up their claims. Real access to land for the freedman had to await the passage of the Southern Homestead Act in 1866, which provided a legal basis and mechanism to promote black landownership. In this legislation public land already designated in the 1862 Homestead Act, which applied only to non-Confederate whites but not blacks, was now opened up to settlement by former slaves in the tradition of homesteading that had helped settle the West. The amount of land involved was substantial, a total of forty-six million acres. Applicants in the first two years of the Homestead Act were limited to only eighty acres, but subsequently this amount increased to 160 acres. The Freedmen's Bureau administered the program, and there was every reason to believe that in reasonable time slaves would be transformed from farm laborers to yeomanry farmers.

This social and economic transformation never occurred. The Southern Homestead Act failed to make newly freed blacks into a landowning class or to provide what Gunnar Myrdal in *An American Dilemma* called "a basis of real democracy in the United States."[3] Indeed, features of the legislation worked against its use as a tool to empower blacks in their quest for land. First, instead of disqualifying former Confederate supporters as the previous act had done, the 1866 legislation allowed all persons who applied for land to swear that they had not taken up arms against the Union or given aid and comfort to the enemies. This opened the door to massive white applications for land. One estimate suggests that over three-quarters (77.1 percent) of the land applicants under the act were white.[4] In addition, much of the land was poor swampland and it was difficult for black or white applicants to meet the necessary homesteading requirements because they could not make a decent living off the land. What is more important, blacks had to face the extra burden of racial prejudice and discrimination along with the charging of illegal fees, expressly discriminatory court challenges and court decisions, and land speculators. While these barriers faced all poor and illiterate applicants, Michael Lanza has stated in his *Agrarianism and Reconstruction Politics* that "The freedmen's badge of color and previous servitude complicated matters to almost incomprehensible proportions."[5]

Gunnar Myrdal's *An American Dilemma* provides the most cogent explanation of the unfulfilled promise of land to the freedman in an anecdotal passage from a white Southerner. Asked, "Wouldn't it have been better for the white man and the Negro" if the land had been provided? the old man remarked emphatically:

"No, for it would have made the Negro 'uppity.' " . . . and "the real reason . . . why it wouldn't do, is that we are having a hard time now keeping the nigger in his place, and if he were a landowner, he'd think he was a bigger man than old Grant, and there would be no living with him in the Black District. . . . Who'd work the land if the niggers had farms of their own?"[6]

Nevertheless, the extent of black landowning was remarkable given the economically deprived backgrounds from which the slaves emerged. Blacks had significant landholdings in the 1870s in South Carolina, Virginia, and Arkansas according to Du Bois's *Black Reconstruction in America*. Michael Lanza has suggested that while the 1866 act did not benefit as many blacks as it should have, it did provide part of the basis for the fact that by 1900 one-quarter of Southern black farmers owned their own farms. One could add that if the Freedmen's Bureau had succeeded, black landowners would have been much more prevalent in the South by 1900, and their wealth much more substantial.

John Rock, abolitionist, pre–Civil War orator, successful Boston dentist and lawyer, and the first African American attorney to plead before the U.S. Supreme Court, expressed great hope in 1858 that property and wealth could be the basis of racial justice:

> When the avenues of wealth are opened to us we will become educated and wealthy, and then the roughest-looking colored man that you ever saw . . . will be pleasanter than the harmonies of Orpheus, and black will be a very pretty color. It will make our jargon, wit—our words, oracles; flattery will then take the place of slander, and you will find no prejudice in the Yankee whatsoever.[7]

THE SUBURBANIZATION OF AMERICA

The Making of the Ghetto

> *Because of racial discrimination, blacks were unable to enter the housing market on the same terms as other groups before them. Thus, the most striking feature of black life was not slum conditions, but the barriers that middle-class blacks encountered trying to escape the ghetto.*
> —KENNETH T. JACKSON, *CRABGRASS FRONTIER*

> *A government offering such bounty to builders and lenders could have required compliance with nondiscriminatory policy. . . . Instead, FHA adopted a racial policy that could well have been culled from the Nuremberg laws. From its inception FHA set itself up as the protector of the all-white neighborhood. It sent its agents into the field to keep Negroes and other minorities from buying houses in white neighborhoods.*
> —CHARLES ABRAMS, *FORBIDDEN NEIGHBORS*

The suburbanization of America was principally financed and encouraged by actions of the federal government, which supported suburban growth from the 1930s through the 1960s by way of taxation, transportation, and housing policy.[8] Taxation policy, for example, provided greater tax savings for businesses relocating to the suburbs than to those who stayed and made capital improvements to plants in central city locations. As a consequence, employment opportunities steadily rose in the suburban rings of the nation's major metropolitan areas. In addition, transportation policy encouraged freeway construction and subsidized cheap fuel and mass-produced automobiles. These factors made living on the outer edges of cities both affordable and relatively convenient. However, the most important government policies encouraging and subsidizing suburbanization focused on housing. In particular, the incentives that government programs gave for the acquisition of single-family detached housing spurred both the development and financing of the tract home, which became the hallmark of suburban living. While these governmental policies collectively enabled over thirty-five million families between 1933 and 1978 to participate in homeowner equity accumulation, they also had the adverse effect of constraining black Americans' residential opportunities to central-city ghettos of major U.S. metropolitan communities and denying them access to one of the most successful generators of wealth in American history—the suburban tract home.[9]

This story begins with the government's initial entry into home financing. Faced with mounting foreclosures, President Roosevelt urged passage of a bill that authorized the Home Owners Loan Corporation (HOLC). According to Kenneth Jackson's *Crabgrass Frontier,* the HOLC "refinanced tens of thousands of mortgages in danger of default or foreclosure."[10] Of more importance to this story, however, it also introduced standardized appraisals of the fitness of particular properties and communities for both individual and group loans. In creating "a formal and uniform system of appraisal, reduced to writing, structured in defined procedures, and implemented by individuals only after intensive training, government appraisals institutionalized in a rational and bureaucratic framework a racially discriminatory practice that all but eliminated black access to the suburbs and to government mortgage money." Charged with the task of determining the "useful or productive life of housing" they considered to finance, government agents methodically included in their procedures the evaluation of the racial composition or potential racial composition of the community. Communities that were changing racially or were already black were deemed undesirable and placed in the lowest category. The categories, assigned various colors on a map ranging from green for the most desirable, which included new, all-white housing that was always in demand, to red, which included already racially mixed or all-black, old, and undesirable areas, subsequently were used by Federal Housing Authority (FHA) loan officers who made loans on the basis of these designations.

Established in 1934, the FHA aimed to bolster the economy and increase employment by aiding the ailing construction industry. The FHA ushered in the modern mortgage system that enabled people to buy homes on small down payments and at reasonable interest rates, with lengthy repayment periods and full loan amortization. The FHA's success was remarkable: housing starts jumped from 332,000 in 1936 to 619,000 in 1941. The incentive for home ownership increased to the point where it became, in some cases, cheaper to buy a home than to rent one. As one former resident of New York City who moved to suburban New Jersey pointed out, "We had been paying $50 per month rent, and here we come up and live for $29.00 a month."[11] This included taxes, principal, insurance, and interest.

This growth in access to housing was confined, however, for the most part to suburban areas. The administrative dictates outlined in the original act, while containing no antiurban bias, functioned in practice to the neglect of central cities. Three reasons can be cited: first, a bias toward the financing of single-family detached homes over multifamily projects favored open areas outside of the central city that had yet to be developed over congested central-city areas; second, a bias toward new purchases over repair of existing homes prompted people to move out of the city rather than upgrade or improve their existing residences; and third, the continued use of the "unbiased professional estimate" that made older homes and communities in which blacks or undesirables were located less likely to receive approval for loans encouraged purchases in communities where race was not an issue.

While the FHA used as its model the HOLC's appraisal system, it provided more precise guidance to its appraisers in its *Underwriting Manual.* The most basic sentiment underlying the FHA's concern was its fear that property values would decline if a rigid black and white segregation was not maintained. The *Underwriting Manual* openly stated that "if a neighborhood is to retain stability, it is necessary that properties shall continue to be occupied by the same social and racial classes" and further recommended that "subdivision regulations and suitable restrictive covenants" are the best way to ensure such neighborhood stability. The FHA's recommended use of restrictive covenants continued until 1949, when, responding to the Supreme Court's outlawing of such covenants in 1948 (*Shelly v. Kraemer*), it announced that "as of February 15, 1950, it would not insure mortgages on real estate subject to covenants."[12]

Even after this date, however, the FHA's discriminatory practices continued to have an impact on the continuing suburbanization of the white population and the deepening ghettoization of the black population. While exact figures regarding the FHA's discrimination against blacks are not available, data by county show a clear pattern of "redlining"[13] in central-city counties and abundant loan activity in suburban counties.

The FHA's actions have had a lasting impact on the wealth portfolios of black Americans. Locked out of the greatest mass-based opportunity for wealth accumulation in American history, African Americans who desired and were able to afford home ownership found themselves consigned to central-city communities where their investments were affected by the "self-fulfilling prophecies" of the FHA appraisers: cut off from sources of new investment their homes and communities deteriorated and lost value in comparison to those homes and communities that FHA appraisers deemed desirable. One infamous housing development of the period— Levittown— provides a classic illustration of the way blacks missed out on this asset-accumulating opportunity. Levittown was built on a mass scale, and housing there was eminently affordable, thanks to the FHA's and VHA's accessible financing, yet as late as 1960 "not a single one of the Long Island Levittown's 82,000 residents was black."[14]

CONTEMPORARY INSTITUTIONAL RACISM

Access to Mortgage Money and Redlining

> *It can now no longer be doubted that banks are discriminating against blacks who try to get home mortgages in city after city across the United States. . . . In many cities, high-income blacks are denied mortgage loans more frequently than low-income whites. This is a persuasive index of bias, whether conscious or not. . . . Construction of single-family housing is practically nonexistent, and much of the older housing is in disrepair. Some desperate homeowners, forced out of the conventional mortgage market, have fallen prey to unscrupulous lenders charging usurious rates of interest.*
>
> —BOSTON GLOBE, 22 OCTOBER 1991

> *For years, racial discrimination in mortgage lending has been considered an issue of geographic "redlining" by banks reluctant to lend in minority neighborhoods. But new evidence raises the specter of an even more insidious form of discrimination, one that follows blacks wherever they live and no matter how much they earn.*
>
> —BOSTON GLOBE, 27 OCTOBER 1991

In May of 1988 the issue of banking discrimination and redlining exploded onto the front pages of the *Atlanta Journal and Constitution*.[15] This Pulitzer Prize–winning series, "The Color of Money," described the wide disparity in mortgage-lending practices in black and white neighborhoods of Atlanta, finding black applicants rejected at a greater rate than whites, even when economic situations were comparable. The practice of geographic redlining of minority neighborhoods detailed in the articles had long been suspected, but one city's experience was not taken as conclusive evidence of a national pattern. Far more comprehensive evidence was soon forthcoming.

A 1991 Federal Reserve study of 6.4 million home mortgage applications by race and income confirmed suspicions of bias in lending by reporting a widespread and systemic pattern of institutional discrimination in the nation's banking system. This study disclosed that commercial banks rejected black applicants twice as often as whites nationwide. In some cities, like Boston, Philadelphia, Chicago, and Minneapolis, it reported a more pronounced pattern of minority loan rejections, with blacks being rejected three times more often than whites.

The argument that financial considerations—not discrimination—are the reason minorities get fewer loans appears to be totally refuted by the Federal Reserve study. The poorest white applicant, according to this report, was more likely to get a mortgage loan approved than a black in the highest income bracket. In Boston, for example, blacks in the highest income levels faced loan rejections three times more often than whites. These findings and reactions from bankers and community activists appeared in newspapers across the country. Bankers refuted the study's findings, labeling it unfair because "creditworthiness" was not considered. A later Federal Reserve study in 1992, taking creditworthiness into account, tempered the severity of bias but not the basic conclusion. We discuss this report more thoroughly in chapter 6.

The problem goes beyond redlining. Not only were banks reluctant to lend in minority communities, but the Federal Reserve study indicates that discrimination follows blacks no matter where they want to live and no matter how much they earn. A 1993 *Washington Post* series highlighted banks' reluctance to lend even in the wealthiest black neighborhoods.[16] One of the capital's most affluent black neighborhoods is the suburban community of Kettering in Prince George's County, Maryland. The average household income is $65,000 a year and the typical Kettering home has four or five bedrooms, a two-car garage, and a spacious lot. Local banks granted proportionately more loans in low-income white communities than they did in Kettering or any other high-income black neighborhoods. In Boston high-income blacks seeking homes outside the city's traditional black community confronted mortgage refusals far more often than whites who live on the same streets and who earn similar incomes. Previously banks responded to allegations of redlining by saying that it is only natural to have higher loan-rejection rates in minority communities because a greater proportion of low-income families live there. The lending patterns disclosed in the 1991 Federal Reserve study shows, however, that disproportionate mortgage denial rates for blacks have little, if any, relation to neighborhood or income. The *Boston Globe* of 22 October 1991 cites Massachusetts congressman Joe Kennedy to the effect that the study's results "portray an America where credit is a privilege of race and wealth, not a function of ability to pay back a loan."

These findings gave credence to the allegations of housing and community activists that banks have been strip-mining minority neighborhoods of housing equity through unscrupulous backdoor loans for home repairs. Homes bought during the 1960s and 1970s in low-income areas had acquired some equity but were also in need of repair. Mainstream banks refused to approve such loans at "normal" rates, but finance companies made loans that,

according to activists, preyed on minority communities by charging exorbi-
tant, pawnshop-style interest rates with unfavorable conditions. Rates of 34
percent and huge balloon payments were not uncommon. Mainstream banks
repurchased many of these loans, and the subsequent foreclosure rates were
very high. Civil rights activists noted, as reported in the 23 January 1989 *Los
Angeles Times,* that this "rape" of minority communities was aided and abetted by the Reagan administration's weakening of the regulatory system built
up in the 1960s and 1970s to combat redlining.

In Atlanta Christine Hill's story is typical. It started with a leaky roof and
ended in personal bankruptcy, foreclosure, and eviction. Using Hill's home
as collateral, the lender charged interest that, according to Rob Wells's piece
in the 10 January 1993 *Chicago Tribune* "made double-digit pawnshop rates
look like bargains." The Hills couldn't pay. The lender was a small and un-
regulated mortgage firm, similar to those often chosen by low-income borrowers because mainstream banks consider them too poor or financially
unstable to qualify for a normal bank loan. Approximately twenty thousand
other low-income Georgian homeowners found themselves in a similar
predicament. The attorney representing some of them is quoted in Wells's
Tribune article as saying: "This is a system of segregation, really. We don't
have separate water fountains, but we have separate lending institutions."
Senator Donald Riegle of Michigan in announcing a Senate Banking Committee hearing on abuse in home equity and second mortgage lending
pointed to "reverse redlining."[17] This means providing credit in low-income
neighborhoods on predatory terms and "taking advantage of unsophisti-
cated borrowers."

In Boston more than one-half of the families who relied on these kinds of
high-interest loans lost their homes through foreclosure. One study charted
every loan between 1984 and mid-1991 made by two high-interest lenders.[18]
Families lost their homes or were facing foreclosure in over three-quarters of
the cases. Only fifty-five of the 406 families still possessed their homes and
did not face foreclosure. The study also showed that the maps of redlined areas and high-interest loans overlapped.

Across the country a strikingly similar pattern emerged regarding home-
repair loans. Banks redlined extensive sections of minority communities,
denying people not only access to home mortgages but access to home-repair
loans as well. States inexplicably failed to license or regulate home-repair
contractors. Home-repair sales people went door to door in the redlined areas "soliciting" business, and their subsequent billing routinely far exceeded
their estimates. Finally, the high-interest mortgages needed to procure the
home-repair work were secured through finance companies, often using existing home equity as collateral in a second mortgage. Mainstream banks
then often bought these high-interest loans.

Even briefly recalled, the three historical moments evoked in the pages
above illustrate the powerful dynamics generating structured inequality in
America. Several common threads link the three scenarios. First, whether it
be a question of homesteading, suburbanization, or redlining, we have seen

how governmental, institutional, and private-sector discrimination enhances the ability of different segments of the population to accumulate and build on their wealth assets and resources, thereby raising their standard of living and securing a better future for themselves and their children. The use of land grants and mass low-priced sales of government lands created massive and unparalleled opportunities for Americans in the nineteenth century to secure title to land in the westward expansion. Likewise, government backing of millions of low-interest loans to returning soldiers and low-income families enabled American cities to suburbanize and their inhabitants to see tremendous home value growth after World War II. Quite clearly, black Americans for the most part were unable to secure the same degree of benefits from these government programs as whites were. Indeed, in many of these programs the government made explicit efforts to exclude blacks from participating in them, or to limit their participation in ways that deeply affected their ability to gain the maximum benefits. As our discussion indicates, moreover, contemporary patterns of institutional bias continue to directly inhibit the ability of blacks to buy homes in black communities, or elsewhere. As a result of this discrimination, blacks have been blocked from home ownership altogether or they have paid higher interest rates to secure residential loans.

Second, disparities in access to housing created differential opportunities for blacks and whites to take advantage of new and more lucrative opportunities to secure the good life. White families who were able to secure title to land in the nineteenth century were much more likely to finance education for their children, provide resources for their own or their children's self-employment, or secure their political rights through political lobbies and the electoral process. Blocked from low-interest government-backed loans, redlined out by financial institutions, or barred from home ownership by banks, black families have been denied the benefits of housing inflation and the subsequent vast increase in home equity assets. Black Americans who failed to secure this economic base were much less likely to be able to provide educational access for their children, secure the necessary financial resources for self-employment, or participate effectively in the political process. . . .

NOTES

1. Is it purely a result? This is a modified version of the question generated by Wilson's *The Declining Significance of Race* in 1978. Much of the literature on race in American society since then has been an attempt to address Wilson's question via empirical test and theoretical argument. The proponents of the class argument concentrate on how race is less important than class and impersonal forces like economic restructuring (see, e.g., Kasarda 1990; Smith and Welch 1989; Wilson 1987); opponents quickly respond that race has endured in significance (Oliver 1980; Willie 1979) and in some cases become more important, especially for the black middle class (Feagin and Sikes 1994; Landry 1987). Others have attempted to map out the ways in which race and class interact to produce racial inequality (Franklin 1991; Fainstein 1993).

2. The quote on "the accumulation of disadvantages . . ." is from Wilson 1987, 120.
3. The quote on the "basis of real democracy . . ." is from Myrdal 1944, 223.
4. For the percentage of white applicants for Southern Homestead Land Act see Lanza 1990.
5. The quote on "the freedman's badge of color . . ." is from Lanza 1990, 87.
6. " 'No,' he said emphatically . . ." The quote is from Myrdal 1944, 226–27.
7. "When the avenues of wealth opened" is from John Rock's Address to the Boston Antislavery Society, March 5, 1858.
8. For discussions of the suburbanization of America see Feagin and Parker 1990; Jackson 1985; Lipsitz 1995; and Squires 1994.
9. On the constrainment of black American's residential opportunities see Jackson 1985.
10. For quotations from *Crabgrass Frontier* on the discriminatory impact of HOLC standards see Jackson 1985, 196.
11. "We had been paying . . ." The quote is from Jackson 1985, 206.
12. The quote on "real estate subject to covenants" is from Jackson 1985, 208. See also Bell 1992b, 691–94.
13. On FHA "redlining" see Lipsitz 1995.
14. Levittown's exclusion of blacks. The quote is from Jackson 1985, 241.
15. On banking discrimination and redlining in Atlanta see Dedman 1988.
16. On lending bias in the nation's capital see Brenner and Spayd 1993.
17. On "reverse redlining" see Zuckoff 1993.
18. For the study of high-interest loans in Boston see *Boston Globe* 1991a.

REFERENCES

Bell, Derrick. 1992b. *Race, Racism, and American Law.* 3d ed. Boston: Little Brown.

Boston Globe. 1991a. "Risk Perception Burdens Minorities." 28 May, 21.

Brenner, Joel, and Liz Spayd. 1993. "Separate and Unequal: Racial Discrimination in Area Home Lending." *Washington Post.* 6–8 June: A1.

Dedman, Bill. 1988. "The Color of Money." *Atlanta Journal and Constitution* (May): 15–19.

Du Bois, W. E. B. 1935. *Black Reconstruction in America.* New York: Harcourt, Brace.

Fainstein, Norman I. 1993. "Race, Class, and Segregation." *International Journal of Urban and Regional Research* 17:384–93.

Feagin, Joe R., and Robert Parker. 1990. *Building American Cities: The Urban Real Estate Game.* Englewood Cliffs, NJ: Prentice Hall.

Feagin, Joe R., and Melvin P. Sikes. 1994. *Living with Racism: The Black Middle-Class Experience.* Boston: Beacon Press.

Franklin, Raymond S. 1991. *Shadows of Race and Class.* Minneapolis: University of Minnesota Press.

Jackson, Kenneth T. 1985. *Crabgrass Frontier: The Suburbanization of the United States.* New York: Oxford University Press.

Kasarda, John D. 1990. "Structural Factors Affecting the Location and Timing of Underclass Growth." *Urban Geography* 11, no. 3:234–64.

Landry, Bart. 1987. *The New Black Middle Class.* Berkeley: University of California Press.

Lanza, Michael L. 1990. *Agrarianism and Reconstruction Politics: The Southern Homestead Act.* Baton Rouge: Louisiana State University Press.

Lipsitz, George. 1995. "The Possessive Investment in Whiteness: The 'White' Problem in American Studies." *American Quarterly* (Fall).

Myrdal, Gunnar. 1944. *An American Dilemma.* New York: Harper.

Oliver, Melvin L. 1980. "The Enduring Significance of Race." *Journal of Ethnic Studies* 7, no. 4:79–91.

Rock, John S. 1858. "Address to Boston Antislavery Society, March 5." *Antislavery Collection.* Rare Book Division, Boston Public Library.

Smith, James, and Finis Welch. 1989. "Black Economic Progress after Myrdal." *Journal of Economic Literature* 27: 519–64.

Squires, Gregory D. 1994. *Capital and Communities in Black and White.* Albany: State University of New York Press.

Willie, Charles Vert, ed. 1979. *The Class-Caste Controversy.* Bayside, NY: General Hill.

Wilson, William J. 1978. *The Declining Significance of Race.* Chicago: University of Chicago Press.

———. 1987. *The Truly Disadvantaged.* Chicago: University of Chicago Press.

Zuckoff, Mitchell. 1993. "Senator Says Feb. 17 Hearing to Look at 'Reverse Redlining.' " *Boston Globe,* 28 January, Economy sec., 37.

6

MEDIA MAGIC
Making Class Invisible

GREGORY MANTSIOS

Of the various social and cultural forces in our society, the mass media is arguably the most influential in molding public consciousness. Americans spend an average twenty-eight hours per week watching television. They also spend an undetermined number of hours reading periodicals, listening to the radio, and going to the movies. Unlike other cultural and socializing institutions, ownership and control of the mass media is highly concentrated. Twenty-three corporations own more than one-half of all the daily newspapers, magazines, movie studios, and radio and television outlets in the United States.[1] The number of media companies is shrinking and their control of the industry is expanding. And a relatively small number of media outlets is producing and packaging the majority of news and enter-tainment programs. For the most part, our media is national in nature and single-minded (profit-oriented) in purpose. This media plays a key role in defining our cultural tastes, helping us locate ourselves in history, establish-ing our national identity, and ascertaining the range of national and social possibilities. In this essay, we will examine the way the mass media shapes how people think about each other and about the nature of our society.

The United States is the most highly stratified society in the industrial-ized world. Class distinctions operate in virtually every aspect of our lives, determining the nature of our work, the quality of our schooling, and the health and safety of our loved ones. Yet remarkably, we, as a nation, retain il-lusions about living in an egalitarian society. We maintain these illusions, in large part, because the media hides gross inequities from public view. In those instances when inequities are revealed, we are provided with messages that obscure the nature of class realities and blame the victims of class-dominated society for their own plight. Let's briefly examine what the news media, in particular, tells us about class.

ABOUT THE POOR

The news media provides meager coverage of poor people and poverty. The coverage it does provide is often distorted and misleading.

The Poor Do Not Exist

For the most part, the news media ignores the poor. Unnoticed are forty mil-lion poor people in the nation—a number that equals the entire population of Maine, Vermont, New Hampshire, Connecticut, Rhode Island, New Jersey, and New York combined. Perhaps even more alarming is that the rate of poverty is increasing twice as fast as the population growth in the United States. Ordinarily, even a calamity of much smaller proportion (e.g., flooding in the Midwest) would garner a great deal of coverage and hype from a me-dia usually eager to declare a crisis, yet less than one in five hundred articles in the *New York Times* and one in one thousand articles listed in the *Readers Guide to Periodic Literature* are on poverty. With remarkably little attention to them, the poor and their problems are hidden from most Americans.

When the media does turn its attention to the poor, it offers a series of contradictory messages and portrayals.

The Poor Are Faceless

Each year the Census Bureau releases a new report on poverty in our society and its results are duly reported in the media. At best, however, this coverage emphasizes annual fluctuations (showing how the numbers differ from pre-vious years) and ongoing debates over the validity of the numbers (some ar-gue the number should be lower, most that the number should be higher).

Coverage like this desensitizes us to the poor by reducing poverty to a number. It ignores the human tragedy of poverty—the suffering, indignities, and misery endured by millions of children and adults. Instead, the poor become statistics rather than people.

The Poor Are Undeserving

When the media does put a face on the poor, it is not likely to be a pretty one. The media will provide us with sensational stories about welfare cheats, drug addicts, and greedy panhandlers (almost always urban and Black). Compare these images and the emotions evoked by them with the media's treatment of middle-class (usually white) "tax evaders," celebrities who have a "chemical dependency," or wealthy businesspeople who use unscrupulous means to "make a profit." While the behavior of the more affluent offenders is considered an "impropriety" and a deviation from the norm, the behavior of the poor is considered repugnant, indicative of the poor in general, and worthy of our indignation and resentment.

The Poor Are an Eyesore

When the media does cover the poor, they are often presented through the eyes of the middle class. For example, sometimes the media includes a story about community resistance to a homeless shelter or storekeeper annoyance with panhandlers. Rather than focusing on the plight of the poor, these stories are about middle-class opposition to the poor. Such stories tell us that the poor are an inconvenience and an irritation.

The Poor Have Only Themselves to Blame

In another example of media coverage, we are told that the poor live in a personal and cultural cycle of poverty that hopelessly imprisons them. They routinely center on the Black urban population and focus on perceived personality or cultural traits that doom the poor. While the women in these stories typically exhibit an "attitude" that leads to trouble or a promiscuity that leads to single motherhood, the men possess a need for immediate gratification that leads to drug abuse or an unquenchable greed that leads to the pursuit of fast money. The images that are seared into our mind are sexist, racist, and classist. Census figures reveal that most of the poor are white not Black or Hispanic, that they live in rural or suburban areas not urban centers, and hold jobs at least part of the year.[2] Yet, in a fashion that is often framed in an understanding and sympathetic tone, we are told that the poor have inflicted poverty on themselves.

The Poor Are Down on Their Luck

During the Christmas season, the news media sometimes provides us with accounts of poor individuals or families (usually white) who are down on their luck. These stories are often linked to stories about soup kitchens or other charitable activities and sometimes call for charitable contributions. These "Yule time" stories are as much about the affluent as they are about the poor: they tell us that the affluent in our society are a kind, understanding, giving people—which we are not.* The series of unfortunate circumstances that have led to impoverishment are presumed to be a temporary condition that will improve with time and a change in luck.

Despite appearances, the messages provided by the media are not entirely disparate. With each variation, the media informs us what poverty is not (i.e., systemic and indicative of American society) by informing us what it is. The media tells us that poverty is either an aberration of the American way of life (it doesn't exist, it's just another number, it's unfortunate but temporary) or an end product of the poor themselves (they are a nuisance, do not deserve better, and have brought their predicament upon themselves).

By suggesting that the poor have brought poverty upon themselves, the media is engaging in what William Ryan has called "blaming the victim."[3] The media identifies in what ways the poor are different as a consequence of deprivation, then defines those differences as the cause of poverty itself. Whether blatantly hostile or cloaked in sympathy, the message is that there is something fundamentally wrong with the victims—their hormones, psychological makeup, family environment, community, race, or some combination of these—that accounts for their plight and their failure to lift themselves out of poverty.

But poverty in the United States is systemic. It is a direct result of economic and political policies that deprive people of jobs, adequate wages, or legitimate support. It is neither natural nor inevitable: there is enough wealth in our nation to eliminate poverty if we chose to redistribute existing wealth or income. The plight of the poor is reason enough to make the elimination of poverty the nation's first priority. But poverty also impacts dramatically on the nonpoor. It has a dampening effect on wages in general (by maintaining a reserve army of unemployed and underemployed anxious for any job at any wage) and breeds crime and violence (by maintaining conditions that invite private gain by illegal means and rebellion-like behavior, not entirely unlike the urban riots of the 1960s). Given the extent of poverty in the nation and the impact it has on us all, the media must spin considerable magic to keep the poor and the issue of poverty and its root causes out of the public consciousness.

---

*American households with incomes of less than $10,000 give an average of 5.5 percent of their earning to charity or to a religious organization, while those making more than $100,000 a year give only 2.9 percent. After changes in the 1986 tax code reduced the benefits of charitable giving, taxpayers earning $500,000 or more slashed their average donation by nearly one-third. Furthermore, many of these acts of benevolence do not help the needy. Rather than provide funding to social service agencies that aid the poor, the voluntary contributions of the wealthy go to places and institutions that entertain, inspire, cure, or educate wealthy Americans—art museums, opera houses, theaters, orchestras, ballet companies, private hospitals, and elite universities. (Robert Reich, "Secession of the Successful," *New York Times Magazine*, February 17, 1991, p. 43.)

ABOUT EVERYONE ELSE

Both the broadcast and the print news media strive to develop a strong sense of "we-ness" in their audience. They seek to speak to and for an audience that is both affluent and like-minded. The media's solidarity with affluence, that is, with the middle and upper class, varies little from one medium to another. Benjamin DeMott points out, for example, that the *New York Times* understands affluence to be intelligence, taste, public spirit, responsibility, and a readiness to rule and "conceives itself as spokesperson for a readership awash in these qualities."[4] Of course, the flip side to creating a sense of "we," or "us," is establishing a perception of the "other." The other relates back to the faceless, amoral, undeserving, and inferior "underclass." Thus, the world according to the news media is divided between the "underclass" and everyone else. Again the messages are often contradictory.

The Wealthy Are Us

Much of the information provided to us by the news media focuses attention on the concerns of a very wealthy and privileged class of people. Although the concerns of a small fraction of the populace, they are presented as though they were the concerns of everyone. For example, while relatively few people actually own stock, the news media devotes an inordinate amount of broadcast time and print space to business news and stock market quotations. Not only do business reports cater to a particular narrow clientele, so do the fashion pages (with $2,000 dresses), wedding announcements, and the obituaries. Even weather and sports news often have a class bias. An all news radio station in New York City, for example, provides regular national ski reports. International news, trade agreements, and domestic policies issues are also reported in terms of their impact on business climate and the business community. Besides being of practical value to the wealthy, such coverage has considerable ideological value. Its message: the concerns of the wealthy are the concerns of us all.

The Wealthy (as a Class) Do Not Exist

While preoccupied with the concerns of the wealthy, the media fails to notice the way in which the rich as a class of people create and shape domestic and foreign policy. Presented as an aggregate of individuals, the wealthy appear without special interests, interconnections, or unity in purpose. Out of public view are the class interests of the wealthy, the interlocking business links, the concerted actions to preserve their class privileges and business interests (by running for public office, supporting political candidates, lobbying, etc.). Corporate lobbying is ignored, taken for granted, or assumed to be in the public interest. (Compare this with the media's portrayal of the "strong arm of labor" in attempting to defeat trade legislation that is harmful to the interests of working people.) It is estimated that two-thirds of the U.S. Senate is composed of millionaires.[5] Having such a preponderance of millionaires in the Senate, however, is perceived to be neither unusual nor anti-democratic; these millionaire senators are assumed to be serving "our" collective interests in governing.

The Wealthy Are Fascinating and Benevolent

The broadcast and print media regularly provide hype for individuals who have achieved "super" success. These stories are usually about celebrities and superstars from the sports and entertainment world. Society pages and gossip columns serve to keep the social elite informed of each others' doings, allow the rest of us to gawk at their excesses, and help to keep the American dream alive. The print media is also fond of feature stories on corporate empire builders. These stories provide an occasional "insider's" view of the private and corporate life of industrialists by suggesting a rags to riches account of corporate success. These stories tell us that corporate success is a series of smart moves, shrewd acquisitions, timely mergers, and well thought out executive suite shuffles. By painting the upper class in a positive light, innocent of any wrongdoing (labor leaders and union organizations usually get the opposite treatment), the media assures us that wealth and power are benevolent. One person's capital accumulation is presumed to be good for all. The elite, then, are portrayed as investment wizards, people of special talent and skill, whom even their victims (workers and consumers) can admire.

The Wealthy Include a Few Bad Apples

On rare occasions, the media will mock selected individuals for their personality flaws. Real estate investor Donald Trump and New York Yankees owner George Steinbrenner, for example, are admonished by the media for deliberately seeking publicity (a very un–upper class thing to do); hotel owner Leona Helmsley was caricatured for her personal cruelties; and junk bond broker Michael Milkin was condemned because he had the audacity to rob the rich. Michael Parenti points out that by treating business wrongdoings as isolated deviations from the socially beneficial system of "responsible capitalism," the media overlooks the features of the system that produce such abuses and the regularity with which they occur. Rather than portraying them as predictable and frequent outcomes of corporate power and the business system, the media treats abuses as if they were isolated and atypical. Presented as an occasional aberration, these incidents serve not to challenge, but to legitimate, the system.[6]

The Middle Class Is Us

By ignoring the poor and blurring the lines between the working people and the upper class, the news media creates a universal middle class. From this perspective, the size of one's income becomes largely irrelevant: what matters is that most of "us" share an intellectual and moral superiority over the disadvantaged. As *Time* magazine once concluded, "Middle America is a state of mind."[7] "We are all middle class," we are told, "and we all share the same concerns": job security, inflation, tax burdens, world peace, the cost of food and housing, health care, clean air and water, and the safety of our streets. While the concerns of the wealthy are quite distinct from those of the middle class (e.g., the wealthy worry about investments, not jobs), the media convinces us that "we [the affluent] are all in this together."

The Middle Class Is a Victim

For the media, "we" the affluent not only stand apart from the "other"—the poor, the working class, the minorities, and their problems—"we" are also victimized by the poor (who drive up the costs of maintaining the welfare rolls), minorities (who commit crimes against us), and by workers (who are greedy and drive companies out and prices up). Ignored are the subsidies to the rich, the crimes of corporate America, and the policies that wreak havoc on the economic well-being of middle America. Media magic convinces us to fear, more than anything else, being victimized by those less affluent than ourselves.

The Middle Class Is Not a Working Class

The news media clearly distinguishes the middle class (employees) from the working class (i.e., blue collar workers) who are portrayed, at best, as irrelevant, outmoded, and a dying breed. Furthermore, the media will tell us that the hardships faced by blue-collar workers are inevitable (due to progress), a result of bad luck (chance circumstances in a particular industry), or a product of their own doing (they priced themselves out of a job). Given the media's presentation of reality, it is hard to believe that manual, supervised, unskilled, and semiskilled workers actually represent more than 50 percent of the adult working population.[8] The working class, instead, is relegated by the media to "the other."

In short, the news media either lionizes the wealthy or treats their interests and those of the middle class as one in the same. But the upper class and the middle class do not share the same interests or worries. Members of the upper class worry about stock dividends (not employment), they profit from inflation and global militarism, their children attend exclusive private schools, they eat and live in a royal fashion, they call on (or are called upon by) personal physicians, they have few consumer problems, they can escape whenever they want from environmental pollution, and they live on streets and travel to other areas under the protection of private police forces.*[9]

---

*The number of private security guards in the United States now exceeds the number of public police officers. (Robert Reich, "Secession of the Successful," *New York Times Magazine,* February 17, 1991, p. 42.)

The wealthy are not only a class with distinct life-styles and interests, they are a ruling class. They receive a disproportionate share of the country's yearly income, own a disproportionate amount of the country's wealth, and contribute a disproportionate number of their members to governmental bodies and decision-making groups—all traits that William Domhoff, in his classic work *Who Rules America,* defined as characteristic of a governing class.[10]

This governing class maintains and manages our political and economic structures in such a way that these structures continue to yield an amazing proportion of our wealth to a minuscule upper class. While the media is not above referring to ruling classes in other countries (we hear, for example, references to Japan's ruling elite),[11] its treatment of the news proceeds as though there were no such ruling class in the United States.

Furthermore, the news media inverts reality so that those who are working class and middle class learn to fear, resent, and blame those below, rather than those above them in the class structure. We learn to resent welfare, which accounts for only two cents out of every dollar in the federal budget (approximately $10 billion) and provides financial relief for the needy,* but learn little about the $11 billion the federal government spends on individuals with incomes in excess of $1,000,000 (not needy),[12] or the $17 billion in farm subsidies, or the $214 billion (twenty times the cost of welfare) in interest payments to financial institutions.

Middle-class whites learn to fear African Americans and Latinos, but most violent crime occurs within poor and minority communities and is neither interracial† nor interclass. As horrid as such crime is, it should not mask the destruction and violence perpetrated by corporate America. In spite of the fact that 14,000 innocent people are killed on the job each year, 100,000 die prematurely, 400,000 become seriously ill, and 6 million are injured from work-related accidents and diseases, most Americans fear government regulation more than they do unsafe working conditions.

Through the media, middle-class—and even working class—Americans learn to blame blue-collar workers and their unions for declining purchasing power and economic security. But while workers who managed to keep their jobs and their unions struggled to keep up with inflation, the top 1 percent of American families saw their average incomes soar 80 percent in the last decade.[13] Much of the wealth at the top was accumulated as stockholders and

---

*A total of $20 billion is spent on welfare when you include all state funding. But the average state funding also comes to only two cents per state dollar.
†In 92 percent of the murders nationwide the assailant and the victim are of the same race (46 percent are white/white, 46 percent are black/black), 5.6 percent are black on white, and 2.4 percent are white on black. (FBI and Bureau of Justice Statistics, 1985–1986, quoted in Raymond S. Franklin, *Shadows of Race and Class,* University of Minnesota Press, Minneapolis, 1991, p. 108.)

corporate executives moved their companies abroad to employ cheaper labor (56 cents per hour in El Salvador) and avoid paying taxes in the United States. Corporate America is a world made up of ruthless bosses, massive layoffs, favoritism and nepotism, health and safety violations, pension plan losses, union busting, tax evasions, unfair competition, and price gouging, as well as fast buck deals, financial speculation, and corporate wheeling and dealing that serve the interests of the corporate elite, but are generally wasteful and destructive to workers and the economy in general.

It is no wonder Americans cannot think straight about class. The mass media is neither objective, balanced, independent, nor neutral. Those who own and direct the mass media are themselves part of the upper class, and neither they nor the ruling class in general have to conspire to manipulate public opinion. Their interest is in preserving the status quo, and their view of society as fair and equitable comes naturally to them. But their ideology dominates our society and justifies what is in reality a perverse social order— one that perpetuates unprecedented elite privilege and power on the one hand and widespread deprivation on the other. A mass media that did not have its own class interests in preserving the status quo would acknowledge that inordinate wealth and power undermines democracy and that a "free market" economy can ravage a people and their communities.

NOTES

1. Martin Lee and Norman Solomon, *Unreliable Sources,* Lyle Stuart (New York, 1990), p. 71. See also Ben Bagdikian, *The Media Monopoly,* Beacon Press (Boston, 1990).
2. Department of Commerce, Bureau of the Census, "Poverty in the United States: 1992," *Current Population Reports, Consumer Income,* Series P60–185, pp. xi, xv, 1.
3. William Ryan, *Blaming the Victim,* Vintage (New York, 1971).
4. Benjamin Demott, *The Imperial Middle,* William Morrow (New York, 1990), p. 123.
5. Fred Barnes, "The Zillionaires Club," *The New Republic,* January 29, 1990, p. 24.
6. Michael Parenti, *Inventing Reality,* St. Martin's Press (New York, 1986), p. 109.
7. *Time,* January 5, 1979, p. 10.
8. Vincent Navarro, "The Middle Class—A Useful Myth," *The Nation,* March 23, 1992, p. 1.
9. Charles Anderson, *The Political Economy of Social Class,* Prentice Hall (Englewood Cliffs, N.J., 1974), p. 137.
10. William Domhoff, *Who Rules America?,* Prentice Hall (Englewood Cliffs, N.J., 1967), p. 5.
11. Lee and Solomon, *Unreliable Sources,* p. 179.
12. *Newsweek,* August 10, 1992, p. 57.
13. *Business Week,* June 8, 1992, p. 86.

7

THE GROWING WEALTH GAP
The median household net worth matches the sticker price of the new Ford Excursion

HOLLY SKLAR • CHUCK COLLINS
BETSY LEONDAR-WRIGHT

The booming economy has been a bust for millions of Americans. Most households have lower inflation-adjusted net worth now than they did in 1983, when the Dow was still at 1,000.

The top 1 percent of households has soared while most Americans have been working harder to stay in place, if they have not fallen further behind. Since the 1970s, the top 1 percent of households has doubled their share of the national wealth to 40 percent. The top 1 percent of households has more wealth than the entire bottom 95 percent. Financial wealth is even more concentrated. The top 1 percent of households has nearly half of all financial wealth (net worth minus net equity in owner-occupied housing), says economist Edward Wolff of New York University. Wealth is further concentrated at the top of the top 1 percent. The richest 0.5 percent of households has 42 percent of the financial wealth.

The total net worth of the median American household just about matches the projected sticker price of Ford's new supersized sports utility vehicle, the Excursion. Adjusting for inflation, the net worth of the household in the middle (the median household) fell from $54,600 in 1989 to $49,900 in 1997. Median financial wealth fell from $13,000 in 1989 to $11,700 in 1997.

The percentage of households with zero or negative net worth (greater debts than assets) increased from 15.5 percent in 1983 to 18.5 percent in 1995—nearly one out of five households. That's nearly double the rate in 1962 when the comparable figure was 9.8 percent—one out of ten households. The net worth of the poorest fifth of households averaged −$5,600 in 1997. That's down from −$3,000 in 1983.

Many households are deeper in debt. Debt as a percentage of personal income rose from 58 percent in 1973 to 76 percent in 1989 to an estimated 85 percent in 1997.

This article is based on the authors' new book *Shifting Fortunes: The Perils of the Growing American Wealth Gap*, published by the Boston-based United for a Fair Economy; www.stw.org.

The growth in household debt has helped keep the economy growing despite wage stagnation at home and economic turmoil abroad—at a significant cost to many families and the nation's long-term economic health. "The unsustainable growth in debt," says John Schmitt of the Economic Policy Institute, "undermines the stability of the recovery and threatens to magnify the impact of any downturn." A rise in interest rates "could put some newly indebted households over the edge. Even a mild increase in unemployment could produce a substantial rise in bad debts, private bankruptcies, and mortgage foreclosures."

The stock market boom has sent the fortunes of some Americans soaring while leaving many others in the dust. At a 15 percent annual return—big by historical standards—investments double about every five years. The recent stock market has done much better than that.

From 1983 to 1998, the Standard & Poor's 500 Index (S&P 500), a much broader gauge of the stock market than the Dow, grew a cumulative 1,336 percent with dividends reinvested. If you had put $10,000 in the stock market in 1983 you could have more than $143,000 today. Unfortunately, most Americans didn't have the $10,000 to invest then, and they don't have it today. A million dollars invested by a wealthy American in S&P 500 index stocks in 1983 would have ballooned to $14.4 million by the end of 1998.

Between 1983 and 1995, the S&P 500 delivered a huge cumulative return of 582 percent (with dividends reinvested). At the same time, the median household net worth dropped 11 percent and the bottom 40 percent lost an incredible 80 percent. The top 1 percent, meanwhile, gained 17 percent.

Between 1995 and 1998, S&P 500 stocks had an annualized return of 30 percent. Most of it went to the top 10 percent of households.

Four out of ten households now own stock directly and indirectly, but most still don't own much. Almost 90 percent of the value of all stocks and mutual funds owned by households is in the hands of the top 10 percent. According to Edward Wolff, an estimated 42 percent of the benefits of the increase in the stock market between 1989 and 1997 went to the richest 1 percent alone. The bottom 80 percent of households split 11 percent of the gains.

THE WAGE GAP

Nine years into the longest peacetime expansion in U.S. history, average workers are still earning less, adjusting for inflation, than they did when Richard Nixon was president. Despite long-overdue wage growth since 1996, hourly wages for average workers in 1998 were still 6.2 percent below 1973, adjusting for inflation; weekly wages were 12 percent lower than in 1973. Nonfarm business productivity grew nearly 33 percent in the same period, according to the Economic Policy Institute.

What if wages had kept rising with productivity? What if they were 33 percent higher in 1998 than they were in 1973? The average hourly wage in

1998 would have been $18.10, rather than $12.77. That's a difference of $5.33 an hour—more than $11,000 for a full-time, year-round worker. The 30 cents workers gained in their hourly wages between 1997 and 1998 pales by comparison.

The pace of recent wage growth has already slowed despite tight labor markets in many parts of the country. The cumulative wages lost since 1973 will never be recovered—much less their lost investment potential.

The minimum wage has become a poverty wage. It was 19 percent lower in 1998 at $5.15 than it was in 1979, when it was worth $6.39, adjusted for inflation. The minimum wage used to bring a family of three, with a full-time worker, above the official poverty line. Now it doesn't bring a full-time worker with one child above the official poverty line.

Many Americans can't make ends meet today, much less build assets for the future. A recent study by the Urban Institute, *Snapshots of America's Families,* found that many families with incomes up to 200 percent of the federal poverty level—which they call lower-income families—had trouble supporting themselves and their families. Nearly three in ten lower-income families were unable to pay the mortgage, rent or utility bills at some point in the prior year. Nearly half of lower-income families reported worrying about or having difficulty affording food.

Low-income workers are turning increasingly to food banks and homeless shelters, which cannot keep up with the rising demand. In its 1998 survey of 30 major cities, the U.S. Conference of Mayors found that requests for emergency shelter by homeless families had risen 15 percent during the past year; 30 percent of the requests went unmet. The mayors also found that more than one-fifth of the urban homeless were employed. The mayors found that requests for emergency food increased an average of 14 percent during the past year. One out of five requests for food assistance went unmet.

A survey by Second Harvest, the nation's largest private network of food charities, found that nearly 40 percent of the households who received Second Harvest food in 1997 had at least one employed person. Recent visitors to a Greenwich, Connecticut, food bank included "a cook from a local French restaurant, a construction worker, housekeepers from nearby estates who made the minimum wage, $5.15 an hour, and a woman who cared for the children of housekeepers" (*New York Times,* February 26, 1999).

According to the Washington-based Wider Opportunities for Women and the Boston-based Women's Educational and Industrial Union, the self-sufficiency standard (the level of income necessary to meet all basic needs, including taxes) for an adult and preschooler in high-cost Boston is $32,279—nearly twice the official poverty line for a family of four. In lower-cost Berkshire County, Massachusetts, it's $24,678. No wonder many low-income workers—including growing numbers of former welfare recipients—can't make ends meet. Recent studies of former recipients and those combining work and welfare have found they typically earn between $8,000 and

$10,800 annually. Most do not receive paid vacation, sick leave, or health benefits from their employers.

Retired people's incomes have long been said to rest on a "three-legged stool" of Social Security (and Medicare), private savings, and employer pensions. The stool is wobbling for some retirees and collapsing for others, as savings decline and pension coverage deteriorates.

Fewer than half of all workers (47 percent) were covered by pensions in 1996—down from 51 percent in 1979. To make matters worse, there has been a shift away from traditional "defined benefit" pension plans, which guarantee workers fixed retirement payments based on pre-retirement wages and years of service, toward "defined contribution" plans, such as 401(k)s, that take a chunk out of workers' paychecks and saddle employees with all the investment risk. According to the Economic Policy Institute, defined contribution plans accounted for 42 percent of all pension plans in 1997, up from 13 percent in 1975.

Lower-wage workers are far less likely than high-wage workers to be covered by any employer-sponsored retirement plan, further exacerbating the wealth gap. Only 16 percent of the lowest-wage workers (the bottom fifth by income) were covered by employer-provided pension plans in 1996, versus 73 percent of workers in the top fifth. In addition to placing the investment risk on employees, defined contribution plans require employee contributions in order to receive company matching contributions, if offered. Many low-wage workers, faced with the dilemma of choosing between feeding and housing their family today and saving for retirement in the future, do not participate in defined contribution plans even when given the option.

HOME $WEET HOME

As the Children's Defense Fund observes, "Homeownership has long been a central part of the American dream. It is also a major source of financial security and stability for young families, and an essential means of accumulating the equity that has enabled countless families later to borrow money in order to stave off a crisis, send a child to college, or help start a family business."

Fueled by low mortgage interest rates, the U.S. homeownership rate hit a record 66 percent in 1998, but for people under age 55, the rates were actually lower in 1998 than in 1982.

The biggest government support for homeownership comes in the form of the tax deduction for mortgage interest on owner-occupied first and second homes. Unfortunately, much of the tax write-off goes to higher-income families. The more you can already afford to spend, the more the government subsidizes you. As the *New York Times* reports (January 10, 1999), for each dollar in tax savings from the mortgage-interest deduction "going to the average taxpayer making $200,000 or more, the average taxpayer in all lower income groups combined saves just 6 cents."

For the fiscal year ending September 30, 1999, the mortgage deduction will add up to about $53.7 billion. That's $23 billion more than total 1998 federal spending by the Department of Housing and Urban Development (under $31 billion). The mortgage deduction costs 23 times as much as the credit for low-income housing investment ($2.3 billion).

While tax subsidies for affluent homeowners remained high, federal funding for low-income housing was cut by 80 percent from 1978 to 1991, adjusting for inflation. Not surprisingly, shortages of affordable housing have increased greatly.

THE RACIAL WEALTH GAP

While the racial income gap is terribly wide, the racial wealth gap is even worse. According to Edward Wolff, the median black household had a net worth of just $7,400 in 1995—about 12 percent of the $61,000 in median wealth for whites. Median black financial wealth (net worth minus home equity) was just $200—a mere 1 percent of the $18,000 in median financial wealth for whites. In the same year, nearly one out of three black households had zero or negative net worth, twice the rate among whites.

Hispanic households have even less wealth than blacks. The median Hispanic household had a net worth of only $5,000 in 1995—just 8 percent of whites. Median financial wealth was actually zero.

Because of employment, housing, insurance, and other discrimination, black and Latino families are far less likely than whites to own the homes in which they live. In 1995, the homeownership rate was 47 percent for blacks and 44 percent for Hispanics, about two-thirds the rate for white households (69 percent).

In 1999, the *Kansas City Star* analyzed mortgage applications taken by more than 500 area banks and mortgage companies from 1992 to 1997. As reported by Ted Sickinger, a former commercial loan officer, "lenders still reject minority mortgage applicants far more frequently than they do whites. Even high-income minorities are rejected more frequently than whites with lower incomes."

Moreover, "most loans made in minority neighborhoods refinance existing debt and are made by companies that often charge higher interest rates and fees. In white neighborhoods, by contrast, most loans are made at market rates and go to buy homes—the kind of lending that helps borrowers build wealth." Unlike the overt redlining of the past, the *Kansas City Star* found "discrimination with a smile."

Melvin Oliver and Thomas Shapiro analyzed the asset gap in their book, *Black Wealth/White Wealth*. Even if differences in income, occupation, education, and other factors are removed from the equation, a difference of $43,143 in average net worth remained in 1988. They call it "the costs of being black." For married couples, the difference was greater: $46,294. Housing discrimination is a major factor; inheritance is another. White parents generally have far greater resources to pay for their children's college education, help them with their first home purchase, and bequeath them assets at death.

As Oliver and Shapiro observe, "Wealth signifies the command over financial resources that a family has accumulated over its lifetime along with those resources that have been inherited across generations."

Inequality is a matter of life and death—and not just for the poor. In the words of the University of Washington International Health Program and Health Alliance International, "the greater the income differences within populations (whether of whole countries or of cities or larger administrative areas within countries), the worse their health. This helps explain why the United States, the richest and most powerful country in the world (spending more than any other on health care), ranks below 25th in the league of countries ordered by life expectancy. Income differences between rich and poor are bigger in the United States than in any other developed nation."

A July 1998 report in the *American Journal of Public Health* found that higher income inequality is associated with increased mortality at all per capita income levels. "Given the mortality burden associated with income inequality," the report concludes, "business, private, and public sector initiatives to reduce economic inequalities should be a high priority."

CLOSING THE WEALTH GAP

Increased inequality is not the result of natural phenomena like sun spots or shifting winds. It is the result of over two decades of public policies and private corporate practices that have benefited asset owners at the expense of wage earners.

Where are we headed? "The Atlanta-based Affluent Market Institute predicts that by 2005 America's millionaires will control 60 percent of the nation's purchasing dollars," notes Jeff Gates in *The Ownership Solution*.

"Money makes money," said Adam Smith, author of *The Wealth of Nations*, long ago. Immediate steps are needed to enable low- and moderate-income families to earn, save, and invest more money, and build asset security. . . .

8

CORPORATE WELFARE

DONALD L. BARLETT • JAMES B. STEELE

How would you like to pay only a quarter of the real estate taxes you owe on your home? And buy everything for the next 10 years without spending a single penny in sales tax? Keep a chunk of your paycheck free of income taxes? Have the city in which you live lend you money at rates cheaper than any bank charges? Then have the same city install free water and sewer lines to your house, offer you a perpetual discount on utility bills—and top it all off by landscaping your front yard at no charge?

Fat chance. You can't get any of that, of course. But if you live almost anywhere in America, all around you are taxpayers getting deals like this. These taxpayers are called corporations, and their deals are usually trumpeted as "economic development" or "public-private partnerships." But a better name is corporate welfare. It's a game in which governments large and small subsidize corporations large and small, usually at the expense of another state or town and almost always at the expense of individual and other corporate taxpayers.

Two years after Congress reduced welfare for individuals and families, this other kind of welfare continues to expand, penetrating every corner of the American economy. It has turned politicians into bribery specialists, and smart business people into con artists. And most surprising of all, it has rarely created any new jobs.

While corporate welfare has attracted critics from both the left and the right, there is no uniform definition. By [our] definition, it is this: any action by local, state or federal government that gives a corporation or an entire industry a benefit not offered to others. It can be an outright subsidy, a grant, real estate, a low-interest loan or a government service. It can also be a tax break—a credit, exemption, deferral or deduction, or a tax rate lower than the one others pay. . . .

. . . The Federal Government alone shells out $125 billion a year in corporate welfare, this in the midst of one of the more robust economic periods in the nation's history. Indeed, thus far in the 1990s, corporate profits have totaled $4.5 trillion—a sum equal to the cumulative paychecks of 50 million working Americans who earned less than $25,000 a year, for those eight years.

"Special Report, Corporate Welfare." From *Time* 152, no. 19, November 9, 1998.

That makes the Federal Government America's biggest sugar daddy, dispensing a range of giveaways from tax abatements to price supports for sugar itself. Companies get government money to advertise their products; to help build new plants, offices and stores; and to train their workers. They sell their goods to foreign buyers that make the acquisitions with tax dollars supplied by the U.S. government, engage in foreign transactions that are insured by the government, and are excused from paying a portion of their income tax if they sell products overseas. They pocket lucrative government contracts to carry out ordinary business operations, and government grants to conduct research that will improve their profit margins. They are extended partial tax immunity if they locate in certain geographical areas, and they may write off as business expenses some of the perks enjoyed by their top executives.

The justification for much of this welfare is that the U.S. government is creating jobs. Over the past six years, Congress appropriated $5 billion to run the Export-Import Bank of the United States, which subsidizes companies that sell goods abroad. James A. Harmon, president and chairman, puts it this way: "American workers . . . have higher-quality, better-paying jobs, thanks to Eximbank's financing." But the numbers at the bank's five biggest beneficiaries—AT&T, Bechtel, Boeing, General Electric and McDonnell Douglas (now a part of Boeing)—tell another story. At these companies, which have accounted for about 40% of all loans, grants and long-term guarantees in this decade, overall employment has fallen 38%, as more than a third of a million jobs have disappeared.

The picture is much the same at the state and local level, where a different kind of feeding frenzy is taking place. Politicians stumble over one another in the rush to arrange special deals for select corporations, fueling a growing economic war among the states. The result is that states keep throwing money at companies that in many cases are not serious about moving anyway. The companies are certainly not reluctant to take the money, though, which is available if they simply utter the word relocation. And why not? Corporate executives, after all, have a fiduciary duty to squeeze every dollar they can from every locality waving blandishments in their face.

State and local governments now give corporations money to move from one city to another—even from one building to another—and tax credits for hiring new employees. They supply funds to train workers or pay part of their wages while they are in training, and provide scientific and engineering assistance to solve workplace technical problems. They repave existing roads and build new ones. They lend money at bargain-basement interest rates to erect plants or buy equipment. They excuse corporations from paying sales and property taxes and relieve them from taxes on investment income.

There are no reasonably accurate estimates on the amount of money states shovel out. That's because few want you to know. Some say they maintain no records. Some say they don't know where the files are. Some say the information is not public. All that's certain is that the figure is in the many billions of dollars each year—and it is growing, when measured against the subsidy per job.

- In 1989 Illinois gave $240 million in economic incentives to Sears, Roebuck & Co. to keep its corporate headquarters and 5,400 workers in the state by moving from Chicago to suburban Hoffman Estates. That amounted to a subsidy of $44,000 for each job.
- In 1991 Indiana gave $451 million in economic incentives to United Airlines to build an aircraft-maintenance facility that would employ as many as 6,300 people. Subsidy: $72,000 for each job.
- In 1993 Alabama gave $253 million in economic incentives to Mercedes-Benz to build an automobile-assembly plant near Tuscaloosa and employ 1,500 workers. Subsidy: $169,000 for each job.
- And in 1997 Pennsylvania gave $307 million in economic incentives to Kvaerner ASA, a Norwegian global engineering and construction company, to open a shipyard at the former Philadelphia Naval Shipyard and employ 950 people. Subsidy: $323,000 for each job.

This kind of arithmetic seldom adds up. Let's say the Philadelphia job pays $50,000. And each new worker pays $6,700 in local and state taxes. That means it will take nearly a half-century of tax collections from each individual to earn back the money granted to create his or her job. And that assumes all 950 workers will be recruited from outside Philadelphia and will relocate in the city, rather than move from existing jobs within the city, where they are already paying taxes.

All this is in service of a system that may produce jobs in one city or state, thus fostering the illusion of an uptick in employment. But it does not create more jobs in the nation as a whole. Market forces do that, and that's why 10 million jobs have been created since 1990. But most of those jobs have been created by small- and medium-size companies, from high-tech start-ups to franchised cleaning services. FORTUNE 500 companies, on the other hand, have erased more jobs than they have created this past decade, and yet they are the biggest beneficiaries of corporate welfare.

To be sure, some economic incentives are handed out for a seemingly worthwhile public purpose. The tax breaks that companies receive to locate in inner cities come to mind. Without them, companies might not invest in those neighborhoods. However well intended, these subsidies rarely produce lasting results. They may provide short-term jobs but not long-term employment. And in the end, the costs outweigh any benefits.

And what are those costs? The equivalent of nearly two weekly paychecks from every working man and woman in America—extra money that would stay in their pockets if it didn't go to support some business venture or another.

If corporate welfare is an unproductive end game, why does it keep growing in a period of intensive government cost cutting? For starters, it has good P.R. and an army of bureaucrats working to expand it. A corporate-welfare bureaucracy of an estimated 11,000 organizations and agencies has grown up, with access to city halls, statehouses, the Capitol and the White House. They conduct seminars, conferences and training sessions. They have their own trade associations. They publish their own journals and newsletters. They create attractive websites on the Internet. And they never call it "welfare." They call it "economic incentives" or "empowerment zones" or "enterprise zones."

Whatever the name, the result is the same. Some companies receive public services at reduced rates, while all others pay the full cost. Some companies are excused from paying all or a portion of their taxes due, while all others must pay the full amount imposed by law. Some companies receive grants, low-interest loans and other subsidies, while all others must fend for themselves.

In the end, that's corporate welfare's greatest flaw. It's unfair. One role of government is to help ensure a level playing field for people and businesses. Corporate welfare does just the opposite. It tilts the playing field in favor of the largest or the most politically influential or most aggressive businesses. . . .

SEX AND GENDER

9

THE SOCIAL CONSTRUCTION OF GENDER

JUDITH LORBER

Talking about gender for most people is the equivalent of fish talking about water. Gender is so much the routine ground of everyday activities that questioning its taken-for-granted assumptions and presuppositions is like thinking about whether the sun will come up.[1] Gender is so pervasive that in our society we assume it is bred into our genes. Most people find it hard to believe that gender is constantly created and re-created out of human interaction, out of social life, and is the texture and order of that

Judith Lorber, (1994). "Night to His Day: The Social Construction of Gender." From *Paradoxes of Gender*, Yale University Press, 1994, pp. 13–15, 32–36. Reprinted by permission of Yale University Press.

social life. Yet gender, like culture, is a human production that depends on everyone constantly "doing gender" (West and Zimmerman 1987).

And everyone "does gender"without thinking about it. Today, on the subway, I saw a well-dressed man with a year-old child in a stroller. Yesterday, on a bus, I saw a man with a tiny baby in a carrier on his chest. Seeing men taking care of small children in public is increasingly common—at least in New York City. But both men were quite obviously stared at—and smiled at, approvingly. Everyone was doing gender—the men who were changing the role of fathers and the other passengers, who were applauding them silently. But there was more gendering going on that probably fewer people noticed. The baby was wearing a white crocheted cap and white clothes. You couldn't tell if it was a boy or a girl. The child in the stroller was wearing a dark blue T-shirt and dark print pants. As they started to leave the train, the father put a Yankee baseball cap on the child's head. Ah, a boy, I thought. Then I noticed the gleam of tiny earrings in the child's ears, and as they got off, I saw the little flowered sneakers and lace-trimmed socks. Not a boy after all. Gender done.

Gender is such a familiar part of daily life that it usually takes a deliberate disruption of our expectations of how women and men are supposed to act to pay attention to how it is produced. Gender signs and signals are so ubiquitous that we usually fail to note them—unless they are missing or ambiguous. Then we are uncomfortable until we have successfully placed the other person in a gender status; otherwise, we feel socially dislocated. In our society, in addition to man and woman, the status can be *transvestite* (a person who dresses in opposite-gender clothes) and *transsexual* (a person who has had sex-change surgery). Transvestites and transsexuals construct their gender status by dressing, speaking, walking, gesturing in the ways prescribed for women or men—whichever they want to be taken for—and so does any "normal" person.

For the individual, gender construction starts with assignment to a sex category on the basis of what the genitalia look like at birth.[2] Then babies are dressed or adorned in a way that displays the category because parents don't want to be constantly asked whether their baby is a girl or a boy. A sex category becomes a gender status through naming, dress, and the use of other gender markers. Once a child's gender is evident, others treat those in one gender differently from those in the other, and the children respond to the different treatment by feeling different and behaving differently. As soon as they can talk, they start to refer to themselves as members of their gender. Sex doesn't come into play again until puberty, but by that time, sexual feelings and desires and practices have been shaped by gendered norms and expectations. Adolescent boys and girls approach and avoid each other in an elaborately scripted and gendered mating dance. Parenting is gendered, with different expectations for mothers and for fathers, and people of different genders work at different kinds of jobs. The work adults do as mothers and fathers and as low-level workers and high-level bosses, shapes women's and men's life experiences, and these experiences produce different feelings, consciousness, relationships, skills—ways of being that we call feminine or masculine.[3] All of these processes constitute the social construction of gender.

Gendered roles change—today fathers are taking care of little children, girls and boys are wearing unisex clothing and getting the same education, women and men are working at the same jobs. Although many traditional social groups are quite strict about maintaining gender differences, in other social groups they seem to be blurring. Then why the one-year-old's earrings? Why is it still important to mark a child as a girl or a boy, to make sure she is not taken for a boy or he for a girl? What would happen if they were? They would, quite literally, have changed places in their social world.

To explain why gendering is done from birth, constantly and by everyone, we have to look not only at the way individuals experience gender but at gender as a social institution. As a social institution, gender is one of the major ways that human beings organize their lives. Human society depends on a predictable division of labor, a designated allocation of scarce goods, assigned responsibility for children and others who cannot care for themselves, common values and their systematic transmission to new members, legitimate leadership, music, art, stories, games, and other symbolic productions. One way of choosing people for the different tasks of society is on the basis of their talents, motivations, and competence—their demonstrated achievements. The other way is on the basis of gender, race, ethnicity—ascribed membership in a category of people. Although societies vary in the extent to which they use one or the other of these ways of allocating people to work and to carry out other responsibilities, every society uses gender and age grades. Every society classifies people as "girl and boy children," "girls and boys ready to be married," and "fully adult women and men," constructs similarities among them and differences between them, and assigns them to different roles and responsibilities. Personality characteristics, feelings, motivations, and ambitions flow from these different life experiences so that the members of these different groups become different kinds of people. The process of gendering and its outcome are legitimated by religion, law, science, and the society's entire set of values.

GENDER AS PROCESS, STRATIFICATION, AND STRUCTURE

As a social institution, gender is a process of creating distinguishable social statuses for the assignment of rights and responsibilities. As part of a stratification system that ranks these statuses unequally, gender is a major building block in the social structures built on these unequal statuses.

As a *process*, gender creates the social differences that define "woman" and "man." In social interaction throughout their lives, individuals learn what is expected, see what is expected, act and react in expected ways, and thus simultaneously construct and maintain the gender order: "The very injunction to be given gender takes place through discursive routes: to be a good mother, to be a heterosexually desirable object, to be a fit worker, in sum, to signify a multiplicity of guarantees in response to a variety of different demands all at once" (J. Butler 1990, 145). Members of a social group neither make up gender as they go along nor exactly replicate in rote fashion what was done before. In almost every encounter, human beings produce gender, behaving in the ways they learned were appropriate for their gender status, or resisting or rebelling against these norms. Resistance and rebellion have altered gender norms, but so far they have rarely eroded the statuses.

Gendered patterns of interaction acquire additional layers of gendered sexuality, parenting, and work behaviors in childhood, adolescence, and adulthood. Gendered norms and expectations are enforced through informal sanctions of gender-inappropriate behavior by peers and by formal punishment or threat of punishment by those in authority should behavior deviate too far from socially imposed standards for women and men.

Everyday gendered interactions build gender into the family, the work process, and other organizations and institutions, which in turn reinforce gender expectations for individuals.[4] Because gender is a process, there is room not only for modification and variation by individuals and small groups but also for institutionalized change (J. W. Scott 1988, 7).

As part of a *stratification* system, gender ranks men above women of the same race and class. Women and men could be different but equal. In practice, the process of creating difference depends to a great extent on differential evaluation. As Nancy Jay (1981) says: "That which is defined, separated out, isolated from all else is A and pure. Not-A is necessarily impure, a random catchall, to which nothing is external except A and the principle of order that separates it from Not-A" (45). From the individual's point of view, whichever gender is A, the other is Not-A; gender boundaries tell the individual who is like him or her, and all the rest are unlike. From society's point of view, however, one gender is usually the touchstone, the normal, the dominant, and the other is different, deviant, and subordinate. In Western society, "man" is A, "wo-man" is Not-A. (Consider what a society would be like where woman was A and man Not-A.)

The further dichotomization by race and class constructs the gradations of a heterogeneous society's stratification scheme. Thus, in the United States, white is A, African American is Not-A; middle class is A, working class is Not-A, and "African-American women occupy a position whereby the inferior half of a series of these dichotomies converge" (P. H. Collins 1990, 70). The dominant categories are the hegemonic ideals, taken so for granted as the way things should be that white is not ordinarily thought of as a race, middle class as a class, or men as a gender. The characteristics of these categories define the Other as that which lacks the valuable qualities the dominants exhibit.

In a gender-stratified society, what men do is usually valued more highly than what women do because men do it, even when their activities are very similar or the same. In different regions of southern India, for example, harvesting rice is men's work, shared work, or women's work: "Wherever a task is done by women it is considered easy, and where it is done by [men] it is considered difficult" (Mencher 1988, 104). A gathering and hunting society's survival usually depends on the nuts, grubs, and small animals brought in by the women's foraging trips, but when the men's hunt is successful, it is the occasion for a celebration. Conversely, because they are the superior group, white men do not have to do the "dirty work," such as housework; the most inferior group does it, usually poor women of color (Palmer 1989).

Freudian psychoanalytic theory claims that boys must reject their mothers and deny the feminine in themselves in order to become men: "For boys the major goal is the achievement of personal masculine identification with their father and sense of secure masculine self, achieved through superego formation and disparagement of women" (Chodorow 1978, 165). Masculinity may be the outcome of boys' intrapsychic struggles to separate their identity from that of their mothers, but the proofs of masculinity are culturally shaped and usually ritualistic and symbolic (Gilmore 1990).

The Marxist feminist explanation for gender inequality is that by demeaning women's abilities and keeping them from learning valuable technological skills, bosses preserve them as a cheap and exploitable reserve army of labor. Unionized men who could easily be replaced by women collude in this process because it allows them to monopolize the better-paid, more interesting, and more autonomous jobs: "Two factors emerge as helping men maintain their separation from women and their control of technological occupations. One is the active gendering of jobs and people. The second is the continual creation of sub-divisions in the work processes, and levels in work hierarchies, into which men can move in order to keep their distance from women" (Cockburn 1985, 13).

Societies vary in the extent of the inequality in social status of their women and men members, but where there is inequality, the status "woman" (and its attendant behavior and role allocations) is usually held in lesser esteem than the status "man." Since gender is also intertwined with a society's other constructed statuses of differential evaluation—race, religion, occupation, class, country of origin, and so on—men and women members of the favored groups command more power, more prestige, and more property than the members of the disfavored groups. Within many social groups, however, men are advantaged over women. The more economic resources, such as education and job opportunities, are available to a group, the more they tend to be monopolized by men. In poorer groups that have few resources (such as working-class African Americans in the United States), women and men are more nearly equal, and the women may even outstrip the men in education and occupational status (Almquist 1987).

As a *structure*, gender divides work in the home and in economic production, legitimates those in authority, and organizes sexuality and emotional life (Connell 1987, 91–142). As primary parents, women significantly influence children's psychological development and emotional attachments, in the process reproducing gender. Emergent sexuality is shaped by heterosexual, homosexual, bisexual, and sadomasochistic patterns that are gendered—different for girls and boys, and for women and men—so that sexual statuses reflect gender statuses.

When gender is a major component of structured inequality, the devalued genders have less power, prestige, and economic rewards than the valued genders. In countries that discourage gender discrimination, many major roles are still gendered; women still do most of the domestic labor and child rearing, even while doing full-time paid work; women and men are segregated on the job and each does work considered "appropriate"; women's work is usually paid less than men's work. Men dominate the positions of authority and leadership in government, the military, and the law; cultural productions, religions, and sports reflect men's interests.

In societies that create the greatest gender difference, such as Saudi Arabia, women are kept out of sight behind walls or veils, have no civil rights, and often create a cultural and emotional world of their own (Bernard 1981). But even in societies with less rigid gender boundaries, women and men spend much of their time with people of their own gender because of the way work and family are organized. This spatial separation of women and men reinforces gendered differences, identity, and ways of thinking and behaving (Coser 1986).

Gender inequality—the devaluation of "women" and the social domination of "men"—has social functions and social history. It is not the result of sex, procreation, physiology, anatomy, hormones, or genetic predispositions. It is produced and maintained by identifiable social processes and built into the general social structure and individual identities deliberately and purposefully. The social order as we know it in Western societies is organized around racial, ethnic, class, and gender inequality. I contend, therefore, that the continuing purpose of gender as a modern social institution is to construct women as a group to be the subordinates of men as a group.

THE PARADOX OF HUMAN NATURE

To say that sex, sexuality, and gender are all socially constructed is not to minimize their social power. These categorical imperatives govern our lives in the most profound and pervasive ways, through the social experiences and social practices of what Dorothy Smith calls the "everday/evernight world" (1990, 31–57). The paradox of human nature is that it is *always* a manifestation of cultural meanings, social relationships, and power politics; "not biology, but culture, becomes destiny" (J. Butler 1990, 8). Gendered people emerge not from physiology or sexual orientations but from the exigencies of the social order, mostly from the need for a reliable division of the work of food production and the social (not physical) reproduction of new members. The moral imperatives of religion and cultural representations guard the boundary lines among genders and ensure that what is demanded, what is permitted, and what is tabooed for the people in each gender is well known and followed by most (C. Davies 1982). Political power, control of scarce resources, and, if necessary, violence uphold the gendered social order in the face of resistance and rebellion. Most people, however, voluntarily go along with their society's prescriptions for those of their gender status, because the norms and expectations get built into their sense of worth and identity as [the way we] think, the way we see and hear and speak, the way we fantasy, and the way we feel.

There is no core or bedrock in human nature below these endlessly looping processes of the social production of sex and gender, self and other, identity and psyche, each of which is a "complex cultural construction" (J. Butler 1990, 36). *For humans, the social is the natural.* Therefore, "in its feminist senses, gender cannot mean simply the cultural appropriation of biological sexual difference. Sexual difference is itself a fundamental—and scientifically contested—construction. Both 'sex' and 'gender' are woven of multiple, asymmetrical strands of difference, charged with multifaceted dramatic narratives of domination and struggle" (Haraway 1990, 140).

NOTES

1. Gender is, in Erving Goffman's words, an aspect of *Felicity's Condition:* "any arrangement which leads us to judge an individual's . . . acts not to be a manifestation of strangeness. Behind Felicity's Condition is our sense of what it is to be sane" (1983:27). Also see Bem 1993; Frye 1983, 17–40; Goffman 1977.
2. In cases of ambiguity in countries with modern medicine, surgery is usually performed to make the genitalia more clearly male or female.
3. See J. Butler 1990 for an analysis of how doing gender is gender identity.
4. On the "logic of practice," or how the experience of gender is embedded in the norms of everyday interaction and the structure of formal organizations, see Acker 1990; Bourdieu [1980] 1990; Connell 1987; Smith 1987.

REFERENCES

Acker, Joan. 1990. "Hierarchies, jobs, and bodies: A theory of gendered organizations," *Gender & Society* 4: 139–158.

Almquist, Elizabeth M. 1987. "Labor market gendered inequality in minority groups," *Gender & Society* 1: 400–14.

Bem, Sandara Lipsitz. 1993. *The Lenses of Gender: Transforming the Debate on Sexual Inequality.* New Haven: Yale University Press.

Bernard, Jessie. 1981. *The Female World.* New York: Free Press.

Bourdieu, Pierre. [1980] 1990. *The Logic of Practice.* Stanford, Calif.: Stanford University Press.

Butler, Judith. 1990. *Gender Trouble: Feminism and the Subversion of Identity.* New York and London: Routledge.

Chodorow, Nancy, 1978. *The Reproduction of Mothering.* Berkeley: University of California Press.

Cockburn, Cynthia. 1985. *Machinery of Dominance: Women, Men and Technical Know-how.* London: Pluto Press.

Collins, Patricia Hill. 1989. "The social construction of black feminist thought," *Signs* 14: 745–73.

Connell, R. [Robert] W. 1987. *Gender and Power: Society, the Person, and Sexual Politics.* Stanford, Calif.: Stanford University Press.

Coser, Rose Laub. 1986. "Cognitive structure and the use of social space," *Sociological Forum* 1: 1–26.

Davies, Christie. 1982. "Sexual taboos and social boundaries," *American Journal of Sociology* 87: 1032–63.

Dwyer, Daisy, and Judith Bruce (eds.). 1988. *A Home Divided: Women and Income in the Third World.* Palo Alto, Calif.: Stanford University Press.

Frye, Marilyn. 1983. *The Politics of Reality: Essays in Feminist Theory.* Trumansburg, N.Y.: Crossing Press.

Gilmore, David D. 1990. *Manhood in the Making: Cultural Concepts of Masculinity.* New Haven: Yale University Press.

Goffman, Erving. 1977. "The arrangement between the sexes," *Theory and Society* 4: 301–33.

Haraway, Donna. 1990. "Investment strategies for the evolving portfolio of primate females," in *Jacobus, Keller, and Shuttleworth.*

Jacobus, Mary, Evelyn Fox Keller, and Sally Shuttleworth (eds.). (1990). *Body/politics: Women and the Discourse of Science.* New York and London: Routledge.

Jay, Nancy. 1981. "Gender and dichotomy," *Feminist Studies* 7: 38–56.

Mencher, Joan. 1988. "Women's work and poverty: Women's contribution to household maintenance in South India," in *Dwyer and Bruce.*

Palmer, Phyllis. 1989. *Domesticity and Dirt: Housewives and Domestic Servants in the United States, 1920–1945.* Philadelphia: Temple University Press.

Scott, Joan Wallach. 1988. *Gender and the Politics of History.* New York: Columbia University Press.

Smith, Dorothy. 1987. *The Everyday World as Problematic: A Feminist Sociology.* Toronto: University of Toronto Press.

———. 1990. *The Conceptual Practices of Power: A Feminist Sociology of Knowledge.* Toronto: University of Toronto Press.

West, Candace, and Don Zimmerman. 1987. "Doing gender." *Gender & Society* 1: 125–51.

10

THE FIVE SEXES
Why Male and Female Are Not Enough

ANNE FAUSTO-STERLING

In 1843 Levi Suydam, a twenty-three-year-old resident of Salisbury, Connecticut, asked the town board of selectmen to validate his right to vote as a Whig in a hotly contested local election. The request raised a flurry of objections from the opposition party, for reasons that must be rare in the annals of American democracy: it was said that Suydam was more female than male and thus (some eighty years before suffrage was extended to women) could not be allowed to cast a ballot. To settle the dispute a physician, one William James Barry, was brought in to examine Suydam. And, presumably upon encountering a phallus, the good doctor declared the prospective voter male. With Suydam safely in their column the Whigs won the election by a majority of one.

Barry's diagnosis, however, turned out to be somewhat premature. Within a few days he discovered that, phallus notwithstanding, Suydam menstruated regularly and had a vaginal opening. Both his/her physique and his/her mental predispositions were more complex than was first suspected. S/he had narrow shoulders and broad hips and felt occasional sexual yearnings for women. Suydam's "feminine propensities, such as a fondness for gay colors, for pieces of calico, comparing and placing them together, and an aversion for bodily labor, and an inability to perform the same, were remarked by many," Barry later wrote. It is not clear whether Suydam lost or retained the vote, or whether the election results were reversed.

Western culture is deeply committed to the idea that there are only two sexes. Even language refuses other possibilities; thus to write about Levi Suydam I have had to invent conventions—*s/he* and *his/her*—to denote someone who is clearly neither male nor female or who is perhaps both sexes at once. Legally, too, every adult is either man or woman, and the difference, of course, is not trivial. For Suydam it meant the franchise; today it means being available for, or exempt from, draft registration, as well as being subject, in various ways, to a number of laws governing marriage, the family and human intimacy. In many parts of the United States, for instance, two people legally registered as men cannot have sexual relations without violating anti-sodomy statutes.

In *The Sciences,* Vol. 33, March/April 1993, pp. 20–24. Reprinted by permission of The Sciences.

But if the state and the legal system have an interest in maintaining a two-party sexual system, they are in defiance of nature. For biologically speaking, there are many gradations running from female to male; and depending on how one calls the shots, one can argue that along that spectrum lie at least five sexes—and perhaps even more.

For some time medical investigators have recognized the concept of the intersexual body. But the standard medical literature uses the term *intersex* as a catch-all for three major subgroups with some mixture of male and female characteristics: the so-called true hermaphrodites, whom I call herms, who possess one testis and one ovary (the sperm- and egg-producing vessels, or gonads); the male pseudohermaphrodites (the "merms"), who have testes and some aspects of the female genitalia but no ovaries; and the female pseudohermaphrodites (the "ferms"), who have ovaries and some aspects of the male genitalia but lack testes. Each of those categories is in itself complex; the percentage of male and female characteristics, for instance, can vary enormously among members of the same subgroup. Moreover, the inner lives of the people in each subgroup—their special needs and their problems, attractions and repulsions—have gone unexplored by science. But on the basis of what is known about them I suggest that the three intersexes, herm, merm and ferm, deserve to be considered additional sexes each in its own right. Indeed, I would argue further that sex is a vast, infinitely malleable continuum that defies the constraints of even five categories.

Not surprisingly, it is extremely difficult to estimate the frequency of intersexuality, much less the frequency of each of the three additional sexes; it is not the sort of information one volunteers on a job application. The psychologist John Money of Johns Hopkins University, a specialist in the study of congenital sexual-organ defects, suggests intersexuals may constitute as many as 4 percent of births. As I point out to my students at Brown University, in a student body of about 6,000 that fraction, if correct, implies there may be as many as 240 intersexuals on campus—surely enough to form a minority caucus of some kind.

In reality though, few such students would make it as far as Brown in sexually diverse form. Recent advances in physiology and surgical technology now enable physicians to catch most intersexuals at the moment of birth. Almost at once such infants are entered into a program of hormonal and surgical management so that they can slip quietly into society as "normal" heterosexual males or females. I emphasize that the motive is in no way conspiratorial. The aims of the policy are genuinely humanitarian, reflecting the wish that people be able to "fit in" both physically and psychologically. In the medical community, however, the assumptions behind that wish—that there be only two sexes, that heterosexuality alone is normal, that there is one true model of psychological health—have gone virtually unexamined.

The word *hermaphrodite* comes from the Greek names Hermes, variously known as the messenger of the gods, the patron of music, the controller of dreams or the protector of livestock, and Aphrodite, the goddess of sexual love and beauty. According to Greek mythology, those two gods parented Hermaphroditus, who at age fifteen became half male and half female when his body fused with the body of a nymph he fell in love with. In some true hermaphrodites the testis and the ovary grow separately but bilaterally; in others they grow together within the same organ, forming an ovo-testis. Not infrequently, at least one of the gonads functions quite well, producing either sperm cells or eggs, as well as functional levels of the sex hormones—androgens or estrogens. Although in theory it might be possible for a true hermaphrodite to become both father and mother to a child, in practice the appropriate ducts and tubes are not configured so that egg and sperm can meet.

In contrast with the true hermaphrodites, the pseudohermaphrodites possess two gonads of the same kind along with the usual male (XY) or female (XX) chromosomal makeup. But their external genitalia and secondary sex characteristics do not match their chromosomes. Thus merms have testes and XY chromosomes, yet they also have a vagina and a clitoris, and at puberty they often develop breasts. They do not menstruate, however. Ferms have ovaries, two X chromosomes and sometimes a uterus, but they also have at least partly masculine external genitalia. Without medical intervention they can develop beards, deep voices and adult-size penises. . . .

Intersexuality itself is old news. Hermaphrodites, for instance, are often featured in stories about human origins. Early biblical scholars believed Adam began life as a hermaphrodite and later divided into two people—a male and a female—after falling from grace. According to Plato there once were three sexes—male, female, and hermaphrodite—but the third sex was lost with time.

Both the Talmud and the Tosefta, the Jewish books of law, list extensive regulations for people of mixed sex. The Tosefta expressly forbids hermaphrodites to inherit their fathers' estates (like daughters), to seclude themselves with women (like sons) or to shave (like men). When hermaphrodites menstruate they must be isolated from men (like women); they are disqualified from serving as witnesses or as priests (like women), but the laws of pederasty apply to them.

In Europe a pattern emerged by the end of the Middle Ages that, in a sense, has lasted to the present day: hermaphrodites were compelled to choose an established gender role and stick with it. The penalty for transgression was often death. Thus in the 1600s a Scottish hermaphrodite living as a woman was buried alive after impregnating his/her master's daughter.

For questions of inheritance, legitimacy, paternity, succession to title and eligibility for certain professions to be determined, modern Anglo-Saxon legal systems require that newborns be registered as either male or female. In the U.S. today sex determination is governed by state laws. Illinois permits adults to change the sex recorded on their birth certificates should a physician attest to having performed the appropriate surgery. The New York Academy of Medicine, on the other hand, has taken an opposite view. In spite of surgical alterations of the external genitalia, the academy argued in 1966, the chromosomal sex remains the same. By that measure, a person's wish to conceal his or her original sex cannot outweigh the public interest in protection against fraud.

During this century the medical community has completed what the legal world began—the complete erasure of any form of embodied sex that does not conform to a male-female, heterosexual pattern. Ironically, a more sophisticated knowledge of the complexity of sexual systems has led to the repression of such intricacy.

In 1937 the urologist Hugh H. Young of Johns Hopkins University published a volume titled *Genital Abnormalities, Hermaphroditism and Related Adrenal Diseases.* The book is remarkable for its erudition, scientific insight and open-mindedness. In it Young drew together a wealth of carefully documented case histories to demonstrate and study the medical treatment of such "accidents of birth." Young did not pass judgment on the people he studied, nor did he attempt to coerce into treatment those intersexuals who rejected that option. And he showed unusual even-handedness in referring to those people who had had sexual experiences as both men and women as "practicing hermaphrodites."

One of Young's more interesting cases was a hermaphrodite named Emma who had grown up as a female. Emma had both a penis-size clitoris and a vagina, which made it possible for him/her to have "normal" heterosexual sex with both men and women. As a teenager Emma had had sex with a number of girls to whom s/he was deeply attracted; but at the age of nineteen s/he had married a man. Unfortunately, he had given Emma little sexual pleasure (though *he* had had no complaints), and so throughout that marriage and subsequent ones Emma had kept girlfriends on the side. With some frequency s/he had pleasurable sex with them. Young describes his subject as appearing "to be quite content and even happy." In conversation Emma occasionally told him of his/her wish to be a man, a circumstance Young said would be relatively easy to bring about. But Emma's reply strikes a heroic blow for self-interest:

> Would you have to remove that vagina? I don't know about that
> because that's my meal ticket. If you did that, I would have to
> quit my husband and go to work, so I think I'll keep it and stay
> as I am. My husband supports me well, and even though I don't
> have any sexual pleasure with him, I do have lots with my girl-
> friends.

Yet even as Young was illuminating intersexuality with the light of scientific reason, he was beginning its suppression. For his book is also an extended treatise on the most modern surgical and hormonal methods of changing intersexuals into either males or females. Young may have differed from his successors in being less judgmental and controlling of the patients and their families, but he nonetheless supplied the foundation on which current intervention practices were built.

By 1969, when the English physicians Christopher J. Dewhurst and Ronald R. Gordon wrote *The Intersexual Disorders,* medical and surgical approaches to intersexuality had neared a state of rigid uniformity. It is hardly surprising that such a hardening of opinion took place in the era of the feminine mystique—of the post–Second World War flight to the suburbs and the strict division of family roles according to sex. That the medical consensus was not quite universal (or perhaps that it seemed poised to break apart again) can be gleaned from the near-hysterical tone of Dewhurst and Gordon's book, which contrasts markedly with the calm reason of Young's founding work. Consider their opening description of an intersexual newborn:

> One can only attempt to imagine the anguish of the parents. That a newborn should have a deformity . . . [affecting] so fundamental an issue as the very sex of the child . . . is a tragic event which immediately conjures up visions of a hopeless psychological misfit doomed to live always as a sexual freak in loneliness and frustration.

Dewhurst and Gordon warned that such a miserable fate would, indeed, be a baby's lot should the case be improperly managed; "but fortunately," they wrote, "with correct management the outlook is infinitely better than the poor parents—emotionally stunned by the event—or indeed anyone without special knowledge could ever imagine."

Scientific dogma has held fast to the assumption that without medical care hermaphrodites are doomed to a life of misery. Yet there are few empirical studies to back up that assumption, and some of the same research gathered to build a case for medical treatment contradicts it. Francies Benton, another of Young's practicing hermaphrodites, "had not worried over his condition, did not wish to be changed, and was enjoying life." The same could be said of Emma, the opportunistic hausfrau. Even Dewhurst and Gordon, adamant about the psychological importance of treating intersexuals at the infant stage, acknowledged great success in "changing the sex" of older patients. They reported on twenty cases of children reclassified into a different sex after the supposedly critical age of eighteen months. They asserted that all the reclassifications were "successful," and they wondered then whether reregistration could be "recommended more readily than [had] been suggested so far."

The treatment of intersexuality in this century provides a clear example of what the French historian Michel Foucault has called biopower. The knowledge developed in biochemistry, embryology, endocrinology, psychology and surgery has enabled physicians to control the very sex of the human body. The multiple contradictions in that kind of power call for some scrutiny. On the one hand, the medical "management" of intersexuality certainly developed as part of an attempt to free people from perceived psychological pain (though whether the pain was the patient's, the parents' or the physician's is unclear). And if one accepts the assumption that in a sex-divided culture people can realize their greatest potential for happiness and productivity only if they are sure they belong to one of only two acknowl-edged sexes, modern medicine has been extremely successful.

On the other hand, the same medical accomplishments can be read not as progress but as a mode of discipline. Hermaphrodites have unruly bodies. They do not fall naturally into a binary classification; only a surgical shoe-horn can put them there. But why should we care if a "woman," defined as one who has breasts, a vagina, a uterus and ovaries and who menstruates also has a clitoris large enough to penetrate the vagina of another woman? Why should we care if there are people whose biological equipment enables them to have sex "naturally" with both men and women? The answers seem to lie in a cultural need to maintain clear distinctions between the sexes. Society mandates the control of intersexual bodies because they blur and bridge the great divide. Inasmuch as hermaphrodites literally embody both sexes, they challenge traditional beliefs about sexual difference: they possess the irritat-ing ability to live sometimes as one sex and sometimes the other, and they raise the specter of homosexuality.

But what if things were altogether different? Imagine a world in which the same knowledge that has enabled medicine to intervene in the manage-ment of intersexual patients has been placed at the service of multiple sexu-alities. Imagine that the sexes have multiplied beyond currently imaginable limits. It would have to be a world of shared powers. Patient and physician, parent and child, male and female, heterosexual and homosexual—all those oppositions and others would have to be dissolved as sources of division. A new ethic of medical treatment would arise, one that would permit ambigu-ity in a culture that had overcome sexual division. The central mission of medical treatment would be to preserve life. Thus hermaphrodites would be concerned primarily not about whether they can conform to society, but about whether they might develop potentially life-threatening conditions—hernias, gonadal tumors, salt imbalance caused by adrenal malfunction—that sometimes accompany hermaphroditic development. In my ideal world medical intervention for intersexuals would take place only rarely before the age of reason; subsequent treatment would be a cooperative venture between physician, patient and other advisers trained in issues of gender multiplicity.

I do not pretend that the transition to my utopia would be smooth. Sex, even the supposedly "normal," heterosexual kind, continues to cause untold anxieties in Western society. And certainly a culture that has yet to come to grips—religiously and, in some states, legally—with the ancient and rela-tively uncomplicated reality of homosexual love will not readily embrace in-tersexuality. No doubt the most troublesome arena by far would be the rearing of children. Parents, at least since the Victorian era, have fretted, sometimes to the point of outright denial, over the fact that their children are sexual beings.

All that and more amply explains why intersexual children are generally squeezed into one of the two prevailing sexual categories. But what would be the psychological consequences of taking the alternative road—raising children as unabashed intersexuals? On the surface that tack seems fraught with peril. What, for example, would happen to the intersexual child amid the unrelenting cruelty of the school yard? When the time came to shower in gym class, what horrors and humiliations would await the intersexual as his/her anatomy was displayed in all its nontraditional glory? In whose gym class would s/he register to begin with? What bathroom would s/he use? And how on earth would Mom and Dad help shepherd him/her through the mine field of puberty?

In the past thirty years those questions have been ignored, as the scientific community has, with remarkable unanimity, avoided contemplating the alternative route of unimpeded intersexuality. But modern investigators tend to overlook a substantial body of case histories, most of them compiled between 1930 and 1960, before surgical intervention became rampant. Almost without exception, those reports describe children who grew up knowing they were intersexual (though they did not advertise it) and adjusted to their unusual status. Some of the studies are richly detailed—described at the level of gym-class showering (which most intersexuals avoided without incident); in any event, there is not a psychotic or a suicide in the lot.

Still, the nuances of socialization among intersexuals cry out for more sophisticated analysis. Clearly, before my vision of sexual multiplicity can be realized, the first openly intersexual children and their parents will have to be brave pioneers who will bear the brunt of society's growing pains. But in the long view—though it could take generations to achieve—the prize might be a society in which sexuality is something to be celebrated for its subtleties and not something to be feared or ridiculed.

11

THE TRANSGENDER PARADIGM SHIFT TOWARD FREE EXPRESSION

HOLLY BOSWELL

What is transgender? What is it like to be transgendered? How many forms might this actually take? Is this paradigm shift new, and if so, how? What will it mean, not only for transgendered people, but for everyone?

Up until this decade, the emerging transgender community consisted of three recognizable components: transsexuals, cross-dressers (usually heterosexual), and our seldom-acknowledged cousins of gay drag. While the need to challenge culturally imposed stereotypes remains just as strong today, these three models have proven to be far too restrictive of the true range of transgender expression, ironically reinforcing the very myth that there are only two genders, as defined by most contemporary assimilationist cultures. This is changing (Boswell 1991).

In the primary cases of transsexualism and cross-dressing, notions of femininity and masculinity are thoroughly emulated—even to the point of undergoing radical surgery, or at least by challenging conformance to societal expectations of gender expression. The transgenderist, as defined by Virginia Prince, is usually no different from the non-operative transsexual who expresses only one of two genders. Still, this is risky business, often involving the loss of marriages, children, parents, family, friends, and livelihood. Such is the depth of the quest for selfhood, struggling to survive against social stigmatization and rejection.

What we are now beginning to experience is a new—yet anciently rooted—way of being that defies and transcends the absurd linkage between biological sex and gender expression. While biological sex manifests between our legs, the complexity of sexual and gender expression occurs between our ears. Even so, the concept of sex itself must be challenged as an artificial construct (Rothblatt 1995), especially in view of recurrent hermaphroditism and a host of other persistent psycho/social deviations from so-called male or female characteristics. Sex, in spite of how we have been conditioned to perceive it, is far from black or white, and is as much a state of mind—distinct from

From *Gender Blending,* Bonnie Bullough, Vern Bullough, and James Elias, eds., Amherst, NY: Prometheus Books. Copyright © 1997 Prometheus Books. Reprinted by permission of the publisher.

anatomy—as the outward expression we call gender. It is time to move beyond the bipolar masculine/feminine model of sex and gender based solely on anatomy. Manifesting our true humanity has much more to do with the rainbow of possibilities emanating from within our hearts, minds, and spirits.

It is important to recognize that this new paradigm of gender is coming from, and is finally being articulated by, the very people who are living it. For us, the experience comes first, then our conceptual explanation of it—unlike the academic approach of postulating a hypothesis that must then be proven. Many of us have become living proof of transgender reality. Some of us have been the willing subjects of research, but we are also recognizing the need to assert our own voices—some voices dialogue within our transgender community, and other voices remind us evermore of our rich diversity.

We are discovering how difficult it is to describe to others what it is like to be transgendered. I used to be amazed that, despite my elaborate explanations, no one could ever quite understand my experience of transgender, until I finally realized that neither have I ever understood what it is to be a man or a woman (Bornstein 1994). I seem to be neither, or maybe both, yet ultimately only myself. So, is transgender simply a result of being more honest with oneself and resistant to socialization, or is it chromosomally or hormonally induced, or better described as spirit taking precedence over form? All I know is that I could no longer live any other way, and have since found many others who share this experience.

So the word "transgender" describes much more than crossing between the poles of masculinity and femininity. It more aptly refers to the transgressing of gender norms, or being freely gendered, or transcending gender altogether in order to become more fully human. Transgender has to do with reinventing and realizing oneself more fully outside of the current systems of gender (Williams 1995). There are probably as many genders as there are people. Gender may be nothing more than a personal matrix of personality traits.

In fact, once the concept of gender is freed from various cultural and biological expectations of sex, the terms "masculine" and "feminine" become so relative that they are virtually meaningless. The Bem Sex Role Inventory lists two hundred personality characteristics such as analytical, gentle, independent, sympathetic, idealistic, and worldly. It is understood that each culture assigns different groupings of traits to each anatomical sex and leaves some in a neutral category. No trait is intrinsically masculine or feminine, though a few are more commonly attributable. As a culture evolves, it defines and re-defines which traits are appropriate for each sex through the contrived linkage of anatomy with gender. But imagine a non-polarized culture without this linkage, where each person would be free to explore and express his or her own unique set of traits. So much human potential could be unleashed that both the individual and the culture as a whole might self-actualize en masse.

Therapists today acknowledge that androgyny is a healthier gender model for self-actualization and fulfillment than either of the binary genders.

This entails a process of transcending social conditioning in order to more fully become ourselves. Jung's process of individuation, with its reconciliation of animus and anima, leads to "wholeness"—a word that is related to health and holiness. If most people were more honest about it, they would probably find themselves somewhere in the middle of the bell-shaped curve of gender distribution rather than at the Rambo/bimbo extremes.

So while many people have androgynous potential, the traditions of alternative gender expression involve a minority within which these tendencies are much more pronounced. These are the profoundly transgendered, who have real difficulty conforming to the polarized codes of gender, and whose gender identities stray far beyond the normal expectations of their biological sex. This has always been so.

Despite all the new advances in hormonal and surgical procedures, many of us are choosing to customize the program to suit our individual self-definitions and expression (Mackenzie 1994). This hearkens back to the many "two-spirit" traditions throughout human history (though some of these did involve castration) and enlivens a growing awareness among transgendered people that passing is becoming passé. Only within the last few decades have transgendered people become so seduced by the ability to assimilate, made possible by recent hormonal and surgical advances (Feinberg 1992). This has relieved society of its responsibility to recognize more than two genders. All of us—transgendered and otherwise—continue to live under the constant "tyranny of passing" (Williams 1985), of questioning our sense of belonging against our self-worth. Are we living up to the societal roles and expectations that are imposed on us? Are we accepted and valued by others? How much should we care? How much societal rejection can we endure to achieve honest self-expression before we are undermined or destroyed in the process?

Diverse manifestations of transgender, however, are certainly not new. We have existed throughout history all over the planet (Williams 1986; Roscoe 1993). We are a normal, recurring expression of human nature. As a Lakota shaman explained, "To us a man is what nature, or his dreams, makes him. We accept him for what he wants to be. That's up to him." Various cultures in the past have honored our unique ability to make special contributions to society as shamans, spiritual leaders, visionaries, healers, mediators, counselors, teachers, and in other specific ways. Within these value systems, weeds don't exist. Every being has its sacred purpose, and none are to be wasted (Swifthawk 1992). Anthropologists are continually unearthing more evidence of such multifarious traditions as the *berdache* in native North America, shamans in Siberia and the Arctic, *hijiras* in India, *xanith* in the Middle East, *gallae* in the Roman Empire, certain Druid priestesses in Old Europe, the *mahu* of Polynesia, one-breasted Amazons, and many more. Ancient goddess religions, and other natural spiritual world-views, respected men and women as equals, regarded Nature as divine, revered diversity, and loved all manifestations of life. But since the replacement of Mother Nature with God the Father (about five thousand years ago), the constructs of gender have been defined more narrowly and rigidly to suit the purposes of those in control of each particular society.

So what impact does all this have on the transgender community and all of us as human beings? Because of Western civilization's emphasis on materialism and its inherently polarized value system, most transgendered people have been manifesting as their assumed opposite, either through cross-dressing or sex reassignment surgery. This is often motivated more by a need to assimilate than a quest toward truly becoming oneself, which would otherwise support the notion of gender as a many-splendored thing. Whereas cross-dressing may vicariously lead to gender insights, and transsexualism appropriately correct those who see their gender/anatomy variance as a problem, the newly emerging paradigm of gender will lead to a potent activation of healthy and renewable alternative gender expression.

Yes, this shift is new. Never before have we had so many options, yet chosen to manifest—despite our culture—our *true selves.* We are choosing to define ourselves outside of our cultures, and virtually outside of the very system of gender as we have known it. Transgendered people are redefining gender. This will no doubt be perceived as a radical course by the prevailing cultural consciousness for perhaps another generation or so, but it will be increasingly embraced on a personal level as the simple, honest human expression of Nature that it ultimately is. Gender liberation is a crucial key to human evolution, promoting the idea that we should strive to be *whole gendered,* cultivating all our gender traits to meet the critical challenges of our time.

Is this not a timely universal message, emanating deeply from within our collective consciousness? Are we not connected by our "continuous common humanity" (Bolin 1994), in exploring fully what it is to be ourselves—infinitely unique, yet united by the undeniable commonality of our human experience? This is the very bridge of transgender: connecting the myth of polarity into a whole, healing the illusions of our separateness, and celebrating the diversity of what it is to be fully human.

The mass media, especially cinema—after TV talk shows ad nauseam—seem to be acknowledging the revelatory human truth of transgender. This needs little documentation. Professional caregivers are gradually becoming more educated about the breadth and depth of transgender phenomena, and how they might more appropriately help their transgendered clients. This is happening at the pervasive grassroots level, and now even more extensively at this first International Congress on Gender, Cross-Dressing and Sex Issues, February 1995. There has also been an increasing influx of updated educational programming at certain annual transgender conferences, such as Southern Comfort, International Foundation for Gender Education (IFGE), and International Conference on Transgender Law and Employment Policy's (ICTLEP) law conference.

With all this newly emerging awareness comes new resolve among transgendered people to be honest, to be "out," to endeavor to educate, to be politically active, to support young people joining our ranks with new issues, to venture into the cyberspace of "virtual gender," and to gather into our own circles for the intimate, spiritual processing of who we are truly becoming (Boswell 1994).

All this is very exciting and ought to serve as a catalyst to inspire the rest of humanity. Becoming truly oneself, on any level, is a most beautiful and worthwhile process. Yet how few actually venture into this territory? Transgendered people can serve as a bridge to help others find their own way. As avid students make the best teachers, we are living advocates for the profound experience of exploring one's true humanity—nothing less. And as we are each in need of healing ourselves on this essential level, we may then be able to hope for a world that reflects the dazzling rainbow of our immense wholeness, along with our long sought harmony, and the true beauty of our natural grace.

REFERENCES

Bolin, A. 1994. Transcending and transgendering: Male-to-female transsexuals, dichotomy and diversity. In *Third sex, third gender: Beyond sexual dimorphism in culture and history,* edited by G. Herdt, 448–85. New York: Zone Books.

Bornstein, K. 1994. *Gender outlaw: On men, women and the rest of us.* New York and London: Routledge.

Boswell, H. 1991. The transgender alternative. *Chrysalis Quarterly,* 1, no. 2.

———. 1994. New berdache circling. *Tapestry,* 68.

Feinberg, L. 1992. *Transgender liberation.* New York: World View Forum.

Mackenzie, G. 1994. *Transgender nation.* Bowling Green: Bowling Green University Popular Press.

Roscoe, W. 1993. *Priests of the goddess: Gender transgression in the ancient world.* Palo Alto, Calif.: Stanford University Women's Studies.

Rothblatt, M. 1995. *The apartheid of sex.* New York: Crown.

Swifthawk, R. 1992. *We have a duty to the earth.* Houston: International Foundation for Gender Education.

Williams, C. 1985. TIGC newsletter: Albany, N.Y.

———. 1995. Why transgender? *Gender Quest* (March-April).

Williams, W. 1986. *The spirit and the flesh.* Boston: Beacon Press.

12

MASCULINITY AS HOMOPHOBIA
Fear, Shame, and Silence in the Construction of Gender Identity

MICHAEL S. KIMMEL

"Funny thing," [Curley's wife] said. "If I catch any one man, and he's alone, I get along fine with him. But just let two of the guys get together an' you won't talk. Jus' nothin' but mad." She dropped her fingers and put her hands on her hips. "You're all scared of each other, that's what. Ever' one of you's scared the rest is goin' to get something on you."

JOHN STEINBECK
OF MICE AND MEN (1937)

We think of manhood as eternal, a timeless essence that resides deep in the heart of every man. We think of manhood as a thing, a quality that one either has or doesn't have. We think of manhood as innate, residing in the particular biological composition of the human male, the result of androgens or the possession of a penis. We think of manhood as a transcendent tangible property that each man must manifest in the world, the reward presented with great ceremony to a young novice by his elders for having successfully completed an arduous initiation ritual. In the words of poet Robert Bly (1990), "the structure at the bottom of the male psyche is still as firm as it was twenty thousand years ago" (p. 230).

In this chapter, I view masculinity as a constantly changing collection of meanings that we construct through our relationships with ourselves, with each other, and with our world. Manhood is neither static nor timeless; it is historical. Manhood is not the manifestation of an inner essence; it is socially constructed. Manhood does not bubble up to consciousness from our biological makeup; it is created in culture. Manhood means different things at different times to different people. We come to know what it means to be a man in our culture by setting our definitions in opposition to a set of "others"— racial minorities, sexual minorities, and, above all, women.

Our definitions of manhood are constantly changing, being played out on the political and social terrain on which the relationships between women and men are played out. In fact, the search for the transcendent, timeless definition of manhood is itself a sociological phenomenon—we tend to search for the timeless and eternal during moments of crisis, those points of transition when old definitions no longer work and new definitions are yet to be firmly established.

This idea that manhood is socially constructed and historically shifting should not be understood as a loss, that something is being taken away from men. In fact, it gives us something extraordinarily valuable—agency, the capacity to act. It gives us a sense of historical possibilities to replace the despondent resignation that invariably attends timeless, ahistorical essentialisms. Our behaviors are not simply "just human nature," because "boys will be boys." From the materials we find around us in our culture—other people, ideas, objects—we actively create our worlds, our identities. Men, both individually and collectively, can change.

In this chapter, I explore this social and historical construction of both hegemonic masculinity and alternate masculinities, with an eye toward offering a new theoretical model of American manhood.[1] To accomplish this I first uncover some of the hidden gender meanings in classical statements of social and political philosophy, so that I can anchor the emergence of contemporary manhood in specific historical and social contexts. I then spell out the ways in which this version of masculinity emerged in the United States, by tracing both psychoanalytic developmental sequences and a historical trajectory in the development of marketplace relationships. . . .

MASCULINITY AS HISTORY AND THE HISTORY OF MASCULINITY

The idea of masculinity . . . is the product of historical shifts in the grounds on which men rooted their sense of themselves as men. To argue that cultural definitions of gender identity are historically specific goes only so far; we have to specify exactly what those models were. In my historical inquiry into the development of these models for manhood[2] I chart the fate of two models for manhood at the turn of the 19th century and the emergence of a third in the first few decades of that century.

In the late 18th and 19th centuries, two models of manhood prevailed. The *Genteel Patriarch* derived his identity from landownership. Supervising his estate, he was refined, elegant, and given to casual sensuousness. He was a doting and devoted father, who spent much of his time supervising the estate and with his family. Think of George Washington or Thomas Jefferson as examples. By contrast, the *Heroic Artisan* embodied the physical strength and republican virtue that Jefferson observed in the yeoman farmer, independent urban craftsman, or shopkeeper. Also a devoted father, the Heroic Artisan taught his son his craft, bringing him through ritual apprenticeship to status as master craftsman. Economically autonomous, the Heroic Artisan also cherished his democratic community, delighting in the participatory democracy of the town meeting. Think of Paul Revere at his pewter shop, shirtsleeves rolled up, a leather apron—a man who took pride in his work.

Heroic Artisans and Genteel Patriarchs lived in casual accord, in part because their gender ideals were complementary (both supported participatory democracy and individual autonomy, although patriarchs tended to support more powerful state machineries and also supported slavery) and because they rarely saw one another: Artisans were decidedly urban and the Genteel Patriarchs ruled their rural estates. By the 1830s, though, this casual symbiosis was shattered by the emergence of a new vision of masculinity, *Marketplace Manhood.*

Marketplace Man derived his identity entirely from his success in the capitalist marketplace, as he accumulated wealth, power, status. He was the urban entrepreneur, the businessman. Restless, agitated, and anxious, Marketplace Man was an absentee landlord at home and an absent father with his children, devoting himself to his work in an increasingly homosocial environment—a male-only world in which he pits himself against other men. His efforts at self-making transform the political and economic spheres, casting aside the Genteel Patriarch as an anachronistic feminized dandy—sweet, but ineffective and outmoded, and transforming the Heroic Artisan into a dispossessed proletarian, a wage slave.

As Tocqueville would have seen it, the coexistence of the Genteel Patriarch and the Heroic Artisan embodied the fusion of liberty and equality. Genteel Patriarchy was the manhood of the traditional aristocracy, the class that embodied the virtue of liberty. The Heroic Artisan embodied democratic community, the solidarity of the urban shopkeeper or craftsman. Liberty and democracy, the patriarch and the artisan, could, and did, coexist. But Marketplace Man is capitalist man, and he makes both freedom and equality problematic, eliminating the freedom of the artisocracy and proletarianizing the equality of the artisan. In one sense, American history has been an effort to restore, retrieve, or reconstitute the virtues of Genteel Patriarchy and Heroic Artisanate as they were being transformed in the capitalist marketplace.

Marketplace Manhood was a manhood that required proof, and that required the acquisition of tangible goods as evidence of success. It reconstituted itself by the exclusion of "others"—women, nonwhite men, nonnative-born men, homosexual men—and by terrified flight into a pristine mythic homosocial Eden where men could, at last, be real men among other men. The story of the ways in which Marketplace Man becomes American Everyman is a tragic tale, a tale of striving to live up to impossible ideals of success leading to chronic terrors of emasculation, emotional emptiness, and a gendered rage that leave a wide swath of destruction in [their] wake.

MASCULINITIES AS POWER RELATIONS

Marketplace Masculinity describes the normative definition of American masculinity. It describes his characteristics—aggression, competition, anxiety—and the arena in which those characteristics are deployed—the public sphere, the marketplace. If the marketplace is the arena in which manhood is tested and proved, it is a gendered arena, in which tensions between women and men and tensions among different groups of men are weighted with meaning. These tensions suggest that cultural definitions of gender are played out in a contested terrain and are themselves power relations.

All masculinities are not created equal; or rather, we are all *created* equal, but any hypothetical equality evaporates quickly because our definitions of masculinity are not equally valued in our society. One definition of manhood continues to remain the standard against which other forms of manhood are measured and evaluated. Within the dominant culture, the masculinity that defines white, middle class, early middle-aged, heterosexual men is the masculinity that sets the standards for other men, against which other men are measured and, more often than not, found wanting. Sociologist Erving Goffman (1963) wrote that in America, there is only "one complete, unblushing male":

> a young, married, white, urban, northern heterosexual, Protestant
> father of college education, fully employed, of good complexion,
> weight and height, and a recent record in sports. Every American
> male tends to look out upon the world from this perspective. . . .
> Any male who fails to qualify in any one of these ways is likely to
> view himself . . . as unworthy, incomplete, and inferior. (p. 128)

This is the definition that we will call "hegemonic" masculinity, the image of masculinity of those men who hold power, which has become the standard in psychological evaluations, sociological research, and self-help and advice literature for teaching young men to become "real men" (Connell, 1987). The hegemonic definition of manhood is a man *in* power, a man *with* power, and a man *of* power. We equate manhood with being strong, successful, capable, reliable, in control. The very definitions of manhood we have developed in our culture maintain the power that some men have over other men and that men have over women.

Our culture's definition of masculinity is thus several stories at once. It is about the individual man's quest to accumulate those cultural symbols that denote manhood, signs that he has in fact achieved it. It is about those standards being used against women to prevent their inclusion in public life and their consignment to a devalued private sphere. It is about the differential access that different types of men have to those cultural resources that confer manhood and about how each of these groups then develop their own modifications to preserve and claim their manhood. It is about the power of these definitions themselves to serve to maintain the real-life power that men have over women and that some men have over other men.

This definition of manhood has been summarized cleverly by psychologist Robert Brannon (1976) into four succinct phrases:

1. "No Sissy Stuff!" One may never do anything that even remotely suggests femininity. Masculinity is the relentless repudiation of the feminine.
2. "Be a Big Wheel." Masculinity is measured by power, success, wealth, and status. As the current saying goes, "He who has the most toys when he dies wins."
3. "Be a Sturdy Oak." Masculinity depends on remaining calm and reliable in a crisis, holding emotions in check. In fact, proving you're a man depends on never showing your emotions at all. Boys don't cry.
4. "Give 'em Hell." Exude an aura of manly daring and aggression. Go for it. Take risks.

These rules contain the elements of the definition against which virtually all American men are measured. Failure to embody these rules, to affirm the power of the rules and one's achievement of them is a source of men's confusion and pain. Such a model is, of course, unrealizable for any man. But we keep trying, valiantly and vainly, to measure up. American masculinity is a relentless test.[3] The chief test is contained in the first rule. Whatever the variations by race, class, age, ethnicity, or sexual orientation, being a man means "not being like women." This notion of anti-femininity lies at the heart of contemporary and historical conceptions of manhood, so that masculinity is defined more by what one is not rather than who one is.

MASCULINITY AS THE FLIGHT FROM THE FEMININE

Historically and developmentally, masculinity has been defined as the flight from women, the repudiation of femininity. Since Freud, we have come to understand that developmentally the central task that every little boy must confront is to develop a secure identity for himself as a man. As Freud had it, the oedipal project is a process of the boy's renouncing his identification with and deep emotional attachment to his mother and then replacing her with the father as the object of identification. Notice that he reidentifies but never reattaches. This entire process, Freud argued, is set in motion by the boy's sexual desire for his mother. But the father stands in the son's path and will not yield his sexual property to his puny son. The boy's first emotional experience, then, the one that inevitably follows his experience of desire, is fear—fear of the bigger, stronger, more sexually powerful father. It is this fear, experienced symbolically as the fear of castration, Freud argues, that forces the young boy to renounce his identification with mother and seek to identify with the being who is the actual source of his fear, his father. In so doing, the boy is now symbolically capable of sexual union with a mother-like substitute, that is, a woman. The boy becomes gendered (masculine) and heterosexual at the same time.

Masculinity, in this model, is irrevocably tied to sexuality. The boy's sexuality will now come to resemble the sexuality of his father (or at least the way he imagines his father)—menacing, predatory, possessive, and possibly punitive. The boy has come to identify with his oppressor; now he can become the oppressor himself. But a terror remains, the terror that the young man will be unmasked as a fraud, as a man who has not completely and irrevocably separated from mother. It will be other men who will do the unmasking. Failure will de-sex the man, make him appear as not fully a man. He will be seen as a wimp, a Mama's boy, a sissy.

After pulling away from his mother, the boy comes to see her not as a source of nurturance and love, but as an insatiably infantilizing creature, capable of humiliating him in front of his peers. She makes him dress up in uncomfortable and itchy clothing, her kisses smear his cheeks with lipstick, staining his boyish innocence with the mark of feminine dependency. No wonder so many boys cringe from their mothers' embraces with groans of "Aw, Mom! Quit it!" Mothers represent the humiliation of infancy, helplessness, dependency. "Men act as though they were being guided by (or rebelling against) rules and prohibitions enunciated by a moral mother," writes psychohistorian Geoffrey Gorer (1964). As a result, "all the niceties of masculine behavior—modesty, politeness, neatness, cleanliness—come to be regarded as concessions to feminine demands, and not good in themselves as part of the behavior of a proper man" (pp. 56, 57).

The flight from femininity is angry and frightened, because mother can so easily emasculate the young boy by her power to render him dependent, or at least to remind him of dependency. It is relentless; manhood becomes a lifelong quest to demonstrate its achievement, as if to prove the unprovable to others, because we feel so unsure of it ourselves. Women don't often feel compelled to "prove their womanhood"—the phrase itself sounds ridiculous. Women have different kinds of gender identity crises; their anger and frustration, and their own symptoms of depression, come more from being excluded than from questioning whether they are feminine enough.[4]

The drive to repudiate the mother as the indication of the acquisition of masculine gender identity has three consequences for the young boy. First, he pushes away his real mother, and with her the traits of nurturance, compassion, and tenderness she may have embodied. Second, he suppresses those traits in himself, because they will reveal his incomplete separation from mother. His life becomes a lifelong project to demonstrate that he possesses none of his mother's traits. Masculine identity is born in the renunciation of the feminine, not in the direct affirmation of the masculine, which leaves masculine gender identity tenuous and fragile.

Third, as if to demonstrate the accomplishment of these first two tasks, the boy also learns to devalue all women in his society, as the living embodiments of those traits in himself he has learned to despise. Whether or not he was aware of it, Freud also described the origins of sexism—the systematic devaluation of women—in the desperate efforts of the boy to separate from mother. We may *want* "a girl just like the girl that married dear old Dad," as the popular song had it, but we certainly don't want to *be like* her.

This chronic uncertainty about gender identity helps us understand several obsessive behaviors. Take, for example, the continuing problem of the school-yard bully. Parents remind us that the bully is the *least* secure about his manhood, and so he is constantly trying to prove it. But he "proves" it by choosing opponents he is absolutely certain he can defeat; thus the standard taunt to a bully is to "pick on someone your own size." He can't, though, and after defeating a smaller and weaker opponent, which he was sure would prove his manhood, he is left with the empty gnawing feeling that he has not proved it after all, and he must find another opponent, again one smaller and weaker, that he can again defeat to prove it to himself.[5]

One of the more graphic illustrations of this lifelong quest to prove one's manhood occurred at the Academy Awards presentation in 1992. As aging, tough guy actor Jack Palance accepted the award for best supporting actor for his role in the cowboy comedy *City Slickers,* he commented that people, especially film producers, think that because he is 71 years old, he's all washed up, that he's no longer competent. "Can we take a risk on this guy?" he quoted them as saying, before he dropped to the floor to do a set of one-armed push-ups. It was pathetic to see such an accomplished actor still having to prove that he is virile enough to work and, as he also commented at the podium, to have sex.

When does it end? Never. To admit weakness, to admit frailty or fragility, is to be seen as a wimp, a sissy, not a real man. But seen by whom?

MASCULINITY AS A HOMOSOCIAL ENACTMENT

Other men: We are under the constant careful scrutiny of other men. Other men watch us, rank us, grant our acceptance into the realm of manhood. Manhood is demonstrated for other men's approval. It is other men who evaluate the performance. Literary critic David Leverenz (1991) argues that "ideologies of manhood have functioned primarily in relation to the gaze of male peers and male authority" (p. 769). Think of how men boast to one another of their accomplishments—from their latest sexual conquest to the size of the fish they caught—and how we constantly parade the markers of manhood—wealth, power, status, sexy women—in front of other men, desperate for their approval.

That men prove their manhood in the eyes of other men is both a consequence of sexism and one of its chief props. "Women have, in men's minds, such a low place on the social ladder of this country that it's useless to define yourself in terms of a woman," noted playwright David Mamet. "What men need is men's approval." Women become a kind of currency that men use to improve their ranking on the masculine social scale. (Even those moments of heroic conquest of women carry, I believe, a current of homosocial evaluation.) Masculinity is a *homosocial* enactment. We test ourselves, perform heroic feats, take enormous risks, all because we want other men to grant us our manhood.

Masculinity as a homosocial enactment is fraught with danger, with the risk of failure, and with intense relentless competition. "Every man you meet has a rating or an estimate of himself which he never loses or forgets," wrote Kenneth Wayne (1912) in his popular turn-of-the-century advice book. "A man has his own rating, and instantly he lays it alongside of the other man" (p. 18). Almost a century later, another man remarked to psychologist Sam Osherson (1992) that "[b]y the time you're an adult, it's easy to think you're always in competition with men, for the attention of women, in sports; at work" (p. 291).

MASCULINITY AS HOMOPHOBIA

If masculinity is a homosocial enactment, its overriding emotion is fear. In the Freudian model, the fear of the father's power terrifies the young boy to renounce his desire for his mother and identify with his father. This model links gender identity with sexual orientation: The little boy's identification with father (becoming masculine) allows him to now engage in sexual relations with women (he becomes heterosexual). This is the origin of how we can "read" one's sexual orientation through the successful performance of gender identity. Second, the fear that the little boy feels does not send him scurrying into the arms of his mother to protect him from his father. Rather, he believes he will overcome his fear by identifying with its source. We become masculine by identifying with our oppressor.

But there is a piece of the puzzle missing, a piece that Freud, himself, implied but did not follow up.[6] If the pre-oedipal boy identifies with mother, he *sees the world through mother's eyes.* Thus, when he confronts father during his great oedipal crisis, he experiences a split vision: He sees his father as his mother sees his father, with a combination of awe, wonder, terror, *and desire.* He simultaneously sees the father as he, the boy, would like to see him—as the object not of desire but of emulation. Repudiating mother and identifying with father only partially answer his dilemma. What is he to do with that homoerotic desire, the desire he felt because he saw father the way that his mother saw father?

He must suppress it. Homoerotic desire is cast as feminine desire, desire for other men. Homophobia is the effort to suppress that desire, to purify all relationships with other men, with women, with children of its taint, and to ensure that no one could possibly ever mistake one for a homosexual. Homophobic flight from intimacy with other men is the repudiation of the homosexual within—never completely successful and hence constantly reenacted in every homosocial relationship. "The lives of most American men are bounded, and their interests daily curtailed by the constant necessity to prove to their fellows, and to themselves, that they are not sissies, not homosexuals," writes psychoanalytic historian Geoffrey Gorer (1964). "An interest or pursuit which is identified as a feminine interest or pursuit becomes deeply suspect for men" (p. 129).

Even if we do not subscribe to Freudian psychoanalytic ideas, we can still observe how, in less sexualized terms, the father is the first man who evaluates the boy's masculine performance, the first pair of male eyes before whom he tries to prove himself. Those eyes will follow him for the rest of his life. Other men's eyes will join them—the eyes of role models such as teachers, coaches, bosses, or media heroes; the eyes of his peers, his friends, his workmates; and the eyes of millions of other men, living and dead, from whose constant scrutiny of his performance he will never be free. "The tradition of all the dead generations weighs like a nightmare on the brain of the living," was how Karl Marx put it over a century ago (1848/1964, p. 11). "The birthright of every American male is a chronic sense of personal inadequacy," is how two psychologists describe it today (Woolfolk & Richardson, 1978, p. 57).

That nightmare from which we never seem to awaken is that those other men will see that sense of inadequacy, they will see that in our own eyes we are not who we are pretending to be. What we call masculinity is often a hedge against being revealed as a fraud, an exaggerated set of activities that keep others from seeing through us, and a frenzied effort to keep at bay those fears within ourselves. Our real fear "is not fear of women but of being ashamed or humiliated in front of other men, or being dominated by stronger men" (Leverenz, 1986, p. 451).

This, then, is the great secret of American manhood: *We are afraid of other men.* Homophobia is a central organizing principle of our cultural definition of manhood. Homophobia is more than the irrational fear of gay men, more than the fear that we might be perceived as gay. "The word 'faggot' has nothing to do with homosexual experience or even with fears of homosexuals," writes David Leverenz (1986). "It comes out of the depths of manhood: a label of ultimate contempt for anyone who seems sissy, untough, uncool" (p. 455). Homophobia is the fear that other men will unmask us, emasculate us, reveal to us and the world that we do not measure up, that we are not real men. We are afraid to let other men see that fear. Fear makes us ashamed, because the recognition of fear in ourselves is proof to ourselves that we are not as manly as we pretend, that we are, like the young man in a poem by Yeats, "one that ruffles in a manly pose for all his timid heart." Our fear is the fear of humiliation. We are ashamed to be afraid.

Shame leads to silence—the silences that keep other people believing that we actually approve of the things that are done to women, to minorities, to gays and lesbians in our culture. The frightened silence as we scurry past a woman being hassled by men on the street. That furtive silence when men make sexist or racist jokes in a bar. That clammy-handed silence when guys in the office make gay-bashing jokes. Our fears are the sources of our silences, and men's silence is what keeps the system running. This might help to explain why women often complain that their male friends or partners are often so understanding when they are alone and yet laugh at sexist jokes or even make those jokes themselves when they are out with a group.

The fear of being seen as a sissy dominates the cultural definitions of manhood. It starts so early. "Boys among boys are ashamed to be unmanly," wrote one educator in 1871 (cited in Rotundo, 1993, p. 264). I have a standing bet with a friend that I can walk onto any playground in America where 6-year-old boys are happily playing and by asking one question, I can provoke a fight. That question is simple: "Who's a sissy around here?" Once posed, the challenge is made. One of two things is likely to happen. One boy will accuse another of being a sissy, to which that boy will respond that he is not a sissy, that the first boy is. They may have to fight it out to see who's lying. Or a whole group of boys will surround one boy and all shout "He is! He is!" That boy will either burst into tears and run home crying, disgraced, or he will have to take on several boys at once, to prove that he's not a sissy. (And what will his father or older brothers tell him if he chooses to run home crying?) It will be some time before he regains any sense of self-respect.

Violence is often the single most evident marker of manhood. Rather it is the willingness to fight, the desire to fight. The origin of our expression that one has a chip on one's shoulder lies in the practice of an adolescent boy in the country or small town at the turn of the century, who would literally walk around with a chip of wood balanced on his shoulder—a signal of his readiness to fight with anyone who would take the initiative of knocking the chip off (see Gorer, 1964, p. 38; Mead, 1965).

As adolescents, we learn that our peers are a kind of gender police, constantly threatening to unmask us as feminine, as sissies. One of the favorite tricks when I was an adolescent was to ask a boy to look at his fingernails. If he held his palm toward his face and curled his fingers back to see them, he passed the test. He'd looked at his nails "like a man." But if he held the back of his hand away from his face, and looked at his fingernails with arm outstretched, he was immediately ridiculed as a sissy.

As young men we are constantly riding those gender boundaries, checking the fences we have constructed on the perimeter, making sure that nothing even remotely feminine might show through. The possibilities of being unmasked are everywhere. Even the most seemingly insignificant thing can pose a threat or activate that haunting terror. On the day the students in my course "Sociology of Men and Masculinities" were scheduled to discuss homophobia and male-male friendships, one student provided a touching illustration. Noting that it was a beautiful day, the first day of spring after a brutal northeast winter, he decided to wear shorts to class. "I had this really nice pair of new Madras shorts," he commented. "But then I thought to myself, these shorts have lavender and pink in them. Today's class topic is homophobia. Maybe today is not the best day to wear these shorts."

Our efforts to maintain a manly front cover everything we do. What we wear. How we talk. How we walk. What we eat. Every mannerism, every movement contains a coded gender language. Think, for example, of how you would answer the question: How do you "know" if a man is homosexual? When I ask this question in classes or workshops, respondents invariably provide a pretty standard list of stereotypically effeminate behaviors. He walks a certain way, talks a certain way, acts a certain way. He's very emotional; he shows his feelings. One woman commented that she "knows" a man is gay if he really cares about her; another said she knows he's gay if he shows no interest in her, if he leaves her alone.

Now alter the question and imagine what heterosexual men do to make sure no one could possibly get the "wrong idea" about them. Responses typically refer to the original stereotypes, this time as a set of negative rules about behavior. Never dress that way. Never talk or walk that way. Never show your feelings or get emotional. Always be prepared to demonstrate sexual interest in women that you meet, so it is impossible for any woman to get the wrong idea about you. In this sense, homophobia, the fear of being perceived as gay, as not a real man, keeps men exaggerating all the traditional rules of masculinity, including sexual predation with women. Homophobia and sexism go hand in hand.

The stakes of perceived sissydom are enormous—sometimes matters of life and death. We take enormous risks to prove our manhood, exposing ourselves disproportionately to health risks, workplace hazards, and stress-related illnesses. Men commit suicide three times as often as women. Psychiatrist Willard Gaylin (1992) explains that it is "invariably because of perceived social humiliation," most often tied to failure in business:

> Men become depressed because of loss of status and power in the
> world of men. It is not the loss of money, or the material advan-
> tages that money could buy, which produces the despair that leads
> to self-destruction. It is the "shame," the "humiliation," the sense of
> personal "failure." . . . A man despairs when he has ceased being a
> man among men. (p. 32)

In one survey, women and men were asked what they were most afraid of. Women responded that they were most afraid of being raped and murdered. Men responded that they were most afraid of being laughed at (Noble, 1992, pp. 105–106).

HOMOPHOBIA AS A CAUSE OF SEXISM, HETEROSEXISM, AND RACISM

Homophobia is intimately interwoven with both sexism and racism. The fear—sometimes conscious, sometimes not—that others might perceive us as homosexual propels men to enact all manner of exaggerated masculine behaviors and attitudes to make sure that no one could possibly get the wrong idea about us. One of the centerpieces of that exaggerated masculinity is putting women down, both by excluding them from the public sphere and by the quotidian put-downs in speech and behaviors that organize the daily life of the American man. Women and gay men become the "other" against which heterosexual men project their identities, against whom they stack the decks so as to compete in a situation in which they will always win, so that by suppressing them, men can stake a claim for their own manhood. Women threaten emasculation by representing the home, workplace, and familial responsibility, the negation of fun. Gay men have historically played the role of the consummate sissy in the American popular mind because homosexuality is seen as an inversion of normal gender development. There have been other "others." Through American history, various groups have represented the sissy, the non-men against whom American men played out their definitions of manhood, often with vicious results. In fact, these changing groups provide an interesting lesson in American historical development.

At the turn of the 19th century, it was Europeans and children who provided the contrast for American men. The "true American was vigorous, manly, and direct, not effete and corrupt like the supposed Europeans," writes Rupert Wilkinson (1986). "He was plain rather than ornamented, rugged rather than luxury seeking, a liberty loving common man or natural gentleman rather than an aristocratic oppressor or servile minion" (p. 96). The "real man" of the early 19th century was neither noble nor serf. By the middle of the century, black slaves had replaced the effete nobleman. Slaves were seen as dependent, helpless men, incapable of defending their women and children, and therefore less than manly. Native Americans were cast as foolish and naive children, so they could be infantilized as the "Red Children of the Great White Father" and therefore excluded from full manhood.

By the end of the century, new European immigrants were also added to the list of the unreal men, especially the Irish and Italians, who were seen as too passionate and emotionally volatile to remain controlled sturdy oaks, and Jews, who were seen as too bookishly effete and too physically puny to truly measure up. In the mid-20th century, it was also Asians—first the Japanese during the Second World War, and more recently, the Vietnamese during the Vietnam War—who have served as unmanly templates against which American men have hurled their gendered rage. Asian men were seen as small, soft, and effeminate—hardly men at all.

Such a list of "hyphenated" Americans—Italian-, Jewish-, Irish-, African-, Native-, Asian-, gay—composes the majority of American men. So manhood is only possible for a distinct minority, and the definition has been constructed to prevent the others from achieving it. Interestingly, this emasculation of one's enemies has a flip side—and one that is equally gendered. These very groups that have historically been cast as less than manly were also, often simultaneously, cast as hypermasculine, as sexually aggressive, violent rapacious beasts, against whom "civilized" men must take a decisive stand and thereby rescue civilization. Thus black men were depicted as rampaging sexual beasts, women as carnivorously carnal, gay men as sexually insatiable, southern European men as sexually predatory and voracious, and Asian men as vicious and cruel torturers who were immorally disinterested in life itself, willing to sacrifice their entire people for their whims. But whether one saw these groups as effeminate sissies or as brutal uncivilized savages, the terms with which they were perceived were gendered. These groups become the "others," the screens against which traditional conceptions of manhood were developed.

Being seen as unmanly is a fear that propels American men to deny manhood to others, as a way of proving the unprovable—that one is fully manly. Masculinity becomes a defense against the perceived threat of humiliation in the eyes of other men, enacted through a "sequence of postures"—things we might say, or do, or even think, that, if we thought carefully about them, would make us ashamed of ourselves (Savran, 1992, p. 16). After all, how many of us have made homophobic or sexist remarks, or told racist jokes, or made lewd comments to women on the street? How many of us have translated those ideas and those words into actions, by physically attacking gay men, or forcing or cajoling a woman to have sex even though she didn't really want to because it was important to score?

POWER AND POWERLESSNESS IN THE LIVES OF MEN

I have argued that homophobia, men's fear of other men, is the animating condition of the dominant definition of masculinity in America, that the reigning definition of masculinity is a defensive effort to prevent being emasculated. In our efforts to suppress or overcome those fears, the dominant culture exacts a tremendous price from those deemed less than fully manly: women, gay men, nonnative-born men, men of color. This perspective may help clarify a paradox in men's lives, a paradox in which men have virtually all the power and yet do not feel powerful (see Kaufman, 1993).

Manhood is equated with power—over women, over other men. Everywhere we look, we see the institutional expression of that power—in state and national legislatures, on the boards of directors of every major U.S. corporation or law firm, and in every school and hospital administration. Women have long understood this, and feminist women have spent the past three decades challenging both the public and the private expressions of men's power and acknowledging their fear of men. Feminism as a set of theories both explains women's fear of men and empowers women to confront it both publicly and privately. Feminist women have theorized that masculinity is about the drive for domination, the drive for power, for conquest.

This feminist definition of masculinity as the drive for power is theorized from women's point of view. It is how women experience masculinity. But it assumes a symmetry between the public and the private that does not conform to men's experiences. Feminists observe that women, as a group, do not hold power in our society. They also observe that individually, they, as women, do not feel powerful. They feel afraid, vulnerable. Their observation of the social reality and their individual experiences are therefore symmetrical. Feminism also observes that men, as a group, *are* in power. Thus, with the same symmetry, feminism has tended to assume that individually men must feel powerful.

This is why the feminist critique of masculinity often falls on deaf ears with men. When confronted with the analysis that men have all the power, many men react incredulously. "What do you mean, men have all the power?" they ask. "What are you talking about? My wife bosses me around. My kids boss me around. My boss bosses me around. I have no power at all! I'm completely powerless!"

Men's feelings are not the feelings of the powerful, but of those who see themselves as powerless. These are the feelings that come inevitably from the discontinuity between the social and the psychological, between the aggregate analysis that reveals how men are in power as a group and the psychological fact that they do not feel powerful as individuals. They are the feelings of men who were raised to believe themselves entitled to feel that power, but do not feel it. No wonder many men are frustrated and angry.

This may explain the recent popularity of those workshops and retreats designed to help men to claim their "inner" power, their "deep manhood," or their "warrior within." Authors such as Bly (1990), Moore and Gillette (1991, 1992, 1993a, 1993b), Farrell (1986, 1993), and Keen (1991) honor and respect men's feelings of powerlessness and acknowledge those feelings to be both true and real. "They gave white men the semblance of power," notes John Lee, one of the leaders of these retreats (quoted in *Newsweek,* p. 41). "We'll let you run the country, but in the meantime, stop feeling, stop talking, and continue swallowing your pain and your hurt." (We are not told who "they" are.)

Often the purveyors of the mythopoetic men's movement, that broad umbrella that encompasses all the groups helping men to retrieve this mythic deep manhood, use the image of the chauffeur to describe modern man's position. The chauffeur appears to have the power—he's wearing the uniform, he's in the driver's seat, and he knows where he's going. So, to the observer, the chauffeur looks as though he is in command. But to the chauffeur himself, they note, he is merely taking orders. He is not at all in charge.[7]

Despite the reality that everyone knows chauffeurs do not have the power, this image remains appealing to the men who hear it at these weekend workshops. But there is a missing piece to the image, a piece concealed by the framing of the image in terms of the individual man's experience. That missing piece is that the person who is giving the orders is also a man. Now we have a relationship *between* men—between men giving orders and other men taking those orders. The man who identifies with the chauffeur is entitled to be the man giving the orders, but he is not. ("They," it turns out, are other men.)

The dimension of power is now reinserted into men's experience not only as the product of individual experience but also as the product of relations with other men. In this sense, men's experience of powerlessness is *real*—the men actually feel it and certainly act on it—but it is not *true*, that is, it does not accurately describe their condition. In contrast to women's lives, men's lives are structured around relationships of power and men's differential access to power, as well as the differential access to that power of men as a group. Our imperfect analysis of our own situation leads us to believe that we men need *more* power, rather than leading us to support feminists' efforts to rearrange power relationships along more equitable lines.

Philosopher Hannah Arendt (1970) fully understood this contradictory experience of social and individual power:

> Power corresponds to the human ability not just to act but to act in concert. Power is never the property of an individual; it belongs to a group and remains in existence only so long as the group keeps together. When we say of somebody that he is "in power" we actually refer to his being empowered by a certain number of people to act in their name. The moment the group, from which the power originated to begin with . . . disappears, "his power" also vanishes. (p. 44)

Why, then, do American men feel so powerless? Part of the answer is because we've constructed the rules of manhood so that only the tiniest fraction of men come to believe that they are the biggest of wheels, the sturdiest of oaks, the most virulent repudiators of femininity, the most daring and aggressive. We've managed to disempower the overwhelming majority of American men by other means—such as discriminating on the basis of race, class, ethnicity, age, or sexual preference.

Masculinist retreats to retrieve deep, wounded, masculinity are but one of the ways in which American men currently struggle with their fears and their shame. Unfortunately, at the very moment that they work to break down the isolation that governs men's lives, as they enable men to express those fears and that shame, they ignore the social power that men continue to exert over women and the privileges from which they (as the middle-aged, middle-class white men who largely make up these retreats) continue to benefit—regardless of their experiences as wounded victims of oppressive male socialization.

Others still rehearse the politics of exclusion, as if by clearing away the playing field of secure gender identity of any that we deem less than manly—

women, gay men, nonnative-born men, men of color—middle-class, straight, white men can reground their sense of themselves without those haunting fears and that deep shame that they are unmanly and will be exposed by other men. This is the manhood of racism, of sexism, of homophobia. It is the manhood that is so chronically insecure that it trembles at the idea of lifting the ban on gays in the military, that is so threatened by women in the workplace that women become the targets of sexual harassment, that is so deeply frightened of equality that it must ensure that the playing field of male competition remains stacked against all newcomers to the game.

Exclusion and escape have been the dominant methods American men have used to keep their fears of humiliation at bay. The fear of emasculation by other men, of being humiliated, of being seen as a sissy, is the leitmotif in my reading of the history of American manhood. Masculinity has become a relentless test by which we prove to other men, to women, and ultimately to ourselves, that we have successfully mastered the part. The restlessness that men feel today is nothing new in American history; we have been anxious and restless for almost two centuries. Neither exclusion nor escape has ever brought us the relief we've sought, and there is no reason to think that either will solve our problems now. Peace of mind, relief from gender struggle, will come only from a politics of inclusion, not exclusion, from standing up for equality and justice, and not by running away.

NOTES

1. Of course, the phrase "American manhood" contains several simultaneous fictions. There is no single manhood that defines all American men; "America" is meant to refer to the United States proper, and there are significant ways in which this "American manhood" is the outcome of forces that transcend both gender and nation, that is, the global economic development of industrial capitalism. I use it, therefore, to describe the specific hegemonic version of masculinity in the United States, that normative constellation of attitudes, traits, and behaviors that became the standard against which all other masculinities are measured and against which individual men measure the success of their gender accomplishments.
2. Much of this work is elaborated in *Manhood: The American Quest* (in press).
3. Although I am here discussing only American masculinity, I am aware that others have located this chronic instability and efforts to prove manhood in the particular cultural and economic arrangements of Western society. Calvin, after all, inveighed against the disgrace "for men to become effeminate," and countless other theorists have described the mechanics of manly proof. (See, for example, Seidler, 1994.)
4. I do not mean to argue that women do not have anxieties about whether they are feminine enough. Ask any woman how she feels about being called aggressive; it sends a chill into her heart because her femininity is suspect. (I believe that the reason for the enormous recent popularity of sexy lingerie among women is that it enables women to remember they are still feminine underneath their corporate business suit—a suit that apes masculine styles.) But I think the stakes are not as great for women and that women have greater latitude in defining their identities around these questions than men do. Such are the ironies of sexism: The powerful

have a narrower range of options than the powerless, because the powerless can *also* imitate the powerful and get away with it. It may even enhance status, if done with charm and grace—that is, not threatening. For the powerful, any hint of behaving like the powerless is a fall from grace.

5. Such observations also led journalist Heywood Broun to argue that most of the attacks against feminism came from men who were shorter than 5 ft. 7 in. "The man who, whatever his physical size, feels secure in his own masculinity and in his own relation to life is rarely resentful of the opposite sex" (cited in Symes, 1930, p. 139).

6. Some of Freud's followers, such as Anna Freud and Alfred Adler, did follow up on these suggestions. (See especially Adler, 1980.) I am grateful to Terry Kupers for his help in thinking through Adler's ideas.

7. The image is from Warren Farrell, who spoke at a workshop I attended at the First International Men's Conference, Austin, Texas, October 1991.

REFERENCES

Adler, A. (1980). *Cooperation between the sexes: Writings on women, love and marriage, sexuality and its disorders* (H. Ansbacher & R. Ansbacher, Eds. & Trans.). New York: Jason Aronson.

Arendt, H. (1970). *On revolution.* New York: Viking.

Bly, R. (1990). *Iron John: A book about men.* Reading, MA: Addison-Wesley.

Brannon, R. (1976). The male sex role—and what it's done for us lately. In R. Brannon & D. David (Eds.), *The forty-nine percent majority* (pp. 1–40). Reading, MA: Addison-Wesley.

Connell, R. W. (1987). *Gender and power.* Stanford, CA: Stanford University Press.

Farrell, W. (1986). *Why men are the way they are.* New York: McGraw-Hill.

Farrell, W. (1993). *The myth of male power: Why men are the disposable sex.* New York: Simon & Schuster.

Gaylin, W. (1992). *The male ego.* New York: Viking.

Goffman, E. (1963). *Stigma.* Englewood Cliffs, NJ: Prentice Hall.

Gorer, G. (1964). *The American people: A study in national character.* New York: Norton.

Kaufman, M. (1993). *Cracking the armour: Power and pain in the lives of men.* Toronto: Viking Canada.

Keen, S. (1991). *Fire in the belly.* New York: Bantam.

Kimmel, M. S. (in press). *Manhood: The American quest.* New York: HarperCollins.

Leverenz, D. (1986). Manhood, humiliation and public life: Some stories. *Southwest Review* 71, Fall.

Leverenz, D. (1991). The last real man in America: From Natty Bumppo to Batman. *American Literary Review* 3.

Marx, K., & F. Engels. (1848/1964). The communist manifesto. In R. Tucker (Ed.), *The Marx-Engels reader.* New York: Norton.

Mead, M. (1965). *And keep your powder dry.* New York: William Morrow.

Moore, R., & Gillette, D. (1991). *King, warrior, magician, lover.* New York: HarperCollins.

Moore, R., & Gillette, D. (1992). *The king within: Accessing the king in the male psyche.* New York: William Morrow.

Moore, R., & Gillette, D. (1993a). *The warrior within: Accessing the warrior in the male psyche.* New York: William Morrow.

Moore, R., & Gillette, D. (1993b). *The magician within: Accessing the magician in the male psyche.* New York: William Morrow.

Noble, V. (1992). A helping hand from the guys. In K. L. Hagan (Ed.), *Women respond to the men's movement.* San Francisco: HarperCollins.

Osherson, S. (1992). *Wrestling with love: How men struggle with intimacy, with women, children, parents, and each other.* New York: Fawcett.

Rotundo, E. A. (1993). *American manhood: Transformations in masculinity from the revolution to the modern era.* New York: Basic Books.

Savran, D. (1992). *Communists, cowboys and queers: The politics of masculinity in the work of Arthur Miller and Tennessee Williams.* Minneapolis: University of Minnesota Press.

Seidler, V. J. (1994). *Unreasonable men: Masculinity and social theory.* New York: Routledge.

Symes, L. (1930). The new masculinism. *Harper's Monthly* 161, January.

Wayne, K. (1912). *Building the young man.* Chicago: A. C. McClurg.

What men need is men's approval. (1993, January 3). *The New York Times*, p. C-11.

Wilkinson, R. (1986). *American tough: The tough-guy tradition and American character.* New York: Harper & Row.

Woolfolk, R. L., & Richardson, F. (1978). *Sanity, stress and survival.* New York: Signet.

SEXUALITY

13

THE INVENTION OF HETEROSEXUALITY

JONATHAN NED KATZ

Heterosexuality is old as procreation, ancient as the lust of Eve and Adam. That first lady and gentleman, we assume, perceived themselves, behaved, and felt just like today's heterosexuals. We suppose that heterosexuality is unchanging, universal, essential: ahistorical.

Contrary to that common sense conjecture, the concept of heterosexuality is only one particular historical way of perceiving, categorizing, and imag-

Katz, Jonathan Ned. "The Invention of Heterosexuality." *Socialist Review,* vol. 20, no. 1, Jan.–Mar. 1990, pp. 7–34.

ining the social relations of the sexes. Not ancient at all, the idea of heterosexuality is a modern invention, dating to the late nineteenth century. The
heterosexual belief, with its metaphysical claim to eternity, has a particular,
pivotal place in the social universe of the late nineteenth and twentieth centuries that it did not inhabit earlier. This essay traces the historical process by
which the heterosexual idea was created as ahistorical and taken-for-
granted. . . .

By not studying the heterosexual idea in history, analysts of sex, gay and
straight, have continued to privilege the "normal" and "natural" at the expense of the "abnormal" and "unnatural." Such privileging of the norm ac-
cedes to its domination, protecting it from questions. In making the normal
the object of a thorough-going historical study we simultaneously pursue a
pure truth and a sex-radical and subversive goal: we upset basic preconceptions. We discover that the heterosexual, the normal, and the natural have a
history of changing definitions. Studying the history of the term challenges
its power.

Contrary to our usual assumption, past Americans and other peoples
named, perceived, and socially organized the bodies, lusts, and intercourse
of the sexes in ways radically different from the way we do. If we care to understand this vast past sexual diversity, we need to stop promiscuously projecting our own hetero and homo arrangement. Though lip-service is often
paid to the distorting, ethnocentric effect of such conceptual imperialism, the
category heterosexuality continues to be applied uncritically as a universal
analytical tool. Recognizing the time-bound and culturally-specific character
of the heterosexual category can help us begin to work toward a thoroughly
historical view of sex. . . .

BEFORE HETEROSEXUALITY: EARLY VICTORIAN TRUE LOVE, 1820–1860

In the early nineteenth-century United States, from about 1820 to 1860, the
heterosexual did not exist. Middle-class white Americans idealized a True
Womanhood, True Manhood, and True Love, all characterized by "purity"—
the freedom from sensuality.[1] Presented mainly in literary and religious texts,
this True Love was a fine romance with no lascivious kisses. This ideal contrasts strikingly with late-nineteenth and twentieth century American incite-
ments to a hetero sex.*

---

*Some historians have recently told us to revise our idea of sexless Victorians: their ex-
perience and even their ideology, it is said, were more erotic than we previously
thought. Despite the revisionists, I argue that "purity" was indeed the dominant,
early Victorian, white, middle-class standard. For the debate on Victorian sexuality
see John D'Emilio and Estelle Freedman, *Intimate Matters: A History of Sexuality in
America* (New York: Harper & Row, 1988), p. xii.

Early Victorian True Love was only realized within the mode of proper procreation, marriage, the legal organization for producing a new set of correctly
gendered women and men. Proper womanhood, manhood, and progeny—not
a normal male-female eros—was the main product of this mode of engendering
and of human reproduction.

The actors in this sexual economy were identified as manly men and
womanly women and as procreators, not specifically as erotic beings or heterosexuals. Eros did not constitute the core of a heterosexual identity that in-
hered, democratically, in both men and women. True Women were defined by
their distance from lust. True Men, though thought to live closer to carnality,
and in less control of it, aspired to the same freedom from concupiscence.

Legitimate natural desire was for procreation and a proper manhood or
womanhood; no heteroerotic desire was thought to be directed exclusively
and naturally toward the other sex; lust in men was roving. The human body
was thought of as a means towards procreation and production; penis and
vagina were instruments of reproduction, not of pleasure. Human energy,
thought of as a closed and severely limited system, was to be used in producing children and in work, not wasted in libidinous pleasures.

The location of all this engendering and procreative labor was the sacred
sanctum of early Victorian True Love, the home of the True Woman and True
Man—a temple of purity threatened from within by the monster masturbator,
an archetypal early Victorian cult figure of illicit lust. The home of True Love
was a castle far removed from the erotic exotic ghetto inhabited most notoriously then by the prostitute, another archetypal Victorian erotic monster. . . .

LATE VICTORIAN SEX-LOVE: 1860–1892

"Heterosexuality" and "homosexuality" did not appear out of the blue in the
1890s. These two eroticisms were in the making from the 1860s on. In late Victorian America and in Germany, from about 1860 to 1892, our modern idea of
an eroticized universe began to develop, and the experience of a heterolust
began to be widely documented and named. . . .

In the late nineteenth-century United States, several social factors con-
verged to cause the eroticizing of consciousness, behavior, emotion, and
identity that became typical of the twentieth-century Western middle class.
The transformation of the family from producer to consumer unit resulted in
a change in family members' relation to their own bodies; from being an instrument primarily of work, the human body was integrated into a new economy, and began more commonly to be perceived as a means of consumption
and pleasure. Historical work has recently begun on how the biological human body is differently integrated into changing modes of production, procreation, engendering, and pleasure so as to alter radically the identity,
activity, and experience of that body.[2]

The growth of a consumer economy also fostered a new pleasure ethic. This imperative challenged the early Victorian work ethic, finally helping to usher in a major transformation of values. While the early Victorian work ethic had touted the value of economic production, that era's procreation ethic had extolled the virtues of human reproduction. In contrast, the late Victorian economic ethic hawked the pleasures of consuming, while its sex ethic praised an erotic pleasure principle for men and even for women.

In the late nineteenth century, the erotic became the raw material for a new consumer culture. Newspapers, books, plays, and films touching on sex, "normal" and "abnormal," became available for a price. Restaurants, bars, and baths opened, catering to sexual consumers with cash. Late Victorian entrepreneurs of desire incited the proliferation of a new eroticism, a commoditized culture of pleasure.

In these same years, the rise in power and prestige of medical doctors allowed these upwardly mobile professionals to prescribe a healthy new sexuality. Medical men, in the name of science, defined a new ideal of male-female relationships that included, in women as well as men, an essential, necessary, normal eroticism. Doctors, who had earlier named and judged the sex-enjoying woman a "nymphomaniac," now began to label women's *lack* of sexual pleasure a mental disturbance, speaking critically, for example, of female "frigidity" and "anesthesia."*

By the 1880s, the rise of doctors as a professional group fostered the rise of a new medical model of Normal Love, replete with sexuality. The new Normal Woman and Man were endowed with a healthy libido. The new theory of Normal Love was the modern medical alternative to the old Cult of True Love. The doctors prescribed a new sexual ethic as if it were a morally neutral, medical description of health. The creation of the new Normal Sexual had its counterpart in the invention of the late Victorian Sexual Pervert. The attention paid the sexual abnormal created a need to name the sexual normal, the better to distinguish the average him and her from the deviant it.

HETEROSEXUALITY: THE FIRST YEARS, 1892–1900

In the periodization of heterosexual American history suggested here, the years 1892 to 1900 represent "The First Years" of the heterosexual epoch, eight key years in which the idea of the heterosexual and homosexual were initially and tentatively formulated by U.S. doctors. The earliest-known American use

---

*This reference to females reminds us that the invention of heterosexuality had vastly different impacts on the histories of women and men. It also differed in its impact on lesbians and heterosexual women, homosexual and heterosexual men, the middle class and working class, and on different religious, racial, national, and geographic groups.

of the word "heterosexual" occurs in a medical journal article by Dr. James G. Kiernan of Chicago, read before the city's medical society on March 7, 1892, and published that May—portentous dates in sexual history.[3] But Dr. Kiernan's heterosexuals were definitely not exemplars of normality. Heterosexuals, said Kiernan, were defined by a mental condition, "psychical hermaphroditism." Its symptoms were "inclinations to both sexes." These heterodox sexuals also betrayed inclinations "to abnormal methods of gratification," that is, techniques to insure pleasure without procreation. Dr. Kiernan's heterogeneous sexuals did demonstrate "traces of the normal sexual appetite" (a touch of procreative desire). Kiernan's normal sexuals were implicitly defined by a monolithic other-sex inclination and procreative aim. Significantly, they still lacked a name.

Dr. Kiernan's article of 1892 also included one of the earliest-known uses of the word "homosexual" in American English. Kiernan defined "Pure homosexuals" as persons whose "general mental state is that of the opposite sex." Kiernan thus defined homosexuals by their deviance from a gender norm. His heterosexuals displayed a double deviance from both gender and procreative norms.

Though Kiernan used the new words "heterosexual" and "homosexual," an old procreative standard and a new gender norm coexisted uneasily in his thought. His word heterosexual defined a mixed person and compound urge, abnormal because they wantonly included procreative and non-procreative objectives, as well as same-sex and different-sex attractions.

That same year, 1892, Dr. Krafft-Ebing's influential *Psychopathia Sexualis* was first translated and published in the United States.[4] But Kiernan and Krafft-Ebing by no means agreed on the definition of the heterosexual. In Krafft-Ebing's book, "hetero-sexual" was used unambiguously in the modern sense to refer to an erotic feeling for a different sex. "Homo-sexual" referred unambiguously to an erotic feeling for a "same sex." In Krafft-Ebing's volume, unlike Kiernan's article, heterosexual and homosexual were clearly distinguished from a third category, a "psycho-sexual hermaphroditism," defined by impulses toward both sexes.

Krafft-Ebing hypothesized an inborn "sexual instinct" for relations with the "opposite sex," the inherent "purpose" of which was to foster procreation. Krafft-Ebing's erotic drive was still a reproductive instinct. But the doctor's clear focus on a different-sex versus same-sex sexuality constituted a historic, epochal move from an absolute procreative standard of normality toward a new norm. His definition of heterosexuality as other-sex attraction provided the basis for a revolutionary, modern break with a centuries-old procreative standard.

It is difficult to overstress the importance of that new way of categorizing. The German's mode of labeling was radical in referring to the biological sex, masculinity or femininity, and the pleasure of actors (along with the procreant purpose of acts). Krafft-Ebing's heterosexual offered the modern world a new norm that came to dominate our idea of the sexual universe, helping to change it from a mode of human reproduction and engendering to a mode of pleasure. The heterosexual category provided the basis for a move from a production-oriented, procreative imperative to a consumerist pleasure principle—an institutionalized pursuit of happiness. . . .

Only gradually did doctors agree that heterosexual referred to a normal, "other-sex" eros. This new standard-model heterosex provided the pivotal term for the modern regularization of eros that paralleled similar attempts to standardize masculinity and femininity, intelligence, and manufacturing.[5] The idea of heterosexuality as the master sex from which all others deviated was (like the idea of the master race) deeply authoritarian. The doctors' normalization of a sex that was hetero proclaimed a new heterosexual separatism—an erotic apartheid that forcefully segregated the sex normals from the sex perverts. The new, strict boundaries made the emerging erotic world less polymorphous—safer for sex normals. However, the idea of such creatures as heterosexuals and homosexuals emerged from the narrow world of medicine to become a commonly accepted notion only in the early twentieth century. In 1901, in the comprehensive *Oxford English Dictionary,* "heterosexual" and "homosexual" had not yet made it.

THE DISTRIBUTION OF THE HETEROSEXUAL MYSTIQUE: 1900–1930

In the early years of this heterosexual century the tentative hetero hypothesis was stabilized, fixed, and widely distributed as the ruling sexual orthodoxy: The Heterosexual Mystique. Starting among pleasure-affirming urban working-class youths, southern blacks, and Greenwich-Village bohemians as defensive subculture, heterosex soon triumphed as dominant culture.[6]

In its earliest version, the twentieth-century heterosexual imperative usually continued to associate heterosexuality with a supposed human "need," "drive," or "instinct" for propagation, a procreant urge linked inexorably with carnal lust as it had not been earlier. In the early twentieth century, the falling birth rate, rising divorce rate, and "war of the sexes" of the middle class were matters of increasing public concern. Giving vent to heteroerotic emotions was thus praised as enhancing baby-making capacity, marital intimacy, and family stability. (Only many years later, in the mid-1960s, would heteroeroticism be distinguished completely, in practice and theory, from procreativity and male-female pleasure sex justified in its own name.)

The first part of the new sex norm—hetero—referred to a basic gender divergence. The "oppositeness" of the sexes was alleged to be the basis for a universal, normal, erotic attraction between males and females. The stress on the sexes' "oppositeness," which harked back to the early nineteenth century, by no means simply registered biological differences of females and males. The early twentieth-century focus on physiological and gender dimorphism reflected the deep anxieties of men about the shifting work, social roles, and power of men over women, and about the ideals of womanhood and manhood. That gender anxiety is documented, for example, in 1897, in *The New York Times'* publication of the Reverend Charles Parkhurst's diatribe against female "andromaniacs," the preacher's derogatory, scientific-sounding name for women who tried to "minimize distinctions by which manhood and womanhood are differentiated."[7] The stress on gender difference was a conservative response to the changing social-sexual division of activity and feeling which gave rise to the independent "New Woman" of the 1880s and eroticized "Flapper" of the 1920s.

The second part of the new hetero norm referred positively to sexuality. That novel upbeat focus on the hedonistic possibilities of male-female conjunctions also reflected a social transformation—a revaluing of pleasure and procreation, consumption and work in commercial, capitalist society. The democratic attribution of a normal lust to human females (as well as males) served to authorize women's enjoyment of their own bodies and began to undermine the early Victorian idea of the pure True Woman—a sex-affirmative action still part of women's struggle. The twentieth-century Erotic Woman also undercut nineteenth-century feminist assertion of women's moral superiority, cast suspicions of lust on women's passionate romantic friendships with women, and asserted the presence of a menacing female monster, "the lesbian."[8] . . .

In the perspective of heterosexual history, this early twentieth century struggle for the more explicit depiction of an "opposite-sex" eros appears in a curious new light. Ironically, we find sex-conservatives, the social purity advocates of censorship and repression, fighting against the depiction not just of sexual perversity but also of the new normal heterosexuality. That a more open depiction of normal sex had to be defended against forces of propriety confirms the claim that heterosexuality's predecessor, Victorian True Love, had included no legitimate eros. . . .

THE HETEROSEXUAL STEPS OUT: 1930–1945

In 1930, in *The New York Times,* heterosexuality first became a love that dared to speak its name. On April 30th of that year, the word "heterosexual" is first known to have appeared in *The New York Times Book Review.* There, a critic described the subject of André Gide's *The Immoralist* proceeding "from a heterosexual liaison to a homosexual one." The ability to slip between sexual categories was referred to casually as a rather unremarkable aspect of human possibility. This is also the first known reference by *The Times* to the new hetero/homo duo.[9]

The following month the second reference to the hetero/homo dyad appeared in *The New York Times Book Review,* in a comment on Floyd Dell's *Love in the Machine Age.* This work revealed a prominent antipuritan of the 1930s using the dire threat of homosexuality as his rationale for greater heterosexual freedom. *The Times* quoted Dell's warning that current abnormal social conditions kept the young dependent on their parents, causing "infantilism, prostitution and homosexuality." Also quoted was Dell's attack on the "inculcation of purity" that "breeds distrust of the opposite sex." Young people, Dell said, should be "permitted to develop normally to heterosexual adulthood." "But," *The Times* reviewer emphasized, "such a state already exists, here and now." And so it did. Heterosexuality, a new gender-sex category, had been distributed from the narrow, rarified realm of a few doctors to become a nationally, even internationally, cited aspect of middle-class life.[10] . . .

HETEROSEXUAL HEGEMONY: 1945–1965

The "cult of domesticity" following World War II—the reassociation of women with the home, motherhood, and child-care; men with fatherhood and wage work outside the home—was a period in which the predominance of the hetero norm went almost unchallenged, an era of heterosexual hegemony. This was an age in which conservative mental-health professionals reasserted the old link between heterosexuality and procreation. In contrast, sex-liberals of the day strove, ultimately with success, to expand the heterosexual ideal to include within the boundaries of normality a wider-than-ever range of nonprocreative, premarital, and extra-marital behaviors. But sex-liberal reform actually helped to extend and secure the dominance of the heterosexual idea, as we shall see when we get to Kinsey.

The post-war sex-conservative tendency was illustrated in 1947, in Ferdinand Lundberg and Dr. Marnia Farnham's book, *Modern Woman: The Lost Sex.* Improper masculinity and femininity was exemplified, the authors decreed, by "engagement in heterosexual relations . . . with the complete intent to see to it that they do not eventuate in reproduction."[11] Their procreatively-defined heterosex was one expression of a postwar ideology of fecundity that, internalized and enacted dutifully by a large part of the population, gave rise to the postwar baby boom.

The idea of the feminine female and masculine male as prolific breeders was also reflected in the stress, specific to the late 1940s, on the homosexual as sad symbol of "sterility"—that particular loaded term appears incessantly in comments on homosex dating to the fecund forties.

In 1948, in *The New York Times Book Review,* sex liberalism was in ascendancy. Dr. Howard A. Rusk declared that Alfred Kinsey's just published report on *Sexual Behavior in the Human Male* had found "wide variations in sex concepts and behavior." This raised the question: "What is 'normal' and 'abnormal'?" In particular, the report had found that "homosexual experience is much more common than previously thought," and "there is often a mixture of both homo and hetero experience."[12]

Kinsey's counting of orgasms indeed stressed the wide range of behaviors and feelings that fell within the boundaries of a quantitative, statistically accounted heterosexuality. Kinsey's liberal reform of the hetero/homo dualism widened the narrow, old hetero category to accord better with the varieties of social experience. He thereby contradicted the older idea of a monolithic, qualitatively defined, natural procreative act, experience, and person.[13]

Though Kinsey explicitly questioned "whether the terms 'normal' and 'abnormal' belong in a scientific vocabulary," his counting of climaxes was generally understood to define normal sex as majority sex. This quantified norm constituted a final, society-wide break with the old qualitatively defined reproductive standard. Though conceived of as purely scientific, the statistical definition of the normal as the-sex-most-people-are-having substituted a new, quantitative moral standard for the old, qualitative sex ethic—another triumph for the spirit of capitalism.

Kinsey also explicitly contested the idea of an absolute, either/or antithesis between hetero and homo persons. He denied that human beings "represent two discrete populations, heterosexual and homosexual." The world, he ordered, "is not to be divided into sheep and goats." The hetero/homo division was not nature's doing: "Only the human mind invents categories and tries to force facts into separated pigeon-holes. The living world is a continuum."[14]

With a wave of the taxonomist's hand, Kinsey dismissed the social and historical division of people into heteros and homos. His denial of heterosexual and homosexual personhood rejected the social reality and profound subjective force of a historically constructed tradition which, since 1892 in the United States, had cut the sexual population in two and helped to establish the social reality of a heterosexual and homosexual identity.

On the one hand, the social construction of homosexual persons has led to the development of a powerful gay liberation identity politics based on an ethnic group model. This has freed generations of women and men from a deep, painful, socially induced sense of shame, and helped to bring about a society-wide liberalization of attitudes and responses to homosexuals.[15] On the other hand, contesting the notion of homosexual and heterosexual persons was one early, partial resistance to the limits of the hetero/homo construction. Gore Vidal, rebel son of Kinsey, has for years been joyfully proclaiming:

> there is no such thing as a homosexual or a heterosexual person. There are only homo- or heterosexual acts. Most people are a mixture of impulses if not practices, and what anyone does with a willing partner is of no social or cosmic significance.
>
> So why all the fuss? In order for a ruling class to rule, there must be arbitrary prohibitions. Of all prohibitions, sexual taboo is the most useful because sex involves everyone. . . . we have allowed our governors to divide the population into two teams. One team is good, godly, straight; the other is evil, sick, vicious.[16]

. . .

HETEROSEXUALITY QUESTIONED: 1965–1982

By the late 1960s, anti-establishment counterculturalists, fledgling feminists, and homosexual-rights activists had begun to produce an unprecedented critique of sexual repression in general, of women's sexual repression in particular, of marriage and the family—and of some forms of heterosexuality. This critique even found its way into *The New York Times.*

In March 1968, in the theater section of that paper, freelancer Rosalyn Regelson cited a scene from a satirical review brought to New York by a San Francisco troupe:

> a heterosexual man wanders inadvertently into a homosexual bar. Before he realizes his mistake, he becomes involved with an aggressive queen who orders a drink for him. Being a broadminded liberal and trying to play it cool until he can back out of the situation gracefully, he asks, "How do you like being a ah homosexual?" To which the queen drawls drily, "How do you like being ah whatever it is you are?"

Regelson continued:

> The Two Cultures in confrontation. The middle-class liberal, challenged today on many fronts, finds his last remaining fixed value, his heterosexuality, called into question. The theater . . . recalls the strategies he uses in dealing with this ultimate threat to his world view.[17]

. . .

HETEROSEXUAL HISTORY: OUT OF THE SHADOWS

Our brief survey of the heterosexual idea suggests a new hypothesis. Rather than naming a conjunction old as Eve and Adam, heterosexual designates a word and concept, a norm and role, an individual and group identity, a behavior and feeling, and a peculiar sexual-political institution particular to the late nineteenth and twentieth centuries.

Because much stress has been placed here on heterosexuality as word and concept, it seems important to affirm that heterosexuality (and homosexuality) came into existence before it was named and thought about. The formulation of the heterosexual idea did not create a heterosexual experience or behavior; to suggest otherwise would be to ascribe determining power to labels and concepts. But the titling and envisioning of heterosexuality did play an important role in consolidating the construction of the heterosexual's social existence. Before the wide use of the word heterosexual, I suggest, women and men did not mutually lust with the same profound, sure sense of normalcy that followed the distribution of "heterosexual" as universal sanctifier.

According to this proposal, women and men make their own sexual histories. But they do not produce their sex lives just as they please. They make their sexualities within a particular mode of organization given by the past and altered by their changing desire, their present power and activity, and their vision of a better world. That hypothesis suggests a number of good reasons for the immediate inauguration of research on a historically specific heterosexuality.

The study of the history of the heterosexual experience will forward a great intellectual struggle still in its early stages. This is the fight to pull heterosexuality, homosexuality, and all the sexualities out of the realm of nature and biology [and] into the realm of the social and historical. Feminists have explained to us that anatomy does not determine our gender destinies (our masculinities and femininities). But we've only recently begun to consider that *biology does not settle our erotic fates.* The common notion that biology determines the object of sexual desire, or that physiology and society together cause sexual orientation, are determinisms that deny the break existing between our bodies and situations and our desiring. Just as the biology of our hearing organs will never tell us why we take pleasure in Bach or delight in Dixieland, our female or male anatomies, hormones, and genes will never tell us why we yearn for women, men, both, other, or none. That is because desiring is a self-generated project of individuals within particular historical cultures. Heterosexual history can help us see the place of values and judgments in the construction of our own and others' pleasures, and to see how our erotic tastes—our aesthetics of the flesh—are socially institutionalized through the struggle of individuals and classes.

The study of heterosexuality in time will also help us to recognize the *vast historical diversity of sexual emotions and behaviors*—a variety that challenges the monolithic heterosexual hypothesis. John D'Emilio and Estelle Freedman's *Intimate Matters: A History of Sexuality in America* refers in passing to numerous substantial changes in sexual activity and feeling: for example, the widespread use of contraceptives in the nineteenth century, the twentieth-century incitement of the female orgasm, and the recent sexual conduct changes by gay men in response to the AIDS epidemic. It's now a commonplace of family history that people in particular classes feel and behave in substantially different ways under different historical conditions.[18] Only when we stop assuming an invariable essence of heterosexuality will we begin the research to reveal the full variety of sexual emotions and behaviors.

The historical study of the heterosexual experience can help us *understand the erotic relationships of women and men in terms of their changing modes of social organization.* Such modal analysis actually characterizes a sex history well underway.[19] This suggests that the eros-gender-procreation system (the social ordering of lust, femininity and masculinity, and baby-making) has been linked closely to a society's particular organization of power and production. To understand the subtle history of heterosexuality we need to look carefully at correlations between (1) society's organization of eros and pleasure; (2) its mode of engendering persons as feminine or masculine (its making of women and men); (3) its ordering of human reproduction; and (4) its dominant political economy. This General Theory of Sexual Relativity proposes that substantial historical changes in the social organization of eros, gender, and procreation have basically altered the activity and experience of human beings within those modes.[20]

A historical view locates heterosexuality and homosexuality in time, helping us distance ourselves from them. This distancing can help us formulate new questions that clarify our long-range sexual-political goals: What has been and is the social function of sexual categorizing? Whose interests have been served by the division of the world into heterosexual and homosexual? Do we dare not draw a line between those two erotic species? Is some sexual naming socially necessary? Would human freedom be enhanced if the sex-biology of our partners in lust was of no particular concern, and had no name? In what kind of society could we all more freely explore our desire and our flesh?

As we move toward [the year 2000], a new sense of the historical making of the heterosexual and homosexual suggests that these are ways of feeling, acting, and being with each other that we can together unmake and radically remake according to our present desire, power, and our vision of a future political-economy of pleasure.

REFERENCES

1. Barbara Welter, "The Cult of True Womanhood: 1820–1860," *American Quarterly,* vol. 18 (Summer 1966); Welter's analysis is extended here to include True Men and True Love.

2. See, for example, Catherine Gallagher and Thomas Laqueur, eds., "The Making of the Modern Body: Sexuality and Society in the Nineteenth Century," *Representations,* no. 14 (Spring 1986) (republished, Berkeley: University of California Press, 1987).

3. Dr. James G. Kiernan, "Responsibility in Sexual Perversion," *Chicago Medical Recorder,* vol. 3 (May 1892), pp. 185–210.

4. R. von Krafft-Ebing, *Psychopathia Sexualis, with Especial Reference to Contrary Sexual Instinct: A Medico-Legal Study,* trans. Charles Gilbert Chaddock (Philadelphia: F. A. Davis, 1892), from the 7th and revised German ed. Preface, November 1892.

5. For the standardization of gender see Lewis Terman and C. C. Miles, *Sex and Personality, Studies in Femininity and Masculinity* (New York: McGraw-Hill, 1936). For the standardization of intelligence see Lewis Terman, *Stanford-Binet Intelligence Scale* (Boston: Houghton Mifflin, 1916). For the standardization of work, see "scientific management" and "Taylorism" in Harry Braverman, *Labor and Monopoly Capital: The Degradation of Work in the Twentieth Century* (New York: Monthly Review Press, 1974).

6. See D'Emilio and Freedman, *Intimate Matters,* pp. 194–201, 231, 241, 295–96; Ellen Kay Trimberger, "Feminism, Men, and Modern Love: Greenwich Village, 1900–1925," in *Powers of Desire: The Politics of Sexuality,* eds. Ann Snitow, Christine Stansell, Sharon Thompson (New York: Monthly Review Press, 1983), pp. 131–52; Kathy Peiss, " 'Charity Girls' and City Pleasures: Historical Notes on Working Class Sexuality, 1880–1920," in *Powers of Desire,* pp. 74–87; and Mary P. Ryan, "The

Sexy Saleslady: Psychology, Heterosexuality, and Consumption in the Twentieth Century," in her *Womanhood in America*, 2nd ed. (New York: Franklin Watts: 1979), pp. 151–82.

7. [Rev. Charles Parkhurst], "Woman. Calls Them Andromaniacs. Dr. Parkhurst So Characterizes Certain Women Who Passionately Ape Everything That Is Mannish. Woman Divinely Preferred. Her Supremacy Lies in Her Womanliness, and She Should Make the Most of It—Her Sphere of Best Usefulness the Home," *The New York Times*, May 23, 1897, p. 16:1.

8. See Lisa Duggan, "The Social Enforcement of Heterosexuality and Lesbian Resistance in the 1920s," in *Class, Race, and Sex: The Dynamics of Control*, ed. Amy Swerdlow and Hanah Lessinger (Boston: G. K. Hall, 1983), pp. 75–92; Rayna Rapp and Ellen Ross, "The Twenties Backlash: Compulsory Heterosexuality, the Consumer Family, and the Waning of Feminism," in Swerdlow and Lessinger; Christina Simmons, "Companionate Marriage and the Lesbian Threat," *Frontiers*, vol. 4, no. 3 (Fall 1979), pp. 54–59; and Lillian Faderman, *Surpassing the Love of Men* (New York: William Morrow, 1981).

9. Louis Kronenberger, review of André Gide, *The Immoralist, New York Times Book Review*, April 20, 1930, p. 9.

10. Henry James Forman, review of Floyd Dell, *Love in the Machine Age* (New York: Farrar & Rinehart), *New York Times Book Review*, September 14, 1930, p. 9.

11. Ferdinand Lundberg and Dr. Marnia F. Farnham, *Modern Woman the Lost Sex* (NY: Harper, 1947).

12. Dr. Howard A. Rusk, *New York Times Book Review*, January 4, 1948, p. 3.

13. Alfred Kinsey, Wardell B. Pomeroy, Clyde E. Martin, *Sexual Behavior in the Human Male* (Philadelphia: W. B. Saunders, 1948), pp. 199–200.

14. Kinsey, *Sexual Behavior*, pp. 637, 639.

15. See Steven Epstein, "Gay Politics, Ethnic Identity: The Limits of Social Constructionism," *Socialist Review* 93/93 (1987), pp. 9–54.

16. Gore Vidal, "Someone to Laugh at the Squares With" [Tennessee Williams], *New York Review of Books*, June 13, 1985; reprinted in his *At Home: Essays, 1982–1988* (New York: Random House, 1988), p. 48.

17. Rosalyn Regelson, "Up the Camp Staircase," *The New York Times*, March 3, 1968, Section II, p. 1:5.

18. D'Emilio and Freedman, *Intimate Matters*, pp. 57–63, 268, 356.

19. Ryan, *Womanhood*; John D'Emilio, "Capitalism and Gay Identity" in *Powers of Desire*, pp. 100–13; Jeffrey Weeks, *Coming Out: Homosexual Politics in Britain from the Nineteenth Century to the Present* (London: Quartet Books, 1977); D'Emilio and Freedman, *Intimate Matters*; Katz, "Early Colonial Exploration, Agriculture, and Commerce: The Age of Sodomitical Sin, 1607–1740," *Gay/Lesbian Almanac*, pp. 23–65.

20. This tripartite system is intended as a revision of Gayle Rubin's pioneering work on the social-historical organization of eros and gender. See "The Traffic in Women: Notes on the Political-Economy of Sex," in *Toward an Anthropology of Women*, ed. Rayna R. Reiter (New York: Monthly Review Press, 1975), pp. 157–210, and "Thinking Sex: Notes for a Radical Theory of the Politics of Sexuality," in *Pleasure and Danger: Exploring Female Sexuality*, ed. Carole S. Vance (Boston: Routledge & Kegan Paul, 1984), pp. 267–329.

14

PILLS AND POWER TOOLS

SUSAN BORDO

Viagra. "The Potency Pill," as *Time* magazine's cover describes it. Since it went on sale, it has had "the fastest takeoff of a new drug" that the RiteAid drugstore chain has ever seen. It is all over the media. Users are jubilant, claiming effects that last through the night, youth restored, better "quality" erections. "This little pill is like a package of dynamite," says one.

Some even see Viagra as a potential cure for social ills. Bob Guccione, publisher of *Penthouse*, hails the drug as "freeing the American male libido" from the emasculating clutches of feminism. This diagnosis does not sit very comfortably with current medical wisdom, which has declared impotence to be a physiological problem. I, like Guccione, am skeptical of that declaration—but would suggest a deeper meditation on what has put the squeeze on male libido.

Think, to begin with, of the term *impotence.* It rings with disgrace, humiliation—and it was not the feminists who invented it. Writer Philip Lopate, in an essay on his body, says that merely to say the word out loud makes him nervous. Yet remarkably, *impotence*—rather than the more forgiving, if medicalized, *erectile dysfunction*—is still a common nomenclature among medical researchers. *Frigidity,* with its suggestion that the woman is cold, like some barren tundra, went by the board a while ago. But *impotence,* no less loaded with ugly gender implications, remains. Lenore Tiefer, who researches medical terminology, suggests that we cannot let go of *impotence* because to do so would force us to also let go of *potency* and the cultural mythology that equates male sexuality with power. But to hold on to that mythology, men must pay a steep price.

Impotence. Unlike other disorders, impotence implicates the whole man, not merely the body part. He is impotent. Would we ever say about a man with a headache "He is a headache?" Yet this is just what we do with impotence, as Warren Farrell notes in *Why Men Are the Way They Are.* "We make no attempt to separate impotence from the total personality." Then, we expect the personality to perform like a machine.

That expectation of men is embedded throughout our culture. Think of our slang terms, so many of which encase the penis, like a cyborg, in various sorts of metal or steel armor. Big rig. Blow torch. Bolt. Cockpit. Crank. Crowbar. Destroyer. Dipstick. Drill. Engine. Hammer. Hand tool. Hardware. Hose. Power tool. Rod. Torpedo. Rocket. Spear. Such slang—common among teenage boys—is violent in what it suggests the machine penis can do to another, "softer" body. But the terms are also metaphorical protection against the failure of potency. A human organ of flesh and blood is subject to anxiety, ambivalence, uncertainty. A torpedo or rocket, on the other hand, would never let one down.

Contemporary urologists have taken the metaphor of man the machine even further. Erectile functioning is "all hydraulics," says Irwin Goldstein of the Boston University Medical Center, scorning a previous generation of researchers who stressed psychological issues. But if it is all a matter of fluid dynamics, why keep the term *impotent,* whose definitions (according to *Webster's Unabridged*) are "want of power," "weakness," "lack of effectiveness, helplessness" and (appearing last) "lack of ability to engage in sexual intercourse." In keeping the term *impotence,* the drug companies, it seems, get to have it both ways: reduce a complex human condition to a matter of chemistry while keeping the old shame machine working, helping to assure the flow of men to their doors.

We live in a culture that encourages men to think of their sexuality as residing in their penises and that gives men little encouragement to explore the rest of their bodies. The beauty of the male body has finally been brought out of the cultural closet by Calvin Klein, Versace, and other designers. But notice how many of those new underwear ads aggressively direct our attention to the (often extraordinary) endowments of the models. Many of the models stare coldly, challengingly at the viewer, defying the viewer's gaze to define them in any way other than how they have chosen to present themselves: powerful, armored, emotionally impenetrable. "I am a rock," their bodies seem to proclaim. Commercial advertisements depict women stroking their necks, their faces, their legs, lost in sensual reverie, taking pleasure in touching themselves—all over. Similar poses with men are very rare. Touching oneself languidly, lost in the sensual pleasure of the body, is too feminine, too "soft," for a real man. Crotch-grabbing, thrusting, putting it "in your face"— that is another matter.

There is a fascinating irony in the fact that although it is women whose bodies are most sexually objectified by this culture, women's bodies are permitted much greater sexual expression in our cultural representations than men's. In sex scenes, the moaning and writhing of the female partner have become the conventional cinematic code for heterosexual ecstasy and climax. The male's participation largely gets represented via caressing hands, humping buttocks, and—on rare occasions—a facial expression of intense concentration. She is transported to another world; he is the pilot of the ship that takes her there. When men are shown being transported themselves, it is usually being played for comedy (as in Al Pacino's shrieks in *Frankie and Johnny,* Eddie Murphy's moaning in *Boomerang,* Kevin Kline's contortions in *A Fish Called Wanda*), or it is coded to suggest that something is not quite normal with the man—he is sexually enslaved, for example (as with Jeremy Irons in *Damage*). Men's bodies in the movies are action-hero toys, power tools—wind them up and watch them perform.

Thankfully, the equation between penis and power tool is now being questioned in other movies. Earlier this year, *The Full Monty* brought us a likable group of unemployed workers in Sheffield, England, who hatch the moneymaking scheme of displaying all in a male strip show and learn what it is like to be what feminist theorists call "the object of the gaze." Paul Thomas Anderson's *Boogie Night* told the story of the rise and fall (so to speak) of a mythically endowed young porn star, Dirk Diggler, who does fine so long as he is the most celebrated stallion in the stable but loses his grip in the face of competition. On the surface, the film is about a world far removed from the lives of most men, a commercial underground where men pray for "wood" and lose their jobs unless they can achieve erection on command. On a deeper level, however, the world of the porn actor is simply the most literalized embodiment—and a perfect metaphor—for a masculinity that demands constant performance from men.

Even before he takes up a career that depends on it, Diggler's sense of self is constellated around his penis; he pumps up his ego by looking in the mirror and—like a coach mesmerizing the team before a game—intoning mantras about his superior gifts. That works well, so long as he believes it. But unlike a real power tool, the motor of male self-worth cannot simply be switched on and off. In the very final shot of the movie, we see Diggler's fabled organ itself. It is a prosthesis, actually (a fact that annoyed several men I know until I pointed out that it was no more a cheat than implanted breasts passing for the real thing). But prosthesis or not and despite its dimensions, it is no masterful tool. It points downward, weighted with expectation, with shame, looking tired and used.

Beginning with the French film *Ridicule* (in which an aristocrat, using his penis as an instrument of vengeance, urinates on the lap of another man), we have seen more unclothed penises in films this year than ever before. But what is groundbreaking about *Boogie Nights* is not that it displays a nude penis, but that it so unflinchingly exposes the job that the mythology of unwavering potency does on the male body. As long as the fortress holds, the sense of power may be intoxicating; but when it cracks—as it is bound to do at some point—the whole structure falls to pieces. Those of whom such constancy is expected (or who require it of themselves) are set up for defeat and humiliation.

Unless, of course, he pops his little pill whenever "failure" threatens. I have no desire to withhold Viagra from the many men who have been deprived of the ability to get an erection by accidents, diabetes, cancer, and other misfortunes to which the flesh—or psyche—is heir. I would just like

CNN and *Time* to spend a fraction of the time they devote to describing "how Viagra cures" to looking at how our culture continues to administer the poison for whose effects we now claim a cure. Let us note, too, that the official medical definition of erectile dysfunction (like the definitions of depression and attention deficit disorder) has broadened coincident with the development of new drugs. Dysfunction is no longer defined as "inability to get an erection" but inability to get an erection that is adequate for "satisfactory sexual performance." Performance. Not pleasure. Not feeling. Performance.

Some of what we now call impotence may indeed be physiological in origin; some may be grounded in deep psychic fears and insecurities. But sometimes, too, a man's penis may simply be instructing him that his feelings are not in synch with the job he is supposed to do—or with the very fact that it's a "job." So, I like Philip Lopate's epistemological metaphor for the penis much better than the machine images. Over the years, he has come to appreciate, he writes, that his penis has its "own specialized form of intelligence." The penis knows that it is not a torpedo, no matter what a culture expects of it or what drugs are relayed to its blood vessels. If we accept that, the notion that a man requires understanding and tolerance when he does not "perform" would go by the wayside ("It's OK. It happens" still assumes that there is something to be excused.) So, too, would the idea that there ought to be one model for understanding nonarousal. Sometimes, the penis's "specialized intelligence" should be listened to rather than cured.

Viagra, unfortunately, seems to be marketed—and used—with the opposite message in mind. Now men can perform all night! Do their job no matter how they feel! (The drug does require some degree of arousal, but minimal.) The hype surrounding the drug encourages rather than deconstructs the expectation that men perform like power tools with only one switch—on or off. Until this expectation is replaced by a conception of manhood that permits men and their penises a full range of human feeling, we will not yet have the kind of "cure" we really need.

15

SEXUAL IDENTITY AND BISEXUAL IDENTITIES
The Struggle for Self-Description in
a Changing Sexual Landscape

PAULA C. RUST

As we look back over our lives, we construct them as stories. A story has a conclusion, and the story line leads inexorably to the conclusion; events and details that are irrelevant to the conclusion are irrelevant to the story and distract the listener from the "real" story. When we construct our life stories, we tend to forget the irrelevant details of our pasts. We identify the relevant experiences and interpret them as the building blocks that made us into the people we are today, and we understand our past changes as the twists and turns in the road we took to reach our current selves. Even if we recognize that we have not yet completed our personal journeys and that we will continue to rewrite our stories until we reach the final draft at death, we still perceive our pasts as the paths by which we arrived at our present selves. Most of us who identify our present selves as gay, lesbian, or bisexual have constructed "coming out stories" that explain—to ourselves and to others—how we arrived at our sexual self-definitions.

Social scientists in the 1970s, seeking to redress the scientific sins that had been committed against lesbian and gay people in the past, sought to understand the lives of lesbian and gay people as they (we) understood their (our) own lives. Taking the cue from their lesbian and gay subjects, many sociologists and psychologists set out to study the process of coming out, i.e., the process of lesbian or gay identity formation. Researchers soon discovered "milestone events," or life events that lesbian and gay people had identified as relevant to their development and incorporated into their coming out stories. Typical milestone events were the first experience of a feeling of sexual attraction for someone of the same sex, the first sexual experience with someone of the same sex, the first labeling of one's self as homosexual, the first public expression of one's homosexual identity to significant others, the symbolic switch from a homosexual to a lesbian or gay identity as one's self-acceptance increased and, eventually, the integration of one's private and public identities as one came out of the closet.

Rust, Paula C. "Sexual Identity and Bisexual Identities: The Struggle for Self-Description in a Changing Sexual Landscape." From Brett Beeyman and Mickey Eliason (eds.) *Queer Studies: A Lesbian, Gay, Bisexual, and Transgender Anthology.* New York: New York University Press, 1996, pp. 64–86.

Based on these observations, scientists elaborated developmental models of coming out that construct it as a linear process of self-discovery in which a false, socially imposed heterosexual identity is replaced with a lesbian or gay identity that accurately reflects the essence of the individual. These models rarely account for bisexual identity as an authentic identity; when they acknowledge bisexual identity at all, they usually cast it as a phase one might pass through on the way to adopting a lesbian or gay identity.[1] Researchers operating within these linear developmental models of coming out asked respondents for the ages at which they experienced each milestone, and then, reporting the average ages, described coming out as an ordered sequence of events. From this research, we learned that lesbians first experience sexual attraction to other women at an average age of twelve or thirteen, but do not become aware of these sexual feelings until late adolescence. They begin suspecting that they are lesbian at an average age of eighteen, but do not adopt lesbian identities until their early twenties. We learned that gay men experience these events at younger ages and in more rapid sequence than lesbians, and—from the few studies that treated bisexual identity as authentic—we learned that bisexuals come out later and more slowly than gays and lesbians.[2] Based on these findings, researchers began theorizing about why men come out more quickly than women and why bisexuals come out more slowly than monosexuals.

The portrait of sexual identity formation that is painted by these average ages is not only grossly simplified but factually inaccurate. Based on research with lesbian-identified and bisexual-identified women,[3] I have shown that average ages conceal a great deal of variation in the coming out process, both among and between lesbian and bisexual women.[4] In contrast to the linear portrait painted by average ages, lesbian and bisexual women experience each milestone event at a wide range of ages; many women do not experience all of the so-called milestone events; women who do experience these events experience them in various orders, and some women experience some events repeatedly.

Moreover, I discovered that the "finding" that bisexual women come out more slowly than lesbians is an artifact of the statistical methods used in studies based on linear models of coming out. When I calculated average ages for the over 400 women in my first study, the results confirmed earlier findings that bisexual women come out at later ages and more slowly than lesbian women. Bisexual women first felt attracted to women at an average age of 18.1, compared to 15.4 for lesbian women. Bisexual women first questioned their heterosexual identity 1.9 years later, at an average of 20.0 years, whereas lesbians first questioned their heterosexual identity 1.6 years later, at an average age of 17.0. But a closer look at the data revealed that lesbian women were twice as likely as bisexual women to have questioned their heterosexual identity before they felt attracted to women (28% vs. 14%), probably because some women were encouraged by lesbian feminist arguments about the political nature of lesbianism to identify themselves as lesbian even in the absence of sexual feelings toward women. Among women who questioned their heterosexual identities only after feeling attracted to other women, bisexual women actually did so sooner—not later—than lesbian women. In other words, the original finding that bisexual women come out more slowly than lesbian women was an artifact resulting from a failure to recognize variations in the coming out process as equally authentic patterns, rather than as deviations from an underlying linear course.

I also discovered that bisexual women had changed sexual identities more frequently in the past than lesbian women, often alternating repeatedly between lesbian and bisexual identities. Under linear developmental models, this finding would be taken as an indication of the instability of bisexual identity and the sociopsychological immaturity of bisexual-identified individuals.[5] Under more sophisticated, but still linear, social interactionist understandings of the creation of identity, this finding would be taken as evidence of the difficulty of constructing a bisexual identity in a social world that offers only two authenticated categories, heterosexual and homosexual.[6] But I also discovered that, at any given moment, a bisexual woman was as likely to be satisfied with her current sexual identity as a lesbian was with hers. This finding disproves the hypothesis that bisexual women are engaged in a constant struggle to establish a satisfactory sexual identity and suggests instead that bisexual women find different sexual identities satisfactory at different times and under different circumstances. Bisexual women's frequent identity changes do not indicate a state of searching immaturity, but a mature state of mutability.

Previous researchers have attempted to modify the linear model of coming out by introducing feedback loops, alternate routes, and contingencies.[7] Although these modifications produce models with ample room for deviation, they do not effectively describe the formation of sexual identity. They are unable to account for the findings that bisexual women incorporate their same-sex feelings into sexual identities more quickly than lesbians and that bisexual women are as satisfied with their sexual identities as lesbians are. This inability highlights the need to develop a new model of the identity formation process.

To accommodate the empirical reality of identity change processes, linear developmental models of coming out must be abandoned in favor of a social constructionist view of identity as a description of the location of the self in relation to other individuals, groups, and institutions. The individuals, groups, and institutions to which we relate are landmarks on a sexual landscape that is itself socially constructed. From this perspective, identity change would be understood as a process of modifying one's self-description in response to changes in either the location of the self or the socially constructed landscape on which one is located. Identity change would be a necessary outcome of one's efforts to maintain an accurate self-description, not an indication that one has not yet achieved an accurate self-description. "Coming out" would not be a process of essential discovery leading to a mature and stable identity, but merely one story constructed around one of the myriad identity changes we all go through as mature adults attempting to maintain accurate self-descriptions in a changing social environment. Research on the so-called "coming out process" would be reconceptualized as research on the social contexts of identity changes that take place throughout life, and the goal of this research would be to discover the types of contextual changes that motivate individual identity change.

In the spring of 1993, I began a second study guided by the concept of sexual identity as a description of the self in relation to other individuals, groups, and institutions.[8] The overall goal of the study is to document the development of bisexual identity, community, and politics in the United States, the United Kingdom, and other, primarily English-speaking, countries. A specific goal of the study is to explore the types of contextual changes that lead individuals to change their sexual identities, with an eye toward understanding why currently bisexual-identified individuals tend to have changed their sexual identities frequently in the past. The study includes people of all gender and sexual identities, including transsexuals and transgenderists.

CHANGES IN ONE'S LOCATION ON THE SEXUAL LANDSCAPE

The most common type of change reported by individuals is change in their own locations on the sexual landscape. Change is relative, and can only be defined in relation to objects other than the self; these objects might be other individuals, social groups, or social and political institutions. Many respondents recalled that they changed their sexual identities when they developed new relationships with particular people, usually romantic or sexual relationships with people whose genders were different from the genders of the people with whom they had expected to become intimately involved. For example, a White American[9] woman who used to identify herself as a Lesbian[10] explained why she began to identify herself as Bisexual:

> About two years ago, I had been in a sexual relationship with a wonderful woman for one year, and I was identifying as lesbian at the time. I found myself attracted to a man who was interested in me. I had a sense of being at a crossroads: lesbian or "something else." She wanted a monogamous relationship and . . . I didn't want that conservatism. We broke up and I began a sexual relationship with the man.[11]

Her previous Lesbian identity represented her sexual relationship with a woman. It also represented her lack of relationship with a man, as evidenced by the fact that it had to change when she began to feel attracted to a man. The conflict between her Lesbian identity and her attraction to a man created, for her, a crossroads, i.e., the moment of change. When this attraction led to a sexual relationship with the man, she adopted a Bisexual identity that apparently represents both her (ex-)relationship to a woman and her current relationship to a man. The new identity represents her new location on the sexual landscape, a location that is described in relation to two other individuals, a woman and a man.

Sometimes the new relationship is not an actual sexual or physical one but merely a feeling of attraction toward another person, as was the case with an Irish woman who identified herself as Bisexual when she "[r]ealiz[ed] I was experiencing a sexual fantasy about a female friend." Or the relationships represented by an identity might be potential relationships. For example, a White man explained that he began identifying as a Gay Bisexual when he "recognized the reality of my past (and potential future) relationships."

For some respondents, a single relationship with an individual—whether actual, desired, or potential—is not enough to motivate a complete identity change. These respondents' identities represent their relationships to entire social groups, and they do not change their sexual identities until their relationships with individuals lead them to perceive changes in their relationships to entire social groups. For example, a Jewish Lesbian said that she fell in love with "a woman," but it was not until she realized she "was sexually attracted to women" that she "suddenly saw the possibility and even inevitability of a different (i.e., lesbian) erotic self-definition." In other words, noting that the individual with whom she had developed a relationship belonged to the social group "women," she generalized her feelings to the entire social group by "realizing" that she could potentially be attracted to any member of that group. She then adopted a Lesbian identity to represent her new relationship to this social group. Another woman explained that she did not begin to call herself Bi until her relationship to an individual man led to the realization that she was attracted to men as a social group. She wrote,

> I had been involved with a man for about two years, during which time I identified as "a lesbian who happens to be seeing a man until something else comes along." After a while I realized that I was really deeply committed to my other-sex relationship. . . . Also I became aware that I was starting to feel more generalized attraction to men other than just my lover. So "bi" seemed more accurate.

Lesbian-identified, gay-identified, and heterosexual-identified respondents often described their identities as representing a single relationship to either an individual, a group, or an institution, whereas bisexual-identified respondents usually said that their identities represent multiple relationships to various individuals, social groups, and institutions. The larger number of relationships needed to anchor bisexual identity is a function of two facts. First, landmarks in the mainstream Euro-American sexual landscape are gendered. For example, individuals are recognized as either female or male, woman or man. Social groups include "men," "women," and "lesbians," and institutions include "gay male society," "legally recognized marriage," and "the feminist movement." Second, Euro-American sexual categories are defined in reference to gender; heterosexuality is defined in terms of relationships between persons of different gender, and homosexuality is defined in terms of relationships between persons of same gender. Thus, on the gendered sexual landscape, a minimum of one landmark is necessary to anchor a monosexual identity such as lesbian, gay, or heterosexual. But in this system of dichotomous sexuality based on dichotomous gender, bisexuality can only be understood as a hybrid combination of heterosexuality and homosexuality. Thus to maintain a *bi*sexual self-description on the gendered landscape, one needs to locate oneself with respect to both female and male, or lesbian/gay and heterosexual, landmarks.

For example, a bisexual identity might represent relationships to two individuals of different genders, as it does to the White man who explained that he adopted his Bisexual identity because he "dated a man and woman at the same time." Or, it might represent relationships to two social groups, men and women, as it does to the Asian-American/Caucasian individual who wrote, "I realized I have always loved men. . . . At the same time I did not cease to love or feel attracted to women, so I discovered I was bisexual." Many bisexuals' identities represent an attraction to one gender as a social group and an actual physical or emotional relationship with a particular individual of the other gender. As one man explained, the incident that led him to adopt a Bisexual identity was "My first same-sex experience, but I realized I was still attracted to women." Although the particular landmarks varied, most bisexual-identified respondents were able to support their bisexual identities only by maintaining relationships to multiple landmarks of both genders.

CHANGES IN THE SEXUAL LANDSCAPE

Whether or not an individual changes co's[12] location on the sexual landscape, the sexual landscape itself might change, creating new opportunities for self-description while transforming or eliminating existing possibilities. The types of landscape change reported by respondents included the appearance of previously invisible landmarks on the sexual landscape and historical changes in the sexual landscape.

Newly visible landmarks might consist of a single individual. For example, one Heterosexual-identified, Bisexual American woman wrote that she "had to sharpen up my own fuzzy feeling about my own bisexuality" when her daughter came out to her as bisexual. The appearance of a bisexual person in her life forced her to consider her relationship to this person, and in the process, to clarify her thoughts about her own sexuality. Conversely, the disappearance of an individual can eliminate the need for an identity that represents one's relationship to that individual, as it did for this Australian woman:

I really craved to be a "lesbian" or "bisexual"—but somehow I couldn't take this label unless I had sexual encounters with women. . . . My period of confusion and questioning my heterosexuality passed away [when] the woman I was attracted to left—so I told myself I was hetero again.

Historical changes, such as the development of social and political movements, create new social groups and institutions and modify or destroy others. As these historical forces transform the sexual landscape, individuals whose identities located them on the old landscape find that they have to relate themselves to their new environment. For example, in the very early days of the second wave of the (predominantly white) feminist movement, lesbianism was labeled a "lavender herring," and feminist lesbians were encouraged to demonstrate their commitment to the feminist movement by remaining in the closet.[13] But the reconstruction of the relationship between lesbianism and feminism in the early 1970s resulted in the creation of the category of the "political lesbian" and led many women to adopt lesbian identities as an expression of commitment to the newly reconstituted feminist movement.[14] One respondent wrote that in 1977 she adopted her Lesbian identity because "Thru feminist politics I began to understand that my primary emotional/energetic commitment was with women." Several years earlier, a lesbian identity would not have served to express her feminist "emotional/energetic commitment" to women.

More recently, the development of a small but growing bisexual culture and social structure has created new social and political landmarks with which individuals can anchor bisexual identities. For example, an American woman mentioned that she had realized that she was bisexual since 1976, but that she only adopted a Bisexual identity "in the last five years since there was a movement." Another woman said that she "had previously identified as a Lesbian," but she "became aware of the Bi option" because "there was a growing, visible Bi community." As the number of bisexual social and political institutions continues to increase, more and more people will identify themselves as bisexual, abandoning the identities that they had considered satisfactory only a few years earlier—identities that became unsatisfactory because the landmarks to which they referred changed and new landmarks arose.

Individuals often experience changes in their personal social contexts. It is only later, when individuals look back over their lives and the lives of others, that they will see the changes they experienced as part of more global, historical contexts that had similar effects on other people. Therefore, few respondents referred to the effect of history on their sexual identities, but this lack of reference to historical change was complemented by an abundance of references to changes in respondents' individual social contexts. These alterations in social context were usually significant because they brought with them changes in the language available for self-description.

CHANGES IN THE LANGUAGE AVAILABLE
FOR SELF-DESCRIPTION

The distinction between changes in the sexual landscape—whether historical or personal—and changes in language is largely theoretical; in practice, they are usually interdependent and virtually indistinguishable. The relevant distinction between different constructions of the sexual landscape is in the language available for self-description, and the relevant distinctions between various languages are the different landmarks and the different relationships to these landmarks that are created by each language, i.e., in the various ways that they construct the sexual landscape.

Some people intentionally put themselves in new social contexts in the hope of finding a new language for self-description. For example, a White American woman said that she went to Coming Out Day in 1990 because she was unsure about her sexuality, but by the time she left, she was a Dyke. Several respondents mentioned that they had read the book *Bi Any Other Name: Bisexual People Speak Out,* and that this book had helped them develop bisexual identities. A Latino-American man explained that he was able to come out as Bisexual after he joined a therapy group in which a bisexual identity was available.

> I joined a bisexual men's therapy group (while still with my female
> partner). I had always heard the term but never really claimed it
> until I joined this group. I think I knew that that's what I was but
> when you're living in a straight environment, you don't talk about it.

Other people, through no conscious intent of their own, find themselves in social contexts where they become involved in new relationships or encounter new identities, and then discover that they can use these identities to describe themselves. For example, a Native American/Caucasian man reexamined his own "repressed bisexuality" when he observed culturally approved intimacy among men while working in the Middle East. A Caucasian man became a "punk" while serving time in a U.S. jail; he explained that he "got used to it and they treated me well so I got emotionally involved with them and dependent on them for security. There was no other term for that role." An Indian woman living in the U.S. was introduced to the Kinsey scale during a seminar on religion and sexuality. She learned that everyone "existed somewhere on this continuum" and scored herself right in the middle. Reflecting on the experience, she stated: "From that moment on, I have thought of myself continuously as someone who is what I would call today 'bisexual.' " An English man explained that he "never really 'began' to think of myself as bisexual, any more than I guess most straights begin to think of themselves as straight." He had begun to use the word "bisexual" after seeing it appear more and more frequently on electronic mail postings.

Because the terms "lesbian" and "gay" are now nearly household words, they are available as self-descriptors even outside lesbian and gay social contexts. In contrast, the concept of an authentic bisexual identity is still limited to particular social contexts, and many bisexual-identified respondents reported that they had adopted their current sexual identities only after encountering the term "bisexual" for the first time when they joined a bisexual support group, therapy group, or political group. Before they encountered the concept of bisexuality, the only terms that were available to them were synonyms for heterosexual and homosexual. Most had chosen one of these two available identities based on their conceptions of the types of relationships that could be represented by each. For example, one man called himself heterosexual, although he had a male sexual partner, because he preferred his wife as a sexual partner. For him, a heterosexual identity was an accurate description of his location on the sexual landscape because it did not deny his relationship to his male lover; it merely indicated that his relationship to his female lover was stronger. When his male partner introduced him to the term "bisexual," he discovered that bisexual identity could also describe his location by representing both of his relationships, and he changed his identity accordingly.

Language also changes when familiar terms take on new meanings or change in meaning. Many respondents reported that they had been familiar with the term "bisexual" for some time but had understood it as a temporary phase that one passed through when coming out as lesbian or gay or as an identity used by those who wish to deny their homosexuality. Once they encountered the term as a reference to a stable set of relationships involving both female and male landmarks, they became comfortable describing themselves as bisexual. For example, one woman encountered a new meaning for "bisexual" when she began associating with a new group of people:

> [I] went to a bisexual convention. Though I'd known that I liked
> women and I like men, meeting a group of people who had
> chosen this as a viable identity—not just a resting place between
> gay and straight—gave me a word to use with myself and a sense
> of legitimacy.

In contrast, another woman felt that the meaning of the word had changed over time, eventually enabling her to adopt it as an identity:

> For a long time, I was afraid to say I was bisexual, because it was
> largely regarded as a term for a lesbian who didn't want to "fess
> up" and I knew women who were like this and who used the term
> this way. I've only started calling myself "bisexual" in the last five
> years, because the term seems to have lost the "closeted lesbian"
> connotation.

For some individuals, a change in the meaning of a term allowed them to maintain an identity that might otherwise have had to change or forced them to change an identity that they might otherwise have been able to keep. An Anglo-American man explained that his concept of "gay" had recently broadened; previously, if he had had a heterosexual encounter, he would have given up his gay identity, but now he says, "If I were to have an occasional heterosexual encounter, I'd still call myself gay, not bisexual." Conversely, a woman who used to identify herself "solely as a Lesbian" was "distressed at the trend of women who used the word "Lesbian" to be femme, hetero-appearing career women with closet politics." Because of this trend, she no longer feels that the word "lesbian" adequately describes herself; she now calls herself a Dyke, among other things, and is "still sad over the loss of the label Lesbian."

CHANGES IN SOCIAL CONTEXT

The fact that different relationships and languages for self-description are available in different social contexts means that individuals who live their lives in multiple social contexts—which most people do, particularly those who identify as sexual minorities and/or as members of racial or ethnic minorities—have to describe themselves differently in different social contexts. The act of moving from one context to another entails a change in sexual identity simply to maintain an accurate description of one's location on the sexual landscape. At the very least, an individual might have to use different terms to describe coself in a heterosexual context than co uses in a sexual minority context and different terms in a Euro-American cultural context than in other racial and ethnic contexts.

For example, a Jewish-American man explained that he often describes himself as "queer" in gay circles because "it expresses my political identity," but that he "generally use[s] 'bi' in straight circles, since 'queer' is generally considered pejorative." In heterosexual contexts, the term "queer" does not accurately convey his sexual location because the political institution to which it refers—a radical sexual movement—is largely unknown. In contrast to Euro-American sexual culture, which emphasizes the genders of one's sexual partners, the Chicano cultures described by Joseph Carrier incorporate the Mexican cultural emphasis on the role one plays in the sex act over the gender of one's partner.[15] Thus, for Chicanos, the development of a gay identity requires a measure of assimilation to Euro-American culture, and this identity is only viable in contexts in which Euro-American concepts of sexuality operate. A Chicano, therefore, would have to describe his sexuality differently depending on the particular ethnic context he is in.

Even within LesBiGayTrans communities, there are contextual variations that necessitate identity changes as one moves from one part of a community to another. Some women identify themselves as bisexual only among other bisexuals and avoid identifying themselves as bisexual among lesbians, because a positive bisexual identity is often not available in lesbian contexts. Among lesbians, they might identify themselves as "lesbians," or they might call themselves "queer," because they feel that this is the most accurate identity available in that context. An Asian-American woman explained that she calls herself "bi" proudly—but only in certain contexts, because in other contexts her bi identity would be misunderstood and, hence, not accurately describe her location on the sexual landscape:

> [I]n a college environment, there are a few "fakes"—bi women who really do embody lots of bad bi stereotypes. In order not to be lumped in with them, I avoid that term here. However, when I go somewhere more Bi-aware . . . more aware of the diversity of us Bi women, I proudly use the term. . . . I think context is very important.

CHANGES IN THE ACCURACY OF SELF-DESCRIPTION

Individuals do not always describe their locations accurately, and identity changes occur as individuals become more accurate or more honest about describing their locations on the sexual landscape. There are many reasons that individuals might intentionally misrepresent their locations, but the most common reason is a belief that other people would disapprove of their true location. Lesbians and gay men often misrepresent their sexual locations when in heterosexual contexts, and bisexual women often misrepresent their location when in lesbian contexts. For example, a White American woman reported that she thinks of herself as a "bi dyke," but until recently, she called herself "queer," because she was afraid "bi dyke" would offend lesbians. She explained that "queer" was a word that she could "use among gay men and lesbians without them knowing I'm bisexual." Unlike the Asian-American woman quoted above, this White woman avoided identifying herself as bisexual in gay and lesbian contexts, not because she thought the term would be misunderstood and hence not accurately represent her, but because she wanted to mislead gay men and lesbians who would disapprove of her true bisexual identity. She also reported that she "just recently felt justified in calling [her]self a 'bi dyke' " among lesbians. In other words, she recently changed the identity she uses in lesbian contexts; this change represented, not a change in her location on the sexual landscape, but a change in her honesty about that location.

Although the politics surrounding bisexual identities are not as intense in gay male communities as they are in lesbian communities, men are also sometimes reluctant to identify themselves as bisexual rather than gay. A Latino man reported that he had known he was bisexual since childhood, but for eleven years he dated women secretly and called himself gay, because he didn't want to lose his friends in the gay community.

It is common for individuals to feel that their previous sexual identities were the result of their own lack of honesty with themselves, even if they did not experience these identities as dishonest at the time. Because "coming out" is traditionally conceptualized as a developmental process of discovering and coming to terms with one's essential sexuality, many people perceive their changes in identity as processes of becoming honest with themselves about their sexuality. For example, a Caucasian man wrote, "I began to question my sexuality and finally admitted that I was in denial about my feelings towards men." Whether the identity changes that these individuals experienced were the result of growing self-honesty, or whether they were the result of actual changes in their relationships or in the languages available to describe their relationships, which in hindsight they interpreted in terms of honesty, is a question that involves a discussion of essential existence that is outside the scope of this article.

Any attempt to create stable bisexual identities or bisexual communities will eventually encounter the same problems that lesbian and gay identities and communities now face. As David Bell points out, despite the theoretical attractiveness and exciting revolutionary potential of conceptualizing bisexuality as something that exists outside fixed categories, individuals seeking a "home" attempt to create positively defined bisexual identities and communities.[16] Indeed, success within current modes of political discourse might necessitate the creation of a bisexual "ethnicity."[17] Creating a bisexual "home" or "ethnicity" is difficult, and during the formative stage these difficulties are easily attributed to the adverse conditions afforded by the current gendered, monosexual construction of sexual identity. But, if some people eventually succeed in convincing themselves that they have managed to give a specific and definable form to bisexual identity and bisexual community, they will discover that bisexual identity and community, like their monosexual counterparts, need constant defense. At that point, in accordance with the principles of dialectic change, a new antagonist will arise, and the defenders of bisexual identities and communities will be able to attribute their difficulties to the new antagonist, who will be constructed as a threat. But the new antagonist will no more be the real threat to bisexual identities and communities than a bisexual identity is the real threat to monosexual identities and communities. The real threat to all identity-based communities is the dynamic nature of identity itself; the appearance of a new antagonist will merely be the symptom of the tension inherent in attempting to build stable identities and communities on dynamic self-descriptions. The revolutionary potential of a bisexual identity is the potential to expose the dynamic nature of sexuality, and it has this potential only insofar as the current landscape is predominantly monosexual and gendered. If we succeed in reconstructing the sexual landscape to support a bisexual identity, we will have destroyed its revolutionary potential. We will have, in effect, created a new aristocracy and postponed the revolutionization of sexual identity until the arrival of the next antagonist.

Fortunately, bisexual political ideology is not yet moving toward the solidification of a definition of bisexuality. On the contrary, the current tendency is to resist efforts to agree on a definition.[18] If we continue on this path and refuse to follow in the footsteps of lesbian and gay movements toward the creation of a bisexual ethnicity, then we will preserve the revolutionary potential of bisexuality.

NOTES

Acknowledgments: This research was supported in part by a grant from the Horace H. Rackham School of Graduate Studies of the University of Michigan in Ann Arbor, by research funding from Hamilton College in Clinton, New York, and by a grant from the Society for the Psychological Study of Social Issues. I am grateful to Jackie Vargas, Ana Morel, Sandy Siemoens, and Michael Peluse for their help in tabulating the data. I am solely responsible for the content of this paper.

1. For example, Beata E. Chapman and JoAnn C. Brannock, "Proposed Model of Lesbian Identity Development: An Empirical Examination," *Journal of Homosexuality* 14, nos. 3/4 (1987): 69–80.

2. Alan P. Bell, Martin S. Weinberg, and Sue Kiefer Hammersmith, *Sexual Preference: Its Development in Men and Women* (Bloomington: Indiana University Press, 1981); Pat Califia, "Lesbian Sexuality," *Journal of Homosexuality* 4, no. 3 (Spring 1979): 255–66; Denise M. Cronin, "Coming Out among Lesbians," in *Sexual Deviance and Sexual Deviants,* ed. Erich Goode and Richard R. Troiden (New York: Morrow, 1974), 268–77; Karla Jay and Allen Young, eds., *The Gay Report: Lesbians and Gay Men Speak Out about Sexual Experiences and Lifestyles* (New York: Simon and Schuster, 1979); Harold D. Kooden, Stephen F. Morin, Dorothy I. Riddle, Martin Rogers, Barbara E. Sang, and Fred Strassburger, *Removing the Stigma: Final Report of the Board of Social and Ethical Responsibility for Psychology's Task Force on the Status of Lesbian and Gay Male Psychologists* (Washington, D.C.: American Psychological Association, 1979); Gary J. McDonald, "Individual Differences in the Coming Out Process for Gay Men: Implications for Theoretical Models," *Journal of Homosexuality* 8, no. 1 (Fall 1982): 47–60; Carmen de Monteflores and Stephen J. Schultz, "Coming Out: Similarities and Differences for Lesbians and Gay Men," *Journal of Social Issues* 34, no. 3 (1978): 59–72; Dorothy Riddle and Stephen Morin, "Removing the Stigma: Data from Institutions," *APA Monitor* (November 1977): 16–28; Siegrid Schäfer, "Sexual and Social Problems of Lesbians," *Journal of Sex Research* 12, no. 1 (February 1976): 50–69; Richard R. Troiden, *Gay and Lesbian Identity: A Sociological Analysis* (Dix Hills, NY: General Hall, 1988).

3. Henceforth, I will use the terms "bisexual" and "lesbian" to refer to women who were, respectively, self-identified as bisexual and as lesbian at the time of this earlier study.

4. Paula C. Rust, " 'Coming Out' in the Age of Social Constructionism: Sexual Identity Formation among Lesbian and Bisexual Women," *Gender and Society* 7, no. 1 (March 1993): 50–77.

5. For example, Chapman and Brannock, "Proposed Model of Lesbian Identity Development."

6. For example, Philip Blumstein and Pepper Schwartz, "Intimate Relationships and the Creation of Sexuality," in *Homosexuality/Heterosexuality: Concepts of Sexual Orientation,* ed. David P. McWhirter, Stephanie A. Sanders, and June M. Reinisch (New York: Oxford University Press, 1990), 307–20; and Kenneth Plummer, *Sexual Stigma: An Interactionist Account* (London: Routledge and Kegan Paul, 1975).

7. For example, Vivienne C. Cass, "Homosexual Identity Formation: A Theoretical Model," *Journal of Homosexuality* 4, no. 3 (Spring 1979): 219–35; Vivienne C. Cass,

"The Implications of Homosexual Identity Formation for the Kinsey Model and Scale of Sexual Preference," in *Homosexuality/ Heterosexuality,* 239–66; Eli Coleman, "Developmental Stages of the Coming Out Process," *Journal of Homosexuality* 7, nos. 2/3 (Winter 1981/Spring 1982): 31–43; McDonald, "Individual Differences in the Coming Out Process for Gay Men."

8. I am collecting data via an anonymous self-administered questionnaire containing a postage-paid return envelope inside the U.S. or postal coupons outside the U.S. The cover of the questionnaire tells potential respondents that

> You can fill out this questionnaire if you are bisexual or if you call yourself bisexual, if you are coming out or questioning your sexuality, if you prefer not to label your sexual orientation, if you used to identify as bisexual, if you are lesbian or gay but have felt attracted to or had a sexual or romantic relationship with someone of the other sex at any time in your life, or if you are heterosexual but have felt attracted to or had a sexual or romantic relationship with someone of your own sex at any time in your life.

The cover of the questionnaire encouraged non-eligible individuals to give the questionnaire to an eligible friend. Respondents are, therefore, self-selected. The questionnaire is being distributed through bisexual and bisexual-inclusive social and political organizations; community centers and counseling services for gay, lesbian, and bisexual people and people exploring their sexuality; institutions dedicated to sexuality education and information dissemination; advertisements in bisexual newsletters and alternative community newspapers; fliers in alternative bookstores; conferences on topics related to sexuality and/or gender; electronic mail networks; and friendship networks. More detailed information about the methodology will be forthcoming in later publications.

Distribution began in the United States in April 1993 and in the United Kingdom in September 1993. To date, questionnaires have been completed and returned by over 450 individuals in the United States, 46 in the United Kingdom, and 22 in Australia and New Zealand. Men and women are equally represented in all countries, except the United States, where women constitute 63% of the sample. Slightly under 4% of respondents are transgendered, including postoperative male-to-female transsexuals, non-transsexual transgenderists, and crossdressers. The age distribution is broader among respondents in the United States than the U.K. The ages of U.S. respondents range from eighteen to eighty-two, with 39% in their twenties, 30% in their thirties, 19% in their forties, and 10% fifty years or older. The oldest respondent from the U.K. is fifty-nine years old, and 67% of respondents from the U.K. are in their twenties. The incomes of respondents in both countries follow normal distribution curves. In the U.S., the median income is in the range of $20–29,999 with 18% earning less than $10,000 and 21% earning $50,000 or more. In the U.K., the mean income is £14,000, with 20% earning under £5,000 and 20% earning over £25,000. Eleven percent of respondents from the United States are people of color, including African-Americans, Asian-Americans, Indigenous Peoples, and Latinas/os.

9. The terms used to describe respondents' racial and ethnic identities are the terms used by respondents themselves when they were asked, "What is your race and/or ethnicity?" Throughout this chapter, capitalization of identity terms indicates that these are the terms used by respondents themselves. Some respondents belong to small racial or ethnic groups with only a few representatives in this

study; more general terms are used to describe their racial/ethnic identity in order to protect their anonymity. For example, respondents descended from indigenous tribes of North America are referred to collectively as Native Americans.

This is an international study, and respondents are occasionally described in terms of their citizenship or country of residence as well as their racial or ethnic identities. For example, "Irish" indicates that a respondent resides in Ireland, "English" indicates that a respondent resides in England, "Australian" indicates that a respondent resides in Australia, and "American" indicates that a respondent resides in the United States This usage of "American" to describe residents of the United States is consistent with usage by citizens of other North, Central, and South American countries, who refer to citizens of the United States as "Americans" or "Americanos/as," and is not intended to imply that citizens of these other American countries are not also Americans in the continental, rather than the national, sense of the term.

10. Terms representing particular individuals' sexual identities are capitalized. However, when these terms are used to refer to sexual identities in general rather than to the identities of specific individuals, or when they are used as identity descriptors, even if in reference to particular individuals, they are not capitalized. In respondent quotes, respondents' choices regarding capitalization are retained.

11. Quotes from respondents have been edited for space. Identifying personal details have been omitted and obvious spelling errors have been corrected.

12. "Co" is a generic pronoun that refers to a person who might be female, male, or intersexed, and woman, man, or transgendered. It is used in some alternative communities in the United States whose members believe that gendered language, including the use of the masculine pronoun "he" as a generic pronoun, reinforces gender hierarchies. I use it here because it seems particularly appropriate in a paper that discusses the difficulties that gendered language poses for bisexual-identified people. "Co" is less disruptive to the appearance of written language than slashed formations like "s/he" and "his/hers" and avoids the problems of numerical agreement that arise when "they" is used as a generic pronoun for referring to a single individual.

I invite the reader to use this chapter as an exercise in non-gendered language. Observe your emotional reactions to the non-gendered pronoun "co," and notice how it changes your understanding of the written word. In this paper, I discuss the importation of non-gendered concepts from one social context to another; the paper itself is an example of this process.

13. Toby Marotta attributed "lavender herring" to Susan Brownmiller, who referred to lesbians as "a lavender herring, perhaps, but surely no clear and present danger." See Toby Marotta, *The Politics of Homosexuality* (Boston: Houghton Mifflin, 1981), 236; and Susan Brownmiller, "Sisterhood Is Powerful!" *New York Times Magazine* (15 March 1970): 140.

14. Paula C. Rust, *Bisexuality and the Challenge to Lesbian Politics: Sex, Loyalty, and Revolution* (New York: New York University Press, 1995).

15. Joseph M. Carrier, " 'Sex-Role Preference' as an Explanatory Variable in Homosexual Behavior," *Archives of Sexual Behavior* 6, no. 1 (January 1977): 53–65; Joseph M. Carrier, "Miguel: Sexual Life History of a Gay Mexican American," in *Gay Culture in America: Essays from the Field,* ed. Gilbert Herdt (Boston: Beacon Press, 1992), 202–24; J. R. Magaña and J. M. Carrier, "Mexican and Mexican American Male Sexual Behavior and Spread of AIDS in California," *Journal of Sex Research* 28, no. 3 (August 1991): 425–41.

16. David Bell, "The Trouble with Bisexuality," paper presented at the IBG, Nottingham, U.K., 1994.
17. Paula C. Rust, "Who Are We and Where Do We Go from Here? Conceptualizing Bisexuality," in *Closer to Home*, 281–310.

  The term bisexual "ethnicity" refers to the notion of bisexuality as a group identity analogous to racial or ethnic group identities. It involves, for example, the concepts of group heritage and group pride. The concept of sexual ethnicity is drawn from Steven Epstein, "Gay Politics, Ethnic Identity: The Limits of Social Constructionism," *Socialist Review* 93, no. 4 (1987): 9–53, and Richard K. Herrell, "The Symbolic Strategies of Chicago's Gay and Lesbian Pride Day Parade," in *Gay Culture in America*, 225–52. Epstein and Herrell argue that the gay and lesbian movement, which is modeled after earlier racial and ethnic movements, is based on the notion of gayness as an ethnicity.

18. Rust, *Bisexuality and the Challenge to Lesbian Politics.*

BIBLIOGRAPHY

Baker, Karin. "Bisexual Feminist Politics: Because Bisexuality Is Not Enough." *Closer to Home: Bisexuality and Feminism.* Ed. Elizabeth Reba Weise. Seattle, WA: Seal Press, 1992. 255–67.

Bell, Alan P., Martin S. Weinberg, and Sue Kiefer Hammersmith. *Sexual Preference: Its Development in Men and Women.* Bloomington: Indiana University Press, 1981.

Bell, David. "The Trouble with Bisexuality." Paper presented at the IBG, Nottingham, U.K., 1994.

Bennett, Kathleen. "Feminist Bisexuality: A Both/And Option for an Either/Or World." *Closer to Home: Bisexuality and Feminism.* Ed. Elizabeth Reba Weise. Seattle, WA: Seal Press, 1992. 205–31.

Blumstein, Philip, and Pepper Schwartz. "Intimate Relationships and the Creation of Sexuality." *Homosexuality/Heterosexuality: Concepts of Sexual Orientation.* Ed. David P. McWhirter, Stephanie A. Sanders, and June M. Reinisch. New York: Oxford University Press, 1990. 307–20.

Califia, Pat. "Lesbian Sexuality." *Journal of Homosexuality* 4, no. 3 (Spring 1979): 255–66.

Carrier, Joseph M. " 'Sex-Role Preference' as an Explanatory Variable in Homosexual Behavior." *Archives of Sexual Behavior* 6, no. 1 (January 1977): 53–65.

———. "Miguel: Sexual Life History of a Gay Mexican American." *Gay Culture in America: Essays from the Field.* Ed. Gilbert Herdt. Boston: Beacon Press, 1992. 202–24.

Cass, Vivienne C. "Homosexual Identity Formation: A Theoretical Model." *Journal of Homosexuality* 4, no. 3 (Spring 1979): 219–35.

———. "The Implications of Homosexual Identity Formation for the Kinsey Model and Scale of Sexual Preference." *Homosexuality/Heterosexuality: Concepts of Sexual Orientation.* Ed. David P. McWhirter, Stephanie A. Sanders, and June M. Reinisch. New York: Oxford University Press, 1990. 239–66.

Chapman, Beata E., and JoAnn C. Brannock. "Proposed Model of Lesbian Identity Development: An Empirical Examination." *Journal of Homosexuality* 14, nos. 3/4 (1987): 69–80.

Coleman, Eli: "Developmental Stages of the Coming Out Process." *Journal of Homosexuality* 7, nos. 2/3 (Winter 1981/Spring 1982): 31–43.

Cronin, Denise M. "Coming Out among Lesbians." *Sexual Deviance and Sexual Deviants.* Ed. Erich Good and Richard R. Troiden. New York: William Morrow, 1974. 268–77.

de Monteflores, Carmen, and Stephen J. Schultz. "Coming Out: Similarities and Differences for Lesbians and Gay Men." *Journal of Social Issues* 34, no. 3 (1978): 59–72.

Eadie, Jo. "Activating Bisexuality: Towards a Bi/Sexual Politics." *Activating Theory: Lesbian, Gay, Bisexual Politics.* Ed. Joseph Bristow and Angelia R. Wilson. London: Lawrence and Wishart, 1993. 139–70.

Epstein, Steven. "Gay Politics, Ethnic Identity: The Limits of Social Constructionism." *Socialist Review* 93, no. 4 (1987): 9–53.

Freimuth, Marilyn J., and Gail A. Hornstein. "A Critical Examination of the Concept of Gender." *Sex Roles* 8, no. 5 (May 1982): 515–32.

Gibian, Ruth. "Refusing Certainty: Toward a Bisexuality of Wholeness." *Closer to Home: Bisexuality and Feminism.* Ed. Elizabeth Reba Weise. Seattle, WA: Seal Press, 1992. 3–16.

Hedblom, Jack H. "Dimensions of Lesbian Sexual Experience." *Archives of Sexual Behavior* 2, no. 4 (December 1973): 329–41.

Hemmings, Clare. "Resituating the Bisexual Body: From Identity to Difference." *Activating Theory: Lesbian, Gay, Bisexual Politics.* Ed. Joseph Bristow and Angelia R. Wilson. London: Lawrence and Wishart, 1993. 118–38.

Herrell, Richard K. "The Symbolic Strategies of Chicago's Gay and Lesbian Pride Day Parade." *Gay Culture in America: Essays from the Field.* Ed. Gilbert Herdt. Boston: Beacon Press, 1992. 225–52.

Hoffman, Richard J. "Vices, Gods, and Virtues: Cosmology as a Mediating Factor in Attitudes toward Male Homosexuality." *Journal of Homosexuality* 9, nos. 2/3 (Winter 1983/Spring 1984): 27–44.

Hutchins, Loraine, and Lani Kaahumanu, eds. *Bi Any Other Name: Bisexual People Speak Out.* Boston, MA: Alyson, 1991.

Jay, Karla, and Allen Young, eds. *The Gay Report: Lesbians and Gay Men Speak Out about Sexual Experiences and Lifestyles.* New York: Simon and Schuster, 1979.

Kooden, Harold D., Stephen F. Morin, Dorothy I. Riddle, Martin Rogers, Barbara E. Sang, and Fred Strassburger. *Removing the Stigma: Final Report of the Board of Social and Ethical Responsibility for Psychology's Task Force on the Status of Lesbian and Gay Male Psychologists.* Washington, DC: American Psychological Association, 1979.

Lavender, Abraham D., and Lauren C. Bressler. "Nondualists as Deviants: Female Bisexuals Compared to Female Heterosexuals-Homosexuals." *Deviant Behavior: An Interdisciplinary Journal* 2, no. 2 (January–March 1981): 155–65.

Magaña, J. R., and J. M. Carrier. "Mexican and Mexican American Male Sexual Behavior and Spread of AIDS in California." *Journal of Sex Research* 28, no. 3 (August 1991): 425–41.

Marotta, Toby. *The Politics of Homosexuality.* Boston: Houghton Mifflin, 1981.

McDonald, Gary J. "Individual Differences in the Coming Out Process for Gay Men: Implications for Theoretical Models." *Journal of Homosexuality* 8, no. 1 (Fall 1982): 47–60.

Plummer, Kenneth. *Sexual Stigma: An Interactionist Account.* London: Routledge and Kegan Paul, 1975.

Riddle, Dorothy, and Stephen Morin. "Removing the Stigma: Data from Institutions." *APA Monitor* (November 1977): 16–28.

Rust, Paula C. "The Politics of Sexual Identity: Sexual Attraction and Behavior among Lesbian and Bisexual Women." *Social Problems* 39, no. 4 (November 1992) 366–86.

———. "Who Are We and Where Do We Go from Here? Conceptualizing Bisexuality." *Closer to Home: Bisexuality and Feminism.* Ed. Elizabeth Reba Weise. Seattle, WA: Seal Press, 1992. 281–310.

———. " 'Coming Out' in the Age of Social Constructionism: Sexual Identity Formation among Lesbian and Bisexual Women." *Gender and Society* 7, no. 1 (March 1993): 50–77.

———. *Bisexuality and the Challenge to Lesbian Politics: Sex, Loyalty, and Revolution.* New York: New York University Press, 1995.

Saghir, Marcel T., and Eli Robins. *Male and Female Homosexuality: A Comprehensive Investigation.* Baltimore, MD: Williams and Wilkins, 1973.

Schäfer, Siegrid. "Sexual and Social Problems of Lesbians." *Journal of Sex Research* 12, no. 1 (February 1976): 50–69.

Troiden, Richard R. *Gay and Lesbian Identity: A Sociological Analysis.* Dix Hills, NY: General Hall, 1988.

Udis-Kessler, Amanda. "Present Tense: Biphobia as a Crisis of Meaning." *Bi Any Other Name: Bisexual People Speak Out.* Ed. Loraine Hutchins and Lani Kaahumanu. Boston, MA: Alyson, 1991. 350–58.

16

NAMING ALL THE PARTS

KATE BORNSTEIN

For the first thirty-or-so years of my life, I didn't listen, I didn't ask questions, I didn't talk, I didn't deal with gender—I avoided the dilemma as best I could. I lived frantically on the edge of my white male privilege, and it wasn't 'til I got into therapy around the issue of my transsexualism that I began to take apart gender and really examine it from several sides. As I looked at each facet of gender, I needed to fix it with a definition, just long enough for me to realize that each definition I came up with was entirely inadequate and needed to be abandoned in search of deeper meaning.

Bornstein, Kate. "Naming All the Parts." From *Gender Outlaw: On Men, Women and the Rest of Us.* New York: Routledge, 1994, pp. 21–40.

> Definitions have their uses in much the same way that road signs
> make it easy to travel: they point out the directions. But you don't
> get where you're going when you just stand underneath some sign,
> waiting for it to tell you what to do.

I took the first steps of my journey by trying to define the phenomenon I was
daily becoming.

> There's a real simple way to look at gender: Once upon a time,
> someone drew a line in the sands of a culture and proclaimed with
> great self-importance, "On this side, you are a man; on the other
> side, you are a woman." It's time for the winds of change to blow
> that line away. Simple.

Gender means *class.* By calling gender a system of classification, we can dis-
mantle the system and examine its components. Suzanne Kessler and Wendy
McKenna in their landmark 1978 book, *Gender: An Ethnomethodological Approach,* open the door to viewing gender as a social construct. They pinpoint
various phenomena of gender, as follows:

GENDER ASSIGNMENT

Gender assignment happens when the culture says, "This is what you are."
In most cultures, we're assigned a gender at birth. In our culture, once you've
been assigned a gender, that's what you are; and for the most part, it's doctors who dole out the gender assignments, which shows you how emphatically gender has been medicalized. These doctors look down at a newly-born
infant and say, "It has a penis; it's a boy." Or they say, "It doesn't have a penis; it's a girl." It has little or nothing to do with vaginas. It's all penises or no
penises: gender assignment is both phallocentric and genital. Other cultures
are not or have not been so rigid.

In the early nineteenth century, Kodiak Islanders would occasionally
assign a female gender to a child with a penis: this resulted in a woman
who would bring great good luck to her husband, and a larger dowry to
her parents. The European umbrella term for this and any other type of Native American transgendered person is *berdache.* Walter Williams in *The
Spirit and the Flesh* chronicles nearly as many types of *berdache* as there were
nations.

> *Even as early as 1702, a French explorer who lived for four years among the
> Illinois Indians noted that berdaches were known "from their childhood, when
> they are seen frequently picking up the spade, the spindle, the ax [women's
> tools], but making no use of the bow and arrow as all the other small boys do."*
> —Pierre Liette, *Memoir of Pierre Liette on the Illinois Country*

When the gender of a child was in question in some Navajo tribes, they reached a decision by putting a child inside a *tipi* with loom and a bow and arrow—female and male implements, respectively. They set fire to the *tipi*, and whatever the child grabbed as he/she ran out determined the child's gender. It was perfectly natural to these Navajo that the child had some say in determining its own gender. Compare this method with the following modern example:

> [*The Montana Educational Telecommunications Network, a computer bulletin board,*] *enabled students in tiny rural schools to communicate with students around the world. Cynthia Denton, until last year a teacher at the only public school in Hobson, Montana (population 200), describes the benefit of such links. "When we got our first messages from Japan, a wonderful little fifth-grade girl named Michelle was asked if she was a boy or a girl. She was extraordinarily indignant at that, and said, 'I'm Michelle—I'm a girl of course.' Then I pointed out the name of the person who had asked the question and said, 'Do you know if this is a boy or a girl?' She said, 'No, how am I supposed to know that?' I said, 'Oh, the rest of the world is supposed to know that Michelle is a girl, but you have no social responsibility to know if this is a boy or a girl?' She stopped and said, 'Oh.' And then she rephrased her reply considerably."*
>
> —JACQUES LESLIE, THE CURSOR COWBOY, 1993

Is the determination of one another's gender a "social responsibility"?

Do we have the legal or moral right to decide and assign our own genders?

Or does that right belong to the state, the church, and the medical profession?

If gender is classification, can we afford to throw away the very basic right to classify ourselves?

GENDER IDENTITY

Gender identity answers the question, "who am I?" Am I a man or a woman or a what? It's a decision made by nearly every individual, and it's subject to any influence: peer pressure, advertising, drugs, cultural definitions of gender, whatever.

Gender identity is assumed by many to be "natural"; that is someone can feel "like a man," or "like a woman." When I first started giving talks about gender, this was the one question that would keep coming up: "Do you feel like a woman now?" "Did you ever feel like a man?" "How did you know what a woman would feel like?"

I've no idea what "a woman" feels like. I never did feel like a girl or a woman; rather, it was my unshakable conviction that I was not a boy or a man. It was the absence of a feeling, rather than its presence, that convinced me to change my gender.

> What **does** a man feel like?
> What does a woman feel like?
> Do **you** feel "like a man?"
> Do you feel "like a woman?"
> I'd really like to know that from people.

Gender identity answers another question: "to which gender (class) do I want to belong?" Being and belonging are closely related concepts when it comes to gender. I felt I was a woman (being), and more importantly I felt I belonged with the other women (belonging). In this culture, the only two sanctioned gender clubs are "men" and "women." If you don't belong to one or the other, you're told in no uncertain terms to sign up fast. . . .

> . . . I remember a dream I had when I was no more than seven or eight years old—I might have been younger. In this dream, two lines of battle were drawn up facing one another on a devastated plain: I remember the earth was dry and cracked. An army of men on one side faced an army of women on the other. The soldiers on both sides were exhausted. They were all wearing skins—I remember smelling the untanned leather in my dream. I was a young boy, on the side of the men, and I was being tied down to a roughly-hewn cart. I wasn't struggling. When I was completely secured the men attached a long rope to the cart, and tossed the other end of the rope over to the women. The soldiers of the women's army slowly pulled me across the empty ground between the two armies, as the sun began to rise. I could see only the sun and the sky. When I'd been pulled over to the side of the women, they untied me, turned their backs to the men, and we all walked away. I looked back, and saw the men walking away from us. We were all silent.
>
> I wonder about reincarnation. I wonder how a child could have had a dream like that in such detail. I told this dream to the psychiatrist at the Army induction center in Boston in 1969—they'd asked if I'd ever had any strange dreams, so I told them this one. They gave me a 1-Y, deferred duty due to psychiatric instability.

GENDER ROLES

Gender roles are collections of factors which answer the question, "How do I need to function so that society perceives me as belonging or not belonging to a specific gender?" Some people would include appearance, sexual orientation, and methods of communication under the term, but I think it makes more sense to think in terms of things like jobs, economic roles, chores, hobbies; in other words, positions and actions specific to a given gender as defined by a culture. Gender roles, when followed, send signals of membership in a given gender.

GENDER ATTRIBUTION

Then there's gender attribution, whereby we look at somebody and say, "that's a man," or "that's a woman." And this is important because the way we perceive another's gender affects the way we relate to that person. Gender attribution is the sneaky one. It's the one we do all the time without thinking about it; kinda like driving a sixteen-wheeler down a crowded highway . . . without thinking about it.

In this culture, gender attribution, like gender assignment, is phallocentric. That is, one is male until perceived otherwise. According to a study done by Kessler and McKenna, one can extrapolate that it would take the presence of roughly four female cues to outweigh the presence of one male cue: one is assumed male until proven otherwise. That's one reason why many women today get "sirred" whereas very few men get called "ma'am."

Gender attribution depends on cues given by the attributee, and perceived by the attributer. The categories of cues as I have looked at them apply to a man/woman bi-polar gender system, although they could be relevant to a more fluidly-gendered system. I found these cues to be useful in training actors in cross-gender role-playing.

Physical cues include body, hair, clothes, voice, skin, and movement.

> I'm nearly six feet tall, and I'm large-boned. Like most people born "male," my hands, feet, and forearms are proportionally larger to my body as a whole than those of people born "female." My hair pattern included coarse facial hair. My voice is naturally deep—I sang bass in a high school choir and quartet. I've had to study ways and means of either changing these physical cues, or drawing attention away from them if I want to achieve a female attribution from people.

Susan Brownmiller's book, *Femininity,* is an excellent analysis of the social impact of physical factors as gender cues.

Behavioral cues include manners, decorum, protocol, and deportment. Like physical cues, behavioral cues change with time and culture. *Dear Abby* and other advice columnists often freely dispense gender-specific manners. Most of the behavioral cues I can think of boil down to how we occupy space, both alone and with others.

Some points of manners are not taught in books of etiquette. They are, instead, signals we learn from one another, mostly signals acknowledging membership to an upper (male) or lower (female) class. But to commit some of *these* manners in writing in terms of gender-specific behavior would be an acknowledgment that gender exists as a class system.

Here's one: As part of learning to pass as a woman, I was taught to avoid eye contact when walking down the street; that looking someone in the eye was a male cue. Nowadays, sometimes I'll look away, and sometimes I'll look someone in the eye—it's a behavior pattern that's more fun to play with than to follow rigidly. A femme cue (not "woman," but "femme") is to meet someone's eyes (usually a butch), glance quickly away, then slowly look back into the butch's eyes and hold that gaze: great hot fun, that one!

In many transsexual and transvestite meetings I attended, when the subject of the discussion was "passing," a lot of emphasis was given to manners: who stands up to shake hands? who exits an elevator first? who opens doors? who lights cigarettes? These are all cues I had to learn in order to pass as a woman in this culture. It wasn't 'til I began to read feminist literature that I began to question these cues or to see them as oppressive.

Textual cues include histories, documents, names, associates, relationships— true or false—which support a desired gender attribution. Someone trying to be taken for male in this culture might take the name Bernard, which would probably get a better male attribution than the name Brenda.

Changing my name from Al to Kate was no big deal in Pennsylvania. It was a simple matter of filing a form with the court and publishing the name change in some unobtrusive "notices" column of a court-approved newspaper. Bingo—done. The problems came with changing all my documents. The driver's license was particularly interesting. Prior to my full gender change, I'd been pulled over once already dressed as a woman, yet holding my male driver's license—it wasn't something I cared to repeat.

Any changes in licenses had to be done in person at the Department of Motor Vehicles. I was working in corporate America: Ford Aerospace. On my lunch break, I went down to the DMV and waited in line with the other folks who had changes to make to their licenses. The male officer at the desk was flirting with me, and I didn't know what to do with that, so I kept looking away. When I finally got to the desk, he asked "Well, young lady, what can we do for you?"

"I've got to make a name change on my license," I mumbled.

"Just get married?" he asked jovially.

"Uh, no," I replied.

"Oh! Divorced!" he proclaimed with just a bit of hope in his voice, "Let's see your license." I handed him my old driver's license with my male name on it. He glanced down at the card, apparently not registering what he saw. "You just go on over there, honey, and take your test. We'll have you fixed up soon. Oh," he added with a wink, "if you need anything special, you just come back here and ask old Fred."

I left old Fred and joined the line for my test. I handed the next officer both my license and my court order authorizing my name change. This time, the officer didn't give my license a cursory glance. He kept looking at me, then down at the paper, then me, then the paper. His face grim, he pointed over to the direction of the testing booths. On my way over to the booths, old Fred called out, "Honey, they treating you all right?" Before I could reply, the second officer snarled at old Fred to "get his butt over" to look at all my paperwork.

I reached the testing booths and looked back just in time to see a quite crestfallen old Fred looking at me, then the paper, then me, then the paper.

Mythic cues include cultural and sub-cultural myths which support membership in a given gender. This culture's myths include archetypes like: weaker sex, dumb blonde, strong silent type, and better half. Various waves of the women's movement have had to deal with a multitude of myths of male superiority.

Power dynamics as cue include modes of communication, communication techniques, and degrees of aggressiveness, assertiveness, persistence, and ambition.

Sexual orientation as cue highlights, in the dominant culture, the heterosexual imperative (or in the lesbian and gay culture, the homosexual imperative). For this reason, many male heterosexual transvestites who wish to pass as female will go out on a "date" with another man (who is dressed as a man)—the two seem to be a heterosexual couple. In glancing at the "woman" of the two, an inner dialogue might go, "It's wearing a dress, and it's hanging on the arm of a man, so it must be a woman." For the same man to pass as a female in a lesbian bar, he'd need to be with a woman, dressed as a woman, as a "date."

I remember one Fourth of July evening in Philadelphia, about a year after my surgery. I was walking home arm in arm with Lisa, my lover at the time, after the fireworks display. We were leaning in to one another, walking like lovers walk. Coming towards us was a family of five: mom, dad, and three teenage boys. "Look, it's a coupla faggots," said one of the boys. "Nah, it's two girls," said another. "That's enough outa you," bellowed the father, "one of 'em's got to be a man. This is America!"

So sex (the act) and gender (the classification) are different, and depending on the qualifier one is using for gender differentiation, they may or may not be dependent on one another. There are probably as many types of gender (gender systems) as could be imagined. Gender by clothing, gender by divine right, gender by lottery—these all make as much sense as any other criteria, but in our Western civilization, we bow down to the great god Science. No other type of gender holds as much sway as:

Biological gender, which classifies a person through any combination of body type, chromosomes, hormones, genitals, reproductive organs, or some other corporal or chemical essence. Belief in biological gender is in fact a belief in the supremacy of the body in the determination of identity. It's biological gender that most folks refer to when they say *sex*. By calling something "sex," we grant it seniority over all the other types of gender—by some right of biology.

So, there are all these *types* of gender which in and of themselves are *not* gender, but criteria for systemic classification. And there's sex, which somehow winds up on top of the heap. Add to this room full of seeds the words *male, female, masculine, feminine, man, woman, boy, girl.* These words are not descriptive of any sexual act, so all these words fall under the category of gender and are highly subjective, depending on which system of gender one is following.

But none of this explains why there is such a widespread insistence upon the conflation of *sex* and *gender.* I think a larger question is why Eurocentric culture needs to see *so much* in terms of sex.

> It's not like gender is the **only** thing we confuse with sex. As a culture, we're encouraged to equate sex (the act) with money, success, and security; and with the products we're told will help us attain money, success and security. We live in a culture that succeeds in selling products (the apex of accomplishment in capitalism) by aligning those products with the attainment of one's sexual fantasies.
>
> Switching my gender knocked me for a time curiously out of the loop of ads designed for men or women, gays or straights. I got to look at sex without the hype, and ads without the allure. None of them, after all, spoke to me, although all of them beckoned.

KINDS OF SEX

It's important to keep *gender* and *sex* separated as, respectively, *system* and *function.* Since function is easier to pin down than system, sex is a simpler starting place than gender.

Sex does have a primary factor to it which is germane to a discussion of gender: *sexual orientation,* which is what people call it, if they believe you're born with it, or *sexual preference,* which is what people call it if they believe you have more of a choice and more of a say in the matter.

[W]e do not need a sophisticated methodology or technology to confirm that the gender component of identity is the most important one articulated during sex. Nearly everyone (except for bisexuals, perhaps) regards it as the prime criterion for choosing a sex partner.
—MURRAY S. DAVIS, SMUT: EROTIC REALITY/OBSCENE IDEOLOGY, 1983

The Basic Mix-Up

A gay man who lived in Khartoum
Took a lesbian up to his room.
They argued all night
Over who had the right
To do what, and with what, to whom.

—Anonymous Limerick

Here's the tangle that I found: sexual orientation/preference is based in this culture solely on the gender of one's partner of choice. Not only do we confuse the two words, we make them dependent on one another. The only choices we're given to determine the focus of our sexual desire are these:

- *Heterosexual model:* in which a culturally-defined male is in a relationship with a culturally-defined female.
- *Gay male model:* two culturally-defined men involved with each other.
- *Lesbian model:* two culturally-defined women involved with each other.
- *Bisexual model:* culturally-defined men and women who could be involved with either culturally-defined men or women.

Variants to these gender-based relationship dynamics would include heterosexual female with gay male, gay male with lesbian woman, lesbian woman with heterosexual woman, gay male with bisexual male, and so forth. People involved in these variants know that each dynamic is different from the other. A lesbian involved with another lesbian, for example, is a very different relationship than that of a lesbian involved with a bisexual woman, and *that's* distinct from being a lesbian woman involved with a heterosexual woman. What these variants have in common is that each of these combinations forms its own clearly-recognizable dynamic, and none of these are acknowledged by the dominant cultural binary of sexual orientation: heterosexuality/homosexuality.

Despite the non-recognition of these dynamics by the broader culture, *all these models depend on the gender of the partner.* This results in minimizing, if not completely dismissing, other dynamic models of a relationship which could be more important than gender and are often more telling about the real nature of someone's desire. There are so many factors on which we *could* base sexual orientation. The point is there's more to sex (the act) than gender (one classification of identity).

Try making a list of ways in which sexual preference or orientation could be measured, and then add to that list (or subtract from it) every day for a month, or a year (or for the rest of your life). Could be fun!

SEX WITHOUT GENDER

There are plenty of instances in which sexual attraction can have absolutely nothing to do with the gender of one's partner.

> *When Batman and Catwoman try to get it on sexually, it only works when they are both in their caped crusader outfits. Naked heterosexuality is a miserable failure between them. . . . When they encounter each other in costume however something much sexier happens and the only thing missing is a really good scene where we get to hear the delicious sound of Catwoman's latex rubbing on Batman's black rubber/leather skin. To me their flirtation in capes looked queer precisely because it was not heterosexual, they were not man and woman, they were bat and cat, or latex and rubber, or feminist and vigilante: gender became irrelevant and sexuality was dependent on many other factors. . . .*
>
> *You could also read their sexual encounters as the kind of sex play between gay men and lesbians that we are hearing so much about recently: in other words, the sexual encounter is queer because both partners are queer and the genders of the participants are less relevant. Just because Batman is male and Catwoman is female does not make their interactions heterosexual—think about it, there is nothing straight about two people getting it on in rubber and latex costumes, wearing eyemasks and carrying whips and other accoutrements.*
>
> —JUDITH HALBERSTAM, "QUEER CREATURES,"
> ON OUR BACKS, NOV./DEC., 1992

Sexual preference *could* be based on genital preference. (This is not the same as saying preference for a specific gender, unless you're basing your definition of gender on the presence or absence of some combination of genitals.) Preference could also be based on the kind of sex *acts* one prefers. But despite the many variations possible, sexual orientation/preference remains culturally linked to our gender system (and by extension to gender identity) through the fact that it's most usually based on the gender of one's partner. This link probably accounts for much of the tangle between sex and gender.

The confusion between sex and gender affects more than individuals and relationships. The conflation of sex and gender contributes to the linking together of the very different subcultures of gays, lesbians, bisexuals, leather sexers, sex-workers, and the transgendered.

A common misconception is that male cross-dressers are both gay
and prostitutes, whereas the truth of the matter is that most cross-
dressers that I've met hold down more mainstream jobs, careers, or
professions, are married, and are practicing heterosexuals.

A dominant culture tends to combine its subcultures into manageable units.
As a result, those who practice non-traditional sex are seen by members of the
dominant culture (as well as by members of sex and gender subcultures) as a
whole with those who don non-traditional gender roles and identities. Any
work to deconstruct the gender system needs to take into account the artificial amalgam of subcultures, which might itself collapse if the confusion of
terms holding it together were to be settled.

In any case, if we buy into categories of sexual orientation based solely
on gender—heterosexual, homosexual, or bisexual—we're cheating ourselves of a searching examination of our real sexual preferences. In the same
fashion, by subscribing to the categories of gender based solely on the
male/female binary, we cheat ourselves of a searching examination of our
real gender identity. And now we can park sex off to the side for a while, and
bring this essay back around to gender.

DESIRE

I was not an unattractive man. People's reactions to my gender change often included the remonstrative, "But you're such a good-looking guy!" Nowadays, as
I navigate the waters between male and female, there are still people attracted to
me. At first, my reaction was fear: "What kind of pervert," I thought, "would be
attracted to a freak like me?" As I got over that internalized phobia of my transgender status, I began to get curious about the nature of desire, sex, and identity.
When, for example, I talk about the need to do away with gender, I always get
looks of horror from the audience: "What about desire and attraction!" they
want to know, "How can you have desire with no gender?" They've got a good
point: the concepts of sex and gender seem to overlap around the phenomenon
of desire. So I began to explore my transgendered relationship to desire.

> About five months into living full-time as a woman, I woke up one
> morning and felt really good about the day. I got dressed for work,
> and checking the mirror before I left, I liked what I saw—at last! I
> opened the door to leave the building, only to find two workmen
> standing on the porch, the hand of one poised to knock on the door.
> This workman's face lit up when he saw me. "Well!" he said, "Don't
> you look beautiful today." At that moment, I realized I didn't know
> how to respond to that. I felt like a deer caught in the headlights of
> an oncoming truck. I really wasn't prepared for people to be
> attracted to me. To this day, I don't know how to respond to a man
> who's attracted to me—I never learned the rituals.

To me, desire is a wish to experience someone or something that I've never experienced, or that I'm not currently experiencing. Usually, I need an identity appropriate (or appropriately inappropriate) to the context in which I want to experience that person or thing. This context could be anything: a romantic involvement, a tennis match, or a boat trip up a canal. On a boat trip up the canal, I could appropriately be a passenger or a crew member. In a tennis match, I could be a player, an audience member, a concessionaire, a referee, a member of the grounds staff. In the context of a romantic involvement, it gets less obvious about what I need to be in order to have an appropriate identity, but I would need to have *some* identity. Given that most romantic or sexual involvements in this culture are defined by the genders of the partners, the *most* appropriate identity to have in a romantic relationship would be a gender identity, or something that passes for gender identity, like a gender role. A gender role might be butch, femme, top, and bottom—these are all methods of acting. So, even without a gender identity *per se,* some workable identity can be called up and put into motion within a relationship, and when we play with our identities, we play with desire. Some identities stimulate desire; others diminish desire. To make ourselves attractive to someone, we modify our identity, or at least the appearance of an identity—and this includes gender identity.

I love the idea of being without an identity; it gives me a lot of room to play around; but it makes me dizzy, having nowhere to hang my hat. When I get too tired of not having an identity, I take one on: it doesn't really matter what identity I take on, as long as it's recognizable. I can be a writer, a lover, a confidante, a femme, a top, or a woman. I retreat into definition as a way of demarcating my space, a way of saying "Step back, I'm getting crowded here." By saying "I am the (fill in the blank)," I also say, "You are *not,* and so you are not in my space." Thus, I achieve privacy. Gender identity is a form of self-definition: something into which we can withdraw, from which we can glean a degree of privacy from time to time, and with which we can, to a limited degree, manipulate desire.

Our culture is obsessed with desire: it drives our economy. We come right out and say we're going to stimulate desire for goods and services, and so we're bombarded daily with ads and commercial announcements geared to make us desire things. No wonder the emphasis on desire spills over into the rest of our lives. No wonder I get panicked reactions from audiences when I suggest we eliminate gender as a system; gender defines our desire, and we don't know what to do if we don't have desire. Perhaps the more importance a culture places on desire, the more conflated become the concepts of sex and gender.

As an exercise, can you recall the last time you saw someone whose gender was ambiguous? Was this person attractive to you? And if you knew they called themselves neither a man nor a woman, what would it make you if you're attracted to that person? And if you were to kiss? Make love? What would you be?

PART II
Maintaining Inequalities: Systems of Oppression and Privilege

INTRODUCTION

On September 17, 2001, Ashraf Khan, bearing a first-class ticket, boarded Delta Airlines flight 1469 to Dallas. This was to be the first part of a two-day trip to Pakistan to attend his brother's wedding. Khan, an 11-year U.S. resident, was approached by the pilot, who asked to speak with him in the gate area. There the pilot informed Mr. Khan that he and the crew did not feel safe flying with him on board. Further, the pilot questioned Khan about how he had obtained a first-class ticket.

On September 20, 2001, Kareem Alasady, a U.S. citizen, and his two companions, were denied flight on a Northwest Airlines flight from Minneapolis to Salt Lake City. A spokesperson for the airline stated that the crew took the appropriate action because the majority of the passengers felt uncomfortable flying with them.

In Tampa, Florida, Mohamed el-Sayed, a U.S. citizen of Egyptian origin, was denied boarding on a United Airlines flight to Washington on September 21, 2001. An airport manager told him apologetically that the pilot refused to fly with him on board, explaining, "We've reviewed your profile; your name is Mohamed."

Since the events of September 11, 2001, passengers who are perceived to be Arab—which has included people who are South Asian, Latino, and Mexican—have been removed from airplanes due to the refusal by crew members and passengers to fly with them. Calling it "Flying While Arab," Michel Shehadeh, West Coast regional director of the American-Arab Anti-Discrimination Committee (ADC), asserts that any Arab (or person perceived to be Arab) is thought to be a terrorist. This form of racial profiling is certainly nothing new.[1] Rather, it is based on a long history of U.S. government anti-Arab programs and policies, as Hussein Ibish discussed in "They Are Absolutely Obsessed with US" in Part I. However, racial profiling of people perceived to be Arab or Muslim has increased greatly due to a September 12, 2001, directive from the FAA to the nation's airlines instructing security to immediately conduct "random identification checks," stating:

> Extremist groups, with a history of targeting civil action, are
> actively targeting U.S. interests, particularly in the Middle East.

---

[1]The phrase "Flying While Arab" or "Flying While Muslim" was likely coined at the June 1999 meeting of the American Muslim Political Coordination Council.

They retain a capability to conduct airline bombings, hijackings, suicide attacks, and possess surface-to-air missiles.

Such profiling is similar to that experienced by blacks and Latinos for some time. For example, in May 1992 the Maryland State Police stopped a car in the early morning hours just outside of Cumberland, Maryland. The occupants—Washington, D.C., attorney Robert Wilkins and members of his family—were questioned, ticketed, and made to stand in the rain while a dog sniffed for drugs in their car. Mr. Wilkins sued, and the resulting litigation uncovered a memorandum instructing police to watch for "predominantly black" drug couriers.

In Illinois, a defense attorney hired a Latino private investigator to drive across certain counties to test the validity of assertions that the state police stopped Latinos and African Americans in disproportionate numbers. Peso Chavez, a 20-year veteran investigator and a former elected official from Santa Fe, New Mexico, was followed by an assistant to verify the legality of his driving. Even though the assistant saw no violation, state police officers stopped Chavez for a traffic offense. They asked him for permission to search his car and, when he asked whether he had to allow the search, a drug-sniffing dog was brought to the scene. Despite Chavez's unmistakable objection and his request that he be permitted to leave, the police used the dog on his car. The officers then told Chavez that the dog had "alerted" them to the presence of drugs. Chavez was put into the back of a patrol car and probed with questions as he watched the police search every part of his vehicle, open his luggage, and go through all of his personal possessions.

These are examples of a practice known as **pretext stops**—the use of traffic stops as an excuse to stop African Americans, Latinos, and other people of color in order to search their cars and question the occupants about possession of drugs. There is considerable evidence of the pervasiveness of this practice. For example, in Volusia County, Florida, a review of 1,100 video-taped traffic stops made during a drug interdiction effort revealed that approximately 70 percent of the drivers stopped were black. Black drivers were more likely to have their cars searched after being stopped than were whites, and their stops usually lasted twice as long (Harris, 1998). An investigation of drivers stopped by Maryland State troopers from January 1995 to December 1997 showed that 70 percent of drivers stopped on Interstate 95 were black. According to a survey by the ACLU, only 17.5 percent of the drivers (and likely traffic violators) on that road were black (Cole, 1999). Pretext stops are so common that members of black and Latino communities refer to them as DWB: driving while black or driving while brown. (Fletcher, 1996).

These examples illustrate the way in which institutions maintain inequality based on categories of difference. Police officers and airline crew members, acting not on the basis of their own attitudes but on institutional policies (e.g., memorandums instructing to watch for "predominantly black" drug couriers, directives to conduct random checks mentioning "extremist groups . . . particularly in the Middle East"), help to maintain racial inequality. Individuals are stopped because of their **status,** the socially defined position that they occupy in society. Note that only one status is important here. Although Mr. Wilkins occupied different statuses (lawyer, spouse, father, etc.) as did Mr. Chavez (investigator, former elected official, etc.), what mattered to the police was their presumed membership in a racial or ethnic group. Thus their **master status**—the most important status they occupied— was their race or ethnicity.

Each of us occupies a variety of statuses at any given moment in terms of our race, class, gender, sexuality, age, religion, (dis)ability, height, weight, and so on. While we may feel that one status is more important to ourselves than another, we don't always get to pick which is most important to others. Just as Mr. Wilkins and Mr. Chavez were singled out for their race, each of us has likely been singled out by other individuals for some aspect of ourselves. In this section we will investigate how institutions—family, education, economy, the state, and media—support this practice and thus maintain inequality based on categories of difference.

CATEGORIES OF DIFFERENCE MAINTAINED AS A SYSTEM OF OPPRESSION AND PRIVILEGE

The value of the statuses that we occupy is determined by how they have been defined. When our statuses are defined as having value within the social structure, we experience **privilege**—a set of (not necessarily) earned rights or assets belonging to a certain status. If our statuses are devalued, the result is **oppression,** defined in Part I as a relationship of domination and subordination in which the dominant group benefits from the *systematic* abuse, exploitation, and injustice directed at a subordinate group. Oppression occurs in three forms: **institutionalized oppression**—that which is built into, supported by, and perpetuated by social institutions; **interpersonal oppression**—that which is manifested between individuals; and **internalized oppression**—that which is directed at oneself.

THE ROLE OF IDEOLOGY

Maintaining systems of inequality relies on a foundation constructed of several components. Central to this foundation is the presence of an **ideology**— a set of cultural values, beliefs, and attitudes that provide the basis for inequality and thus, in part, endorse and justify the interests of the dominant group. Systems of racial inequality in the United States rely on ideologies that include judgments about racial differences in order to maintain white privilege. Similarly, systems of class inequality rely on ideologies that include valuing the rich over the poor to uphold class privilege. Furthermore, ideologies based in **androcentrism**—the notion that males are superior to females—preserves systems of sex and gender inequality. Finally, an ideology that includes moral or religious judgments about what is and is not an appropriate sexual orientation is used to justify a system of inequality on the basis of sexuality.

The readings in this section demonstrate that the ideologies that maintain systems of inequality are built into the rules, policies, and practices of our social institutions. In addition, these ideologies often depend on one another, further illustrating the matrix of domination discussed in Part I. For example, as several of the readings in this section illustrate, the foundation of class inequality in the United States is an ideology based in capitalism. More than just the private ownership of goods, capitalism, according to some social theorists, involves exploitation because those who control the ownership of goods use the labor of workers to make a profit. Profit making, they argue, is based on paying workers less than the full value of what they produce. In order to justify paying one group less than another, we establish ideologies in which one group is viewed as less valuable than others. Thus, ideologies justifying inequality in terms of race/ethnicity, sex/gender, and sexuality perpetuate class inequality.

These interdependent ideologies and the resulting interlocking systems of inequality illustrate that oppression is *systematic.* According to Marilyn Frye, **oppression** involves:

> a system of interrelated barriers and forces which reduce, immobilize and mold people who belong to a certain group, and effect their subordination to another group. (1983, p. 33)

Thus, our circumstances are shaped not by accidental or avoidable events but by systematically related forces. To illustrate how pervasive and institutionalized oppression is, Frye offers the following analogy:

> Consider a birdcage. If you look very closely at just one wire in the cage, you cannot see the other wires. If your conception of what is before you is determined by this myopic focus, you could look at that one wire, up and down the length of it and be unable to see why a bird would not just fly around the wire any time it wanted to go somewhere . . . There is no physical property of any one wire, *nothing* that the closest scrutiny could discover, that will reveal how a bird could be inhibited or harmed by it except in the most accidental way. It is only when you step back, stop looking at the wires one by one, microscopically, and take a macroscopic view of the whole cage, that you see why the bird doesn't go anywhere; and then you will see it in a moment . . . It is perfectly *obvious* that the bird is surrounded by a network of systematically related barriers, no one of which could be the least hindrance to its flight, but

which, by their relations to each other, are as confining as the walls of a dungeon. (Frey 1983:35)

As this analogy illustrates, comprehensive systems of oppression maintain the inequality that many experience in our culture. To fully comprehend this system, we need to employ a macro-rather than microscopic perspective, using a systemic frame of analysis to understand how each form of oppression is interrelated and maintained by our social institutions.

DEFINING FORMS OF OPPRESSION

Employing a systemic frame of analysis requires that we redefine the ways we categorize issues of discrimination. To label unjust ideas and actions, many of us usually think in terms of **prejudice**—a negative attitude toward members of a group or social category—and **discrimination**—the unequal treatment of people determined by their membership in a group. However, these concepts do not acknowledge the ways in which inequality is institutionalized. The definitions of forms of oppression that follow incorporate a more systematic perspective.

To understand issues of racial oppression within the United States, we must examine **institutional racism.** This refers to the systematic and institutionalized policy or practice by which people of color are exploited or controlled because of their perceived physical characteristics. Racism is part of our institutional structure, not simply the product of individual actions. In the previous examples, racism does not simply consist of the actions of the individual officers. Rather, it is the fact that these actions are supported by police *policy* that defines them as racist behaviors.

Furthermore, to fully understand racism we need to see how white people in the United States benefit from institutionalized racism regardless of their own individual actions. For example, as Stanley Eitzen and Maxine Baca Zinn discuss in "The Dark Side of Sports Symbols" (Reading 40), some institutions of higher education make use of Native American images and symbols in creating "mascots" for their sport teams. Despite the protest of a substantial number of American Indian individuals and organizations, places such as the University of Illinois, the home of the "Fighting Illini," institutionalize racist notions of American Indians by continuing to use these images. White students at that university benefit from this practice, regardless of their participation in it, by *not* having their race objectified and dehumanized at each sporting event and on numerous University souvenirs.

Similar to racism, oppression based on social class also relies on the rules, policies, and practices of social institutions. As discussed in Part I, social class is a great deal more than individual characteristics. Rather, it is determined by a variety of factors in our social structure. Social institutions, including the state and the economy, relying on a capitalist system, create class structures that benefit some at the expense of others. The result is a heavily skewed distribution of income and wealth. According to the U.S. Census Bureau's *Current Population Report* the median household income in 2000 was $42,100. The 20 percent of households with the highest earnings (with mean earnings of about $141,621) received 49.7 percent of all income, while the bottom 20 percent (with mean earnings of $10,188) received only about 3.6 percent. The distribution of income is illustrated in Figure 1. The distribution of wealth is even more concentrated than income. According to economist Edward Wolf (2000), in 1998 the top 10 percent of the population of the United States owned 71 percent of the wealth. As Figure 2 illustrates, 1 percent of the United States owned 38 percent of the wealth in 1998 (with their average net worth topping $10 million), while the bottom 90 percent possessed just 29 percent of the nation's wealth. What makes this unequal distribution even more significant is the difference in kind of wealth at various places in the social class system. For example, the majority of the net worth of the bottom 90 percent consists of assets tied up in the family home, while the distribution of stocks and bonds is concentrated in the richest 10 percent of the population (see Figure 3). Government programs that grant a disproportionate amount of subsidies and tax breaks to corporations and the wealthy help to perpetuate a skewed distribution of income and wealth (See Figure 4).

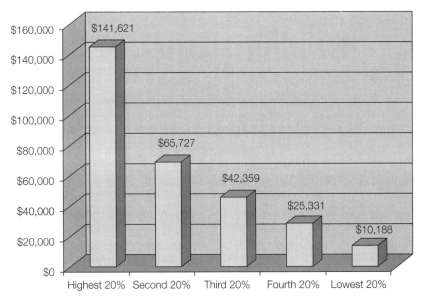

FIGURE 1   2000 Distribution of Family Income (*Source:* U.S. Census Bureau *Current Population Report.* World Wide Web Site: http://www.census.gov/hhes/www/income00.html)

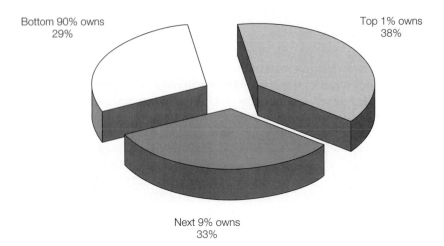

Bottom 90% owns
29%

Top 1% owns
38%

Next 9% owns
33%

FIGURE 2 Distribution of Wealth, 1998: Share of Total Net Worth (*Source:* Wolf, Edward N. "Recent Trends in Wealth Ownership, 1983–1998," Unpublished Working Paper No. 300, Jerome Levy Economics Institute, April 2000. World Wide Web Site: http://levy.org/docs/wrkpap/papers/300.html)

Such systematic class inequality is defined as **classism**—a system of beliefs rooted in the institutions of society where the wealthy are privileged with a higher status at the expense of the oppression of the poor. The ways in which this system is maintained, as well as how issues of class intersect with race/ethnicity and sex/gender, will be discussed later.

Using a systemic analysis to understand issues of sex/gender oppression and privilege requires that we incorporate the role of institutions in definitions of sexism. Thus, for the purposes of this discussion, **sexism** is a systematic and institutionalized policy or practice in which women are exploited or controlled due to perceptions that their sex or gender characteristics are inferior. Again, in recognizing that sexism is systematic we acknowledge that it is a product of our institutional structure, not necessarily individual actions. As a result, men do not need to individually behave in a sexist manner in order to benefit from a sexist system. For example, many physical requirements for occupations (such as height) advantage men while they disadvantage women, even though they may have little to do with the actual requirements for the job. Additional ways in which sex and gender inequality is reinforced by social institutions will be discussed later.

Finally, inequality with regard to sexuality is also institutionalized. Thus, privilege experienced by heterosexuals and the oppression experienced by those who are or are perceived to be lesbian, gay, bisexual, or transgender is perpetuated through the practices and policies of social institutions. For example, the rejection of the **Employment Non-Discrimination Act** (ENDA)—a bill to prohibit employment discrimination on the basis of sexual orientation—perpetuates the advantage experienced by heterosexuals and the stigma expe-

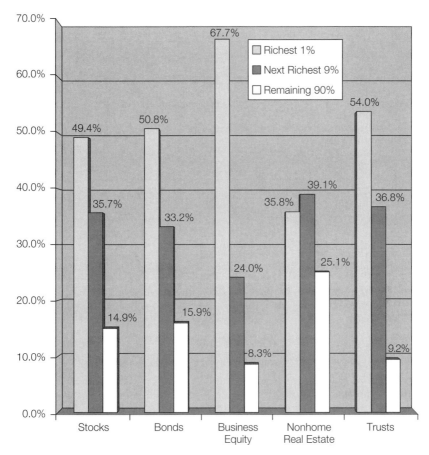

FIGURE 3   Distribution of Assets (*Source:* Wolf, Edward N. "Recent Trends in Wealth Ownership, 1983–1998," Unpublished Working Paper No. 300, Jerome Levy Economics Institute, April 2000. World Wide Web Site: http://levy.org/docs/wrkpap/papers/300.html)

rienced by lesbian, gay, bisexual, and transgender individuals. **Heterosexism,** as defined by Cherríe Moraga, applies directly to this example:

> The view that heterosexuality is the "norm" for all social/sexual relationships and as such the heterosexist imposes the model on all individuals through **homophobia** (fear of homosexuality). S/he supports and/or advocates this continued institutionalization of heterosexuality in all aspects of society—including legal and social discrimination against homosexuals and the denial of homosexual rights as a political concern. (1983:105)

Moraga indicates here that a person who is heterosexist is an active participant in oppressing those who are or are perceived to be lesbian, gay, bisexual, or transgender. However, as with all other forms of oppression it is not

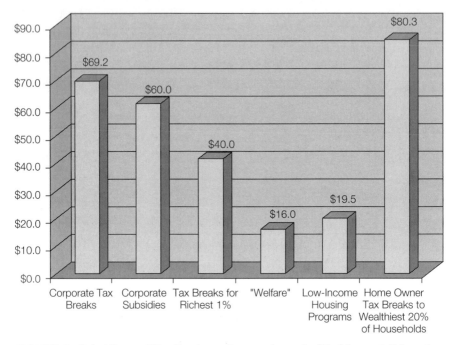

FIGURE 4   Subsidies and Tax Breaks to Corporations, the Wealthy, and Others in 1996 (in Billions of Dollars) (*Source:* Budget of the United States Government, FY '97, Citizens for Tax Justice, Cato Institute, National Low Income Housing Coalition. Copyright © 1996, The National Priorities Project, 17 New South St., #302, Northampton, MA 01060, (413) 584-9558 (phone), (413) 586-9647 (fax) World Wide Web Source: http://www.natprior.org)

necessary to actively participate in discrimination against others in order to benefit from their systematic exploitation. For example, as Peter Nardi discusses in "Changing Gay and Lesbian Images in the Media" (Reading 35), mainstream media continues to render lesbian, gay, bisexual, and transgender individuals invisible while they present a varied representation of heterosexuality. Thus, a heterosexual seeking to find images in the media of someone who represents her or his own sexuality is likely to find numerous examples. This ability to find representations of self is a benefit that is not only often overlooked by those who are privileged but also does not require any direct discrimination on the part of the individual who benefits.

As each of these examples illustrates, oppression on the basis of race, class, gender, and sexuality does not require the overt discrimination of bigots that we often think of when examining issues of inequality. Acts of oppression in interpersonal contexts maintain systems of inequality by engaging in oppressive practices that are a reflection of oppressive social institutions.

In summary, our experiences of oppression and privilege occur within a comprehensive system of interconnected social institutions. Thus, issues of prejudice and discrimination are transformed into experiences of institutionalized *oppression*. The remainder of this section will explore the ways in which the social institutions of family, education, work and the economy, the state, and media, along with the social forces of language and social control, maintain systems of inequality. As you consider the following, remember to keep in mind how the ideologies depend on one another, forming interlocking systems of oppression.

SOCIAL INSTITUTIONS: MAINTAINING SYSTEMS OF OPPRESSION AND PRIVILEGE

As an intangible aspect of the social structure, the role of social institutions in maintaining inequality often goes largely unnoticed. Rather, we tend to view institutionalized oppression or privilege as "the way things are." For example, when we hear of racist acts on the part of individuals, such as in the brutal killing of James Byrd in Jasper, Texas[2], we are often rightfully outraged and horrified. At the same time, however, few of us are likely to notice the residential segregation that systematically excludes blacks from certain neighborhoods. Although the federal government eliminated overtly racially biased housing, tax, and transportation policies in the 1960s, as a recent *New York Times* article documented, a high level of racial segregation nevertheless continues to exist (Schmitt, 2001). Feagin and Sikes (1994) note that practices such as redlining (the systematic refusal on the part of some lenders to make loans in certain areas due to racial composition), racial steering, animosity on the part of whites, and discriminatory practices by mortgage lenders help maintain this segregation. In this section we will examine the practices and policies of institutions in order to understand the ways in which they maintain systems of oppression.

As discussed in Part I, social institutions play a significant role in creating inequality. They define race, class, gender, and sexuality not only in terms of what does and does not exist, but also in terms of the values that we associate with each category. Thus, they confer privilege on some while oppressing others. This is done through the establishment and enforcement of policies constructed by these institutions.

The readings in this section illustrate how social institutions maintain systems of oppression and privilege and how they in turn impact access to

---

[2]James Byrd, 49, was beaten unconscious, then dragged by a chain from the back of a pickup truck to his death after accepting a ride from three white men in Jasper, Texas in June 1998. One of the men, John William King, was found guilty and given the death penalty for his role in the killing. Another man, Lawrence Brewer, was also found guilty and sentenced to death. The third suspect, Shawn Berry, was sentenced to life in prison. Byrd's body was dismembered in the assault, and many of his body parts were found about a mile from his torso. When he was found, his body was so badly disfigured that Byrd had to be identified by fingerprints.

resources. Ranging from money and property to medical care and education, **resources** are anything that is valued in society. Resources are generally considered scarce due to their unequal distribution among different groups. For example, the unequal distribution of income and wealth, as illustrated earlier, results in the perception that resources such as money and property are scarce.

The ways in which resources are distributed greatly impact an individual's **life chances**—the material advantages or disadvantages that a particular member of a social category can expect to receive based on his or her status (Weber 1946; Dahrendorf 1979). One of the most significant of life chances is the distribution of health care and the resulting impact on one's quality of life. For example, according to a recent article in the *New York Times* by Erica Goode (1999), social class is one of the most powerful predictors of health—more powerful than genetics and even more than smoking. As a result of an unequal distribution of resources, the higher one's rung on the socioeconomic ladder, as Alejandro Reuss illustrates in "Cause of Death: Inequality" (Reading 28), the lower the risk of poor health. Furthermore, experiences of being marginalized, residing in racially segregated areas, and other forms of institutionalized racism were also found to magnify the impact of social class on health.

This example illustrates that social institutions, with their unequal distribution of valuable resources, perpetuate a cycle of disparate life chances. Obviously, if someone experiences poor health due to occupying a lower social class or living in a racially segregated neighborhood, she or he is going to be less able to fully participate in the social system, and less able to develop skills and achieve career goals than is someone who belongs to a higher social class with correspondingly better health.

Family

As a primary social institution, the family is central to maintaining systems of oppression and privilege based on race, class, gender, and sexuality. In addition, because it is so closely connected with other social institutions, such as the state and the economy, the structure of the family significantly influences and is influenced by the structure and actions of these institutions. While many of the ways systems of inequality are maintained are interconnected, perhaps the strongest connection is the relationship of family to the social structure.

For example, Lillian Rubin in "Families on the Fault Line" (Reading 18) illustrates how changes in our economic system resulted in a "crisis" in the family. Out of economic necessity, many women in white working-class families are now participating more fully in the paid workforce. When both parents attempt to work full-time, they need to find ways to pay for their child care. However, these families lack the economic resources that middle- and upper-class families have to seek quality child care. Rubin illustrates that social institutions such as the economy and the state have not responded in ways that support working-class families. As a result, they maintain systems of class inequality.

Our notions regarding what constitutes a family also maintains systems of oppression in a variety of ways. As Nan Hunter explains in "Sexual Dissent and the Family" (Reading 20), in efforts to obtain equality for lesbian, gay, bisexual, and transgender individuals in the United States, "no obstacle has proved tougher to surmount than the cluster of issues surrounding 'the family.' " The determination of who gets to be considered a family and whose "family values" are used as the standard against which all others are judged maintains inequality. As Hunter illustrates, these debates have significant impact on the amount of social equality or inequality experienced by various family structures.

Education

The institution of education also maintains systems of oppression and privilege. This institution reproduces the existing race, class, and gender structure through a variety of mechanisms, including the distribution of cultural capital and the existence of a hidden curriculum. In "Savage Inequalities" (Reading 21), Jonathan Kozol clearly illustrates how the institution of education perpetuates race and class inequalities through the way it is structured. His discussion of the divergent experiences of students in resource-rich and resource-poor educational systems demonstrates a difference in the distribution of **cultural capital**—social assets that include beliefs, values, attitudes, and competencies in language and culture. A concept proposed by Bordieu and Paseron (1977), cultural capital consists of ideas and knowledge people draw upon as they participate in social life, including "proper" attitudes toward education; socially approved dress and manners; and knowledge about books, music, and other forms of high and popular culture. Because cultural capital is essential for succeeding, children with less cultural capital often have fewer opportunities. In addition, the dominance of white, patriarchal, affluent class notions of what *counts* as cultural capital generally excludes the ideas and beliefs of the poor and people of color. Kozol illustrates that schools with fewer economic resources, which are often disproportionately attended by African-American, Latina/o, or Native American students, are less able to provide students with what is viewed by the dominant culture as important cultural capital, thus affecting their opportunities in the future. On the other hand, as Peter Cookson and Caroline Persell illustrate in "Preparing for Power" (Reading 22), children of higher social class have better access to this valued cultural capital and are thus better able to maintain their privilege. As a result, the educational system with its unequal distribution of cultural capital perpetuates a system of stratification based not only on race but also on class.

The institution of education also maintains race and class inequality through the existence of a **hidden curriculum**—the transmission of cultural values and attitudes, such as conformity and obedience to authority, through implied demands found in rules, routines, and regulations of schools. Because of the existence of a hidden curriculum, the values and attitudes that are reinforced in one school are not necessarily those that are promoted at another. For example, curriculum directed toward working-class students often focuses on rote memorization without much decision making, choice, or explanation of why something is done. Curriculum directed at middle-class students, however, emphasizes figuring and decision making in getting the right answer. The curriculum directed at affluent students often stresses the expression of ideas and creative activities, while that directed at elite students stresses critical thinking skills and developing analytical powers to apply abstract principles to problem solving. The readings of Cookson and Persell and Kozol provide clear contrasts of the extremes of the hidden curriculum and how they maintain systems of oppression. As each of these readings illustrates, our education system is largely segregated on the basis of class. In addition, there is also significant evidence of *de facto* racial segregation. As a result, the hidden curriculum maintains class as well as racial inequality.

Mary Crow Dog and Richard Erdoes further illustrate in "Civilize Them with a Stick" (Reading 23) the ways policies in the institution of education perpetuate racial inequality. In combination with policies of the state, Native American children were forced to leave their reservations and attend boarding or day schools. These efforts to assimilate members of this group are but one example of how the institution of education maintains racial inequality.

The institution of education also constructs and perpetuates categories of difference on the basis of sex and gender. Various studies have shown how teachers pay more attention to boys in the classroom than to girls, and the ramifications of this differential treatment are numerous. For example, in "Missing in Interaction" (Reading 24), Myra and David Sadker examine a variety of ways the elementary classroom setting maintains sex and gender inequality. For example, teachers often force boys to work out problems that they don't understand but tell girls what to do, go easier on girls when disciplining their students, and reward girls for non-academic achievements such as neat penmanship or getting along with others. These and other behaviors on the part of teachers and students maintain clear sex and gender divisions that contribute to differential ways of viewing and valuing males and females in our culture as well as the inequalities that females experience in our society.

Finally, the policies and practices of the institution of education can also maintain a system of stratification in which students who are perceived to be heterosexual are deemed more important and are thus more embraced by the institution than those that are perceived to be lesbian, gay, bisexual, or transgender. Examples of heterosexism can be found in what may be viewed as harmless school traditions (e.g., proms and other social events), but it can also be seen in more overt and meaningful ways. For example, in recent years the U.S. Congress has voted on proposals to eliminate federal aid to schools which "promote" homosexuality. In addition, a policy enacted by the Merrimack, New Hampshire, School Board stated:

> The Merrimack School District shall neither implement nor carry out any program or activity that has either the purpose or effect of encouraging or supporting homosexuality as a positive lifestyle alternative. A program or activity, for purposes of this item, includes the distribution of instructional materials, instruction, counseling, or other services on school grounds, or referral of a pupil to an organization that affirms a homosexual lifestyle.

Although this policy was later repealed, similar policies have been passed in other school districts. Some of the policies are phrased more bluntly than the one above and simply forbid any discussion of homosexuality at all—be it positive or negative. Regardless, the ramifications of official policies such as these, as well as implicit practices based on heterosexism, are severe.

Because of heterosexist school traditions and policies like those described above, lesbian, gay, bisexual, transgender, or questioning students are likely to experience feelings of alienation and self-alienation. For example, a 1989 U.S. Department of Health and Human Services report on youth suicide indicated that over 30 percent of all completed youth suicides each year are by gay and lesbian youth, and that gay youth are two to three times more likely to have attempted or seriously considered suicide than their heterosexual peers. Lesbian, gay, and bisexual youth, as well as students who are questioning their sexuality, often need counseling that is only available in the schools. Official and unofficial policies and practices based on heterosexism ignore these concerns and maintain inequality based on sexuality.

Work and the Economy

The institution of work and the economy is perhaps the most fundamental in maintaining systems of inequality. As already noted, changes in the structure of the economy significantly impact other institutions. At times, these changes offer new opportunities and privilege to some, and at others these changes foster continued oppression. In "Jobless Ghettos" (Reading 25), William Julius Wilson illustrates that the poor conditions in some segregated neighborhoods are made worse when places of employment no longer exist. Indeed, increases in the jobless rate disproportionately affect those who are on the low end of the economic spectrum as they are less likely to have other sources of support (e.g., savings, social networks leading to new jobs, etc.).

Joleen Kirschenman and Kathryn Neckerman in " 'We'd Love to Hire Them, But . . .' " (Reading 26), offer additional examples of how policies within the institution of work and the economy maintain a system of inequality. Through selective recruitment and biased hiring strategies, employers favor white applicants at the expense of others. As Figure 5 indicates,

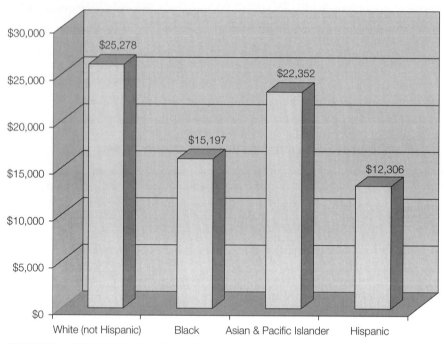

FIGURE 5   2000 Median Per-Capita Income (*Source:* U.S. Census Bureau *Current Population Survey.* World Wide Web Site: http://www.census.gov/hhes/income/histinc/histinctb.html)

there is a significant wage gap with regard to race in the United States. Policies such as those discussed by Kirschenman and Neckerman maintain this gap. Finally, policies of the social institution of work and the economy also perpetuate inequality with regard to sex and gender. As Christine Williams discusses in "The Glass Escalator" (Reading 27), sex segregation continues to exist within the U.S. labor force. She also reveals policies and practices with regard to hiring and supervising. These maintain a gap in the incomes of women and men, as illustrated in Figure 6, and as a result, they maintain a system of inequality.

The State and Public Policy

The state and public policy is another social institution that contributes to inequality. Often confused with the government, the state acts as a blueprint for how various procedures of the government should be carried out. In maintaining inequality, it acts in the interest of the dominant group or groups in society, reinforcing policies that work in their favor.

Currently, social policies regarding welfare "reform" have been the subject of much debate. As a result of the myths and stereotypes regarding people who receive aid within the welfare system, U.S. policies regarding

Medium Income of Year-Round, Full-Time Workers, by Sex and Age, 2000			
Age	**Males**	**Females**	**Female Income as Percentage of Male Income**
All Ages	$39,020	$28,823	73.9%
15–24	20,825	18,960	91.0
25–34	34,218	27,953	81.7
35–44	41,560	30,471	73.3
45–54	46,674	31,981	68.5
55–64	46,752	30,282	64.8
65 and Over	47,985	34,159	71.2

FIGURE 6   Median Income of Full-Time Workers by Sex and Age, 2000 (*Source:* U.S. Census Bureau, World Wide Web Site: http://www.census.gov/hhes/income/income00/inctab7.html)

Aid to Families with Dependent Children (AFDC) and similar entitlement programs have undergone considerable change in recent years. Randy Albelda and Chris Tilly explain in "It's a Family Affair" (Reading 29) that state policies often ignore how issues of race and class intersect. As Figure 7 illustrates, poverty is unequally distributed according to race, with people of color disproportionately representing those who are poor. Issues of poverty are exacerbated by stratification on the basis of sex, with women being more likely to be poor than men (21.6 percent as compared to 16 percent according to 2000 census data). In addition, female-headed households are also disproportionately poor, with 24.7 percent living in poverty. Albelda and Tilly explain that the recent changes in welfare reform only maintain these economic inequalities.

The criminal justice system, also ruled by state policies, reinforces inequality, particularly with regard to race and class. As David Cole illustrates in "No Equal Justice" (Reading 30), the criminal justice system depends on unequal racial and class patterns in prosecution and incarceration. The evidence of such continuing institutionalized racism can serve as a justification for the need of corrective programs such as affirmative action. While such programs have often been accused of discriminating against those in the majority, as Barbara Reskin discusses in "The Effects of Affirmative Action on Other Stakeholders" (Reading 31), such policies rarely do this. Rather, they tend to enhance productivity and encourage improved employment practices.

Finally, as stated earlier, public policies established by the state maintain the interest of the majority. For example, state policies prohibiting concepts of multiraciality were established during the colonial period in an effort to sustain the distinction between master and slave. George Lipsitz illustrates this notion in his discussion in "The Possessive Investment in Whiteness" (Reading 32). The establishment of these and other public policies were created, he argues, to maintain the control of whites over others. This motivation is reflected

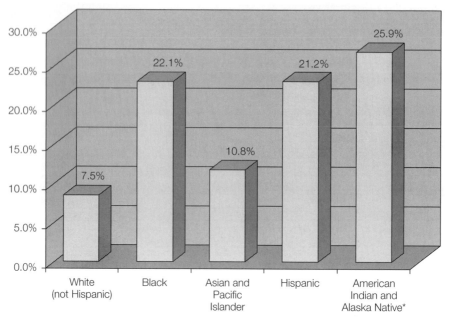

FIGURE 7   Poverty Rates by Race, 2000 (*Source:* U.S. Census Bureau *Current Population Report.* World Wide Web Site: http://www.census.gov/prod/2001pubs/p60-214.pdf)

*Denotes 1998–2000 average poverty rate. The average is used because the American Indian and Alaska Native population is relatively small and multiyear averages provide more reliable estimates.

in contemporary policies as well, and whites continue to benefit from such a system in the United States.

Media

Like other social institutions, the media conveys dominant ideologies about systems of inequality. Often the images reflected in the media represent the policies, practices, and prevailing attitudes of other social institutions. We can see policies of inclusion and exclusion regarding lesbian, gay, bisexual, and transgender individuals reflected in our television media. For example, when the Employment Non-Discrimination Act (ENDA) was rejected, denying lesbian, gay, bisexual, and transgender individuals the right to be free from employment discrimination on the basis of sexual orientation, *Ellen*, the first prime-time series to feature an out lesbian as the main character, was canceled. As Peter Nardi explains in "Changing Gay and Lesbian Images in the Media" (Reading 35), television has failed to accurately reflect the diversity of sexuality present in the United States.

Television is perhaps the most influential form of media today, with people in the United States watching an average of 24 hours each week, according to a December 1999 Gallup poll. As a result, this form of media possesses the power not only to influence but also to maintain our perceptions of reality. Richard Butsch, in "Ralph, Fred, Archie, and Homer" (Reading 33), discusses the inaccurate image of the "white male working-class buffoon," and Robert Lichter and Daniel Anderson discuss in "Distorted Reality" (Reading 34) the absence or misrepresentation of Chicana/o and Latina/o characters on television. Such distorted images perpetuate not only our stereotypes of these groups but also their continued oppression.

The institution of the media also maintains systems of oppression on the basis of sex and gender. For example, images in music, movies, television, and advertising degrade women. One of the ways this is accomplished is through the process of **objectification,** which Catharine MacKinnon defines as:

> the primary process of subjugation of women. It unites act with word, construction with expression, perception with enforcement, myth with reality (1982, p. 541).

Through such a process, the media supports the privileges of men and the oppression of women.

As the preceding discussion illustrates, social institutions, often acting in tandem, play a significant role in maintaining inequality. As you read the selections in this section, keep in mind the earlier discussions of the matrix of domination and look closely to see the ways in which these social institutions work together to maintain interlocking systems of oppression and privilege.

LANGUAGE AND MAINTAINING INEQUALITY

One significant, yet often unexplored mechanism for maintaining inequality is language. Functioning in a manner similar to a social institution, the ways in which we use language can maintain the values, roles, norms, and ideologies of the dominant culture. The readings on language in this section demonstrate that it is a powerful tool of culture, determining how members of a society interpret their environment. According to social construction theory, our social world has no inherent meaning. Rather, the meaning of the social world is constructed, in part, through language. Language serves as the link between all of the different elements of culture and maintains a system of inequality.

There are those who feel that examining the role of language in the maintenance of inequality is trivial or misplaced. However, as Gloria Anzaldúa explains in "How to Tame a Wild Tongue" (Reading 39), issues of language are particularly significant, especially when one doesn't speak the language of the dominant culture. In addition, one of the significant functions of language is to serve the purpose of **cultural transmission**—the passing of culture (values, beliefs, symbols, behaviors) from one generation to the next. Through language, children learn about their cultural heritage and develop a sense of personal identity in relation to their group. In addition, language also helps them learn about socially constructed categories of difference and the meanings associated with them.

Language consists of words that are symbols with meaning and serves as a tool for interpreting our environment. The power of words lies in the fact that the members of a culture share their meanings and valuations. It is our common language that allows us to communicate and understand one another, and this makes for order in society. Philosopher Ernst Cassirer (1978) identified several different functions of the ability of humans to use symbols, explaining that they help to define, organize, and evaluate experiences of people. Julia Wood (1997) uses the assertions of Cassirer to illustrate the ways in which we use language to indicate cultural values and views of women and men, thereby maintaining inequality.

First, Wood argues that language *defines sex and gender.* It serves to define women and men as well as what can and cannot exist. For example, "generic" language (e.g., using the pronoun *he* to refer to both women and men or using words like *fireman, mankind, man-hour,* etc.) excludes women and dismisses their importance. As a result, men and their experiences are presented as the norm while women and their experiences are seen as deviant. In addition to establishing *who* exists, Wood argues that language defines *what* exists. For example, since we use the masculine word as the base to make compounds in the English language, it might appear that women's ability to rule or own may seem impossible in that we can have a kingdom but not a *queendom.* Does this mean that only men can have land over which they rule? Certainly not. Rather, it illustrates that we attend to what we name and tend not to recognize that which we don't name. For example, words like *sexual harassment* or *date rape* are rather recent creations. That does not mean that these are new phenomena; rather, they are phenomena that we have only recently attended to and been willing to acknowledge.

Additional ways that language is used to define our perceptions of women and men can be seen in how women are defined by their relationships. Consider, for example, the commonly used titles of respect for men and women in our society. Men are addressed as Mr., which reveals nothing about their relationship to women. But how are women typically addressed? The titles Miss and Mrs. define women in terms of their relationship to men. Even when women have earned a higher status title, such as Dr., she is still likely to be addressed as Miss or Mrs. On an interesting note, many states in the United States have required women to take their husband's name on marrying. It was only in 1975 that a Hawaiian statute requiring women to give up their birth names on marriage was ruled unconstitutional.

The second way that language illustrates our perceptions of women and men, according to Wood, is that it *organizes our perceptions of sex and gender.*

The ability of language to organize our experiences and perceptions enables us to express cultural views of sex and gender by stereotyping men and women. In addition, the ways in which we talk about women and men in the English language encourage dualistic notions of sex and gender. For example, when we stereotype women as emotional and men as rational, we limit our abilities to recognize rationality in women and men's abilities to express emotion. Furthermore, due to the heavy emphasis that the English language places on polarity (good-bad, wrong-right, male-female), it is often difficult for us to think of things such as gender as existing along a continuum. In reality, very few of us fit on the polar ends of what a male or female is supposed to be like. Rather, most of us are somewhere in the middle. Yet we are all expected to conform to the two polar ends or suffer the consequences for not being seen as "gender appropriate."

Third, Wood argues that language *evaluates our perceptions of women and men*. Language is ideological, reflecting the values that are important in our culture. In the case of our use of the English language, we can find a great deal of evidence of linguistic sexism—the ways in which a language devalues members of one sex, almost invariably women. To illustrate this concept, consider the following word pairs: *brothers* and *sisters, husband* and *wife, men* and *women, hostess* and *host, madam* and *sir, Eve* and *Adam.* As you read these word pairs, it is likely that those in which the female term preceded the male term sounded awkward or incorrect. This is not coincidental; rather, it is a practice based on a long tradition. As Baron (1986) notes, 18th-century grammarians established the rule precisely to assert that "the supreme Being . . . is in all languages Masculine, in as much as the masculine sex is the superior and more excellent" (p. 3). According to these grammarians, to place women before men was to violate the "natural" order.

In addition, the English language often trivializes or diminishes women and things defined as feminine. As Eitzen and Baca Zinn note in Reading 40, there is a debate in college athletic associations regarding whether the names generally applied to female sports teams trivialize or diminish the role of women in sport. While male teams are generally set as the standard, being assigned team names with little or no gender meaning (e.g., the Polar Cats, the Volunteers), female teams generally receive "feminized" team names (e.g., the Polar Kittens, the Lady Volunteers). Many argue that such a practice devalues the role of women in sport and thus in society.

An additional example of how language trivializes things that are feminine is in the use of diminutive suffixes for occupations held by women (e.g., actress, waitress, stewardess) and through the use of terms like *girls* for adult females. Furthermore, when we consider word pairs like *governor* and *governess, master* and *mistress,* or *bachelor* and *spinster,* it becomes clear that the words associated with men have very different implied meanings than those associated with women, with the latter consistently negative or demeaning. The male words suggest power or positively valued status, whereas the female words have negative connotations. Although many of these words originally had neutral connotations, over time these words declined in value, a process known as **semantic derogation.** Smith notes that "once a word or term becomes associated with women, it often acquires semantic characteristics that are congruent with social stereotypes and evaluations of women as a group" (1985, p. 48). Because such values about women are reflected in our language, our perception that women have less value than men is perpetuated. According to the **Sapir-Whorf hypothesis,** "people perceive the world through the cultural lens of language" (Sapir, 1949, p. 162). Thus, language shapes our reality.

As the preceding discussion illustrates, language plays a significant role in maintaining inequality. The readings in this section expand upon this illustration. For example, Robert Moore in "Racism in the English Language" (Reading 37) discusses the symbolism of white as positive and black as negative in the English language. As a result, language maintains racial inequality. In addition, Irving Kenneth Zola argues in "Self, Identity, and the Naming Question" (Reading 38) that those who occupy marginalized groups are not often given the opportunity to name themselves. Rather, names are generally imposed upon them by those with social power, maintaining a system in which the marginalized group is oppressed. Finally, Stanley Eitzen and Maxine Baca Zinn discuss in "The Dark Side of Sports Symbols" (Reading 40) the use of American Indian names and images in sports. Their discussion explains that such a practice maintains a system of stratification in which Native Americans are not only seen as less valuable than whites but are often objectified and seen as less than human. Each of the readings demonstrates that language is a pervasive tool of culture. In maintaining cultural values, roles, norms, and ideologies, language maintains inequality.

VIOLENCE AND SOCIAL CONTROL

Increasing violence in the United States—particularly evident in the school shootings most recently in Fort Gibson, Oklahoma; Deming, New Mexico; Conyers, Georgia; Littleton, Colorado; Pearl, Mississippi; West Paducah, Kentucky; Jonesboro, Arkansas; and Springfield, Oregon—has resulted in considerable discussion regarding the causes of and solutions to this problem. While some have been quick to blame the media or lax gun-control laws, focusing on violence as an act of individuals, it is important that we understand violence as a pervasive form of **social control**—the regulation of human behavior in any social group. As the findings of a May 1999 Gallup Poll linking antigay and racist attitudes with student-on-student violence illustrates, violence used as a mechanism for social control maintains inequality.

Several of the readings in this section illustrate how violence is used as a means of social control. For example, Helen Zia in "Where Race and Gender Meet" (Reading 41) examines the role of pornography in perpetuating violence against women, particularly women of color. The role of violence in controlling women is further demonstrated in "Fraternities and Collegiate Rape Culture" (Reading 42). In their discussion, A. Ayres Boswell and Joan Spade discuss the role of a **rape culture**—a set of values and beliefs that create an environment conducive to rape—in perpetuating violence against women. Furthermore, connections between homophobia, sexism, and heterosexism are evident in Suzanne Pharr's discussion of "Homophobia as a Weapon of Sexism" (Reading 44). Each of these examples illustrates that violence is used as a mechanism of social control to reinforce interlocking systems oppression.

Michael Kaufman, in "The Construction of Masculinity and the Triad of Men's Violence" (Reading 43), explains how members of dominant groups, in this case men, are taught to be violent so that they may participate in the oppression of others. As this reading demonstrates, the impact of all forms of violence has a severe impact on an individual's ability to participate fully in society. As a result, violence perpetuates inequality.

Examining violence and social control further illustrates the interconnectedness of race, class, gender, and sexuality oppression. In working to understand the escalating violence within the United States and the world, it is important also to understand how systems of oppression interconnect. In so doing we will gain a better understanding of how violence is used to maintain interlocking systems of inequality.

CONCLUSION

As discussed in this section, constructions of difference regarding race, class, gender, and sexuality are transformed into interlocking systems of oppression and privilege. As a result, it is important that we understand how one system relies on another. The readings in this section examine the ways in which the social institutions of family, education, the economy, the state, and media work together with language and violence and social control to maintain inequality. Once we are aware of this process, we will have a greater understanding of how to transform systems of inequality.

REFERENCES

Baron, Dennis E. 1986. *Grammar and Gender*. New Haven, CT: Yale University Press.

Bordieu, Pierre, and Jean-Claude Paseron. 1977. *Society, Culture, and Education*. Beverly Hills, CA: Sage Publications.

Cassirer, Ernst. 1978. *An Essay on Man*. New Haven, CT: Yale University Press.

Cole, David. 1999. *No Equal Justice: Race and Class in the American Criminal Justice System*. New York: The New Press.

Collins, Patricia Hill. 1991. *Black Feminist Thought: Knowledge, Consciousness, and the Politics of Empowerment*. New York: Routledge.

Dahrendorf, Ralf. 1979. *Life Chances*. London: Weidenfeld & Nicolson.

Feagin, Joe R. and Melvin P. Sikes. 1994. *Living with Racism: The Black Middle-Class Experience.* Boston: Beacon Press.

Fletcher, Michael A. 1996. "Driven to Extremes: Black Men Take Steps to Avoid Police Stops," *Washington Post,* March 29: A1.

Frye, Marilyn. 1983. *The Politics of Reality: Essays in Feminist Theory.* Trumansburg, New York: The Crossing Press.

Gibson, Paul. 1989. "Gay Male and Lesbian Youth Suicide," in Marcia R. Feinleib (ed.), *Report of the Secretary's Task Force on Youth Suicide.* Washington, D.C.: U.S. Department of Health and Human Services.

Goode, Erica. 1999, "For Good Health, It Helps to Be Rich and Important." *New York Times,* June 1: D-1;D-9.

Harris, David A. 1998. "The Use of Traffic Stops against African Americans: What Can Be Done?" *American Civil Liberties Freedom Network,* <http://www.aclu.org/issues/policepractices/harris_statement.html>.

MacKinnon, Catharine A. 1982. "Feminism, Marxism, Method, and the State: An Agenda for Theory." *Signs* 7(3):515–44.

Moraga, Cherríe. 1983. *Loving in the War Years.* Boston: South End Press.

Petruno, Tom. 1991. "A Bigger Piece of the Pie." *Los Angeles Times,* May 22: D-1.

Sapir, Edward. 1949. *Selected Writings of Edward Sapir in Language, Culture, and Personality,* edited by David G. Mandelbaum. Berkeley: University of California Press.

Schmitt, Eric. 2001. "Analysis of Census Finds Segregation along with Diversity." *New York Times,* Wednesday, April 4.

Smith, Philip M. 1985. *Language, the Sexes, and Society.* NY: Blackwell.

Weber, Max. 1946. From *Max Weber: Essays in Sociology.* Edited and translated by Hans Gerth and C. Wright Mills. New York: Oxford University Press.

Wolf, Edward N. 2000. "Recent Trends in Wealth Ownership, 1983–1998." Unpublished Working Paper No. 300, Jerome Levy Economics Institute, April. <http://levy.org/docs/wrkpap/papers/300.html>.

Wood, Julia T. 1997. *Gendered Lives: Communication, Gender, and Culture.* 2nd ed. Belmont, CA: Wadsworth.

17

OUR MOTHERS' GRIEF
Racial-Ethnic Women and the
Maintenance of Families

BONNIE THORNTON DILL

REPRODUCTIVE LABOR[1] FOR WHITE WOMEN
IN EARLY AMERICA

In eighteenth- and nineteenth-century America, the lives of white[2] women in the United States were circumscribed within a legal and social system based on patriarchal authority. This authority took two forms: public and private. The social, legal, and economic position of women in this society was controlled through the private aspects of patriarchy and defined in terms of their relationship to families headed by men. The society was structured to confine white wives to reproductive labor within the domestic sphere. At the same time, the formation, preservation, and protection of families among white settlers was seen as crucial to the growth and development of American society. Building, maintaining, and supporting families was a concern of the State and of those organizations that prefigured the State. Thus, while white women had few legal rights as women, they were protected through public forms of patriarchy that acknowledged and supported their family roles of wives, mothers, and daughters because they were vital instruments for building American society.

The groundwork for public support of women's family roles was laid during the colonial period. As early as 1619, the London Company began planning for the importation of single women into the colonies to marry colonists, form families, and provide for a permanent settlement. The objective was to make the men "more settled and less moveable . . . instability would breed a dissolution, and so an overthrow of the Plantation" (cited in Spruill 1972, p. 8).

From: *Journal of Family History* 13 (1988): 415–31. Reprinted by permission of Sage Publications.

In accordance with this recognition of the importance of families, the London Company provided the economic basis necessary for the development of the family as a viable and essential institution within the nascent social structure of the colonies. Shares of land were allotted for both husbands and wives in recognition of the fact that "in a new plantation it is not known whether men or women be the most necessary" (cited in Spruill 1972, p. 9).

This pattern of providing an economic base designed to attract, promote, and maintain families was followed in the other colonial settlements. Lord Baltimore of Maryland ". . . offered to each adventurer a hundred acres for himself, a hundred for his wife, fifty for each child, a hundred for each man servant, and sixty for a woman servant. Women heads of families were treated just as men" (Spruill 1972, p. 11).

In Georgia, which appealed to poorer classes for settlers more than did Virginia or Maryland, Maryland, ". . . among the advantages they offered men to emigrate was the gainful employment of their wives and children" (Spruill 1972, p. 16).

In colonial America, white women were seen as vital contributors to the stabilization and growth of society. They were therefore accorded some legal and economic recognition through a patriarchal family structure.

> While colonial life remained hard, . . . American women married earlier [than European women], were less restricted by dowries, and often had legal protection for themselves and their children in antenuptial contracts (Kennedy 1979, p. 7).

Throughout the colonial period, women's reproductive labor in the family was an integral part of the daily operation of small-scale family farms or artisan's shops. According to Kessler-Harris (1981), a gender-based division of labor was common, but not rigid. The participation of women in work that was essential to family survival reinforced the importance of their contributions to both the protection of the family and the growth of society.

Between the end of the eighteenth and mid-nineteenth century, what is labeled the "modern American family" developed. The growth of industrialization and an urban middle class, along with the accumulation of agrarian wealth among Southern planters, had two results that are particularly pertinent to this discussion. First, class differentiation increased and sharpened, and with it, distinctions in the content and nature of women's family lives.

Second, the organization of industrial labor resulted in the separation of home and family and the assignment to women of a separate sphere of activity focused on childcare and home maintenance. Whereas men's activities became increasingly focused upon the industrial competitive sphere of work, "women's activities were increasingly confined to the care of children, the nurturing of the husband, and the physical maintenance of the home" (Degler 1980, p. 26).

This separate sphere of domesticity and piety became both an ideal for all white women as well as a source of important distinctions between them.

As Matthaei (1982) points out, tied to the notion of wife as homemaker is a definition of masculinity in which the husband's successful role performance was measured by his ability to keep his wife in the homemaker role. The entry of white women into the labor force came to be linked with the husband's assumed inability to fulfill his provider role.

For wealthy and middle-class women, the growth of the domestic sphere offered a potential for creative development as homemakers and mothers. Given ample financial support from their husband's earnings, some of these women were able to concentrate their energies on the development and elaboration of the more intangible elements of this separate sphere. They were also able to hire other women to perform the daily tasks such as cleaning, laundry, cooking, and ironing. Kessler-Harris cautions, however, that the separation of productive labor from the home did not seriously diminish the amount of physical drudgery associated with housework, even for middle-class women.

> It did relegate the continuing hard work to second place, transforming the public image of the household by the 1820s and 1830s from a place where productive labor was performed to one whose main goals were the preservation of virtue and morality. . . . Many of the "well-run" homes of the pre-Civil War period seem to have been the dwelling of overworked women. Short of household help, without modern conveniences, and frequently pregnant, these women complained bitterly of their harsh existence (Kessler-Harris 1981, p. 39).

In effect, household labor was transformed from economic productivity done by members of the family group to home maintenance, childcare and moral uplift done by an isolated woman who perhaps supervised some servants.

Working-class white women experienced this same transformation but their families' acceptance of the domestic code meant that their labor in the home intensified. Given the meager earnings of working-class men, working-class families had to develop alternative strategies to both survive and keep the wives at home. The result was that working-class women's reproductive labor increased to fill the gap between family need and family income. Women increased their own production of household goods through things such as canning and sewing; and by developing other sources of income, including boarders and homework. A final and very important source of other income was wages earned by the participation of sons and daughters in the labor force. In fact, Matthaei argues that "the domestic homemaking of married women was supported by the labors of their daughters" (1982, p. 130).

The question arises: Why did white working-class families sacrifice other aspects of this nineteenth-century notion of family, such as privacy and the protection of children, to keep wives as homemakers within the home? Zaretsky (1978) provides a possible answer.

The Victorian emphasis on the sanctity of the family and on the autonomy of women within the family marked an advance for women of all classes over the interdependent but male dominated subsistence farm of the 18th century . . . most of women's adult life was taken up with childrearing. As a result, a special respect for her place within the home, and particularly for her childrearing activities was appreciated by working-class women (p. 211).

Another way in which white women's family roles were socially acknowledged and protected was through the existence of a separate sphere for women. The code of domesticity, attainable for affluent women, became an ideal toward which nonaffluent women aspired. Notwithstanding the personal constraints placed on women's development, the notion of separate spheres promoted the growth and stability of family life among the white middle class and became the basis for working-class men's efforts to achieve a family wage, so that they could keep their wives at home. Also, women gained a distinct sphere of authority and expertise that yielded them special recognition.

During the eighteenth and nineteenth centuries, American society accorded considerable importance to the development and sustenance of European immigrant families. As primary laborers in the reproduction and maintenance of family life, women were acknowledged and accorded the privileges and protections deemed socially appropriate to their family roles. This argument acknowledges the fact that the family structure denied these women many rights and privileges and seriously constrained their individual growth and development. Because women gained social recognition primarily through their membership in families, their personal rights were few and privileges were subject to the will of the male head of the household. Nevertheless, the recognition of women's reproductive labor as an essential building block of the family, combined with a view of the family as the cornerstone of the nation, distinguished the experiences of the white, dominant culture from those of racial ethnics.

Thus, in its founding, American society initiated legal, economic, and social practices designed to promote the growth of family life among European colonists. The reception colonial families found in the United States contrasts sharply with the lack of attention given to the families of racial-ethnics. Although the presence of racial-ethnics was equally as important for the growth of the nation, their political, economic, legal, and social status was quite different.

REPRODUCTIVE LABOR AMONG RACIAL-ETHNICS IN EARLY AMERICA

Unlike white women, racial-ethnic women experienced the oppressions of a patriarchal society but were denied the protections and buffering of a patriarchal family. Their families suffered as a direct result of the organization of the labor systems in which they participated.

Racial-ethnics were brought to this country to meet the need for a cheap and exploitable labor force. Little attention was given to their family and community life except as it related to their economic productivity. Labor, and not the existence or maintenance of families, was the critical aspect of their role in building the nation. Thus they were denied the social structural supports necessary to make *their* families a vital element in the social order. Family membership was not a key means of access to participation in the wider society. The lack of social, legal, and economic support for racial-ethnic families intensified and extended women's reproductive labor, created tensions and strains in family relationships, and set the stage for a variety of creative and adaptive forms of resistance.

AFRICAN-AMERICAN SLAVES

Among students of slavery, there has been considerable debate over the relative "harshness" of American slavery, and the degree to which slaves were permitted or encouraged to form families. It is generally acknowledged that many slave-owners found it economically advantageous to encourage family formation as a way of reproducing and perpetuating the slave labor force. This became increasingly true after 1807 when the importation of African slaves was explicitly prohibited. The existence of these families and many aspects of their functioning, however, were directly controlled by the master. In other words, slaves married and formed families but these groupings were completely subject to the master's decision to let them remain intact. One study has estimated that about 32 percent of all recorded slave marriages were disrupted by sale, about 45 percent by death of a spouse, about 10 percent by choice, with the remaining 13 percent not disrupted at all (Blassingame 1972, pp. 90–92). African slaves thus quickly learned that they had a limited degree of control over the formation and maintenance of their marriages and could not be assured of keeping their children with them. The threat of disruption was perhaps the most direct and pervasive cultural assault[3] on families that slaves encountered. Yet there were a number of other aspects of the slave system which reinforced the precariousness of slave family life.

In contrast to some African traditions and the Euro-American patterns of the period, slave men were not the main provider or authority figure in the family. The mother-child tie was basic and of greatest interest to the slave-owner because it was critical in the reproduction of the labor force.

In addition to the lack of authority and economic autonomy experienced by the husband-father in the slave family, use of the rape of women slaves as a weapon of terror and control further undermined the integrity of the slave family.

> It would be a mistake to regard the institutionalized pattern of rape
> during slavery as an expression of white men's sexual urges,
> otherwise stifled by the specter of the white womanhood's chastity

... Rape was a weapon of domination, a weapon of repression,
whose covert goal was to extinguish slave women's will to resist,
and in the process, to demoralize their men (Davis 1981, pp. 23–24).

The slave family, therefore, was at the heart of a peculiar tension in the master-slave relationship. On the one hand, slaveowners sought to encourage familial ties among slaves because, as Matthaei (1982) states: "... these provided the basis of the development of the slave into a self-conscious socialized human being" (p. 81). They also hoped and believed that this socialization process would help children learn to accept their place in society as slaves. Yet the master's need to control and intervene in the familial life of the slaves is indicative of the other side of this tension. Family ties had the potential for becoming a competing and more potent source of allegiance than the slavemaster himself. Also, kin were as likely to socialize children in forms of resistance as in acts of compliance.

It was within this context of surveillance, assault, and ambivalence that slave women's reproductive labor took place. She and her menfolk had the task of preserving the human and family ties that could ultimately give them a reason for living. They had to socialize their children to believe in the possibility of a life in which they were not enslaved. The slave woman's labor on behalf of the family was, as David (1971) has pointed out, the only labor the slave engaged in that could not be directly appropriated by the slaveowner for his own profit. Yet, its indirect appropriation, as labor crucial to the reproduction of the slaveowner's labor force, was the source of strong ambivalence for many slave women. Whereas some mothers murdered their babies to keep them from being slaves, many sought within the family sphere a degree of autonomy and creativity denied them in other realms of the society. The maintenance of a distinct African-American culture is testimony to the ways in which slaves maintained a degree of cultural autonomy and resisted the creation of a slave family that only served the needs of the master.

Gutman (1976) provides evidence of the ways in which slaves expressed a unique Afro-American culture through their family practices. He provides data on naming patterns and kinship ties among slaves that flies in the face of the dominant ideology of the period. That ideology argued that slaves were immoral and had little concern for or appreciation of family life.

Yet Gutman demonstrated that within a system which denied the father authority over his family, slave boys were frequently named after their fathers, and many children were named after blood relatives as a way of maintaining family ties. Gutman also suggested that after emancipation a number of slaves took the names of former owners in order to reestablish family ties that had been disrupted earlier. On plantation after plantation, Gutman found considerable evidence of the building and maintenance of extensive kinship ties among slaves. In instances where slave families had been disrupted, slaves in new communities reconstituted the kinds of family and kin ties that came to characterize black family life throughout the South. These patterns included, but were not limited to, a belief in the importance of marriage as a long-term commitment, rules of exogamy that included marriage between first cousins, and acceptance of women who had children outside of marriage. Kinship networks were an important source of resistance to the organization of labor that treated the individual slave, and not the family, as the unit of labor (Caulfield 1974).

Another interesting indicator of the slaves' maintenance of some degree of cultural autonomy has been pointed out by Wright (1981) in her discussion of slave housing. Until the early 1800s, slaves were often permitted to build their housing according to their own design and taste. During that period, housing built in an African style was quite common in the slave quarters. By 1830, however, slaveowners had begun to control the design and arrangement of slave housing and had introduced a degree of conformity and regularity to it that left little room for the slave's personalization of the home. Nevertheless, slaves did use some of their own techniques in construction and often hid it from their masters.

> Even the floors, which usually consisted of only tamped earth, were evidence of a hidden African tradition: slaves cooked clay over a fire, mixing in ox blood or cow dung, and then poured it in place to make hard dirt floors almost like asphalt . . . In slave houses, in contrast to other crafts, these signs of skill and tradition would then be covered over (Wright 1981, p. 48).

Housing is important in discussions of family because its design reflects sociocultural attitudes about family life. The housing that slaveowners provided for their slaves reflected a view of Black family life consistent with the stereotypes of the period. While the existence of slave families was acknowledged, it certainly was not nurtured. Thus, cabins were crowded, often containing more than one family, and there were no provisions for privacy. Slaves had to create their own.

> Slave couples hung up old clothes or quilts to establish boundaries; others built more substantial partitions from scrap wood. Parents sought to establish sexual privacy from children. A few ex-slaves described modified trundle beds designed to hide parental lovemaking . . . Even in one-room cabins, sexual segregation was carefully organized (Wright 1981, p. 50).

Perhaps most critical in developing an understanding of slave women's reproductive labor is the gender-based division of labor in the domestic sphere. The organization of slave labor enforced considerably equality among men and women. The ways in which equality in the labor force was translated into the family sphere is somewhat speculative. David (1981), for example, suggests that egalitarianism between males and females was a direct result of slavery when she says:

> Within the confines of their family and community life, therefore, Black people managed to accomplish a magnificent feat. They

transformed that negative equality which emanated from the equal oppression they suffered as slaves into a positive quality: the egalitarianism characterizing their social relations (p. 18).

It is likely, however, that this transformation was far less direct than Davis implies. We know, for example, that slave women experienced what has recently been called the "double day" before most other women in this society. Slave narratives (Jones 1985; White 1985; Blassingame 1977) reveal that women had primary responsibility for their family's domestic chores. They cooked (although on some plantations meals were prepared for all of the slaves), sewed, cared for their children, and cleaned house, all after completing a full day of labor for the master. Blassingame (1972) and others have pointed out that slave men engaged in hunting, trapping, perhaps some gardening, and furniture making as ways of contributing to the maintenance of their families. Clearly, a gender-based division of labor did exist within the family and it appears that women bore the larger share of the burden for housekeeping and child care.

By contrast to white families of the period, however, the division of labor in the domestic sphere was neither reinforced in the relationship of slave women to work nor in the social institutions of the slave community. The gender-based division of labor among the slaves existed within a social system that treated men and women as almost equal, independent units of labor.[4] Thus Mattaei (1982) is probably correct in concluding that

> Whereas . . . the white homemaker interacted with the public
> sphere through her husband, and had her work life determined by
> him, the enslaved Afro-American homemaker was directly subordi-
> nated to and determined by her owner . . . The equal enslavement
> of husband and wife gave the slave marriage a curious kind of
> equality, an equality of oppression (p. 94).

Black men were denied the male resources of a patriarchal society and therefore were unable to turn gender distinctions into female subordination, even if that had been their desire. Black women, on the other hand, were denied support and protection for their roles as mothers and wives and thus had to modify and structure those roles around the demands of their labor. Thus, reproductive labor for slave women was intensified in several ways: by the demands of slave labor that forced them into the double-day of work; by the desire and need to maintain family ties in the face of a system that gave them only limited recognition; by the stresses of building a family with men who were denied the standard social privileges of manhood; and by the struggle to raise children who could survive in a hostile environment.

This intensification of reproductive labor made networks of kin and quasi-kin important instruments in carrying out the reproductive tasks of the slave community. Given an African cultural heritage where kinship ties formed the basis of social relations, it is not at all surprising that African

American slaves developed an extensive system of kinship ties and obligations (Gutman 1976; Sudarkasa 1981). Research on Black families in slavery
provides considerable documentation of participation of extended kin in
childrearing, childbirth, and other domestic, social, and economic activities
(Gutman 1976; Blassingame 1972; Genovese 1974).

After slavery, these ties continued to be an important factor linking individual household units in a variety of domestic activities. While kinship ties
were also important among native-born whites and European immigrants,
Gutman (1976) has suggested that these ties

> were comparatively more important to Afro-Americans than to
> lower-class native white and immigrant Americans, the result of
> their distinctive low economic status, a condition that denied them
> the advantages of an extensive associational life beyond the kin
> group and the advantages and disadvantages resulting from
> mobility opportunities (p. 213).

His argument is reaffirmed by research on Afro-American families after
slavery (Shimkin et al. 1978; Aschenbrenner 1975; Davis 1981; Stock 1974).
Sudarkasa (1981) takes this argument one step further and links this pattern
to the African cultural heritage:

> historical realities require that the derivation of this aspect of Black
> family organization be traced to its African antecedents. Such a
> view does not deny the adaptive significance of consanguineal (kin)
> networks. In fact, it helps to clarify why these networks had the
> flexibility they had and why, they, rather than conjugal relation-
> ships came to be the stabilizing factor in Black families (p. 49).

With individual households, the gender-based division of labor experienced some important shifts during emancipation. In their first real opportunity to establish family life beyond the controls and constraints imposed
by a slavemaster, family life among Black sharecroppers changed radically.
Most women, at least those who were wives and daughters of able-bodied
men, withdrew from field labor and concentrated on their domestic duties
in the home. Husbands took primary responsibility for the fieldwork and for
relations with the owners, such as signing contracts on behalf of the family.
Black women were severely criticized by whites for removing themselves
from field labor because they were seen to be aspiring to a model of womanhood that was considered inappropriate for them. This reorganization of
female labor, however, represented an attempt on the part of Blacks to protect women from some of the abuses of the slave system and to thus secure
their family life. It was more likely a response to the particular set of circumstances that the newly freed slaves faced than a reaction to the lives of
their former masters. Jones (1985) argues that these patterns were "particularly significant" because at a time when industrial development was introducing a labor system that divided male and female labor, the freed Black

family was establishing a pattern of joint work and complementary tasks between males and females that was reminiscent of the preindustrial American families. Unfortunately, these former slaves had to do this without the institutional supports that white farm families had in the midst of a sharecropping system that deprived them of economic independence.

CHINESE SOJOURNERS

An increase in the African slave population was a desired goal. Therefore, Africans were permitted and even encouraged at times to form families subject to the authority and whim of the master. By sharp contrast, Chinese people were explicitly denied the right to form families in the United States through both law and social practice. Although male laborers began coming to the United States in sizable numbers in the middle of the nineteenth century, it was more than a century before an appreciable number of children of Chinese parents were born in America. Tom, a respondent in Nee and Nee's (1973) book, *Longtime Californ'* says: "One thing about Chinese men in America was you had to be either a merchant or a big gambler, have lot of side money to have a family here. A working man, an ordinary man, just can't!" (p. 80).

Working in the United States was a means of gaining support for one's family with an end of obtaining sufficient capital to return to China and purchase land. The practice of sojourning was reinforced by laws preventing Chinese laborers from becoming citizens, and by restrictions on their entry into this country. Chinese laborers who arrived before 1882 could not bring their wives and were prevented by law from marrying whites. Thus, it is likely that the number of Chinese-American families might have been negligible had it not been for two things: the San Francisco earthquake and fire in 1906, which destroyed all municipal records; and the ingenuity and persistence of the Chinese people who used the opportunity created by the earthquake to increase their numbers in the United States. Since relatives of citizens were permitted entry, American-born Chinese (real and claimed) would visit China, report the birth of a son, and thus create an entry slot. Years later the slot could be used by a relative or purchased. The purchasers were called "paper sons." Paper sons became a major mechanism for increasing the Chinese population, but it was a slow process and the sojourner community remained predominantly male for decades.

The high concentration of males in the Chinese community before 1920 resulted in a split-household form of family. As Glenn observes:

> In the split-household family, production is separated from other
> functions and is carried out by a member living far from the rest of the
> household. The rest—consumption, reproduction and socialization—
> are carried out by the wife and other relatives from the home
> village. . . . The split-household form makes possible maximum

exploitation of the workers . . . The labor of prime-age male workers can be bought relatively cheaply, since the cost of reproduction and family maintenance is borne partially by unpaid subsistence work of women and old people in the home village (Glenn 1981, pp. 14–15).

The women who were in the United States during this period consisted of a small number who were wives and daughters of merchants and a larger percentage who were prostitutes. Hirata (1979) has suggested that Chinese prostitution was an important element in helping to maintain the split-household family. In conjunction with laws prohibiting intermarriage, Chinese prostitution helped men avoid long-term relationships with women in the United States and ensured that the bulk of their meager earnings would continue to support the family at home.

The reproductive labor of Chinese women, therefore, took on two dimensions primarily because of the split-household family form. Wives who remained in China were forced to raise children and care for in-laws on the meager remittances of their sojourning husband. Although we know few details about their lives, it is clear that the everyday work of bearing and maintaining children and a household fell entirely on their shoulders. Those women who immigrated and worked as prostitutes performed the more nurturant aspects of reproductive labor, that is, providing emotional and sexual companionship for men who were far from home. Yet their role as prostitute was more likely a means of supporting their families at home in China than a chosen vocation.

The Chinese family system during the nineteenth century was a patriarchal one wherein girls had little value. In fact, they were considered only temporary members of their father's family because when they married, they became members of their husband's families. They also had little social value: girls were sold by some poor parents to work as prostitutes, concubines, or servants. This saved the family the expense of raising them, and their earnings also became a source of family income. For most girls, however, marriages were arranged and families sought useful connections through this process.

With the development of a sojourning pattern in the United States, some Chinese women in those regions of China where this pattern was more prevalent would be sold to become prostitutes in the United States. Most, however, were married off to men whom they saw only once or twice in the 20- or 30-year period during which he was sojourning in the United States. Her status as wife ensured that a portion of the meager wages he earned would be returned to his family in China. This arrangement required considerable sacrifice and adjustment on the part of wives who remained in China and those who joined their husbands after a long separation.

Kingston (1977) tells the story of the unhappy meeting of her aunt, Moon Orchid, with her husband from whom she had been separated for 30 years.

For thirty years she had been receiving money from him from America. But she had never told him that she wanted to come to the United States. She waited for him to suggest it, but he never did (p. 144).

His response to her when she arrived unexpectedly was to say:

"Look at her. She'd never fit into an American household. I have important American guests who come inside my house to eat." He turned to Moon Orchid, "You can't talk to them. You can barely talk to me." Moon Orchid was so ashamed, she held her hands over her face. She wished she could also hide her dappled hands (p. 178).

Despite these handicaps, Chinese people collaborated to establish the opportunity to form families and settle in the United States. In some cases it took as long as three generations for a child to be born on United States soil.

In one typical history, related by a 21-year-old college student, great-grandfather arrived in the States in the 1890s as a "paper son" and worked for about 20 years as a laborer. He then sent for the grandfather, who worked alongside greatgrandfather in a small business for several years. Greatgrandfather subsequently returned to China, leaving grandfather to run the business and send remittance. In the 1940s, grandfather sent for father; up to this point, none of the wives had left China. Finally, in the late 1950s father returned to China and brought his wife back with him. Thus, after nearly 70 years, the first child was born in the United States (Glenn 1981, p. 14).

CHICANOS

Africans were uprooted from their native lands and encouraged to have families in order to increase the slave labor force. Chinese people were immigrant laborers whose "permanent" presence in the country was denied. By contrast, Mexican-Americans were colonized and their traditional family life was disrupted by war and the imposition of a new set of laws and conditions of labor. The hardships faced by Chicano families, therefore, were the result of the United States colonization of the indigenous Mexican population, accompanied by the beginnings of industrial development in the region. The treaty of Guadalupe Hidalgo, signed in 1848, granted American citizenship to Mexicans living in what is now called the Southwest. The American takeover, however, resulted in the gradual displacement of Mexicans from the land and their incorporation into a colonial labor force (Barrera 1979). In addition, Mexicans who immigrated into the United States after 1848 were also absorbed into the labor force.

Whether natives of Northern Mexico (which became the United States after 1848) or immigrants from Southern Mexico, Chicanos were a largely peasant population whose lives were defined by a feudal economy and a daily struggle on the land for economic survival. Patriarchal families were important instruments of community life and nuclear family units were linked together through an elaborate system of kinship and godparenting. Traditional life was characterized by hard work and a fairly distinct pattern of sex-role segregation.

> Most Mexican women were valued for their household qualities, men by their ability to work and to provide for a family. Children were taught to get up early, to contribute to the family's labor to prepare themselves for adult life . . . Such a life demanded discipline, authority, deference—values that cemented the working of a family surrounded and shaped by the requirements of Mexico's distinctive historical pattern of agricultural development, especially its pervasive debt peonage (Saragoza 1983, p. 8).

As the primary caretakers of hearth and home in a rural environment, *Las Chicanas* labor made a vital and important contribution to family survival. A description of women's reproductive labor in the early twentieth century can be used to gain insight into the work of the nineteenth-century rural women.

> For country women, work was seldom a salaried job. More often it was the work of growing and preparing food, of making adobes and plastering houses with mud, or making their children's clothes for school and teaching them the hymns and prayers of the church, or delivering babies and treating sicknesses with herbs and patience. In almost every town there were one or two women who, in addition to working in their own homes, served other families in the community as *curanderas* (healers), *parteras* (midwives), and schoolteachers (Elasser 1980, p. 10).

Although some scholars have argued that family rituals and community life showed little change before World War I (Saragoza 1983), the American conquest of Mexican lands, the introduction of a new system of labor, the loss of Mexican-owned land through the inability to document ownership, plus the transient nature of most of the jobs in which Chicanos were employed resulted in the gradual erosion of this pastoral way of life. Families were uprooted as the economic basis for family life changed. Some immigrated from Mexico in search of a better standard of living and worked in the mines and railroads. Others who were native to the Southwest faced a job market that no longer required their skills and moved into mining, railroad, and agricultural labor in search of a means of earning a living. According to Camarillo (1979), the influx of Anglo[5] capital into the pastoral economy of Santa Barbara rendered obsolete the skills of many Chicano males who had worked as ranch-hands and farmers prior to the urbanization of that economy. While some women and children accompanied their husbands to the railroad and mine camps, they often did so despite prohibitions against it. Initially many of these camps discouraged or prohibited family settlement.

The American period (post-1848) was characterized by considerable transiency for the Chicano population. Its impact on families is seen in the growth of female-headed households, which was reflected in the data as early as 1860. Griswold del Castillo (1979) found a sharp increase in female-headed households in Los Angeles, from a low of 13 percent in 1844 to 31 percent in 1880. Camarillo (1979, p. 120) documents a similar increase in Santa Barbara from 15 percent in 1844 to 30 percent by 1880. These increases appear to be due not so much to divorce, which was infrequent in this Catholic population, but to widowhood and temporary abandonment in search of work. Given the hazardous nature of work in the mines and railroad camps, the death of a husband, father or son who was laboring in these sites was not uncommon. Griswold del Castillo (1979) reports a higher death rate among men than women in Los Angeles. The rise in female-headed households, therefore, reflects the instabilities and insecurities introduced into women's lives as a result of the changing social organization of work.

One outcome, the increasing participation of women and children in the labor force was primarily a response to economic factors that required the modification of traditional values. According to Louisa Vigil, who was born in 1890:

> The women didn't work at that time. The man was supposed to marry that girl and take [care] of her . . . Your grandpa never did let me work for nobody. He always had to work, and we never did have really bad times (Elasser 1980, p. 14).

Señora Vigil's comments are reinforced in Garcia's (1980) study of El Paso. In the 393 households he examined in the 1900 census, he found 17.1 percent of the women to be employed. The majority of this group were daughters, mothers with no husbands, and single women. In the cases of Los Angeles and Santa Barbara, where there were even greater work opportunities for women than in El Paso, wives who were heads of household worked in seasonal and part-time jobs and lived from the earnings of children and relatives in an effort to maintain traditional female roles.

Slowly, entire families were encouraged to go to railroad workcamps and were eventually incorporated into the agricultural labor market. This was a response both to the extremely low wages paid to Chicano laborers and to the preferences of employers who saw family labor as a way of stabilizing the workforce. For Chicanos, engaging all family members in agricultural work was a means of increasing their earnings to a level close to subsistence for the entire group and of keeping the family unit together. Camarillo (1979, p. 93) provides a picture of the interplay of work, family, and migration in the Santa Barbara area in the following observation:

The time of year when women and children were employed in the fruit cannery and participated in the almond and olive harvests coincided with the seasons when the men were most likely to be engaged in seasonal migratory work. There were seasons, however, especially in the early summer when the entire family migrated from the city to pick fruit. This type of family seasonal harvest was evident in Santa Barbara by the 1890s. As walnuts replaced almonds and as the fruit industry expanded, Chicano family labor became essential.

This arrangement, while bringing families together, did not decrease the hardships that Chicanas had to confront in raising their families. We may infer something about the rigors of that life from Jesse Lopez de la Cruz's description of the workday of migrant farm laborers in the 1940s. Work conditions in the 1890s were as difficult, if not worse.

We always went where the women and men were going to work, because if it were just the men working it wasn't worth going out there because we wouldn't earn enough to support a family . . . We would start around 6:30 A.M. and work for four or five hours, then walk home and eat and rest until about three-thirty in the afternoon when it cooled off. We would go back and work until we couldn't see. Then I'd clean up the kitchen. I was doing the housework and working out in the fields and taking care of two children (quoted in Goldman 1981, pp. 119–120).

In the towns, women's reproductive labor was intensified by the congested and unsanitary conditions of the *barrios* in which they lived. Garcia (1980) described the following conditions in El Paso:

Mexican women had to haul water for washing and cooking from the river or public water pipes. To feed their families, they had to spend time marketing, often in Ciudad Juarez across the border, as well as long, hot hours cooking meals and coping with the burden of desert sand both inside and outside their homes. Besides the problem of raising children, unsanitary living conditions forced Mexican mothers to deal with disease and illness in their families. Diphtheria, tuberculosis, typhus and influenza were never too far away. Some diseases could be directly traced to inferior city services . . . As a result, Mexican mothers had to devote much energy to caring for sick children, many of whom died (pp. 320–321).

While the extended family has remained an important element of Chicano life, it was eroded in the American period in several ways. Griswold del Castillo (1979), for example, points out that in 1845 about 71 percent of Angelenos lived in extended families and that by 1880, fewer than half did. This decrease in extended families appears to be a response to the changed economic conditions and to the instabilities generated by the new sociopolitical structure. Additionally, the imposition of American law and custom ignored and ultimately undermined some aspects of the extended family. The extended family in traditional Mexican life consisted of an important set of familial, religious, and community obligations. Women, while valued primarily for their domesticity, had certain legal and property rights that acknowledged the importance of their work, their families of origin and their children. In California, for example:

> Equal ownership of property between husband and wife had been one of the mainstays of the Spanish and Mexican family systems. Community-property laws were written into the civil codes with the intention of strengthening the economic controls of the wife and her relatives. The American government incorporated these Mexican laws into the state constitution, but later court decisions interpreted these statutes so as to undermine the wife's economic rights. In 1861, the legislature passed a law that allowed the deceased wife's property to revert to her husband. Previously it had been inherited by her children and relatives if she died without a will (Griswold del Castillo 1979, p. 69).

The impact of this and other similar court rulings was to "strengthen the property rights of the husband at the expense of his wife and children" (Griswold del Castillo 1979, p. 69).

In the face of the legal, social, and economic changes that occurred during the American period, Chicanas were forced to cope with a series of dislocations in traditional life. They were caught between conflicting pressures to maintain traditional women's roles and family customs and the need to participate in the economic support of their families by working outside the home. During this period the preservation of some traditional customs became an important force for resisting complete disarray.

According to Saragoza (1983), transiency, the effects of racism and segregation, and proximity to Mexico aided in the maintenance of traditional family practices. Garcia has suggested that women were the guardians of Mexican cultural traditions within the family. He cites the work of anthropologist Manuel Gamio, who identified the retention of many Mexican customs among Chicanos in settlements around the United States in the early 1900s.

> These included folklore, songs and ballads, birthday celebrations, saints' day, baptism, weddings, and funerals in the traditional style. Because of poverty, a lack of physicians in the barrios, and adherence to traditional customs, Mexicans continued to use medicinal herbs. Gamio also identified the maintenance of a number of oral traditions, and Mexican style cooking (Garcia 1980, p. 322).

Of vital importance to the integrity of traditional culture was the perpetuation of the Spanish language. Factors that aided in the maintenance of
other aspects of Mexican culture also helped in sustaining the language.
However, entry into English-language public schools introduced the children
and their families to systematic efforts to erase their native tongue. Griswold
del Castillo reports that in the early 1880s there was considerable pressure
against the speaker of Spanish in the public school. He also found that some
Chicano parents responded to this kind of discrimination by helping support
independent bilingual schools. These efforts, however, were short-lived.

Another key factor in conserving Chicano culture was the extended family network, particularly the system of *compadrazgo* or godparenting. Although the full extent of the impact of the American period on the Chicano
extended family is not known, it is generally acknowledged that this family
system, though lacking many legal and social sanctions, played an important
role in the preservation of the Mexican community (Camarillo 1979, p. 13). In
Mexican society, godparents were an important way of linking family and
community through respected friends or authorities. Named at the important
rites of passage in a child's life, such as birth, confirmation, first communion,
and marriage, *compadrazgo* created a moral obligation for godparents to act as
guardians, to provide financial assistance in times of need, and to substitute
in case of the death of a parent. Camarillo (1979) points out that in traditional
society these bonds cut across class and racial lines.

> The rites of baptism established kinship networks between rich and
> poor—between Spanish, mestizo and Indian—and often carried
> with them political loyalty and economic-occupational ties. The
> leading California patriarchs in the pueblo played important roles
> in the compadrazgo network. They sponsored dozens of children
> for their workers or poor relatives. The kindness of the *padrino* and
> *madrina* was repaid with respect and support from the *pobladores*
> (pp. 12–13).

The extended family network—which included godparents—expanded
the support groups for women who were widowed or temporarily abandoned and for those who were in seasonal, part-, or full-time work. It suggests, therefore, the potential for an exchange of services among poor people
whose income did not provide the basis for family subsistence. Griswold del
Castillo (1980) argues that family organization influenced literacy rates and
socioeconomic mobility among Chicanos in Los Angeles between 1850 and
1880. His data suggest that children in extended families (defined as those
with at least one relative living in a nuclear family household) had higher literacy rates than those in nuclear families. He also argues that those in larger
families fared better economically, and experienced less downward mobility.
The data here are too limited to generalize to the Chicano experience as a
whole but they do reinforce the actual and potential importance of this family form to the continued cultural autonomy of the Chicano community.

CONCLUSION: OUR MOTHERS' GRIEF

Reproductive labor for Afro-American, Chinese-American, and Mexican-American women in the nineteenth century centered on the struggle to maintain family units in the face of a variety of cultural assaults. Treated primarily as individual units of labor rather than as members of family groups, these women labored to maintain, sustain, stabilize, and reproduce their families while working in both the public (productive) and private (reproductive) spheres. Thus, the concept of reproductive labor, when applied to women of color, must be modified to account for the fact that labor in the productive sphere was required to achieve even minimal levels of family subsistence. Long after industrialization had begun to reshape family roles among middle-class white families, driving white women into a cult of domesticity, women of color were coping with an extended day. This day included subsistence labor outside the family and domestic labor within the family. For slaves, domestics, migrant farm laborers, seasonal factory-workers, and prostitutes, the distinctions between labor that reproduced family life and which economically sustained it were minimized. The expanded workday was one of the primary ways in which reproductive labor increased.

Racial-ethnic families were sustained and maintained in the face of various forms of disruption. Yet racial-ethnic women and their families paid a high price in the process. High rates of infant morality, a shortened life span, the early onset of crippling and debilitating disease provided some insight into the costs of survival.

The poor quality of housing and the neglect of communities further increased reproductive labor. Not only did racial-ethnic women work hard outside the home for a mere subsistence, they worked very hard inside the home to achieve even minimal standards of privacy and cleanliness. They were continually faced with disease and illness that directly resulted from the absence of basic sanitation. The fact that some African women murdered their children to prevent them from becoming slaves is an indication of the emotional strain associated with bearing and raising children while participating in the colonial labor system.

We have uncovered little information about the use of birth control, the prevalence of infanticide, or the motivations that may have generated these or other behaviors. We can surmise, however, that no matter how much children were accepted, loved, or valued among any of these groups of people, their futures in a colonial labor system were a source of grief for their mothers. For those children who were born, the task of keeping them alive, of helping them to understand and participate in a system that exploited them, and the challenge of maintaining a measure—no matter how small—of cultural integrity, intensified reproductive labor.

Being a racial-ethnic woman in nineteenth-century American society meant having extra work both inside and outside the home. It meant having a contradictory relationship to the norms and values about women that were being generated in the dominant white culture. As pointed out earlier, the notion of separate spheres of male and female labor had contradictory outcomes for the nineteenth-century whites. It was the basis for the confinement of women to the household and for much of the protective legislation that subsequently developed. At the same time, it sustained white families by providing social acknowledgment and support to women in the performance of their family roles. For racial-ethnic women, however, the notion of separate spheres served to reinforce their subordinate status and became, in effect, another assault. As they increased their work outside the home, they were forced into a productive labor sphere that was organized for men and "desperate" women who were so unfortunate or immoral that they could not confine their work to the domestic sphere. In the productive sphere, racial-ethnic women faced exploitative jobs and depressed wages. In the reproductive sphere, however, they were denied the opportunity to embrace the dominant ideological definition of "good" wife or mother. In essence, they were faced with a double-bind situation, one that required their participation in the labor force to sustain family life but damned them as women, wives, and mothers because they did not confine their labor to the home. Thus, the conflict between ideology and reality in the lives of racial-ethnic women during the nineteenth century sets the stage for stereotypes, issues of self-esteem, and conflicts around gender-role prescriptions that surface more fully in the twentieth century. Further, the tensions and conflicts that characterized their lives during this period provided the impulse for community activism to jointly address the inequities, which they and their children and families faced.

ACKNOWLEDGMENTS

The research in this study is the result of the author's participation in a larger collaborative project examining family, community, and work lives of racial-ethnic women in the United States. The author is deeply indebted to the scholarship and creativity of members of the group in the development of this study. Appreciation is extended to Elizabeth Higginbotham, Cheryl Townsend Gilkes, Evelyn Nakano Glenn, and Ruth Zambrana (members of the original working group), and to the Ford Foundation for a grant that supported in part the work of this study.

NOTES

1. The term *reproductive labor* is used to refer to all of the work of women in the home. This includes but is not limited to: the buying and preparation of food and clothing, provision of emotional support and nurturance for all family members, bearing children, and planning, organizing, and carrying out a wide variety of tasks associated with their socialization. All of these activities are necessary for the growth of patriarchal capitalism because they maintain, sustain, stabilize, and *reproduce* (both biologically and socially) the labor force.

2. The term *white* is a global construct used to characterize peoples of European descent who migrated to and helped colonize America. In the seventeenth century, most of these immigrants were from the British Isles. However, during the time period covered by this article, European immigrants became increasingly diverse. It is a limitation of this article that time and space does not permit a fuller discussion of the variations in the white European immigrant experience. For the purposes of the argument made herein and of the contrast it seeks to draw between the experiences of mainstream (European) cultural groups and that of racial/ethnic minorities, the differences among European settlers are joined and the broad similarities emphasized.

3. Cultural assaults, according to Caulfield (1974), are benign and systematic attacks on the institutions and forms of social organization that are fundamental to the maintenance and flourishing of a group's culture.

4. Recent research suggests that there were some tasks that were primarily assigned to males and some others to females. Whereas some gender-role distinctions with regard to work may have existed on some plantations, it is clear that slave women were not exempt from strenuous physical labor.

5. This term is used to refer to white Americans of European ancestry.

REFERENCES

Aschenbrenner, Joyce. 1975. *Lifelines: Black Families in Chicago.* New York, NY: Holt, Rinehart, and Winston.

Barrera, Mario. 1979. *Race and Class in the Southwest.* South Bend, IN: Notre Dame University Press.

Blassingame, John. 1972. *The Slave Community: Plantation Life in the Antebellum South.* New York: Oxford University Press.

———. 1977. *Slave Testimony: Two Centuries of Letters, Speeches, Interviews, and Autobiographies.* Baton Rouge, LA: Louisiana State University Press.

Camarillo, Albert. 1979. *Chicanos in a Changing Society.* Cambridge, MA: Harvard University Press.

Caulfield, Mina Davis. 1974. "Imperialism, the Family, and Cultures of Resistance." *Socialist Review* 4(2)(October): 67–85.

Davis, Angela. 1971. "The Black Woman's Role in the Community of Slaves." *Black Scholar* 3(4)(December): 2–15.

———. 1981. *Women, Race and Class.* New York: Random House.

Degler, Carl. 1980. *At Odds.* New York: Oxford University Press.

Elasser, Nan Kyle MacKenzie, and Yvonne Tixier Y. Vigil. 1980. *Las Mujeres.* New York: The Feminist Press.

Garcia, Mario T. 1980. "The Chicano in American History: The Mexican Women of El Paso, 1880–1920—A Case Study." *Pacific Historical Review* 49(2)(May): 315–358.

Genovese, Eugene D., and Elinor Miller, eds. 1974. *Plantation, Town, and County: Essays on the Local History of American Slave Society.* Urbana: University of Illinois Press.

Glenn, Evelyn Nakano. 1981. "Family Strategies of Chinese-Americans: An Institutional Analysis." Paper presented at the Society for the Study of Social Problems Annual Meetings.

Goldman, Marion S. 1981. *Gold Diggers and Silver Miners.* Ann Arbor: The University of Michigan Press.

Griswold del Castillo, Richard. 1979. *The Los Angeles Barrio: 1850–1890.* Los Angeles: The University of California Press.

Gutman, Herbert. 1976. *The Black Family in Slavery and Freedom: 1750–1925.* New York: Pantheon.

Hirata, Lucie Cheng. 1979. "Free, Indentured, Enslaved: Chinese Prostitutes in Nineteenth-Century America." *Signs* 5 (Autumn): 3–29.

Jones, Jacqueline. 1985. *Labor of Love, Labor of Sorrow.* New York: Basic Books.

Kennedy, Susan Estabrook. 1979. *If All We Did Was to Weep at Home: A History of White Working-Class Women in America.* Bloomington: Indiana University Press.

Kessler-Harris, Alice. 1981. *Women Have Always Worked.* Old Westbury: The Feminist Press.

———. 1982. *Out to Work.* New York: Oxford University Press.

Kingston, Maxine Hong. 1977. *The Woman Warrior.* Vintage Books.

Matthaei, Julie. 1982. *An Economic History of Women in America.* New York: Schocken Books.

Nee, Victor G., and Brett de Bary Nee. 1973. *Longtime Californ'.* New York: Pantheon Books.

Saragoza, Alex M. 1983. "The Conceptualization of the History of the Chicano Family: Work, Family, and Migration in Chicanos." Research Proceedings of the Symposium on Chicano Research and Public Policy. Stanford, CA: Stanford University, Center for Chicano Research.

Shimkin, Demetri, E. M. Shimkin, and D. A. Frate, eds. 1978. *The Extended Family in Black Societies.* The Hague: Mouton.

Spruill, Julia Cherry. 1972. *Women's Life and Work in the Southern Colonies.* New York: W. W. Norton and Company (first published in 1938, University of North Carolina Press).

Stack, Carol S. 1974. *All Our Kin: Strategies for Survival in a Black Community.* New York: Harper and Row.

Sudarkasa, Niara. 1981. "Interpreting the African Heritage in Afro-American Family Organization." Pp. 37–53 in *Black Families,* edited by Harriette Pipes McAdoo. Beverly Hills, CA: Sage Publications.

White, Deborah Gray. 1985. *Ar'n't I a Woman?: Female Slaves in the Plantation South.* New York: W. W. Norton.

Wright, Gwendolyn. 1981. *Building the Dream: A Social History of Housing in America.* New York: Pantheon Books.

Zaretsky, Eli. 1978. "The Effects of the Economic Crisis on the Family." Pp. 209–218 in *U.S. Capitalism in Crisis,* edited by Crisis Reader Editorial Collective. New York: Union of Radical Political Economists.

18

FAMILIES ON THE FAULT LINE
America's Working Class Speaks about the Family,
the Economy, Race, and Ethnicity

LILLIAN B. RUBIN

Not surprisingly, there are generational differences in what fuels the conflict around the division of labor in families. For the older couples—those who grew up in a different time, whose marriages started with another set of ground rules—the struggle is not simply around how much men do or about whether they take responsibility for the daily tasks of living without being pushed, prodded, and reminded. That's the overt manifestation of the discord, the trigger that starts the fight. But the noise of the explosion when it comes serves to conceal the more fundamental issue underlying the dissension: legitimacy. What does she have a *right* to expect? "What do I know about doing stuff around the house?" asks Frank Moreno, a forty-eight-year-old foreman in a warehouse. "I wasn't brought up like that. My pop, he never did one damn thing, and my mother never complained. It was her job; she did it and kept quiet. Besides, I work my ass off every day. Isn't that enough?"

For younger couples, those under forty, the problem is somewhat different. The men may complain about the expectation that they'll participate more fully in the care and feeding of the family, but talk to them about it quietly and they'll usually admit that it's not really unfair, given that their wives also work outside the home. In these homes, the issue between husband and wife isn't only who does what. That's there and it's a source of more or less conflict, depending upon what the men actually do and how forceful their wives are in their demands. But in most of these families there's at least a verbal consensus that men *ought* to participate in the tasks of daily life. Which raises the next and perhaps more difficult issue in contest between them: Who feels responsible for getting the tasks done? Who regards them as a duty, and for whom are they an option? On this, tradition rules.

Even in families where husbands now share many of the tasks, their wives still bear full responsibility for the organization of family life. A man may help cook the meal these days, but a woman is most likely to be the one

From *Families on the Fault Line: America's Working Class Speaks about the Family, the Economy, Race, and Ethnicity*. New York: Harper Collins. 1994, pp. 89–102. © 1994 by Lillian B. Rubin. With permission from the Rhoda Weyr Agency, New York.

who has planned it. He may take the children to child care, but she virtually always has had to arrange it. It's she also who is accountable for the emotional life of the family, for monitoring the emotional temperature of its members and making the necessary corrections. It's this need to be responsible for it all that often feels as burdensome as the tasks themselves. "It's not just doing all the stuff that needs doing," explains Maria Jankowicz, a white twenty-eight-year-old assembler in an electronics factory. "It's worrying all the time about everything and always having to arrange everything, you know what I mean. It's like I run the whole show. If I don't stay on top of it all, things fall apart because nobody else is going to do it. The kids can't and Nick, well, forget it," she concludes angrily.

If, regardless of age, life stage, or verbal consensus, women usually still carry the greatest share of the household burdens, why is it important to notice that younger men grant legitimacy to their wives' demands and older men generally do not? Because men who believe their wives have a right to expect their participation tend to suffer guilt and discomfort when they don't live up to those expectations. And no one lives comfortably with guilt.

It's possible, of course, that the men who speak of guilt and rights are only trying to impress me by mouthing the politically correct words. But even if true, they display a sensitivity to the issue that's missing from the men who don't speak those words. For words are more than just words. They embody ideas; they are the symbols that give meaning to our thoughts; they shape our consciousness. New ideas come to us on the wings of words. It's words that bring those ideas to life, that allow us to see possibilities unrecognized before we gave them words. Indeed, without words, there is no conscious thought, no possibility for the kind of self-reflection that lights the path of change.[1]

True, there's often a long way between word and deed. But the man who feels guilty when he disappoints his wife's expectations has a different consciousness than the one who doesn't—a difference that usually makes for at least some small change in his behavior. Although the emergence of this changing male consciousness is visible in all the racial groups in this study, there also are differences among them that are worthy of comment.

Virtually all the men do some work inside the family—tending the children, washing dishes, running the vacuum, going to the market. And they generally also remain responsible for those tasks that have always been traditionally male—mowing the lawn, shoveling the snow, fixing the car, cleaning the garage, doing repairs around the house. Among the white families in this study, 16 percent of the men share the family work relatively equally, almost always those who live in families where they and their wives work different shifts or where the men are unemployed. "What choice do I have?" asks Don Bartlett, a thirty-year-old white handyman who works days while his wife is on the swing shift. "I'm the only one here, so I do what's got to be done."

Asian and Latino men of all ages, however, tend to operate more often on the old male model, even when they work different shifts or are unemployed, a finding that puzzled me at first. Why, I wondered, did I find only two Asian men and one Latino who are real partners in the work of the family? Aren't these men subject to the same social and personal pressures others experience?

The answer is both yes and no. The pressures are there but, depending upon where they live, there's more or less support for resisting them. The Latino and Asian men who live in ethnic neighborhoods—settings where they are embedded in an intergenerational community and where the language and culture of the home country is kept alive by a steady stream of new immigrants—find strong support for clinging to the old ways. Therefore, change comes much more slowly in those families. The men who live outside the ethnic quarter are freer from the mandates and constraints of these often tight-knit communities, therefore are more responsive to the winds of change in the larger society.

These distinctions notwithstanding, it's clear that Asian and Latino men generally participate least in the work of the household and are the least likely to believe they have much responsibility there beyond bringing home a paycheck. "Taking care of the house and kids is my wife's job, that's all," says Joe Gomez flatly.

"A Chinese man mopping a floor? I've never seen it yet," says Amy Lee angrily. Her husband, Dennis, trying to make a joke of the conflict with his wife, says with a smile, "In Chinese families men don't do floors and windows. I help with the dishes sometimes if she needs me to or," he laughs, "if she screams loud enough. The rest, well, it's pretty much her job."

The commonly held stereotype about black men abandoning women and children, however, doesn't square with the families in this study. In fact, black men are the most likely to be real participants in the daily life of the family and are more intimately involved in raising their children than any of the others. True, the men's family workload doesn't always match their wives', and the women are articulate in their complaints about this. Nevertheless, compared to their white, Asian, or Latino counterparts, the black families look like models of egalitarianism.

Nearly three-quarters of the men in the African-American families in this study do a substantial amount of the cooking, cleaning, and child care, sometimes even more than their wives. All explain it by saying one version or another of: "I just figure it's my job, too." Which simply says what is, without explaining how it came to be that way.

To understand that, we have to look at family histories that tell the story of generations of African-American women who could find work and men who could not, and to the family culture that grew from this difficult and painful reality. "My mother worked six days a week cleaning other people's houses, and my father was an ordinary laborer, when he could find work, which wasn't very often," explains thirty-two-year-old Troy Payne, a black waiter and father of two children. "So he was home a lot more than she was, and he'd do what he had to around the house. The kids all had to do their share, too. It seemed only fair, I guess."

Difficult as the conflict around the division of labor is, it's only one of the many issues that have become flash points in family life since mother went to work. Most important, perhaps, is the question: Who will care for the children? For the lack of decent, affordable facilities for the care of the children creates unbearable problems and tensions for these working-class families.

It's hardly news that child care is an enormous headache and expense for all two-job families. In many professional middle-class families, where the child-care bill can be $1,500–2,000 a month, it competes with the mortgage payment as the biggest single monthly expenditure. Problematic as this may be, however, these families are the lucky ones when compared to working-class families, many of whom don't earn much more than the cost of child care in these upper middle-class families. Even the families in this study at the highest end of the earnings scale, those who earn $42,000 a year, can't dream of such costly arrangements.

For most working-class families, therefore, child care often is patched together in ways that leave parents anxious and children in jeopardy. "Care for the little ones, that's a real big problem," says Beverly Waldov, a thirty-year-old white mother of three children, the youngest two, products of a second marriage, under three years old. "My oldest girl is nine, so she's not such a problem. I hate the idea of her being a latchkey kid, but what can I do? We don't even have the money to put the little ones in one of those good day-care places, so I don't have any choice with her. She's just *got* to be able to take care of herself after school," she says, her words a contest between anxiety and hope.

"We have a kind of complicated arrangement for the little kids. Two days a week, my mom takes care of them. We pay her, but at least I don't have to worry when they're with her; I know it's fine. But she works the rest of the time, so the other days we take them to this woman's house. It's the best we can afford, but it's not great because she keeps too many kids, and I know they don't get good attention. Especially the little one; she's just a baby, you know." She pauses and looks away, anguished. "She's so clingy when I bring her home; she can't let go of me, like nobody's paid her any mind all day. But it's not like I have a choice. We barely make it now; if I stop working, we'd be in real trouble."

Even such makeshift solutions don't work for many families. Some speak of being unable to afford day care at all. "We couldn't pay our bills if we had to pay for somebody to take care of the kids."

Some say they're unwilling to leave the children in the care of strangers. "I just don't believe someone else should be raising our kids, that's all."

Some have tried a variety of child-care arrangements, only to have them fail in a moment of need. "We tried a whole bunch of things, and maybe they work for a little while," says Faye Ensey, a black twenty-eight-year-old office worker. "But what happens when your kid gets sick? Or when the baby sitter's kids get sick? I lost two jobs in a row because my kids kept getting sick and I couldn't go to work. Or else I couldn't take my little one to the baby sitter because her kids were sick. They finally fired me for absenteeism. I didn't really blame them, but it felt terrible anyway. It's such a hassle, I sometimes think I'd be glad to just stay home. But we can't afford for me not to work, so we had to figure out something else."

For such families, that "something else" is the decision to take jobs on different shifts—a decision made by one-fifth of the families in this study. With one working days and the other on swing or graveyard, one parent is home with the children at all times. "We were getting along okay before Daryl junior was born, because Shona, my daughter, was getting on. You know, she didn't need somebody with her all the time, so we could both work days," explains Daryl Adams, a black thirty-year-old postal clerk with a ten-year-old daughter and a nine-month-old son. "I used to work the early shift—seven to three—so I'd get home a little bit after she got here. It worked out okay. But then this here big surprise came along." He stops, smiles down fondly at his young son and runs his hand over his nearly bald head.

"Now between the two of us working, we don't make enough money to pay for child care and have anything left over, so this is the only way we can manage. Besides, both of us, Alesha and me, we think it's better for one of us to be here, not just for the baby, for my daughter, too. She's growing up and, you know, I think maybe they need even more watching than when they were younger. She's coming to the time when she could get into all kinds of trouble if we're not here to put the brakes on."

But the cost such arrangements exact on marriage can be very high. When I asked these husbands and wives when they have time to talk, more often than not I got a look of annoyance at a question that, on its face, seemed stupid to them. "Talk? How can we talk when we hardly see each other?" "Talk? What's that?" "Talk? Ha, that's a joke."

Mostly, conversation is limited to the logistics that take place at shift-changing time when children and chores are handed off from one to the other. With children dancing around underfoot, the incoming parent gets a quick summary of the day's or night's events, a list of reminders about things to be done, perhaps about what's cooking in the pot on the stove. "Sometimes when I'm coming home and it's been a hard day, I think: Wouldn't it be wonderful if I could just sit down with Leon for half an hour and we could have a quiet beer together?" thirty-one-year-old Emma Guerrero, a Latina baker, says wistfully.

But it's not to be. If the arriving spouse gets home early enough, there may be an hour when both are there together. But with the pressures of the workday fresh for one and awaiting the other, and with children clamoring for parental attention, this isn't a promising moment for any serious conversation.

Some of the luckier couples work different shifts on the same days, so they're home together on weekends. But even in these families there's so little time for normal family life that there's hardly any room for anyone or anything outside.

For those whose days off don't match, the problems of sustaining both the couple relationship and family life are magnified enormously. "The last two years have been hell for us," says thirty-five-year-old Tina Mulvaney, a white mother of two teenagers. "My son got into bad company and had some trouble, so Mike and I decided one of us had to be home. But we can't make it without my check, so I can't quit.

"Mike drives a cab and I work in a hospital, so we figured one of us could transfer to nights. We talked it over and decided it would be best if I was here during the day and he was here at night. He controls the kids, especially my son, better than I do. When he lays down the law, they listen." She interrupts her narrative to reflect on the difficulty of raising children. "You know, when they were little, I used to think about how much easier it would be when they got older. But now I see it's not true; that's when you really have to begin to worry about them. This is when they need someone to be here all the time to make sure they stay out of trouble."

She stops again, this time fighting tears, then takes up where she left off. "So now Mike works days and I work graveyard. I hate it, but it's the only answer; at least this way somebody's here all the time. I get home about 8:30 in the morning. The kids and Mike are gone. It's the best time of the day because it's the only time I have a little quiet here. I clean up the house a little, do the shopping and the laundry and whatever, then I go to sleep for a couple of hours until the kids come home from school.

"Mike gets home at five; we eat; then he takes over for the night, and I go back to sleep for another couple of hours. I try to get up by 9 so we can all have a little time together, but I'm so tired that I don't make it a lot of times. And by 10, he's sleeping because he has to be up by 6 in the morning. So if I don't get up, we hardly see each other at all. Mike's here on weekends, but I'm not. Right now I have Tuesday and Wednesday off. I keep hoping for a Monday–Friday shift, but it's what everybody wants, and I don't have the seniority yet. It's hard, very hard; there's no time to live or anything," she concludes with a listless sigh.

Even in families where wife and husband work the same shift, there's less time for leisure pursuits and social activities than ever before, not just because both parents work full-time but also because people work longer hours now than they did twenty years ago.[2] Two decades ago, weekends saw occasional family outings, Friday evening bowling, a Saturday trip to the shopping mall, a Sunday with extended family, once in a while an evening out without the children. In summer, when the children weren't in school, a week night might find the family paying a short visit to a friend, a relative, or a neighbor. Now almost everyone I speak with complains that it's hard to find time for even these occasional outings. Instead, most off-work hours are spent trying to catch up with the dozens of family and household tasks that were left undone during the regular work week. When they aren't doing chores, parents guiltily try to do in two days a week what usually takes seven—that is, to establish a sense of family life for themselves and their children.

"Leisure," snorts Peter Pittman, a twenty-eight-year-old African-American father of two, married six years. "With both of us working like we do, there's no time for anything. We got two little kids; I commute better than an hour each way to my job. Then we live here for half rent because I take care of the place for the landlord. So if somebody's got a complaint, I've got to take care of it, you know, fix it myself or get the landlord to get somebody out to do it if I can't. Most things I can do myself, but it takes time. I sometimes wonder what this life's all about, because this sure ain't what I call living. We don't go anyplace; we don't do anything; Christ, we hardly have time to go to the toilet. There's always some damn thing that's waiting that you've got to do."

Clearly, such complaints aren't unique to the working class. The pressures of time, the impoverishment of social life, the anxieties about child care, the fear that children will live in a world of increasing scarcity, the threat of divorce—all these are part of family life today, regardless of class. Nevertheless, there are important differences between those in the higher reaches of the class structure and the families of the working class. The simple fact that middle-class families have more discretionary income is enough to make a big difference in the quality of their social life. For they generally have enough money to pay for a babysitter once in a while so that parents can have some time to themselves; enough, too, for a family vacation, for tickets to a concert, a play, or a movie. At $7.50 a ticket in a New York or San Francisco movie house, a working-class couple will settle for a $3.00 rental that the whole family can watch together.

Finding time and energy for sex is also a problem, one that's obviously an issue for two-job families of any class. But it's harder to resolve in working-class families because they have so few resources with which to buy some time and privacy for themselves. Ask about their sex lives and you'll be met with an angry, "What's that?" or a wistful, "I wish." When it happens, it is, as one woman put it, "on the run"—a situation that's particularly unsatisfactory for most women. For them, the pleasure of sex is related to the whole of the interaction—to a sense of intimacy and connection, to at least a few relaxed, loving moments. When they can't have these, they're likely to avoid sex altogether—a situation the men find equally unsatisfactory.

"Sex?" asks Lisa Scranton, a white twenty-nine-year-old mother of three who feigns a puzzled frown, as if she doesn't quite know the meaning of the word. "Oh yeah, that; I remember now," she says, her lips smiling, her eyes sad. "At the beginning, when we first got together, it was WOW, real hot, great. But after a while it cools down, doesn't it? Right now, it's down the toilet. I wonder, does it happen to everybody like that?" she asks dejectedly.

"I guess the worst is when you work different shifts like we do and you get to see each other maybe six minutes a day. There's no time for sex. Sometimes we try to steal a few minutes for ourselves but, I don't know, I can't get into it that way. He can. You know how men are; they can do it any time. Give them two minutes, and they can get off. But it takes me time; I mean, I like to feel close, and you can't do that in three minutes. And there's the kids; they're right here all the time. I don't want to do it if it means being interrupted. Then he gets mad, so sometimes I do. But it's a problem, a real problem."

The men aren't content with these quick sexual exchanges either. But for them it's generally better than no sex at all, while for the women it's often the other way around. "You want to talk about sex, huh?" asks Lisa's husband, Chuck, his voice crackling with anger. "Yeah, I don't mind; it's fine, only I got nothing to talk about. Far as I'm concerned, that's one of the things I found out about marriage. You get married, you give up sex. We hardly ever do it anymore, and when we do, it's like she's doing me a favor."

"Christ, I know the way we've got to do things now isn't great," he protests, running a hand through his hair agitatedly. "We don't see each other but a few minutes a day, but I don't see why we can't take five and have a little fun in the sack. Sure, I like it better when we've got more time, too. But for her, if it can't be perfect, she gets all wound and uptight and it's like . . ." He stops, groping for words, then explodes, "It's like screwing a cold fish."

She isn't just a "cold fish," however. The problems they face are deeper than that. For once such conflicts arise, spontaneity takes flight and sex becomes a problem that needs attention rather than a time out for pleasure and renewal. Between times, therefore, he's busy calculating how much time has passed: "It's been over two weeks"; nursing his wounds: "I don't want to have to beg her"; feeling deprived and angry: "I don't know why I got married." When they finally do come together, he's disappointed. How could it be otherwise, given the mix of feelings he brings to the bed with him—the frustration and anger, the humiliation of feeling he has to beg her, the wounded sense of manhood.

Meanwhile, she, too, is preoccupied with sex, not with thoughts of pleasure but with figuring out how much time she has before, as she puts it, "he walks around with his mouth stuck out. I know I'm in real big trouble if we don't do it once a week. So I make sure we do, even if I don't want to." She doesn't say those words to him, of course. But he knows. And it's precisely this, the knowledge that she's servicing him rather than desiring him that's so hard for him to take.

The sexual arena is one of the most common places to find a "his and her" marriage—one marriage, two different sex lives.[3] Each partner has a different story to tell; each is convinced that his or her version is the real one. A husband says mournfully, "I'm lucky if we get to make love once a week." His wife reports with irritation, "It's two, sometimes three times a week." It's impossible to know whose account is closest to the reality. And it's irrelevant. If that's what they were after, they could keep tabs and get it straight. But facts and feelings are often at war in family life. And nowhere does right or wrong, true or false count for less than in their sexual interactions. It isn't that people arbitrarily distort the truth. They simply report their experience, and it's feeling, not fact, that dominates that experience; feeling, not fact, that is their truth.

But it's also true that, especially for women, the difference in frequency of sexual desire can be a response—sometimes conscious, sometimes not— to other conflicts in the marriage. It isn't that men never withhold sex as a weapon in the family wars, only that they're much more likely than women to be able to split sex from emotion, to feel their anger and still experience sexual desire. For a man, too, a sexual connection with his wife can relieve the pressures and tensions of the day, can make him feel whole again, even if they've barely spoken a word to each other.

For a woman it's different. What happens—or, more likely, what doesn't happen—in the kitchen, the living room, and the laundry room profoundly affects what's possible in the bedroom. When she feels distant, unconnected, angry; when her pressured life leaves her feeling fragmented; when she hasn't had a real conversation with her husband for a couple of days, sex is very far from either her mind or her loins. "I run around busy all the time, and he just sits there, so by the time we go to bed, I'm too tired," explains Linda Bloodworth, a white thirty-one-year-old telephone operator.

"Do you think your lack of sexual response has something to do with your anger at your husband's refusal to participate more fully in the household?" I ask.

Her eyes smoldering, her voice tight, she snaps, "No, I'm just tired, that's all." Then noticing something in my response, she adds, "I know what you're thinking; I saw that look. But really, I don't think it's *because* I'm angry; I really am tired. I have to admit, though, that I tell him if he helped more, maybe I wouldn't be so tired all the time. And," she adds defiantly, "maybe I wouldn't be."

Some couples, of course, manage their sexual relationship with greater ease. Often that's because they have less conflict in other areas of living. But whether they accommodate well or poorly, for all two-job families, sex requires a level of attention and concern that leaves most people wanting much of the time. "It's a problem, and I tell you, it has to be well planned," explains thirty-four-year-old Dan Stolman, a black construction worker. "But we manage okay; we make dates or try to slip it in when the baby's asleep and my daughter's out with a friend or something. I don't mean things are great in that department. I'm not always satisfied and neither is Lorraine. But what can you do? We try to do the best we can. Sex isn't all there is to a marriage, you know. We get along really well, so that makes up for a lot.

"What I really miss is that we don't ever make love anymore. I mean, we have sex like I said, but we don't have the kind of time you need to make love. We talk about getting away for an overnight by ourselves once in a while. Lorraine's mother would come watch the kids if we asked her; the problem is we don't have any extra cash to spare right now."

Time and money—precious commodities in short supply. These are the twin plagues of family life, the missing ingredients that combine to create families that are both frantic and fragile. Yet there's no mystery about what would alleviate the crisis that now threatens to engulf them: A job that pays a living wage, quality child-care facilities at rates people can pay, health care for all, parental leave, flexible work schedules, decent and affordable housing, a shorter work week so that parents and children have time to spend together, tax breaks for those in need rather than for those in greed, to mention just a few. These are the policies we need to put in place if we're to have any hope of making our families stable and healthy.

What we have, instead, are families in which mother goes to work to relieve financial distress, only to find that time takes its place next to money as a source of strain, tension, and conflict. Time for the children, time for the couple's relationship, time for self, time for social life—none of it easily available for anyone in two-job families, not even for the children, who are hurried along at every step of the way.[4] And money! Never enough, not for the clothes children need, not for the doctor's bill, not for a vacation, not even for the kind of child care that would allow parents to go to work in peace. But large as these problems loom in the lives of working-class families, difficult as they are to manage, they pale beside those they face when unemployment strikes, especially if it's father who loses his job.

NOTES

1. See Daniel Stern, *The Interpersonal World of the Infant* (New York: Basic Books, 1985), who argues that a child's capacity for self-reflection coincides with the development of language.
2. For an excellent analysis of the increasing amount of time Americans spend at work and the consequences to family and social life, see Juliet B. Schor, *The Overworked American* (New York: Basic Books, 1992). See also Carmen Sirianni and Andrea Walsh, "Through the Prism of Time: Temporal Structures in Postindustrial America," in Alan Wolfe, ed., *America at Century's End* (Berkeley: University of California Press, 1991), for their discussion of the "time famine."
3. For the origin of the term "his and her marriage," see Jessie Bernard, *The Future of Marriage* (New York: Bantam Books, 1973).
4. David Elkind, *The Hurried Child* (New York: Addison-Wesley, 1981).

19

STABILITY AND CHANGE IN CHICANO
MEN'S FAMILY LIVES

SCOTT COLTRANE

One of the most popular pejorative American slang terms to emerge in the 1980s was "macho," used to describe men prone to combative posturing, relentless sexual conquest, and other compulsive displays of masculinity. Macho men continually guard against imputations of being soft or feminine and thus tend to avoid domestic tasks and family activities that are considered "women's work." Macho comes from the Spanish *machismo,* and although the behaviors associated with it are clearly not limited to one ethnic group, Latino men are often stereotyped as especially prone toward macho displays.[1] This chapter uses in-depth interviews with twenty Chicano couples to explore how paid work and family work are divided. As in other contemporary American households, divisions of labor in these Chicano families were far from balanced or egalitarian, and husbands tended to enjoy special privileges simply because they were men. Nevertheless, many couples were allocating household chores without reference to gender, and few of the Chicano men exhibited stereotypical macho behavior.

Chicanos, or Mexican-Americans, are often portrayed as living in poor farm-worker families composed of macho men, subservient women, and plentiful children. Yet these stereotypes have been changing, as diverse groups of people with Mexican and Latin-American heritage are responding to the same sorts of social and economic pressures faced by families of other ethnic backgrounds. For example, most Chicano families in the United States now live in urban centers or their suburbs rather than in traditional rural farming areas, and their patterns of marital interaction appear to be about as egalitarian as those of other American families. What's more, Chicanos will

This article is based on a study of Dual-Earner Chicano Couples conducted in 1990–1992 by Scott Coltrane with research assistance from Elsa Valdez and Hilda Cortez. Partial funding was provided by the Academic Senate of the University of California, Riverside, and the UCR Minority Student Research Internship Program. Included here are analyses of unpublished interview excerpts along with selected passages from three published sources: (1) Coltrane, *Family Man: Fatherhood, Housework, and Gender Equity* (New York: Oxford University Press, 1994); (2) Coltrane and Valdez, "Reluctant Compliance: Work/Family Role Allocation in Dual-Earner Chicano Families," in Jane C. Hood (ed.), *Men, Work, and Family* (Newbury Park, CA: Sage, 1994); and (3) Valdez and Coltrane, "Work, Family, and the Chicana: Power, Perception and Equity," in Judith Frankel (ed.), *Employed Mothers and the Family Context* (New York: Springer, 1993).

no longer be a numerical minority in the near future. Because of higher-than-average birth rates and continued in-migration, by the year 2015 Chicano children will outnumber Anglos in many southwest states, including California, Texas, Arizona, and New Mexico.[2]

When family researchers study white couples, they typically focus on middle-class suburban households, usually highlighting their strengths. Studies of ethnic minority families, in contrast, have tended to focus on the problems of poor or working-class households living in inner-city or rural settings. Because most research on Latino families in the United States has not controlled for social class, wife's employment status, or recency of immigration, a narrow and stereotyped view of these families as patriarchal and culturally backward has persisted. In addition, large-scale studies of "Hispanics" have failed to distinguish between divergent groups of people with Mexican, Central American, South American, Cuban, Puerto Rican, Spanish, or Portuguese ancestry. In contrast, contemporary scholars are beginning to look at some of the positive aspects of minority families and to focus on the economic and institutional factors that influence men's lives within these families.[3]

In 1990 and 1991, Elsa Valdez and I interviewed a group of twenty middle-class Chicano couples with young children living in Southern California. We were primarily interested in finding out if they were facing the same sorts of pressures experienced by other families, so we selected only families in which both the husband and the wife were employed outside the home—the most typical pattern among young parents in the United States today. We wanted to see who did what in these families and find out how they talked about the personal and financial pushes and pulls associated with raising a family. We interviewed wives and husbands separately in their homes, asking them a variety of questions about housework, child care, and their jobs. Elsewhere, we describe details of their time use and task performance, but here I analyze the couples' talk about work, family, and gender, exploring how feelings of entitlement and obligation are shaped by patterns of paid and unpaid labor.[4]

When we asked husbands and wives to sort sixty-four common household tasks according to who most often performed them, we found that wives in most families were responsible for housecleaning, clothes care, meal preparation, and clean-up, whereas husbands were primarily responsible for home maintenance and repair. Most routine child care was also performed by wives, though most husbands reported that they made substantial contributions to parenting. Wives saw the mundane daily housework as an ever-present burden that they had to shoulder themselves or delegate to someone else. While many wives did not expect the current division of labor to change, they did acknowledge that it was unbalanced. The men, although acknowledging that things weren't exactly fair, tended to minimize the asymmetry by seeing many of the short repetitive tasks associated with housekeeping as shared activities. Although there was tremendous diversity among the couples we talked to, we observed a general pattern of disagreement over how much family work the other spouse performed.

The sociologist Jesse Bernard provides us with a useful way to understand why this might be. Bernard suggested that every marital union contains two marriages—"his" and "hers."[5] We discovered from our interviews and observations that most of the husbands and wives were, indeed, living in separate marriages or separate worlds. Her world centered around keeping track of the countless details of housework and child care even though she was employed. His world centered around his work and his leisure activities so that he avoided noticing or anticipating the details of running a home. Husbands "helped out" when wives gave them tasks to do, and because they almost always complied with requests for help, most tended to assume that they were sharing the household labor. Because much of the work the women did was unseen or taken for granted by the men, they tended to underestimate their wives' contributions and escaped the full range of tensions and strains associated with family work.

Because wives remained in control of setting schedules, generating lists for domestic chores, and worrying about the children, they perceived their husbands as contributing relatively little. A frequent comment from wives was that their husbands "just didn't see" the domestic details, and that the men would not often take responsibility for anticipating and planning for what needed to be done. Although many of the men we interviewed maintained their favored position within the family by "not seeing" various aspects of domestic life and leaving the details and planning to their wives, other couples were in the process of ongoing negotiations and, as described below, were successful at redefining some household chores as shared endeavors.

Concerning their paid work, the families we interviewed reported that both husbands and wives had jobs because of financial necessity. The men made comments like, "we were pretty much forced into it," or "we didn't really have any choice." Although most of the husbands and wives were employed full-time, only a few accepted the wife as an equal provider or true breadwinner. Using the type of job, employment schedule, and earnings of each spouse, along with their attitudes toward providing, I categorized the couples into main-provider families and co-provider families.[6] Main-provider couples considered the husband's job to be primary and the wife's job to be secondary. Co-provider couples, in contrast, tended to accept the wife's job as permanent, and some even treated the wife's job as equally important to her husband's. Accepting the wife as an equal provider, or considering the husband to have failed as a provider, significantly shaped the couples' divisions of household labor.

MAIN-PROVIDER FAMILIES

In just under half of the families we interviewed, the men earned substantially more money than their wives and were assumed to be "natural" breadwinners, whereas the women were assumed to be innately better equipped to deal with home and children. Wives in all of these main-provider families were employed, but the wife's job was often considered temporary, and her income was treated as "extra" money and earmarked for special purposes.[7] One main-provider husband said, "I would prefer that my wife did not have to work, and could stay at home with my daughter, but finances just don't permit that." Another commented that his wife made just about enough to cover the costs of child care, suggesting that the children were still her primary responsibility, and that any wages she earned should first be allocated to cover "her" tasks.

The main-provider couples included many wives who were employed part-time, and some who worked in lower-status full-time jobs with wages much lower than their husband's. These women took pride in their homemaker role and readily accepted responsibility for managing the household, although they occasionally asked for help. One part-time bookkeeper married to a recent law-school graduate described their division of labor by saying, "It's a given that I take care of children and housework, but when I am real tired, he steps in willingly." Main-provider husbands typically remained in a helper role: in this case, the law clerk told his wife," Just tell me what to do and I'll do it." He said that if he came home and she was gone, he might clean house, but that if she was home, he would "let her do it." This reflects a typical division of labor in which the wife acts as household manager and the husband occasionally serves as her helper.[8]

This lawyer-to-be talked about early negotiations between him and his wife that seemed to set the tone for current smoldering arguments about housework:

> When we were first married, I would do something and she
> wouldn't like the way that I did it. So I would say, "OK, then, you
> do it, and I won't do it again." That was like in our first few years
> of marriage when we were first getting used to each other, but now
> she doesn't discourage me so much. She knows that if she does,
> she's going to wind up doing it herself.

His resistance and her reluctance to press for change reflect an unbalanced economy of gratitude.[9] When he occasionally contributed to housework or child care, she was indebted to him. She complimented him for being willing to step in when she asked for help, but privately lamented the fact that she had to negotiate for each small contribution. Firmly entrenched in the main-provider role and somewhat oblivious to the daily rituals of housework and child care, he felt justified in needing prodding and encouragement. When she did ask him for help, she was careful to thank him for dressing the children or for giving her a ten-minute break from them. While these patterns of domestic labor and inequities in the exchange of gratitude were long-standing, tension lurked just below the surface for this couple. He commented, "My wife gets uptight with me for agreeing to help out my mom, when she feels she can't even ask me to go to the store for her."

Another main-provider couple reflected a similar pattern of labor allocation, but claimed that the arrangement was fair to them both. The woman, a part-time teacher's aide, acknowledged that she loved being a wife and mother and "naturally" took charge of managing the household. She commented, "I have the say so on the running of the house, and I also decide on the children's activities." Although she had a college degree, she described her current part-time job as "ideal" for her. She was able to work twenty hours per week at a neighborhood school and was home by the time her own children returned home from their school. While she earned only $6,000 per year, she justified the low salary because the job fit so well with "the family's schedule." Her husband's administrative job allowed them to live comfortably since he earned almost $50,000 annually.

This secondary-provider wife said that they divided household tasks in a conventional manner: She did most all of the cleaning, cooking, clothes-care, and child-care tasks, while he did the yard work, home repairs, and finances. Her major complaints were that her husband didn't notice things, that she had to nag him, and that he created more housework for her. "The worst part about the housework and child care is the amount of nagging I have to do to get him to help. Also, for example, say I just cleaned the house; he will leave the newspaper scattered all over the place or he will leave wet towels on the bathroom floor."

When asked whether there had been any negotiation over who would do what chores, the husband responded, "I don't think a set decision was made; it was a necessity." His wife's response was similar, "It just evolved that way; we never really talked about it." His provider role was taken for granted, but occasionally she voiced some muted resentment. For example, she commented that it upset her when he told her that she should not be working because their youngest child was only five years old. As an afterthought, she mentioned that she was sometimes bothered by the fact that she had not advanced her career, or worked overtime, since that would have interfered with "the family's" schedule.

In general, wives of main-providers not only performed virtually all housework and child care, but both spouses accepted this as "natural" or "normal." Main-provider husbands assumed that financial support was their "job" or their "duty." When one man was asked about how it felt to make more money than his wife, he responded by saying: "It's my job; I wouldn't feel right if I didn't make more money. . . . Any way that I look at it, I have to keep up my salary, or I'm not doing my job. If it costs $40,000 to live nowadays and I'm not in a $40,000-a-year job, then I'm not gonna be happy."

This same husband, a head mechanic who worked between 50 and 60 hours per week, also showed how main-provider husbands sometimes felt threatened when women begin asserting themselves in previously all-male occupational enclaves:

> As long as women mind their own business, no problem with
> me. . . . There's nothing wrong with them being in the job, but they

shouldn't try to do more than that. Like, if you get a secretary that's nosy and wants to run the company, hey, well, we tell her where to stick it. . . . When you can't do my job, don't tell me how to do it.

The mechanic's wife, also a part-time teacher's aide, subtly resisted by "spending as little time on housework as I can get away with." Nevertheless, she still considered it her sole duty to cook, and only when her husband was away at National Guard training sessions did she feel she could "slack off" by not placing "regular meals" on the family's table each night.

THE PROVIDER ROLE AND FAILED ASPIRATIONS

Wives performed most of the household labor in main-provider couples, but if main-provider husbands had failed career aspirations, more domestic work was shared. What appeared to tip the economy of gratitude away from automatic male privilege was the wife's sense that the husband had not fulfilled his occupational potential. For example, one main-provider husband graduated from a four-year college and completed two years of post-graduate study without finishing his Master's Thesis. At the time of the interview, he was making about $30,000 a year as a self-employed house painter, and his wife was making less than half that amount as a full-time secretary. His comments show how her evaluation of his failed or postponed career aspirations led to more bargaining over his participation in routine housework:

> She reminds me that I'm not doing what we both think I should be doing, and sometimes that's a discouragement. I might have worked a lot of hours, and I'll come home tired, for example, and she'll say, "You've gotta clean the house," and I'll say, "Damn I'm tired; I'd like to get a little rest in," but she says "you're only doing this because it's been your choice." She tends to not have sympathy for me in my work because it was more my choice than hers.

He acknowledged that he should be doing something more "worthwhile," and hoped that he would not be painting houses for more than another year. Still, as long as he stayed in his current job, considered beneath him by both of them, she would not allow him to use fatigue from employment as a way to get out of doing housework:

> I worked about 60 hours a week the last couple of weeks. I worked yesterday [Saturday], and today—if it had been my choice—I would have drank beer and watched TV. But since she had a baby shower to go to, I babysitted my nephews. And since we had you coming, she kind of laid out the program: "You've gotta clean the floors, and wash the dishes and do the carpets. So get to it buddy!" [Laughs.]

This main-provider husband capitulated to his wife's demands, but she still had to set tasks for him and remind him to perform them. In responding to her "program," he used the strategy of claimed incompetence that other main-provider husbands also used. While he admitted that he was proficient at the "janitorial stuff," he was careful to point out that he was incapable of dusting or doing the laundry:

> It's amazing what you can do when you have little time and you just get in and do it. And I'm good at that. I'm good at the big cleaning, I'm good at the janitorial stuff. I can do the carpet, do the floors, do all that stuff. But I'm no good on the details. She wants all the details just right, so she handles dusting, the laundry, and stuff like that. . . . You know, like I would have everything come out one color.

By re-categorizing some of the housework as "big cleaning," this husband rendered it accountable as men's work. He drew the line at laundry and dusting, but he had transformed some household tasks, like vacuuming and mopping, into work appropriate for men to do. He was complying, albeit reluctantly, to many of his wife's requests because they agreed that he had not fulfilled "his" job as sole provider. He still yearned to be the "real" breadwinner and shared his hope that getting a better paying job would mean that he could ignore the housework:

> Sharing the house stuff is usually just a necessity. If, as we would hope in the future, she didn't have to work outside the home, then I think I would be comfortable doing less of it. Then she would be the primary house-care person and I would be the primary financial-resource person. I think roles would change then, and I would be comfortable with her doing more of the dishes and more of the cleaning, and I think she would too. In that sense, I think traditional relationships—if traditional means the guy working and the woman staying home—is a good thing. I wouldn't mind getting a taste of it myself!

A similar failed aspirations pattern was found in another main-provider household, in spite of the fact that the husband had a college degree and a job as an elementary-school teacher. While his wife earned less than a sixth of what he did, she was working on an advanced degree and coordinated a non-profit community program. In this family, unlike most of the others, the husband performed more housework than he did child care, though both he and his wife agreed that she did more of both. Nevertheless, he performed these household chores reluctantly and only in response to prodding from his wife: "Housework is mostly her responsibility. I like to come home and kick back. Sometimes she has to complain before I do anything around the house. You know when she hits the wall, then I start doing things."

This main-provider husband talked about how his real love was art, and how he had failed to pursue his dream of being a graphic artist. The blocked occupational achievement in his case was not that he didn't make good money in a respected professional job, but that he was not fulfilling his "true" potential. His failed career goals increased her willingness to make demands on him, influenced their division of household labor, and helped shape feelings of entitlement between them: "I have talents that she doesn't have. I guess that's one of my strongest strengths, that I'm an artist. But she's very disappointed in me that I have not done enough of it . . ."

Another main-provider husband held a job as a telephone lineman, and his wife ran a family day-care center out of their home, which earned her less than a third of what he made. She talked about her regrets that he didn't do something "more important" for a living, and he talked about her frequent reminders that he was "too smart for what I'm doing." Like the other failed-aspirations husbands, he made significant contributions to domestic chores, but his resentment showed when he talked about "the wife" holding a job far from home:

> What I didn't like about it was that I used to get home before the wife, because she had to commute, and I'd have to pop something to eat. Most of the time it was just whatever I happened to find in the fridge. Then I'd have to go pick up the kids immediately from the babysitter, and sometimes I had evening things to do, so what I didn't like was that I had to figure out a way to schedule baby watch or baby sitting.

Even when main-provider husbands began to assume responsibility for domestic work in response to "necessity" or "nagging," they seemed to cling to the idea that these were still "her" chores. Coincidentally, most of the secondary-provider wives reported that they received little help unless they "constantly" reminded their husbands. What generally kept secondary-provider wives from resenting their husband's resistance was their own acceptance of the homemaker role and their recognition of his superior financial contributions. When performance of the male-provider role was deemed to be lacking in some way—i.e., failed aspirations or low occupational prestige—wives' resentment appeared closer to the surface, and they were more persistent in demanding help from their husbands.

AMBIVALENT CO-PROVIDERS

Over half of the couples we interviewed were classified as co-providers. The husbands and wives in these families had more equal earnings and placed a higher value on the wife's employment than those in main-provider families, but there was considerable variation in terms of their willingness to accept the woman as a full and equal provider. Five of the twelve husbands in the co-provider group were ambivalent about sharing the provider role and were also reluctant to share most household tasks. Compared to their wives, ambivalent co-provider husbands usually held jobs that were roughly equivalent in terms of occupational prestige and worked about the same number of hours per week, but because of gender bias in the labor market, the men earned significantly more than their wives. Compared to main-provider husbands, they considered their wives' jobs to be relatively permanent and important, but they continued to use their own job commitments as justification for doing little at home. Ambivalent co-provider husbands' family obligations rarely intruded into their work lives, whereas their wives' family obligations frequently interfered with their paid work. Such asymmetrically permeable work/family boundaries are common in single-earner and main-provider families, but must be supported with subtle ideologies and elaborate justifications when husbands and wives hold similar occupational positions.[10]

Ambivalent co-provider husbands remained in a helper role at home, perceiving their wives to be more involved parents and assuming that housework was also primarily their wives' responsibility. The men used their jobs to justify their absence from home, but most also lamented not being able to spend more time with their families. For instance, one husband who worked full time as a city planner was married to a woman who worked an equal number of hours as an office manager. In talking about the time he put in at his job, he commented, "I wish I had more time to spend with my children, and to spend with my wife too, of course, but it's a fact of life that I have to work." His wife, in contrast, indicated that her paid job, which she had held for fourteen years, did not prohibit her from adequately caring for her three children, or taking care of "her" household chores. Ambivalent co-provider husbands did not perform significantly more housework and child care than main-provider husbands, and generally did fewer household chores than main-provider husbands with failed career aspirations.

Not surprisingly, ambivalent co-provider husbands tended to be satisfied with their current divisions of labor, even though they usually admitted that things were "not quite fair." One junior-high-school teacher married to a bilingual-education program coordinator described his reactions to their division of family labor:

> To be honest, I'm totally satisfied. When I had a first-period conference, I was a little more flexible; I'd help her more with changing 'em, you know, getting them ready for school, since I didn't have to be at school right away. Then I had to switch because they had some situation out at fifth-period conference, so that now she does it a little bit more than I do, and I don't help out with the kids as much in the morning because I have to be there an hour earlier.

This ambivalent co-provider clearly saw himself as "helping" his wife with the children, yet made light of her contributions by saying she does "a little bit more than I do." He went on to reveal how his wife did not enjoy similar special privileges due to her employment, since she had to pick up the children from day care every day, as well as taking them to school in the mornings:

She gets out a little later than I do, because she's an administrator but I have other things outside. I also work out, I run, and that sort of gives me a time away, to do that before they all come here. I have community meetings in the evenings sometimes, too. So, I mean, it might not be totally fair—maybe 60/40—but I'm thoroughly happy with the way things are.

While he was "thoroughly happy" with the current arrangements, she thought that it was decidedly unfair. She said, "I don't like the fact that it's taken for granted that I'm available. When he goes out he just assumes I'm available, but when I go out I have to consult with him to make sure he is available." For her, child care was a given; for him, it was optional. He commented, "If I don't have something else to do, then I'll take the kids."

Ambivalent co-provider husbands also tended to talk about regretting that their family involvements limited their careers or personal activities. For instance the schoolteacher discussed above lamented that he could not do what he used to before he had children:

Having children keeps me away from thinking a lot about my work. You know, it used to be, before we had kids, I could have my mind geared to work—you know how ideas just pop in; you really get into it. But with kids it doesn't get as—you know, you can't switch. It gets more difficult; it makes it hard to get into it. I don't have that freedom of mind, you know, and it takes away from aspects of my work, like doing a little bit more reading or research that I would like to do. Or my own activities, I mean, I still run, but not as much as I used to. I used to play basketball, I used to coach, this and that . . .

Other ambivalent co-provider husbands talked about the impact of children on their careers and personal lives with less bitterness and more appreciation for establishing a relationship with their children. Encouraged by their wives to alter their priorities, some reinterpreted the relative importance of career and family commitments:

I like the way things are going. Let's put it this way. I mean, it's just that once you become a parent, it's a never-ending thing. I coach my kid for example; this past week we had four games. . . . I just think that by having a family that your life becomes so involved after awhile with your own kids, that it's very difficult. I coached at the varsity level for one year, but I had to give it up. I would leave in the morning when they were asleep, and I would get out of coaches' meetings at ten or eleven at night. My wife said to me, "Think about your priorities, man; you leave when the kids are asleep, come back when they are asleep." So I decided to change that act. So I gave it up for one year, and I was home all the time. Now I am going to coach again, but it's at lower levels, and I'll be home every day. I have to make adjustments for my family. Your attitude changes; it's not me that counts anymore.

Whereas family labor was not shared equally in this ambivalent co-provider couple, the husband, at his wife's urging, was beginning to accept and appreciate that his children were more important than his job. He was evaluating his attachment to his children on his wife's terms, but he was agreeing with her, and he had begun to take more responsibility for them.

Many of these husbands talked about struggles over wanting to spend more time on their careers, and most did not relinquish the assumption that the home was the wife's domain. For example, some ambivalent co-provider couples attempted to alleviate stress on the wife by hiring outside help. In response to a question about whether their division of labor was fair, a self-employed male attorney said, "Do you mean fair like equal? It's probably not equal, so probably it wouldn't be fair, but that's why we have a housekeeper." His wife, a social worker earning only ten percent less than he, said that the household was still her responsibility, but that she now had fewer tasks to do: "When I did not have help, I tended to do everything, but with a housekeeper, I don't have to do so much." She went on to talk about how she wished he would do more with their five- and eight-year-old children, but speculated that he probably would as they grew older.

Another couple paid a live-in babysitter/housekeeper to watch their three children during the day while he worked full-time in construction and she worked full-time as a psychiatric social worker. While she labeled the outside help as "essential," she noted that her husband contributed more to the mess than he did to its cleanup. He saw himself as an involved father because he played with his children, and she acknowledged this, but she also complained that he competed with them in games as if he were a child himself. His participation in routine household labor was considered optional, as evidenced by his comment, "I like to cook once in a while."

CO-PROVIDERS

In contrast, about a third of the couples we interviewed fully accepted the wife's long-term employment, considered her career to be just as important as his, and were in various stages of redefining household labor as men's work. Like the ambivalent couples discussed above, full co-provider spouses worked about the same number of hours as each other, but on the whole, these couples worked more total hours than their more ambivalent counterparts, though their annual incomes were a bit lower. According to both husbands and wives, the sharing of housework and child care was substantially greater for full co-providers than for ambivalent co-providers, and also much more balanced than for main-providers.

Like ambivalent co-providers, husbands in full co-provider families discussed conflicts between work and family and sometimes alluded to the ways that their occupational advancement was limited by their commitments to their children. One husband and wife spent the same number of hours on the job, earned approximately the same amount of money, and were employed as engineering technicians for the same employer. When we asked him how his family involvement had affected his job performance, he responded by saying, "It should, OK, because I really need to spend a lot more time learning my work, and I haven't really put in the time I need to advance in the profession. I would like to spend, I mean I *would* spend, more time if I didn't have kids. I'd like to be able to play with the computer or read books more often." Although he talked about conflicts between job and family, he also emphasized that lost work time was not really a sacrifice because he valued time with his children so highly. He did not use his job as an excuse to get out of doing child care or housework, and he seemed to value his wife's career at least as much as his own:

> I think her job is probably more important than mine because she's been at that kind of work a lot longer than I have. And at the level she is—it's awkward the way it is, because I get paid just a little bit more than she does; I have a higher position. But she definitely knows the work a lot more, she's been doing the same type of work for about nine years already, and I've only been doing this type of engineering work for about two-and-a-half years, so she knows a lot more. We both have to work; that's for sure.

Recognition of their roughly equivalent professional status and the need for two equal providers affected this couple's division of parenting and housework. The husband indicated that he did more child care and housework than his wife, and she gave him much credit for his efforts, but in her interview, she indicated that he still did less than half. She described her husband's relationship with their seven-year-old son as "very caring," and noted that he assists the boy with homework more than she does. She also said that her husband did most of the heavy cleaning and scrubbing, but also commented that he doesn't clean toilets and doesn't always notice when things get dirty. The husband described their allocation of housework by saying, "Maybe she does less than I do, but some of the things she does, I just will not do. I will not dust all the little things in the house. That's one of my least favorite things, but I'm more likely to do the mopping and vacuuming." This husband's comments also revealed some ongoing tension about whose housework standards should be maintained. He said, "She has high standards for cleanliness that you would have to be home to maintain. Mine tend to acknowledge that you don't always get to this stuff because you have other things to do. I think I have a better acceptance that one priority hurts something else in the background."

While this couple generally agreed about how to raise their son, standards for child care were also subject to debate. He saw himself as doing more with his son than his wife, as reflected in comments such as "I tend to think of myself as the more involved parent, and I think other people have noticed that, too." While she had only positive things to say about his parenting, he offered both praise and criticism of her parenting:

> She can be very playful. She makes up fun games. She doesn't always put enough into the educational part of it, though, like exploring or reading. . . . She cherishes tune-up time [job-related study or preparation], and sometimes I feel she should be using that time to spend with him. Like at the beach, I'll play with him, but she'll be more likely to be under the umbrella reading.

Like many of the other husbands, he went on to say that he thought their division of labor was unfair. Unlike the others, however, he indicated that he thought their current arrangements favored *her* needs, not his:

> I think I do more housework. It's probably not fair, because I do more of the dirtier tasks. . . . Also, at this point, our solution tends to favor her free time more than my free time. I think that has more to do with our personal backgrounds. She has more personal friends to do things with, so she has more outside things to do whereas I say I'm not doing anything.

In this family, comparable occupational status and earnings, coupled with a relatively egalitarian ideology, led to substantial sharing of both child care and housework. While the husband tended to take more credit for his involvement than his wife gave him, we can see a difference between their talk and that of some of the families discussed above. Other husbands sometimes complained about their wife's high standards, but they also treated housework, and even parenting, as primarily *her* duty. They usually resented being nagged to do more around the house and failed to move out of a helper role. Rarely did such men consider it *their* duty to anticipate, schedule, and take care of family and household needs. In this co-provider household, in contrast, the gendered allocation of responsibility for child care and housework was not assumed. Because of this, negotiations over housework and parenting were more frequent than in the other families. Since they both held expectations that each would fulfill both provider and caretaker roles, resentments came from both spouses—not just from the wife.

Our interviews suggest that it might be easier for couples to share both provider and homemaker roles when, like the family above, the wife's earnings and occupational prestige equal or exceed those of her husband. For instance, in one of the couples reporting the most sharing of child care and housework, the wife earned $36,000 annually as the executive director of a non-profit community organization and a consultant, and her husband earned $30,000 as a self-employed general contractor. This couple started off their marriage with fairly conventional gender-role expectations and an unbalanced division of labor. While the husband's ideology had changed somewhat, he still talked like most of the main-provider husbands:

As far the household is concerned, I divide a house into two categories: one is the interior and the other is the exterior. For the interior, my wife pushes me to deal with that. The exterior, I'm left to it myself. So, what I'm basically saying is that generally speaking, a woman does not deal with the exterior. The woman's main concern is with the interior, although there is a lot of deviation.

In this family, an egalitarian belief system did not precede the sharing of household labor. The wife was still responsible for setting the "interior" household agenda and had to remind her husband to help with housework and child care. When asked whether he and his wife had arguments about housework, this husband laughed and said, "All the time; doesn't everybody?"

What differentiated this couple from most others is that she made more money than he did and had no qualms about demanding help from him. While he had not yet accepted the idea that interior chores were equally his, he reluctantly performed them. She ranked his contributions to child care to be equal to hers, and rated his contributions to housework only slightly below her own. While not eagerly rushing to do the cooking, cleaning, or laundry, he complied with occasional reminders and according to his wife, was "a better cleaner" than she was.

His sharing stemmed, in part, from her higher earnings and their mutual willingness to reduce his "outside chores" by hiring outside help. Unlike the more ambivalent co-providers who hired housekeepers to do "her" chores, this couple hired a gardener to work on the yard so they could both spend more time focusing on the children and the house. Rather than complaining about their division of labor, he talked about how he has come to appreciate his situation:

> Ever since I've known my wife, she's made more money than I have. Initially—as a man—I resented it. I went through a lot of head trips about it. But as time developed, I appreciated it. Now I respect it. The way I figure it is, I'd rather have her sharing the money with me than sharing it with someone else. She has her full-time job and then she has her part-time job as a consultant. The gardener I'm paying $75 per week, and I'm paying someone else $25 per week to make my lunch, so I'm enjoying it! It's self-interest.

The power dynamic in this family, coupled with their willingness to pay for outside help to reduce his chores, and the flexibility of his self-employed work schedule, led to substantial sharing of cooking, cleaning, and child care. Because she was making more money and working more hours than he was, he could not emulate other husbands in claiming priority for his provider activities.

A similar dynamic was evident in other co-provider couples with comparable earnings and career commitments. One male IRS officer married to a school teacher now made more money than his wife, but talked about his feelings when she was the more successful provider:

> It doesn't bother me when she makes more money than me. I don't think it has anything to do with being a man. I don't have any hangups about it, I mean, I don't equate those things with manhood. It takes a pretty simple mind to think that way. First of all, she doesn't feel superior when she has made more money.

The woman in this couple commented that her husband was "better" at housework than she was, but that she still had to nag him to do it. Although only two wives in our sample of Chicano families earned more than their husbands, the reversal of symbolic provider status seemed to raise expectations for increased family work from husbands. The husbands who made less than their wives performed significantly more of the housework and child care than the other husbands.

Even when wives' earnings did not exceed the husbands', some co-providers shared the homemaker role. A male college-admissions recruiter and his executive-secretary wife shared substantial housework and child care according to mutual ratings. He made $29,000 per year working a 50-hour week, while she made $22,000 working a 40-hour week. She was willing to give him more credit than he was willing to claim for child care, reflecting her sincere appreciation for his parenting efforts, which were greater than those of other fathers she knew. He placed a high value on her mothering and seemed to downplay the possibility that they should be considered equal parents. Like most of the men in this study, the college-recruiter husband was reluctant to perform house-cleaning chores. Like many co-providers, however, he managed to redefine some routine household chores as a shared responsibility. For instance, when we asked him what he liked least about housework, he laughingly replied, "Probably those damn toilets, man, and the showers, the bathrooms, gotta scrub 'em, argghh! I wish I didn't have to do any of that, you know the vacuuming and all that. But it's just a fact of life."

Even though he did more than most husbands, he acknowledged that he did less than his wife, and admitted that he sometimes tried to use his job to get out of doing more around the house. But whereas other wives often allowed husbands to use their jobs as excuses for doing less family work, or assumed that their husbands were incapable of performing certain chores like cooking or laundry, the pattern in this family resembled that of the failed-aspirations couples. In other words, the wife did not assume that housework was "her" job, did not accept her husband's job demands as justification for his doing less housework, and sometimes challenged his interpretation of how much his job required of him. She also got her husband to assume more responsibility by refraining from performing certain tasks. He commented:

> Sometimes she just refuses to do something. . . . An example would be the ironing, you know, I never used to do the ironing, hated it. Now it's just something that happens. You need something ironed,

you better iron it or you're not gonna have it in the morning. So, I think, you know, that kinda just evolved. I mean, she just gradually quit doing it so everybody just had to do their own. My son irons his own clothes, I iron my own clothes, my daughter irons her own clothes; the only one that doesn't iron is the baby, and next year she'll probably start.

The sociologist Jane Hood, whose path-breaking family research highlighted the importance of provider role definition to marital power, describes this strategy as "going on strike," and suggests that it is most effective when husbands feel the specific task *must* be done.[11] Since appearing neat and well-dressed was a priority for this husband, when his wife stopped ironing his clothes, he started doing it himself. Because he felt it was important for his children to be "presentable" in public, he also began to remind them to iron their own clothes before going visiting or attending church.

While many co-provider couples reported that sharing housework was contingent upon ongoing bargaining and negotiation, others focused on how it evolved "naturally." One co-provider husband, director of a housing agency, reported that he and his wife didn't negotiate; "we pretty much do what needs to be done." His wife, an executive secretary, confirmed his description, and echoed the ad-hoc arrangements of many of the role-sharing couples: "We have not had to negotiate. We both have our specialties. He is great with dishes, I like to clean bathrooms. He does most of the laundry. It has worked out that we each do what we like best."

Although sharing tasks sometimes increases conflict, when both spouses assume that household tasks are a shared responsibility, negotiation can also become less necessary or contentious. For example, a co-provider husband who worked as a mail carrier commented, "I get home early and start dinner, make sure the kids do their homework, feed the dogs, stuff like that." He and his wife, an executive secretary, agreed that they rarely talk about housework. She said, "When I went back to work we agreed that we both needed to share, and so we just do it." While she still reminded him to perform chores according to her standards or on her schedule, she summed up her appreciation by commenting, "At least he does it without complaining." Lack of complaint was a common feature of co-provider families. Whereas many main-provider husbands complained of having to do "her" chores, the co-providers rarely talked about harboring resentments. Main-provider husbands typically lamented not having the services of a stay-at-home wife, but co-provider husbands almost never made such comparisons.

SUMMARY AND DISCUSSION

For these dual-earner Chicano couples, we found conventional masculine privilege as well as considerable sharing in several domains. First, as in previous studies of ethnic minority families, wives were employed a substantial number of hours and made significant contributions to the household income. Second, like some who have studied Chicano families, we found that couples described their decision-making to be relatively fair and equal.[12] Third, fathers in these families were more involved in child rearing than their own fathers had been, and many were rated as sharing a majority of child care tasks. Finally, while no husband performed fully half of the housework, a few made substantial contributions in this area as well.

One of the power dynamics that appeared to undergird the household division of labor in these families was the relative earning power of each spouse, though this was modified by factors such as occupational prestige, provider role status, and personal preference. In just under half of the families, the wife earned less than a third of the family income, and in all of these families the husband performed little of the routine housework or child care. In two families, wives earned more than their husbands, and these two households reported sharing more domestic labor than others. Among the other couples who shared housework and child care, there was a preponderance of relatively balanced incomes. In the two families with large financial contributions from wives, but little household help from husbands, couples hired housekeepers to reduce the wives' household workload.

While relative income appeared to make a significant difference in marital power, we observed no simple or straightforward exchange of market resources for domestic services. Other factors like failed career aspirations or occupational status influenced marital dynamics and helped explain why some wives were willing to push a little harder for change in the division of household labor. In almost every case, husbands reluctantly responded to requests for help from wives. Only when wives explicitly took the initiative to shift some of the housework burden to husbands did the men begin to assume significant responsibility for the day-to-day operation of the household. Even when they began to share the housework and child care, men tended to do some of the less onerous tasks like playing with the children or washing the dinner dishes. When we compared these men to their own fathers, or their wives' fathers, however, we could see that they were sharing more domestic chores than the generation that preceded them.

Acceptance of wives as co-providers and wives' delegation of a portion of the homemaker role to husbands were especially important to creating more equal divisions of household labor in these families. If wives made lists for their husbands or offered them frequent reminders, they were more successful than if they waited for husbands to take the initiative. Remaining responsible for managing the home and children was cause for resentment on the part of many wives, however. Sometimes wives were effective in getting husbands to perform certain chores, like ironing, by stopping doing it altogether. For other wives, sharing evolved more "naturally," as both spouses agreed to share tasks or performed the chores that they preferred.

Economies of gratitude continually shifted as the ideology, career attachments, and feelings of entitlement of each spouse changed over time. For some main-provider families, this meant that wives were grateful for husbands' "permission" to hold a job, or that wives worked harder at home because they felt guilty for making their husbands do any of the housework. Main-provider husbands usually let their job commitments limit their family work, whereas their wives took time off from work to care for a sick child or to attend a parent-teacher conference.

Even in families where co-provider wives had advanced degrees and earned high incomes, some wives' work/family boundaries were more permeable than their husbands', like the program director married to a teacher who was a "perpetual" graduate student and attended "endless" community meetings. While she was employed more hours than he, and made about the same amount of money, she had to "schedule him" to watch the children if she wanted to leave the house alone. His stature as a "community leader" provided him with subterranean leverage in the unspoken struggle over taking responsibility for the house and children. His "gender ideology," if measured with conventional survey questions, would undoubtedly have been characterized as "egalitarian," because he spoke in broad platitudes about women's equality and was washing the dishes when we arrived for the interviews. He insisted on finishing the dishes as he answered my questions, but in the other room, his wife confided to Elsa in incredulous tones, "He *never* does that!"

In other ambivalent co-provider families, husbands gained unspoken advantage because they had more prestigious jobs than their wives, and earned more money. While these highly educated attorneys and administrators talked about how they respected their wives' careers, and expressed interest in spending more time with their children, their actions showed that they did not fully assume responsibility for sharing the homemaker or parenting role. To solve the dilemma of too little time and too many chores, two of these families hired housekeepers. Wives were grateful for this strategy, though it did not alter inequities in the distribution of housework and child care, nor in the allocation of worry.

In other families, the economy of gratitude departed dramatically from conventional notions of husband as economic provider and wife as nurturing homemaker. When wives' earnings approached or exceeded their husbands', economies of gratitude shifted toward more equal expectations, with husbands beginning to assume that they must do more around the house. Even in these families, husbands rarely began doing more chores without prodding from wives, but they usually did them "without complaining." Similarly, when wives with economic leverage began expecting more from their husbands, they were usually successful in getting them to do more.

Another type of leverage that was important, even in main-provider households, was the existence of failed aspirations. If wives expected husbands to "make more" of themselves, pursue "more important" careers, or follow "dream" occupational goals, then wives were able to get husbands to do more around the house. This perception of failed aspirations, if held by both spouses, served as a reminder that husbands had no excuse for not help-ing out at home. In these families, wives were not at all reluctant to demand assistance with domestic chores, and husbands were rarely able to use their jobs as excuses for getting out of housework.

The economies of gratitude in these families were not equally balanced, but many exhibited divisions of household labor that contradicted cultural stereotypes of macho men and male-dominated families. Particularly salient in these families was the lack of fit between their own class position and that of their parents. Most of the parents were Mexican immigrants with little ed-ucation and low occupational mobility. The couples we interviewed, in con-trast, were well-educated and relatively secure in middle-class occupations. The couples could have compared themselves to their parents, evaluating themselves to be egalitarian and financially successful. While some did just that, most compared themselves to their Anglo and Chicano friends and coworkers, many of whom shared as much or more than they did. Implicitly comparing their earnings, occupational commitments, and perceived apti-tudes, husbands and wives negotiated new patterns of work/family bound-aries and developed novel justifications for their emerging arrangements. These were not created anew, but emerged out of the popular culture in which they found themselves. Judith Stacey labels such developments the making of the "postmodern family," because they signal "the contested, am-bivalent, and undecided character of contemporary gender and kinship arrangements."[13] Our findings confirm that families are an important site of new struggles over the meaning of gender and the rights and obligations of men and women in each other and over each other's labor.

One of the most provocative findings from our study has to do with the class position of Chicano husbands and wives who shared household labor: white-collar, working-class families shared more than upper-middle-class professionals. Contrary to findings from nationwide surveys predicting that higher levels of education for either husbands or wives will be associated with more sharing, the most highly educated of our well-educated sample of Chicano couples shared only moderate amounts of child care and little housework.[14] Contrary to other predictions, neither was it the working-class women in this study who achieved the most balanced divisions of labor.[15] It was the middle occupational group of women, the executive secretaries, clerks, technicians, teachers, and mid-level administrators who extracted the most help from husbands. The men in these families were similarly in the middle in terms of occupational status for this sample—administrative assis-tants, a builder, a mail carrier, a technician—and in the middle in terms of in-come. What this means is that the highest status wives—the program coordinators, nurses, social workers, and office managers—were not able to, or chose not to, transform their salaries or occupational status into more par-ticipation from husbands. This was probably because their husbands had even higher incomes and more prestigious occupations than they did. The lawyers, program directors, ranking bureaucrats, and "community leaders" parlayed their status into extra leisure at home, either by paying for house-keepers or ignoring the housework. Finally, Chicana wives at the lowest end of the occupational structure fared least well. The teacher's aides, entry-level secretaries, day-care providers, and part-time employees did the bulk of the work at home whether they were married to mechanics or lawyers. When wives made less than a third of what their husbands did, they were only able to get husbands to do a little more if the men were working at jobs considered "below" them—a telephone lineman, a painter, an elementary-school teacher.

Only Chicano couples were included in this study, but results are similar to findings from previous interviews with Anglo couples.[16] My interpretation is that the major processes shaping divisions of labor in middle-class Chicano couples are approximately the same as those shaping divisions of labor in other middle-class couples. This is not to say that ethnicity did not make a difference to the Chicano couples we interviewed. They grew up in recently immigrating working-class families, watched their parents work long hours for minimal wages, and understood firsthand the toll that various forms of racial discrimination can take. Probably because of some of these experiences, and their own more recent ones, our informants looked at job security, fertility decisions, and the division of household labor somewhat differently than their Anglo counterparts. In some cases, this can give Chicano husbands in working-class or professional jobs license to ignore more of the housework, and might temper the anger of some working-class or professional Chicanas who are still called on to do most of the domestic chores. If these findings are generalizable, however, it is those in between the blue-collar working-class and the upper-middle-class professionals that might be more likely to share housework and childcare.

Assessing whether these findings apply to other dual-earner Chicano couples will require the use of larger, more representative samples. If the limited sharing observed here represents a trend—however slow or reluctant—it could have far-reaching consequences. More and more Chicana mothers are remaining full-time members of the paid labor force. With the "postindustrial" expansion of the service and information sectors of the economy, Chicanos and Chicanas will be increasingly likely to enter white-collar middle-class occupations. As more Chicano families fit the occupational profile of those we studied, we may see more assumption of housework and child care by Chicano men. Regardless of the specific changes that the economy will undergo, we can expect Chicano men and women, like their Anglo counterparts, to continue to negotiate for change in their work and family roles.

NOTES

1. For a discussion of how the term *machismo* can also reflect positive attributes of respect, loyalty, responsibility and generosity, see Alfredo Mirandé "Chicano Fathers: Traditional Perceptions and Current Realities," pp. 93–106, in *Fatherhood Today*, P. Bronstein and C. Cowan, eds. (New York: Wiley, 1988).

2. For reviews of literature on Latin-American families and projections on their future proportionate representation in the population, see Randall Collins and Scott Coltrane, *Sociology of Marriage and the Family* (Chicago: Nelson Hall, 1994); William A. Vega, "Hispanic Families in the 1980s," *Journal of Marriage and the Family* 52(1990): 1015–1024; and Norma Williams, *The Mexican-American Family* (New York: General Hall, 1990).

3. Maxine Baca Zinn, "Family, Feminism, and Race in America," *Gender & Society* 4(1990): 68–82; Mirandé, "Chicano Fathers"; Vega, "Hispanic Families"; and Williams, *The Mexican-American Family.*

4. See Coltrane, *Family Man: Fatherhood, Housework, and Gender Equity* (New York: Oxford University Press, 1994); Coltrane and Valdez, "Reluctant Compliance: Work/Family Role Allocation in Dual-Earner Chicano Families," in *Men, Work, and Family,* Jane C. Hood, ed. (Newbury Park, CA: Sage, 1994) and Valdez and Coltrane, "Work, Family, and the Chicana: Power, Perception and Equity," in *Employed Mothers and the Family Context.* Judith Frankel, ed. (New York: Springer, 1993). I thank Hilda Cortez, a summer research intern at the University of California, for help in transcribing some of the interviews and for providing insight into some of the issues faced by these families.

5. Jessie Bernard, *The Future of Marriage* (New York: World, 1972).

6. See Jane Hood, 1986. "The Provider Role: Its Meaning and Measurement." *Journal of Marriage and the Family* 48: 349–359.

7. Hood, "The Provider Role."

8. See Coltrane, "Household Labor and the Routine Production of Gender." *Social Problems* 36: 473–490.

9. I am indebted to Arlie Hochschild, who first used this term in *The Second Shift* (New York: Viking, 1987). See also Karen Pyke and Scott Coltrane, "Entitlement, Obligation, and Gratitude in Remarriage: Toward a Gendered Understanding of Household Labor Allocation."

10. I am indebted to Joseph Pleck for his conceptualization of "asymmetrically permeable" work/family boundaries ("The Work-Family Role System." *Social Problems* 24: 417–427).

11. Jane Hood, *Becoming a Two-Job Family,* p. 131.

12. See, for example, V. Cromwell and R. Cromwell, 1978. "Perceived Dominance in Decision Making and Conflict Resolution among Anglo, Black, and Chicano Couples." *Journal of Marriage and the Family* 40: 749–760; G. Hawkes and M. Taylor, 1975, "Power Structure in Mexican and Mexican-American Farm Labor Families." *Journal of Marriage and the Family* 37: 807–811; L. Ybarra, 1982. "When Wives Work: The Impact on the Chicano Family." *Journal of Marriage and the Family* 44: 169–178.

13. Judith Stacey, 1990. *Brave New Families.* New York: Basic Books, p. 17.

14. See, for instance, Donna H. Berardo, Constance Shehan, and Gerald R. Leslie, "A Residue of Tradition: Jobs, Careers, and Spouses' Time in Housework." *Journal of Marriage and the Family* 49(1987) 381–390; Catherine E. Ross, "The Division of Labor at Home." *Social Forces* 65(1987): 816–833.

15. Patricia Zavella, 1987. *Women's Work and Chicano Families.* Ithaca, NY: Cornell University Press; Stacey, *Brave New Families.*

16. See, for example, Hochschild, *Second Shift;* Hood, *Two-Job Family;* Coltrane, *Family Man.*

20

SEXUAL DISSENT AND THE FAMILY
The Sharon Kowalski Case

NAN D. HUNTER

"No connection between family, marriage, or procreation on the one hand and homosexual activity on the other has been demonstrated."
—SUPREME COURT, BOWERS V. HARDWICK, 1986

"Sharon Kowalski is the child of a divorce between her consanguineous family and her family of affinity, the petitioner Karen Thompson. . . . That Sharon's family of affinity has not enjoyed societal recognition in the past is unfortunate."
—MINNESOTA STATE DISTRICT COURT IN RE: GUARDIANSHIP
OF SHARON KOWALSKI, WARD, 1991

In the effort to end second-class citizenship for lesbian and gay Americans, no obstacle has proved tougher to surmount than the cluster of issues surrounding "the family." The concept of family functions as a giant cultural screen. Projected onto it, contests over race, gender, sexuality and a range of other "domestic" issues from crime to taxes constantly create and recreate a newly identified zone of social combat, the politics of the family. Activists of all persuasions eagerly seek to enter the discursive field, ever ready to debate and discuss: Who counts as a family? Which "family values" are the authentic ones? Is there a place in the family for queers? As battles are won and lost in this cultural war, progressives and conservatives agree on at least one thing—the family is highly politicized terrain.

For lesbians and gays, these debates have dramatic real-life consequences, probably more so than with any other legal issue. Relationship questions touch almost every person's life at some point, in a way that military issues, for example, do not. Further, the unequal treatment is blatant, *de jure* and universal, as compared with the employment arena, where discrimination may be more subtle and variable. No state allows a lesbian or gay couple to marry. No state recognizes (although a number of counties and cities do) domestic partnership systems under which unmarried couples (gay or

Hunter, Nan D. "Sexual Dissent and the Family: The Sharon Kowalski Case." *The Nation*, October 7, 1991. Reprinted with permission from the publisher.

straight) can become eligible for certain benefits usually available only to spouses. The fundamental inequity is that, barring mental incompetence or consanguinity, virtually any straight couple has the option to marry and thus establish a next-of-kin relationship that the state will enforce. No lesbian or gay couple can. Under the law, two women or two men are forever strangers, regardless of their relationship.

One result is that every lesbian or gay man's nightmare is to be cut off from one's primary other, physically incapacitated, stranded, unable to make contact, without legal recourse. It is a nightmare that could not happen to a married couple. But it did happen to two Minnesota women, Sharon Kowalski and Karen Thompson, in a remarkable case that threaded its way through the courts for seven years.

Sharon Kowalski, notwithstanding the Minnesota State District Court's characterization of her as a "child of divorce," is an adult with both a committed life partner and parents who bitterly refuse to acknowledge either her lesbianism or her lover. Kowalski is a former physical education teacher and amateur athlete, whose Minnesota women's high school shot-put record still stands. In 1983, she was living with her lover, Thompson, in the home they had jointly purchased in St. Cloud. Both women were deeply closeted; they exchanged rings with each other but told virtually no one of their relationship. That November, Kowalski suffered devastating injuries in a car accident, which left her unable to speak or walk, with arms deformed and with major brain damage, including seriously impaired short-term memory.

After the accident, both Thompson and Kowalski's father petitioned to be appointed Sharon's guardian; initially, an agreement was entered that the father would become guardian on the condition that Thompson retain equal rights to visit and consult with doctors. By the summer of 1985, after growing hostilities, the father refused to continue the arrangement, and persuaded a local court that Thompson's visits caused Kowalski to feel depressed. One doctor hired by the father wrote a letter stating that Kowalski was in danger of sexual abuse. Within twenty-four hours after being named sole guardian, the father cut off all contact between Thompson and Kowalski, including mail. By this time, Kowalski had been moved to a nursing home near the small town where she grew up in the Iron Range, a rural mining area in northern Minnesota.

Surely one reason the Kowalski case is so compelling is that, for millions of parents, learning that one's son is gay or daughter is lesbian would be *their* worst nightmare. That is all the more true in small-town America, among people who are religiously observant and whose expectations for a daughter are primarily marriage and motherhood. "The good Lord put us here for reproduction, not that kind of way," Donald Kowalski told the *Los Angeles Times* in 1988. "It's just not a normal life style. The Bible will tell you that." Karen Thompson, he told other reporters, was "an animal" and was lying about his daughter's life. "I've never seen anything that would make me believe" that his daughter is lesbian, he said to *The New York Times* in 1989. How much less painful it must be to explain a lesbian daughter's life as seduction, rather than to experience it as betrayal.

In 1988, Thompson's stubborn struggle to "bring Sharon home" entered a new stage. A different judge, sitting in Duluth, ordered Kowalski moved to a new facility for medical evaluation. Soon thereafter, based on staff recommendations from the second nursing facility, the court ordered that Thompson be allowed to visit. The two women saw each other again in the spring of 1989, after three and a half years of forced separation. Kowalski, who can communicate by typing on a special keyboard, said that she wanted to live in "St. Cloud with Karen."

In May 1990, citing a heart condition for which he had been hospitalized, Donald Kowalski resigned as his daughter's guardian. This resignation set the stage for Thompson to file a renewed petition for appointment as guardian, which she did. But in an April 1991 ruling, Minnesota State District Court Judge Robert Campbell selected as guardian Karen Tomberlin—a friend of both Kowalski and her parents, who supported Tomberlin's request. On the surface, the court sought balance. The judge characterized the Kowalski parents and Karen Thompson as the "two wings" of Sharon Kowalski's family. He repeatedly asserted that both must have ample access to visitation with Kowalski. He described Tomberlin as a neutral third party who would not exclude either side. But the biggest single reason behind the decision, the one that he characterized as "instrumental," seemed to be the judge's anger at Thompson for ever telling Kowalski's parents (in a private letter), and then the world at large, that she and Kowalski were lovers.

The court condemned Thompson's revelation of her own relationship as the "outing" of Sharon Kowalski. Thompson did write the letter to Kowalski's parents without telling Kowalski (who was at the time just emerging from a three-month coma after the accident) and did build on her own an active political organization around the case, composed chiefly of disability and lesbian and gay rights groups. Of course, for most of that period, she could not have consulted Kowalski because the two were cut off from each other.

In truth, though, the judge's concern seemed to be more for the outing of Kowalski's parents. He describes the Kowalskis as "outraged and hurt by the public invasion of Sharon's privacy and their privacy," and he blames this outing for the bitterness between Thompson and the parents. Had Thompson simply kept this to herself, the court implies, none of these nasty facts would ever have had to be discussed. The cost, of course, would have been the forfeiture of Thompson's relationship with her lover.

An openly stated preference for ignorance over knowledge is remarkable in a judicial opinion. One imagines the judge silently cursing Thompson for her arrogance in claiming the role of spouse, and for her insistence on shattering the polite fiction of two gym teachers living and buying a house together as just good friends. Women, especially, aren't supposed to be so stubborn or uppity. One can sense the court's empathetic response of shared embarrassment with the parents, of the desire not to be told and thus not to be forced to speak on this subject.

The final chapter in the Kowalski case vindicated Karen Thompson's long struggle. The Minnesota Court of Appeals granted Thompson's guardianship petition in December, 1991, reversing the trial judge on every point.

The conflict in the Kowalski case illustrates one of the prime contradictions underlying all the cases seeking legal protection for lesbian and gay couples. This culture is deeply invested with a notion of the ideal family as not only a zone of privacy and a structure of authority (preferably male in the conservative view) but also as a barrier against sexuality unlicensed by the state. Even many leftists and progressives, who actively contest male authority and at least some of the assumptions behind privacy, are queasy about constructing a family politics with queerness on the inside rather than the outside.

When such sexuality is culturally recognized *within* family bounds, "the family" ceases to function as an enforcer of sexual norms. That is why the moms and dads in groups like P-FLAG, an organization primarily of parents supportive of their lesbian and gay children, make such emotionally powerful spokespersons for the cause of civil rights. Parents who welcome sexual dissenters within the family undermine the notion that such dissent is intrinsically antithetical to deep human connection.

The theme of cultural anxiety about forms of sexuality not bounded and controlled by the family runs through a series of recent judicial decisions. In each case, the threat to norms did not come from an assault on the prerogatives of family by libertarian outsiders, a prospect often cited by the right wing to trigger social anxieties. Instead, each court faced the dilemma of how to repress, at least in the law, the anomaly of unsanctioned sexuality within the family.

In a stunning decision in 1989, the Supreme Court ruled in *Michael H. v. Gerald D.* that a biological father had no constitutionally protected right to a relationship with his daughter, despite both paternity (which was not disputed) and a psychological bond that the two had formed. Instead, the Court upheld the rule that because the child's mother—who had had an affair with the child's biological father—was married to another man, the girl would be presumed to be the husband's child. It was more important, the Court declared, to protect the "unitary family," that is, the marriage, than to subject anyone to "embarrassment" by letting the child and her father continue to see each other. The Court ruled that a state could properly force the termination of that bond rather than "disrupt an otherwise harmonious and apparently exclusive marital relationship." We are not bound, the Court said, to protect what it repeatedly described as "adulterous fathers."

In *Hodgson v. Minnesota*, the Supreme Court upheld a Minnesota requirement that a pregnant teenager had to notify both of her parents—even if they were divorced or if there was a threat of violence from her family—prior to obtaining an abortion, so long as she had the alternative option to petition a court. The decision was read primarily as an abortion decision and a ruling on the extent of privacy protection that will be accorded a minor who decides to have an abortion. But the case was also, at its core, about sex in the family and specifically about whether parents could rely on the state for assistance in learning whether a daughter is sexually active.

In two very similar cases in 1991, appellate courts in New York and California ruled that a lesbian partner who had coparented a child with the biological mother for some years had no standing to seek visitation after the couple split up. Both courts acknowledged that the best interests of the child would be served by allowing a parental relationship to continue, but both also ruled that the law would not recognize what the New York court called "a biological stranger." Such a person could be a parent only if there had been a marriage or an adoption.

Indeed, perhaps the most important point in either decision was the footnote in the California ruling that invited lesbian and gay couples to adopt children jointly: "We see nothing in these [statutory] provisions that would preclude a child from being jointly adopted by someone of the same sex as the natural parent." This opens the door for many more such adoptions, at least in California, which is one of six states where lesbian- or gay-couple adoption has occurred, although rarely. The New York court made no such overture.

The effort to legalize gay marriage will almost certainly emerge as a major issue in the next decade. Lawsuits seeking a right to marry have been filed in the District of Columbia and Hawaii, and activists in other states are contemplating litigation. In 1989, the Conference of Delegates of the State Bar of California endorsed an amendment of that state's law to permit lesbian and gay couples to marry.

The law's changes to protect sexual dissent within the family will occur at different speeds in different places, which might not be so bad. Family law has always been a province primarily of state rather than federal regulation, and often has varied from state to state; grounds for divorce, for example, used to differ dramatically depending on geography. What seems likely to occur in the next wave of family cases is the same kind of variability in the legal definition of the family itself. Those very discrepancies may help to denaturalize concepts like "marriage" and "parent," and to expose the utter contingency of the sexual conventions that, in part, construct the family.

21

SAVAGE INEQUALITIES
Children in America's Schools

JONATHAN KOZOL

Most academic studies of school finance, sooner or later, ask us to consider the same question: "How can we achieve more equity in education in America?" A variation of the question is a bit more circumspect: "How can we achieve both equity and excellence in education?" Both questions, however, seem to value equity as a desired goal. But, when the recommendations of such studies are examined, and when we look as well at the solutions that innumerable commissions have proposed, we realize that they do not quite mean "equity" and that they have seldom asked for "equity." What they mean, what they prescribe, is *something that resembles equity but never reaches it:* something close enough to equity to silence criticism by approximating justice, but far enough from equity to guarantee the benefits enjoyed by privilege. The differences are justified by telling us that equity must always be "approximate" and cannot possibly be perfect. But the imperfection falls in almost every case to the advantage of the privileged.

In Maryland, for instance, one of several states in which the courts have looked at fiscal inequalities between school districts, an equity suit filed in 1978, although unsuccessful, led the state to reexamine the school funding system. When a task force set up by the governor offered its suggestions five years later, it argued that 100 percent equality was too expensive. The goal, it said, was *75 percent equality*—meaning that the poorest districts should be granted no less than three quarters of the funds at the disposal of the average district. But, as the missing 25 percent translates into differences of input (teacher pay, provision of books, class size, etc.), we discover it is just enough to demarcate the difference between services appropriate to different social classes, and to formalize that difference in their destinies.

Kozol, Jonathan. "Savage Inequalities: Children in America's Schools." From *Savage Inequalities*. New York: Harper Collins. 1991, pp. 175–184. © 1991 by Jonathan Kozol. Reprinted by permission of Crown Publishers, Inc.

"The equalized 75 percent," says an educator in one of the state's low-income districts, "buys just enough to keep all ships afloat. The unequal 25 percent assures that they will sail in opposite directions."

It is a matter of national pride that every child's ship be kept afloat. Otherwise our nation would be subject to the charge that we deny poor children public school. But what is now encompassed by the one word ("school") are two very different kinds of institutions that, in function, finance and intention, serve entirely different roles. Both are needed for our nation's governance. But children in one set of schools are educated to be governors; children in the other set of schools are trained for being governed. The former are given the imaginative range to mobilize ideas for economic growth; the latter are provided with the discipline to do the narrow tasks the first group will prescribe.

Societies cannot be all generals, no soldiers. But, by our schooling patterns, we assure that soldiers' children are more likely to be soldiers and that the offspring of the generals will have at least the option to be generals. If this is not so, if it is just a matter of the difficulty of assuring perfect fairness, why does the unfairness never benefit the children of the poor?

. . .

"Children in a true sense," writes John Coons of Berkeley University, "are all poor" because they are dependent on adults. There is also, he says, "a sameness among children in the sense of [a] substantial uncertainty about their potential role as adults." It could be expressed, he says, "as an equality of innocence." The equality of adults, by comparison, "is always problematical; even social and economic differences among them are plausibly ascribed to their own deserts. . . . In any event, adults as a class enjoy no presumption of homogeneous virtue and their ethical demand for equality of treatment is accordingly attenuated. The differences among children, on the other hand, cannot be ascribed even vaguely to fault without indulging in an attaint of blood uncongenial to our time."

Terms such as "attaint of blood" are rarely used today, and, if they were, they would occasion public indignation; but the rigging of the game and the acceptance, which is nearly universal, of uneven playing fields reflect a dark unspoken sense that other people's children are of less inherent value than our own. Now and then, in private, affluent suburbanites concede that certain aspects of the game may be a trifle rigged to their advantage. "Sure, it's a bit unjust," they may concede, "but that's reality and that's the way the game is played. . . .

"In any case," they sometimes add in a refrain that we have heard now many times, "there's no real evidence that spending money makes much difference in the outcome of a child's education. We have it. So we spend it. But it's probably a secondary matter. Other factors—family and background—seem to be a great deal more important."

In these ways they fend off dangers of disturbing introspection; and this, in turn, enables them to give their children something far more precious than the simple gift of pedagogic privilege. They give them uncontaminated satisfaction in their victories. Their children learn to shut from mind the possibility that they are winners in an unfair race, and they seldom let themselves lose sleep about the losers. There are, of course, unusual young people who, no matter what their parents tell them, do become aware of the inequities at stake. We have heard the voices of a few such students. But the larger numbers of these favored children live with a remarkable experience of ethical exemption. Cruelty is seldom present in the thinking of such students, but it is contained within insouciance.

Sometimes the residents of affluent school districts point to certain failings in their own suburban schools, as if to say that "all our schools" are "rather unsuccessful" and that "minor differentials" between urban and suburban schools may not therefore be of much significance. "You know," said the father of two children who had gone to school in Great Neck, "it isn't just New York. We have our problems on Long Island too. My daughter had some high school teachers who were utterly inept and uninspired. She has had a devil of a time at Sarah Lawrence. . . ." He added that she had friends who went to private school and who were given a much better preparation. "It just seems terribly unfair," he said.

Defining unfairness as the difficulty that a Great Neck graduate encounters at a topflight private college, to which any child in the South Bronx would have given her right arm to be admitted, strikes one as a way of rendering the term so large that it means almost nothing. "What is unfair," he is saying in effect, "is what I *determine* to be unfair. What I find unfair is what affects my child, not somebody else's child in New York."

Competition at the local high school, said another Great Neck parent, was "unhealthy." He described the toll it took on certain students. "Children in New York may suffer from too little. Many of our children suffer from too much." The loss of distinctions in these statements serves to blur the differences between the inescapable unhappiness of being human and the needless misery created by injustice. It also frees the wealthy from the obligation to concede the difference between inconvenience and destruction.

·   ·   ·

Poor people do not need to be reminded that the contest is unfair. "My children," says Elizabeth, a friend of mine who lives in a black neighborhood of Boston, "know very well the system is unfair. They also know that they are living in a rich society. They see it on TV, and in advertisements, and in the movies. They see the president at his place in Maine, riding around the harbor in his motor boat and playing golf with other wealthy men. They know that men like these did not come out of schools in Roxbury or Harlem. They know that they were given something extra. They don't know exactly what it is, but they have seen enough, and heard enough, to know that men don't speak like that and look like that unless they have been fed with silver spoons—and went to schools that had a lot of silver spoons and other things that cost a lot. . . .

"So they know this other world exists, and, when you tell them that the government can't find the money to provide them with a decent place to go to school, they don't believe it and they know that it's a *choice* that has been made—a choice about how much they matter to society. They see it as a message: 'This is to tell you that you don't much matter. You are ugly to us so we crowd you into ugly places. You are dirty so it will not hurt to pack you into dirty places.' My son says this: 'By doing this to you, we teach you how much you are hated.' I like to listen to the things my children say. They're not so-phisticated so they speak out of their hearts."

One of the ideas, heard often in the press, that stirs the greatest sense of anger in a number of black parents that I know is that the obstacles black children face, to the extent that "obstacles" are still conceded, are attributable, at most, to "past injustice"—something dating maybe back to slavery or maybe to the era of official segregation that came to its close during the years from 1954 to 1968—but not, in any case, to something recent or contemporary or ongoing. The nostrum of a "past injustice"—an expression often spoken with sarcasm—is particularly cherished by conservatives because it serves to un-dercut the claim that young black people living now may have some right to preferential opportunities. Contemporary claims based on a "past injustice," after all, begin to seem implausible if the alleged injustice is believed to be a generation, or six generations, in the past. "We were not alive when these in-justices took place," white students say. "Some of us were born to parents who came here as immigrants. None of these things are our responsibility, and we should not be asked to suffer for them."

But the hundreds of classrooms without teachers in Chicago's public schools, the thousands of children without classrooms in the schools of Irv-ington and Paterson and East Orange, the calculated racial segregation of the children in the skating rink in District 10 in New York City, and the lifelong poisoning of children in the streets and schools of East St. Louis are not mat-ters of anterior injustice. They are injustices of 1991.

Over 30 years ago, the city of Chicago purposely constructed the high-speed Dan Ryan Expressway in such a way as to cut off the section of the city in which housing projects for black people had been built. The Robert Taylor Homes, served by Du Sable High, were subsequently constructed in that iso-lated area as well; realtors thereafter set aside adjoining neighborhoods for rental only to black people. The expressway is still there. The projects are still there. Black children still grow up in the same neighborhoods. There is noth-ing "past" about most "past discrimination" in Chicago or in any other north-ern city.

In seeking to find a metaphor for the unequal contest that takes place in public school, advocates for equal education sometimes use the image of a tainted sports event. We have seen, for instance, the familiar image of the playing field that isn't level. Unlike a tainted sports event, however, a childhood cannot be played again. We are children only once; and, after those few years are gone, there is no second chance to make amends. In this respect, the consequences of unequal education have a terrible finality. Those who are denied cannot be "made whole" by a later act of government. Those who get the unfair edge cannot be later stripped of what they've won. Skills, once attained—no matter how unfairly—take on a compelling aura. Effectiveness seems irrefutable, no matter how acquired. The winners in this race *feel* meritorious. Since they also are, in large part, those who govern the discussion of this issue, they are not disposed to cast a cloud upon the means of their ascent. People like Elizabeth are left disarmed. Their only argument is justice. But justice, poorly argued, is no match for the acquired ingenuity of the successful. The fruits of inequality, in this respect, are self-confirming.

. . .

There are "two worlds of Washington," the *Wall Street Journal* writes. One is the Washington of "cherry blossoms, the sparkling white monuments, the magisterial buildings of government . . ., of politics and power." In the Rayburn House Office Building, the *Journal* writes, "a harpist is playing Schumann's 'Traumerei,' the bartenders are tipping the top brands of Scotch, and two huge salmons sit on mirrored platters." Just over a mile away, the other world is known as Anacostia.

In an elementary school in Anacostia, a little girl in the fifth grade tells me that the first thing she would do if somebody gave money to her school would be to plant a row of flowers by the street. "Blue flowers," she says. "And I'd buy some curtains for my teacher." And she specifies again: "Blue curtains."

I ask her, "Why blue curtains?"

"It's like this," she says. "The school is dirty. There isn't any playground. There's a hole in the wall behind the principal's desk. What we need to do is first rebuild the school. Another color. Build a playground. Plant a lot of flowers. Paint the classrooms. Blue and white. Fix the hole in the principal's office. Buy doors for the toilet stalls in the girls' bathroom. Fix the ceiling in this room. It looks like somebody went up and peed over our heads. Make it a beautiful clean building. Make it *pretty*. Way it is, I feel ashamed."

Her name is Tunisia. She is tall and thin and has big glasses with red frames. "When people come and see our school," she says, "they don't say nothing, but I know what they are thinking."

"Our teachers," says Octavia, who is tiny with red sneakers and two beaded cornrows in her hair, "shouldn't have to eat here in the basement. I would like for them to have a dining room. A nice room with a salad bar. Serve our teachers big thick steaks to give them energy."

A boy named Gregory tells me that he was visiting in Fairfax County on the weekend. "Those neighborhoods are different," Gregory reports. "They got a golf course there. Big houses. Better schools."

I ask him why he thinks they're better schools.

"We don't know why," Tunisia says. "We are too young to have the information."

"You live in certain areas and things are different," Gregory explains.

Not too long ago, the basement cafeteria was flooded. Rain poured into the school and rats appeared. Someone telephoned the mayor: "You've got dead rats here in the cafeteria."

The principal is an aging, slender man. He speaks of generations of black children lost to bitterness and failure. He seems worn down by sorrow and by anger at defeat. He has been the principal since 1959.

"How frustrating it is," he says, "to see so many children going hungry. On Fridays in the cafeteria I see small children putting chicken nuggets in their pockets. They're afraid of being hungry on the weekend."

A teacher looks out at her class: "These children don't smile. Why should they learn when their lives are so hard and so unhappy?"

Seven children meet me in the basement cafeteria. The flood that brought the rats is gone, but other floods have streaked the tiles in the ceiling.

The school is on a road that runs past several boarded buildings. Gregory tells me they are called "pipe" houses. "Go by there one day—it be vacant. Next day, they bring sofas, chairs. Day after that, you see the junkies going in."

I ask the children what they'd do to get rid of the drugs.

"Get the New Yorkers off our streets," Octavia says. "They come here from New York, perturbed, and sell our children drugs."

"Children working for the dealers," Gregory explains.

A teacher sitting with us says, "At eight years old, some of the boys are running drugs and holding money for the dealers. By 28, they're going to be dead."

Tunisia: "It makes me sad to see black people kill black people."

"Four years from now," the principal says when we sit down to talk after the close of school, "one-third of the little girls in this fifth grade are going to be pregnant."

I look into the faces of these children. At this moment they seem full of hope and innocence and expectation. The little girls have tiny voices and they squirm about on little chairs and lean way forward with their elbows on the table and their noses just above the table's surface and make faces at each other and seem mischievous and wise and beautiful. Two years from now, in junior high, there may be more toughness in their eyes, a look of lessened expectations and increased cynicism. By the time they are 14, a certain rawness and vulgarity may have set in. Many will be hostile and embittered by that time. Others will coarsen, partly the result of diet, partly self-neglect and self-dislike. Visitors who meet such girls in elementary school feel tenderness; by junior high, they feel more pity or alarm.

But today, in Anacostia, the children are young and whimsical and playful. If you hadn't worked with kids like these for 20 years, you would have no reason to feel sad. You'd think, "They have the world before them."

"The little ones come into school on Monday," says the teacher, "and they're hungry. A five-year-old. Her laces are undone. She says, 'I had to dress myself this morning.' I ask her why. She says, 'They took my mother off to jail.' Their stomachs hurt. They don't know why. We feed them something hot because they're hungry."

I ask the children if they go to church. Most of them say they do. I ask them how they think of God.

"He has a face like ours," Octavia says.

A white face or a black face?

"Mexican," she says.

Tunisia: "I don't know the answer to that question."

"When you go to God," says Gregory, "He'll remind you of everything you did. He adds it up. If you were good, you go to Heaven. If you were selfish, then He makes you stand and wait awhile—over there. Sometimes you get a second chance. You need to wait and see."

We talk about teen-agers who get pregnant. Octavia explains: "They want to be like rock stars. Grow up fast." She mentions a well-known singer. "She left school in junior high, had a baby. Now she got a swimming pool and car."

Tunisia says, "That isn't it. Their lives are sad."

A child named Monique goes back to something we discussed before: "If I had a lot of money, I would give it to poor children."

The statement surprises me. I ask her if the children in this neighborhood are poor. Several children answer, "No."

Tunisia (after a long pause): "We are all poor people in this school."

The bell rings, although it isn't three o'clock. The children get up and say goodbye and start to head off to the stairs that lead up from the basement to the first floor. The principal later tells me he released the children early. He had been advised that there would be a shooting in the street this afternoon.

I tell him how much I liked the children and he's obviously pleased. Tunisia, he tells me, lives in the Capital City Inn—the city's largest homeless shelter. She has been homeless for a year, he says; he thinks that this may be one reason she is so reflective and mature.

22

PREPARING FOR POWER
Cultural Capital and Curricula in America's Elite Boarding Schools

PETER W. COOKSON, JR. • CAROLINE HODGES PERSELL

Borrowing from the British, early American headmasters and teachers advocated a boarding school curriculum that was classical, conservative, and disciplined. It wasn't until the latter part of the nineteenth century that such "soft" subjects as English, history, and mathematics were given a place beside Latin, Greek, rhetoric, and logic in the syllabus. It was the early schoolmasters' belief that young minds, especially boys' minds, if left to their own devices, were undisciplined, even anarchic. The only reliable antidote to mental flabbiness was a rigorous, regular regime of mental calisthenics. A boy who could not flawlessly recite long Latin passages was required to increase his mental workouts. Classical languages were to the mind what cold showers were to the body: tonics against waywardness.

Girls, with some exceptions, were not thought of as needing much mental preparation for their future roles as wives and mothers. Their heads were best left uncluttered by thought; too much book learning could give a girl ideas about independence. Besides, the great majority of them were not going on to college, where even more classical languages were required.

As an intellectual status symbol, the classical curriculum helped distinguish gentlemen from virtually everyone else and thus defined the difference between an "educated" man and an untutored one, as well as the difference between high culture and popular culture. Such a division is critical to exclude nonmembers from groups seeking status. For a long time a classical curriculum was the only path to admission to a university, as Harvard and many others required candidates to demonstrate proficiency in Latin and Greek (Levine 1980). Thus, the curriculum of boarding schools has long served both social and practical functions.

Culture, much like real estate or stocks, can be considered a form of capital. As the French scholars Pierre Bourdieu and Jean-Claude Passeron (1977) have indicated, the accumulation of cultural capital can be used to reinforce class differences. Cultural capital is socially created: What constitutes the "best in western civilization" is not arrived at by happenstance, nor was it decided upon by public election. The more deeply embedded the values, the more likely they will be perceived as value free and universal.

Thus curriculum is the nursery of culture and the classical curriculum is the cradle of high culture. The definition of what is a classical course of study has evolved, of course, since the nineteenth century. Greek and Latin are no longer required subjects in most schools—electives abound. But the disciplined and trained mind is still the major objective of the boarding school curriculum.

> The Groton curriculum is predicated on the belief that certain qualities of mind are of major importance: precise and articulate communication; the ability to compute accurately and to reason quantitatively; a grasp of scientific approaches to problem-solving; an understanding of the cultural, social, scientific, and political background of Western civilization; and the ability to reason carefully and logically and to think imaginatively and sensitively. Consequently the School puts considerable emphasis on language, mathematics, science, history, and the arts. (*Groton School* 1981–82:15)

The contrast between the relatively lean curricula of many public schools and the abundant courses offered by boarding schools is apparent. In catalogues of the boarding school's academic requirements, courses are usually grouped by subject matter, and at the larger schools course listings and descriptions can go on for several dozen pages. Far from sounding dreary, the courses described in most catalogues are designed to whet the intellectual appetite. Elective subjects in particular have intriguing titles such as "Hemingway: The Man and His Work," "Varieties of the Poetic Experience," "Effecting Political Change," "Rendezvous with Armageddon," and for those with a scientific bent, "Vertebrate Zoology" and "Mammalian Anatomy and Physiology."

Boarding school students are urged to read deeply and widely. A term course on modern American literature may include works from as many as 10 authors, ranging from William Faulkner to Jack Kerouac. Almost all schools offer a course in Shakespeare in which six or seven plays will be read.

In history, original works are far more likely to be assigned than excerpts from a textbook. A course on the presidency at one school included the following required readings: Rossiter, *The American Presidency*; Hofstadter, *The American Political Tradition*; Hargrove, *Presidential Leadership*; Schlesinger, *A Thousand Days*; Kearns, *Lyndon Johnson and the American Dream*; and White, *Breach of Faith*. Courses often use a college-level text, such as Garraty's *The American Nation* or Palmer's *A History of the Modern World*. Economic history is taught as well—in one school we observed a discussion of the interplay between politics and the depression of 1837—and the idea that there are multiple viewpoints in history is stressed. It is little wonder that many prep school graduates find their first year of college relatively easy.

An advanced-placement English class uses a collection of *The Canterbury Tales* by Geoffrey Chaucer that includes the original middle English on the left page and a modern English translation on the right. An advanced third-year French course includes three or four novels as well as two books of grammar and readings. Even social science courses require a great deal of reading. In a course called "An Introduction to Human Behavior" students are assigned 11 texts including works from B. F. Skinner, Sigmund Freud, Erich Fromm, Jean Piaget, and Rollo May.

Diploma requirements usually include: four years of English, three years of math, three years in one foreign language, two years of history or social science, two years of laboratory science, and one year of art. Many schools require a year of philosophy or religion and also may have such noncredit diploma requirements as four years of physical education, a library skills course, introduction to computers, and a seminar on human sexuality. On average, American public high school seniors take one year less English and math, and more than a year less foreign language than boarding school students (Coleman, Hoffer, and Kilgore 1982:90). Moreover, in the past two decades there has been a historical decline in the number of academic subjects taken by students in the public schools (Adleman 1983).

Because success on the Scholastic Aptitude Test is so critical for admission to a selective college, it is not uncommon for schools to offer English review classes that are specifically designed to help students prepare for the tests. Most schools also offer tutorials and remedial opportunities for students who are weak in a particular subject. For foreign students there is often a course in English as a second language.

As the arts will be part of the future roles of boarding school students, the music, art, and theater programs at many schools are enriching, with special courses such as "The Sound and Sense of Music," "Advanced Drawing," and "The Creative Eye in Film." Student art work is usually on display, and almost every school will produce several full-length plays each year, for example, *Arsenic and Old Lace, A Thurber Carnival, Dracula,* and *The Mousetrap.*

Music is a cherished tradition in many boarding schools, in keeping with their British ancestry. The long-standing "Songs" at Harrow, made famous because Winston Churchill liked to return to them for solace during World War II, are a remarkable display of school solidarity. All 750 boys participate, wearing identical morning coats with tails. Every seat is filled in the circular, sharply tiered replica of Shakespeare's Globe Theater as the boys rise in unison, their voices resonating in the rotunda.

The belief that a well-rounded education includes some "hands-on" experience and travel runs deep in the prep view of learning. Virtually every boarding school provides opportunities for its students to study and work off campus. As volunteers, Taft students, for instance, can "tutor on a one-to-one basis in inner-city schools in Waterbury, act as teachers' helpers in Waterbury Public Schools and work with retarded children at Southbury Training School." They can also work in convalescent homes, hospitals, and day-care centers, and act as "apprentices to veterinarians and help with Girl Scout troops" (*Taft* 1981–82:21). At the Ethel Walker School in Connecticut, girls can go on whale watches, trips to the theater, or work in the office of a local politician. The Madeira School in Virginia has a co-curriculum program requiring students to spend every Wednesday participating in volunteer or internship situations.

Generally speaking, the schools that take the position that manual labor and firsthand experience are good for the soul as well as the mind and body, are more progressive in orientation than other schools. At the Putney School every student has to take a tour of duty at the cow barn, starting at 5:30 A.M. In their own words, "Putney's work program is ambitious. We grow much of our own food, mill our own lumber, pick up our own trash, and have a large part in building our buildings. . . . Stoves won't heat until wood is cut and split" (*The Putney School* 1982:3).

Various styles of student-built structures dot the campus of the Colorado Rocky Mountain School, and at the tiny Midland School in California, there is no service staff, except for one cook. When the water pump breaks, faculty and students fix it, and when buildings are to be built, faculty and students pitch in. "We choose to live simply, to distinguish between our needs and our wants, to do without many of the comforts which often obscure the significant things in life" (*Midland School* 1983:1). The creed of self-reliance is reenacted every day at Midland. When a trustee offered to buy the school a swimming pool, he was turned down. Lounging around a pool is not part of the Midland philosophy.

Travel is very much part of the prep way of life and is continued right through the school year. Not only are semesters or a year abroad (usually in France or Spain) offered, but at some of the smaller schools, everyone goes on an extensive field trip. Every March at the Verde Valley School in Arizona the students travel to "Hopi, Navajo and Zuni reservations, to small villages in northern Mexico, to isolated Spanish-American communities in northern New Mexico and to ethnic neighborhoods of Southwestern cities. They live with native families, attend and teach in schools, work on ranches, and participate in the lives of the host families and their communities" (*Verde Valley School* 1982–83:9). Not all boarding schools, of course, place such a high value on rubbing shoulders with the outside world. At most of the academies, entrepreneurial, and girls' schools the emphasis is on service rather than sharing.

While boarding schools may vary in their general philosophy, the actual curricula do not widely differ. The pressures exerted on prep schools to get their students into good colleges means that virtually all students must study the same core subjects. Although not quick to embrace educational innovation, many boarding schools have added computers to their curricula. This has no doubt been encouraged by announcements by a number of Ivy League and other elite colleges that they want their future applicants to be "computer literate." While people at most boarding schools, or anywhere else for that matter, are not quite sure what is meant by computer literate, they are trying to provide well-equipped computer rooms and teachers who can move their students toward computer proficiency.

For students who have particular interests that cannot be met by the formal curriculum, almost all schools offer independent study, which gives students and teachers at boarding schools a great deal of intellectual flexibility. At Groton, for example, independent study can cover a diverse set of topics including listening to the works of Wagner, conducting a scientific experiment, or studying a special aspect of history.

The boarding school curriculum offers students an abundant buffet of regular course work, electives, volunteer opportunities, travel, and independent study, from which to choose a course of study. By encouraging students to treat academic work as an exciting challenge rather than just a job to be done, the prep schools not only pass on culture but increase their students' competitive edge in the scramble for admission to selective colleges.

THE IMPORTANCE OF SPORTS

Even the most diligent student cannot sit in classrooms all day, and because the prep philosophy emphasizes the whole person, boarding schools offer an impressive array of extracurricular activities, the most important of which is athletics. At progressive schools, the competitive nature of sport is deemphasized. The "afternoon out-of-door program" at Putney, for example, allows for a wide variety of outdoor activities that are noncompetitive; in fact, "skiing is the ideal sport for Putney as one may ski chiefly to enjoy himself, the air, the snow" (*The Putney School*, 1982;15).

Putney's sense that sport should be part of a communion with nature is not shared by most other schools, however. At most prep schools sport is about competition, and even more important, about winning. An athletically powerful prep school will field varsity, junior varsity, and third-string teams in most major sports. A typical coed or boys' school will offer football, soccer, cross-country, water polo, ice hockey, swimming, squash, basketball, wrestling, winter track, gymnastics, tennis, golf, baseball, track, and lacrosse. For the faint-hearted there are alternative activities such as modern dance, cycling, tai chi, yoga, ballet, and for the hopelessly unathletic, a "fitness" class. A truly traditional prep school will also have crew like their English forebears at Eton and Harrow. Certain schools have retained such British games as "Fives," but most stop short of the mayhem masquerading as a game called rugby.

Prep teams compete with college freshmen teams, other prep teams, and occasionally with public schools, although public school competitors are picked with care. Not only is there the possible problem of humiliation on the field, there is the even more explosive problem of fraternization in the stands when prep meets townie. Some schools, known as "jock" schools, act essentially as farm teams for Ivy League colleges, consistently providing them with athletes who have been polished by the prep experience. Many prep schools take public high school graduates for a postgraduate year, as a way of adding some size and weight to their football teams.

Prep girls also love sports; they participate as much as the boys, often in the same sports, and with as much vigor. A girls' field hockey game between Exeter and Andover is as intense as when the varsity football teams clash. Horseback riding at girls' schools is still popular; a number of the girls go on to ride in the show or hunt circuit. Unlike many of the girls in public schools, the boarding-school girl is discouraged from being a spectator. Loafing is considered to be almost as bad for girls as it is for boys.

During the school year the halls of nearly all prep schools are decorated with either bulletins of sporting outcomes or posters urging victory in some upcoming game. Pep rallies are common, as are assemblies when awards are given and competitive spirit is eulogized. Often the whole school will be bussed to an opponent's campus if the game is considered to be crucial or if the rivalry is long-standing.

Alumni return to see games, and there are frequent contests between alumni and varsity teams. Because preps retain the love of fitness and sports, it is not uncommon for the old warriors to give the young warriors a thrashing. Similarly, the prep life also invariably includes ritual competitions between, say, the girls' field hockey team and a pick-up faculty team.

Nowhere is the spirit of victory more pronounced than on the ice of the hockey rink. Few public schools can afford a hockey rink so prep schools can attract the best players without much competition. Some prep schools import a few Canadians each year to fill out the roster. Speed, strength, endurance, and fearlessness are the qualities that produce winning hockey and more than one freshman team from an Ivy League college has found itself outskated by a prep team. Whatever else may be, in Holden Caulfield's term, "phony" about prep schools, sports are for real. This emphasis on sport is not without its critics. At the Harrow School in London, the new headmaster, who was an all-England rugby player, has begun a program to reward artistic and musical prowess as well as athletic and academic skills.

The athletic facilities at prep schools are impressive, and at the larger schools, lavish. Acres and acres of playing fields, scores of tennis courts, one or more gyms, a hockey rink, a golf course, swimming pools, squash courts, workout rooms—all can be found on many prep school campuses. Generally, the facilities are extremely well maintained. The equipment most preps use is the best, as are the uniforms. One boy described how "when your gym clothes get dirty, you simply turn them in at the locker room for a fresh set." The cost of all this, of course, is extraordinary, but considered necessary, because excellence in sport is part of the definition of a gentleman or gentlewoman.

The pressure for athletic success is intense on many campuses, and a student's, as well as a school's, social standing can ride on the narrow margin between victory and defeat. Perhaps because of this, schools generally take great pains to play schools of their own size and social eliteness. A study of who plays whom among prep schools reveals that schools will travel great distances, at considerable expense, to play other prep schools whose students and traditions are similar to their own.

EXTRACURRICULARS AND PREPARATION FOR LIFE

Not all prep school extracurricular activities require sweating, however. Like public school students, preps can work on the school newspaper or yearbook, help to organize a dance, or be part of a blood donor drive, and are much more likely than their public school counterparts to be involved in such activities. For example, one in three boarding school students is involved in student government compared to one in five public school students, and two in five are involved in the school newspaper or yearbook compared to one in five. This evidence is consistent with other research. Coleman, Hoffer, and Kilgore (1982) found that private school students participate more in extracurricular activities than do public school students. The fact that more boarding school students than public school students are involved in activities provides additional opportunities for them to practice their verbal, interpersonal, and leadership skills.

The catalogue of clubs at prep schools is nearly endless. The opportunity for students to develop special nonacademic interests is one of the qualities of life at prep schools that distinguishes them from many public schools. Special interest clubs for chess, sailing, bowling, or gun clubs are popular at boys' schools. One elite boys' school has a "war games" club. As the boys at this school are feverishly calculating their country's next strategic arms move, the girls in a Connecticut school are attending a meeting of Amnesty International. Girls, in general, tend to spend their off hours studying the gentler arts such as gourmet cooking and art history. One girls' school has a club with a permanent service mission to the governor's office.

At some schools students can learn printing, metalwork, or woodworking. The shop for the latter at Groton is amply equipped and much of the work turned out by the students is of professional quality. The less traditional schools offer clubs for vegetarian cooking, weaving, quilting, folk music, and—in subtle juxtaposition to the Connecticut girls' school—international cooking. At western schools, the horse still reigns supreme and many students spend endless hours riding, training, cleaning, and loving their own horse, or a horse they have leased from the school.

With the prep emphasis on music, choirs, glee clubs, madrigals, chamber music groups, as well as informal ensembles are all given places to practice. Most schools also have individual practice rooms, and like athletic teams, many prep musicians travel to other schools for concerts and performances.

Some schools offer a five-week "Winterim," during which students and faculty propose and organize a variety of off- and on-campus activities and studies. Such a program breaks the monotony of the usual class routine in the middle of winter, a season teachers repeatedly told us was the worst time at boarding school. It also enables students and faculty to explore new areas or interests in a safe way, that is, without grades.

In prep schools there is a perceived need for students to exercise authority as apprentice leaders early in their educational careers. The tradition of delegating real authority to students has British roots, where head boys and prefects have real power within the public schools. Head boys can discipline other boys by setting punishments and are treated by headmaster and house-masters alike as a part of the administration. In the United States, student power is generally more limited, although at the progressive schools students can be quite involved in the administrative decision-making process.

Virtually all prep schools have a student government. The formal structure of government usually includes a student body president, vice president, treasurer, secretary, class presidents, and dorm prefects, representatives, or "whips," as they are called at one school. Clubs also have presidents and there are always committees to be headed. Some schools have student-faculty senates and in schools like Wooster, in Connecticut, students are expected to play a major part in the disciplinary system. An ambitious student can obtain a great deal of experience in committee work, developing transferable skills for later leadership positions in finance, law, management, or politics.

The office of student body president or head prefect is used by the administration primarily as an extension of the official school culture, and most of the students who fill these offices are quite good at advancing the school's best public relations face. A successful student body president, like a good head, is artful in developing an easy leadership style, which is useful because he or she is in a structural political dilemma. Elected by the students but responsible to the school administration, the student politician is a classic go-between, always running the danger of being seen as "selling out" by students and as "uncooperative" by the administration. Occasionally students rebel against too much pandering to the administration and elect a rebel leader, who makes it his or her business to be a thorn in the side of the administration. A number of heads and deans of students watch elections closely, because if elections go "badly" it could mean a difficult year for them.

The actual content of real power varies by school. At some, authority is more apparent than real; at others, student power can affect important school decisions. At Putney, the "Big Committee" is composed of the school director, student leaders, and teachers. The powers of the Big Committee are laid out in the school's constitution, and students at Putney have real input into the decision-making process. At the Thacher School in California, the Student Leadership Council, which is composed of the school chairman, presidents of the three lower classes, and head prefects, is not only responsible for student activities and events, but also grants funds to groups who petition for special allocations. The power of the purse is learned early in the life of a prep school student. At the Westtown School in Pennsylvania, the student council arrives at decisions not by voting yea or nay, "but by following the Quaker custom of arriving at a 'sense of the meeting' " (*Westtown School* 1982–83:25).

Not all students, of course, participate in school politics; it may well be that many of the students most admired by their peers never run, or never would run, for a political position. The guerrilla leaders who emerge and flourish in the student underlife—or counterculture—may have far greater real power than the "superschoolies" that tend to get elected to public office.

In most coeducational schools boys tend to monopolize positions of power. The highest offices are generally held by boys; girls are found in the vice presidential and secretarial positions. Politics can be important to prep families and we suspect that a number of prep boys arrive at boarding school with a good supply of political ambition. One of the reasons advanced in support of all-girls' schools is that girls can gain important leadership experience there.

Some schools try to capture what they see as the best aspects of single-sex and coed schools. They do this by having boys and girls elect distinct school leaders, by having certain customs, places, and events that they share only with members of their own sex, and by having classes, certain other activities, and social events be coeducational. These schools, often called coordinate schools, see themselves as offering the chance to form strong single-sex bonds, to build self-confidence in adolescents, and to provide experience in working and relating to members of both sexes. Girls at coed schools more generally are likely to say they think in 10 years they will find the social skills they learned to be the most valuable part of their boarding-school experience.

LEARNING BY EXAMPLE

Part of the social learning students obtain is exposure to significant public personalities. Virtually all the schools have guest speaker programs in which well-known people can be seen and heard. Some of the speakers that have appeared at Miss Porter's School in the last several years include Alex Haley, author; Russell Baker, humorist; Arthur Miller, playwright; and Dick Gregory, comedian. At the boys' schools there is a tendency to invite men who are successful in politics and journalism. Recent speakers at the Hill School include James A. Baker III, Secretary of the Treasury (Hill class of 1948); James Reston, columnist; Frank Borman, astronaut and president of Eastern Airlines; and William Proxmire, United States senator (Hill class of 1934).

Inviting successful alumni to return for talks is one of the ways boarding schools can pass on a sense of the school's efficacy. Throughout the year panels, assemblies, and forums are organized for these occasions. Often the alumni speakers will also have informal sessions with students, visit classrooms, and stay for lunch, tea, or supper.

In keeping with cultural environments of prep schools, especially the select 16 schools, professional musicians, actors, and dancers are regularly invited to perform. Art and sculpture exhibits are common and some schools, such as Andover and Exeter, have permanent art galleries. The art at prep schools is generally either original works by artists such as Toulouse-Lautrec, Matisse, or Daumier, or the work of established contemporary artists such as

Frank Stella, who graduated from Andover. At a large school there may be so much cultural activity that it is unnecessary to leave campus for any kind of high cultural event.

Those who come to elite boarding schools to talk or perform are the makers of culture. For adolescents seeking to be the best, these successful individuals give them a sense of importance and empowerment. All around them are the symbols of their special importance—in Groton's main hallway hangs a personal letter from Ronald Reagan to the headmaster, reminding the students that Groton "boasts a former President of the United States and some of America's finest statesmen." Five or six books a year will be published by a school's alumni; Exeter in particular has many alumni authors, including James Agee, Nathaniel G. Benchley, John Knowles, Dwight Macdonald, Jr., Arthur M. Schlesinger, Jr., Sloan Wilson, and Gore Vidal. Roger L. Stevens, Alan Jay Lerner, and Edward Albee are all Choate-Rosemary Hall alumni, adding luster to a theater program that trains many professional actresses and actors. A student at an elite school is part of a world where such success is expected, and celebrity and power are part of the unfolding of life. Not every school is as culturally rich as the elite eastern prep schools, but in the main, most schools work hard to develop an appreciation for high culture. At the Orme School in Arizona, a week is set aside each year in which the whole school participates in looking at art, watching art being made, and making art.

Nowhere is the drive for athletic, cultural, and academic excellence more apparent than in the awards, honors, and prizes that are given to outstanding teams or students at the end of each year. Sporting trophies are often large silver cups with the names of annual champions engraved on several sides. At some schools the triumphs have come with enough regularity to warrant building several hundred yards of glass casing to hold the dozens of medals, trophies, and other mementos that are the victors' spoils. Pictures of past winning teams, looking directly into the camera, seem frozen in time.

Academic prizes tend to be slightly less flashy but no less important. Much like British schoolmasters, American schoolmasters believe in rewarding excellence, so most schools give a number of cultural, service, and academic prizes at the end of each year. There is usually at least one prize in each academic discipline, as well as prizes for overall achievement and effort. There are service prizes for dedicated volunteers, as well as debating and creative writing prizes. Almost all schools have cum laude and other honor societies.

Sitting through a graduation ceremony at a boarding school can be an endurance test—some schools give so many prizes that one could fly from New York to Boston and back in the time it takes to go from the classics prize to the prize for the best woodworking or weaving project. But of course, the greatest prize of all is graduation, and more than a few schools chisel, paint, etch, or carve the names of the graduates into wood, stone, or metal to immortalize their passage from the total institution into the world.

REFERENCES

Adleman, Clifford. 1983. "Devaluation, Diffusion and the College Connection: A Study of High School Transcripts, 1964–1981." Washington, D.C.: National Commission on Excellence in Education.

Bourdieu, Pierre and Jean-Claude Passeron. 1977. *Reproduction: In Education, Society, and Culture.* Beverly Hills, CA: Sage.

Coleman, James S., Thomas Hoffer, and Sally Kilgore. 1982. *High School Achievement.* New York: Basic Books, p. 90.

Levine, Steven B. 1980. "The Rise of American Boarding Schools and the Development of a National Upper Class." *Social Problems* 28:63–94.

23

CIVILIZE THEM WITH A STICK

MARY CROW DOG • RICHARD ERDOES

. . . Gathered from the cabin, the wickiup, and the tepee,
partly by cajolery and partly by threats;
partly by bribery and partly by force,
they are induced to leave their kindred
to enter these schools and take upon themselves
the outward appearance of civilized life.
—ANNUAL REPORT OF THE DEPARTMENT OF INTERIOR, 1901

It is almost impossible to explain to a sympathetic white person what a typical old Indian boarding school was like; how it affected the Indian child suddenly dumped into it like a small creature from another world, helpless, defenseless, bewildered, trying desperately and instinctively to survive and sometimes not surviving at all. I think such children were like the victims of Nazi concentration camps trying to tell average, middle-class Americans what their experience had been like. Even now, when these schools are much improved, when the buildings are new, all gleaming steel

---

and glass, the food tolerable, the teachers well trained and well intentioned, even trained in child psychology—unfortunately the psychology of white children, which is different from ours—the shock to the child upon arrival is still tremendous. Some just seem to shrivel up, don't speak for days on end, and have an empty look in their eyes. I know of an 11-year-old on another reservation who hanged herself, and in our school, while I was there, a girl jumped out of the window, trying to kill herself to escape an unbearable situation. That first shock is always there.

Although the old tiyospaye has been destroyed, in the traditional Sioux families, especially in those where there is no drinking, the child is never left alone. It is always surrounded by relatives, carried around, enveloped in warmth. It is treated with the respect due to any human being, even a small one. It is seldom forced to do anything against its will, seldom screamed at, and never beaten. That much, at least, is left of the old family group among full-bloods. And then suddenly a bus or car arrives, full of strangers, usually white strangers, who yank the child out of the arms of those who love it, taking it screaming to the boarding school. The only word I can think of for what is done to these children is kidnapping.

Even now, in a good school, there is impersonality instead of close human contact; a sterile, cold atmosphere, an unfamiliar routine, language problems, and above all the maza-skan-skan, that damn clock—white man's time as opposed to Indian time, which is natural time. Like eating when you are hungry and sleeping when you are tired, not when that damn clock says you must. But I was not taken to one of the better, modern schools. I was taken to the old-fashioned mission school at St. Francis, run by the nuns and Catholic fathers, built sometime around the turn of the century and not improved a bit when I arrived, not improved as far as the buildings, the food, the teachers, or their methods were concerned.

In the old days, nature was our people's only school and they needed no other. Girls had their toy tipis and dolls, boys their toy bows and arrows. Both rode and swam and played the rough Indian games together. Kids watched their peers and elders and naturally grew from children into adults. Life in the tipi circle was harmonious—until the whiskey peddlers arrived with their wagons and barrels of "Injun whiskey." I often wished I could have grown up in the old, before-whiskey days.

Oddly enough, we owed our unspeakable boarding schools to the do-gooders, the white Indian-lovers. The schools were intended as an alternative to the outright extermination seriously advocated by generals Sherman and Sheridan, as well as by most settlers and prospectors overrunning our land. "You don't have to kill those poor benighted heathen," the do-gooders said, "in order to solve the Indian Problem. Just give us a chance to turn them into useful farmhands, laborers, and chambermaids who will break their backs for you at low wages." In that way the boarding schools were born. The kids were taken away from their villages and pueblos, in their blankets and moccasins, kept completely isolated from their families—sometimes for as long as ten years—suddenly coming back, their short hair slick with pomade, their necks raw from stiff, high collars, their thick jackets always short in the sleeves and pinching under the arms, their tight patent leather shoes giving them corns, the girls in starched white blouses and clumsy, high-buttoned boots—caricatures of white people. When they found out—and they found out quickly—that they were neither wanted by whites nor by Indians, they got good and drunk, many of them staying drunk for the rest of their lives. I still have a poster I found among my grandfather's stuff, given to him by the missionaries to tack up on his wall. It reads:

1. Let Jesus save you.
2. Come out of your blanket, cut your hair, and dress like a white man.
3. Have a Christian family with one wife for life only.
4. Live in a house like your white brother. Work hard and wash often.
5. Learn the value of a hard-earned dollar. Do not waste your money on giveaways. Be punctual.
6. Believe that property and wealth are signs of divine approval.
7. Keep away from saloons and strong spirits.
8. Speak the language of your white brother. Send your children to school to do likewise.
9. Go to church often and regularly.
10. Do not go to Indian dances or to the medicine men.

The people who were stuck upon "solving the Indian Problem" by making us into whites retreated from this position only step by step in the wake of Indian protests.

The mission school at St. Francis was a curse for our family for generations. My grandmother went there, then my mother, then my sisters and I. At one time or other every one of us tried to run away. Grandma told me once about the bad times she had experienced at St. Francis. In those days they let students go home only for one week every year. Two days were used up for transportation, which meant spending just five days out of 365 with her family. And that was an improvement. Before grandma's time, on many reservations they did not let the students go home at all until they had finished school. Anybody who disobeyed the nuns was severely punished. The building in which my grandmother stayed had three floors, for girls only. Way up in the attic were little cells, about five by five by ten feet. One time she was in church and instead of praying she was playing jacks. As punishment they took her to one of those little cubicles where she stayed in darkness because the windows had been boarded up. They left her there for a whole week with only bread and water for nourishment. After she came out she promptly ran away, together with three other girls. They were found and brought back. The nuns stripped them naked and whipped them. They used a horse buggy whip on my grandmother. Then she was put back into the attic—for two weeks.

My mother had much the same experiences but never wanted to talk about them, and then there I was, in the same place. The school is now run by the BIA—the Bureau of Indian Affairs—but only since about 15 years ago. When I was there, during the 1960s, it was still run by the Church. The Jesuit fathers ran the boys' wing and the Sisters of the Sacred Heart ran us—with the help of the strap. Nothing had changed since my grandmother's days. I have been told recently that even in the '70s they were still beating children at that school. All I got out of school was being taught how to pray. I learned quickly that I would be beaten if I failed in my devotions or, God forbid, prayed the wrong way, especially prayed in Indian to Wakan Tanka, the Indian Creator.

The girls' wing was built like an F and was run like a penal institution. Every morning at five o'clock the sisters would come into our large dormitory to wake us up, and immediately we had to kneel down at the sides of our beds and recite the prayers. At six o'clock we were herded into the church for more of the same. I did not take kindly to the discipline and to marching by the clock, left-right, left-right. I was never one to like being forced to do something. I do something because I feel like doing it. I felt this way always, as far as I can remember, and my sister Barbara felt the same way. An old medicine man once told me: "Us Lakotas are not like dogs who can be trained, who can be beaten and keep on wagging their tails, licking the hand that whipped them. We are like cats, little cats, big cats, wildcats, bobcats, mountain lions. It doesn't matter what kind, but cats who can't be tamed, who scratch if you step on their tails." But I was only a kitten and my claws were still small.

Barbara was still in the school when I arrived and during my first year or two she could still protect me a little bit. When Barb was a seventh grader she ran away together with five other girls, early in the morning before sunrise. They brought them back in the evening. The girls had to wait for two hours in front of the mother superior's office. They were hungry and cold, frozen through. It was wintertime and they had been running the whole day without food, trying to make good their escape. The mother superior asked each girl, "Would you do this again?" She told them that as punishment they would not be allowed to visit home for a month and that she'd keep them busy on work details until the skin on their knees and elbows had worn off. At the end of her speech she told each girl, "Get up from this chair and lean over it." She then lifted the girls' skirts and pulled down their underpants. Not little girls either, but teenagers. She had a leather strap about a foot long and four inches wide fastened to a stick, and beat the girls, one after another, until they cried. Barb did not give her that satisfaction but just clenched her teeth. There was one girl, Barb told me, the nun kept on beating and beating until her arm got tired.

I did not escape my share of the strap. Once, when I was 13 years old, I refused to go to Mass. I did not want to go to church because I did not feel well. A nun grabbed me by the hair, dragged me upstairs, made me stoop over, pulled my dress up (we were not allowed at the time to wear jeans), pulled my panties down, and gave me what they called "swats"—25 swats with a board around which Scotch tape had been wound. She hurt me badly.

My classroom was right next to the principal's office and almost every day I could hear him swatting the boys. Beating was the common punishment for not doing one's homework, or for being late to school. It had such a bad effect upon me that I hated and mistrusted every white person on sight, because I met only one kind. It was not until much later that I met sincere white people I could relate to and be friends with. Racism breeds racism in reverse.

The routine at St. Francis was dreary. Six A.M., kneeling in church for an hour or so; seven o'clock, breakfast; eight o'clock, scrub the floor, peel spuds, make classes. We had to mop the dining room twice every day and scrub the tables. If you were caught taking a rest, doodling on the bench with a fingernail or knife, or just rapping, the nun would come up with a dish towel and just slap it across your face, saying, "You're not supposed to be talking; you're supposed to be working!" Monday mornings we had cornmeal mush, Tuesday oatmeal, Wednesday rice and raisins, Thursday cornflakes, and Friday all the leftovers mixed together or sometimes fish. Frequently the food had bugs or rocks in it. We were eating hot dogs that were weeks old, while the nuns were dining on ham, whipped potatoes, sweet peas, and cranberry sauce. In winter our dorm was icy cold while the nuns' rooms were always warm.

I have seen little girls arrive at the school, first graders, just fresh from home and totally unprepared for what awaited them, little girls with pretty braids, and the first thing the nuns did was chop their hair off and tie up what was left behind their ears. Next they would dump the children into tubs of alcohol, a sort of rubbing alcohol, "to get the germs off." Many of the nuns were German immigrants, some from Bavaria, so that we sometimes speculated whether Bavaria was some sort of Dracula country inhabited by monsters. For the sake of objectivity I ought to mention that two of the German fathers were great linguists and that the only Lakota-English dictionaries and grammars which are worth anything were put together by them.

At night some of the girls would huddle in bed together for comfort and reassurance. Then the nun in charge of the dorm would come in and say, "What are the two of you doing in bed together? I smell evil in this room. You girls are evil incarnate. You are sinning. You are going to hell and burn forever. You can act that way in the devil's frying pan." She would get them out of bed in the middle of the night, making them kneel and pray until morning. We had not the slightest idea what it was all about. At home we slept two and three in a bed for animal warmth and a feeling of security.

The nuns and the girls in the two top grades were constantly battling it out physically with fists, nails, and hair-pulling. I myself was growing from a kitten into an undersized cat. My claws were getting bigger and were itching for action. About 1969 or 1970 a strange young white girl appeared on the reservation. She looked about 18 or 20 years old. She was pretty and had long, blond hair down to her waist, patched jeans, boots, and a backpack. She was different from any other white person we had met before. I think her name was Wise. I do not know how she managed to overcome our reluctance and distrust, getting us into a corner, making us listen to her, asking us how we were treated. She told us that she was from New York. She was the first real hippie or Yippie we had come across. She told us of people called the Black Panthers, Young Lords, and Weathermen. She said, "Black people are getting it on. Indians are getting it on in St. Paul and California. How about you?" She also said, "Why don't you put out an underground paper, mimeograph it. It's easy. Tell it like it is. Let it all hang out." She spoke a strange lingo but we caught on fast.

Charlene Left Hand Bull and Gina One Star were two full-blood girls I used to hang out with. We did everything together. They were willing to join me in a Sioux uprising. We put together a newspaper which we called the *Red Panther.* In it we wrote how bad the school was, what kind of slop we had to eat—slimy, rotten, blackened potatoes for two weeks—the way we were beaten. I think I was the one who wrote the worst article about our principal of the moment, Father Keeler. I put all my anger and venom into it. I called him a goddam wasicŭn of a bitch. I wrote that he knew nothing about Indians and should go back to where he came from, teaching white children whom he could relate to. I wrote that we knew which priests slept with which nuns and that all they ever could think about was filling their bellies and buying a new car. It was the kind of writing which foamed at the mouth, but which also lifted a great deal of weight from one's soul.

On Saint Patrick's Day, when everybody was at the big powwow, we distributed our newspapers. We put them on windshields and bulletin boards, in desks and pews, in dorms and toilets. But someone saw us and snitched on us. The shit hit the fan. The three of us were taken before a board meeting. Our parents, in my case my mother, had to come. They were told that ours was a most serious matter, the worst thing that had ever happened in the school's long history. One of the nuns told my mother, "Your daughter really needs to be talked to." "What's wrong with my daughter?" my mother asked. She was given one of our *Red Panther* newspapers. The nun pointed out its name to her and then my piece, waiting for mom's reaction. After a while she asked, "Well, what have you got to say to this? What do you think?"

My mother said, "Well, when I went to school here, some years back, I was treated a lot worse than these kids are. I really can't see how they can have any complaints, because we was treated a lot stricter. We could not even wear skirts halfway up our knees. These girls have it made. But you should forgive them because they are young. And it's supposed to be a free country, free speech and all that. I don't believe what they done is wrong." So all I got out of it was scrubbing six flights of stairs on my hands and knees, every day. And no boy-side privileges.

The boys and girls were still pretty much separated. The only time one could meet a member of the opposite sex was during free time, between 4 and 5:30, in the study hall or on benches or the volleyball court outside, and that was strictly supervised. One day Charlene and I went over to the boys' side. We were on the ball team and they had to let us practice. We played three extra minutes, only three minutes more than we were supposed to. Here was the nuns' opportunity for revenge. We got 25 swats. I told Charlene, "We are getting too old to have our bare asses whipped that way. We are old enough to have babies. Enough of this shit. Next time we fight back." Charlene only said, "Hoka-hay!"

. . .

In a school like this there is always a lot of favoritism. At St. Francis it was strongly tinged with racism. Girls who were near-white, who came from what the nuns called "nice families," got preferential treatment. They waited on the faculty and got to eat ham or eggs and bacon in the morning. They got the easy jobs while the skins, who did not have the right kind of background—myself among them—always wound up in the laundry room sorting out 10-bushel baskets of dirty boys' socks every day. Or we wound up scrubbing the floors and doing all the dishes. The school therefore fostered fights and antagonism between whites and breeds, and between breeds and skins. At one time Charlene and I had to iron all the robes and vestments the priests wore when saying Mass. We had to fold them up and put them into a chest in the back of the church. In a corner, looking over our shoulders, was a statue of the crucified Savior, all bloody and beaten up. Charlene looked up and said, "Look at that poor Indian. The pigs sure worked him over." That was the closest I ever came to seeing Jesus.

I was held up as a bad example and didn't mind. I was old enough to have a boyfriend and promptly got one. At the school we had an hour and a half for ourselves. Between the boys' and the girls' wings were some benches where one could sit. My boyfriend and I used to go there just to hold hands and talk. The nuns were very uptight about any boy-girl stuff. They had an exaggerated fear of anything having even the faintest connection with sex. One day in religion class, an all-girl class, Sister Bernard singled me out for some remarks, pointing me out as a bad example, an example that should be shown. She said that I was too free with my body. That I was holding hands which meant that I was not a good example to follow. She also said that I wore unchaste dresses, skirts which were too short, too suggestive, shorter than regulations permitted, and for that I would be punished. She dressed me down before the whole class, carrying on and on about my unchastity.

. . .

We got a new priest in English. During one of his first classes he asked one of the boys a certain question. The boy was shy. He spoke poor English, but he had the right answer. The priest told him, "You did not say it right. Correct yourself. Say it over again." The boy got flustered and stammered. He could hardly get out a word. But the priest kept after him: "Didn't you hear? I told you to do the whole thing over. Get it right this time." He kept on and on.

I stood up and said, "Father, don't be doing that. If you go into an Indian's home and try to talk Indian, they might laugh at you and say, 'Do it over correctly. Get it right this time!' "

He shouted at me, "Mary, you stay after class. Sit down right now!"

I stayed after class, until after the bell. He told me, "Get over here!" He grabbed me by the arm, pushing me against the blackboard, shouting, "Why are you always mocking us? You have no reason to do this."

I said, "Sure I do. You were making fun of him. You embarrassed him. He needs strengthening, not weakening. You hurt him. I did not hurt you."

He twisted my arm and pushed real hard. I turned around and hit him in the face, giving him a bloody nose. After that I ran out of the room, slamming the door behind me. He and I went to Sister Bernard's office. I told her, "Today I quit school. I'm not taking any more of this, none of this shit anymore. None of this treatment. Better give me my diploma. I can't waste any more time on you people."

Sister Bernard looked at me for a long, long time. She said, "All right, Mary Ellen, go home today. Come back in a few days and get your diploma." And that was that. Oddly enough, that priest turned out okay. He taught a class in grammar, orthography, composition, things like that. I think he wanted more respect in class. He was still young and unsure of himself. But I was in there too long. I didn't feel like hearing it. Later he became a good friend of the Indians, a personal friend of myself and my husband. He stood up for us during Wounded Knee and after. He stood up to his superiors, stuck his neck way out, became a real people's priest. He even learned our language. He died prematurely of cancer. It is not only the good Indians who die young, but the good whites, too. It is the timid ones who know how to take care of themselves who grow old. I am still grateful to that priest for what he did for us later and for the quarrel he picked with me—or did I pick it with him?—because it ended a situation which had become unendurable for me. The day of my fight with him was my last day in school.

24

MISSING IN INTERACTION

MYRA SADKER • DAVID SADKER

"Candid Camera" would have a field day in elementary school. There would be no need to create embarrassing situations. Just set the camera to take a photograph every sixty seconds. Since classroom action moves so swiftly, snapshots slow down the pace and reveal subliminal gender lessons.

Snapshot #1	Tim answers a question.
Snapshot #2	The teacher reprimands Alex.
Snapshot #3	Judy and Alice sit with hands raised while Brad answers a question.
Snapshot #4	Sally answers a question.
Snapshot #5	The teacher praises Marcus for skill in spelling.
Snapshot #6	The teacher helps Sam with a spelling mistake.
Snapshot #7	The teacher compliments Alice on her neat paper.
Snapshot #8	Students are in lines for a spelling bee. Boys are on one side of the room and girls are on the other.

As the snapshots continue, the underlying gender messages become clear. The classroom consists of two worlds: one of boys in action, the other of girls' inaction. Male students control classroom conversation. They ask and answer more questions. They receive more praise for the intellectual quality of their ideas. They get criticized. They get help when they are confused. They are the heart and center of interaction. Watch how boys dominate the discussion in this upper elementary class about presidents.

The fifth-grade class is almost out of control. "Just a minute," the teacher admonishes. "There are too many of us here to all shout out at once. I want you to raise your hands, and then I'll call on you. If you shout out, I'll pick somebody else."

Order is restored. Then Stephen, enthusiastic to make his point, calls out.

STEPHEN: I think Lincoln was the best president. He held the country together during the war.

TEACHER: A lot of historians would agree with you.

From *Failing at Fairness: How America's Schools Cheat Girls*. New York: Scribner & Sons. 1994. p. 42–76. © 1994 by Myra Sadker and David Sadker. Reprinted with permission from Scribner, a division of Simon & Schuster.

MIKE: (seeing that nothing happened to Stephen, calls out):   I don't. Lincoln was okay, but my Dad liked Reagan. He always said Reagan was a great president.

DAVID: (calling out):   Reagan? Are you kidding?

TEACHER: Who do you think our best president was, Dave?

DAVID: FDR. He saved us from the depression.

MAX: (calling out):   I don't think it's right to pick one best president. There were a lot of good ones.

TEACHER: That's interesting.

KIMBERLY: (calling out):   I don't think the presidents today are as good as the ones we used to have.

TEACHER: Okay, Kimberly. But you forgot the rule. You're supposed to raise your hand.

The classroom is the only place in society where so many different, young, and restless individuals are crowded into close quarters for an extended period of time day after day. Teachers sense the undertow of raw energy and restlessness that threatens to engulf the classroom. To preserve order, most teachers use established classroom conventions such as raising your hand if you want to talk.

Intellectually, teachers know they should apply this rule consistently, but when the discussion becomes fast-paced and furious, the rule is often swept aside. When this happens and shouting out begins, it is an open invitation for male dominance. Our research shows that boys call out significantly more often than girls. Sometimes what they say has little or nothing to do with the teacher's questions. Whether male comments are insightful or irrelevant, teachers respond to them. However, when girls call out, there is a fascinating occurrence: Suddenly the teacher remembers the rule about raising your hand before you talk. And then the girl, who is usually not as assertive as the male students, is deftly and swiftly put back in her place.

Not being allowed to call out like her male classmates during the brief conversation about presidents will not psychologically scar Kimberly; however, the system of silencing operates covertly and repeatedly. It occurs several times a day during each school week for twelve years, and even longer if Kimberly goes to college, and, most insidious of all, it happens subliminally. This micro-inequity eventually has a powerful cumulative impact.

On the surface, girls appear to be doing well. They get better grades and receive fewer punishments than boys. Quieter and more conforming, they are the elementary school's ideal students. "If it ain't broke, don't fix it" is the school's operating principle as girls' good behavior frees the teacher to work with the more difficult-to-manage boys. The result is that girls receive less time, less help, and fewer challenges. Reinforced for passivity, their independence and self-esteem suffer. As victims of benign neglect, girls are penalized for doing what they should and lose ground as they go through school. In contrast, boys get reinforced for breaking the rules; they are rewarded for grabbing more than their fair share of the teacher's time and attention.

Even when teachers remember to apply the rules consistently, boys are still the ones who get noticed. When girls raise their hands, it is often at a right angle, arm bent at the elbow, a cautious, tentative, almost insecure gesture. At other times they raise their arms straight and high, but they signal silently. In contrast, when boys raise their hands, they fling them wildly in the air, up and down, up and down, again and again. Sometimes these hand signals are accompanied by strange noises, "Ooh! Ooh! Me! Me! Ooooh!" Occasionally they even stand beside or on top of their seats and wave one or both arms to get attention. "Ooh! Me! Mrs. Smith, call on me." In the social studies class about presidents, we saw boys as a group grabbing attention while girls as a group were left out of the action.

When we videotape classrooms and play back the tapes, most teachers are stunned to see themselves teaching subtle gender lessons along with math and spelling. The teacher in the social studies class about presidents was completely unaware that she gave male students more attention. Only after several viewings of the videotape did she notice how she let boys call out answers but reprimanded girls for similar behavior. Low-achieving boys also get plenty of attention, but more often it's negative. No surprise there. In general, girls receive less attention, but there's another surprise: Unlike the smart boy who flourishes in the classroom, the smart girl is the student who is least likely to be recognized.

When we analyzed the computer printouts for information about gender and race, an intriguing trend emerged. The students most likely to receive teacher attention were white males; the second most likely were minority males; the third, white females; and the least likely, minority females. In elementary school, receiving attention from the teacher is enormously important for a student's achievement and self-esteem. Later in life, in the working world, the salary received is important, and the salary levels parallel the classroom: white males at the top and minority females at the bottom. In her classroom interaction studies, Jacqueline Jordan Irvine found that black girls were active, assertive, and salient in the primary grades, but as they moved up through elementary school, they became the most invisible members of classrooms.

THE "OKAY" CLASSROOM IS NOT

In our studies of sexism in classroom interaction, we have been particularly fascinated by the ways teachers react to student work and comments because this feedback is crucially important to achievement and self-esteem. We found that teachers typically give students four types of responses.

TEACHER   *praises:* "Good job." "That was an excellent paper." "I like the way you're thinking."

TEACHER   *remediates,* encouraging a student to correct a wrong answer or expand and enhance thinking: "Check your addition." "Think about what you've just said and try again."

TEACHER   *criticizes,* giving an explicit statement that something is not correct: "No, you've missed number four." This category also includes statements that are much harsher: "This is a terrible report."

TEACHER   *accepts,* offering a brief acknowledgement that an answer is accurate: "Uh-huh." "Okay."

Teachers praise students only 10 percent of the time. Criticism is even rarer—only 5 percent of comments. In many classrooms teachers do not use any praise or criticism at all. About one-third of teacher interactions are comprised of remediation, a dynamic and beneficial form of feedback.

More than half the time, however, teachers slip into the routine of giving the quickest, easiest, and least helpful feedback—a brief nonverbal nod, a quick "Okay." They rely more on acceptance than on praise, remediation, and criticism combined. The bland and neutral "Okay" is so pervasive that we doubt the "Okay Classroom" is, in fact, okay.

In our research in more than one hundred classrooms, we found that while boys received more of all four reactions, the gender gap was greatest in the most precise and valuable feedback. Boys were more likely to be praised, corrected, helped, and criticized—all reactions that foster student achievement. Girls received the more superficial "Okay" reaction, one that packs far less educational punch. In her research, Jacqueline Jordan Irvine found that black females were least likely to receive clear academic feedback.

At first teachers are surprised to see videotapes where girls are "Okay'd" and boys gain clear feedback. Then it begins to make sense. "I don't like to tell a girl anything is wrong because I don't want to upset her," many say. This vision of females as fragile is held most often by male teachers." What if she cries? I wouldn't know how to handle it."

The "Okay" response is well meaning, but it kills with kindness. If girls don't know when they are wrong, if they don't learn strategies to get it right, then they never will correct their mistakes. And if they rarely receive negative feedback in school, they will be shocked when they are confronted by it in the workplace.

PRETTY IS—HANDSOME DOES

Ashley Reiter, National Winner of the 1991 Westinghouse Talent Competition for her sophisticated project on math modeling, remembers winning her first math contest. It happened at the same time that she first wore her contact lenses. Triumphant, Ashley showed up at school the next day without glasses and with a new medal. "Everybody talked about how pretty I looked," Ashley remembers. "Nobody said a word about the math competition."

The one area where girls are recognized more than boys is appearance. Teachers compliment their outfits and hairstyles. We hear it over and over again—not during large academic discussions but in more private moments, in small groups, when a student comes up to the teacher's desk, at recess, in hallways, at lunchtime, when children enter and exit the classroom: "Is that a new dress?" "You look so pretty today." "I love your new haircut. It's so cute." While these comments are most prevalent in the early grades, they continue through professional education: "That's a great outfit." "You look terrific today."

Many teachers do not want to emphasize appearance. "They pull you in," a preschool teacher says. "The little girls come up to you with their frilly dresses and hair ribbons and jewelry. 'Look what I have,' they say and wait for you to respond. What are you supposed to do? Ignore them? Insult them? They look so happy when you tell them they're pretty. It's a way of connecting. I think it's what they're used to hearing, the way they are rewarded at home."

When teachers talk with boys about appearance, the exchanges are brief—quick recognition and then on to something else. Or teachers use appearance incidents to move on to a physical skill or academic topic. In one exchange, a little boy showed the teacher his shiny new belt buckle. Her response: "Cowboys wore buckles like that. They were rough and tough and they rode horses. Did you know that?"

When teachers talk to girls about their appearance, the conversations are usually longer, and the focus stays on how pretty the girl looks. Sometimes the emphasis moves from personal appearance to papers and work. When boys are praised, it is most often for the intellectual quality of their ideas. Girls are twice as likely to be praised for following the rules of form. "I love your margins" is the message.

THE BOMBING RATE

"How long do you wait for students to answer a question?" When we ask teachers to describe what they do hundreds of times daily in the classroom, their answers are all over the map: One minute. Ten seconds. Five seconds. Twenty-five seconds. Three seconds.

Mary Budd Rowe was the first researcher to frame this question and then try to answer it. Following her lead, many others conducted wait time studies and uncovered an astonishingly hurried classroom. On average, teachers wait only nine-tenths of a second for a student to answer a question. If a student can't answer within that time, teachers call on another student or answer the question themselves.

When questions are hurled at this bombing rate, some students get lost, confused, or rattled, or just drop out of the discussion. "Would you repeat that?" "Say it again." "Give me a minute. I can get it." Requests such as these are really pleas for more time to think. Nobody has enough time in the bombing rate classroom, but boys have more time than girls.

Waiting longer for a student to answer is one of the most powerful and positive things a teacher can do. It is a vote of confidence, a way of saying, "I have high expectations for you, so I will wait a little longer. I know you can get it if I give you a chance." Since boys receive more wait time, they try harder to achieve. As girls struggle to answer under the pressure of time, they may flounder and fail. Watch how it happens:

> "Okay, class, get ready for your next problem. Mr. Warren has four cash registers. Each register weighs thirteen kilograms. How many kilograms do the registers weigh altogether? Linda?"
>
> The teacher waits half a second. Linda looks down at her book and twists her hair. She says nothing in the half-second allotted to her.
>
> "Michael?"
>
> The teacher waits two seconds. Michael is looking down at his book. The teacher waits two more seconds. Michael says, "Fifty-two?"
>
> "Good. Exactly right."

Less assertive in class and more likely to think about their answers and how to respond, girls may need *more* time to think. In the real world of the classroom, they receive less. For female achievement and self-esteem, it is a case of very bad timing.

BOY BASTIONS—GIRL GHETTOS

Raphaela Best spent four years as an observer in an elementary school in one of Maryland's most affluent counties. She helped the children with schoolwork, ate lunch with them, and played games with them in class and at recess. As an anthropologist, she also took copious notes. After more than one thousand hours of living with the children, she concluded that elementary school consists of separate and unequal worlds. She watched segregation in action firsthand. Adult women remember it well.

A college student recalled, "When I was in elementary school, boys were able to play basketball and kick ball. They had the side of the playground with the basketball hoops." Another college woman remembers more formal segregation: "I went to a very small grammar school. At recess and gym the boys played football and the girls jumped rope. All except one girl and one boy—they did the opposite. One day they were pulled aside. I'm not exactly sure what they were told, but the next day the schoolyard was divided in two. The boys got the middle and the girls got the edge, and neither sex was allowed on the other's part."

A third grader described it this way: "Usually we separate ourselves, but my teacher begins recess by handing a jump rope to the girls and a ball to the boys." Like the wave of a magic wand, this gesture creates strict gender lines. "The boys always pick the biggest areas for their games," she says. "We have what's left over, what they don't want."

Every morning at recess in schoolyards across the country, boys fan out over the prime territory to play kick ball, football, or basketball. Sometimes girls join them, but more often it's an all-male ball game. In the typical schoolyard, the boys' area is ten times bigger than the girls'. Boys never ask if it is their right to take over the territory, and it is rarely questioned. Girls huddle along the sidelines, on the fringe, as if in a separate female annex. Recess becomes a spectator sport.

Teachers seldom intervene to divide space and equipment more evenly, and seldom attempt to connect the segregated worlds—not even when they are asked directly by the girls.

"The boys won't let us play," a third grader said, tugging at the arm of the teacher on recess duty. "They have an all-boys club and they won't let any girls play."

"Don't you worry, honey," the teacher said, patting the little girl's hair. "When you get bigger, those boys will pay you all the attention you want. Don't you bother about them now."

As we observed that exchange, we couldn't help but wonder how the teacher would have reacted if the recess group had announced "No Catholics" or if white children had blatantly refused to play with Asians.

Barrie Thorne, a participant observer in elementary schools in California and Michigan whose students are mainly from working-class families, captured the tiny incidents that transform integrated classes into gender-divided worlds: Second-grade girls and boys eat lunch together around a long rectangular table. A popular boy walks by and looks the scene over. "Oooh, too many girls," he says, and takes a place at another table. All the boys immediately pick up their trays and abandon the table with girls, which has now become taboo.

Although sex segregation becomes more pervasive as children get older, contact points remain. School life has its own gender rhythm as girls and boys separate, come together, and separate again. But the points of contact, the together games that girls and boys play, often serve to heighten and solidify the walls of their separate worlds.

"You can't get me!" "Slobber Monster!" With these challenges thrown out, the game begins. It maybe called "Girls Chase the Boys" or "Boys Chase the Girls" or "Chase and Kiss." It usually starts out one on one, but then the individual boy and girl enlist same-sex peers. "C'mon, let's get that boy." "Help, a girl's gonna get me!"

Pollution rituals are an important part of these chases. Children treat one another as if they were germ carriers. "You've got cooties" is the cry. (Substitute other terms for different cultures or different parts of the country.) Elaborate systems are developed around the concept of cooties. Transfer occurs when one child touches another. Prepared for such attack, some protect themselves by writing C.V. (cooties vaccination) on their arms.

Sometimes boys give cooties to girls, but far more frequently girls are the polluting gender. Boys fling taunts such as "girl stain" or "girl touch" or "cootie girl." The least-liked girls, the ones who are considered fat or ugly or poor, become "cootie queens," the real untouchables of the class, the most contaminating females of all.

Chasing, polluting, and invasions, where one gender attacks the play area of the other, all function as gender intensifiers, heightening perceived differences between female and male to an extreme degree. The world of children and the world of adults is composed of *different* races, but each gender is socially constructed as so different, so alien that we use the phrase "the *opposite* sex."

It is boys who work hardest at raising the walls of sex segregation and intensifying the difference between genders. They distance themselves, sending the message that girls are not good enough to play with them. Watch which boys sit next to the girls in informally sex-segregated classrooms and lunchrooms; they are the ones most likely to be rejected by male classmates. Sometimes they are even called "girls." A student at The American University remembers his school lunchroom in Brooklyn:

> At lunch our class all sat together at one long table. All the girls sat
> on one side, and the boys sat on the other. This was our system.
> Unfortunately, there were two more boys in my class than seats on
> the boys' side. There was no greater social embarrassment for a boy
> in the very hierarchical system we had set up in our class than to
> have to sit on the girls' side at lunch. It happened to me once,
> before I moved up the class social ladder. Boys climbed the rungs of
> that ladder by beating on each other during recess. To this day,
> twenty years later, I remember that lunch. It was horrible.

Other men speak, also with horror, of school situations when they became "one of the girls." The father of a nine-year-old daughter remembered girls in elementary school as "worse than just different. We considered them a subspecies." Many teachers who were victims of sexist schooling themselves understand this system and collaborate with it; they warn noisy boys of a humiliating punishment: "If you don't behave, I'm going to make you sit with the girls."

Most little girls—five, six, seven, or eight—are much too young to truly understand and challenge their assignment as the lower-caste gender. But without challenge over the course of years, this hidden curriculum in second-class citizenship sinks in. Schools and children need help—intervention by adults who can equalize the playing field.

We have found that sex segregation in the lunchroom and schoolyard spills over into the classroom. In our three-year, multi-state study of one hundred classrooms, our raters drew "gender geography" maps of each class they visited. They found that more than half of the classes were segregated by gender. There is more communication across race than across gender in elementary schools.

We have seen how sex segregation occurs when children form self-selected groups. Sometimes the division is even clearer, and so is the impact on instruction.

> The students are seated formally in rows. There are even spaces between the rows, except down the middle of the room where the students have created an aisle large enough for two people standing side by side to walk down. On one side of the aisle, the students are all female; on the other side, all male. Black, white, Hispanic, and Asian students sit all around the room, but no student has broken the gender barrier.
>
> The teacher in the room is conducting a math game, with the right team (boys) against the left team (girls). The problems have been put on the board, and members of each team race to the front of the room to see who can write the answer first. Competition is intense, but eventually the girls fall behind. The teacher keeps score on the board, with two columns headed "Good Girls" and "Brilliant Boys."

The gender segregation was so formal in this class that we asked if the teacher had set it up. "Of course not." She looked offended. "I wouldn't think of doing such a thing. The students do it themselves." It never occurred to the well-meaning teacher to raise the issue or change the seats.

In our research we have found that gender segregation is a major contributor to female invisibility. In sex-segregated classes, teachers are pulled to the more talkative, more disruptive male sections of the classroom or pool. There they stay, teaching boys more actively and directly while the girls fade into the background.

THE CHARACTER(S) OF THE CURRICULUM

At a workshop on sexism in the curriculum, we asked participants, "Have you ever read the book *I'm Glad I'm a Boy! I'm Glad I'm a Girl!*?" Since most of the teachers, principals, and parents had not read it, we showed it to them. *I'm Glad I'm a Boy! I'm Glad I'm a Girl!* is for very young children. One page shows the jobs and activities that boys can do, and the following page shows what is appropriate for girls.

The book announces that boys can be doctors and shows a large male cartoon character with a stethoscope around his neck.

"What do girls do?" we asked the audience.

"They're nurses," the parents and educators chorused as one. They may not have read this book, but they seemed to know the plot line. A little girl nurse pushing a wheelchair is drawn on the page.

"Obviously a case of occupational stereotyping with the girl receiving less of every kind of reward including money, but do you notice anything else?" we asked. Most of the people were puzzled, but a few spotted the subtlety: "Look at how little the girl is." When we showed both pages at once, the boy doctor, a cartoon version of Doogie Howser, towered over the girl pushing the wheelchair.

The next page shows boys as pilots. "What are girls?" we asked.

"Stewardesses," the audience called back. A cartoon girl with a big smile and a short skirt carries a tray of drinks. The audience chuckled as several people remarked, "Look, her underpants are showing." "A little cheesecake for the younger set," someone joked as the next picture emerged, a boy drawn as a policeman.

"What are girls?"

This one had the group confused. "Mommies?" "Criminals?" "Crossing guards?" "Meter maids?" They found it. A tough-looking female figure is shown writing out a ticket for an obviously miserable motorist caught in a parking violation. "She looks as if she's had a steroid treatment," a teacher joked. "She's very big this time." The images continued: boys as those who eat, and girls as the ones who cook; boys as the builders of homes, and girls as the ones who clean them. The picture accompanying the caption about cleaning is that of a smiling cartoon girl pushing a vacuum cleaner. She and the cleaning machine are drawn very large because there is so much work to do. This image upset the audience. "Oh, no," several groaned. Others hissed and booed.

The next caption identified boys as the ones who fix things.

"Girls break things," the audience chorused back. But this time the author had outsmarted them. "Break" was too active. The parents and educators tried other stereotypes: "Girls clean things?" "Play with things?" "Buy things?" "Girls cry over things?"

"These are great responses, but they're all too active."

"Girls watch boys?" an astute parent suggested. She was on to something. Several studies have shown that in basal readers the activity girls are most often engaged in is watching boys in action. They look at boys play baseball, admire them as they perform magic tricks, wave good-bye from behind windows as boys leave for adventure. But in this case even "watch" was too active. The audience was stumped.

"Girls are things!" a young woman burst out. She had actually outdone the author, so we displayed the page: GIRLS NEED THINGS FIXED. The smiling stationary figure is holding the wheel of her doll carriage in her hand. She isn't doing anything with the wheel; she is just standing there beside her tipped-over vehicle, clearly in need of male help. The audience groaned, but the pictures went on with boys shown as inventing while girls are described as using things boys invent. Accompanying this description is an illustration of a girl lying in a hammock and reading, thanks to a lamp invented by a boy. "Who invented the cotton gin?" we asked. Several people from around the room answered, "Eli Whitney." Like Alexander Graham Bell and Thomas Edison, this name is one of the staples of American education. "Has anyone ever heard of Catherine Littlefield Greene?" The parents and teachers were silent.

We told the story of the woman who, after the death of her husband, Nathaniel, who had been a general in the Revolutionary War, met Eli Whitney. A Yale-educated tutor, Whitney devised a model for the gin while working at Greene's Mulberry Grove Mansion. But his design was flawed; although seeds were pulled from the cotton, they became clogged in the rollers. It was Kitty Greene who came up with the breakthrough idea of using brushes for the seeds. The concept of the machine was so simple that copycat gins sprang up on other plantations. To pay for lawsuits during the fierce battle for patent rights, Kitty Greene sold her estate. It wasn't until seven years later that Eli Whitney won full title to the cotton gin.

"Why wasn't the patent taken out in both names?" a history teacher asked. It was an excellent question, and in the answer is an important lesson for children. At a time when it was unseemly for women to write books (many female authors took male names), it was especially unlikely for a lady to patent an invention. Textbooks tell the story of the names registered in the patent office, but they leave out how sexism and racism denied groups of people access to that registry.

The caricature of gender roles isn't over, and the picture book moves from inventions to politics, showing boys as presidents and girls as their wives.

"Is this some kind of joke?" a teacher asked. "When was it written?"

We threw the question back at the audience.

"The 1920s?" someone called out.

"No, they didn't have stewardesses then. Or meter maids. I think it was the 1950s," another teacher suggested.

Most of the group were stunned to learn that the book was published in 1970 and was in circulation in libraries and schools for years afterward. Few teachers would read a book like this to children today, and if they did, the phone lines would light up in most communities. Twenty-five years ago, books like this were commonplace, and it is a sign of progress that today they are considered outrageous.

"This book is so bad, it's good," a kindergarten teacher said. "I want to show it to my class. A lot of my kids fly on planes and see male flight attendants, and one of my children has a mom who's a doctor."

We agreed that the book with its yesteryear sexism was a good teaching tool. We have shown it to students in every grade level. They had often read it critically and identified the stereotypes, but not always.

BALANCING THE BOOKS

Few things stir up more controversy than the content of the curriculum. Teachers, parents, students—all seem to be aware intuitively that schoolbooks shape what the next generation knows and how it behaves. In this case research supports intuition. When children read about people in nontraditional gender roles, they are less likely to limit themselves to stereotypes. When children read about women and minorities in history, they are more likely to feel these groups have made important contributions to the country. As one sixth grader told us, "I love to read biographies about women. When I learn about what they've done, I feel like a door is opening. If they can do great things, maybe I can, too."

DOUBLE JEOPARDY

During the spring of 1992 we visited sixteen fourth-, fifth-, and sixth-grade classes in Maryland, Virginia, and Washington, D.C., and gave students this assignment:

> In the next five minutes write down the names of as many famous women and men as you can. They can come from anywhere in the world and they can be alive or dead, but they must be real people. They can't be made up. Also—and this is very important—they can't be entertainers or athletes. See if you can name at least ten men and ten women.
>
> At first the students write furiously, but after about three minutes, most run out of names. On average, students generate eleven male names but only three women's. While the male names are drawn directly from the pages of history books, the female names represent far greater student creativity: Mrs. Fields, Aunt Jemima, Sarah Lee, Princess Di, Fergie, Mrs. Bush, Sally Ride, and children's book authors such as Beverly Cleary and Judy Blume. Few names come from the pages of history. Betsy Ross, Harriet Tubman, Eleanor Roosevelt, Amelia Earhart, Sojourner Truth, Sacajawea, Rosa Parks, Molly Pitcher, and Annie Oakley are sometimes mentioned.
>
> Several students cannot think of a single woman's name. Others have to struggle to come up with a few. In one sixth-grade class, a boy identified as the star history student is stumped by the assignment and obviously frustrated:
>
> "Have you got any girls?" he asks, turning to a classmate.
> "Sure. I got lots."
> "I have only one."
> "Think about the presidents."
> "There are no lady presidents."
> "Of course not. There's a law against it. But all you gotta do is take the presidents' names and put Mrs. in front of them."
>
> In a fourth-grade class, a girl is drawing a blank. She has no names under her Women column. A female classmate leans over to help.

"What about Francis Scott Key? She's famous." The girl immediately writes the name down. "Thanks," she says. "I forgot about her."

As we are leaving this class, one girl stops us. "I don't think we did very well on that list," she says. "It was too bad you didn't let us put in entertainers. We could've put in a lot of women then. I wrote down Madonna anyway."

Given a time line extending from the earliest days of human history to current events, and given no geographic limits whatsoever, these upper-elementary schoolchildren came up with only a handful of women. The most any single child wrote was nine. In one class the total number of women's names given didn't equal ten. We were stunned!

Something was very wrong—was it with the textbooks? We decided to look at them more closely. During the summer of 1992 we analyzed the content of fifteen math, language arts, and history textbooks used in Maryland, Virginia, and the District of Columbia. When we counted pictures of males and females, we were surprised to find that the 1989 language arts textbooks from Macmillan and D.C. Heath had twice as many boys and men as girls and women. In some readers the ratio was three to one. A 1989 upper-elementary history textbook had four times as many males pictures as females. In the 1992 D.C. Heath *Exploring Our World, Past and Present,* a text for sixth graders, only eleven female names were mentioned, and not a single American adult woman was included. In the entire 631 pages of a textbook covering the history of the world, only seven pages related to women, either as famous individuals or as a general group. Two of the seven pages were about Samantha Smith, a fifth-grade Maine student who traveled to the Soviet Union on a peace mission. While we felt that Samantha Smith's story brought an interesting message to other students, we wondered why Susan B. Anthony didn't rate a single line. No wonder students knew so little about women. Given the content of their history books, it was a tribute to their creativity that they could list any female names at all.

Every day in America little girls lose independence, achievement, and self-esteem in classes like this. Subtle and insidious, the gender-biased lessons result in quiet catastrophes and silent losses. But the casualties—tomorrow's women—are very real.

25

JOBLESS GHETTOS
The Social Implications of the Disappearance of Work in Segregated Neighborhoods

WILLIAM J. WILSON

In 1950, a substantial portion of the urban black population was poor but working. Urban poverty was quite extensive, but people held jobs. However, in many inner-city ghetto neighborhoods in 1990, most adults were not working in a typical week. For example, in 1950, 69 percent of all males 14 and over held jobs in a typical week in the three neighborhoods that represent the historic core of the Black Belt in Chicago—Douglas, Grand Boulevard, and Washington Park. But by 1990, only four in ten in Douglas worked in a typical week, one in three in Washington Park, and one in four in Grand Boulevard. In all, only 37 percent of all males 16 and over held jobs in a typical week in these neighborhoods.

The disappearance of work has had devastating effects not only on individuals and families but also on the social life of neighborhoods as well. Inner-city joblessness is a severe problem that is often overlooked or obscured when the focus is mainly on poverty and its consequences. Despite increases in the concentration of poverty since 1970, inner cities have always featured high levels of poverty, but the levels of inner-city joblessness reached in 1990 were unprecedented.[1]

It should be noted that when I refer to "joblessness" I am not solely referring to official unemployment. The unemployment rate represents only the *official* labor force—that is, those who are actively looking for work. It does not include those who are outside of or have dropped out of the labor market, including the nearly 6 million males age 25–60 who appear in the census statistics but do not show up in the labor statistics.[2]

These uncounted males in the labor market are disproportionately represented in the inner-city ghettos. A more appropriate measure of joblessness that takes into account both official unemployment and non–labor force participation is the employment-to-population ratio, which corresponds to the

From: Marshall, Ra (ed.). 2000. *Back to Shared Prosperity: The Growing Inequality of Wealth and Income in America*. Armonk: New York, M. W. Sharpe.

percentage of adults 16 and older who are working. In 1990, for example, only one in three adults ages 16 and older held a job in the ghetto poverty areas of Chicago, representing roughly 425,000 men, women, and children. And in the ghetto tracts of the nation's 100 largest cities, for every ten adults who did not hold a job in a typical week in 1990, there were only six employed persons.

The consequences of high neighborhood joblessness are more devastating than those of high neighborhood poverty. A neighborhood in which people are poor, but employed, is much different from a neighborhood in which people are poor and jobless. Many of today's problems in the inner-city ghetto neighborhoods—crime, family dissolution, welfare, low levels of social organization, and so on—are fundamentally a consequence of the disappearance of work.

It should be clear that when I speak of the disappearance of work, I am referring to the declining involvement in or lack of attachment to the formal labor market. It could be argued that the general sense of the term "joblessness" does not necessarily mean "non-work." Many people who are officially jobless are nonetheless involved in informal activities, ranging from unpaid housework to income from work in the informal or illegal economies.

Housework is work; baby-sitting is work; even drug dealing is work. However, what contrasts work in the formal economy with work activity in the informal and illegal economies is that work in the formal economy has greater regularity and consistency in schedules and hours. The demands for discipline are greater. It is true that some work activities outside the formal economy also call for discipline and regular schedules. Several studies reveal that the social organization of the drug industry is driven by discipline and a work ethic, however perverse. However, as a general rule, work in the informal and illegal economies is far less governed by norms or expectations that place a premium on discipline and regularity. For all these reasons, when I speak of the disappearance of work, I mean work in the formal economy, work that provides a framework for daily behavior because of the discipline and regularity that it imposes.

Thus, a youngster who grows up in a family with a steady breadwinner and in a neighborhood in which most of the adults are employed will tend to develop some of the disciplined habits associated with stable or steady employment—habits that are reflected in the behavior of his or her parents and of other neighborhood adults. These might include attachment to a routine, a recognition of the hierarchy found in most work situations, a sense of personal efficacy attained through the routine management of financial affairs, endorsement of a system of personal and material rewards associated with dependability and responsibility, and so on. Accordingly, when this youngster enters the labor market, he or she has a distinct advantage over the youngsters who grow up in households without a steady breadwinner and in neighborhoods that are not organized around work—in other words, a milieu in which one is more exposed to the less-disciplined habits associated with casual or infrequent work.

In the absence of regular employment, a person lacks not only a place in which to work and the receipt of regular income but also a coherent organization of the present—that is, a system of concrete expectations and goals. Regular employment provides the anchor for the spatial and temporal aspects of daily life. It determines where you are going to be and when you are going to be there. In the absence of regular employment, life, including family life, becomes less coherent. Persistent unemployment and irregular employment hinder rational planning in daily life, a necessary condition of adaptation to an industrial economy.[3]

EXPLANATIONS OF THE GROWTH OF JOBLESS GHETTOS

What accounts for the growing proportion of jobless adults in inner-city communities? An easy explanation would be racial segregation. However, a race-specific argument is not sufficient to explain recent changes in such neighborhoods. After all, these historical Black Belt neighborhoods were just as segregated by skin color in 1950 as they are today, yet the level of employment was much higher then. One has to account for the ways in which racial segregation interacts with other changes in society to produce the recent escalating rates of joblessness.

The disappearance of work in many inner-city neighborhoods is in part related to the nationwide decline in the fortunes of low-skilled workers. Over the past two decades, wage inequality has increased sharply and gaps in labor market outcomes between the less- and more-skilled workers have risen substantially. Research suggests that these changes are the result of "a substantial decline in the relative demand for the less-educated and those doing more routinized tasks compared to the relative supply of such workers."[4] Two factors appear to have reduced the relative demand for less-skilled workers—the computer revolution (i.e., skill-based technological change) and the internationalization of economic activity. Inner-city workers face an additional problem—the growing suburbanization of jobs. Most ghetto residents cannot afford cars and therefore rely on public transit systems that make the connection between inner-city neighborhoods and suburban job locations difficult and time consuming.

Although the relative importance of the different underlying causes of the growing jobs problems of the less-skilled, including those in the inner city, continues to be debated, there is little disagreement about the underlying trends. They are unlikely to reverse themselves.[5]

Changes in the class, racial, and demographic composition of inner-city neighborhoods have also contributed to the high percentage of jobless adults in these neighborhoods. Because of the steady outmigration of more advantaged families, the proportion of non-poor families and prime-age working adults has decreased sharply in the typical inner-city ghetto since 1970. These changes have made it increasingly difficult to sustain basic neighborhood institutions or to achieve adequate levels of social organization. The declining presence of working- and middle-class blacks has also deprived ghetto neighborhoods of key resources, including structural resources, such as residents with income to sustain neighborhood services, and cultural resources, such as conventional role models for neighborhood children.

It is not surprising therefore that our research in Chicago revealed that inner-city ghetto residents share a feeling of little informal social control of their children. A primary reason is the absence of a strong organizational capacity or an institutional resource base that would provide an extra layer of social organization in their neighborhoods. It is easier for parents to control the behavior of the children in their neighborhoods when a strong institutional resource base exists and when the links between community institutions such as churches, schools, political organizations, businesses, and civic clubs are strong or secure. The higher the density and stability of formal organizations, the less illicit activities such as drug trafficking, crime, prostitution, and the formation of gangs can take root in the neighborhood.

It is within this context that the public policy discussion on welfare reform and family values should be couched. Our Chicago research suggests that, as employment prospects recede, the foundation for stable relationships becomes weaker over time. More permanent relationships such as marriage give way to temporary liaisons that result in broken unions, out-of-wedlock pregnancies and births, and, to a lesser extent, separation and divorce. The changing norms concerning marriage in the larger society reinforce the movement toward temporary liaisons in the inner city, and therefore economic considerations in marital decisions take on even greater weight. The evolving cultural patterns are seen in the sharing of negative outlooks toward marriage and toward the relationships between males and females in the inner city, outlooks that are developed in and influenced by an environment featuring persistent joblessness. This combination of factors has increased out-of-wedlock births, weakened the family structure, expanded the welfare rolls, and, as a result, caused poor inner-city blacks to be even more disconnected from the job market and discouraged about their role in the labor force. The economic marginality of the ghetto poor is cruelly reinforced, therefore, by conditions in the neighborhoods in which they live.

In the eyes of employers in metropolitan Chicago, the social conditions in the ghetto render inner-city blacks less desirable as workers, and therefore many employers are reluctant to hire them. One of the three studies that provided the empirical foundation for *When Work Disappears* included a representative sample of employers in the greater Chicago area who provided entry-level jobs. An overwhelming majority of these employers, both white and black, expressed negative views about inner-city ghetto workers, and many stated that they were reluctant to hire them. For example, a president of an inner-city manufacturing firm expressed a concern about employing residents from certain inner-city neighborhoods:

> If somebody gave me their address, uh, Cabrini Green, I might unavoidably have some concerns. [*Interviewer:* What would your concerns be?] That the poor guy probably would be frequently

unable to get to work and . . . I probably would watch him more carefully, even if it wasn't fair, than I would with somebody else. I know what I should do though is recognize that here's a guy that is trying to get out of his situation and probably will work harder than somebody else who's already out of there and he might be the best one around here. But I, I think I would have to struggle accepting that premise at the beginning.

In addition to qualms about the neighborhood milieu, employers frequently mentioned concerns about applicants' language skills and educational training. An employer from a computer software firm expressed the view "that in many businesses the ability to meet the public is paramount and you do not talk street talk to the buying public. Almost all your black welfare people talk street talk. And who's going to sit them down and change their speech patterns?" A Chicago real estate broker made a similar point:

A lot of times I will interview applicants who are black, who are sort of lower class. . . . They'll come to me and I cannot hire them because their language skills are so poor. Their speaking voice for one thing is poor. . . . They have no verbal facility with the language . . . and these . . . you know, they just don't know how to speak and they'll say "salesmens" instead of "salesmen" and that's a problem. . . . They don't know punctuation, they don't know how to use correct grammar, and they cannot spell. And I can't hire them. And I feel bad about that and I think they're being very disadvantaged by the Chicago public school system.

Another respondent defended his method of screening out most job applicants on the telephone on the basis of their use of "grammar and English."

I have every right to say that that's a requirement for this job. I don't care if you're pink, black, green, yellow, or orange, I demand someone who speaks well. You want to tell me that I'm a bigot, fine, call me a bigot.

Finally, an inner-city banker claimed that many blacks in the ghetto "simply cannot read. When you're talking our type of business, that disqualifies them immediately. We don't have a job here that doesn't require that somebody have minimum reading and writing skills."

How should we interpret the negative attitudes and actions of employers? To what extent do they represent an aversion to blacks per se and to what degree do they reflect judgments based on the job-related skills and training of inner-city blacks in a changing labor market? I should point out that the statements made by the African-American employers concerning the qualifications of inner-city black workers do not differ significantly from those of the white employers. Whereas 74 percent of all the white employers who responded to the open-ended questions expressed negative views of the job-related traits of inner-city blacks, 80 percent of the black employers did so as well.

This raises a question about the meaning and significance of race in certain situations—in other words, how race intersects with other factors. A key hypothesis in this connection is that, given the recent shifts in the economy, employers are looking for workers with a broad range of abilities: "hard" skills (literacy, numeracy, basic mechanical ability, and other testable attributes) and "soft" skills (personalities suitable to the work environment, good grooming, group-oriented work behaviors, etc.). While hard skills are the product of education and training—benefits that are apparently in short supply in inner-city schools—soft skills are strongly tied to culture and are therefore shaped by the harsh environment of the inner-city ghetto. If employers are indeed reacting to the difference in skills between white and black applicants, it becomes increasingly difficult to discuss the motives of employers: are they rejecting inner-city black applicants out of overt racial discrimination or on the basis of qualifications?

Nonetheless, many of the selective recruitment practices do represent what economists call statistical discrimination: employers make assumptions about the inner-city black workers *in general* and reach decisions based on those assumptions before they have had a chance to review systematically the qualifications of an individual applicant. The net effect is that many black inner-city applicants are never given the chance to prove their qualifications on an individual level because they are systematically screened out by the selective recruitment process. Statistical discrimination, although representing elements of class bias against poor workers in the inner city, is clearly a matter of race. The selective recruitment patterns effectively screen out far more black workers from the inner city than Hispanic or white workers from the same types of backgrounds. But race is also a factor, even in those decisions to deny employment to inner-city black workers on the basis of objective and thorough evaluations of their qualifications. The hard and soft skills among inner-city blacks that do not match the current needs of the labor market are products of racially segregated communities, communities that have historically featured widespread social constraints and restricted opportunities.

Thus, the job prospects of inner-city workers have diminished not only because of the decreasing relative demand for low-skilled labor, the suburbanization of jobs, and the social deterioration of ghetto neighborhoods, but also because of negative employer attitudes. This combination of factors presents a real challenge to policy-makers. Indeed, considering the narrow range of social policy options in the "balance-the-budget" political climate, how can we immediately alleviate the inner-city jobs problem—a problem that will undoubtedly grow when the new welfare reform bill takes full effect.

PUBLIC POLICY DILEMMAS

To what extent will the inner-city jobs problem respond to macroeconomic levers that can act to enhance growth and reduce unemployment? I include here fiscal policies that regulate government spending and taxation and monetary policies that influence interest rates and control the money supply. If jobs are plentiful even for less-skilled workers during periods of economic expansion, then labor shortages reduce the likelihood that hiring decisions will be determined by subjective negative judgments concerning a group's job-related traits.

But given the fundamental structural decline in the demand for low-skilled workers, fiscal and monetary policies designed to enhance economic growth will have their greatest impact in the higher-wage sectors of the economy. Many low-wage workers, especially those in high-jobless inner-city neighborhoods who are not in or have dropped out of the labor force and who also face the problem of negative employer attitudes, will not experience any improvement in their job prospects because of such policies.

If firms in the private sector cannot use or refuse to hire low-skilled adults who are willing to take minimum-wage jobs, then the jobs problem for inner-city workers cannot be adequately addressed without considering a policy of public-sector employment of last resort. Indeed, until current changes in the labor market are reversed or until the skills of the next generation can be upgraded before it enters the labor market, many workers, especially those who are not in the official labor force, will not be able to find jobs unless the government becomes an employer of last resort. This argument applies especially to low-skilled inner-city black workers. It is bad enough that they face the problem of shifts in labor-market demand shared by all low-skilled workers; it is even worse that they confront negative employer perceptions about their work-related skills and attitudes.

Prior to the late 1970s, there was less need for the creation of public-sector jobs. Not only was economic growth fairly rapid during periods of expansion, but "the gains from growth were widely shared." Before the late 1970s, public jobs of last resort were thought of in terms of "a counter-cyclical policy to be put in place during recessions and retired during recoveries. It is only since the late 1970s that the disadvantaged have been left behind during recoveries. The labor market changes . . . seem to have permanently reduced private-sector demand for less-skilled workers."[6]

For all these reasons, the passage of the recent welfare reform bill, which did not include a program of job creation, could have negative social consequences in the inner city. Unless something is done to enhance the employment opportunities of inner-city welfare recipients who reach the time limit for the receipt of welfare, they may flood a pool already filled with low-skilled jobless workers.

New research into urban labor markets by Harry Holzer reveals the magnitude of the problem. Surveying 3,000 employers in Atlanta, Boston, and Los Angeles, Holzer found that only 5 to 10 percent of the jobs in central-city areas for non-college graduates require very few work credentials or cognitive skills. This means that most inner-city workers today not only need to have basic reading, writing, and math skills but also need to know how to operate a computer as well. Also, most employers require a high school degree, particular kinds of previous work experience, and job references. Because of the large oversupply of low-skilled workers relative to the number of low-skilled jobs, many low-educated and poorly trained individuals have difficulty finding jobs even when the local labor market is strong.[7]

The problem is that in recent years tight labor markets have been of relatively short duration, frequently followed by a recession which either wiped out previous gains for many workers or did not allow others to fully recover from a previous period of economic stagnation. It would take sustained tight labor markets over many years to draw back those discouraged inner-city workers who have dropped out of the labor market altogether, some for very long periods of time. We are currently in one of the longest economic recoveries in the last half century, a recovery that has lasted eight years and generated more than 14 million net new jobs and the lowest official unemployment rate in twenty-four years. This sustained recovery is beginning to have some positive effect on the hard-core unemployed. The ranks of those out of work for more than six months declined by almost 150,000 over a two-month period in early 1997. And, as reported in early 1998, the unemployment rate for high school dropouts declined by five points since 1992, from 12 to 7 percent. Two-fifths of this decline has come in the last year.[8]

How long this current period of economic recovery will last is anybody's guess. Some economists feel that this period of tight labor markets will last for at least several more years. If it does it will be the best antidote for low-skilled workers whose employment and earning prospects have been diminished in the late twentieth century. For example, in the inner cities the extension of the economic recovery for several more years will significantly lower the overall jobless rate not only for the low-skilled workers who are still in the labor force but for those who have been outside the labor market for many years as well. It will also enhance the job prospects of many of the welfare recipients who reach the time limit for the receipt of welfare. But, given the decreased relative demand for low-skilled labor, what will happen to all of these groups if the economy slows down? Considering the changing nature of the economy, there is little reason to assume that their prospects will be anything but bleak. Why? Simply because the economic trend that has twisted against low-skilled workers is unlikely to reverse itself, thereby diminishing over the long term their job prospects and earnings.

Concerned about these issues, I sent President Clinton a memorandum in August 1996. I pointed out that, although he has long realized the crucial relationship between welfare reform and job creation and that his initial welfare plan emphasized job creation, the bill he signed had no such provision. I pointed out that to remedy the most glaring defects of the bill, a mechanism for state and local governments to respond to widespread joblessness in the inner cities was essential. I was aware that the president was giving some thought to tax credits and wage subsidies to encourage businesses to hire welfare recipients. I pointed out that although giving subsidies and tax credits to private employers may help, research suggests that subsidies and credits are hardly sufficient by themselves to accomplish this goal.

The track record of private employers is not especially encouraging. Past efforts to subsidize employers to hire welfare recipients and other disadvantaged individuals have generally failed to work on a large scale. For example, during the late 1960s and early 1970s, the federal government funded a program by the National Alliance of Business (NAB) in which employers received a $3,200 subsidy for each disadvantaged worker, including welfare recipients, they hired (an amount that would be much higher in inflation-adjusted terms today). That effort resulted in a very low take-up rate among employers. Why? Simply because not enough employers have been willing to hire people whom they view as troublesome or "damaged goods." Indeed, a study by the economist Gary Burtless revealed that the low-income individuals who were supposed to be aided were *less* likely to be hired as a result of a targeted wage subsidy. Employers evidently thought that if the government was willing to subsidize the hiring of these individuals so heavily, they must have serious work-related problems.[9]

Studies also show that when employers do receive a subsidy for hiring such individuals—whether a tax credit or a direct subsidy—the subsidy often rewards employers for hires they would have made anyway. When that occurs, it costs the government money but the number of jobs for this population does not increase.

Although a new study by Lawrence Katz reveals that one tax credit program, the Targeted Jobs Tax Credit, "may have modestly improved the employment rates of economically disadvantaged youth,"[10] an impressive array of other studies over the past two decades suggests that a single approach involving tax credits or wage subsidies will fail to move a significant number of welfare recipients into employment.

In my memorandum to the president, I therefore urged caution in placing too many of his "eggs" in the private-sector job-placement basket. We will need a mix of both private- and public-sector initiatives to enhance employment. In inner cities, where the number of very low-skilled individuals vastly exceeds the number of low-skilled jobs even before welfare reform adds tens of thousands more people to the low-skilled labor pool, a healthy dose of public-sector job creation will be needed. Public jobs can help people shunned by private employers initially to learn acceptable work habits and build an employment record, from which they may be able to graduate to private-sector positions. In order to really make my point clear, I pointed out to President Clinton that I am not suggesting a new federal public works program because I understand the difficulties in getting such a program approved in today's political climate. I am only recommending that he enable governors and mayors to use a mix of private- and public-sector approaches as they see fit, based on local conditions. I pointed out that he could not be criticized for a "big government" approach if he allows state and local officials, so many of whom are now Republicans, to make this choice. Indeed, Governor Tommy Thompson's welfare plan in Wisconsin includes provisions for significant public- as well as private-sector employment.

The president responded that several of my recommendations were already under consideration by his administration. And during the presidential campaign, he outlined a proposal that included both tax credits to companies that hire welfare recipients and $3 billion to create public and private work slots in localities that have high unemployment and welfare dependency.

However, in the tax bill submitted to Congress on February 6, 1997, the president's proposal to strengthen the welfare-to-work initiative did not include language that would allow governors and mayors to create private or public work slots in areas plagued by high rates of unemployment and welfare receipt. Indeed the focus, although stated in vague language, was entirely on initiatives to place recipients in private-sector jobs, including a larger tax credit for businesses that hire long-term welfare recipients. The new tax credit would allow employers to deduct 50 percent of the first $10,000 in wages paid to recipients who had been on welfare for at least eighteen months.

The conclusions I draw from the current evidence is that as the president and the Congress take future steps to address the jobs problem for welfare recipients and other disadvantaged workers, they ought not rely on a stand-alone strategy of employer subsidies—either tax credits or wage subsidies. Instead, they ought to consider a mixed strategy that combines employer subsidies with job creation in the public and non-profit private sectors.

It is especially important that this mixed strategy include a plan to make adequate monies available to localities or communities with high jobless and welfare dependency rates. At the same time that the new welfare law has generated a greater need for work opportunities, high-jobless urban and rural areas will have more difficulty placing individuals in private-sector jobs. To create work opportunities for welfare recipients, these areas will therefore have to "rely more heavily upon job creation strategies in the public and private non-profit sectors."[11] West Virginia, plagued with a severe shortage of work opportunities, has provided community service jobs to welfare recipients for several years. In Wisconsin, Governor Thompson's welfare reform plan envisions community-service jobs for many parents in the more depressed areas of the state, and the New Hope program in Milwaukee provides community-service jobs for those unable to find employment in the private sector.

Thus, we could face a real catastrophe in many urban areas if steps are not taken soon to enhance the job prospects of hundreds of thousands of inner-city youths and adults.

NOTES

1. Parts of this essay are based on my latest book, *When Work Disappears: The World of the New Urban Poor* (New York: Alfred A. Knopf, 1996), which included three research studies conducted in Chicago between 1986 and 1993. The first of these included a random survey of nearly 2,500 poor and non-poor African-American,

Latino, and white residents in Chicago's poor neighborhoods; a subsample of 175 participants from this survey who were reinterviewed and answered open-ended questions; a survey of 179 employers selected to reflect the distribution of employment and firm sizes in the metropolitan area; and comprehensive ethnographic research, including participant-observation research and life-history interviews in a representative sample of inner-city neighborhoods.

The second study included a survey of a representative sample of 546 black mothers and up to two of their adolescent children (ages 11 to 16—or 887 adolescents), in working- and middle-class neighborhoods and high-poverty neighborhoods. Finally, the third study featured a survey of a representative sample of 500 respondents from two high-joblessness neighborhoods on the South Side of Chicago and six focus-group discussions involving the residents and former residents of these neighborhoods.

2. Lester Thurow, "The Crusade That's Killing Prosperity," *American Prospect,* March–April 1995, pp. 54–59.

3. Pierre Bourdieu, *Travail et Travailleurs en Algerio* (Paris: Editions Mouton, 1965).

4. Lawrence Katz, "Wage Subsidies for the Disadvantaged," Working Paper 5679, National Bureau of Economic Research, Cambridge, MA, 1996, p. 2.

5. Ibid.

6. Sheldon Danziger and Peter Gottschalk, *America Unequal* (Cambridge: Harvard University Press, 1995), p. 174.

7. Harry Holzer, *What Employers Want: Job Prospects for Less-Educated Workers* (New York: Russell Sage Foundation, 1995).

8. Sylvia Nasar, "Jobs Juggernaut Continues Surge: 30,000 Find Work," *New York Times,* March 7, 1998, pp. 1A and 1B.

9. Gary Burtless, "Are Targeted Wage Subsidies Harmful? Evidence from a Wage Voucher Experiment," *Industrial and Labor Relations Review* 39, October 1985.

10. Katz, op. cit.

11. Center on Budget and Policy Priorities, "The Administration's $3 Billion Jobs Proposal," Washington, DC, 1996.

26

"WE'D LOVE TO HIRE THEM, BUT . . ."
The Meaning of Race for Employers

JOLEEN KIRSCHENMAN • KATHRYN M. NECKERMAN

In this paper we explore the meaning of race and ethnicity to employers, the ways race and ethnicity are qualified by—and at times reinforce—other characteristics in the eyes of employers, and the conditions under which race seems to matter most. Our interviews at Chicago-area businesses show that employers view inner-city workers, especially black men, as unstable, uncooperative, dishonest, and uneducated. Race is an important factor in hiring decisions. But it is not race alone: rather it is race in a complex interaction with employers' perceptions of class and space, or inner-city residence. Our findings suggest that racial discrimination deserves an important place in analyses of the underclass.

RACE AND EMPLOYMENT

In research on the disadvantages blacks experience in the labor market, social scientists tend to rely on indirect measures of racial discrimination. They interpret as evidence of this discrimination the differences in wages or employment among races and ethnic groups that remain after education and experience are controlled. With a few exceptions they have neglected the processes at the level of the firm that underlie these observed differences.[1] . . .

The theoretical literature conventionally distinguishes two types of discrimination, "pure" and "statistical." In pure discrimination, employers, employees, or consumers have a "taste" for discrimination; that is, they will pay a premium to avoid members of another group.[2] Statistical discrimination is a more recent conception that builds on the discussions of "signaling."[3] In statistical discrimination, employers use group membership as a proxy for aspects of productivity that are relatively expensive or impossible to measure. Those who use the concept disagree about whether employers' perceptions of group differences in productivity must reflect reality. In this discussion, we are concerned with statistical discrimination as a cognitive

Excerpt from "We'd Love to Hire Them, But . . .: The Meaning of Race for Employers," by Joleen Kirschenman and Kathryn M. Neckerman, from *Social Problems,* Vol. 38, no. 4 (1991), pp. 433–447. Reprinted by permission of the University of California Press.

process, regardless of whether the employer is correct or mistaken in his or her views of the labor force. . . .

This distinction between pure and statistical discrimination is a useful one. However, it is also useful to recognize the relationship between the two. There are several ways in which a taste for discrimination in employment practices may lead to perceived and actual productivity differences between groups, making statistical discrimination more likely. Social psychological evidence suggests that expectations about group differences in productivity may bias evaluation of job performance. These expectations may also influence job placement. In particular, workers of lower expected productivity may be given less on-the-job training. Finally, and most important for our study, productivity is not an individual characteristic; rather, it is shaped by the social relations of the workplace. If these relations are strained because of tastes for discrimination on the part of the employer, supervisor, coworkers, or consumers, lower productivity may result. Thus what begins as irrational practice based on prejudice or mistaken beliefs may end up being rational, profit-maximizing behavior.

DATA

This research is based on face-to-face interviews with employers in Chicago and surrounding Cook County between July 1988 and March 1989. Inner-city firms were oversampled; all results here are weighted to adjust for this oversampling. Our overall response rate was 46 percent, and the completed sample of 185 employers is representative of the distribution of Cook County's employment by industry and firm size.[4]

Interviews included both closed- and open-ended questions about employers' hiring and recruitment practices and about their perceptions of Chicago's labor force and business climate. Our initial contacts, and most of the interviews themselves, were conducted with the highest ranking official at the establishment. Because of the many open-ended questions, we taped the interviews.

Most of the structured portion of the interview focused on a sample job, defined by the interview schedule as "the most typical entry-level position" in the firm's modal occupational category—sales, clerical, skilled, semi-skilled, unskilled, or service, but excluding managerial, professional, and technical. The distribution of our sample jobs approximates the occupational distribution in the 1980 census for Cook County, again excluding professional, managerial, and technical categories. In effect, what we have is a sample of the opportunities facing the Chicago job-seeker with minimal skills. . . .

Although we do not present our findings as necessarily representative of the attitudes of all Chicago employers, as the rules of positivist social science would require, they are representative of those Chicago employers who spoke to a particular issue. A standard rule of discourse is that some things are acceptable to say and others are better left unsaid. Silence has the capacity to speak volumes. Thus we were overwhelmed by the degree to which Chicago employers felt comfortable talking with us—in a situation where the temptation would be to conceal rather than reveal—in a negative manner about blacks. In this paper we make an effort to understand the discursive evidence by relating it to the practice of discrimination, using quantitative data to reinforce the qualitative findings.

WE'D LOVE TO HIRE THEM, BUT . . .

. . . Explanations for the high rates of unemployment and poverty among blacks have relied heavily on the categories of class and space.[5] We found that employers also relied on those categories, but they used them to refine the category of race, which for them is primary. Indeed, it was through the interaction of race with class and space that these categories were imbued with new meaning. It was race that made class and space important to employers.

Although some employers regarded Chicago's workers as highly skilled and having a good work ethic, far more thought that the labor force has deteriorated. When asked why they thought business had been leaving Chicago, 35 percent referred to the inferior quality of the work force. . . . Several firms in our sample were relocating or seriously considering a move to the South in a search for cheap skilled labor. Employers of less skilled labor can find an ample supply of applicants, but many complained that it was becoming more difficult to find workers with basic skills and a good work ethic.

These employers coped with what they considered a less qualified work force though various strategies. Some restructured production to require either fewer workers or fewer skills. These strategies included increasing automation and deemphasizing literacy requirements—using color-coded filing systems, for example. But far more widespread were the use of recruiting and screening techniques to help select "good" workers. For instance, employers relied more heavily on referrals from employees, which tend to reproduce the traits and characteristics of the current work force: the Chicago Association of Commerce and Industry has reported a dramatic increase in the use of referral bonuses in the past few years. Or employers targeted newspaper ads to particular neighborhoods or ethnic groups. The rationale underlying these strategies was, in part, related to the productivity employers accorded different categories of workers.

For instance, whether or not the urban underclass is an objective social category, its subjective importance in the discourse of Chicago employers cannot be denied. Their characterizations of inner-city workers mirrored many descriptions of the underclass by social scientists. Common among the traits listed were that workers were unskilled, uneducated, illiterate, dishonest, lacking initiative, unmotivated, involved with drugs and gangs, did not understand work, had no personal charm, were unstable, lacked a work ethic, and had no family life or role models.

Social scientists discover pathologies; employers try to avoid them. After explaining that he hired "the best applicant," the owner of a transportation firm added, "Probably what I'm trying to say is we're not social minded. We're not worried about solving the problems of sociology. We can't afford to." But despite not being worried about the "problems of sociology," employers have become lay social theorists, creating numerous distinctions among the labor force that then serve as bases for statistical discrimination. From their own experiences and biases, those of other employers, and accounts in the mass media, employers have attributed meaning to the categories of race and ethnicity, class, and space. These have then become markers of more or less desirable workers.

These categories were often confounded with each other, as when one respondent contrasted the white youth (with opportunities) from the North Shore with the black one (without opportunities) from the South Side. Although the primary distinction that more than 70 percent of our informants made was based on race and ethnicity, it was frequently confounded with class: black and Hispanic equaled lower class; white equaled middle class. And these distinctions also overlapped with space: "inner-city" and at times "Chicago" equaled minority, especially black; "suburb" equaled white. In fact, race was important in part because it signaled class and inner-city residence, which are less easy to observe directly. But employers also needed class and space to draw distinctions within racial and ethnic groups; race was the distinguishing characteristic most often referred to, followed respectively by class and space. . . .

Race and Ethnicity

When they talked about the work ethic, tensions in the workplace, or attitudes toward work, employers emphasized the color of a person's skin. Many believed that white workers were superior to minorities in their work ethic. A woman who hires for a suburban service firm said, "The Polish immigrants that I know and know of are more highly motivated than the Hispanics. The Hispanics share in some of the problems that the blacks do." These problems included "exposure to poverty and drugs" as well as "a lack of motivation" related to "their environment and background." A man from a Chicago construction company, expressing a view shared by many of our informants, said, "For all groups, the pride [in their work] of days gone by is not there, but what is left, I think probably the whites take more pride than some of the other minorities." (Interviewer: "And between blacks and Hispanics?") "Probably the same."

In the discourse of "work ethic," which looms large among the concerns of employers, whites usually came out on top. But although white workers generally looked good to employers, East European whites were repeatedly praised for really knowing how to work and caring about their work. Several informants cited positive experiences with their Polish domestic help. In the skilled occupations, East European men were sought. One company advertised for its skilled workers in Polish and German-language newspapers, but hired all its unskilled workers, 97 percent of whom were Hispanic, through an employee network.

When asked directly whether they thought there were any differences in the work ethics of whites, blacks, and Hispanics, 37.7 percent of the employers ranked blacks last, 1.4 percent ranked Hispanics last, and no one ranked whites there. Another 7.6 percent placed blacks and Hispanics together on the lowest level; 51.4 percent either saw no difference or refused to categorize in a straightforward way. Many of the latter group qualified their response by saying they saw no differences once one controlled for education, background, or environment, and that any differences were more the result of class or space.

Although blacks were consistently evaluated less favorably than whites, employers' perceptions of Hispanics were more mixed. Some ranked them with blacks; others positioned them between whites and blacks. . . .

They also believed that a homogeneous work force serves to maintain good relations among workers. . . . A personnel manager from a large, once all-white Chicago manufacturing concern lamented the tensions that race and ethnic diversity had created among workers: "I wish we could all be the same, but, unfortunately, we're not." An employer of an all-white work force said that "if I had one [black worker] back there it might be okay, but if I have two or more I would have trouble." But although some employers found a diverse work force more difficult to manage, few actually maintained a homogeneous labor force, at least in terms of race and ethnicity.

Employers worried about tensions not only between white and minority workers but also between Mexicans and blacks, Mexicans and Puerto Ricans, and even African and American blacks. A restaurateur with an all-white staff of waiters and a Hispanic kitchen said, "The Mexican kids that work in the kitchen, they're not, they're not kids anymore, but they don't like to work with black guys. But they don't like to work with Puerto Rican guys either." . . .

Blacks are by and large thought to possess very few of the characteristics of a "good" worker. Over and over employers said, "They don't want to work." "They don't want to stay." "They've got an attitude problem." One compared blacks with Mexicans: "Most of them are not as educated as you might think. I've never seen any of these guys read anything outside of a comic book. These Mexicans are sitting here reading novels constantly, even though they're in Spanish. These guys will sit and watch cartoons while the other guys are busy reading. To me that shows basic laziness. No desire to upgrade yourself." When asked about discrimination against black workers, a Chicago manufacturer related a common view: "Oh, I would in all honesty probably say there is some among most employers. I think one of the reasons, in all honesty, is because we've had bad experience in that sector, and believe me, I've tried. And as I say, if I find—whether he's black or white, if he's good and, you know, we'll hire him. We are not shutting out any black specifically. But I will say that our experience factor has been bad. We've had more bad black employees over the years than we had good." This negative opinion of blacks sometimes cuts across class lines. For instance, a personnel officer of a professional service company in the suburbs commented that "with the professional staff, black males that we've had, some of the skill levels—they're not as orientated to details. They lack some of the leadership skills."

One must also consider the "relevant nots": what were some employers not talking about? They were not talking about how clever black workers were, they were not talking about the cultural richness of the black community, nor were they talking about rising divorce rates among whites. Furthermore, although each employer reserved the right to deny making distinctions along racial lines, fewer than 10 percent consistently refused to distinguish or generalize according to race.

These ways of talking about black workers—they have a bad work ethic, they create tensions in the workplace, they are lazy and unreliable, they have a bad attitude—reveal the meaning race has for many employers. If race were a proxy for expected productivity and the sole basis for statistical discrimination, black applicants would indeed find few job opportunities.

Class

Although some respondents spoke only in terms of race and ethnicity, or conflated class with race, others were sensitive to class distinctions. Class constituted a second, less easily detected signal for employers. Depending somewhat on the demands of the jobs, they used class markers to select among black applicants. The contrasts between their discourse about blacks and Hispanics were striking. Employers sometimes placed Hispanics with blacks in the lower class: an inner-city retailer confounded race, ethnicity, and class when he said, "I think there's a self-defeating prophecy that's maybe inherent in a lot of lower-income ethnic groups or races. Blacks, Hispanics." But although they rarely drew class distinctions among Hispanics, such distinctions were widely made for black workers. As one manufacturer said, "The black work ethic. There's no work ethic. At least at the unskilled. I'm sure with the skilled, as you go up, it's a lot different." Employers generally considered it likely that lower-class blacks would have more negative traits than blacks of other classes.

In many ways black business owners and black personnel managers were the most expressive about class divisions among blacks. A few believed poor blacks were most likely to be dishonest because of the economic pressures they face. A black jeweler said the most important quality he looked for in his help was "a person who doesn't need a job."

(INTERVIEWER: That's what you're looking for?)

That's what we usually try to hire. People that don't need the job.

(INTERVIEWER: Why?)

Because they will tend to be a little more honest. Most of the people
that live in the neighborhoods and areas where my stores are at need
the job. They are low-income, and so, consequently, they're under
more pressure and there's more of a tendency to be dishonest,
because of the pressure. . . .

Other employers mentioned problems that occur in the workplace when
there are class divisions among the workers. These are reminiscent of the tensions created by the racial and ethnic diversity described earlier. One black
businesswoman told of a program wherein disadvantaged youths were sent
to private schools by wealthy sponsors. She herself was a sponsor and held
the program in high regard, but she hired some of these youths and they did
not get along with her other young employees: "Those kids were too smart
'cause they were from a middle-class background." (Interviewer: "So these
were primarily middle-class kids?") "No, they're not middle class, but they
have middle-class values because they're exposed to them all the time." They
made excellent employees, she said, "if you kept your store filled with just
them. They're more outgoing and less afraid of the customers. But they're
very intimidating to the supervisors because they know everything by the
time they get to be a sophomore in high school." . . .

Thus, although many employers assumed that black meant "inner-city
poor," others—both black and white—were quick to see divisions within the
black population. Of course, class itself is not directly observable, but markers that convey middle- or working-class status will help a black job applicant get through race-based exclusionary barriers. Class is primarily signaled
to employers through speech, dress, education levels, skill levels, and place
of residence. Although many respondents drew class distinctions among
blacks, very few made those same distinctions among Hispanics or whites; in
refining these categories, respondents referred to ethnicity and age rather
than class.

Space

Although some employers spoke implicitly or explicitly in terms of class, for
others "inner-city" was the more important category. For most the term immediately connoted black, poor, uneducated, unskilled, lacking in values,
crime, gangs, drugs, and unstable families. "Suburb" connoted white,
middle-class, educated, skilled, and stable families. Conversely, race was
salient in part because it signaled space; black connoted inner city and white
the suburbs. . . . When asked what it would take for their firm to relocate to
the inner city, respondents generally thought it an implausible notion. They

were sure their skilled workers would not consider working in those neighborhoods because they feared for their safety, and the employers saw no alternative labor supply there.

The skepticism that greets the inner-city worker often arises when employers associate their race and residence with enrollment in Chicago's troubled public education system. Being educated in Chicago public schools has become a way of signaling "I'm black, I'm poor, and I'm from the inner city" to employers. Some mentioned that they passed over applicants from Chicago public schools for those with parochial or suburban education. If employers were looking at an applicant's credentials when screening, blacks in the inner city did not do well. As one employer said, "The educational skills they come to the job with are minimal because of the schools in the areas where they generally live."

A vice president of a television station complained of the inner-city work force:

> They are frequently unable to write. They go through the Chicago
> public schools or they dropped out when they were in the eighth
> grade. They can't read. They can't write. They can hardly talk. I
> have another opinion which is strictly my own and that is that
> people who insist on beating themselves to the point where they
> are out of the mainstream of the world suffer the consequences.
> And I'm talking about the languages that are spoken in the ghetto.
> They are not English.

Employers were clearly disappointed, not just in the academic content and level of training students receive, but in the failure of the school system to prepare them for the work force. Because the inner city is heavily associated with a lack of family values, employers wished the schools would compensate and provide students the self-discipline needed for workers' socialization. Additionally, they complained that black workers had no "ability to understand work." . . . It is not only educational content per se that employers were looking for; some were concerned with the educational "experience." One talked about how it just showed "they could finish something." Thus inner city is equated with public school attendance, which in turn signifies insufficient work skills and work ethic.

. . . Another employer used space to refine the category of race: "We have some black women here but they're not inner city. They're from suburbs and . . . I think they're a little bit more willing to give it a shot, you know, I mean they're a little bit more willing [than black men] to give a day's work for a day's pay."

Employers readily distinguished among blacks on the basis of space. They talked about Cabrini Green or the Robert Taylor Homes or referred to the South Side and West Side as a shorthand for black. But they were not likely to make these distinctions among whites and Hispanics. They made no reference to Pilsen (a largely immigrant Mexican neighborhood), Humboldt

Park (largely Puerto Rican), or Uptown (a community of poor whites and new immigrants).

For black applicants, having the wrong combination of class and space markers suggested low productivity and undesirability to an employer. The important findings of this research, then, is not only that employers make hiring decisions based on the color of a person's skin, but the extent to which that act has become nuanced. Race, class, and space interact with each other. Moreover, the precise nature of that interaction is largely determined by the demands of the job. . . .

CONCLUSION

Chicago's employers did not hesitate to generalize about race or ethnic differences in the quality of the labor force. Most associated negative images with inner-city workers, and particularly with black men. "Black" and "inner-city" were inextricably linked, and both were linked with "lower-class."

Regardless of the generalizations employers made, they did consider the black population particularly heterogeneous, which made it more important that they be able to distinguish "good" from "bad" workers. Whether through skills tests, credentials, personal references, folk theories, or their intuition, they used some means of screening out the inner-city applicant. The ubiquitous anecdote about the good black worker, the exception to the rule, testified to their own perceived success at doing this. So did frequent reference to "our" black workers as opposed to "those guys on the street corner."

And black job applicants, unlike their white counterparts, must indicate to employers that the stereotypes do not apply to them. Inner-city and lower-class workers were seen as undesirable, and black applicants had to try to signal to employers that they did not fall into those categories, either by demonstrating their skills or by adopting a middle-class style of dress, manner, and speech or perhaps (as we were told some did) by lying about their address or work history.

By stressing employers' preconceptions about inner-city workers, we do not mean to imply that there are no problems of labor quality in the inner city: the low reading and mathematics test scores of Chicago public school students testify to these problems. But if the quality of the inner-city labor force has indeed deteriorated, then it is incumbent on employers to avoid hiring inner-city workers. This is precisely the result one would expect from William Julius Wilson's account of increased social dislocations in the inner city since the early 1970s. Because race and inner-city residence are so highly correlated, it would not be surprising if race were to become a key marker of worker productivity.

However, productivity is not an individual characteristic. Rather it is embedded in social relations. The qualities most likely to be proxied by race are not job skills but behavioral and attitudinal attributes—dependability, strong work ethic, cooperativeness—that are closely tied to interactions among workers and between workers and employers. Our evidence suggests that more attention should be paid to social relations in the workplace. Antagonisms among workers and between workers and their employers are likely to diminish productivity. Thus employers' expectations may become self-fulfilling prophecies.

NOTES

1. One of the exceptions is Braddock and McPartland (1987).
2. Becker (1957).
3. Phelps (1972); Arrow (1973); and Spence (1973).
4. The sample and survey methods are described in more detail in the "Employer Survey Final Report," available from the authors.
5. Wilson (1980, 1987); and Kasarda (1985). We use the term "space" in the tradition of urban geography. We do this to draw attention to the way people categorize and attach meaning to geographic locations.

REFERENCES

Arrow, Kenneth. 1973. "The Theory of Discrimination." In *Discrimination in Labor Markets*, edited by Orley Aschenfelter and Albert Rees. Princeton University Press.

Braddock, Jomills Henry II, and James M. McPartland. 1987. "How Minorities Continue to Be Excluded from Equal Employment Opportunities: Research on Labor Market and Institutional Barriers." *Journal of Social Issues* 43, pp. 5–39.

Kasarda, John D. 1985. "Urban Change and Minority Opportunities." In *The New Urban Reality*, edited by Paul E. Peterson. Brookings.

Phelps, Edmund S. 1972. "The Statistical Theory of Racism and Sexism." *American Economic Review* 62 (September), pp. 659–61.

Spence, Michael. 1973. "Job Market Signalling." *Quarterly Journal of Economics* 87 (August), pp. 355–74.

Wilson, William Julius. 1980. *The Declining Significance of Race: Blacks and Changing American Institutions.* 2d ed. University of Chicago Press.

———. 1987. *The Truly Disadvantaged: The Inner City, the Underclass, and Public Policy.* University of Chicago Press.

27

THE GLASS ESCALATOR
Hidden Advantages for Men in the "Female" Professions

CHRISTINE L. WILLIAMS

The sex segregation of the U.S. labor force is one of the most perplexing and tenacious problems in our society. Even though the proportion of men and women in the labor force is approaching parity (particularly for younger cohorts of workers) (U.S. Department of Labor 1991:18), men and women are still generally confined to predominantly single-sex occupations. Forty percent of men or women would have to change major occupational categories to achieve equal representation of men and women in all jobs (Reskin and Roos 1990:6), but even this figure underestimates the true degree of sex segregation. It is extremely rare to find specific jobs where equal numbers of men and women are engaged in the same activities in the same industries (Bielby and Baron 1984).

Most studies of sex segregation in the workforce have focused on women's experiences in male-dominated occupations. Both researchers and advocates for social change have focused on the barriers faced by women who try to integrate predominantly male fields. Few have looked at the "flip-side" of occupational sex segregation: the exclusion of men from predominantly female occupations (exceptions include Schreiber 1979; Williams 1989; Zimmer 1988). But the fact is that men are less likely to enter female sex-typed occupations than women are to enter male-dominated jobs (Jacobs 1989). Reskin and Roos, for example, were able to identify 33 occupations in which female representation increased by more than nine percentage points between 1970 and 1980, but only three occupations in which the proportion of men increased as radically (1990: 20–21).

In this paper, I examine men's underrepresentation in four predominantly female occupations—nursing, librarianship, elementary school teaching, and social work. Throughout the twentieth century, these occupations have been identified with "women's work"—even though prior to the Civil War, men were more likely to be employed in these areas. These four occupations, often called the female "semi-professions" (Hodson and Sullivan 1990), today range from 5.5 percent male (in nursing) to 32 percent male (in

From *Social Problems* 39, no. 3 (August 1992):253–67. Reprinted by permission of the University of California Press.

social work). These percentages have not changed substantially in decades. In fact, two of these professions—librarianship and social work—have experienced declines in the proportions of men since 1975. Nursing is the only one of the four experiencing noticeable changes in sex composition, with the proportion of men increasing 80 percent between 1975 and 1990. Even so, men continue to be a tiny minority of all nurses.

. . .

METHODS

I conducted in-depth interviews with 76 men and 23 women in four occupations from 1985 to 1991. Interviews were conducted in four metropolitan areas: San Francisco/Oakland, California; Austin, Texas; Boston, Massachusetts; and Phoenix, Arizona. These four areas were selected because they show considerable variation in the proportions of men in the four professions. For example, Austin has one of the highest percentages of men in nursing (7.7 percent), whereas Phoenix's percentage is one of the lowest (2.7 percent) (U.S. Bureau of the Census 1980). The sample was generated using "snowballing" techniques. Women were included in the sample to gauge their feelings and responses to men who enter "their" professions.

. . .

DISCRIMINATION IN HIRING

Contrary to the experience of many women in the male-dominated professions, many of the men and women I spoke to indicated that there is a *preference* for hiring men in these occupations. A Texas librarian at a junior high school said that his school district "would hire a male over a female."

 I: Why do you think that is?

 R: Because there are so few, and the . . . ones that they do have, the library directors seem to really . . . think they're doing great jobs. I don't know, maybe they just feel they're being progressive or something, [but] I have had a real sense that they really appreciate having a male, particularly at the junior high. . . . As I said, when seven of us lost our jobs from the high schools and were redistributed, there were only four positions at junior high, and I got one of them. Three of the librarians, some who had been here longer than I had with the school district, were put down in elementary schools as librarians. And I definitely think that being male made a difference in my being moved to the junior high rather than an elementary school.

Many of the men perceived their token status as males in predominantly female occupations as an *advantage* in hiring and promotions. I asked an Arizona teacher whether his specialty (elementary special education) was an unusual area for men compared to other areas within education. He said,

> Much more so. I am extremely marketable in special education. That's not why I got into the field. But I am extremely marketable because I am a man.

In several cases, the more female-dominated the specialty, the greater the apparent preference for men. For example, when asked if he encountered any problem getting a job in pediatrics, a Massachusetts nurse said,

> No, no, none. . . . I've heard this from managers and supervisory-type people with men in pediatrics: "It's nice to have a man because it's such a female-dominated profession."

However, there were some exceptions to this preference for men in the most female-dominated specialties. In some cases, formal policies actually barred men from certain jobs. This was the case in some rural Texas school districts, which refused to hire men in the youngest grades (K–3). Some nurses also reported being excluded from positions in obstetrics and gynecology wards, a policy encountered more frequently in private Catholic hospitals.

But often the pressures keeping men out of certain specialties were more subtle than this. Some men described being "tracked" into practice areas within their professions which were considered more legitimate for men. For example, one Texas man described how he was pushed into administration and planning in social work, even though "I'm not interested in writing policy; I'm much more interested in research and clinical stuff." A nurse who is interested in pursuing graduate study in family and child health in Boston said he was dissuaded from entering the program specialty in favor of a concentration in "adult nursing." A kindergarten teacher described the difficulty of finding a job in his specialty after graduation: "I was recruited immediately to start getting into a track to become an administrator. And it was men who recruited me. It was men that ran the system at that time, especially in Los Angeles."

This tracking may bar men from the most female-identified specialties within these professions. But men are effectively being "kicked upstairs" in the process. Those specialties considered more legitimate practice areas for men also tend to be the most prestigious, better paying ones. A distinguished kindergarten teacher, who had been voted citywide "Teacher of the Year," told me that even though people were pleased to see him in the classroom, "there's been some encouragement to think about administration, and there's been some encouragement to think about teaching at the university level or something like that, or supervisory-type position." That is, despite his aptitude and interest in staying in the classroom, he felt pushed in the direction of administration.

The effect of this "tracking" is the opposite of that experienced by women in male-dominated occupations. Researchers have reported that many women encounter a "glass ceiling" in their efforts to scale organizational and professional hierarchies. That is, they are constrained by invisible barriers to promotion in their careers, caused mainly by sexist attitudes of men in the highest positions (Freeman 1990). In contrast to the "glass ceiling," many of the men I interviewed seem to encounter a "glass escalator." Often, despite their intentions, they face invisible pressures to move up in their professions. As if on a moving escalator, they must work to stay in place.

A public librarian specializing in children's collections (a heavily female-dominated concentration) described an encounter with this "escalator" in his very first job out of library school. In his first six-months' evaluation, his supervisors commended him for his good work in storytelling and related activities, but they criticized him for "not shooting high enough."

> Seriously. That's literally what they were telling me. They assumed that because I was a male—and they told me this—and that I was being hired right out of graduate school, that somehow I wasn't doing the kind of management-oriented work that they thought I should be doing. And as a result, really they had a lot of bad marks, as it were, against me on my evaluation. And I said I couldn't believe this!

Throughout his 10-year career, he had had to struggle to remain in children's collections.

The glass escalator does not operate at all levels. In particular, men in academia reported some gender-based discrimination in the highest positions due to their universities' commitment to affirmative action. Two nursing professors reported that they felt their own chances of promotion to deanships were nil because their universities viewed the position of nursing dean as a guaranteed female appointment in an otherwise heavily male-dominated administration. One California social work professor reported his university canceled its search for a dean because no minority male or female candidates had been placed on their short list. It was rumored that other schools on campus were permitted to go forward with their searches—even though they also failed to put forward names of minority candidates—because the higher administration perceived it to be "easier" to fulfill affirmative action goals in the social work school. The interviews provide greater evidence of the "glass escalator" at work in the lower levels of these professions.

Of course, men's motivations also play a role in their advancement to higher professional positions. I do not mean to suggest that the men I talked to all resented the informal tracking they experienced. For many men, leaving the most female-identified areas of their professions helped them resolve internal conflicts involving their masculinity. One man left his job as a school social worker to work in a methadone drug treatment program, not because he was encouraged to leave by his colleagues, but because "I think there was some macho shit there, to tell you the truth, because I remember feeling a little uncomfortable there . . .; it didn't feel right to me." Another social worker, employed in the mental health services department of a large urban area in California, reflected on his move into administration:

> The more I think about it, through our discussion, I'm sure that's a large part of why I wound up in administration. It's okay for a man to do the administration. In fact, I don't know if I fully answered a question that you asked a little while ago about how did being male contribute to my advancing in the field. I was saying it wasn't because I got any special favoritism as a man, but . . . I think . . . because I'm a man, I felt a need to get into this kind of position. I may have worked harder toward it, may have competed harder for it, than most women would do, even women who think about doing administrative work.

Elsewhere I have speculated on the origins of men's tendency to define masculinity through single-sex work environments (Williams 1989). Clearly, personal ambition does play a role in accounting for men's movement into more "male-defined" arenas within these professions. But these occupations also structure opportunities for males independent of their individual desires or motives.

The interviews suggest that men's underrepresentation in these professions cannot be attributed to discrimination in hiring or promotions. Many of the men indicated that they received preferential treatment because they were men. Although men mentioned gender discrimination in the hiring process, for the most part they were channeled into the more "masculine" specialties within these professions, which ironically meant being "tracked" into better-paying and more prestigious specialties.

SUPERVISORS AND COLLEAGUES: THE WORKING ENVIRONMENT

Researchers claim that subtle forms of workplace discrimination push women out of male-dominated occupations (Jacobs 1989; Reskin and Hartmann 1986). In particular, women report feeling excluded from informal leadership and decision-making networks, and they sense hostility from their male co-workers, which makes them feel uncomfortable and unwanted (Carothers and Crull 1984). Respondents in this study were asked about their relationships with supervisors and female colleagues to ascertain whether men also experienced "poisoned" work environments when entering gender atypical occupations.

A major difference in the experience of men and women in nontraditional occupations is that men in these situations are far more likely to be supervised by a member of their own sex. In each of the four professions I studied, men are overrepresented in administrative and managerial capacities, or, as is the case of nursing, their positions in the organizational hierarchy are governed by men (Grimm and Stern 1974; Phenix 1987; Schmuck 1987; Williams 1989; York, Henley and Gamble 1987). Thus, unlike women who enter "male fields," the men in these professions often work under the direct supervision of other men.

Many of the men interviewed reported that they had good rapport with their male supervisors. Even in professional school, some men reported extremely close relationships with their male professors. For example, a Texas librarian described an unusually intimate association with two male professors in graduate school:

> I can remember a lot of times in the classroom there would be discussions about a particular topic or issue, and the conversation would spill over into their office hours, after the class was over. And even though there were . . . a couple of the other women that had been in on the discussion, they weren't there. And I don't know if that was preferential or not . . . it certainly carried over into personal life as well. Not just at the school and that sort of thing. I mean, we would get together for dinner. . . .

. . .

Other men reported similar closeness with their professors. A Texas psychotherapist recalled his relationships with his male professors in social work school:

> I made it a point to make a golfing buddy with one of the guys that was in administration. He and I played golf a lot. He was the guy who kind of ran the research training, the research part of the master's program. Then there was a sociologist who ran the other part of the research program. He and I developed a good friendship.

This close mentoring by male professors contrasts with the reported experience of women in nontraditional occupations. Others have noted a lack of solidarity among women in nontraditional occupations. Writing about military academies, for example, Yoder describes the failure of token women to mentor succeeding generations of female cadets. She argues that women attempt to play down their gender difference from men because it is the source of scorn and derision.

> Because women felt unaccepted by their male colleagues, one of the last things they wanted to do was to emphasize their gender. Some women thought that, if they kept company with other women, this would highlight their gender and would further isolate them from male cadets. These women desperately wanted to be accepted as cadets, not as *women* cadets. Therefore, they did everything from not wearing skirts as an option with their uniforms to avoiding being a part of a group of women. (Yoder 1989:532)

Men in nontraditional occupations face a different scenario—their gender is construed as a *positive* difference. Therefore, they have an incentive to bond together and emphasize their distinctiveness from the female majority.

. . .

Openly gay men may encounter less favorable treatment at the hands of their supervisors. For example, a nurse in Texas stated that one of the physicians he worked with preferred to staff the operating room with male nurses exclusively—as long as they weren't gay. Stigma associated with homosexuality leads some men to enhance, or even exaggerate their "masculine" qualities, and may be another factor pushing men into more "acceptable" specialties for men.

Not all men who work in these occupations are supervised by men. Many of the men interviewed who had female bosses also reported high levels of acceptance—although levels of intimacy with women seemed lower than with other men. In some cases, however, men reported feeling shut out from decision making when the higher administration was constituted entirely by women. I asked an Arizona librarian whether men in the library profession were discriminated against in hiring because of their sex:

> Professionally speaking, people go to considerable lengths to keep that kind of thing out of their [hiring] deliberations. Personally, is another matter. It's pretty common around here to talk about the "old girl network." This is one of the few libraries that I've had any intimate knowledge of which is actually controlled by women. . . . Most of the department heads and upper-level administrators are women. And there's an "old girl network" that works just like the "old boy network," except that the important conferences take place in the women's room rather than on the golf course. But the political mechanism is the same, the exclusion of the other sex from decision making is the same. The reasons are the same. It's somewhat discouraging. . . .

Although I did not interview many supervisors, I did include 23 women in my sample to ascertain their perspectives about the presence of men in their professions. All of the women I interviewed claimed to be supportive of their male colleagues, but some conveyed ambivalence. For example, a social work professor said she would like to see more men enter the social work profession, particularly in the clinical specialty (where they are underrepresented). Indeed, she favored affirmative action hiring guidelines for men in the profession. Yet, she resented the fact that her department hired "another white male" during a recent search.

. . .

Even outside work, most of the men interviewed said they felt fully accepted by their female colleagues. They were usually included in informal socialization occasions with the women—even though this frequently meant attending baby showers or Tupperware parties. Many said that they declined offers to attend these events because they were not interested in "women's things," although several others claimed to attend everything: The minority men I interviewed seemed to feel the least comfortable in these informal contexts. One social worker in Arizona was asked about socializing with his female colleagues:

> I: So in general, for example, if all the employees were going to get together to have a party, or celebrate a bridal shower or whatever, would you be invited along with the rest of the group?
>
> R: They would invite me, I would say, somewhat reluctantly. Being a black male, working with all white females, it did cause some outside problems. So I didn't go to a lot of functions with them. . . .
>
> I: You felt that there was some tension there on the level of your acceptance . . . ?
>
> R: Yeah. It was OK working, but on the outside, personally, there was some tension there. It never came out, that they said, "Because of who you are we can't invite you" (laughs), and I wouldn't have done anything anyway. I would have probably respected them more for saying what was on their minds. But I never felt completely in with the group.

Some single men also said they felt uncomfortable socializing with married female colleagues because it gave the "wrong impression." But in general, the men said that they felt very comfortable around their colleagues and described their work places as very congenial for men. It appears unlikely, therefore, that men's underrepresentation in these professions is due to hostility toward men on the part of supervisors or women workers.

DISCRIMINATION FROM "OUTSIDERS"

The most compelling evidence of discrimination against men in these professions is related to their dealings with the public. Men often encounter negative stereotypes when they come into contact with clients or "outsiders"—people they meet outside of work. For instance, it is popularly assumed that male nurses are gay. Librarians encounter images of themselves as "wimpy" and asexual. Male social workers describe being typecast as "feminine" and "passive." Elementary school teachers are often confronted by suspicions that they are pedophiles. One kindergarten teacher described an experience that occurred early in his career, which was related to him years afterward by his principal:

> He indicated to me that parents had come to him and indicated to him that they had a problem with the fact that I was a male. . . . I recall almost exactly what he said. There were three specific

concerns that the parents had: One parent said, "How can he love my child; he's a man." The second thing that I recall, he said the parent said, "He has a beard." And the third thing was, "Aren't you concerned about homosexuality?"

Such suspicions often cause men in all four professions to alter their work behavior to guard against sexual abuse charges, particularly in those specialties requiring intimate contact with women and children.

Men are very distressed by these negative stereotypes, which tend to undermine their self-esteem and to cause them to second-guess their motivations for entering these fields. A California teacher said,

If I tell men that I don't know, that I'm meeting for the first time, that that's what I do, . . . sometimes there's a look on their faces that, you know, "Oh, couldn't get a real job?"

When asked if his wife, who is also an elementary school teacher, encounters the same kind of prejudice, he said,

No, it's accepted because she's a woman. . . . I think people would see that as a . . . step up, you know. "Oh you're not a housewife; you've got a career. That's great . . . that you're out there working. And you have a daughter, but you're still out there working. You decided not to stay home, and you went out there and got a job." Whereas for me, it's more like I'm supposed to be out working anyway, even though I'd rather be home with [my daughter].

Unlike women who enter traditionally male professions, men's movement into these jobs is perceived by the "outside world" as a step down in status. This particular form of discrimination may be most significant in explaining why men are underrepresented in these professions. Men who otherwise might show interest in and aptitudes for such careers are probably discouraged from pursuing them because of the negative popular stereotypes associated with the men who work in them. This is a crucial difference from the experience of women in nontraditional professions: "My daughter, the physician," resonates far more favorably in most people's ears than "my son, the nurse."

Many of the men in my sample identified the stigma of working in a female-identified occupation as the major barrier to more men entering their professions. However, for the most part, they claimed that these negative stereotypes were not a factor in their own decisions to join these occupations. Most respondents didn't consider entering these fields until well into adulthood, after working in some related occupation. Several social workers and librarians even claimed they were not aware that men were a minority in their chosen professions. Either they had no well-defined image or stereotype, or their contacts and mentors were predominantly men. For example, prior to entering library school, many librarians held part-time jobs in university libraries, where there are proportionally more men than in the profession generally. Nurses and elementary school teachers were more aware that mostly women worked in these jobs, and this was often a matter of some concern to them. However, their choices were ultimately legitimized by mentors, or by encouraging friends or family members who implicitly reassured them that entering these occupations would not typecast them as feminine. In some cases, men were told by recruiters there were special advancement opportunities for men in these fields, and they entered them expecting rapid promotion to administrative positions.

> I: Did it ever concern you when you were making the decision to enter nursing school, the fact that it is a female-dominated profession?
>
> R: Not really. I never saw myself working on the floor. I saw myself pretty much going into administration, just getting the background and then getting a job someplace as a supervisor and then working, getting up into administration.

Because of the unique circumstances of their recruitment, many of the respondents did not view their occupational choices as inconsistent with a male gender role, and they generally avoided the negative stereotypes directed against men in these fields.

Indeed, many of the men I interviewed claimed that they did not encounter negative professional stereotypes until they had worked in these fields for several years. Popular prejudices can be damaging to self-esteem and probably push some men out of these professions altogether. Yet, ironically, they sometimes contribute to the "glass escalator" effect I have been describing. Men seem to encounter the most vituperative criticism from the public when they are in the most female-identified specialties. Public concerns sometimes result in their being shunted into more "legitimate" positions for men. A librarian formerly in charge of a branch library's children's collection, who now works in the reference department of the city's main library, describes his experience:

> R: Some of the people [who frequented the branch library] complained that they didn't want to have a man doing the storytelling scenario. And I got transferred here to the central library in an equivalent job. . . . I thought that I did a good job. And I had been told by my supervisor that I was doing a good job.
>
> I: Have you ever considered filing some sort of lawsuit to get that other job back?
>
> R: Well, actually, the job I've gotten now . . . well, it's a reference librarian; it's what I wanted in the first place. I've got a whole lot more authority here. I'm also in charge of the circulation desk. And I've recently been promoted because of my new stature, so . . . no, I'm not considering trying to get that other job back.

The negative stereotypes about men who do "women's work" can push men out of specific jobs. However, to the extent that they channel men into more "legitimate" practice areas, their effects can actually be positive. Instead of being a source of discrimination, these prejudices can add to the "glass escalator effect" by pressuring men to move *out* of the most female-identified areas, and *up* to those regarded more legitimate and prestigious for men.

Author's Note: This research was funded in part by a faculty grant from the University of Texas at Austin. I also acknowledge the support of the sociology departments of the University of California, Berkeley; Harvard University; and Arizona State University. I would like to thank Judy Auerbach, Martin Button, Robert Nye, Teresa Sullivan, Debra Umberson, Mary Waters, and the reviewers at *Social Problems* for their comments on earlier versions of this paper. ©1992 by the Society for the Study of Social Problems. Reprinted from *Social Problems,* Vol. 39, No. 3, August 1992, pp. 253–67 by permission.

REFERENCES

Bielby, William T. and James N. Baron. 1984. "A Woman's Place Is with Other Women: Sex Segregation within Organizations." Pp. 27–55 in *Sex Segregation in the Workplace: Trends, Explanations, Remedies,* edited by Barbara Reskin. Washington, D.C.: National Academy Press.

Carothers, Suzanne C. and Peggy Crull. 1984. "Contrasting Sexual Harassment in Female-Dominated and Male-Dominated Occupations." Pp. 220–27 in *My Troubles Are Going to Have Trouble with Me: Everyday Trials and Triumphs of Women Workers,* edited by Karen B. Sacks and Dorothy Remy. New Brunswick, NJ: Rutgers University Press.

Freeman, Sue J. M. 1990. *Managing Lives: Corporate Women and Social Change.* Amherst, MA: University of Massachusetts Press.

Grimm, James W. and Robert N. Stern. 1974. "Sex Roles and Internal Labor Market Structures: The Female Semi-Professions." *Social Problems* 21: 690–705.

Hodson, Randy and Teresa Sullivan. 1990. *The Social Organization of Work.* Belmont, CA: Wadsworth Publishing Co.

Jacobs, Jerry. 1989. *Revolving Doors: Sex Segregation and Women's Careers.* Stanford, CA: Stanford University Press.

Phenix, Katherine. 1987. "The Status of Women Librarians." *Frontiers* 9:36–40.

Reskin, Barbara and Heidi Hartmann. 1986. *Women's Work, Men's Work: Sex Segregation on the Job.* Washington, D.C.: National Academy Press.

Reskin, Barbara and Patricia Roos. 1990. *Job Queues, Gender Queues: Explaining Women's Inroads into Male Occupations.* Philadelphia: Temple University Press.

Schmuck, Patricia A. 1987. "Women School Employees in the United States." Pp. 75–97 in *Women Educators: Employees of Schools in Western Counties,* edited by Patricia A. Schmuck. Albany: State University of New York Press.

Schrieber, Carol. 1979. *Men and Women in Transitional Occupations.* Cambridge, MA: MIT Press.

U.S. Bureau of the Census. 1980. *Detailed Population Characteristics,* vol. 1, Ch. D. Washington, D.C.: Government Printing Office.

U.S. Department of Labor. Bureau of Labor Statistics. 1991. *Employment and Earnings.* Washington, D.C.: Government Printing Office.

Williams, Christine L. 1989. *Gender Differences at Work: Women and Men in Non-traditional Occupations.* Berkeley: University of California Press.

Yoder, Janice D. 1989. "Women at West Point: Lessons for Token Women in Male-Dominated Occupations." Pp. 523–37 in *Women: A Feminist Perspective,* edited by Jo Freeman, Mountain View, CA: Mayfield Publishing Company.

York, Reginald O., H. Carl Henley, and Dorothy N. Gamble. 1987. "Sexual Discrimination in Social Work: Is It Salary or Advancement?" *Social Work* 32:336–40.

Zimmer, Lynn. 1988. "Tokenism and Women in the Workplace." *Social Problems* 35: 64–77.

28

CAUSE OF DEATH: INEQUALITY

ALEJANDRO REUSS

INEQUALITY KILLS

You won't see inequality on a medical chart or a coroner's report under "cause of death." You won't see it listed among the top killers in the United States each year. All too often, however, it is social inequality that lurks behind a more immediate cause of death, be it heart disease or diabetes, accidental injury or homicide. Few of the top causes of death are "equal opportunity killers." Instead, they tend to strike poor people more than rich people, the less educated more than the highly educated, people lower on the occupational ladder more than those higher up, or people of color more than white people.

Statistics on mortality and life expectancy do not provide a perfect map of social inequality. For example, the life expectancy for women in the United States is about six years longer than the life expectancy for men, despite the many ways in which women are subordinated to men. Take most indicators of socioeconomic status, however, and most causes of death, and it's a strong bet that you'll find illness and injury (or "morbidity") and mortality increasing as status decreases.

Men with less than 12 years of education are more than twice as likely to die of chronic diseases (e.g., heart disease), more than three times as likely to

Alejandro Reuss is co-editor of *Dollars & Sense.* Dollars & Sense, May/June 2001 pp. 10–12.

die as a result of injury, and nearly twice as likely to die of communicable diseases, compared to those with 13 or more years of education. Women with family incomes below $10,000 are more than three times as likely to die of heart disease and nearly three times as likely to die of diabetes, compared to those with family incomes above $25,000. African Americans are more likely than whites to die of heart disease; stroke; lung, colon, prostate, and breast cancer, as well as all cancers combined; liver disease; diabetes; AIDS; accidental injury; and homicide. In all, the lower you are in a social hierarchy, the worse your health and the shorter your life are likely to be.

THE WORSE OFF IN THE UNITED STATES ARE NOT WELL OFF BY WORLD STANDARDS

You often hear it said that even poor people in rich countries like the United States are rich compared to ordinary people in poor countries. While that may be true when it comes to consumer goods like televisions or telephones, which are widely available even to poor people in the United States, it's completely wrong when it comes to health.

In a 1996 study published in the *New England Journal of Medicine,* University of Michigan researchers found that African-American females living to age 15 in Harlem had a 65% chance of surviving to age 65, about the same as women in India. Meanwhile, Harlem's African-American males had only a 37% chance of surviving to age 65, about the same as men in Angola or the Democratic Republic of Congo. Among both African-American men and women, infectious diseases and diseases of the circulatory system were the prime causes of high mortality.

It takes more income to achieve a given life expectancy in a rich country like the United States than it does to achieve the same life expectancy in a less affluent country. So the higher money income of a low-income person in the United States, compared to a middle-income person in a poor country, does not necessarily translate into a longer life span. The average income per person in African-American families, for example, is more than five times the per capita income of El Salvador. The life expectancy for African-American men in the United States, however, is only about 67 years, the same as the average life expectancy for men in El Salvador.

HEALTH INEQUALITIES IN THE UNITED STATES ARE NOT JUST ABOUT ACCESS TO HEALTH CARE

Nearly one sixth of the U.S. population lacks health insurance, including about 44% of poor people. A poor adult with a health problem is only half as likely to see a doctor as a high-income adult. Adults living in low-income areas are more than twice as likely to be hospitalized for a health problem that could have been effectively treated with timely outpatient care, compared with adults living in high-income areas. Obviously, lack of access to health care is a major health problem.

But so are environmental and occupational hazards; communicable diseases; homicide and firearm-related injuries; and smoking, alcohol consumption, lack of exercise, and other risk factors. These dangers all tend to affect lower-income people more than higher-income, less-educated people more than more-educated, and people of color more than whites. African-American children are more than twice as likely as white children to be hospitalized for asthma, which is linked to air pollution. Poor men are nearly six times as likely as high-income men to have elevated blood-lead levels, which reflect both residential and workplace environmental hazards. African-American men are more than seven times as likely to fall victim to homicide as white men; African-American women, more than four times as likely as white women. The less education someone has, the more likely they are to smoke or to drink heavily. The lower someone's income, the less likely they are to get regular exercise.

Michael Marmot, a pioneer in the study of social inequality and health, notes that so-called diseases of affluence—disorders, like heart disease, associated with high-calorie and high-fat diets, lack of physical activity, etc.—are most prevalent among the *least affluent* people in rich societies. While recognizing the role of such "behavioral" risk factors as smoking in producing poor health, he argues, "It is not sufficient . . . to ask what contribution smoking makes to generating the social gradient in ill health, but we must ask, why is there a social gradient in smoking?" What appear to be individual "lifestyle" decisions often reflect a broader *social* epidemiology.

GREATER INCOME INEQUALITY GOES HAND IN HAND WITH POORER HEALTH

Numerous studies suggest that the more unequal the income distribution in a country, state, or city, the lower the life expectancies for people at all income levels. One study published in the *American Journal of Public Health,* for example, shows that U.S. metropolitan areas with low per capita incomes and low levels of income inequality have lower mortality rates than areas with high median incomes and high levels of income inequality. Meanwhile, for a given per capita income range, mortality rates always decline as inequality declines.

R. G. Wilkinson, perhaps the researcher most responsible for relating health outcomes to overall levels of inequality (rather than individual income levels), argues that greater income inequality causes worse health outcomes independent of its effects on poverty. Wilkinson and his associates suggest several explanations for this relationship. First, the bigger the income gap between rich and poor, the less inclined the well off are to pay taxes for public services they either do not use or use in low proportion to the taxes they pay. Lower spending on public hospitals, schools, and other basic services does not affect wealthy people's life expectancies very much, but it affects poor people's life expectancies a great deal. Second, the bigger the income gap, the lower the overall level of social cohesion. High levels of social cohesion are associated with good health outcomes for several reasons. For example, people in highly cohesive societies are more likely to be active in their communities, reducing social isolation, a known health risk factor. (See Thad Williamson, "Social Movements are Good for Your Health," p. 7.)

Numerous researchers have criticized Wilkinson's conclusions, arguing that the real reason income inequality tends to be associated with worse health outcomes is that it is associated with higher rates of poverty. But even if they are right and income inequality causes worse health *simply by bringing about greater poverty*, that hardly makes for a defense of inequality. Poverty and inequality are like partners in crime. "[W]hether public policy focuses primarily on the elimination of poverty or on reduction in income disparity," argue Wilkinson critics Kevin Fiscella and Peter Franks, "neither goal is likely to be achieved in the absence of the other."

DIFFERENCES IN STATUS MAY BE JUST AS IMPORTANT AS INCOME LEVELS

Even after accounting for differences in income, education, and other factors, the life expectancy for African Americans is less than that for whites. U.S. researchers are beginning to explore the relationship between high blood pressure among African Americans and the racism of the surrounding society. African Americans tend to suffer from high blood pressure, a risk factor for circulatory disease, more often than whites. Moreover, studies have found that, when confronted with racism, African Americans suffer larger and longer-lasting increases in blood pressure than when faced with other stressful situations. Broader surveys relating blood pressure in African Americans to perceived instances of racial discrimination have yielded complex results, depending on social class, gender, and other factors.

Stresses cascade down social hierarchies and accumulate among the least empowered. Even researchers focusing on social inequality and health, however, have been surprised by the large effects on mortality. Over 30 years ago, Michael Marmot and his associates undertook a landmark study, known as Whitehall I, of health among British civil servants. Since the civil servants shared many characteristics regardless of job classification—an office work environment, a high degree of job security, etc.—the researchers expected to find only modest health differences among them. To their surprise, the study revealed a sharp increase in mortality with each step down the job hierarchy—even from the highest grade to the second highest. Over ten years, employees in the lowest grade were three times as likely to die as those in the highest grade. One factor was that people in lower grades showed a higher incidence of many "lifestyle" risk factors, like smoking, poor diet, and lack of exercise. Even when the researchers controlled for such factors, however, more than half the mortality gap remained.

Marmot noted that people in the lower job grades were less likely to describe themselves as having "control over their working lives" or being "satisfied with their work situation," compared to those higher up. While people in higher job grades were more likely to report "having to work at a fast pace," lower-level civil servants were more likely to report feelings of hostility, the main stress-related risk factor for heart disease. Marmot concluded that "psycho-social" factors—the psychological costs of being lower in the hierarchy—played an important role in the unexplained mortality gap. Many of us have probably said to ourselves, after a trying day on the job, "They're killing me." Turns out it's not just a figure of speech. Inequality kills—and it starts at the bottom.

Resources: Lisa Berkman, "Social Inequalities and Health: Five Key Points for Policy-Makers to Know," February 5, 2001, Kennedy School of Government, Harvard University; *Health, United States, 1998, with Socioeconomic Status and Health Chartbook,* National Center for Health Statistics <www.cdc.gov/nchs>; Ichiro Kawachi, Bruce P. Kennedy, and Richard G. Wilkinson, eds., *The Society and Population Health Reader, Volume I: Income Inequality and Health,* 1999; Michael Marmot, "Social Differences in Mortality: The Whitehall Studies," *Adult Mortality in Developed Countries: From Description to Explanation,* Alan D. Lopez, Graziella Caselli, and Tapani Valkonen, eds., 1995; Michael Marmot, "The Social Pattern of Health and Disease," *Health and Social Organization: Towards a Health Policy for the Twenty-First Century,* David Blane, Eric Brunner, and Richard Wilkinson, eds., 1996; Arline T. Geronimus, et al., "Excess Mortality Among Blacks and Whites in the United States," *The New England Journal of Medicine* 335 (21), November 21, 1996; Nancy Krieger, Ph.D., and Stephen Sidney, M.D., "Racial Discrimination and Blood Pressure: The CARDIA Study of Young Black and White Adults," *American Journal of Public Health* 86(10), October 1996; *Human Development Report 2000,* UN Development Programme; *World Development Indicators 2000,* World Bank.

29

IT'S A FAMILY AFFAIR
Women, Poverty, and Welfare

RANDY ALBELDA ● CHRIS TILLY

Hating poor women for being poor is all the rage—literally. Radio talk show hosts, conservative think tanks, and many elected officials bash poor single mothers for being too "lazy," too "dependent," and too fertile. Poor mothers are blamed for almost every imaginable economic and social ill under the sun. Largely based on anecdotal information, mythical characterizations, and a recognition that the welfare system just isn't alleviating poverty, legislatures across the land and the federal government are proposing and passing draconian welfare "reform" measures.

It is true that current welfare policies do not work well—but not for the reasons usually presented. Welfare "reform" refuses to address the real issues facing single-mother families, and is heavily permeated by myths.

Aid to Families with Dependent Children (AFDC), the government income transfer program for poor non-elder families in the United States, serves only about 5 percent of the population at any given time, with over 90 percent of those receiving AFDC benefits being single mothers and their children. In 1993, 14 million people (two-thirds of them children) in the United States received AFDC. That same year, just under 40 million people were poor. Despite garnering a lion's share of political discussion, AFDC receives a minuscule amount of funding: It accounts for less than 1 percent of the federal budget and less than 3 percent of the state budgets.

Single mothers work. Not only do they do the unpaid work of raising children, they also average the same number of hours in the paid labor force as other mothers do—about 1,000 hours a year (a full-time, year-round job is about 2,000 hours a year).[1] And while close to 80 percent of all AFDC

From Dujon, Diane & Ann Withorn (eds.) *For Crying Out Loud: Women's Poverty in the United States.* Boston: South End Press, 1996, p. 79–85. Reprinted by permission of the publisher.

recipients are off in two years, over half of those return at some later point—usually because their wages in the jobs that got them off welfare just didn't match the cost of health care and childcare needed so they could keep the jobs. In fact, most AFDC recipients "cycle" between relying on families, work, and AFDC benefits to get or keep their families afloat.[2] That means that, for many single mothers, AFDC serves the same function as unemployment insurance does for higher-paid, full-time workers.

And, contrary to a highly volatile stereotype, welfare mothers, on average, have fewer kids than other mothers. And once on AFDC, they are less likely to have another child.

POVERTY AND THE "TRIPLE WHAMMY"

Poverty is a persistent problem in the United States. People without access to income are poor. In the United States, most people get access to income by living in a family with one or more wage-earners (either themselves or others). Income from ownership (rent, dividends, interest, and profits) provides only a few families with a large source of income. Government assistance is limited—with elders getting the bulk of it. So wages account for about 80 percent of all income generated in the United States. Not surprisingly, people whose labor market activity is limited, or who face discrimination, are the people most at risk for poverty. Children, people of color, and single mothers are most likely to be poor (see Boxes).

In 1993, 46 percent of single-mother families in the United States were living in poverty, but only 9 percent of two-adult families with children were poor.[3]

Why are so many single-mother families poor? Are they lazy, do they lack initiative, or are they just unlucky? The answer to all of these is a resounding "No." Single-mother families have a very hard time generating enough income to keep themselves above the poverty line for a remarkably straightforward reason: One female adult supports the family—and one female adult usually does not earn enough to provide both childcare expenses and adequate earnings.

To spell it out, single mothers face a "triple whammy." First, like all women, when they do paid work they often face low wages—far lower than men with comparable education and experience. In 1992, the median income (the midpoint) for all women who worked full-time was $13,677. That means that about 40 percent of all working women (regardless of their marital status) would not have made enough to support a family of three above the poverty line. Even when women work year-round full-time, they make 70 percent of what men do.

Second, like all mothers, single mothers must juggle paid and unpaid work. Taking care of healthy and, sometimes, sick children, and knowing

BOX 1
Who's Poor in the United States?

In 1993, one person in six was living below the official poverty line. The poverty line is an income threshold determined annually by the Department of Commerce's Census Bureau. The dollar amount is based on the price-adjusted determination of the 1960s cash value of a minimum adequate diet for families of different sizes multiplied by three (at the time, budget studies indicated that low-income families spent one-third of their incomes on food). In 1993, the poverty threshold for a family of four is about $11,631.

While 10 percent of all men are poor, 16 percent of women and 25 percent—a full quarter—of all children in the United States are poor. Further, 36 percent of all black persons and 34 percent of Latinos are poor, versus 17 percent of Asians and 13 percent of white persons. Does education help stave off poverty? Yes—but not very evenly. Consider the table in Box 2. Those with low levels of education are much more likely to be poor—but gender matters. For men, getting a high school diploma cuts the chances of being poor by half—20 percent versus 10 percent. For women, poverty rates are more than halved by getting that degree, but the rates are still high—15 percent. For women to lower their likelihood of poverty to that of men with high school diplomas means getting some college education.

**Percent Poor Persons in the United States
(All Ages) by Selected Characteristics, 1993**

	All	Men	Women	Children
All	16.4%	10.2%	16.1%	25.2%
By race				
White	13.2%	8.6%	13.2%	19.8%
Black	35.9%	20.6%	34.5%	50.8%
Asian	17.0%	14.3%	17.4%	20.0%
By ethnicity				
Non-Latino	14.5%	8.9%	14.5%	22.0%
Latino	33.7%	22.2%	32.5%	45.2%
By residence				
City	24.1%	14.4%	22.6%	38.8%
Suburb	11.4%	7.1%	11.2%	17.4%
Rural	18.1%	11.8%	18.4%	25.9%

Source: U.S. Census Bureau, Current Population Survey, 1994.

BOX 2
Poverty Rates for Adults in the United States
by Educational Attainment, 1993

Years of Education	All Adults	Men	Women
8 or less	31.6%	26.4%	36.7%
9–11	27.5%	19.9%	34.3%
12	13.1%	10.0%	15.6%
13–15	9.0%	6.8%	10.9%
16	4.3%	3.8%	4.8%
17+	2.9%	2.8%	3.1%

Source: U.S. Census Bureau, Current Population Survey, 1994.

where they are when at work, requires time and flexibility that few full-time jobs afford. All mothers are more likely to earn less and work less than other women workers because of it.

Finally, *unlike* married mothers, many single mothers must juggle earning income and taking care of children without the help of another adult. Single-mother families have only one adult to send into the labor market. And that same adult must also make sure children get through their day.

The deck is stacked—but not just for single mothers. All women with children face a job market which has little sympathy for their caregiving responsibilities and at the same time places no economic value on their time spent at home. The economic activity of raising children is one that no society can do without. In our society, we do not recognize it as work worth paying mothers for. For a married mother, this contradiction is the "double day." For a single mother, the contradiction frequently results in poverty for her and her children.

DENYING THE REAL PROBLEMS

The lack of affordable childcare, the large number of jobs that fail to pay living wages, and the lack of job flexibility are the real problems that face all mothers (and increasingly everyone). For single mothers, these problems compound into crisis.

But instead of tackling these problems head on, politicians and pundits attack AFDC. Why? One reason is that non-AFDC families themselves are becoming more desperate, and resent the limited assistance that welfare provides to the worst-off. With men's wages falling over the last 30 years, fewer and fewer families can get by with only one wage earner. The government is not providing help for many low-income families who are struggling but are still above the AFDC eligibility threshold. This family "speed-up" has helped contribute to the idea that if both parents in a two-parent household can work (in order to be poor), then all AFDC recipients should have to work too.

Instead of facing the real problems, debates about welfare reform are dominated by three dead ends. First, politicians argue that single mothers must be made to work in the paid labor market. But most single mothers already work as much as they can. Studies confirm that AFDC recipients already do cycle in and out of the labor force. Further, as surveys indicate, mothers receiving AFDC would like to work. The issue is not whether or not to work, but whether paid work is available, how much it pays, and how to balance work and childcare.

Second, there is a notion of replacing the social responsibilities of government assistance with individual "family" responsibilities: Make men pay child support, demand behavioral changes of AFDC recipients, or even pressure single women to get married. While child support can help, for most single mothers it offers a poor substitute for reliable government assistance. Penalizing women and their children for ascribed behaviors (such as having more children to collect welfare) that are supported by anecdotes but not facts is at best mean-spirited.

Third, there is an expectation that people only need support for a limited amount of time—many states and some versions of federal welfare reform limit families to 24 months of aid over some period of time (from a lifetime to five years). Yet limiting the amount of time women receive AFDC will not reduce or limit the need for support. Children do not grow up in 24 months, nor will many women with few skills and little education necessarily become job ready. But more important, many women who do leave AFDC for the workplace will not make enough to pay for childcare or the health insurance they need to go to work.

In short, welfare "reform" that means less spending and no labor market supports will do little beyond making poor women's lives more miserable.

BEYOND WELFARE REFORM

What could be done instead? Welfare reform in a vacuum can solve only a small part of the problem. To deal with poverty among single-mother families, to break the connection between gender and poverty, requires changing the world of work, socializing the costs of raising children, and providing low-wage supports.

If we as a nation are serious about reducing the poverty of women and children, we need to invest in seven kinds of institutional changes:

- *Create an income-maintenance system that recognizes the need for full-time childcare.* Policies that affect families must acknowledge the reality of children's needs. To truly value families means to financially support those (women or men) who must provide full-time childcare at home or to provide dependable, affordable, and caring alternative sources of childcare for those who work outside the home.

- *Provide support for low-wage workers.* If leaving welfare and taking a job means giving up health benefits and childcare subsidies, the loss to poor families can be devastating. Although high-salary workers receive (or can afford) these benefits, low-wage workers often don't. Government should provide these supports; universal health care and higher earned income tax credits (EITC) are a first step in the right direction.

- *Close the gender pay gap.* One way to achieve pay equity is to require employers to re-evaluate the ways that they compensate comparable skills. Poor women need pay equity the most, but all women need it. Another way to close the pay gap is to increase the minimum wage. Most minimum-wage workers are women. An increase from the current $4.25 an hour to $5.50 would bring the minimum wage to 50 percent of the average wage.

- *Create jobs.* Create the opportunity to work, for poor women and poor men as well. Full employment is an old idea that still makes sense.

- *Create jobs that don't assume you have a "wife" at home to perform limitless unpaid work.* It's not just the welfare system that has to come to terms with family needs; it's employers as well. With women making up 46 percent of the workforce—and men taking on more childcare responsibilities as well—a change in work styles is overdue.

- *Make education and training affordable and available for all.* In an economy where the premium on skills and education is increasing, education and training are necessary for young people and adults, women and men.

- *Fix the tax structure.* Many of these proposals require government spending consistent with the ways our industrial counterparts spend money. Taxes must be raised to pay for these programs: the alternative—not funding child allowances, health care, and training—will prove more costly to society in the long run. But it is critically important to make the programs universal, and to fund them with a *fairer* tax system. Federal, state, and local governments have taxed middle- and low-income families for too long without assuring them basic benefits. Taxes paid by the wealthiest families as a percentage of their income have fallen dramatically over the last 15 years, while the burden on the bottom 80 percent has risen; it's time to reverse these trends.

The changes proposed are sweeping, but no less so than those proposed by the Republican Contract with America. With one out of every four children in this nation living in poverty, all our futures are at stake.

NOTES

1. These data, and others throughout the paper, were calculated by the authors using current population survey tapes.
2. Five recent studies have looked at welfare dynamics and all come to these conclusions. LaDonna Pavetti, "The Dynamics of Welfare and Work: Exploring the Process by Which Young Women Work Their Way Off Welfare," paper presented at the APPAM Annual Research Conference, 1992; Kathleen Harris, "Work and Welfare Among Single Mothers in Poverty," *American Journal of Sociology,* vol. 99 (2), September 1993, pp. 317–52; Roberta Spalter-Roth, Beverly Burr, Heidi Hartmann, and Lois Shaw, "Welfare That Works: The Working Lives of AFDC Recipients," Institute for Women's Policy Research, 1995; Rebecca Blank and Patricia Ruggles, "Short-Term Recidivism Among Public Assistance Recipients," *American Economic Review,* vol. 84 (2), May 1994, pp. 49–53; and Peter David Brandon, "Vulnerability to Future Dependence Among Former AFDC Mothers," Institute for Research on Poverty discussion paper DP1005-95, University of Wisconsin, Madison, Wis., 1995.
3. U.S. Department of Commerce, Census Bureau, "Income, Poverty and Valuation of Noncash Benefits," *Current Populations Reports,* 1995, pp. 60–188, p. D-22.

30

NO EQUAL JUSTICE
Race and Class in the American
Criminal Justice System

DAVID COLE

In April 1992, federal and state agents on a joint drug crime task force raided Room 203 of La Mirage, a seedy motel in Los Angeles, and arrested Christopher Lee Armstrong and four of his companions. That month, a federal grand jury in Los Angeles indicted the men for conspiracy to distribute more than fifty grams of crack cocaine. All five were black. To the public defenders who were assigned to represent the men, the pattern was all too familiar. Of the twenty-four crack cocaine cases the public defender office closed in the prior year, all the defendants were black. And of the fifty-three

From: David Cole, *No Equal Justice: Race and Class in the American Criminal Justice System.* New York: The New Press, 1999, pp. 158–168. © 1999 David Cole. Reprinted by permission of the publisher.

crack cases the office completed over the prior three years, forty-eight defendants were black, five Hispanic, and none white. At the same time, they knew that many whites used crack, and that white defendants had been tried for crack cocaine charges in California's state court system, where the penalties are much less harsh. Armstrong's lawyers suspected that the authorities might be routing black defendants through the federal system, while directing white defendants into the more lenient state court system. If prosecutors were treating defendants differently based on their race, they reasoned, that conduct would violate equal protection and should require dismissal of the cases. However, the best evidence of what the prosecutors were doing and why they were doing it was in the prosecutors' control. So the defense lawyers submitted to the court the evidence of racial disparity that they had, and asked for the right to conduct "discovery" of the prosecution's files to determine whether their suspicions were in fact well-founded.

SELECTIVE PROSECUTION

In making their charge of "selective prosecution," Armstrong's lawyers were not advancing a new theory. The Supreme Court had recognized long before that selective enforcement of the laws based on race violates equal protection. In *Yick Wo v. Hopkins*,[1] the Court in 1886 unanimously overturned convictions of two Chinese men for operating laundries without a license. San Francisco authorities had arrested about 150 persons for operating laundries without a license—every one of them Chinese. They had denied licenses to all Chinese applicants. And they had granted licenses to all but one of the eighty or so non-Chinese laundry operators who applied. In a unanimous decision invalidating Yick Wo's conviction, the Supreme Court stated, "Though the law itself be fair on its face, and impartial in appearance, yet, if it is applied and administered by public authority with an evil eye and an unequal hand, so as practically to make unjust and illegal discriminations, between persons in similar circumstances, material to their rights, the denial of equal justice is still within the prohibition of the constitution."[2]

The principle the Court established in *Yick Wo* is straightforward: where the government discriminates based on race in its enforcement of the criminal law, it denies equal protection of the laws. Yet at the time Christopher Armstrong's lawyers made their selective prosecution claim, there had been no reported federal or state cases since 1886 that had dismissed a criminal prosecution on the ground that the prosecutor acted for racial reasons. It seems unlikely that this is because no federal or state prosecutor in over 100 years had engaged in racial discrimination. The more likely explanation is that it is virtually impossible to prove such a claim in court.

Criminal defendants making selective prosecution claims face a classic catch-22. To establish selective prosecution, a defendant must prove that the prosecutor singled him out for prosecution because of his race, and did not prosecute others engaged in the same conduct. The best—and usually the only—evidence on these issues is in the prosecutor's control. But the courts have ruled that defendants have no right to see the prosecutor's files until they first make a "colorable showing" of selective prosecution. Thus, a defendant must provide evidence of selective prosecution *before* he gets any access to the documents and other evidence necessary to establish the claim. In the vast majority of cases, this is an insurmountable hurdle. Absent a public admission from the prosecutor of racial animus, or a remarkable racial pattern of prosecutions, defendants are not likely even to obtain discovery, much less dismissal of their claims.

The pattern Armstrong's lawyers presented to the court was quite remarkable: no white crack defendants prosecuted in federal court over a three-year period. In addition, defendants submitted two sworn statements. The first related a halfway house intake coordinator's observation that in his experience treating crack cocaine addicts, whites and blacks dealt and used the drug in equal proportions. (The United States Sentencing Commission subsequently reported in 1995 that 65 percent of those who have used crack are white.) Another, from a defense attorney experienced in state prosecutions, stated that many nonblack defendants were prosecuted for crack cocaine offenses in state court. The government's own evidence seemed to support the defendants' suspicions: it submitted a list of some 2,400 persons charged with federal crack cocaine violations over a three-year period, of which all but eleven were black, and none were white.

The trial court deemed this evidence enough to justify discovery, to determine whether the allegations of racial selectivity were in fact well-founded. But the prosecutors refused to submit to the discovery, and appealed. In May 1996, the Supreme Court reversed.[3] It stated that Armstrong's evidence was insufficient because he had failed to identify any similarly situated white defendants who had been prosecuted in state court. The Court seemed to go out of its way to ensure that Armstrong's claims of race discrimination would not see the light of day. It dismissed the criminal defense attorney's affidavit, which presented precisely the information the Court said was missing, as "hearsay" that "reported personal conclusions based on anecdotal evidence." Yet the prosecutors had never objected to the evidence in the trial court, and the general rule—which the Supreme Court enforces rigorously against criminal defendants—is that if one fails to object when evidence is introduced, the objection is waived. Only a single Justice, John Paul Stevens, dissented.

As the *Armstrong* decision suggests, and as the absence of any successful claims over more than a century confirms, the selective-prosecution defense is available in theory, but unattainable in practice. Much like the guarantee of effective assistance of counsel, the nominal availability of the selective-prosecution defense does more to legitimate the status quo as nondiscriminatory than it does to protect defendants from discrimination. The Court's tactic for dealing with the issue—effectively blocking at the threshold the very investigation necessary to establish the claim—ensures that the courts will rarely if ever be forced to confront evidence of race discrimination in criminal prosecutions.

STANDING TO CHALLENGE RACIAL DISCRIMINATION IN CRIMINAL LAW ENFORCEMENT

The tactic of burying race discrimination claims before they can be made is not limited to selective prosecution; it is a consistent theme throughout virtually all of the Supreme Court's doctrine governing legal challenges to discrimination in the administration of criminal justice. The Court has imposed nearly insurmountable barriers to persons challenging race discrimination at all stages of the criminal justice system, from policing to judging to sentencing. With the exception of jury discrimination, the barriers are so high that few claims are even filed, notwithstanding shocking racial disparities and widespread belief among minority groups that criminal justice is enforced in a discriminatory manner. The few suits involving claims of criminal justice abuses along racial lines that have reached the Supreme Court have almost all been dismissed on technical grounds before the issue of discrimination could even be aired. This frees the Court from having to address the messy and troubling reality of racial inequality in criminal justice, but it is also likely to breed distrust and cynicism among those who feel that the system is unfairly administered.

Adolph Lyons, a twenty-four-year-old black man, filed such a suit, and his experience is illustrative. While driving his car in Los Angeles early in the morning of October 6, 1976, Lyons was pulled over by four police officers for a burnt-out taillight. Drawing their guns, the police ordered Lyons out of his car. He complied. They told him to face the car and spread his legs. He did so. They told him to put his hands on his head. Again, he followed their orders. After they subjected him to a patdown search, Lyons dropped his hands, at which point an officer slammed Lyons's hands back on his head. When Lyons complained of pain from the car keys he was holding, the officer applied a chokehold. Lyons lost consciousness and fell to the ground. When he came to, he was spitting up blood and dirt, had urinated and defecated, and had suffered permanent damage to his larynx. The officers issued a traffic ticket for the burnt-out taillight and sent him on his way.

Lyons sued to challenge the use of the chokehold in such circumstances. Between 1975 and 1980, the LAPD had applied the chokehold on 975 occasions. By the time Lyons's case reached the Supreme Court, sixteen persons had been killed by police use of the chokehold; twelve of the victims were black men. The Supreme Court, however, dismissed the case, ruling that Lyons lacked "standing" to seek an injunction against this practice.

The "standing" doctrine holds that courts may provide relief only where they are presented with a specific and concrete dispute. At a minimum, an individual must identify some injury caused by the defendant that will be remedied through the lawsuit. Lyons sought a court order limiting the LAPD's use of chokeholds in the future. The Supreme Court said he had no right to bring such a suit, because he could not show that he would encounter another chokehold again. That Lyons had been victimized by a chokehold in the past did not mean that he faced a threat of being subjected to one in the future. In the absence of a threat of future harm, the Court concluded, there was no concrete dispute between the parties justifying judicial intervention. In essence, the Court deemed the case too abstract to decide.

The matter was hardly abstract to Lyons. He argued that, as a black man, he could not drive his car in Los Angeles without fearing that he would be pulled over again and subjected to another chokehold. Because the police had applied the chokehold even though Lyons had cooperated fully, there was nothing short of a lawsuit he could do to protect himself. Yet the Court held that in order to have standing,

> Lyons would have had not only to allege that he would have
> another encounter with the police but also to make the incredible
> assertion either (1) that *all* police officers in Los Angeles *always*
> choke any citizen with whom they happen to have an encounter,
> whether for the purpose of arrest, issuing a citation or for ques-
> tioning, or (2) that the City ordered or authorized police officers to
> act in such manner.[4]

Lyons did not explicitly allege race discrimination, although the statistics on chokehold deaths suggest that black men had particular reason to fear its application. But the Court's holding makes it difficult to challenge any discriminatory applications of criminal law authority. Because criminal law is by its nature enforced selectively and intermittently, individuals will rarely be able to satisfy the Court's requirement that they show that an encounter with the police, a prosecutor, or judge, is sufficiently likely to recur to them in the future.

Two racially charged precursors to *Lyons* illustrate the point. *O'Shea v. Littleton*[5] arose out of the civil rights struggle in Cairo, Illinois, in the early 1970s. The plaintiffs were seventeen blacks and two whites who had been engaged in peaceful demonstrations and boycotts against racially discriminatory stores. They alleged that Cairo's criminal justice authorities were conducting a race war in retaliation for their political activities. They specifically charged that the state prosecutor, investigator, and police commissioner sought harsher penalties against black criminal defendants, and impeded black citizens' ability to have the law enforced against whites who harmed them. They also charged the local judges with setting bail rates higher for black than for white defendants. Several plaintiffs had been subject to the practices they complained of, which they claimed were motivated both by their race and by their continuing involvement in civil rights activities.

As in *Lyons,* the Supreme Court ruled that the case should be dismissed for lack of a "case or controversy." Although some of the plaintiffs had been victimized in the past, the Court stated, "past exposure to illegal conduct does not in itself show a present case or controversy regarding injunctive relief . . . if unaccompanied by any continuing, present adverse effects."[6]

Two years later, the Court reaffirmed its resistance to judicial oversight of criminal law enforcement. *Rizzo v. Goode*[7] involved the notorious Philadelphia police department, and the equally notorious Frank Rizzo, who was police chief when the case began and mayor when it ended. Rizzo prided himself on being tough on crime. During his mayoral campaign he vowed, "I'm gonna make Attila the Hun look like a faggot after this election's over," and stated that "the way to treat criminals is *spacco il capa*"—to bust their heads.[8] During his eight years as mayor, fatal shootings by Philadelphia police officers increased by about 20 percent *per year.*[9] The *Rizzo* case involved two consolidated class action lawsuits, both of which charged that the Philadelphia police force had engaged in a pattern and practice of police misconduct, and had adopted a civilian complaint procedure that was more effective at deterring civilians from filing complaints than at controlling or punishing police abuse. The district court heard 250 witnesses over the course of twenty-one days, and made detailed factual findings on approximately forty incidents of alleged police abuse. The district court found that "it is impossible to avoid the conclusion that, in the absence of probable cause for arrest, at least two classes of individuals are particularly likely to be subjected to [abuse]: poor blacks, and individuals who question or protest the initial police action."[10] It also concluded that the constitutional violations it found "cannot be dismissed as rare isolated instances."[11] Finding that the civilian complaint procedure was grossly inadequate, the court ordered the police department to implement an improved complaint procedure.

The Supreme Court reversed. Citing *O'Shea*, it expressed serious doubts as to whether the case presented a case or controversy, again because there was insufficient likelihood that the plaintiffs would be subjected to police misconduct in the future. After the Supreme Court issued its decision in *Rizzo*, the Civil Rights Division of the Justice Department launched an eight-month federal investigation into allegations of police brutality in Philadelphia. At the close of that investigation, the Justice Department itself sued the City of Philadelphia, claiming that it had discovered an extensive pattern of constitutional violations, that the police department exercised inadequate supervision, and that the misconduct was disproportionately directed at black and Hispanic citizens.[12] Backed by resources not available to private plaintiffs, the Justice Department was armed with evidence of hundreds of incidents of misconduct and abuse. It found that blacks and Hispanics comprised about a third of Philadelphia's population, but accounted for about 60 to 70 percent of the complaints of physical abuse, illegal searches and seizures, and unlawful detentions.[13] Nonetheless, the district court, reading the signs from *Rizzo* and *O'Shea*, dismissed the complaint on its own initiative.[14] The court of appeals affirmed. If the Justice Department itself could not prevail in such a suit, there is little hope for anyone else to do so.

In *Lyons*, *O'Shea*, and *Rizzo*, the Supreme Court repeatedly turned back legal challenges to constitutional violations in the administration of criminal justice, each of which involved claims of racial discrimination or racially disparate impact. It did so, moreover, not on the merits, but by barring such suits at the threshold. It defined standing to sue in such narrow terms that few will ever be able to satisfy its requirements in connection with a challenge to criminal law enforcement. Much like the selective prosecution cases, these rulings have the effect of foreclosing claims of discrimination before they are even aired. Because the bars operate at the threshold of the lawsuit, cases are frequently dismissed before the allegations of discrimination can even be developed. They never see the light of day. In this way, the illusion is maintained that the system forbids discrimination; the reality is that the system for all practical purposes forbids discrimination *cases.*

LIMITS ON SUITS FOR DAMAGES

The restrictions erected in *O'Shea*, *Rizzo*, and *Lyons* apply only to suits for injunctive relief. Thus, the Supreme Court stated that Adolph Lyons could have sued the LAPD for money damages for the injuries he suffered. But suits for monetary compensation face their own set of hurdles, in many instances more formidable even than those that apply to requests for injunctions. Consider a situation faced by many black parents: your son is stopped without cause by a state police officer, ordered out of his car, and searched illegally. You want to challenge the conduct, which appeared to be predicated on nothing more than your son's race. You can't sue for injunctive relief, because you can't show that he will be stopped again, so you want to sue for damages. Who can you sue?

Not the state and not the state police. The Supreme Court has held that the state and its offices are immune from federal suits for damages under the Eleventh Amendment to the Constitution.[15] The Eleventh Amendment literally protects states only from being sued in federal court "by citizens of another state," but the Supreme Court has interpreted it broadly to bar *any* federal suits for damages against states absent their consent. The Court has also held that states cannot be sued for damages for constitutional rights violations in state court.[16] Thus, the state, the defendant with the deepest pocket, is immune.

If the police officer were employed by a city rather than by the state, you could sue the city, but only if you could point to a city policy or custom authorizing such illegal stops and searches.[17] Because most cities do not have such policies, and "custom" is notoriously hard to prove, suing the city is often not a realistic option either.

That leaves the individual officer. But the Supreme Court has also granted government officials substantial protection from suit. Some officials are absolutely immune: judges, for example, can't be sued for damages for discrimination in the courtroom, nor can prosecutors be sued for damages for discriminatory prosecutions, no matter how strong the evidence of wrongdoing. Police officers and other government officials may be sued, but they, too, have a form of immunity: under the judicially created doctrine of "qualified immunity," they may be held liable for constitutional violations only if it was clearly established at the time the conduct occurred that their actions were illegal.[18] The idea behind this doctrine makes some sense standing alone: individual officers should not be held personally liable for their wrongdoing if they could not reasonably have known that their conduct was illegal. But the Supreme Court has interpreted this immunity so broadly that, in its own words, "all but the plainly incompetent or those who knowingly violate the law" are immune.[19] As a result, shockingly few damages actions for government misconduct succeed. For example, of some 12,000 actions filed against federal officials for constitutional violations from 1971 to 1985, only four led to a successful judgment or settlement for the plaintiff.[20] When the qualified immunity rule is combined with the bars on suits against states and cities, the result often means that *no one* can be sued for a constitutional violation. The victim is made to bear the cost of the violation himself.

In addition to these legal barriers to relief, there are numerous practical hurdles to bringing a suit for damages. In many instances the violation of constitutional rights does not lead to any tangible harm. An illegal search motivated by race, for example, may be extremely intrusive and humiliating, but as long as the police do no physical damage, it will be difficult to point to harm for which one should be compensated. In addition, many such suits reduce to a swearing match between a police officer and the individual stopped. Because those who are stopped are disproportionately poor and members of minority groups, they may find it difficult to convince a judge or jury to accept their word over a police officer's.

Finally, as the *McCleskey* case demonstrated, to establish an equal protection violation, one must prove *intentional* discrimination, and it is extremely difficult to do so. Government officials do not commonly admit that their actions were motivated by prejudice. Indeed, because there is such a strong social sanction against racial prejudice, few people are even willing to admit to themselves that they have acted for racial reasons. Yet racial stereotypes affect all of us in subtle and not-so-subtle ways. The Court's prohibition of intentional discrimination weeds out the bigots who admit they are racist, but ignores (and thereby effectively legitimates) all other discrimination.

Thus, despite the Supreme Court's assurances to Lyons that he could seek damages, the likelihood of obtaining any relief in any case challenging discriminatory law enforcement is slim. This is true whether one seeks to raise selective prosecution as a defense to a particular criminal prosecution, whether one seeks injunctive relief to forestall future violations, or whether one seeks only monetary compensation for an individual case. In each setting, the Court has constructed a set of all-but-impassable barriers. And in each area, the hurdles operate at the threshold, stopping the complaint from even being aired. In this way, the illusion of a constitutional prohibition against discrimination in criminal justice is maintained, but the avenue left open for enforcing it is so narrow and difficult that few will succeed in navigating its course. At one level, that may have the effect of legitimating the system; the courts can say that they abhor and forbid race discrimination, but that they simply do not see it. But I suggest at a deeper level this strategy eats away at the system's legitimacy. The charade cannot be maintained forever. Ultimately members of minority groups are likely to conclude that the courts and the law cannot be counted on to guarantee equal protection.

NOTES

1. 118 U.S. 356 (1886).
2. Id. at 373–74.
3. *United States v. Armstrong,* 517 U.S. 456 (1996).
4. *City of Los Angeles v. Lyons,* 461 U.S. 95, 105 (1983).
5. 414 U.S. 488 (1974).
6. 414 U.S. at 495–96.
7. *Rizzo v. Goode,* 423 U.S. 362 (1976).
8. Ralph Cipriano & Tom Infield, "You Either Loved Him or Hated Him," *Phila. Inquirer,* 17 July 1991, 1A.
9. Jerome H. Skolnick & James J. Fyfe, *Above the Law: Police and the Excessive Use of Force,* 140 (1993).
10. *COPPAR v. Rizzo,* 357 F. Supp. 1289, 1317 (E.D. Pa. 1973).
11. Id. at 1319.
12. *United States v. City of Philadelphia,* 644 F.2d 187 (3d Circ. 1980).
13. 644 F.2d at 210 (Gibbons, J., dissenting from denial of petition for rehearing).
14. Id. at 209.
15. *Quern v. Jordan,* 440 U.S. 332 (1979).
16. *Will v. Mich. Dept. of State Police,* 491 U.S. 58 (1989).
17. *Monell v. Dept. of Social Services,* 436 U.S. 658 (1978).
18. *Harlow v. Fitzgerald,* 457 U.S. 800 (1982).
19. *Malley v. Briggs,* 475 U.S. 335, 341 (1986).
20. Written Statement of John J. Farley, III, Director, Torts Branch, Civil Division, U.S. Dept. of Justice, to the Litigation Section of the Bar of the District of Columbia (May 1985); cited in Cornelia Pillard, *Taking Fiction Seriously,* manuscript on file with author.

31

THE EFFECTS OF AFFIRMATIVE ACTION
ON OTHER STAKEHOLDERS
BARBARA RESKIN

Affirmative action policies and practices reduce job discrimination against minorities and white women, although their effects have not been large. Some critics charge that affirmative action's positive effects have been offset by its negative effects on white men, on productivity, and on the merit system. The research examined in this chapter shows that affirmative action rarely entails reverse discrimination, and neither hampers business productivity nor unduly increases the costs of doing business. Both theoretical and empirical research suggest that it enhances productivity by encouraging employment practices that better utilize workers' skills.

REVERSE DISCRIMINATION

For many people, the most troubling aspect of affirmative action is that it may discriminate against majority-group members (Lynch 1997). According to 1994 surveys, 70 to 80 percent of whites believed that affirmative action sometimes discriminates against whites (Steeh and Krysan 1996, p. 139). Men are more likely to believe that a woman will get a job or promotion over an equally or more qualified man than they are to believe that a man will get a promotion over an equally or more qualified woman (Davis and Smith 1996). In short, many whites, especially white men, feel that they are vulnerable to reverse discrimination (Bobo and Kluegel 1993). When asked whether African Americans or whites were at greater risk of discrimination at work, respondents named whites over African Americans by a margin of two to one (Steeh and Krysan 1996, p. 140). In addition, 39 percent of respondents to a 1997 *New York Times*/CBS News poll said that whites losing out because of affirmative action was a bigger problem than African Americans losing out because of discrimination (Verhovek 1997, p. 32).

From *The Realities of Affirmative Action in Employment*. Washington, D.C.: The American Sociological Association, 1998, pp. 74–84. © 1998 Barbara F. Reskin. Reprinted by permission of the American Sociological Association.

Several kinds of evidence indicate that whites' fears of reverse discrimination are exaggerated. Reverse discrimination is rare both in absolute terms and relative to conventional discrimination.[1] The most direct evidence for this conclusion comes from employment-audit studies: On every measured outcome, African-American men were much more likely than white men to experience discrimination, and Latinos were more likely than non-Hispanic men to experience discrimination (Heckman and Siegelman 1993, p. 218). Statistics on the numbers and outcomes of complaints of employment discrimination also suggest that reverse discrimination is rare.

According to national surveys, relatively few whites have experienced reverse discrimination. Only 5 to 12 percent of whites believe that their race has cost them a job or promotion, compared to 36 percent of African Americans (Steeh and Krysan 1996, pp. 139–40). Of 4,025 Los Angeles workers, 45 percent of African Americans and 16 percent of Latinos said that they had been refused a job because of their race, and 16 percent of African Americans and 8 percent of Latinos reported that they had been discriminated against in terms of pay or a promotion (Bobo and Suh 1996, table 1). In contrast, of the 863 whites surveyed, less than 3 percent had ever experienced discrimination in pay or promotion, and only one mentioned reverse discrimination. Nonetheless, two-thirds to four-fifths of whites (but just one-quarter of African Americans) surveyed in the 1990s thought it likely that less qualified African Americans won jobs or promotions over more qualified whites (Taylor 1994a; Davis and Smith 1994; Steeh and Krysan 1996, p. 139).[2]

Alfred Blumrosen's (1996, pp. 5–6) exhaustive review of discrimination complaints filed with the Equal Employment Opportunity Commission offers additional evidence that reverse discrimination is rare. Of the 451,442 discrimination complaints filed with the EEOC between 1987 and 1994, only 4 percent charged reverse discrimination (see also Norton 1996, pp. 44–5).[3] Of the 2,189 discrimination cases that Federal appellate courts decided between 1965 and 1985, less than 5 percent charged employers with reverse discrimination (Burstein 1991, p. 518).

Statistics on the more than 3,000 cases that reached district and appeals courts between 1990 and 1994 show an even lower incidence of reverse-discrimination charges: Less than 2 percent charged reverse discrimination (U.S. Department of Labor, Employment Standards Administration n.d., p. 3). The small number of reverse discrimination complaints by white men does not appear to stem from their reluctance to file complaints: They filed more than 80 percent of the age discrimination complaints that the EEOC received in 1994. Instead, as former EEOC chair Eleanor Holmes Norton (1996, p. 45) suggested, white men presumably complain most about the kind of discrimination that they experience most and least about discrimination they rarely encounter.

Allegations of reverse discrimination are less likely than conventional discrimination cases to be supported by evidence. Of the approximately 7,000 reverse-discrimination complaints filed with the EEOC in 1994, the EEOC found only 28 credible (Crosby and Herzberger 1996, p. 55). Indeed, U.S. district and appellate courts dismissed almost all the reverse-discrimination cases they heard between 1990 and 1994 as lacking merit.

Although rare, reverse discrimination does occur. District and appellate courts found seven employers guilty of reverse discrimination in the early 1990s (all involved voluntary affirmative action programs), and a few Federal contractors have engaged in reverse discrimination, according to the Office of Federal Contract Compliance Program's (OFCCP) director for Region II (Stephanopoulos and Edley 1995, section 6.3).[4]

The actions and reports of Federal contractors are inconsistent with the belief that goals are *de facto* quotas that lead inevitably to reverse discrimination. In the first place, the fact that contractors rarely meet their goals means that they do not view them as quotas (Leonard 1990, p. 56). Second, only 2 percent of 641 Federal contractors the OFCCP surveyed in 1994 complained that the agency required quotas or reverse discrimination (Stephanopoulos and Edley 1995, section 6.3).

How can we reconcile the enormous gulf between whites' perceptions that they are likely to lose jobs or promotions because of affirmative action and the small risk of this happening? The white men who brought reverse discrimination suits presumably concluded that their employers' choices of women or minorities could not have been based on merit, because men are accustomed to being selected for customarily male jobs (*New York Times*, March 31, 1995).[5] Most majority-group members who have not had a first-hand experience of competing unsuccessfully with a minority man or woman or a white woman cite media reports as the source of their impression that affirmative action prompts employers to favor minorities and women (Hochschild 1995, pp. 144, 308).[6] It seems likely that politicians' and the media's emphasis on "quotas" has distorted the public's understanding of what is required and permitted in the name of affirmative action (Entman 1997). It is also likely that the public does not distinguish affirmative action in employment from affirmative action in education which may include preferences or in the awarding of contracts which have included set-asides.

AFFIRMATIVE ACTION AND AMERICAN COMMERCE

Does affirmative action curb productivity, as some critics have charged? On the one hand, affirmative action could impede productivity if it forces employers to hire or promote marginally qualified and unqualified workers, or if the paperwork associated with affirmative action programs is burdensome. On the other hand, employers who assign workers to jobs based on their qualifications rather than their sex or race should make more efficient use of workers' abilities and hence should be more productive than those who use discriminatory employment practices (Becker 1971; Leonard 1984c; Donohue

1986). Affirmative action could also increase profitability by introducing varied points of view or helping firms broaden their markets (Cox and Blake 1991; Watson, Kumar, and Michaelsen 1993).

Effects on Productivity

There is no evidence that affirmative action reduces productivity or that workers hired under affirmative action are less qualified than other workers. In the first place, affirmative action plans that compromise valid educational and job requirements are illegal. Hiring unqualified workers or choosing a less qualified person over a more qualified one because of their race or sex is illegal and is not condoned in the name of affirmative action (U.S. Department of Labor, Employment Standards Administration n.d., p. 2). Second, to the extent that affirmative action gives women and minority men access to jobs that more fully exploit their productive capacity, their productivity and that of their employers should increase.

Although many Americans believe that affirmative action means that less qualified persons are hired and promoted (Verhovek 1997, p. 32), the evidence does not bear this out. According to a study of more than 3,000 workers hired in entry-level jobs in a cross-section of firms in Atlanta, Boston, Detroit, and Los Angeles, the performance evaluations of women and minorities hired under affirmative action did not differ from those of white men or female or minority workers for whom affirmative action played no role in hiring (Holzer and Neumark 1998). In addition, Columbus, Ohio, female and minority police officers hired under an affirmative action consent decree performed as well as white men (Kern 1996). Of nearly 300 corporate executives surveyed in 1979, 72 percent believed that minority hiring did not impair productivity (*Wall Street Journal* 1979); 41 percent of CEOs surveyed in 1995 said affirmative action improved corporate productivity (Crosby and Herzberger 1996, p. 86).[7]

Studies assessing the effect of firms' racial makeup on their profits also show no effects of affirmative action on productivity. An analysis of 100 of Chicago's largest firms over a 13-year period found no statistically significant relationship between the firms' share of minority workers and their profit margins or return on equity (McMillen 1995). This absence of an association is inconsistent with companies using lower standards when hiring African American employees. Finally, according to a study that compared the market performance of the 100 firms with best and worst records of hiring and promoting women and minorities, the former averaged an 18-percent return on investments, whereas the latter's average returns were below 8 percent (Glass Ceiling Commission 1995, pp. 14, 61).[8]

Costs to Business

Estimates of the price tag of affirmative action range from a low of hundreds of millions of dollars to a high of $26 billion (Brimelow and Spencer 1993).[9] More realistic estimates put enforcement and compliance costs at about

$1.9 billion (Leonard 1994, p. 34; Conrad 1995, pp. 37–8). According to Andrew Brimmer (1995, p. 12), former Governor of the Federal Reserve Board, the inefficient use of African Americans' productive capacity (as indicated by their education, training, and experience) costs the economy 70 times this much: about $138 billion annually, which is about 2.15 percent of the gross national product. Adding the cost of sex discrimination against white women would substantially increase the estimated cost of discrimination because white women outnumber African American men and women in the labor force by about three to one. The more affirmative action reduces race and sex discrimination, the lower its costs relative to the savings it engenders.

The affirmative action that the Federal executive order requires of Federal contractors adds to their paperwork. Companies with at least $50,000 in Federal contracts that employ at least 50 employees must provide written affirmative action plans that include goals and timetables, based on an annual analysis of their utilization of their labor pool. They must also provide specified information to the OFCCP and keep detailed records on the composition of their jobs and job applicants by race and sex. In response to an OFCCP survey soliciting their criticisms of the program, about one in eight Federal contractors complained about the paperwork burden (Stephanopoulos and Edley 1995, section 6.3). Keeping the records required by the OFCCP encourages the bureaucratization of human resource practices. As noted, informal employment practices, while cheaper in the short run, are also more subject to discriminatory bias and hence cost firms efficiency. Thus, implicit in the logic of the OFCCP's requirements is the recognition that formalizing personnel practices helps to reduce discrimination.

Business Support

U.S. business has supported affirmative action for at least 15 years. The Reagan administration's efforts to curtail the contract compliance program in the early 1980s drew strong opposition from the corporate sector (Bureau of National Affairs 1986a). Among the groups that went on record as opposing cutbacks in Federal affirmative action programs was the National Association of Manufacturers, a major organization of U.S. employers (*The San Diego Union-Tribune* 1985, p. AA-2). All but six of 128 heads of major corporations indicated that they would retain their affirmative action plans if the Federal government ended affirmative action (Noble 1986, p. B4). A 1996 survey showed similar levels of corporate support for affirmative action: 94 percent of CEOs surveyed said that affirmative action had improved their hiring procedures, 53 percent said it had improved marketing, and—as noted above—41 percent said it had improved productivity (Crosby and Herzberger 1996, p. 86). The business community's favorable stance toward affirmative action is also seen in the jump in stock prices for firms recognized by the OFCCP for their effective affirmative action programs (Wright et al. 1995, p. 281).

Perhaps the most telling sign of business support for affirmative action is the diffusion of affirmative action practices from Federal contractors to noncontractors. As noncontractors have recognized the efficiency or market payoffs associated with more objective employment practices and a more diverse workforce, many have voluntarily implemented some affirmative action practices (Fisher 1985).

AFFIRMATIVE ACTION AND OTHER STAKEHOLDERS

The consequences of affirmative action reach beyond workers and employers by increasing the pools of skilled minority and female workers. When affirmative action prompts employers to hire minorities or women for positions that serve the public, it can bring services to communities that would otherwise be underserved. For example, African-American and Hispanic physicians are more likely than whites and Anglos to practice in minority communities (Komaromy et al. 1996). Graduates of the Medical School at the University of California at San Diego who were admitted under a special admissions program were more likely to serve inner-city and rural communities and saw more poor patients than those admitted under the regular procedures (Penn, Russell, and Simon 1986).

Women's and minorities' employment in nontraditional jobs also raises the aspirations of other members of excluded groups by providing role models and by signaling that jobs are open to them. Some minorities and women do not pursue jobs or promotions because they expect to encounter discrimination (Mayhew 1968, p. 313). By reducing the perception that discriminatory barriers block access to certain lines of work, affirmative action curtails this self-selection (Reskin and Roos 1990, p. 305). In addition, the economic gains provided by better jobs permit beneficiaries to invest in the education of the next generation.

AFFIRMATIVE ACTION, MERITOCRACY, AND FAIRNESS

Affirmative action troubles some Americans for the same reasons discrimination does: They see it as unfair and inconsistent with meritocracy (Nacoste 1990). The evidence summarized above indicates that employers very rarely use quotas and that affirmative action does not lead to the employment of unqualified workers. We know too that many employers implement affirmative action by expanding their recruiting efforts, by providing additional training, and by formalizing human resource practices to eliminate bias. By eliminating cronyism, drawing on wider talent pools, and providing for due process, these practices are fairer to all workers than conventional business practices (*Harvard Law Review* 1989, pp. 668–70; Dobbin et al. 1993, pp. 401–6). After all, managers who judge minority and female workers by their race or sex instead of their performance may judge white workers by arbitrary standards as well (Rand 1996, p. 72).

Available research does not address how often employers take into account race and gender in choosing among equally qualified applicants. Although the courts have forbidden race- and gender-conscious practices in layoffs, they have allowed employers to take into account race or gender in selecting among qualified applicants in order to remedy the consequences of having previously excluded certain groups from some jobs. Such programs trouble some Americans, as we can see from the research evidence presented in the next section.

AMERICANS' VIEWS OF AFFIRMATIVE ACTION

The passage of the 1996 California Civil Rights Initiative, which barred this state from engaging in affirmative action, has been interpreted as signaling mounting public opposition to affirmative action. In reality, whites' and African Americans' views of affirmative action are both more nuanced and more positive than the California election result suggests. People's responses to opinion polls depend largely on how pollsters characterize affirmative action (Kravitz et al. 1997).[10] About 70 percent of Americans support affirmative action programs that pollsters describe as not involving "quotas" or "preferences" (Steeh and Krysan 1996, pp. 132, 134; Entman 1997, p. 37). Like a red flag, the term "quota" also triggers strong negative reactions. This happens because people view quotas as inconsistent with merit-based hiring and because quotas provoke fear of unfairly losing a job or promotion by members of groups that are not covered by affirmative action. As a result, most whites and African Americans oppose quotas (Bobo and Kluegel, 1993; Steeh and Krysan 1996, pp. 132–3, 148).

A casual reading of newspaper reports indicates considerable instability in Americans' attitudes toward affirmative action and a fair amount of opposition to affirmative action. For example, fewer than one in eight Americans surveyed in a 1995 Gallup poll approved of affirmative action programs that involve hiring quotas, and only 40 to 50 percent of Americans endorsed affirmative action programs designed to give African Americans or women preferential treatment (Moore 1995). However, polls that show low levels of support for affirmative action in the workplace typically ask about practices that are illegal and hence rare in actual affirmative action programs (Kravitz et al. 1997, p. xi). When pollsters ask about affirmative action in general or about the practices that actual affirmative action programs include, the majority of whites and African Americans are supportive.

In national polls conducted in the mid-1990s, about 70 percent of respondents endorsed affirmative action either as currently practiced or with reforms (Entman 1997, p. 37). For example, almost three-quarters of the respondents to a 1995 Gallup poll approved of employers using outreach efforts to recruit qualified minorities and women (Steeh and Krysan 1996, pp. 132, 134). Most whites and African Americans support such practices as targeted recruitment, open advertising, monitoring diversity, job training, and educational assistance designed to allow minorities to compete as individuals (e.g., training programs). More than three out of four white respondents and 85 percent of African-American respondents to a 1991 Harris survey agreed that "as long as there are no rigid quotas, it makes sense to give special training and advice to women and minorities so that they can perform better on the job" (Bobo and Kluegel 1993; Bruno 1995, p. 24).

In sum, the polls reveal that the majority of whites and African Americans have supported affirmative action since the early 1970s. Most Americans support the affirmative action procedures that employers actually use, such as taking extra efforts to find and recruit minorities and women. The broadest support is for practices that expand the applicant pool, but ignore race or gender in the selection process. Thus, Americans' first choice is enhancing equal opportunity without using race- or gender-conscious mechanisms. What most Americans oppose is quotas, an employment remedy that courts impose only under exceptional circumstances. Thus, the kinds of affirmative action practices most Americans support are in synch with what most affirmative action employers do.

CONCLUSION

Some critics charge that any positive effects of affirmative action come at too high a price. However, the evidence suggests that the predominant effects of affirmative action on American enterprise are neutral, and some are positive. Contrary to popular opinion, reverse discrimination is rare. Workers for whom affirmative action was a hiring consideration are no less productive than other workers. There is no evidence that affirmative action impairs productivity, and there is some evidence that, when properly implemented, affirmative action increases firms' efficiency by rationalizing their business practices. These neutral to positive effects of affirmative action contribute to the broad support it enjoys in corporate America. The affirmative action practices that appear to be most common—such as special training programs or efforts to expand recruitment pools (Bureau of National Affairs 1986)—have the support of the majority of whites and people of color.

Although most affirmative action practices are neutral with respect to race and gender (e.g., eliminating subjectivity from evaluation systems), some employers take into account race and sex as "plus factors" in choosing among qualified candidates in order to reduce imbalances stemming from their past employment practices. Race- and gender-conscious practices are legal if they are part of court-ordered or voluntary affirmative action programs designed to correct a serious imbalance resulting from past exclusionary practices and as long as they are properly structured so that they do not unnecessarily or permanently limit the opportunities of groups not protected under affirmative action. At least one in four Americans opposes such race- and gender-conscious practices. More generally, any departure from strict reliance on merit troubles some Americans. Others favor taking into account group membership in order to eradicate America's occupational caste system, enhance equal opportunity, and strengthen the U.S. democracy (Steinberg 1995).

The tension between affirmative action and merit is the inevitable result of the conflict between our national values and what actually occurs in the nation's workplaces. As long as discrimination is more pervasive than affirmative action, it is the real threat to meritocracy. But because no one will join the debate on behalf of discrimination, we end up with the illusion of a struggle between affirmative action and merit.

NOTES

1. Lynch's (1989, p. 53) search for white male Southern Californians who saw themselves as victims of reverse discrimination turned up only 32 men.
2. Younger whites, those from more privileged backgrounds, and those from areas with larger black populations—especially black populations who were relatively well off—were most likely to believe that blacks benefited from preferential treatment (Taylor 1994b).
3. Two percent were by white men charging sex, race, or national origin discrimination (three-quarters of these charged sex discrimination), and 1.8 percent were by white women charging race discrimination (Blumrosen 1996, p. 5).
4. In the early years of affirmative action, some federal contractors implemented quotas; since then the OFCCP has made considerable effort to ensure that contractors understand that quotas are illegal.
5. Occupational segregation by sex, race, and ethnicity no doubt contribute to this perception by reinforcing the notion that one's sex, color, or ethnicity is naturally related to the ability to perform a particular job.
6. The disproportionate number of court-ordered interventions to curtail race and sex discrimination in cities' police and fire departments (Martin 1991) and the large number of court challenges by white men (Bureau of National Affairs 1995, pp. 5–12) probably contributed to the public's impression that hiring quotas are common.
7. No data were provided on the proportion who believed that affirmative action hampered productivity.
8. Although firms' stock prices fall after the media report a discrimination suit, they rebound within a few days (Hersch 1991; Wright et al. 1995).
9. The $26 billion estimate includes the budgets of the OFCCP, the EEOC, other federal agencies' affirmative action–related activities, and private firms' compliance costs estimated at $20 million for each million of public funds budgeted for enforcement (Brimelow and Spencer 1993). Arguably, the EEOC's budget—indeed all enforcement costs—should be chalked up to the cost of discrimination, not the cost of affirmative action.
10. Several factors affect Americans' response to surveys about affirmative action in the workplace: whether their employer practices affirmative action (Taylor 1995), their own conception of what affirmative action means (one-third of white respondents to a 1995 CBS/*New York Times* poll acknowledged that they were not sure what affirmative action is; Steeh and Krysan 1996, p. 129), whether the ques-

tion also asks about affirmative action in education, whether the question asks about race- or sex-based affirmative action (although contractors are also obliged to provide affirmative action for Vietnam-era veterans and disabled persons, these groups are invisible in opinion polls), the respondents' own race and sex, the reasons respondents think racial inequality exists, and their level of racial prejudice (Bobo and Kluegel 1993). For full reviews, see Steeh and Krysan (1996) and Kravitz et al. (1997).

REFERENCES

Becker, Gary S. 1971. *A Theory of Discrimination.* 2d ed. Chicago, IL: University of Chicago Press.

Blumrosen, Alfred W. 1996. *Declaration.* Statement submitted to the Supreme Court of California in Response to Proposition 209, September 26.

Bobo, Lawrence and James R. Kluegel. 1993. "Opposition to Race Targeting." *American Sociological Review* 58:443–64.

Bobo, Larry and Susan A. Suh. 1996. "Surveying Racial Discrimination: Analyses from a Multi-Ethnic Labor Market." Working Paper No. 75, Russell Sage Foundation, New York.

Brimelow, Peter and Leslie Spencer. 1993. "When Quotas Replace Merit, Everybody Suffers." *Forbes,* February 15, pp. 80–102.

Brimmer, Andrew F. 1995. "The Economic Cost of Discrimination against Black Americans." Pp. 11–29 in *Economic Perspectives on Affirmative Action,* edited by M. C. Simms. Washington, D.C.: Joint Center for Political and Economic Studies.

Bruno, Andorra, 1995. *Affirmative Action in Employment.* CRS Report for Congress. Washington, D.C.: Congressional Research Service.

Bureau of National Affairs. 1986. *Affirmative Action Today: A Legal and Political Analysis. A BNA Special Report.* Washington, D.C.: The Bureau of National Affairs.

———. 1995. *Affirmative Action after Adarand: A Legal, Regulatory, Legislative Outlook.* Washington, D.C.: The Bureau of National Affairs.

Burnstein, Paul. 1991. " 'Reverse Discrimination' Cases in the Federal Courts: Mobilization by a Countermovement." *Sociological Quarterly* 32:511–28.

Conrad, Cecilia. 1995. "The Economic Cost of Affirmative Action." Pp. 33–53 in *Economic Perspectives on Affirmative Action,* edited by M. C. Simms. Washington, D.C.: Joint Center for Political and Economic Studies.

Cox, Taylor H. and Stacy Blake. 1991. "Managing Cultural Diversity: Implications for Organizational Competitiveness." *Academy of Management Executive* 5:45–56.

Crosby, Faye J. and Sharon D. Herzberger. 1996. "For Affirmative Action." Pp. 3–109 in *Affirmative Action: Pros and Cons of Policy and Practice,* edited by R. J. Simon. Washington, D.C.: American University Press.

Davis, James A. and Tom W. Smith. 1994. *General Social Survey* [MRDF]. Chicago IL: National Opinion Research Center [producer, distributor].

———. 1996. *General Social Survey* [MRDF]. Chicago IL: National Opinion Research Center [producer, distributor].

Dobbin, Frank, John Sutton, John Meyer, and W. Richard Scott. 1993. "Equal Opportunity Law and the Construction of Internal Labor Markets." *American Journal of Sociology* 99:396–427.

Donohue, John J. 1986. "Is Title VII Efficient?" *University of Pennsylvania Law Review* 134:1411–31.

Entman, Robert M. 1997. "Manufacturing Discord: Media in the Affirmative Action Debate." *Press/Politics* 2:32–51.

Fisher, Ann B. 1985. "Businessmen Like to Hire by the Numbers." *Fortune Magazine*, September 16, pp. 26, 28–30.

Glass Ceiling Commission. See U.S. Department of Labor, Office of Federal Contract Compliance Programs, Glass Ceiling Commission.

Harvard Law Review. 1989. "Rethinking Weber: The Business Response to Affirmative Action." *Harvard Law Review* 102:658–71.

Heckman, James J. and Peter Siegelman. 1993. "The Urban Institute Audit Studies: Their Methods and Findings." Pp. 187–229 in *Clear and Convincing Evidence: Measurement of Discrimination in America,* edited by M. Fix and R. J. Struyk. Washington, D.C.: The Urban Institute.

Hellerstein, Judith K., David Neumark, and Kenneth R. Troske. 1998. "Market Forces and Sex Discrimination." Department of Sociology, University of Maryland, College Park. Unpublished manuscript.

Hersch, Joni. 1991. "Equal Employment Opportunity Law and Firm Profitability." *Journal of Human Resources* 26:139–53.

Hochschild, Jennifer. 1995. *Facing Up to the American Dream.* Princeton, NJ: Princeton University Press.

Holzer, Harry J. and David Neumark. Forthcoming 1998. "Are Affirmative Action Hires Less Qualified? Evidence from Employer-Employee Data on New Hires." *Journal of Labor Economics.*

Kern, Leesa. 1996. "Hiring and Seniority: Issues in Policing the Post-Judicial Intervention Period." Department of Sociology, Ohio State University, Columbus, OH: Unpublished manuscript.

Kormaromy, Miriam, Kevin Grumbach, Michael Drake, Karen Vranizan, Nicole Lurie, Dennis Keane, and Andrew Bindman. 1996. "The Role of Black and Hispanic Physicians in Providing Health Care in Underserved Populations." *New England Journal of Medicine* 334:1305–10.

Kravitz, David A., David A. Harrison, Marlene E. Turner, Edward L. Levine, Wanda Chaves, Michael T. Brannick, Donna L. Denning, Craig J. Russell, and Maureen A. Conrad. 1997. *Affirmative Action: A Review of Psychological and Behavioral Research.* Bowling Green, OH: Society for Industrial and Organizational Psychology.

Leonard, Jonathan S. 1984c. "Anti-Discrimination or Reverse Discrimination: The Impact of Changing Demographics, Title VII, and Affirmative Action on Productivity" *Journal of Human Resources* 19:145–74.

———. 1990. "The Impact of Affirmative Action Regulation and Equal Employment Law on Black Employment." *Journal of Economic Perspectives* 4:47–63.

———. 1994. "Use of Enforcement Techniques in Eliminating Glass Ceiling Barriers." Report to the Glass Ceiling Commission, April, U.S. Department of Labor, Washington, D.C.

Lovrich, Nicholas P., Brent S. Steel, and David Hood. 1986. "Equity versus Productivity: Affirmative Action and Municipal Police Services." *Public Productivity Review* 39:61–72.

Lynch, Frederick R. 1989. *Invisible Victims: White Males and the Crisis of Affirmative Action.* New York: Greenwood.

———. 1997. *The Diversity Machine: The Drive to Change the White Male Workplace.* New York: Free Press.

Martin, Susan E. 1991. "The Effectiveness of Affirmative Action: The Case of Women in Policing." *Justice Quarterly* 8:489–504.

Mayhew, Leon. 1968. *Law and Equal Opportunity: A Study of Massachusetts Commission against Discrimination.* Cambridge, MA: Harvard University Press.

McMillen, Liz. 1995. "[Affirmative Action] Policies Said to Help Companies Hire Qualified Workers at No Extra Cost." *Chronicle of Higher Education,* November 17, p. A7.

Moore, David W. 1995. "Americans Today Are Dubious about Affirmative Action." *The Gallup Poll Monthly,* March, pp. 36–8.

Nacoste, Rupert Barnes. 1990. "Sources of Stigma: Analyzing the Psychology of Affirmative Action." *Law & Policy* 12:175–95.

New York Times. 1995. "Reverse Discrimination Complaints Rare, Labor Study Reports." *New York Times,* March 31, p. A23.

Noble, Kenneth. 1986. "Employers Are Split on Affirmative Goals." *New York Times,* March 3, p. B4.

Norton, Eleanor Holmes. 1996. "Affirmative Action in the Workplace." Pp. 39–48 in *The Affirmative Action Debate,* edited by G. Curry. Reading, MA: Addison-Wesley.

Penn, Nolan E., Percy J. Russell, and Harold J. Simon. 1986. "Affirmative Action at Work: A Survey of Graduates of the University of California at San Diego Medical School." *American Journal of Public Health* 76:1144–46.

Rand, A. Barry. 1996. "Diversity in Corporate America." Pp. 65–76 in *The Affirmative Action Debate,* edited by G. Curry. Reading, MA: Addison-Wesley.

Reskin, Barbara F. and Patricia Roos. 1990. *Job Queues, Gender Queues,* Philadelphia, PA: Temple University Press.

Roper Center for Public Opinion. 1995. *Poll Database:* Question ID USGALLUP.95MRW1.R32[MRDF]. Storrs, CT: Roper Center for Public Opinion [producer, distributor].

San Diego Union-Tribune. 1995. "Groups at Odds Over Affirmative Action Revisions." *San Diego Union-Tribune,* September 13, p. AA-2.

Steeh, Charlotte, and Maria Krysan. 1996. "The Polls—Trends: Affirmative Action and the Public, 1970–1995." *Public Opinion Quarterly* 60:128–58.

Steel, Brent S. and Nicholas P. Lovrich. 1987. "Equality and Efficiency Tradeoffs in Affirmative Action—Real or Imagined? The Case of Women in Policing." *Social Science Journal* 24:53–70.

Steinberg, Steven. 1995. *Turning Back: Retreat from Racial Justice in American Thought.* Boston, MA: Beacon.

Stephanopoulos, George and Christopher Edley, Jr. 1995. "Affirmative Action Review." Report to the President, Washington, D.C.

Taylor, Marylee C. 1994a. "Beliefs about the Preferential Hiring of Black Applicants: Sure It Happens, But I've Never Seen It." Pennsylvania State University, University Park, PA. Unpublished manuscript.

————. 1994b. "Impact of Affirmative Action on Beneficiary Groups: Evidence from the 1990 General Social Survey." *Basic and Applied Social Psychology* 15:143–78.

————. 1995. "White Backlash to Workplace Affirmative Action: Peril or Myth?" *Social Forces* 73:1385–1414.

U.S. Department of Labor, Employment Standards Administration, Office of Federal Contract Compliance Programs [cited as OFCCP]. n.d. "The Rhetoric and the Reality about Federal Affirmative Action at the OFCCP." Washington, D.C.: U.S. Department of Labor.

U.S. Department of Labor, Office of Federal Contract Compliance Programs, Glass Ceiling Commission. 1995. *Good for Business: Making Full Use of the Nation's Human Capital/The Environmental Scar.* Washington, D.C.: U.S. Government Printing Office.

Verhovek, Sam Howe. 1997. "In Poll, Americans Reject Means but Not Ends of Racial Diversity." *New York Times,* December 14, pp. 1, 32.

Wall Street Journal. 1979. "Labor Letter: A Special News Report on People and Their Jobs in Offices, Fields, and Factories: Affirmative Action Is Accepted by Most Corporate Chiefs." *Wall Street Journal,* April 3, p. 1.

Watson, Warren E., Kamalesh Kumar, and Larry K. Michaelsen. 1993. "Cultural Diversity's Impact on Interaction Process and Performance: Comparing Homogeneous and Diverse Task Groups." *Academy of Management Journal* 36:590–602.

Wright, Peter, Stephen P. Ferris, Janine S. Hiller, and Mark Kroll. 1995. "Competitiveness through Management of Diversity: Effects on Stock Price Valuation." *Academy of Management Journal* 38:272–87.

32

THE POSSESSIVE INVESTMENT IN WHITENESS
Racialized Social Democracy and the "White" Problem in American Studies

GEORGE LIPSITZ

Shortly after World War II, a French reporter asked expatriate Richard Wright his opinion about the "Negro problem" in the United States. The author replied "There isn't any Negro problem; there is only a white problem."[1] By inverting the reporter's question, Wright called attention to its hidden assumptions—that racial polarization comes from the existence of

From *American Quarterly,* Vol. 47, no. 3, September, 1995. © 1995 The American Studies Association. Reprinted by permission of Johns Hopkins University Press.

blacks rather than from the behavior of whites, that black people are a "problem" for whites rather than fellow citizens entitled to justice, and that unless otherwise specified, "Americans" means whites.[2] But Wright's formulation also placed political mobilization by African Americans in context, attributing it to the systemic practices of aversion, exploitation, denigration, and discrimination practiced by people who think of themselves as "white."

Whiteness is everywhere in American culture, but it is very hard to see. As Richard Dyer argues, "white power secures its dominance by seeming not to be anything in particular."[3] As the unmarked category against which difference is constructed, whiteness never has to speak its name, never has to acknowledge its role as an organizing principle in social and cultural relations.[4]

To identify, analyze, and oppose the destructive consequences of whiteness, we need what Walter Benjamin called "presence of mind." Benjamin wrote that people visit fortune-tellers not so much out of a desire to know the future but rather out of a fear of not noticing some important aspect of the present. "Presence of mind," he argued, "is an abstract of the future, and precise awareness of the present moment more decisive than foreknowledge of the most distant events."[5] In our society at this time, precise awareness of the present moment requires an understanding of the existence and the destructive consequences of "white" identity.

In recent years, an important body of American studies scholarship has started to explore the role played by cultural practices in creating "whiteness" in the United States. More than the product of private prejudices, whiteness emerged as a relevant category in American life largely because of realities created by slavery and segregation, by immigration restriction and Indian policy, by conquest and colonialism. A fictive identity of "whiteness" appeared in law as an abstraction, and it became actualized in everyday life in many ways. American economic and political life gave different racial groups unequal access to citizenship and property, while cultural practices including wild west shows, minstrel shows, racist images in advertising, and Hollywood films institutionalized racism by uniting ethnically diverse European-American audiences into an imagined community—one called into being through inscribed appeals to the solidarity of white supremacy.[6] Although cross-ethnic identification and pan-ethnic antiracism in culture, politics, and economics have often interrupted and resisted racialized white supremacist notions of American identity, from colonial days to the present, successful political coalitions serving dominant interests have often relied on exclusionary concepts of whiteness to fuse unity among otherwise antagonistic individuals and groups.[7]

Yet, while cultural expressions have played an important role in the construction of white supremacist political alliances, the reverse is also true (i.e., political activity has also played a constitutive role in racializing U.S. culture). Race is a cultural construct, but one with sinister structural causes and consequences. Conscious and deliberate actions have institutionalized group identity in the United States, not just through the dissemination of cultural stories but also through systematic efforts from colonial times to the present to create a possessive investment in whiteness for European Americans. Studies of culture too far removed from studies of social structure leave us with inadequate explanations for understanding racism and inadequate remedies for combatting it.

From the start, European settlers in North America established structures encouraging possessive investment in whiteness. The colonial and early-national legal systems authorized attacks on Native Americans and encouraged the appropriation of their lands. They legitimated racialized chattel slavery, restricted naturalized citizenship to "white" immigrants, and provided pretexts for exploiting labor, seizing property, and denying the franchise to Asian Americans, Mexican Americans, Native Americans, and African Americans. Slavery and "Jim Crow" segregation institutionalized possessive identification with whiteness visibly and openly, but an elaborate interaction of largely *covert* public and private decisions during and after the days of slavery and segregation also produced a powerful legacy with enduring effects on the racialization of experience, opportunities, and rewards in the United States possessive investment in whiteness pervades public policy in the United States past and present—not just long ago during slavery and segregation but in the recent past and present as well—through the covert but no less systematic racism inscribed within U.S. social democracy.

Even though there has always been racism in American history, it has not always been the same racism. Political and cultural struggles over power shape the contours and dimensions of racism in any era. Mass mobilizations against racism during the Civil War and civil rights eras meaningfully curtailed the reach and scope of white supremacy, but in each case reactionary forces then engineered a renewal of racism, albeit in new forms, during successive decades. Racism changes over time, taking on different forms and serving different social purposes in different eras.

Contemporary racism is not just a residual consequence of slavery and *de jure* segregation but rather something that has been created anew in our own time by many factors including the putatively race-neutral liberal social democratic reforms of the past five decades. Despite hard-fought battles for change that secured important concessions during the 1960s in the form of civil rights legislation, the racialized nature of social democratic policies in the United States since the Great Depression has, in my judgment, actually increased the possessive investment in whiteness among European Americans over the past half-century.

The possessive investment in whiteness is not a simple matter of black and white; all racialized minority groups have suffered from it, albeit to different degrees and in different ways. Most of my argument here addresses relations between European Americans and African Americans because they contain many of the most vivid oppositions and contrasts, but the possessive investment in whiteness always emerges from a fused sensibility drawing on many sources at once—on antiblack racism to be sure, but also on the legacies of racialization left by federal, state, and local policies toward Native Americans, Asian Americans, Mexican Americans, and other groups designated by whites as "racially other."

During the New Deal, both the Wagner Act and the Social Security Act excluded farm workers and domestics from coverage, effectively denying those disproportionately minority sectors of the work force protections and benefits routinely channeled to whites. The Federal Housing Act of 1934 brought home ownership within reach of millions of citizens by placing the credit of the federal government behind private lending to home buyers, but overtly racist categories in the Federal Housing Administration's (FHA's) "confidential" city surveys and appraisers' manuals channeled almost all of the loan money toward whites and away from communities of color.[8] In the post–World War II era, trade unions negotiated contract provisions giving private medical insurance, pensions, and job security largely to the mostly white workers in unionized mass-production industries rather than fighting for full employment, universal medical care, and old age pensions for all or for an end to discriminatory hiring and promotion practices by employers.[9]

Each of these policies widened the gap between the resources available to whites and those available to aggrieved racial communities, but the most damaging long-term effects may well have come from the impact of the racial discrimination codified by the policies of the FHA. By channeling loans away from older inner-city neighborhoods and toward white home buyers moving into segregated suburbs, the FHA and private lenders after World War II aided and abetted the growth and development of increased segregation in U.S. residential neighborhoods. For example, FHA appraisers denied federally supported loans to prospective home buyers in the racially mixed Boyle Heights neighborhood of Los Angeles because it was a " 'melting pot' area literally honeycombed with diverse and subversive racial elements."[10] Similarly, mostly white St. Louis County secured five times as many FHA mortgages as the more racially mixed city of St. Louis between 1943 and 1960. Home buyers in the county received six times as much loan money and enjoyed per capita mortgage spending 6.3 times greater than those in the city.[11]

In concert with FHA support for segregation in the suburbs, federal and state tax monies routinely provided water supplies and sewage facilities for racially exclusive suburban communities in the 1940s and 1950s. By the 1960s, these areas often incorporated themselves as independent municipalities in order to gain greater access to federal funds allocated for "urban aid."[12] At the same time that FHA loans and federal highway building projects subsidized the growth of segregated suburbs, urban renewal programs in cities throughout the country devastated minority neighborhoods.

During the 1950s and 1960s, federally assisted urban renewal projects destroyed 20 percent of the central city housing units occupied by blacks, as opposed to only 10 percent of those inhabited by whites.[13] Even after most major urban renewal programs had been completed in the 1970s, black central city residents continued to lose housing units at a rate equal to 80 percent of what had been lost in the 1960s. Yet white displacement declined back to the relatively low levels of the 1950s.[14] In addition, the refusal first to pass, then to enforce, fair housing laws, has enabled realtors, buyers, and sellers to profit from racist collusion against minorities without fear of legal retribution.

During the decades following World War II, urban renewal helped construct a new "white" identity in the suburbs by helping destroy ethnically specific European-American urban inner-city neighborhoods. Wrecking balls and bulldozers eliminated some of these sites, while others became transformed by an influx of minority residents desperately competing for a declining number of affordable housing units. As increasing numbers of racial minorities moved into cities, increasing numbers of European-American ethnics moved out. Consequently, ethnic differences among whites became a less important dividing line in American culture, while race became more important. The suburbs helped turn European Americans into "whites" who could live near each other and intermarry with relatively little difficulty. But this "white" unity rested on residential segregation and on shared access to housing and life chances largely unavailable to communities of color.[15]

Federally funded highways designed to connect suburban commuters with downtown places of employment destroyed already scarce housing in minority communities and often disrupted neighborhood life as well. Construction of the Harbor Freeway in Los Angeles, the Gulf Freeway in Houston, and the Mark Twain Freeway in St. Louis displaced thousands of residents and bisected previously connected neighborhoods, shopping districts, and political precincts. The process of urban renewal and highway construction set in motion a vicious cycle: population loss led to decreased political power, which made minority neighborhoods more likely to be victimized by further urban renewal and freeway construction, not to mention more susceptible to the placement of prisons, waste dumps, and other projects that further depopulated these areas.

In Houston, Texas—where blacks make up slightly more than one-quarter of the local population—more than 75 percent of municipal garbage incinerators and 100 percent of the city-owned garbage dumps are located in black neighborhoods.[16] A 1992 study by staff writers for the *National Law Journal* examined the Environmental Protection Agency's response to 1,177 toxic waste cases and found that polluters of sites near the greatest white population received penalties 500 percent higher than penalties imposed on polluters in minority areas—an average of $335,566 for white areas contrasted with $55,318 for minority areas. Income did not account for these differences—penalties for low-income areas on average actually exceeded those for areas with the highest median incomes by about 3 percent. The penalties for violating all federal environmental laws about air, water, and waste pollution in minority communities were 46 percent lower than in white communities. In addition, Superfund remedies left minority communities with longer waiting times for being placed on the national priority list, cleanups that begin from 12 to 42 percent later than at white sites, and a 7 percent greater likelihood of "containment" (walling off a hazardous site) than cleanup, while white sites experienced treatment and cleanup 22 percent more often than containment.[17]

When housing prices doubled during the 1970s, white homeowners who had been able to take advantage of discriminatory FHA financing policies received increased equity in their homes, while those excluded from the housing market by earlier policies found themselves facing higher costs of entry into the market in addition to the traditional obstacles presented by the discriminatory practices of sellers, realtors, and lenders. The contrast between European Americans and African Americans is instructive in this regard. Because whites have access to broader housing choices than blacks, whites pay 15 percent less than blacks for similar housing in the same neighborhood. White neighborhoods typically experience housing costs 25 percent less expensive than would be the case if the residents were black.[18]

A recent Federal Reserve Bank of Boston study showed that minority applicants had a 60 percent greater chance of being denied home loans than white applicants with the same credit-worthiness. Boston bankers made 2.9 times as many mortgage loans per one thousand housing units in neighborhoods inhabited by low-income whites than they did to neighborhoods populated by low-income blacks.[19] In addition, loan officers were far more likely to overlook flaws in the credit records of white applicants or to arrange creative financing for them than they were with black applicants.[20]

A Los Angeles study found that loan officers more frequently used dividend income and underlying assets as criteria for judging black applicants than they did for whites.[21] In Houston, the NCNB Bank of Texas disqualified 13 percent of middle-income white loan applicants but disqualified 36 percent of middle-income black applicants.[22] Atlanta's home loan institutions gave five times as many home loans to whites as to blacks in the late 1980s. An analysis of sixteen Atlanta neighborhoods found that home buyers in white neighborhoods received conventional financing four times as often as those in black sections of the city.[23] Nationwide, financial institutions get more money in deposits from black neighborhoods than they invest in them in the form of home mortgage loans, making home lending a vehicle for the transfer of capital away from black savers and toward white investors.[24] In many locations, high-income blacks were denied loans more often than low-income whites.[25]

Federal home loan policies have placed the power of the federal government behind private discrimination. Urban renewal and highway construction programs have enhanced the possessive investment in whiteness directly through government initiatives. In addition, decisions about the location of federal jobs have also systematically supported the subsidy for whiteness. Federal civilian employment dropped by 41,419 in central cities between 1966 and 1973, but total federal employment in metropolitan areas grew by 26,558.[26] While one might naturally expect the location of government buildings that serve the public to follow population trends, the federal government's policies in locating offices and records centers in suburbs helped aggravate the flight of jobs to suburban locations less accessible to inner-city residents. Since racial discrimination in the private sector forces minority workers to seek government positions disproportionate to their numbers, these moves exact particular hardships on them. In addition, minorities who follow their jobs to the suburbs generally encounter increased commuter costs because housing discrimination makes it harder and more expensive for them to relocate than for whites.

The racialized aspects of fifty years of these social democratic policies became greatly exacerbated by the anti–social democratic policies of neoconservatives in the Reagan and Bush administrations during the 1980s and 1990s. They clearly contributed to the reinforcement of possessive investments in whiteness through their regressive policies in respect to federal aid to education and their refusal to challenge segregated education, housing, and hiring, as well as their cynical cultivation of an antiblack, countersubversive consensus through attacks on affirmative action and voting rights legislation. In the U.S. economy, where 86 percent of available jobs do not appear in classified advertisements and where personal connections provide the most important factor in securing employment, attacks on affirmative action guarantee that whites will be rewarded for their historical advantages in the labor market rather than for their individual abilities or efforts.[27]

Yet even seemingly race-neutral policies supported by both neoconservatives and social democrats in the 1980s and 1990s have also increased the absolute value of being white. In the 1980s, changes in federal tax laws decreased the value of wage income and increased the value of investment income—a move harmful to minorities who suffer from an even greater gap between their total wealth and that of whites than in the disparity between their income and white income. Failure to raise the minimum wage between 1981 and 1989 and the more than one-third decline in value of Aid for Families with Dependent Children payments hurt all poor people, but they exacted special costs on nonwhites facing even more constricted markets for employment, housing, and education than poor whites.[28]

Because they are ignorant of even the recent history of the possessive investment in whiteness—generated by slavery and segregation but augmented by social democratic reform—Americans produce largely cultural explanations for structural social problems. The increased possessive investment in whiteness generated by dis-investment in American's cities, factories, and schools since the 1970s disguises the general problems posed to our society by deindustrialization, economic restructuring, and neoconservative attacks on the welfare state as *racial* problems. It fuels a discourse that demonizes people of color for being victimized by these changes, while hiding the privileges of whiteness by attributing them to family values, fatherhood, and foresight—rather than to favoritism.

Many recent popular and scholarly studies have explained clearly the causes for black economic decline over the past two decades.[29] Deindustrialization has decimated the industrial infrastructure that formerly provided high-wage jobs and chances for upward mobility to black workers. Neoconservative attacks on government spending for public housing, health, education, and transportation have deprived African Americans of needed services and opportunities for jobs in the public sector. A massive retreat from responsibility to enforce antidiscrimination laws at the highest levels of government has sanctioned pervasive overt and covert racial discrimination by bankers, realtors, and employers.

Yet public opinion polls conducted among white Americans display little recognition of these devastating changes. Seventy percent of whites in one poll said that African Americans "have the same opportunities to live a middle-class life as whites."[30] Nearly three-fourths of white respondents to a 1989 poll believed that opportunities for blacks had improved during the Reagan presidency.[31]

It is my contention that the stark contrast between black experiences and white opinions during the past two decades cannot be attributed solely to ignorance or intolerance on the part of individuals but stems instead from the overdetermined inadequacy of the language of liberal individualism to describe collective experience.[32] As long as we define social life as the sum total of conscious and deliberate individual activities, then only *individual* manifestations of personal prejudice and hostility will be seen as racist. Systemic, collective, and coordinated behavior disappears from sight. Collective exercises of group power relentlessly channeling rewards, resources, and opportunities from one group to another will not appear to be "racist" from this perspective because they rarely announce their intention to discriminate against individuals. But they work to construct racial identities by giving people of different races vastly different life chances.

The gap between white perceptions and minority experiences can have explosive consequences. Little more than a year after the 1992 Los Angeles rebellion, a sixteen-year-old high school junior shared her opinions with a reporter from the *Los Angeles Times*. "I don't think white people owe anything to black people," she explained. "We didn't sell them into slavery; it was our ancestors. What they did was wrong, but we've done our best to make up for it."[33] A seventeen-year-old senior echoed those comments, telling the reporter:

> I feel we spend more time in my history class talking about what whites owe blacks than just about anything else when the issue of slavery comes up. I often received dirty looks. This seems strange given that I wasn't even alive then. And the few members of my family from that time didn't have the luxury of owning much, let alone slaves. So why, I ask you, am I constantly made to feel guilty?[34]

More ominously, after pleading guilty to bombing two homes and one car, to vandalizing a synagogue, and attempting to start a race war by murdering Rodney King and bombing Los Angeles's First African Methodist

Episcopal Church, twenty-year-old Christopher David Fisher explained that "sometimes whites were picked on because of the color of their skin. . . . Maybe we're blamed for slavery."[35] Fisher's actions were certainly extreme, but his justification of them drew knowingly and precisely on a broadly shared narrative about the victimization of innocent whites by irrational and ungrateful minorities.

The comments and questions raised about the legacy of slavery by these young whites illumine broader currents in our culture that have enormous implications for understanding the enduring significance of race in our country. These young people associate black grievances solely with slavery, and they express irritation at what they perceive as efforts to make them feel guilty or unduly privileged in the present because of things that happened in the distant past. Because their own ancestors may not have been slave owners or because "we've done our best to make up for it," they feel that it is unreasonable for anyone to view them as people who owe "anything" to blacks. On the contrary, Fisher felt that his discomfort with being "picked on" and "blamed" for slavery gave him good reason to bomb homes, deface synagogues, and plot to kill black people.

Unfortunately for our society, these young whites accurately reflect the logic of the language of liberal individualism and its ideological predispositions in discussions of race. They seem to have no knowledge of the disciplined, systemic, and collective *group* activity that has structured white identities in American history. They are not alone in their ignorance; in a 1979 law journal article, future Supreme Court Justice Antonin Scalia argued that affirmative action "is based upon concepts of racial indebtedness and racial entitlement rather than individual worth and individual need" and is thus "racist."[36]

Group interests are not monolithic, and aggregate figures can obscure serious differences within racial groups. All whites do not benefit from the possessive investment in whiteness in precisely the same way; the experiences of members of minority groups are not interchangeable. But the possessive investment in whiteness always affects individual and group life chances and opportunities. Even in cases where minority groups secure political and economic power through collective mobilization, the terms and conditions of their collectivity and the logic of group solidarity are always influenced and intensified by the absolute value of whiteness in American politics, economics, and culture.[37]

In the 1960s, members of the Black Panther Party used to say that "if you're not part of the solution, you're part of the problem." But those of us who are "white" can only become part of the solution if we recognize the degree to which we are already part of the problem—not because of our race, but because of our possessive investment in it. Neither conservative "free market" policies nor liberal social democratic reforms can solve the "white problem" in America because both of them reinforce the possessive investment in whiteness. But an explicitly antiracist pan-ethnic movement that acknowledges the existence and power of whiteness might make some important changes. Pan-ethnic, antiracist coalitions have a long history in the United States—in the political activism of John Brown, Sojourner Truth, and the Magon brothers, among others—but we also have a rich cultural tradition of pan-ethnic antiracism connected to civil rights activism of the kind detailed so brilliantly in rhythm and blues musician Johnny Otis's recent book, *Upside Your Head! Rhythm and Blues on Central Avenue.*[38] These efforts by whites to fight racism, not out of sympathy for someone else but out of a sense of self-respect and simple justice, have never completely disappeared; they remain available as models for the present.[39]

Walter Benjamin's praise for "presence of mind" came from his understanding of how difficult it may be to see the present. But more important, he called for presence of mind as the means for implementing what he called "the only true telepathic miracle"—turning the forbidding future into the fulfilled present.[40] Failure to acknowledge our society's possessive investment in whiteness prevents us from facing the present openly and honestly. It hides from us the devastating costs of disinvestment in America's infrastructure over the past two decades and keeps us from facing our responsibilities to reinvest in human capital by channeling resources toward education, health, and housing—and away from subsidies for speculation and luxury. After two decades of disinvestment, the only further disinvestment we need is to disinvest in the ruinous pathology of whiteness that has always undermined our own best instincts and interests. In a society suffering so badly from an absence of mutuality, an absence of responsibility, and an absence of simple justice, presence of mind might be just what we need.

NOTES

1. Raphael Tardon, "Richard Wright Tells Us: The White Problem in the United States," *Action,* 24 Oct. 1946. Reprinted in Kenneth Kinnamon and Michet Fabre, *Conversations with Richard Wright* (Jackson, Miss., 1993), 99. Malcolm X and others used this same formulation in the 1960s, but I believe that it originated with Wright, or at least that is the earliest citation I have found so far.
2. This is also Toni Morrison's point in *Playing in the Dark: Whiteness in the Literary Imagination* (Cambridge, Mass., 1992).
3. Richard Dyer, "White," *Screen* 29 (fall 1988): 44.
4. I thank Michael Schudson for pointing out to me that since the passage of civil rights legislation in the 1960s whiteness dares not speak its name, cannot speak in its own behalf, but rather advances through a color-blind language radically at odds with the distinctly racialized distribution of resources and life chances in American society.
5. Walter Benjamin, "Madame Ariane: Second Courtyard on the Left." from *One-Way Street* (London, 1969). 98–99.
6. Richard Slotkin, *Gunfighter Nation: The Myth of the Frontier in Twentieth Century America* (New York, 1992); Eric Lott, *Love and Theft* (New York, 1993); David Roediger, *Wages of Whiteness* (New York, 1992); Michael Rogin, "Blackface White Noise: The Jewish Jazz Singer Finds His Voice," *Critical Inquiry* 18 (spring 1992).

7. Robin Kelley, *Hammer and Hoe* (Chapel Hill, N.C., 1990); Lizabeth Cohen, *Making a New Deal* (Cambridge, 1991); George Sanchez, *Becoming Mexican American* (New York, 1993); Edmund Morgan, *American Slavery, American Freedom* (New York, 1975); John Hope Franklin, *The Color Line: Legacy for the Twenty-First Century* (Columbia, Mo., 1993).

8. See Kenneth Jackson. *Crabgrass Frontier: The Suburbanization of the United States,* (New York, 1985); and Douglas S. Massey and Nancy A. Denton, *American Apartheid: Segregation and the Making of the Underclass* (Cambridge, Mass., 1993).

9. I thank Phil Ethington for pointing out to me that these aspects of New Deal policies emerged out of political negotiations between the segregationist Dixiecrats and liberals from the north and west. My perspective is that white supremacy was not a gnawing aberration within the New Deal coalition but rather an essential point of unity between southern whites and northern white ethnics.

10. Records of the Federal Home Loan Bank Board of the Home Owners Loan Corporation. City Survey File, Los Angeles, 1939, Neighborhood D-53, National Archives, Washington, D.C., box 74, records group 195.

11. Massey and Denton, *American Apartheid,* 54.

12. John R. Logan and Harvey Molotch, *Urban Fortunes: The Political Economy of Place* (Berkeley, 1987), 182.

13. Ibid., 114.

14. Ibid., 130.

15. See Gary Gerstle, "Working-Class Racism: Broaden the Focus," *International Labor and Working Class History,* 44 (fall 1993): 36.

16. Logan and Molotch, *Urban Fortunes,* 113.

17. Robert D. Bullard, "Environmental Justice for All," in *Unequal Protection: Environmental Justice and Communities of Color,* ed. Robert Bullard (San Francisco, 1994), 9–10.

18. Logan and Molotch, *Urban Fortunes,* 116.

19. Jim Campen, "Lending Insights: Hard Proof That Banks Discriminate," *Dollars and Sense* 191 (Jan.–Feb. 1991), 17.

20. Mitchell Zuckoff, "Study Shows Racial Bias in Lending," *The Boston Globe,* 9 October 1992, 1, 77, 78.

21. Paul Ong and J. Eugene Grisby III, "Race and Late Cycle Effects on Home Ownership in Los Angeles, 1970 to 1980," *Urban Affairs Quarterly* 23 (June 1998), 605.

22. Massey and Denton, *American Apartheid,* 108.

23. Gary Orfield and Carol Ashkinaze, *The Closing Door: Conservative Policy and Black Opportunity* (Chicago, 1991), 58, 78.

24. Logan and Molotch, *Urban Fortunes.*

25. Campen, "Lending Insights," 18.

26. Gregory Squires, " 'Runaway Plants.' Capital Mobility, and Black Economic Rights," in *Community and Capital in Conflict: Plant Closings and Job Loss,* ed. John C. Raines, Lenora E. Berson, and David Mel Gracie (Philadelphia, 1982), 70.

27. Gertrude Ezorsky, *Racism and Justice: The Case for Affirmative Action* (Ithaca, N.Y., 1991), 15.

28. Orfield and Ashkinaze, *The Closing Door,* 225–26.

29. Melvin Oliver and James Johnson, "Economic Restructuring and Black Male Joblessness in United States Metropolitan Areas," *Urban Geography* 12 (Nov.–Dec. 1991); Gerald David Jaynes and Robin M. Williams, Jr., eds., *A Common Destiny:*

Blacks and American Society (Washington, D.C., 1989); Reynolds Farley and Walter R. Allen, *The Color Line and the Quality of Life in America* (New York, 1987); Melvin Oliver and Tom Shapiro, "Wealth of a Nation: A Reassessment of Asset Inequality in America Shows at Least 1/3 of Households Are Asset Poor," *Journal of Economics and Sociology,* 49 (Apr. 1990); Jonathan Kozol, *Savage Inequalities: Children in America's Schools* (New York, 1991); Cornell West, *Race Matters* (Boston, 1993).

30. Orfield and Ashkinaze, *Closing Door,* 46.

31. Ibid., 206.

32. I borrow the term "overdetermination" here from Louis Althusser, who uses it to show how dominant ideologies become credible to people in part because various institutions and agencies independently replicate them and reinforce their social power.

33. Rogena Schuyler, "Youth: We Didn't Sell Them into Slavery," *Los Angeles Times,* 21 June 1993, B4.

34. Ibid.

35. Jim Newton, "Skinhead Leader Pleads Guilty to Violence, Plot," *Los Angeles Times,* 20 Oct. 1993, A1, A15.

36. Antonin Scalia, Quoted in Cheryl I. Harris, "Whiteness as Property," *Harvard Law Review* 106 (June 1993), 1767.

37. The rise of a black middle class and the setbacks suffered by white workers during deindustrialization may seem to subvert the analysis presented here. Yet the black middle class remains fragile, far less able than other middle-class groups to translate advances in income into advances in wealth and power. Similarly, the success of neoconservatism since the 1970s has rested on securing support from white workers for economic policies that do them objective harm by mobilizing counter-subversive electoral coalitions against busing and affirmative action, while carrying out attacks on public institutions and resources by representing "public" space and black space. See Oliver and Shapiro, "Wealth of a Nation." See also Logan and Harvey, *Urban Fortunes.*

38. Johnny Otis, *Upside Your Head: Rhythm and Blues on Central Avenue* (Hanover, N.H., 1993).

39. Mobilizations against plant shutdowns, for environmental protection, against cutbacks in education spending, and for reproductive rights all contain the potential for pan-ethnic antiracist organizing, but, too often, neglect of race as a central modality for how issues of employment, pollution, education, or reproductive rights are experienced isolates these social movements from their broadest possible base.

40. Walter Benjamin, "Madame Ariane: Second Courtyard on the Left," from *One-Way Street* (London, 1969), 98, 99.

33

RALPH, FRED, ARCHIE AND HOMER
Why Television Keeps Recreating the White Male Working-Class Buffoon

RICHARD BUTSCH

Strewn across our mass media are portrayals of class that justify class relations of modern capitalism. Studies of 50 years of comic strips, radio serials, television drama, movies and popular fiction reveal a very persistent pattern, an underrepresentation of working-class occupations and an overrepresentation of professional and managerial occupations among characters.[1]

My own studies of class in prime-time network television family series from 1946 to 1990 (Butsch, 1992; Butsch & Glennon, 1983; Glennon & Butsch, 1982) indicate that this pattern is persistent over four decades of television, in 262 domestic situation comedies, such as *I Love Lucy, The Brady Bunch, All in the Family,* and *The Simpsons.* In only 11% of the series were heads of house portrayed as working-class, that is, holding occupations as blue-collar, clerical or unskilled or semiskilled service workers. Blue-collar families were most underrepresented: only 4% (11 series) compared with 45% of American families in 1970.

Widespread affluence was exaggerated as well. More lucrative, glamorous or prestigious professions predominated over more mundane ones: 9 doctors to one nurse, 19 lawyers to 2 accountants, 7 college professors to 2 school teachers. Working wives were almost exclusively middle-class and in pursuit of a career. Working-class wives, such as in *Roseanne,* who have to work to help support the family, were very rare. Particularly notable was the prevalence of servants: one of every five series had a maid or butler.

The working class is not only underrepresented; the few men who are portrayed are buffoons. They are dumb, immature, irresponsible or lacking in common sense. This is the character of the husbands in almost every sit-com depicting a blue-collar (white) male head of house, *The Honeymooners*, *The Flintstones*, *All in the Family* and *The Simpsons* being the most famous examples. He is typically well-intentioned, even lovable, but no one to respect or emulate. These men are played against more mature, sensible wives, such as Ralph against Alice in the *Honeymooners*.

In most middle-class series, there is no buffoon. More typically, both parents are wise and work cooperatively to raise their children in practically perfect families, as in *Father Knows Best, The Brady Bunch* and the *Bill Cosby Show*. In the few middle-class series featuring a buffoon, it is the dizzy wife, such as Lucy. The professional/managerial husband is the sensible, mature partner. Inverting gender status in working-class but not middle-class sitcoms is a statement about class.

HOW DOES IT HAPPEN?

The prevalence of such views of working-class men well illustrates ideological hegemony, the dominance of values in mainstream culture that justify and help to maintain the status quo. Blue-collar workers are portrayed as requiring supervision, and managers and professionals as intelligent and mature enough to provide it. But do viewers, and particularly the working class, accept these views? Only a handful of scattered, incidental observations (Blum, 1969; Gans, 1962; Jhally & Lewis, 1992; Vidmar & Rokeach, 1974) consider how people have responded to portrayals of class.

And why does television keep reproducing these caricatures? How does it happen? Seldom have studies of television industries pinpointed how specific content arises. Studies of production have not been linked to studies of content any more than audience studies have. What follows is an effort to make that link between existing production studies and persistent images of working-class men in domestic sitcoms. In the words of Connell (1977), "No evil-minded capitalistic plotters need be assumed because the production of ideology is seen as the more or less automatic outcome of the normal, regular processes by which commercial mass communications work in a capitalist system" (p. 195). The simple need to make a profit is a structural constraint that affects content (see also Ryan, 1992).

Let us then examine how the organization of the industry and television drama production may explain class content in television series. I will look at three levels of organization: (a) network domination of the industry, (b) the organization of decisions within the networks and on the production line, and (c) the work community and culture of the creative personnel. I will trace how these may explain the consistency and persistence of the portrayals, the underrepresentation of the working class and the choice of the particular stereotypes of working-class men in prime-time domestic sitcoms.

Network Domination and Persistent Images

For four decades ABC, CBS, and NBC dominated the television industry. Of television audiences, 90% watched network programs. The networks accounted for over half of all television advertising revenues in the 1960s and 1970s and just under half by the late 1980s (Owen & Wildman, 1992). They therefore had the money and the audience to dominate as almost the sole buyers of drama programming from Hollywood producers and studios.[2]

During the 1980s, the three-network share of the audience dropped from about 90% to 60%; network share of television ad revenues declined from 60% to 47% (Owen & Wildman, 1992). These dramatic changes have generated many news stories of the demise of the big three. Cable networks and multistation owners (companies that own several local broadcast stations) began to challenge the dominance of the big three. They became alternative markets for producers as they began purchasing their own programs.

But program development is costly; even major Hollywood studios are unwilling to produce drama programs without subsidies from buyers. Nine networks have sufficient funds in the 1990s to qualify as buyers of drama programming: the four broadcast networks (ABC, CBS, Fox and NBC) and five cable networks (Disney, HBO, Showtime, TNT and USA Network) (Blumler & Spicer, 1990). But ABC, CBS and NBC still account for the development of the overwhelming majority of new drama series, the programming that presents the same characters week after week—and year after year in reruns.

This is the case in part because the broadcast networks still deliver by far the largest audiences. Even in 1993, the combined ratings for the 20 largest cable audiences would still only rank 48th in ratings for broadcast network shows. The highest rated cable network, USA Network, reached only 1.5% of the audience, compared to an average of 20% for ABC, NBC and CBS. The larger audiences translate into more dollars for program development.

And producers still prefer to work for the broadcast networks. When sold to broadcast networks, their work receives much broader exposure, which enhances their subsequent profits from syndication after the network run and increases the likelihood for future purchases and employment.

Moreover, whether or not dominance by the big three has slipped, many of the same factors that shaped their programming decisions shape the decisions of their competitors as well. The increased number of outlets has not resulted in the innovation and diversity in program development once expected. Jay Blumler and Carolyn Spicer (1990) interviewed over 150 industry personnel concerned with program decision making and found that the promise of more openness to innovation and creativity was short-lived. The cost of drama programming limits buyers to only a handful of large corporations and dictates that programs attract a large audience and avoid risk. How has this affected content?

Using their market power, the networks have maintained sweeping control over production decisions of even highly successful producers from initial idea for a new program to final film or tape (Bryant, 1969, pp. 624–626; Gitlin, 1983; Pekurny, 1977, 1982; Winick, 1961). Their first concern affecting program decisions is risk avoidance. Popular culture success is notoriously unpredictable, making decisions risky. The music recording industry spreads investment over many records so that any single decision is less significant (Peterson & Berger, 1971). Spreading risk is not a strategy available to networks (neither broadcast nor cable), because only a few programming decisions fill the prime-time hours that account for most income. Networks are constrained further from expanding the number of their decisions by their use of the series as the basic unit of programming. The series format increases ratings predictability from week to week. Each decision, then, represents a considerable financial risk, not simply in production costs but in advertising income. For example, ABC increased profits from $35 million in 1975 to $185 million in 1978 by raising its average prime-time ratings from 16.6 to 20.7 (personal communication, W. Behanna, A. C. Nielsen Company, June 1980).

Because programming decisions are risky and costly and network executives' careers rest on their ability to make the right decisions, they are constrained, in their own interest, to avoid innovation and novelty. They stick to tried-and-true formulas and to producers with a track record of success (Brown, 1971; Wakshlag & Adams, 1985). The result is a small, closed community of proven creative personnel (about 500 producers, writers, directors) closely tied to and dependent on the networks (Gitlin, 1983, pp. 115, 135; Pekurny, 1982; Tunstall & Walker, 1981, pp. 77–79). This proven talent then self-censor their work on the basis of a product image their previous experience tells them the networks will tolerate (Cantor, 1971; Pekurny, 1982; Ravage, 1978) creating an "imaginary feedback loop" (DiMaggio & Hirsch, 1976) between producers and network executives.

These same conditions continue to characterize program development in the late 1980s (Blumler & Spicer, 1990), as the new buyers of programming, cable networks, operate under the same constraints as broadcast networks.

To avoid risk, network executives have chosen programs that repeat the same images of class decade after decade. More diverse programming has appeared only in the early days of an industry when there were no past successes to copy—broadcast television in the early 1950s and cable in the early 1980s—or when declining ratings made it clear that past successes no longer worked (Blumler & Spicer, 1990; Turow, 1982b, p. 124). Dominick (1976) found that the lower the profits of the networks, the more variation in program types could be discerned from season to season and the less network schedules resembled each other. For example, in the late 1950s, ABC introduced hour-long western series to prime time to become competitive with NBC and CBS (Federal Communications Commission [FCC], Office of Network Study, 1965, pp. 373, 742). Again, in 1970, CBS purchased Norman Lear's then controversial *All in the Family* (other networks turned it down) to counteract a drift to an audience of undesirable demographics (rural and over 50). Acceptance by networks of innovative programs takes much longer than conventional programs and requires backing by the most successful producers (Turow, 1982b, p. 126). *Roseanne* was introduced by Carsey-Werner, producers of the top-rated *Cosby Show,* when ABC was trying to counter ratings losses (Reeves, 1990, 153–154). Hugh Wilson, the creator of *WKRP* and *Frank's Place,* described CBS in 1987 as desperate about slipping ratings; "Consequently they were the best people to work for from a creative standpoint" (Campbell & Reeves, 1990, p. 8).

NETWORK DECISION MAKING— PROGRAM DEVELOPMENT

The second factor affecting network decisions on content is the need to produce programming suited to advertising. What the audience wants—or what network executives imagine they want—is secondary to ad revenue. (Subscriber-supported, pay cable networks, which do not sell advertising, also do not program weekly drama series.) In matters of content, networks avoid that which will offend or dissatisfy advertisers (Bryant, 1969). For example, ABC contracts with producers in 1977 stipulated that

> no program or pilot shall contain . . . anything . . . which does not conform with the then current business or advertising policies of any such sponsor; or which is detrimental to the good will or the products or services of . . . any such sponsor. (FCC, Network Inquiry, 1980, Appendix C, p. A-2)

Gary Marshall, producer of several highly successful series, stated that ABC rejected a story line for *Mork & Mindy,* the top rated show for 1978, in which Mork takes TV ads literally, buys everything and creates havoc. Despite the series' and Marshall's proven success, the network feared advertisers' reactions to such a story line.

An advertiser's preferred program is one that allows full use of the products being advertised. The program should be a complementary context for the ad. In the 1950s, an ad agency, rejecting a play about working-class life, stated, "It is the general policy of advertisers to glamorize their products, the people who buy them, and the whole American social and economic scene" (Barnouw, 1970, p. 32). Advertisers in 1961 considered it "of key importance" to avoid "irritating, controversial, depressive, or downbeat material" (FCC, Office of Network Study, 1965, p. 373). This requires dramas built around affluent characters for whom consuming is not problematic. Thus affluent characters predominate, and occupational groups with higher levels of consumer expenditure are overrepresented.

A third factor in program decisions is whether it will attract the right audience. Network executives construct a product image of what they *imagine* the audience wants, which surprisingly is not based on actual research of audiences in their homes (Blumler & Spicer, 1990; Pekurny, 1982). For example, Michael Dann, a CBS executive was "concerned the public might not accept a program about a blue-collar worker" when offered the pilot script for *Arnie* in 1969 (before *All in the Family* proved that wrong and after a decade in which the only working-class family appearing in prime time was *The Flintstones*). On the other hand, in 1979 an NBC executive expressed the concern that a couple in a pilot was too wealthy to appeal to most viewers (Turow, 1982b, p. 123).

With the exception of the few anecdotes I have mentioned, almost no research has examined program development or production decisions about class content of programs. My research found no significant differences between characters in sitcom pilots and series from 1973 to 1982, indicating that class biases in content begin very early in the decision-making process, when the first pilot episode is being developed (Butsch, 1984). I therefore conducted a mail survey of the producers, writers or directors of the pilots from 1973 to 1982. I specifically asked how the decisions were made about the occupation of the characters in their pilot. I was able to contact 40 persons concerning 50 pilots. I received responses from 6 persons concerning 12 pilots.

Although this represents only a small portion of the original sample, their responses are strikingly similar. Decisions on occupations of main characters were made by the creators and made early in program development, as part of the program idea. In no case did the occupation become a matter of debate or disagreement with the networks. Moreover, the choice of occupation was incidental to the situation or other aspect of the program idea; thus it was embedded in the creator's conception of the situation. For example, according to one writer, a character was conceived of as an architect "to take advantage of the Century City" location for shooting the series; the father in another pilot was cast as owner of a bakery after the decision was made to do a series about an extended Italian family; in another pilot, the creator thought the actor "looked like your average businessman." The particular occupations and even the classes are not necessitated by the situations that creators offered as explanations. But they do not seem to be hiding the truth; their responses were open and unguarded. It appears they did not think through themselves why this *particular* class or occupation; rather, the occupations seem to them an obvious derivative of the situation or location or actors they choose. The choice of class is thus diffuse, embedded in their culture.

This absence of any awareness of decisions about class is confirmed by Gitlin's (1983) interviews with industry personnel about social issues. Thus the process of class construction seems difficult to document given the unspoken guidelines, the indirect manner in which they suggest class and the absence of overt decisions about class. Class or occupation is not typically an issue for discussion, as are obscenity or race. To examine it further, we need to look at the organization of the production process and the culture of creative personnel.

THE HOLLYWOOD INPUT—PROGRAM PRODUCTION

Within the production process in Hollywood studios and associated organizations, and in the work culture of creative personnel, we find factors that contribute to the use of simple and repetitious stereotypes of working-class men.

An important factor in television drama production is the severe time constraints (Lynch, 1973; Ravage, 1978; Reeves, 1990, p. 150). The production schedule for series requires that a finished program be delivered to the networks each week. Even if the production company had the entire year over which to complete the season's 22 to 24 episodes, an episode would have to be produced on the average every 2 weeks, including script writing, casting, staging, filming and editing. This is achieved through an assembly line process in which several episodes are in various stages of production and being worked on by the same team of producer, writers, director and actors, simultaneously (Lynch, 1973; Ravage, 1978; Reeves, 1990).

Such a schedule puts great pressure on the production team to simplify the amount of work and decisions to be made as much as possible. The series format is advantageous for this reason: When the general story line and main characters are set, the script can be written following a simple formula. For situation comedy, even the sets and the cast do not change from episode to episode.

The time pressures contribute in several ways to the dependence on stereotypes for characterization. First, if ideas for new series are to be noticed, they cannot be "subtle ideas and feelings of depth" but, rather, "have to be attention getters—loud farts," in the words of a successful director (Ravage, 1978, p. 92).

Also, time pressure encourages type-casting to obtain casts quickly. The script is sent to a "breakdown" agency, which reads the script and extracts the description of characters that need to be cast. One such agency, employing six persons, provided this service for the majority of series (Turow, 1978). These brief character descriptions, not the script, are used by the casting agency to recommend actors, particularly for minor characters. Not surprisingly, the descriptions are highly stereotyped (Turow, 1980). Occupation—and by inference, class—was an important part of these descriptions, being identified for 84% of male characters.

Producers, casting directors and casting agencies freely admit the stereotyping but argue its necessity on the basis of time and dramatic constraints. Type-casting is much quicker. They also argue that to diverge from stereotypes would draw attention away from the action, the story line or other characters and destroy dramatic effect. Thus, unless the contradiction of the stereotype is the basic story idea—as in *Arnie*, a blue-collar worker suddenly appointed corporate executive—there is a very strong pressure, for purposes of dramatic effect, to reproduce existing stereotypes.

The time pressures also make it more likely that the creators will stick to what is familiar to them whenever possible. Two of the most frequent occupations of main characters in family series were in entertainment and writing, that is, modeled on the creators' own lives (Butsch & Glennon, 1983). The vast majority of producers grew up in middle-class homes, with little direct experience of working-class life (Cantor, 1971; Gitlin, 1983; Stein, 1979; Thompson & Burns, 1990). Moreover, the tight schedules and deadlines of series production leave no time for becoming familiar enough with a working-class lifestyle to be able to capture it realistically. Those who have done so—for example, Jackie Gleason, Norman Lear—had childhood memories of working-class neighborhoods to draw on.

Thus the time pressure encourages creative personnel to rely heavily on a shared and consistent product image—including diffuse and undifferentiated images of class—embedded in what Elliott (1972) called "the media culture." The small, closed community of those engaged in television production, including Hollywood creators and network executives (Blumler & Spicer, 1990; Gitlin, 1983; Stein, 1979; Tunstall & Walker, 1981; Turow, 1982a), shares a culture that includes certain conceptions of what life is like and what the audience finds interesting. According to Norman Lear, the production community draws its ideas from what filters into it from the mass media (Gitlin, 1983, p. 204). From this, they try to guess what "the public" would like and formulate images of class they think are compatible (Gitlin, 1983, pp. 225–226).

Although the consistency of image, the underrepresentation of the working class and the use of stereotypes can be explained by structural constraints, the particular stereotypes grow from a rather diffuse set of cultural images, constrained and framed by the structure of the industry. Any further specification will require a close examination of the construction of the consciousness of the program creators and network executives from, among other things, their exposure to the same media they create—a closed circle of cultural reproduction. Whether one can indeed extract the process of class image making from the totality of this occupational culture remains a challenge to researchers.

NOTES

1. Subordinate statuses, generally, race and gender as well as class, are underrepresented and/or presented negatively.
2. The sellers, the production companies, on the other hand, are not an oligopoly. Market concentration is low compared to the buyers (broadcast and cable networks); there was high turnover in the ranks of suppliers and great year-to-year fluctuation in market share; and collusion between suppliers is very difficult (FCC Network Inquiry Special Staff, 1980; Owen & Wildman, 1990).

REFERENCES

Barnouw, E. (1970). *The image empire: A history of broadcasting in the U.S. from 1953.* New York: Oxford University Press.

Blum, A. (1969). Lower class Negro television spectators. In A. Shostak (Ed.), *Blue collar world* (pp. 429–435). New York: Random House.

Blumler, J., & Spicer, C. (1990). Prospects for creativity in the new television marketplace. *Journal of Communication, 40*(4), 78–101.

Brown, L. (1971). *Television: The business behind the box.* New York: Harcourt, Brace, Jovanovich.

Bryant, A. (1969). Historical and social aspects of concentration of program control in television. *Law and Contemporary Problems, 34,* 610–635.

Butsch, R. (1984, August). *Minorities from pilot to series: Network selection of character statuses and traits.* Paper presented at the annual meeting of Society for the Study of Social Problems, Washington, DC.

Butsch, R. (1992). Class and gender in four decades of television situation comedy. *Critical Studies in Mass Communication, 9,* 387–399.

Butsch, R., & Glennon, L. M. (1983). Social class: Frequency trends in domestic situation comedy, 1946–1978. *Journal of Broadcasting, 27*(1), 77–81.

Campbell, R., & Reeves, J. (1990). Television authors: The case of Hugh Wilson. In R. Thompson & G. Burns (Eds.), *Making television: Authorship and the production process* (pp. 3–18). New York: Praeger.

Cantor, M. (1971). *The Hollywood TV producer.* New York: Basic Books.

Connell, B. (1978). *Ruling class, ruling culture.* London: Cambridge University Press.

DiMaggio, P., & Hirsch, P. (1976). Production organization in the arts. *American Behavioral Scientist, 19,* 735–752.

Dominick, J. (1976, Winter). Trends in network prime time, 1953–1974. *Journal of Broadcasting, 26,* 70–80.

Elliott, P. (1972). *The making of a television series: A case study in the sociology of culture.* New York: Hastings.

Federal Communications Commission, Network Inquiry Special Staff. (1980). *Preliminary reports.* Washington, DC: Government Printing Office.

Federal Communications Commission, Office of Network Study. (1965). *Second interim report: Television network program procurement* (Part 2). Washington, DC: Government Printing Office.

Gans, H. (1962). *The urban villagers.* New York: Free Press.

Gitlin, T. (1983). *Inside prime time.* New York: Pantheon.

Glennon, L. M., & Butsch, R. (1982). The family as portrayed on television, 1946–78. In National Institute of Mental Health, *Television and social behavior: Ten Years of scientific progress and implications for the eighties* (Vol. 2, Technical Review, 264–271). Washington, DC: Government Printing Office.

Jhally, S., & Lewis J. (1992). *Enlightened racism: The Cosby Show, Audiences and the myth of the American dream.* Boulder, CO: Westview.

Lynch, J. (1973). Seven days with *All in the Family:* A case study of the taped TV drama. *Journal of Broadcasting, 17*(3), 259–274.

Owen, B., & Wildman, S. (1992). *Video economics.* Cambridge, MA: Harvard University Press.

Pekurny, R. (1977). *Broadcast self-regulation: A participant observation study of NBC's broadcast standards department.* Unpublished doctoral dissertation, University of Minnesota.

Pekurny, R. (1982). Coping with television production. In J. S. Ettema & D. C. Whitney (Eds.), *Individuals in mass media organizations*. Beverly Hills, CA: Sage.

Peterson, R. A., & Berger, D. (1971). Entrepreneurship in organizations: Evidence from the popular music industry. *Administrative Science Quarterly, 16*, 97–107.

Ravage, J. (1978). *Television: The director's viewpoint*. New York: Praeger.

Reeves, J. (1990). Rewriting culture: A dialogic view of television authorship. In R. Thompson & G. Burns (Eds.), *Making television: Authorship and the production process* (pp. 147–160). New York: Praeger.

Ryan, B. (1992). *Making capital from culture: The corporate form of capitalist cultural production*. New York: Walter de Gruyter.

Stein, B. (1979). *The view from Sunset Boulevard*. New York: Basic Books.

Thompson, R., & Burns, G. (Eds.). (1990). *Making television: Authorship and the production process*. New York: Praeger.

Tunstall, J., & Walker, D. (1981). *Media made in California*. New York: Oxford University Press.

Turow, J. (1978). Casting for TV parts: The anatomy of social typing. *Journal of Communication, 28*(4), 18–24.

Turow, J. (1980). Occupation and personality in television dramas. *Communication Research, 7*(3), 295–318.

Turow, J. (1982a). Producing TV's world: How important is community? *Journal of Communication, 32*(2), 186–193.

Turow, J. (1982b). Unconventional programs on commercial television. In J. S. Ettema & D. C. Whitney (Eds.), *Individuals in mass media organizations*. Beverly Hills, CA: Sage.

Vidmar, N., & Rokeach, M. (1974). Archie Bunker's bigotry: A study in selective perception and exposure. *Journal of Communication, 24*, 36–47.

Wakshlag, J., & Adams, W. J. (1985). Trends in program variety and prime time access rules. *Journal of Broadcasting and Electronic Media, 29*(1), 23–34.

Winick, C. (1961). Censor and sensibility: A content analysis of the television censor's comments. *Journal of Broadcasting, 5*(2), 117–135.

34

DISTORTED REALITY
Hispanic Characters in TV Entertainment

S. ROBERT LICHTER • DANIEL R. AMUNDSON

THE PAST AS PROLOGUE

It takes diff'rent strokes to move the world.
—"DIFF'RENT STROKES" THEME SONG

W hen Kingfish uttered his last "Holy Mackerel, Andy!" in 1953, it
marked the end of television's most controversial depiction of
blacks. Ironically, the departure of "Amos 'n' Andy" also signaled
the end of a brief period of ethnic diversity that would not reappear in prime
time for two decades. Several of the earliest family sitcoms were transplanted
radio shows set in America's black or white ethnic subcultures. "The Gold-
bergs" followed the lives of a Jewish immigrant family in New York for
twenty years on radio before switching to the new medium in 1949. It featured Gertrude Berg as Molly Goldberg, everyone's favorite Jewish mother.
An even more successful series that premiered the same year was "Mama,"
which chronicled a Norwegian immigrant family in turn-of-the-century San
Francisco. Theme music by Grieg added to the "ethnic" atmosphere, as did
accents that made Aunt "Yenny" into a popular character. These white ethnic
shows were soon joined by the all-black "Amos 'n' Andy" as well as "Beulah," which starred the black maid of a white middle-class family.

All these shows relied on stereotypical dialogue and behavior for much
of their humor. But social standards were changing, and the new medium created its own demands and perceptions. For example, not only Amos and
Andy but even Beulah had been portrayed on radio by white males. When
the popular radio show "Life with Luigi" made the switch to TV in 1952, Italian American groups protested its stereotyped portrayal of Italian immigrants. Black groups were equally outraged over "Amos 'n' Andy," which
had been an institution on radio since 1929. As the program evolved, it centered on the schemes of George "Kingfish" Stevens, who combined the soul

of Sgt. Bilko with the fate of Ralph Kramden. A small-time con man with big plans that never panned out, he became an immensely popular, lovable loser. His schemes usually pulled in the ingenuous cabbie Andy and the slow-moving janitor Lightnin'.

From Kingfish's fractured syntax ("I'se regusted") to Lightnin's shuffle and falsetto "yazzuh," the series drew on overtly racial stereotypes. The NAACP blasted the portrayal of blacks as "inferior, lazy, dumb, and dishonest," and urged a boycott of Blatz beer, the sponsor. The pressure from civil rights groups probably helped bring the series to a premature end, since it attracted sizeable audiences throughout its two year run. . . .

While controversy surrounded "Amos 'n' Andy," little debate attended television's earliest and most high profile Latino portrayal. From 1950 through 1956, Ziv productions sold 156 episodes of "The Cisco Kid" in syndication to individual stations across the country. Resplendent in his heavily embroidered black costume, Cisco rode across the southwest righting wrongs and rescuing damsels in distress. He was accompanied by his portly sidekick, Pancho, who served as a comic foil. Pancho was loyal and brave, but his English was every bit as fractured as the Kingfish's. Further, although Cisco and Pancho were positive and even heroic characters, they were often outnumbered by evil and frequently criminal Latino adversaries. In its simplistic presentation that combined positive and negative ethnic stereotypes, "Cisco" set the tone for the "Zorro" series that would follow it on ABC from 1957 through 1959. Thus, these early high-profile representations of Latinos proved a mixed bag, as television's conventions of the day were applied to both network and syndicated fare.

THE ALL-WHITE WORLD

"Cisco" and "Zorro," which were aimed at children, outlasted the first generation of ethnic sitcoms for general audiences. By the 1954 season "Mama" was the only survivor of this once-thriving genre. Thus, by the time our study period began, TV's first era of ethnic humor had already come and gone. The urban ethnic sitcoms were replaced by homogeneous suburban settings. There was nothing Irish about the life of Chester Riley, nothing Scandinavian about Jim and Margaret Anderson. The new family shows were all-American, which meant vaguely northern European and carefully noncontroversial. The few remaining ethnics were mostly relegated to minor roles or single episodes.

Just how homogeneous was this electronic neighborhood? From 1955 through 1964, our coders could identify only one character in ten as anything other than northern European on the basis of name, language, or appearance. Such a small slice of the pie got cut up very quickly, and many groups got only crumbs. Just one character in fifty was Hispanic, fewer than one in a hundred was Asian, and only one in two hundred was black.

. . .

Hispanics had virtually no starring roles. For most Hispanic characters, life consisted of lounging in the dusty square of a sleepy Latin town, waiting for the stars to come on stage. Occasionally Hispanics would show up as outlaws in the Old West, but even then mostly as members of someone else's gang. Their comic roles were epitomized by Pepino Garcia, a farmhand for "The Real McCoys," who functioned mainly as a target of Grandpa Amos McCoy's tirades. Pepino and "The Real McCoys" were replaced in 1963 by Jose Jimenez in the "Bill Dana Show."

Like their black colleagues, a few stars stood out in a sea of marginal and insignificant roles. A notable exception was Cuban band leader Ricky Ricardo in "I Love Lucy," played by Desi Arnaz. As the co-star of one of the most popular shows on TV (and co-owner of Desilu Productions, along with wife Lucille Ball), Arnaz was a prominent figure in Hollywood. When exasperated by Lucy's schemes and misadventures, Ricky added a comic touch with displays of "Latin" temper and lapses into Spanish. "I Love Lucy" made its mark on television comedy and TV production in general, but it did little for Hispanic characters. The same could be said of another early show with a Hispanic setting, which nonetheless cast Anglos in the major roles. Guy Williams played Don Diego, alias Zorro, the masked champion of the poor and oppressed in old Los Angeles. Their oppressors were evil, greedy Spanish governors and landowners. In one episode Annette Funicello, fresh from the Mickey Mouse Club, showed up as the singing senorita Anita Cabrillo. Despite its "Hispanic" characters, the show was not a generous portrayal of either the people or the culture.

The departure of "Amos 'n' Andy" and "Beulah" all but eliminated black stars. Jack Benny's valet Rochester was one of the few major roles still held by a black in the late 1950s. Black characters didn't even show up in the backgrounds of early shows. Urban settings might feature a black delivery man, porter, or waiter, but black professionals and businessmen were virtually nonexistent. Some westerns like "Rawhide" and "Have Gun, Will Travel" presented a few black cowboys riding the range with their white counterparts. Aside from such occasional and insignificant roles, black characters were simply not a part of the early prime time world.

THE RETURN OF RACE

In the mid-1960s, the portrayal of ethnic and racial minorities underwent major changes. The proportion of non-northern European roles doubled over the next decade. Before 1965, all racial and ethnic groups to the south or east of England, France, and Germany had scrambled for the one role in ten available to them. Now nonwhite characters alone could count on better than one role in ten. From the first to the second decade in our study [1955–1975], the proportion of English characters was cut in half, while Hispanics became half again as numerous and the proportion of Asians doubled. Blacks were the biggest winners, gaining a dramatic fourteen-fold increase in what had been virtually an all-white landscape.

The invisibility of Hispanics during this period remained more than metaphorical. They were simply not part of television's new ethnic "relevance." Latinos had few continuing prime time roles of any sort during the late 1960s, and certainly no major star parts like Bill Cosby's Alexander Scott. In fact, most Latinos who were cast during this period showed up in episodes of international espionage series that used Central and South American locales. "I Spy" had many episodes set in Mexico, bringing the agents into contact with some positive and many more negative Hispanic characters. In other espionage shows, such as "Mission: Impossible," the action often centered on a fictitious Central American country, which was inevitably run by a jack-booted junta that could only be stopped by the enlightened Anglo-led team from north of the border.

One of the few exceptions to this pattern was the western "High Chaparral." Rancher John Cannon had settled in the Arizona territory to found a cattle empire. When his first wife was killed by Apaches, John married Victoria Montoya, the daughter of a wealthy Mexican rancher. The marriage was as much a business move as a romance, since it united the two families. Once tied by marriage, Don Montoya helped John build his herds and produce good breeding stock. Together the two families fought off Apaches and other marauders. Culture clashes between the two families occurred, but usually as a minor part of the plot. Unlike most Mexicans shown in previous westerns, the Montoyas were rich, powerful, sophisticated, and benevolent. In most episodes, Victoria attempted to civilize her more rustic husband and establish a proper home on the range. To be sure, this series still presented semiliterate Hispanic ranchhands, but these portrayals were overshadowed by the Montoyas.

Not only did the proportion of black characters jump to 7 percent between 1965 and 1975, but the range and quality of roles expanded even more dramatically. In adventure series like "I Spy" and "Mission: Impossible," blacks moved into their first starring roles in over a decade. Not only were these roles more prominent, they offered a new style of character. Alexander Scott of "I Spy" and Barney Collier of "Mission: Impossible" were competent, educated professionals. These men were highly successful agents whose racial backgrounds were clearly secondary to their bravery and skill. They opened the way for blacks to appear in roles that did not require the actor to be black. There was no more use of poor English, servile shuffling, or popeyed double takes for comic effect. Instead, Collier was presented as an electronics expert and Scott as a multilingual Rhodes Scholar.

The new visibility of blacks quickly moved beyond the secret agent genre. In 1968 the first of television's relevance series managed to convert a negative stereotype into a positive one by casting a young black rebel as a member of "The Mod Squad." Linc Hayes' militant credentials included an afro haircut, aviator sunglasses, and an arrest during the Watts riots. Not to worry, though. This brooding black rebel was working with the good guys on the L.A.P.D.'s undercover "youth squad," where the dirty dozen met the counterculture every Tuesday at 7:30.

While ABC was coopting the Black Panthers into the establishment, NBC looked to the black middle class for "Julia," the first black-oriented sitcom in fifteen years. As a dedicated nurse and loving mother in an integrated world, the Julia Baker character looked ahead to "The Cosby Show" rather than backward to "Amos 'n' Andy." She certainly had more in common with Claire Huxtable than with Kingfish's nagging wife, Sapphire. Unfortunately, she also lacked the vitality and wit of either Sapphire or future mother figures who would be more firmly rooted in black culture, like "Good Times" Florida Evans.

"Julia" suffered from the dullness of being a prestige series, just as "The Mod Squad" labored under the hype that attended the relevance series. What they had in common with better-written shows like "I Spy" and "Mission: Impossible" was a tendency to replace the old negative black stereotypes with new positive ones. The authors of *Watching TV* wrote with a touch of hyperbole, "They were no longer bumbling, easy-going, po' folk like Beulah, but rather articulate neo-philosophers just descended from Olympus, though still spouting street-wise jargon."[1] Having discovered that blacks didn't have to be cast as valets and janitors, white writers turned them into James Bonds and Mary Tyler Moores. Thus, as blacks suddenly began to appear on the tube after a decade's absence, they remained invisible in Ralph Ellison's sense. The frantic search for positive characters smothered individuality with good intentions.

LET A HUNDRED FLOWERS BLOOM

In the early 1970s TV began to broadcast a different message about minorities. The unlikely agent of change was an equal opportunity bigot named Archie Bunker, who excoriated "spics," "jungle bunnies," "chinks," "yids," and every other minority that ever commanded an epithet. When "All in the Family" became the top-rated show within five months of its 1971 premiere, it attracted a barrage of criticism for making the tube safe for ethnic slurs. The producer of public television's "Black Journal" found it "shocking and racist."[2] Laura Hobson, who wrote "Gentlemen's Agreement," an attack on anti-Semitism, decried its attempt to sanitize bigotry," to clean it up, deodorize it, make millions of people more comfy about indulging in it."[3] Of course, the point of the show was to poke fun at Archie and all he stood for, as the script and laugh track tried to make clear.

Norman Lear's strategy was to educate audiences by entertaining them instead of preaching at them. So he created a kind of politicized Ralph Kramden, whom audiences could like in spite of his reactionary views, not because of them. He intended that the contrast between Archie's basic decency and his unattractive rantings would prod viewers to reexamine the retrograde ideas they permitted themselves. As Lear put it, the show "holds up a mirror to our prejudices. . . . We laugh now, swallowing just the littlest bit of truth about ourselves, and it sits there for the unconscious to toss about later."[4] As a tool for improving race relations, this approach may have been too subtle for its own good. Several studies suggest that liberals watched the show to confirm their disdain for Archie's views, while conservatives identified with him despite his creator's best intentions.[5] But another legacy of the program was to pioneer a more topical and (by television's standards) realistic portrayal of ethnic relations.

An immediate consequence of "All in the Family" was to introduce the first sitcoms populated by black families since "Amos 'n' Andy." A year after demonstrating the audience appeal of a white working class milieu not portrayed successfully since "The Honeymooners," Lear and his partner Bud Yorkin transferred the setting to a black ghetto in "Sanford and Son." Unlike the integrated middle class world of TV blacks in the late 1960s, "Sanford and Son" revolved around the foibles of a junk dealer in a poor black section of Los Angeles. "Sanford" proved so popular that it soon trailed only "All in the Family" in the Nielsen ratings.

Meanwhile, in an irony Archie would not have appreciated, "All in the Family" spawned not one but two additional black family sitcoms. "The Jeffersons" featured Archie's one-time neighbor George Jefferson as an upwardly mobile businessman whose snobbishness and inverted racism made him almost a black Archie Bunker. "Good Times" was actually a second-generation spinoff. When Archie's liberal nemesis Maude got her own show in 1972, the scriptwriters gave her a quick-witted and tart-tongued black maid named Florida Evans. Two years later the popular Florida got her own show as the matriarch of a family living in a Chicago housing project. This series developed the "Sanford" technique of finding sometimes bitter humor among lower status characters trying to cope with life in the ghetto while looking for a way out of it. Scripts featured ward heelers, loan sharks, abused children, and other facets of life on the edge, in sharp contrast to the comfortable middle class world of "Julia" or the glamorous and exotic locales of "I Spy."

By this time, other producers, stimulated by Norman Lear's enormous success, were providing sitcoms that drew their characters from minority settings. "What's Happening!!" followed the adventures of three big city high school kids. "Diff'rent Strokes" created an unlikely "accidental family" in which a wealthy white man raised two black kids from Harlem in his Park Avenue apartment, without any serious clash of cultures. This trend almost never extended from the ghetto to the barrio. The one great exception was "Chico and the Man," a generation-gap sitcom that paired an ebullient young Mexican American with an aging Bunkerish Anglo garage owner. This odd couple clicked with audiences, but the show's success was cut short by the suicide of comedian Freddy Prinze (Chico) in 1977.

Like the black sitcoms, "Chico" used minority culture as a spark to enliven a middle class white world that seemed bland or enervated by comparison. Minority characters of the early 1970s prided themselves not on their similarity to mainstream culture, but on their differences from it. Assimilated characters like Alexander Scott, Barney Collier, and Julia Baker gave way to the racial pride of George Jefferson, Fred of "Sanford and Son," and Rooster on "Starsky and Hutch." Where would Fred Sanford or George Jefferson be without their jive talk and street slang? Language was just one way of stressing the differences between racial and ethnic groups.

Minority characters also picked up flaws as they took on more complete roles. Fred Sanford was domineering and could appear foolish. George Jefferson could be as stubborn and narrow-minded as his onetime next-door neighbor. By badgering the interracial couple living upstairs and labelling their daughter a "zebra," he left no doubt about his views. But the thrust of the ethnic sitcom was not to ridicule minority cultures. Instead, racial and ethnic backgrounds were used as an educational tool. The religious, cultural, and other traditions that differentiate minorities from the mainstream were now treated as beneficial rather than problematic. Removed from the confines of the melting pot, these groups offered new approaches to old problems. Television charged them with the task of teaching new ways to the often obstinate world around them. Blacks and Hispanics participated in this era of racial and cultural re-education. It was Chico Rodriguez who taught Ed Brown to relax and be more tolerant on "Chico and the Man." Benson, the sharp-tongued butler, tried to maintain order amidst the chaos of "Soap," while steering his employers onto the right track. In one episode he even saved young Billy from the clutches of a religious cult.

The most spectacularly successful effort to combine education with entertainment was a hybrid of the miniseries and "big event" genres. Indeed, "Roots" became the biggest event in television history. This adaptation of Alex Haley's best-selling novel traced the history of four generations of a black family in America, beginning with Kunta Kinte, an African tribesman sold into slavery. It ran for eight consecutive nights in January 1977. When it was over, 130 million Americans had tuned in, including 80 million who viewed the final episode. Seven of the eight episodes ranked among the all-time top ten at that point in television's history. "Roots" created a kind of national town meeting comparable to the televised moon landing or the aftermath of President Kennedy's assassination. It was blamed for several racial disturbances but credited for stimulating a productive national debate on the history of American race relations.

While blacks could look to the high-profile presentation of African American history presented by "Roots," there was no similar presentation of Hispanic history. If Anglos relied exclusively on Hollywood for information on Latino contributions to American history, their knowledge would extend little further than John Wayne's defense of "The Alamo" against the Mexican "invaders." Illustrations of Latino culture were equally rare. In fact, the only high-profile Hispanic character during this period was Chico Rodriguez. Despite its popularity, "Chico and the Man" was not known as a series that explored Latino culture or Hispanic contributions to American history and culture.

The late 1970s retained a mix of ethnic heroes and fools in some of the most popular shows of the day. But ethnic characters were beginning to lose their novelty. For instance, "CHiPs" ran from 1977 through 1983 and one of the starring characters was Officer Frank Poncherello. Even though Poncherello was played by the well-known Eric Estrada, Poncherello's Hispanic heritage was all but invisible. It no longer mattered in this series that one of the leads was a Latino. During the 1979 season, three dramatic series were launched with black leads, but none came close to the ratings necessary for renewal. "Paris" starred James Earl Jones as a super-cop who ran the station house during the day and taught criminology at night. "The Lazarus Syndrome" featured Louis Gossett as the chief of cardiology in a large hospital. "Harris and Company" focused on the problems of a single parent raising a family. The twist was that this black family was held together not by a matriarch but a middle-aged widower. Thus, Hollywood was at least trying to create some positive role models for black males. But no such efforts extended to Latinos. There were no network series built around a Latino family, Hispanic high school kids, or any of the other patterns found in sitcoms featuring blacks. It would be several years before the short-lived ABC series "Condo" would prominently cast Latinos as middle class characters.

Overall, the 1980s offered little that was new to racial or ethnic minority portrayals in the wake of TV's ethnic revival. These groups continued to be presented more or less as they were in the late 1970s. Despite the continuing presence of racial and ethnic diversity, however, racial themes were no longer in vogue. Integration was assumed as a backdrop, as the prime time world became less polarized. The age of pluralism had arrived, but the thrill was gone. The riots were over, the battles won, and characters got back to their other plot functions. Among these were crime and other wrongdoing. Comedies like "Taxi," "White Shadow," and "WKRP in Cincinnati" continued to present integrated casts, but ethnic characters in dramatic series were often on the dark side of the law.

Ironically, television's multicultural world of the 1980s provided an updated version of the stereotypical Hispanic banditos who populated the westerns thirty years earlier. In the fall of 1980, ABC's controversial sitcom "Soap" introduced a remake of Frito Bandito. Carlos "El Puerco" Valdez was a South American revolutionary playing a love interest of Jessica Tate. They had met when his band kidnapped her for ransom. This plan failed, but after things took a passionate turn, she became a benefactor of his revolution. "El Puerco" led a bumbling, low-budget revolution, and he was not above taking time out to romance his new gringo benefactor. "El Puerco" was both Latin lover and bandito with a measure of Jerry Lewis buffoonishness thrown in. Thus, it was down this line that the Frito Bandito's sombrero had been passed—to a fatigue-wearing ne'er-do-well.

There were also more sinister turns in Latino portrayals. Crime shows like "Miami Vice," "Hill Street Blues," and "Hunter" presented Hispanic drug lords as a major nemesis. Trafficking in human misery made these characters rich enough to own cities and sometimes even small countries. They were among the nastiest criminals on TV in the 1980s. There were also petty Hispanic criminals in the slums of "Hill Street Blues" and "Cagney & Lacey." These small-time hoods, drug addicts, and pimps were less flamboyant than their big-league counterparts, but no less unsavory. Altogether, TV's latest crop of Hispanics included a cruel and vicious group of criminals.

"Miami Vice" was not only a source of criminal Hispanics—after all the squad was led by the enigmatic Lieutenant Martin Castillo and on the distaff side of the unit was detective Gina Navarro. However inconsistently, the show did attempt to show successful law-abiding Latinos mixed in with the criminal crop. For all of its flaws "Miami Vice" at least attempted to reflect the presence of Latinos in Miami. Contrast this attempt with more contemporary shows like "Baywatch," "Acapulco H.E.A.T.," and others that rarely if ever reference the Hispanic populations in their host cities.

There were occasional attempts to base shows on Hispanic casts, but all proved unsuccessful. In 1983 the Lear-wannabee sitcom "Condo" briefly pitted a bigoted WASP against his Latino next-door neighbors. The following season, the equally short-lived "A.K.A. Pablo" dealt somewhat more seriously with ethnic questions. Focusing on struggling young comic Pablo Rivera and his extended family, the series wrestled with questions about ethnic humor and the preservation of Hispanic culture. Pablo made many jokes about his family and his Mexican American heritage in his nightclub act. This frequently offended his traditionalist parents, who expected him to treat his heritage more respectfully. Despite its brief run, this series was one of the few to deal explicitly with aspects of Latino culture.

Both "A.K.A. Pablo" and "Trial and Error" sprang from the efforts of comedian Paul Rodriguez. It is not uncommon for bankable stars to get their own television series. This is particularly true for stand-up comics, who have taken their nightclub acts into successful series like "Roseanne," "Home Improvement," "Grace Under Fire," and "Seinfeld." This approach has proven to be a very important avenue onto the screen for blacks. Several exclusively black shows currently on the air are the result of the work of a bankable star. Among those who have followed in the footsteps of Bill Cosby and Keenan Ivory Wayans of "In Living Color," Martin Lawrence of "Martin," Mark Curry of "Hangin' with Mr. Cooper," and Charles Dutton of "Roc." Unfortunately, this approach has so far been a dead end for Latinos.

Meanwhile, TV turned out numerous positive black role models as diverse as "The Cosby Show's" Heathcliff Huxtable, Mary Jenkins of "227," Rico Tubbs on "Miami Vice," and Bobby Hill of "Hill Street Blues." These shows suggest the diversity of major roles that were at last becoming available to blacks. "227" and "Amen" continued the sharp-tongued tradition of 1970s sit-coms, without the abrasive or objectionable images that had brought criticism. Tubbs and Hill both carried on the tradition of "salt and pepper" law enforcement teams. Hill also represented the educative function of minorities by helping to wean his partner Renko, a southerner, away from residual racist tendencies.

Of course, "Cosby" was the biggest hit of all. This series further developed the low-key humanistic colorblind approach that Bill Cosby has popularized over two decades as "I Spy's" Alexander Scott, high school teacher Chet Kincaid on "The Bill Cosby Show," and finally in a black version of "Father Knows Best." The enormous success of this venture led some critics to snipe at Cosby for playing black characters in whiteface to maximize audience appeal. Black psychiatrist Alvin Pouissant, retained by the show to review scripts for racial authenticity, notes that the criticisms come from white reporters more often than black viewers: "Sometimes it seems they want the show to be 'culturally black' . . . and sometimes it seems they would be happier to see them cussing out white people, a sort of protest sitcom. Some seem to feel that because the family is middle class with no obvious racial problems, that constitutes a denial or dismissal of the black person."[6]

Compared to the plight of TV's Hispanics, debates over whether the Huxtables are divorced from the black experience may seem a luxury, a sign that a one-time out-group has reached a mature phase in its relationship with the Hollywood community. In 1979 organized opposition even persuaded Norman Lear to withdraw a new comedy series at the last minute. "Mister Dugan," a sitcom about a black congressman, was scheduled to premier on CBS a week after Lear arranged a special screening for the Congressional Black Caucus. The screening was a disaster, with Congressman Mickey Leland calling the lead character "a reversion to the Steppin' Fetchit syndrome."

Lear promptly pulled the show from the schedule. He remarked at the time, "We have a high social conscience, and we want to get the story right. We do not favor the short-term gain over the long-term public interest. Dropping the show was an exercise in that commitment."[7] This was an extraordinary episode in a business often excoriated for caring only about the bottom line. When the medium's most successful producer is willing to withdraw a series on the eve of its broadcast, writing off a $700,000 investment, it shows the power of social commitment in television. The only question is the strength and direction of that commitment.

Moreover, such criticism is belied by the top ten ratings obtained by such diverse families as the Sanfords, Jeffersons, and Evans, not to mention Kunta Kinte and his kin. The success of upper and lower class, matriarchal and patriarchal black family series suggests that television has gone beyond using black characters as a sign of racial diversity. It has begun to show diversity within the black community as well, at last recognizing both the cultural distinctiveness and the universal humanity of this group of Americans. Unfortunately, Hispanics have never played a significant role in television's debate over race relations. When television has explored discrimination, prejudice, or the appropriateness of inter-racial relationships, it has almost always staged them as a black versus white issue. Whatever racial tensions exist between Latinos and other groups in American society, they have very rarely made it to the small screen.

A TALE OF TWO MINORITIES

Black representation continued to increase during the 1990s, as the number of shows with all-black or mostly black casts jumped. Driven largely by the Fox network's quest for new audiences and trademark shows, these new series drew heavily on the struttin' and jivin' characters of the 1970s. Both the 1992 and 1993 seasons featured ten such series, including hits like "Hangin' with Mr. Cooper," "Family Matters," "Martin," and "Fresh Prince of Bel Air." Intense debate has ensued over the quality of these roles and portrayals, which critics disparage as latter-day minstrel show stereotypes. However, such complaints have not diminished the popularity of these shows, particularly among black audiences.

While shows that were exclusively or mainly about blacks comprised about one-eighth of the prime time schedule in 1992–93, only one series in the previous three seasons was based on a Latino family or character. Moreover, that series—the short-lived "Frannie's Turn"—mainly used Hispanic traditions as a comic foil for feminist put-down. This series revolved around the marriage of a Cuban emigré named Joseph Escobar and his wife, Frannie, an Anglo of unclear ethnic origins. Whatever ethnic and cultural differences may have existed between them were rarely played upon, since most of the plots dealt with Frannie's quest for equality. However, when aspects of heritage did come up, they frequently reflected poorly on Latinos. For instance, the first episode dealt with Frannie's discovery that Joseph has been sending money to a Cuban liberation movement while telling her to cut the household budget. At one point in the ensuing argument, she suggests sarcastically, "Who knows, maybe they'll send you the Bay of Pigs decoder ring." In the few episodes that aired, the couple's children seemed oblivious to their heritage, and no effort was made to teach them about their father's culture. Overall, this series made no greater use of ethnicity than "I Love Lucy" did almost forty years earlier.

Otherwise, Latino characters remained largely supporting players or background figures in the prime time schedule. The highest profile in 1992–93 was enjoyed by Daniel Morales, who replaced Victor Sifuentes on "L.A. Law." Most other recent Latino roles involved lower status jobs or far less airtime in low-rated series. Examples include Chuy Castillo, the cook at the "Golden Palace"; Jennifer Clemente, a very junior attorney in the U.S. Justice Department on "The Round Table"; and detective Rafael Martinez on the "Hat Squad." There was also Mahalia Sanchez, a bus station cashier in the "John Larroquette Show," rookie detective James Martinez in "NYPD Blue," and Paco Ortiz in "Nurses," none of them starring roles.

The cultural diversity within the Latino community was almost completely absent from prime time. Most Hispanic characters on television came from a "generic" background without reference to national origin or past. Television has rarely pointed out the cultural, historical, or economic differences among different groups within the Latino community. The few shows to make such distinctions, from "Miami Vice" to "Frannie's Turn," usually did so to place a particular nationality in a negative light. In "Miami Vice," differing national origins were connected with different types of illegal activities, while in "Frannie's Turn" a Cuban heritage was not a badge of honor. Sadly, the highest-profile Latino characters of the season were Eric and Lyle Menendez, whose murder trial was featured in two made-for-television movies.

AN UPDATE

As we have seen, before 1965, prime time was a nearly all-white world populated mainly by generic northern Europeans, save for the occasional black servant or Mexican bandito. Soon thereafter, the spectrum widened to embrace an array of ethnic and cultural traditions. But various minority groups shared unequally in television's new search for ethnic roots.

Some of these disparities are summarized in Table 1. As the table makes clear, between 1955 and 1986, proportionately fewer Hispanic characters were professionals or executives and more were unskilled laborers. Fewer Hispanics had starring roles, were positively portrayed, or succeeded in attaining their goals. Indeed, according to our 1994 study,[8] the more villainous the character, the sharper the group differences that emerged. Hispanic characters were twice as likely as whites and three times as likely as blacks to commit a crime. Once TV's roster of Hispanic stereotypes solely included the grinning bandito criss-crossed with ammunition belts. More recently, as scriptwriter Ben Stein has observed, "Any time a Cuban or Colombian crosses the tube, he leaves a good thick trail of cocaine behind."[9]

In addition, because of their negative and criminal roles, Latinos stood apart from other characters in the methods they adopted to attain their goals. They were more likely than either whites or blacks to use violence and deceit. If Latinos were distinctive in the means they used to pursue their goals, they also differed in their motivations. Hispanic characters were much more likely to be driven by greed than other characters. More broadly, black characters managed to attain whatever they strove for more often than either whites or Hispanics. In fact, the failure rate among Hispanics was more than double that of blacks. Perusing these figures, it is difficult to resist the conclusion that Hollywood has cracked open the door to black concerns while letting Hispanics serve as window dressing.

Examining character portrayals in 1992, we found that compared to both Anglos and African Americans, television's Hispanics were low in number,

TABLE 1   Traits of TV Characters, 1955–1986

	White	Black	Latino
All characters	89%	6%	2%
Social background*			
Attended college	72	44	**
Lacked high school diploma	25	49	**
Low economic status	22	47	40
Professional or executive	22	17	10
Unskilled laborer	13	16	22
Plot functions			
Starring role	17	15	8
Character succeeded	65	72	54
Character failed	23	16	34
Positive portrayal	40	44	32
Negative portrayal	31	24	41
Committed crime	11	7	22

*Characters were coded only if their backgrounds were clearly indicated by the script.
**Too few characters were coded for meaningful comparisons.
Source: Based on a content analysis of 7,639 prime time characters that appeared in 620 entertainment programs between 1955 and 1986.

low in social status, and lowdown in personal character, frequently portraying violent criminals. The worst offenders were "reality" shows, whose version of reality often consisted of white cops chasing black and Hispanic robbers. Utilizing the same scientific content analysis approach, we examined the more recent 1994–95 season. We focused on a composite month of prime time entertainment programs broadcast on the four major broadcast networks and in first-run syndication. We found some welcome progress in television's portrayal of Hispanics, combined with some lingering sins of both omission and commission. (These results reflect our analysis of 5,767 characters who appeared on 528 different episodes of 139 prime time series.)

The proportion of Hispanic characters was up but still far below the proportion of Hispanic Americans in the real world. Latinos were "ghettoized" in a handful of series, few of which are still on the air, and few portrayed prosperous, well-educated, authoritative characters. The most striking and hopeful result, however, was a dramatic decline in the portrayal of Hispanics as criminals. Among the major findings:

- *Visibility.* TV's Hispanic presence doubled from 1992 levels. And these characters were more likely to play major roles when they appeared. But the rise was from only 1 to 2 percent of all characters, far below the 10 percent of Americans with Hispanic ancestry in real life. And a majority appeared in only two series, one of which has been canceled.

- *Criminality.* Hispanic characters were less likely to play villains than they were in the 1992 network prime time schedules. The drop in criminal portrayals was down 63 percent (from 16 percent of all Hispanic characters in 1992 and 6 percent in 1994). But even this level of criminality was higher than the 4 percent we found among whites and 2 percent among blacks.

- *New "Realities."* The most striking changes appeared in the cops-and-robbers "reality" shows, such as "COPS" and "America's Most Wanted." In 1992, a staggering 45 percent of all Hispanics and 50 percent of African Americans who appeared in theses shows committed crimes. In 1994–95, the "crime rate" for both minorities plummeted to less than half the previous levels—down from 45 to 16 percent of Latinos and from 50 to 20 percent of blacks portrayed.

NOTES

1. Harry Castleman and Walter Podrazik, *Watching TV: Four Decades of American Television* (New York: McGraw-Hill, 1982), 208.
2. Ibid., 226.
3. Laura Z. Hobson, quoted in Christopher Lasch, "Archie Bunker and the Liberal Mind," *Channels,* October/November 1981, 34.
4. Quoted in Castleman and Podrazik, *Watching TV,* 227.
5. See Richard Adler, ed., *All in the Family: A Critical Appraisal* (New York: Praeger, 1979).
6. Quoted in William Raspberry, "Cosby Show: Black or White?" *Washington Post,* 5 November 1984.
7. Quoted in *Time,* 19 March 1979, 85.
8. S. Robert Lichter and Daniel R. Amundson, *Distorted Reality: Hispanic Characters in TV Entertainment* (Washington, DC: Center for Media and Public Affairs, 1994).
9. Quoted in *Time,* 19 March 1979, 85.

35

CHANGING GAY AND LESBIAN IMAGES
IN THE MEDIA

PETER M. NARDI

The crowds gathered in the city streets and with anger and action brought the filming to a halt. For several days, protesters shouted and jeered as cameras rolled. The demonstration was a reaction to a script that many felt depicted gay men in negative and distorted ways. The film was *Cruising,* the city was New York, and the year was 1979. For the first time in history, protests by gays took place before the opening of a film (Russo 1987). The same scene was to be repeated in the streets of San Francisco. This time the film was *Basic Instinct,* the negative images were about lesbians, but the year was now 1991. Despite twelve years having passed, gay men and lesbians were still protesting media depictions of homosexuality as violent, pathological, and evil.

However, during these twelve years a growing social movement emerged among lesbians and gays who developed a variety of strategies and organizations to counteract the repeated verbal and visual bashings the media have inflicted. The movement's visibility reached a peak in the weeks leading up to the 1992 Academy Awards when rumors circulated about a possible disruption of the show by lesbian and gay activists protesting *The Silence of the Lambs* and other negative stereotypes in films. An estimated one hundred demonstrators and one hundred police (many in riot gear) stood outside the Dorothy Chandler Pavilion. Ironically, that evening, in front of an estimated billion viewers, Debra Chasnoff, a lesbian, acknowledged her lover after winning an Oscar for best documentary short, and Bill Launch, lover of the late Howard Ashman, who won for the lyrics of *Beauty and the Beast,* said: "Howard and I shared a home and a life together. . . . This is the first Academy Award given to someone we've lost to AIDS" (Wiley and Bona 1993:846). Lesbian and gay people within the media identified themselves publicly for the first time before a massive audience. Clearly, some changes had occurred since the protests against *Cruising.*

By the spring of 1993 the media were covering gay issues as never before, in part as a result of national attention about gays in the military. Within a

From James T. Sears & Walter Williams (eds.) *Overcoming Heterosexism and Homophobia: Strategies That Work.* New York: Columbia University Press, 1997. © 1997 Columbia University Press. Reprinted by permission of the publisher.

two-month period lesbians and gays appeared on the covers of *Newsweek*, *Nation*, *New Republic*, *New York*, *U.S. News and World Report*, and *National Review*, and the coverage of the lesbian and gay march on Washington and of the rising influence of gay political power was unprecedented. This shift and the continuing struggle to maintain accurate and fair media attention through various strategies are the focus of this chapter.

THE WAY WE WERE

In order to develop effective strategies against defamatory media images, the historical and social context of these images first needs to be understood. The history of the depiction of gays and lesbians in movies, on television, and in newspapers and magazines is not a pretty one. Russo (1987:347–49), in an appendix to *The Celluloid Closet* under the heading "Necrology," lists over forty examples of the ways in which gay or lesbian characters in films have died. Almost all were murdered or committed suicide.

From 1930 to the late 1960s the Motion Picture Production Code was the major form of self-regulation of Hollywood movies. And in that code's list of forbidden topics was "any inference of sexual perversion," i.e., homosexuality. Before 1930 many precode films had explicit references to homosexuals and numerous depictions of cross-dressing (Russo 1987). But it wasn't until 1961 that the subject of homosexuality was again allowed on-screen and the tone of the portrayals of gay people shifted. From the humorous, innocent sissy images of failed masculinity typical of the 1930s and 1940s, gay characters became lonely, predatory, and pathological people by the 1960s and 1970s (Russo 1987).

Television also has been "a cultural mirror which has failed to reflect [gays'] images accurately. To be absent from prime time, to be marginally included in it, or to be treated badly by it are seen as serious threats to their rights as citizens" (Montgomery 1989:8). Historically, gay and lesbian characters have been shown in stereotypical ways (men as effeminate and women as masculine), as a social problem, or in terms of how the regular heterosexual characters deal with them. Rarely is it from the perspective of the gay character and rarely is affection displayed between gay characters.

Yet television (and especially British TV) has been much more likely to take risks in the presentation of fair and balanced images of lesbians and gays. Partly in response to pressure from a growing gay activists' movement, ABC in 1973 became the first U.S. network to air a made-for-TV movie about gay men, *That Certain Summer*. Within a few years most major situation comedies, drama shows, and talk shows addressed gay topics, typically as a special issue, rarely in terms of an ongoing character or plot. By the mid-1980s any attention to gay issues was almost always framed in terms of AIDS, and then with gays as victim or villain (Gross 1991).

One of the explanations for the negative media images and the relative invisibility of gays and lesbians historically can be traced to social, economic, and political forces that structure the nature of the entertainment industry and the ways they construct images of people. As profit-making business corporations, media organizations reflect the economic marketplace and political climate of the culture; that is, content is often dictated by what prevents the least erosion of potential consumers. As Gitlin (1985:3) so colorfully phrased it, television's "primary customers are the advertisers whose business is to rent the eyeballs of the audience." Targeting the "typical viewer" who purchases sponsor's goods, the media tailor their products so as not to offend the least common denominator. This is the argument routinely made when the media are asked to include more gay and lesbian characters.

CHANGING IMAGES OF GAYS AND LESBIANS IN THE MEDIA

Many theories can be invoked to explain media depictions of gays and lesbians, but it is also important when developing strategies to combat heterosexism and homophobia in the media to analyze and understand the actual types of portrayals that exist and how they differ. Here are four ways to characterize most gay and lesbian images: (1) overt homophobic and negative stereotypic characterizations, (2) heterosexism and the more subtle forms of stereotyping, (3) invisibility and omission, and (4) accurate, fair, and balanced images.

Overt Homophobic and Negative Stereotypic Characterizations

Combating overtly homophobic images has dominated a good deal of the energies and time of many lesbian and gay activists. Luckily, some of the early strategies of protest and lobbying have resulted in a significant decline of such negative characterizations. Developing successful strategies of reform requires some familiarity with what has been done already.

As mentioned earlier, the history of the movies during the production code era is a history of gay people as one-dimensional, evil, or silly characters who get what they deserve in the end. But in an era when such production codes no longer exist and when increasing visibility of nonstereotypical gays and lesbians is evident, there still remains today overtly homophobic depictions. The repeated use of epithets, such as *faggot, dyke, queer, homo,* and *fruit,* while not used gratuitously as much as in the past, does continue in many media. When they are used they often signify a way of establishing evil or marginality about the character so labeled, although they are occasionally used to demonstrate the ignorance of the person using them. These words become a shorthand for underlining the pathology or villainy of the character.

Linking certain characters with homosexuality through nonverbal cues is a common way of signaling their evilness, even when explicit epithets are not used. This is one area that must be carefully monitored and resisted. The battle over the movie *Basic Instinct* centered on these issues, specifically in the depiction of lesbians and bisexual women as serial killers, using ice picks to murder their predominantly white male heterosexual victims. While the word *dyke* may not have been used, references to a lesbian as masculine were typical. Although some lesbians read this film as a feminist response to patriarchy, many others argued that the historical context of predatory killer lesbian depictions precluded a more positive interpretation. If there were already other depictions of lesbians, then this particular portrayal might not have been so bad. It is the absence of balance and accuracy that becomes the chief contextual concern.

While the use of overtly homophobic expressions in movies and on television dramas and situation comedies has declined significantly in recent years, ad campaigns and videos created and marketed by the radical right groups fighting to overturn antigay discrimination ordinances and to pass repressive legislation against gays and lesbians depend primarily on presenting the most stereotypical images in sensational and negative ways. Many conservative religious programs consistently attack gays and lesbians with bogus research data, misinformation, and fear.

Targeting these groups, however, is probably a Sisyphean task, and many activists would rather not waste their energy fighting the radical right. However, a useful strategy is to target the stations buying and scheduling these shows. Demanding equal time or informing them about the erroneous content can be a more successful technique.

By creating images of lesbians and gays as "other," or as foreign, the media perpetuate and contribute to people's homophobia. While the media may have come a long way from the earlier 1930s' and 1960s' characterizations of homosexuals as genial sissies or unhappy neurotics, there are remnants of these depictions that need continued monitoring.

Strategies   If such a homophobic slur should be broadcast, there are several levels of action that might be taken. A call should be placed immediately to a representative of the medium in which the incident occurred and should be very specific about the details of the incident. Be sure to note the time, date, and context of the occurrence and other relevant information. Ideally, a tape recording of the homophobic remark would be made. If negative remarks continue, organize a phone tree and/or a letter-writing campaign to protest the antigay characterizations.

The call to a senior-level manager should also request that something concrete be done to remedy the situation: a public apology, a request for equal time, and a face-to-face meeting with the parties involved. It is very useful to provide constructive suggestions rather than just a critique. A key idea to remember is that this stage is to inform people about what has happened and why the incident is considered inappropriate.

When meetings, apologies, or equal time are not provided and when monitoring of the medium demonstrates continuing homophobic remarks, several other strategies could be used. If it is a problem with a radio or TV station, one way is to write a letter to the station protesting the incidents; request that the letter be placed in their Federal Communications Commission (FCC) license file, and send a copy to the FCC in Washington, D.C. All stations must be licensed and are open to challenge of that license if discrimination can be demonstrated. Attempts to do this were very common during the 1970s; although few stations lost their license, Montgomery (1989:25) found that "the petition to deny became a powerful weapon of intimidation."

If licenses are not at issue (as in the cases of movies, magazines, or newspapers), suggest that a formal protest take place, as was done at the filming of *Basic Instinct* and *Cruising*. Of course, demonstrations have the risk of publicizing the act that just might have disappeared anyway, but the demise of Andrew Dice Clay's career can be attributed in part to the protests that followed his performances.

Heterosexism and More Subtle Stereotyping

In a response to a minister's question about gays in the military, President Bill Clinton, at a 1993 press conference, replied that he would not be endorsing the "gay lifestyle" by lifting the ban. Clinton framed his response in a way that is probably one of the most common forms of subtle defamation: assuming a heterosexual perspective and presenting gays as "others" whose complex concerns can be reduced to a "lifestyle." In language, images, and the way issues are structured a view that often excludes gays and lesbians or marginalizes them is subtly put forward. It is important to be cognizant of this form of heterosexism in order to develop a more focused strategy of education and reform.

When the media do decide to include lesbian and gay voices and perspectives, there are techniques and words often used that end up reinforcing the dominance of the heterosexual perspective and the outside status of the gay viewpoint. So, for example, calling a lesbian an "avowed homosexual" or nongay people the "general population" perpetuates the "otherness" of the gay person without using traditionally negative stereotypes. While these phrases are not overtly homophobic, note that certain heterosexist assumptions are indicated by them.

In addition to language, the subtle forms of heterosexual dominance can be seen in the ways lesbians and gays are depicted, even positively. The images are almost exclusively white, middle or upper class, disproportionately male, and desexualized. *Making Love, Longtime Companion,* and *An Early Frost* are all examples of the perpetuation of assimilationist images of incorporation in movies and the exclusion of gay (and, especially, lesbian) characters of other races and social classes. Many gay and lesbian characters also appear in sitcoms, usually isolated from other relationships, or in newspaper obituaries without reference to romantic partners, thereby reinforcing some stereotypes about gay people being alone or separate from the ways others lead lives embedded in networks of family and friends (cf. Nardi 1990, 1992).

Furthermore, when lesbians and gays are depicted, the characters usually appear only once and then disappear (Gross 1994). The focus of the stories tends to be "on the acceptance of gay characters by the regular heterosexual characters. Very few gay couples [are] shown, and they [are] not permitted to display physical affection" (Montgomery 1989:93). Usually gay or lesbian characters appear when the topic is a gay one; rarely are they part of the ongoing cast of characters. Typically, they look and act just like everyone else on the show and the humor stems from this misidentification.

These more subtle forms of stereotyping are probably the most common in today's media and deserve special attention and strategic responses. With good intentions the creators of these images and phrases believe they are contributing to the diversity in their work and are helping eliminate discrimination based on sexual orientation. However, we have yet to see many stories dealing with people after they are already openly gay or, more radically, about the ways many lesbians and gays resist dominant heterosexual ideologies.

Strategies   Convincing people in the creative arts to alter their depictions is a difficult process. A typical response from those who are informed that they are using heterosexist language or characterizations is to invoke a charge of political correctness. Yet, the *New York Times* did finally listen to gay activists and dropped the cumbersome and problematic term *homosexual* and its ban against using *gay*. Repeated pressure can indeed be effective.

Again, education is the goal. A media guide was published by GLAAD in 1990 that provided writers with the differences in meanings between various phrases. A clear distinction is made, for example, between "avowed homosexual" and "an openly gay man or lesbian." One strategy, thus, is to compile a list of phrases and words and submit the glossary to the local media with an offer to conduct a workshop explaining the reasons behind the language. When information about the expressions is presented along with the glossary, writers are much more likely to consider the changes as something more than "political correctness."

Calls and letters to writers and producers are useful strategies, since each one usually represents hundreds of others who have not communicated. For example, when Barbara Walters interviewed Martina Navratilova on *20/20*, the ABC newsmagazine show, in 1991, Walters asked her if she could ever see herself married and referred to a husband and children as a "normal" life. Letters were written to the producers and to Walters complaining that she would never think to ask a heterosexual woman if she wished she were lesbian and reminding her that "normal" is not limited to heterosexual families. While no overt homophobic slur was made, the remark is an excellent example of a heterosexist perspective and a more subtle form of stereotyping (in other words, that every lesbian or gay person really wishes to be "normal" and heterosexual). In other segments she did on gay issues later on, Walters generally avoided such heterosexisms.

Critiquing these depictions requires alternative and constructive ways to alleviate the heterosexism. When one sitcom writer remarked at a meeting with GLAAD representatives that he did not know how to communicate quickly to the audience that his character was gay except by using stereotypical signs (more effeminate voice or mannerisms), it was suggested that he review the ways he communicates how characters are heterosexual. By simply allowing people to refer to a same-sex partner, by placing a photo of same-sex couples on a desk, or by having the characters discuss participation in an important gay event, the message could be communicated without resorting to stereotyping or overt declarations. Providing people in the media with specific suggestions and topics is an essential strategy when working with them to correct inaccurate characterizations or situations.

Invisibility and Omission

In 1991 about one hundred Public Broadcasting Service (PBS) stations refused to carry Marlon Riggs's award-winning documentary on African American gay men, *Tongues Untied,* and in 1994 PBS announced it would not financially support a sequel to *Tales of the City,* one of its highest-rated shows of all time. The actions of PBS not only sent a clear message that gay topics are too controversial to schedule but also contributed to keeping lesbians and gays invisible, perhaps the single greatest problem in contemporary media.

Nonreporting of major gay events is a form of distortion that seriously affects lesbian and gay images in the news media. For example, the 1994 Gay Games in New York were ignored in almost all sports coverage, even though they are the largest amateur sporting events in the world. What little was done often appeared in nonsports TV news segments or lifestyle sections of newspapers. Overt cases of omission are matched by routine exclusion from the everyday discourse of entertainment television, movies, newspapers, and magazines. Unless they are an exotic topic on one of the talk shows, a focus of a movie of the week, or a special theme of a sitcom, gays and lesbians are rarely part of the ongoing depiction of everyday life usually portrayed in most movies and TV shows.

With the 1995–1996 television season, there were few continuing gay or lesbian characters on American prime-time TV shows. *Roseanne* and *My So-Called Life* from ABC-TV and *Melrose Place* from Fox-TV were once the only shows with regular lesbian or gay characters. But their characters have been mostly homogenized; in fact, in a show filled with all sorts of sexual escapades, *Melrose Place's* gay man has rarely been seen dating and his kiss with another man was edited from the final version. While appearances of gay characters have occurred on many shows, they have either appeared once or irregularly, thereby emphasizing their invisibility throughout the rest of the series' shows. And, along the way, they have been depoliticized, desexualized, and made nonthreatening to the status quo (Moritz 1994).

As Gitlin (1985) illustrates, however, the production of certain kinds of images is rarely a result of some conscious planned conspiracy; rather, it is a function of corporate bureaucracy and multiple hands involved in a development process that pursues safety and novelty without risk for the benefit of advertisers and economic profit. But, as Gross (1991:21) reminds us, "non-representation maintains the powerless status of groups that do not possess significant material or political power bases." Those in power rarely require media visibility, while those at the bottom are "symbolically annihilated" through relative invisibility and kept distant from the ordinary lives of the majority of viewers.

Strategies   Monitoring invisibility is as elusive as tracking a ghost; it is much easier to deal with what is there than what is not. Thus, organizing to combat omission requires working with those who directly produce and write the material and educating them to see the world from a perspective often outside their own.

One way is to communicate through calls and letters about what was left out. It is very useful to know the names of the people who are in charge rather than to communicate with some anonymous person. But to write a major film studio executive, for example, and suggest that the company make an action film like *Speed* with a lesbian hero may not get very far. Since profits govern decisions, you need to point out other financially successful examples in which gay or lesbian characters were central to the story, such as *The Birdcage, Philadelphia, The Crying Game, Go Fish,* and *Four Weddings and a Funeral.* In fact, gay-themed *The Wedding Banquet* was the most profitable (cost to ticket sales ratio) film of 1993, proportionately outranking *Jurassic Park.*

Television and film are commercial industries and they are not about to jeopardize millions of dollars by doing something too risky. A lead gay or lesbian character is still considered too innovative and fraught with potential political and economic danger. Thus, suggestions to include a lesbian or gay character in secondary and supporting roles are much more likely to be heeded. As Moritz (1994:141) concludes:

> While it may be argued that these scripts are by design relatively
> unconcerned with gay rights and more concerned with ratings, it is
> also true that once-taboo subjects in both cinema and television
> have gained acceptance only gradually. This may not be the first
> choice of feminists and lesbians, but it is a first step in working
> toward at least a small measure of social change.

Thus, it may be an important strategy to work with the media in small but significant steps. Encouraging them to include a gay or lesbian character in any capacity, even as a one-shot event in a secondary role, is still a good start. And it does not hurt to suggest plot lines and ways of doing so. Working with them later on to expand the characters and story lines becomes less difficult.

Accurate and Balanced Portrayals

While invisibility continues to characterize media images, there has been a relative increase in the media representation of gays and lesbians in recent years and a trend toward more accurate and fair images. Some of this is due to an increase in the production of media by gays and lesbians themselves, such as the lesbian and gay film festivals regularly held in many major cities, gay newspapers and magazines that increasingly attract mainstream advertisers, and gay public access television. But nongay media are also increasingly devoting more attention to gay images, especially in light of major social, legal, and political issues that have focused on gays and lesbians.

One of the best examples is ABC-TV's *Roseanne,* which features a lesbian character played by Sandra Bernhart and Martin Mull in the role of Roseanne's gay boss. Their sexual orientation is an integrated aspect of their portrayals, without problematizing. Furthermore, they are depicted as people who have a network of friends and family.

With the exception of Tom Hanks in *Philadelphia* and Whoopi Goldberg in *Boys on the Side* there has not been any major studio feature film with "positive" gay or lesbian characters in lead roles in the past decade. A gay character did appear in *Frankie and Johnny* and another in *The Prince of Tides.* They both were kindly, good supportive neighbors of the lead female character, not too dissimilar to the traditional depictions of the effeminate best friend in the 1930s movies, only more openly acknowledging and stating they were gay. However, many independent films have had gay characters in central roles, in particular *My Beautiful Laundrette, Maurice, My Own Private Idaho, The Adventures of Priscilla, Queen of the Desert, The Sum of Us,* and *Strawberry and Chocolate.*

British television has produced several important gay-themed films, ironically based on American novels, including *Tales of the City, And the Band Played On,* and *The Lost Language of Cranes.* However, in each of these cases a director or writer has been openly gay, lending support to the importance of having open lesbian and gay people in positions of power to produce and regulate images. And while they have been more accurate and balanced in their portrayals, with few exceptions, the representations from Britain continue to emphasize white middle-class men.

Strategies   Essential to changing negative media images is acknowledging when positive ones occur. Too often the media hear only when people complain. Thus, PBS refused to support the production of the *Tales of the City* sequel, perhaps as a result of a barrage of calls from the radical right protesting the original show. Those who supported the miniseries were less likely to call to praise. Hence it is a very important strategy to let the media know when something is good.

However, when writing or calling the media to thank them for a fair appearance of a gay or lesbian character or theme, it is essential to signal that token presentations are insufficient. It is best to acknowledge the depiction and then quickly add an encouragement to do more of the same or to expand the way lesbian and gay characters are portrayed. Providing concrete ideas and situations adds strength to an otherwise dull thank-you letter. Be careful of appearing to accept small crumbs of visible and sanitized gay and lesbian characters.

Since the emergence of more accurate images can be traced in part to more openness among lesbian and gay media people, an indirect method of achieving less heterosexism and homophobia is to work with the media in developing internal policies that make gays and lesbians more likely to be open at work. One example of this is Hollywood Supports, an entertainment industry–founded organization in Los Angeles devoted to countering workplace fears and discrimination based on sexual orientation and HIV status. Through workshops, seminars, employee benefits counseling, and technical advice, this organization has been effective in creating climates supportive of gays and lesbians in the entertainment media. As a result of their work, in 1992, MCA/Universal became the first studio to create benefits for domestic partners.

Many other studios and media organizations now have such benefits, nondiscrimination statements that include sexual orientation, and gay/lesbian employee support groups. In so doing, gay writers, producers, directors, and script readers are much more likely to be open and to speak up when dealing with antigay images. One gay writer told the story about how—when he was closeted because of an antigay climate on the set of a TV sitcom—he was less likely to speak out against inaccurate stereotypes. But when he got a job working on the *Roseanne* show, where the mood was much more supportive, he felt comfortable being open about his sexual orientation and was able to provide important information and advice when the show dealt with gay issues and characters.

So, in addition to praising and encouraging the writers and producers directly about positive depictions of gays and lesbians, it also becomes salient to develop strategies for assisting media in creating a workplace climate that allows gay and lesbian employees to be visibly present and open with their comments and creative skills.

ORGANIZING RESPONSES

While individuals can have a big effect on the media through letters and calls, it often helps to have the clout and legitimacy of larger organizations and media. Several strategies that have been very successful in combating homophobia and heterosexism include the development of media watchdog organizations and the creation of media by and for lesbian and gay people.

In 1973 the Gay Activist Alliance (GAA) in New York was one of the first organizations to take on the media when it confronted executives at ABC-TV about unfavorable treatment of homosexuality (Montgomery, 1989). A group of GAA members later split to form the National Gay Task Force (NGTF), which then formed a Gay Media Task Force (GMTF) in Los Angeles, under the direction of Newt Deiter. The Association of Gay and Lesbian Artists

(AGLA) also started in the early 1980s as a support group of gay media people to lobby the industry, consult on projects, and present awards for positive depictions of gays and lesbians.

Although GMTF and AGLA no longer exist, their efforts led to the formation of the Gay and Lesbian Alliance Against Defamation (GLAAD), begun in New York in 1985, then in 1988 in Los Angeles. Today GLAAD is the largest and most influential national organization, with chapters around the country devoted to monitoring the media's portrayals of gays and lesbians, responding with organized letter-writing actions and protest marches, and consulting with executives and creative staff.

In addition to organizations structured to resist and change stereotypical images, another form of response has been the creation of lesbian and gay media. From cable TV public access shows to computer E-mail, the Internet, newspapers, and slick magazines, gays have developed an impressive communications network.

With the beginning of the modern homophile movement in the early 1950s in Los Angeles, *ONE* became the first widely circulated homosexual magazine, selling two thousand copies a month (D'Emilio 1983), although earlier attempts included a 1924 Chicago newsletter called *Friendship and Freedom,* the 1934 newsletter *Chanticleer,* and *Vice Versa,* a 1947 Los Angeles lesbian magazine (Kepner 1994). Along with the *Ladder,* published by the Daughters of Bilitis from 1956 to 1970, and the *Mattachine Review,* published from 1955 to 1964, these early and important magazines invented a new form of discourse and helped create "an incipient sense of community" (D'Emilio 1983:110). The tradition carries on with such widely circulated national magazines as the *Advocate* (the longest continuously published gay magazine, since 1967) and many local lesbian and gay newspapers.

With the growing power of openly gay and lesbian filmmakers, television and newspaper reporters, and writers, a "most effective form of resistance to the hegemonic force of the dominant media" is occurring, namely "to speak for oneself" (Gross 1991:40). However, there is no lesbian or gay equivalent to the Christian cable networks or the numerous syndicated conservative religious radio and television shows that mobilize thousands of followers to write or call politicians instantly.

For gays and lesbians, access remains limited, especially in the powerful electronic national media. As Russo (1987:323) so forcefully said about homophobia in the movies (but as applicable to television, radio, print, and other media): "This will change only when it becomes financially profitable, and reality will never be profitable until society overcomes its fears and hatred of difference and begins to see that we're all in this together."

NOTE

Comments by Ken Plummer and Beth Schneider on earlier drafts helped shape my arguments. Thanks to them and to the people at GLAAD/Los Angeles who provided me with the opportunity to work with the media in changing gay and lesbian images.

REFERENCES

D'Emilio, J. 1983: *Sexual Politics, Sexual Communities,* Chicago: University of Chicago Press.

Fiske, J. 1987. *Television Culture.* New York: Routledge.

Gay and Lesbian Alliance Against Defamation (GLAAD). 1990. *Media guide to the Lesbian and Gay Community.* New York: GLAAD.

Gitlin, T. 1985. *Inside Prime Time.* New York: Pantheon.

Gross, L. 1984. "The Cultivation of Intolerance." In G. Melischek, K. Rosengren, and J. Stappers, eds., *Cultural Indicators: An International Symposium,* pp. 345–64. Vienna: Austrian Academy of Sciences.

——— 1991. "Out of the Mainstream: Sexual Minorities and the Mass Media." In M. Wolf and A. Kielwasser, eds., *Gay People, Sex, and the Media,* pp. 19–46. New York: Harrington Park.

——— 1994. "What Is Wrong with This Picture? Lesbian Women and Gay Men on Television." In R. J. Ringer, eds., *Queer Words, Queer Images,* pp. 143–56. New York: New York University Press.

Hantzis, D., and V. Lehr. 1994. "Whose Desire? Lesbian (Non)Sexuality and Television's Perpetuation of Hetero/Sexism." In R. J. Ringer, ed., *Queer Words, Queer Images,* pp. 107–21. New York: New York University Press.

Kepner, J. 1994. "Our Movement Before Stonewall." Los Angeles: International Gay and Lesbian Archives.

Montgomery, K. 1989. *Target: Prime Time.* New York: Oxford University Press.

Moritz, M. 1994. "Old Strategies for New Texts: How American Television Is Creating and Treating Lesbian Characters." In R. J. Ringer, ed., *Queer Words, Queer Images,* pp. 122–42. New York: New York University Press.

Nardi, P. M. 1990. "AIDS and Obituaries: The Perpetuation of Stigma in the Press." In D. Feldman, ed., *Culture and AIDS,* pp. 159–68. New York: Praeger.

——— 1992. "That's What Friends Are For: Friends as Family in the Gay and Lesbian Community." In Ken Plummer, ed., *Modern Homosexualities: Fragments of Lesbian and Gay Experience,* pp. 108–20. London: Routledge.

Parenti, M. 1986. *Inventing Reality: The Politics of the Mass Media.* New York: St. Martin's.

Russo, V. 1987. *The Celluloid Closet: Homosexuality in the Movies.* Rev. ed. New York: Harper and Row.

Wiley, M., and D. Bona. 1993. *Inside Oscar: The Unofficial History of the Academy Awards.* New York: Ballantine.

36

THE "F" WORD:
HOW THE MEDIA FRAME FEMINISM

DEBRA BAKER BECK

INTRODUCTION

How did feminism become a national "dirty word"?

For individuals within the American women's movement, this is a troubling question to ponder. The movement's struggles to survive can be traced to several factors, including its own inability at times to deal effectively with the diversity of viewpoints and experiences of American women. However, a strong argument also can be made that the mass media's distaste for active, assertive women—and the way the media portray them—has turned all "feminists" into a frightening fringe element. This article will examine how the mass media frame femininity and how that act of framing affects their portrayal (and the public's perception) of feminism. It will explore the media backlash that occurs when women as a group make significant strides toward independence and equality. Finally, it will discuss how the movement has attempted to deal with the backlash and how alternative media have emerged as a feminist response.

DEFINING FEMININITY IN THE MEDIA

It is useful to begin this discussion with a look at how the mass media shape society's definitions of gender and the appropriate roles of women. John Fiske's work deals primarily with television, but most of the concepts can be carried over to other mass media forms. The media, Fiske (1987) says, use meaning-laden codes that define "reality." A code is a "system of signs, whose rules and conventions are shared amongst members of a culture, and which is used to generate and circulate meanings in and for that culture" (p. 4). Reality is never a universal concept. "What passes for reality in any culture is the product of that culture's codes," Fiske says, "so 'reality' is always already encoded, it is never 'raw' " (p. 5). Even a concept as basic as "woman" is riddled with cultural codes conveyed and interpreted in the various media

NWSA Journal, 3/31/1998 V. 10; N. 1 p. 139.

texts we encounter on a daily basis. There is no objective "feminine," Fiske would argue, only a culturally defined concept created and perpetuated in part by media texts.

REJECTING THE LABEL, NOT THE CAUSE

While most American women support the basic concepts of feminism, they tend to shy from the feminist label. For instance, in a 1989 study, only 33% of women surveyed indicated that they considered themselves to be feminists despite overwhelming support for the issues the movement addresses and the widely held perception that it has helped the status of women overall (Wallis, 1989).

"I'm not a feminist, but . . ." is a common refrain among women who reject the label. The "but" is usually followed by expressions of support/concern for the issues championed by the movement, such as equal pay (94%), day care (90%), job discrimination (82%) and abortion rights (74%) (Wallis, 1989, p. 82).

It is not difficult to see how anyone who indicates she/he wants to change the world, even by an activity as simple as accepting a feminist label, becomes a threat. And not many people want to be known as a threat to everything American.

A primary obstacle for anyone who advocates a position even slightly outside of the norm is that the media world—and Western thought in general—emphasize opposition and dichotomies. Cirksena and Cuklanz (1992) write that "the central organizing principle for much of western thought is the nature of a set of oppositional dualisms" (p. 20). They continue, "Dualisms—either/or, you/me, good/bad, high/low—are so deeply embedded in Western knowledge structures that they often seem like natural categories" (p. 37).

The mass media play on these dichotomies as they perpetuate Western codes. When the world is viewed as a series of dualisms, those who do not fit the "good" qualifications (generally, male/white/middle class/Christian) automatically are cast as "bad." There are no shades of gray in this black-and-white world. For feminists, being cast as outsiders, troublemakers, even evil women, is inevitable since they challenge the very basis of a patriarchal society.

Indeed, the media operate within the bounds of what Marilyn Crafton Smith (1993) calls a "field of allowable images" that limit how outside viewpoints such as feminism are presented—if they are presented at all (p. 76). She describes the "field of allowable images" as

> a core of traditional images and those newly incorporated or on
> their way to incorporation. The process of incorporation is one of
> dilution, whereby images of feminist struggle that are taken in by
> the mass media are made to conform to dominant values and repre-
> sentation. . . . Images on their way to incorporation do not come out

of thin air, but rather arise within the field of the unallowable, those marginalized representations that are directly suppressed, either economically (through limited exhibition, production and distribution) or by the state. Thus, although the mass media may provide a location for feminist issues to be raised for larger audiences, the degree to which the issues and their representations in the mass media conform to the feminist struggle distinguishes them from their oppositional treatment in feminist media (p. 76).

A major strike against feminism's attempt to get a fair shake in media portrayals is the media's attraction to opposition, particularly between men and women (Creedon, 1993a, p. 72). The dualism of masculine/feminine "continues to be most successful in programming us to believe that male is the opposite of female," according to Pamela J. Creedon (p. 72). From there, it is just a short conceptual jump to tagging feminism as "bad" when contrasted against the "good" masculine norm in this society.

Creedon notes, "journalists are taught to think in terms of dichotomies, to develop their stories of right versus wrong, good versus evil. The journalistic obsession with a narrow corridor in an abstract space called 'balance' continues to build this kind of false opposition" (p. 75).

A QUESTION OF OBJECTIVITY

Most journalists place great stock in their ability to maintain "objectivity." On the surface, that would seem to imply an inherent fairness in this approach to news coverage. After all, wouldn't an objective reporter simply convey some set of independent facts as they are without imposing meaning upon them? But Creedon (1993b) says the objectivity so revered by the news media is just a standpoint, one that cannot be separated from factors like gender (p. 77). "Objectivity is a normative ideal," according to Creedon (1993a). "In practice, objectivity is a standpoint—white and male" (p. 15).

Steiner (1992) agrees that since most media decision makers are male, the chance of their changing the dominant gendered standpoint to give women their due is somewhere between slim and none. Despite the fact that more women are entering the field of journalism, those who rule the newsroom are predominantly male (Creedon, 1993a, p. 4).

The reason that news philosophy has not changed despite greater diversity is that the process of gathering news has not changed over the years. Creedon (1993a) has several possible explanations for this. First, mass communication is still driven by the bottom line and supported by the advertising industry which has a lot at stake in maintaining the dominant cultural codes. Women's increased presence in the field has not been powerful enough to overcome the need to make a profit. Second, "the news definers still are predominantly white males, and these editors and owners control the hiring and firing decisions" (p. 13). Making waves could cost a woman her job. Third, "workplace routines and norms force reporters to conform to dominant values, rather than act on empowering values" (p. 13). Though there are more women in the newsroom, they generally are not in a position to influence any of these powerful factors in the mass media. The women's movement has had its media allies over the years, usually other women (Davis, 1991, p. 107). But until the number of women in media management positions increase significantly, no one will know whether they will bring with them their experiences as women (which tend to become more radical with age), and hence a new perspective on news judgment, or whether they will maintain the philosophy into which they were indoctrinated by their male predecessors.

COVERING THE "SISTERHOOD"

So how have the women's movement and the issues it addresses been portrayed in the media over the years? The message has been mixed (Douglas, 1994; Rapping, 1994), though many would say it has been primarily nonexistent or negative (D'Acci, 1994; Douglas, 1994; Gist, 1993; Jones, 1992; Steiner, 1992; Wolfe, 1993).

Most of the sources cited here believe that the contemporary women's movement, which began in the 1960s, was basically ignored by the mainstream media with the exception of a few high-profile incidents such as a protest of the 1968 Miss America pageant. The coverage that protest received must have been both encouraging and frustrating for early women's movement organizers. On the one hand, a feminist event received major news coverage for the first time. On the other hand, though, that coverage was distorted and sensationalized.

It was at this event that the media gave birth to the omnipresent "bra-burner" label for feminists. True, a few protest participants did throw some bras into a trash can. However, no lingerie was singed (Douglas, 1994, p. 139). This protest represented a relatively minor blip on the movement time line and received far more coverage than it really deserved, especially since feminists had been toiling in obscurity for years over such issues as jobs, pay equity, child care, and other far less inflammatory causes.

BATTLING STEREOTYPES

Bra-burners is only one of several less-than-kind labels attached to feminists in the media. Creedon (1993b) writes that "feminists are consistently framed as deviant sexually, a bunch of man-haters out to destroy 'family values.' In the media, the opposite of 'family' often is 'feminist'" (another dualism—feminists can't be "family-women") (p. 75). Other popular stereotypical descriptors of feminists include "bubbleheaded," "Amazons," "angries," "radical," and "hairy." The practice of labeling feminists as lesbians or "dykes" has been a particularly effective means of silencing supporters and scaring away others who share feminist views. This is particularly true of younger heterosexual women (Jones, 1999., p. 59).

Mass rejection of feminism by young women, largely in response to negative images that are at least perpetuated in the media, is a source of concern to many within the movement. After all, these young women are the next generation that must take up the cause if the women's movement is to continue to progress. Many reasons are cited for this generation's hesitancy: young women are turned off by the "man bashers" image of feminists (Jones, 1992, p. 59) and they fear political reprisals (Hogeland, 1994, p. 18). Insofar as they believe the revolution is largely won, young women don't see the struggle for women's rights as relevant to them (Kamen, 1991, p. 36). They believe feminists are "petty and confrontational" (Kamen, 1991, p. 36), that a woman can't be feminist and feminine at the same time (Kamen, 1991, p. 35), and that being a feminist means being anti-motherhood and a lesbian (Kamen, 1991, p. 35). This sampling of reasons young women give for rejecting the women's movement shows how deeply influenced they are by stereotypes commonly found in the mass media—none of them referring to feminism in general versus individuals within the movement.

GETTING SOME "PRESS"

When feminists aren't being portrayed as freaks of nature, these women (and men) and their issues are frequently ignored by the mass media. The effects of seeing their work ignored or distorted in the press can effectively stifle feminism's progress. Wolfe (1993) writes:

> Thought on women's issues goes stale, and the movement stalls.
> The culture's interpretation of history and its manufacture of
> debate, heroes, and prizes are in male hands. So the amount of
> media space that women are not getting bears a ratio to the amount
> of time and energy they must spend spinning their wheels to move
> forward. (pp. 91–92)

The effects can be devastating psychologically to women. Gist (1993) says that, "to the frequent extent that media neglect women, portray them as marginally powerful, or objectify them sexually, these signals become internalized by many women as low self-esteem or an obsession with physical attractiveness" (p. 111).

While most of the sources cited claim that the women's movement has been largely ignored or ridiculed by the mass media, at least one long-time observer of the women's movement has a somewhat different view. In her 1991 book, *Moving the Mountain: The Women's Movement in America Since 1960,* author Flora Davis says the mainstream media originally spotlighted the women's movement when they "discovered" it in 1969 (because the radical feminists were "good copy") (p. 106). Coverage ebbed and flowed over the years, depending upon whether the media were bored with the personalities and their antics. Davis notes, though, that during those publicity spurts reporters and producers routinely sought out the "nuts" to provide more controversy in their stories or programs.

Davis credits the media with actually expanding the women's movement by publicizing its issues, heroines and activities; bringing women to consciousness raising groups; engaging discussions about feminism and women's roles in the world; and organizing women at rallies and demonstrations. She aptly notes that, "social movements need press coverage. That's how they get their message out to the general public" (p. 106). As annoying as the mass media might be, today's feminists would not have a movement without them.

CATFIGHTS

Besides highlighting the extremists, the media typically portray the diversity of women's views and philosophical disagreements between feminists as nothing more than trivial "catfights." According to Douglas (1994).

> The catfight is a staple of American pop culture, and by the 1970s it had evolved into various forms of especially sloppy faux combat between women, like female mud wrestling or Jell-O wrestling. In its purest form, it features two women, one usually a traditional wife (blond), the other a grasping, craven careerist (brunette), who slug it out on a veranda, in a lily pond, or during a mud slide. . . . A metaphor for the struggle between feminism and antifeminism, the catfight provided a symbolic catharsis of women's internal conflict between the desire for liberation and the longing for security. . . . Both women were sullied; no one won. (pp. 221–223)

The catfight could be found in news reports as well as in prime time programming. On the nightly news, we saw Gloria (Steinem) "duke it out" with Phyllis (Schlafly) over the equal rights amendment. We also saw Steinem and other new-wave feminists "wrestle control" of the movement from veterans like Betty Friedan. Today, we see "new" feminists arguing the merits of "power" versus "victim" feminism with their older counterparts. Unanimity among the women's movement has never been possible, given the many different typologies that can be found within feminism (Cirksena & Cuklanz, 1992). Since there are different facets of feminism, disagreements among women are inevitable within the feminist movement. Casting such disagreements as catfights minimizes serious discussion of feminist concerns while also supporting the dualistic bias of media portrayals that has always highlighted conflict. Since women are involved, their disagreements are trivialized as catfights rather than serious philosophical disagreements worthy of further development. Besides the entertainment value of watching women battle each other, the mass media—and society at large—have a lot to gain from this type of portrayal. Dividing women and portraying them as "silly" maintains the status quo that portrays the dominant codes (male) as reasonable and right and the alternative (women fighting for equal rights—or worse) as insignificant.

FEMINISTS IN THE ENTERTAINMENT MEDIA

As women fought for, and attained, greater status within society the entertainment sector's response to feminism has also been rather mixed. In the 1960s, as Betty Friedan's book *The Feminine Mystique* fueled growing dissatisfaction among American adult women, television combined old and new stereotypes of women into some strange hybrids. Examples of this phenomenon were the emergence of such magical characters as Morticia Addams ("The Addams Family"), Jeannie ("I Dream of Jeannie"), Samantha Stevens ("Bewitched") and Sister Bertrille ("The Flying Nun"). Douglas interprets this strange 60s fad as "more than just the ultimate in kitsch or the triumph of special effects" (p. 126). She sees a more interesting trend:

> If we put these TV shows and the impulses behind them on the shrink's couch for a minute, we see that a significant portion of the pop culture moguls were trying to acknowledge the impending release of female sexual and political energy, while keeping it all safely in a straightjacket. Sure, it would be great if women, especially young women, were more sexually liberated. But prefeminist rumblings about economic and political liberation were another matter. You could almost see these guys holding their nuts for dear life. Sensing they were playing with fire, they tried to contain it technologically, through images of levitation, twitching noses and poufs of fake smoke (p. 126).

Though the portrayals of feminist characters and themes were still mixed and far from friendly, the 1970s entertainment media at least made an attempt to deal with their issues. During this period, strong female characters such as Mary Richards ("The Mary Tyler Moore Show") and Maude ("Maude") emerged. Even shows like "All in the Family" and "Green Acres" dealt with feminist subjects from time to time.

Mary Tyler Moore's character was an entertainment heroine for her time and an interesting study, according to Douglas (1994) True, she smiled too much in the beginning and was far more deferential to her boss than her male coworkers were. But Mary Richards was a television rarity—a successful, single career woman who didn't consume herself with finding a man. Early in the series, "The Mary Tyler Moore Show" offered good examples of healthy women's relationships, something that also wasn't so common. Mary regularly interacted with friends Rhoda and Phyllis and they discussed all types of women's issues.

D'Acci (1994) also detects a backlash in the 1970s and early 1980s, which she terms "the jiggle era." Shows such as "Charlie's Angels," "Wonder Woman" and "Three's Company" all fit into her "jiggle" category:

> Each of these programs could be squarely classified under the "jiggle" category, and each promoted sensationalism by providing raw material for setting up the classic "woman in distress" situation. The women protagonists ultimately were either rescued by male colleagues or used superhuman capabilities to resolve their predicaments (p. 15).

D'Acci adds that, "It is, of course, no accident that these representations coincided with the ever-mounting backlash over the concerns and demands of the women's movement" (p. 15).

She notes that the women's movement (and the networks' drive to appeal to young, educated city dwellers) resulted in an expanded representation of women on television. Many programs in the 1970s featured older women, African-American women, divorced women, single mothers and working-class women (p. 14). They covered controversial issues such as rape, equal employment opportunities, abortion and racial and sexual discrimination. However, D'Acci says, "these programs often produced contradictory and troubling representations of femininity and 'independent' women, and most of the social issues raised were domesticated—that is, they were represented as contained and resolvable at the level of the family" (p. 14).

D'Acci's (1994) book, *Defining Women: Television and the Case of "Cagney & Lacey,"* focused on a series that was an exception to the backlash of the early 1980s and challenged the dominant media codes. Cagney & Lacey provided a regular forum for openly feminist discourse, especially that championed by the liberal feminist movement. It portrayed women in a nontraditional career who succeeded despite resistance from male coworkers and other skeptics. It also depicted two nonglamorous women in a strong friendship, both rare in the media world. "Real" women related well to Christine Cagney and Mary Beth Lacey, who were cast outside of the typical sex object roles and portrayed as active participants in the world around them (pp. 177–178).

But several concessions made along the way turned what started out as a straight cop-show into a hybrid genre with far more feminine components and made it more mainstream. For example, both characters were softened because executives felt they were too harsh (and perceived as "dykes"). The series text evolved into a feminine hybrid, with increasing time devoted to characters discussing their personal and professional problems (p. 105). As the series progressed over the years, the protagonists spent less time catching crooks and more time discussing Mary Beth's children and Christine's relationship problems. This parallels Fiske's (1987) definition of a feminine genre, which includes emphasis on dialogue and problem solving not generally found in masculine genres (p. 179). Given television's history of dealing with women characters and given the conservative tenor of the times (1981–88), the survival of the Cagney & Lacey series amidst strong criticism by anti-feminists and media critics is nothing short of miraculous.

Television in the 1990s provides a wider variety of messages and characterizations, more of them bearing a sense of real life. But Hollywood and real life can seldom be used in the same sentence without bringing a chuckle or two. At least we can occasionally see a glimpse of ourselves in current characters. Today, with the flip of a remote, we can find two-parent households ("Home Improvement"), single-parent households (e.g., "Grace Under Fire"), divorced women ("Cybill"), working class families ("Roseanne") and blended families ("Something So Right"). We also are able to identify television families with strong moms who know better than to simply defer to dad (assuming he's around)—especially since mom usually knows best (e.g., "Home Improvement," "Roseanne," "Grace Under Fire," "Family Matters"). On the career front, most television women seem to have a life outside of the household, in jobs ranging from nurses, teachers, and magazine writers to lawyers and crime fighters.

We also see more single women than in the past. While Mary Richards was somewhat of a novelty in her time, today Ellen of "Ellen" can find company with Susan of "Suddenly Susan," Nora of "Naked Truth," and virtually every female working at "ER" and "Chicago Hope." For the most part, like Mary Richards, these women seem to function well enough whether or not there is a man (or woman) in their lives. They may not be totally satisfied with their single status and they have other problems that create story lines, but generally, each individual character manages to get by (some more successfully than others) in their personal and professional lives. In some respect, that can be considered progress—women don't have to spend every waking hour worrying about catching a man.

In the author's view, one of the most important television phenomena in the last 10 years was the sitcom "Designing Women." While not the ultimate feminist mouthpiece, the four original characters were sassy, independent, highly heterosexual, and attractive (simultaneously dispelling many myths about women with strong opinions). Perhaps the best characterization of this was Julia, who, in the smoothest Southern Belle accent, regularly sliced and diced bigots, chauvinists, and other offenders while maintaining a certain feminine dignity. Butler (1993) described the dialog between these characters as "subversion"; they frequently breached the bounds of good taste and politeness as they talked about such taboo topics as sexual harassment, premenstrual syndrome, menopause, single parenting, religion, and women's sexuality (p. 18).

These characterizations were not without their stereotypes: Charlene, the innocent from the backwoods of Missouri, was portrayed as a lovable bumpkin; Suzanne, whose weight fluctuated throughout her tenure on the show, was routinely dismissed as frivolous, loud, and clownish; and even Julia drew rolled eyes when she launched yet another oratory about whatever was wrong with the world.

Today, the hour-long "ER" offers some reasonably interesting character-izations of women. Set in the emergency room of a large public hospital, we find female nurses, doctors, physician assistants, and even an administrator. Focus primarily is on their workplace interactions and professional dilem-mas with which audiences should be able to identify. More time is spent dis-secting the love lives of their male counterparts (particularly those of physicians Mark Green and Doug Ross) than the personal lives of the female characters. One exception is Jeannie, the physician assistant who contracted HIV from her ex-husband. While audiences saw more of her interacting with her coworkers in previous seasons, most of her air time in the 1996–97 series focused on her personal problems and her adjustments to having HIV.

Another exception was resident Susan Lewis, who spent several episodes adapting to single parenthood when her sister left her baby for Su-san to rear. Audiences saw Susan scrambling for child care, trying to balance an erratic work schedule with responsibility for "little Susie." They debated with her when she was offered a challenging position that would require fur-ther demands on her time. Then they agonized with her when her sister, Chloe, re-emerged to claim the child, assuring Susan that she had straight-ened her life out and could now be a good parent. Susan mourned the loss deeply, then eventually gave in to her maternal instincts—which she didn't know she had until left with a baby to care for—and moved to Arizona to be nearer to the baby. (In real life, the actress, Sherry Stringfield, reportedly left the show to be closer to her boyfriend.)

Another interesting portrayal of a female "ER" character is Kerry Weaver, who holds an administrative position within the emergency unit. We know nearly nothing about her personal life, but we do know that she is bossy, cold, tough, and mostly unlikable (very much like the stereotypes we all know of women who dare to rise in a male profession). Still, unlike its CBS rival "Chicago Hope," "ER" offers opportunities for complex female characters and even provides some colorful support roles for women.

No television character is perfect: they wouldn't be "human" (or inter-esting entertainment) if they didn't have a flaw or two. And there are plenty of stereotypes women would rather leave behind. But the author believes there are signs that the television industry is starting to get the message that we're not all homebodies, castrating bitches, or bimbos.

ONLY ONE STANDPOINT

Feminist scholars would argue that the dominant ideological codes represent merely one position that can be countered by alternative standpoint episte-mologies or theories. A "standpoint theory," according to Creedon (1993a),

> uses marginalized lives as the starting point from which to frame
> research questions and concepts, develop designs, define what counts
> as data, and interpret findings . . . standpoint epistemology seeks to
> understand the distinctive features of women's experience as they
> take place in a gender-stratified culture and as they are interpreted by
> women. . . . Standpoint theory argues that individuals interpret their
> own experiences and imbue them with meaning. . . . (pp. 12–13)

Obviously, the idea that the dominant ideological codes are not reality but only one interpretation by one social group is the source of significant conflict between feminists and those who oppose them—including the decision makers in the mass media, who play a significant role in perpetuating the ideological codes. It is especially controversial in its claim that experiences of other groups, such as women or native Americans, are just as valid as the white male viewpoint. But it is the primary point from which feminist criticism of the mass media evolves. The field of communication in general must deal with the concept of gender, according to Cirksena & Cuklanz (1992). They say, "Scholars in this [communication] area have focused on the gendered nature of our language system and the damage done to our understanding of the female through this system" (p. 36). They criticize the methodology of communication studies in general, adding that, "social scientific knowledge until recently was based on limited and distorted information, was tied to norms based on men's experiences of the world, and most significantly, any consideration of the unique aspects of women's experiences was notably absent" (p. 38).

One of the challenges both the women's movement and the media continue to face is that there really is no one "women's voice" or "women's experience" (Wood, 1992). Neither is there one feminism, but several approaches that can diverge greatly on defining the movement's goals and the means of achieving them. Both the women's movement and the mass media err if they try to synthesize "woman," "feminism" or "femininity" into one homogenous mold.

The mass media are far more guilty of this practice. Until the start of the latest wave of feminism, there was no widespread challenge of ideological codes. Women and men simply accepted the dominant codes of gender and family as reality. As women began asserting their power in the 1960s, the question of standpoint began to emerge and challenge ideas about gender relationships at home and at work. Though progress certainly has been made since the 1950s, when gender roles were clearly defined, the move toward equal media representation of women in general and feminism specifically has fallen far short of feminists' goals.

Davis (1991) says the mass media have played an important role in the dilution of feminist ideas, though other factors came into play:

> Though the media were clearly implicated in the eclipse of radical
> feminism, other factors were involved as well. Virtually all social
> movements go through a fairly predictable process of growth and

institutionalization, and in the process some radical ideas are adopted and watered down, and radical voices are apt to be silenced. . . . Throughout the 70s and 80s, the media continued to be a mixed blessing for feminists. On one hand, they educated the American public about a multitude of issues, from wife-beating to the gender gap. On the other hand, they failed to cover much of what happened in the movement and often distorted much of what they did cover. . . . Conflict was news, people with famous names were often news, but ongoing struggles with stubborn problems— and gradual progress—were not. (p. 120)

CREATING AN ALTERNATIVE

Frustrated by continued resistance of the mainstream media to address women's diversity and feminist issues, the women's movement has spawned several alternative media. According to Steiner (1992),

"Massified" media institutions have historically been hostile to women's attempts to negotiate for themselves alternative visions, definitions, ways of being. At worse, mass media ignore, trivialize, or belittle the philosophies and activities of successive waves of the women's movement; at best they dilute or coopt the major concepts. . . . Understanding even before A. J. Leibling said it that "there's freedom of the press for the guy who owns one," women have published books, magazines, newspapers, journals, pamphlets, and newsletters—of various sizes, frequencies, and duration, and with different purposes, audiences, organizations and financing structures. (p. 121)

Not only are the texts found in these alternative media different than in the mainstream, but the structure under which they are produced also differs significantly (Steiner, 1992, pp. 124–126). First, women are involved in all levels of production of these media, including decision making; and they are encouraged to learn other parts of the process. If men are allowed to participate, it is on a limited basis. These publications frequently translate one's experience with grassroots organizing and underground media in the production process. Many of these early publishing groups were collectively owned and operated (Smith, 1993, pp. 63–65). Professional experience or formal training in mass media are not necessary to achieve alternative media's primary goal of "authentic communication" (Steiner, 1992, pp. 124–126). Consequently, publication quality may be rough and amateurish and difficult to market on a wide basis. But that hasn't been a primary concern.

"Feminist communication requires that women not only gain access to the communication tools, but that they actively participate in the communication process," Smith says (1993, p. 66). "A primary role of feminist periodicals has been the establishment of a space where members of the editorial collective and readers are able to exchange views." Hence, another defining characteristic of the alternative feminist media is that readers are encouraged to "speak for themselves" (Smith, p. 66).

Profit is not a primary motivator for most of the alternative media. Naturally, these publications must generate enough revenue to keep the presses running (a problem for many). However, increased revenue beyond that point is not a driving goal. If these publications accept advertising, editorial policy usually limits what is defined as acceptable in terms of type of advertiser and format of the ad itself (Steiner, 1992, p. 125). *Ms.* magazine took a bold step in this area in 1990 when it abandoned the popular magazine format and opted for an ad-free publication (Morgan, 1990, p. 1). It should be noted that *Ms.* is the only major feminist publication to maintain mainstream circulation over the years despite many difficult periods. However, other publications, such as *Working Woman* magazine, do incorporate a generally feminist theme while also reaching a mass audience.

CONCLUSION

Will the women's movement ever see coverage its leaders consider to be a fair portrayal in the mass media? Will the entertainment sector ever provide a view of Americana that more closely resembles how real-life women and their families live and work together? Do feminists even want to be part of the mainstream? These are important questions for both feminists and the mass media to consider in the 1990s, though it is doubtful that one could get them to agree on the answers.

Certainly, it is not unreasonable to expect the mass media—particularly the news sector—to present women's issues in a fair light, without marginalizing them. Women's issues are important to women, their families, their employers and society in general. The media play a major role in framing public opinion and debate. Treating women and their concerns seriously in the media would go a long way to getting society to take them seriously.

Nor is it unreasonable to expect the entertainment media to present a wider range of programming that portrays the diversity of women in this country. Women come from all walks of life and have a wide range of experiences and goals. Women characters should be presented as actors, not just objects of action; and they should be presented in all shapes, sizes, colors, ages and roles—just as women are in real life. While progress has been made since the "Father Knows Best" days of entertainment, women characters still resemble too narrow a range of focus of what is "acceptable" according to cultural codes. There are signs of progress, but women still have some room for growth as capable, multi-dimensional characters.

Whether that range will broaden any time soon is up for debate. The dominant ideological codes that define what is "normal" and "right" still cling too tightly to the white/male/middle-class bias to blithely allow across-the-board shifts in philosophy and programming.

One question begs to be answered: If adult women are the primary consumers of prime time network television, why does programming continue to emphasize masculine genres and outdated stereotypes of women and families? Why don't women's issues receive more widespread, serious portrayal in plots? "Cagney & Lacey" and "Designing Women" offered proof that audiences will stay tuned to quality programming, in both drama and comedy that features realistic women protagonists (even feminist ones) dealing with "women's issues."

Finally, the greatest hope for creating a more "female friendly" media is to put more women in decision making positions. As noted earlier, we don't know whether women who rise to leadership positions in the media will rule more by their experience as women or by the rules they learned as cub reporters and rookie script writers. But if Paula Kamen (1991) is correct in assuming that women become more radical with age as they run up against various kinds of discrimination (pp. 111–112), one would hope that they would create a media atmosphere that welcomes greater diversity of viewpoints and characterizations—including feminism.

REFERENCES

Butler, Jeremy (1993). Redesigning discourse: Feminism, the sitcom, and "Designing Women." *Journal of Film and Video* 45 (1), 13–26.

Cirksena, Kathryn, and Cuklanz, Lisa (1992). Male is to female as——is to——: A guided tour of five feminist frameworks for communication studies. In Lana F. Rakow (Ed.), *Women making meaning: New feminist directions in communication* (pp. 18–44). New York: Routledge, Chapman and Hall, Inc.

Creedon, Pamela J. (1993a). The challenge of re-visioning gender values. In Pamela J. Creedon (Ed.), *Women in Mass Communication* (pp. 3–23). Newbury Park, CA: Sage Publications.

Creedon, Pamela J. (1993b). Framing feminism—A feminist primer for the mass media. *Media Studies Journal* 7 (1/2), 69–80.

D'Acci, Julie (1994). *Defining women: Television and the case of Cagney & Lacey.* Chapel Hill, NC: The University of North Carolina Press.

Davis, Flora (1991). *Moving the mountain: The women's movement in America since 1960.* New York: Simon & Schuster.

Douglas, Susan J. (1994). *Where the girls are: Growing up female with the mass media.* New York: Random House.

Fiske, John (1987). *Television culture.* New York: Routledge.

Gibbs, Nancy, and McDowell, Jeanne (1992, March 9). How to revive a revolution. *Time* magazine, 56–57.

Gist, Marilyn (1993). Through the looking glass: Diversity and reflected appraisals of the self in mass media. In Pamela J. Creedon (Ed.), *Women in mass communication* (pp. 104–117). Newbury Park, CA: Sage Publications.

Hogeland, Lisa Marie (1994, November/December). Fear of feminism: Why young women get the willies. *Ms. Magazine* 18–21.

Jones, Ann (1992, January/February). Backlash and beyond. *Ms. Magazine,* 58–60. Kamen, Paula (1991). *Feminist fatale: Voices from the "twentysomething" generation explore the future of the "women's movement."* New York: Donald I. Fine, Inc.

Morgan, Robin (1990, July/August). Ms. Lives! *Ms. Magazine*, 1–2.

Rapping, Elayne (1994). *Media-tions: Forays into the culture and gender wars*. Boston: South End Press.

Smith, Marilyn Crafton (1993). Feminist media and cultural politics. In Pamela J. Creedon (Ed.), *Women in mass communication* (pp. 61–83). Newbury Park, CA: Sage Publications.

Steiner, Linda (1992). The history and structure of women's alternative media. In Lana F. Rakow (Ed.), *Women making meaning: New feminist directions in communication* (pp. 121–143). New York: Routledge, Chapman and Hall, Inc. Wallis, Claudia (1989, December 4). Onward women! *Time* magazine, 80–89.

Wolfe, Naomi (1993). *Fire with fire: The new female power and how it will change the 21st century*. New York: Random House.

Wood, Julia T. (1992). Gender and moral voice: Moving from women's nature to standpoint epistemology. *Women's Studies in Communication*, 15, 1, 1–24.

LANGUAGE

37

RACISM IN THE ENGLISH LANGUAGE

ROBERT B. MOORE

LANGUAGE AND CULTURE

An integral part of any culture is its language. Language not only develops in conjunction with a society's historical, economic and political evolution; it also reflects that society's attitudes and thinking. Language not only *expresses* ideas and concepts but actually *shapes* thought.[1] If one accepts that our dominant white culture is racist, then one would expect our language—an indispensable transmitter of culture—to be racist as well. Whites, as the dominant group, are not subjected to the same abusive characterization by our language that people of color receive. Aspects of racism in the English language that will be discussed in this essay include terminology, symbolism, politics, ethnocentrism, and context.

Before beginning our analysis of racism in language we would like to quote part of a TV film review which shows the connection between language and culture.[2]

> Depending on one's culture, one interacts with time in a very distinct fashion. One example which gives some cross-cultural insights into the concept of time is language. In Spanish, a watch is said to "walk." In English, the watch "runs." In German, the watch "functions." And in French, the watch "marches." In the Indian culture of the Southwest, people do not refer to time in this way. The value of the watch is displaced with the value of "what time it's getting to be." Viewing these five cultural perspectives of time, one can see some definite emphasis and values that each culture places on time. For example, a cultural perspective may provide a clue to why the negative stereotype of the slow and lazy Mexican who lives in the "Land of Manana" exists in the Anglo value system, where time "flies," the watch "runs" and "time is money."

A SHORT PLAY ON "BLACK" AND "WHITE" WORDS

Some may blackly (angrily) accuse me of trying to blacken (defame) the English language, to give it a black eye (a mark of shame) by writing such black words (hostile). They may denigrate (to cast aspersions; to darken) me by accusing me of being blackhearted (malevolent), of having a black outlook (pessimistic, dismal) on life, of being a blackguard (scoundrel)—which would certainly be a black mark (detrimental fact) against me. Some may blackbrow (scowl at) me and hope that a black cat crosses in front of me because of this black deed. I may become a black sheep (one who causes shame or embarrassment because of deviation from the accepted standards), who will be blackballed (ostracized) by being placed on a blacklist (list of undesirables) in an attempt to blackmail (to force or coerce into a particular action) me to retract my words. But attempts to blackjack (to compel by threat) me will have a Chinaman's chance of success, for I am not a yellow-bellied Indian-giver of words, who will whitewash (cover up or gloss over vices or crimes) a black lie (harmful, inexcusable). I challenge the purity and innocence (white) of the English language. I don't see things in black and white (entirely bad or entirely good) terms, for I am a white man (marked by upright firmness) if there ever was one. However, it would be a black day when I would not "call a spade a spade," even though some will suggest a white man calling the English language racist is like the pot calling the kettle black. While many may be niggardly (grudging, scanty) in their support, others will be honest and decent—and to them I say, that's very white of you (honest, decent).

The preceding is of course a white lie (not intended to cause harm), meant only to illustrate some examples of racist terminology in the English language.

OBVIOUS BIGOTRY

Perhaps the most obvious aspect of racism in language would be terms like "nigger," "spook," "chink," "spic," etc. While they may be facing increasing social disdain, they certainly are not dead. Large numbers of white Americans continue to utilize these terms. "Chink," "gook," and "slant-eyes" were in common usage among U.S. troops in Vietnam. An NBC nightly news broadcast, in February 1972, reported that the basketball team in Pekin, Illinois, was called the "Pekin Chinks" and noted that even though this had been protested by Chinese Americans, the term continued to be used because it was easy, and meant no harm. Spiro Agnew's widely reported "fat Jap" remark and the "little Jap" comment of lawyer John Wilson during the Watergate hearings, are surface indicators of a deep-rooted Archie Bunkerism.

Many white people continue to refer to Black people as "colored," as for instance in a July 30, 1975, *Boston Globe* article on a racist attack by whites on a group of Black people using a public beach in Boston. One white person was quoted as follows:

> We've always welcomed good colored people in South Boston but we will not tolerate radical blacks or Communists. . . . Good colored people are welcome in South Boston; black militants are not.

Many white people may still be unaware of the disdain many African Americans have for the term "colored," but it often appears that whether used intentionally or unintentionally, "colored" people are "good" and "know their place," while "Black" people are perceived as "uppity" and "threatening" to many whites. Similarly, the term "boy" to refer to African American men is now acknowledged to be a demeaning term, though still in common use. Other terms such as "the pot calling the kettle black" and "calling a spade a spade" have negative racial connotations but are still frequently used, as for example when President Ford was quoted in February 1976 saying that even though Daniel Moynihan had left the U.N., the U.S. would continue "calling a spade a spade."

COLOR SYMBOLISM

The symbolism of white as positive and black as negative is pervasive in our culture, with the black/white words used in the beginning of this essay only one of many aspects. "Good guys" wear white hats and ride white horses; "bad guys" wear black hats and ride black horses. Angels are white, and devils are black. The definition of *black* includes "without any moral light or goodness, evil, wicked, indicating disgrace, sinful," while that of *white* includes "morally pure, spotless, innocent, free from evil intent."

A children's TV cartoon program, *Captain Scarlet,* is about an organization called Spectrum, whose purpose is to save the world from an evil extraterrestrial force called the Mysterons. Everyone in Spectrum has a color name—Captain Scarlet, Captain Blue, etc. The one Spectrum agent who has been mysteriously taken over by the Mysterons and works to advance their evil aims is Captain Black. The person who heads Spectrum, the good organization out to defend the world, is Colonel White.

Three of the dictionary definitions of white are "fairness of complexion, purity, innocence." These definitions affect the standards of beauty in our culture, in which whiteness represents the norm. "Blondes have more fun" and "Wouldn't you really rather be a blonde" are sexist in their attitudes toward women generally, but are racist white standards when applied to third world women. A 1971 *Mademoiselle* advertisement pictured a curly-headed, ivory-skinned woman over the caption, "When you go blonde go all the way," and asked: "Isn't this how, in the back of your mind, you always wanted to look? All wide-eyed and silky blonde down to there, and innocent?" Whatever the advertising people meant by this particular woman's innocence, one must remember that "innocent" is one of the definitions of the word white. This standard of beauty when preached to all women is racist. The statement "Isn't this how, in the back of your mind, you always wanted to look?" either ignores third world women or assumes they long to be white.

Time magazine in its coverage of the Wimbledon tennis competition between the black Australian Evonne Goolagong and the white American Chris Evert described Ms. Goolagong as "the dusky daughter of an Australian sheepshearer," while Ms. Evert was "a fair young girl from the middle-class groves of Florida." *Dusky* is a synonym of "black" and is defined as "having dark skin; of a dark color; gloomy; dark; swarthy." Its antonyms are "fair" and "blonde." *Fair* is defined in part as "free from blemish, imperfection, or anything that impairs the appearance, quality, or character; pleasing in appearance, attractive; clean; pretty; comely." By defining Evonne Goolagong as "dusky," *Time* technically defined her as the opposite of "pleasing in appearance; attractive; clean; pretty; comely."

The studies of Kenneth B. Clark, Mary Ellen Goodman, Judith Porter and others indicate that this persuasive "rightness of whiteness" in U.S. culture affects children before the age of four, providing white youngsters with a false sense of superiority and encouraging self-hatred among third world youngsters.

ETHNOCENTRISM OR FROM A WHITE PERSPECTIVE

Some words and phrases that are commonly used represent particular perspectives and frames of reference, and these often distort the understanding of the reader or listener. David R. Burgest[3] has written about the effect of using the terms "slave" or "master." He argues that the psychological impact of the statement referring to "the master raped his slave" is different from the impact of the same statement substituting the words: "the white captor raped an African woman held in captivity."

> Implicit in the English usage of the "master-slave" concept is ownership of the "slave" by the "master"; therefore, the "master" is merely abusing his property (slave). In reality, the captives (slave) were African individuals with human worth, right and dignity and the term "slave" denounces that human quality thereby making the mass rape of African women by white captors more acceptable in the minds of people and setting a mental frame of reference for legitimizing the atrocities perpetuated against African people.

The term "slave" connotes a less than human quality and turns the captive person into a thing. For example, two McGraw-Hill Far Eastern Publishers textbooks (1970) stated, "At first it was the slaves who worked the cane and they got only food for it. Now men work cane and get money." Next time you write about slavery or read about it, try transposing all "slaves" into "African people held in captivity," "Black people forced to work for no pay" or "African people stolen from their families and societies." While it is more cumbersome, such phrasing conveys a different meaning.

PASSIVE TENSE

Another means by which language shapes our perspective has been noted by Thomas Greenfield,[4] who writes that the achievements of Black people—and Black people themselves—have been hidden in

> the linguistic ghetto of the passive voice, the subordinate clause, and the "understood" subject. The seemingly innocuous distinction (between active/passive voice) holds enormous implications for writers and speakers. When it is effectively applied, the rhetorical impact of the passive voice—the art of making the creator or instigator of action totally disappear from a reader's perception—can be devastating.

For instance, some history texts will discuss how European immigrants came to the United States seeking a better life and expanded opportunities, but will note that "slaves *were brought* to America." Not only does this omit the destruction of African societies and families, but it ignores the role of northern merchants and southern slaveholders in the profitable trade in human beings. Other books will state that "the continental railroad *was built*," conveniently omitting information about the Chinese laborers who built much of it or the oppression they suffered.

Another example. While touring Monticello, Greenfield noted that the tour guide

> made all the black people at Monticello disappear through her use of the passive voice. While speaking of the architectural achievement of Jefferson in the active voice, she unfailingly shifted to passive when speaking of the work performed by Negro slaves and skilled servants.

Noting a type of door that after 166 years continued to operate without need for repair, Greenfield remarks that the design aspect of the door was much simpler than the actual skill and work involved in building and installing it. Yet his guide stated: "Mr. Jefferson designed these doors . . ." while "the doors **were installed** in 1809." The workers who installed those doors were African people whom Jefferson held in bondage. The guide's use of the passive tense enabled her to dismiss the reality of Jefferson's slaveholding. It also meant that she did not have to make any mention of the skills of those people held in bondage.

POLITICS AND TERMINOLOGY

"Culturally deprived," "economically disadvantaged" and "underdeveloped" are other terms which mislead and distort our awareness of reality. The application of the term "culturally deprived" and third world children in this society reflects a value judgment. It assumes that the dominant whites are cultured and all others without culture. In fact, third world children generally are bicultural, and many are bilingual, having grown up in their own culture as well as absorbing the dominant culture. In many ways, they are equipped with skills and experiences which white youth have been deprived of, since most white youth develop in a monocultural, monolingual environment. Burgest[5] suggests that the term "culturally deprived" be replaced by "culturally dispossessed," and that the term "economically disadvantaged" be replaced by "economically exploited." Both these terms present a perspective and implication that provide an entirely different frame of reference as to the reality of the third world experience in U.S. society.

Similarly, many nations of the third world are described as "underdeveloped." These less wealthy nations are generally those that suffered under colonialism and neocolonialism. The "developed" nations are those that exploited their resources and wealth. Therefore, rather than referring to these countries as "underdeveloped," a more appropriate and meaningful designation might be "over exploited." Again, transpose this term next time you read about "underdeveloped nations" and note the different meaning that results.

Terms such as "culturally deprived," "economically disadvantaged" and "underdeveloped" place the responsibility for their own conditions on those being so described. This is known as "Blaming the Victim."[6] It places responsibility for poverty on the victims of poverty. It removes the blame from those in power who benefit from, and continue to permit, poverty.

Still another example involves the use of "nonwhite," "minority" or "third world." While people of color are a minority in the U.S., they are part of the vast majority of the world's population, in which white people are a distinct minority. Thus, by utilizing the term "minority" to describe people of color in the U.S., we can lose sight of the global majority/minority reality—a fact of some importance in the increasing and interconnected struggles of people of color inside and outside the U.S.

To describe people of color as "nonwhite" is to use whiteness as the standard and norm against which to measure all others. Use of the term "third world" to describe all people of color overcomes the inherent bias of "minority" and "nonwhite." Moreover, it connects the struggles of third world people in the U.S. with the freedom struggles around the globe.

The term "third world" gained increasing usage after the 1955 Bandung Conference of "non-aligned" nations, which represented a third force outside of the two world superpowers. The "first world" represents the United States, Western Europe and their sphere of influence. The "second world" represents the Soviet Union and its sphere. The "third world" represents, for the most part, nations that were, or are, controlled by the "first world" or West. For the most part, these are nations of Africa, Asia and Latin America.

"LOADED" WORDS AND NATIVE AMERICANS

Many words lead to a demeaning characterization of groups of people. For instance, Columbus, it is said, "discovered" America. The word *discover* is defined as "to gain sight or knowledge of something previously unseen or unknown; to discover may be to find some existent thing that was previously unknown." Thus, a continent inhabited by millions of human beings cannot be "discovered." For history books to continue this usage represents a Eurocentric (white European) perspective on world history and ignores the existence of, and the perspective of, Native Americans. "Discovery," as used in the Euro-American context, implies the right to take what one finds, ignoring the rights of those who already inhabit or own the "discovered" thing.

Eurocentrism is also apparent in the usage of "victory" and "massacre" to describe the battles between Native Americans and whites. *Victory* is defined in the dictionary as "a success or triumph over an enemy in battle or war; the decisive defeat of an opponent." *Conquest* denotes the "taking over of control by the victor, and the obedience of the conquered." *Massacre* is defined as "the unnecessary, indiscriminate killing of a number of human beings, as in barbarous warfare or persecution, or for revenge or plunder." *Defend* is described as "to ward off attack from; guard against assault or injury; to strive to keep safe by resisting attack."

Eurocentrism turns these definitions around to serve the purpose of distorting history and justifying Euro-American conquest of the Native American homelands. Euro-Americans are not described in history books as invading Native American lands, but rather as defending *their* homes against "Indian" attacks. Since European communities were constantly encroaching on land already occupied, then a more honest interpretation would state that it was the Native Americans who were "warding off," "guarding" and "defending" their homelands.

Native American victories are invariably defined as "massacres," while the indiscriminate killing, extermination and plunder of Native American nations by Euro-Americans is defined as "victory." Distortion of history by the choice of "loaded" words used to describe historical events is a common racist practice. Rather than portraying Native Americans as human beings in highly defined and complex societies, cultures and civilizations, history books use such adjectives as "savages," "beasts," "primitive," and "backward." Native people are referred to as "squaw," "brave," or "papoose" instead of "woman," "man," or "baby."

Another term that has questionable connotations is *tribe.* The Oxford English Dictionary defines this noun as "a race of people; now applied especially to a primary aggregate of people in a primitive or barbarous condition, under a headman or chief." Morton Fried,[7] discussing "The Myth of Tribe," states that the word "did not become a general term of reference to American Indian society until the nineteenth century. Previously, the words commonly used for Indian populations were 'nation' and 'people.' " Since "tribe" has assumed a connotation of primitiveness or backwardness, it is suggested that the use of "nation" or "people" replace the term whenever possible in referring to Native American peoples.

The term *tribe* invokes even more negative implications when used in reference to American peoples. As Evelyn Jones Rich[8] has noted, the term is "almost always used to refer to third world people and it implies a stage of development which is, in short, a put-down."

"LOADED" WORDS AND AFRICANS

Conflicts among diverse peoples within African nations are often referred to as "tribal warfare," while conflicts among the diverse peoples within European countries are never described in such terms. If the rivalries between the Ibo and the Hausa and Yoruba in Nigeria are described as "tribal," why not the rivalries between Serbs and Slavs in Yugoslavia, or Scots and English in Great Britain, Protestants and Catholics in Ireland, or the Basques and the Southern Spaniards in Spain? Conflicts among African peoples in a particular nation have religious, cultural, economic and/or political roots. If we can analyze the roots of conflicts among European peoples in terms other than "tribal warfare," certainly we can do the same with African peoples, including correct reference to the ethnic groups or nations involved. For example, the terms "Kaffirs," "Hottentot" or "Bushmen" are names imposed by white Europeans. The correct names are always those by which a people refer to themselves. (In these instances Xhosa, Khoi-Khoin and San are correct.[9])

The generalized application of "tribal" in reference to Africans—as well as the failure to acknowledge the religious, cultural and social diversity of African peoples—is a decidedly racist dynamic. It is part of the process whereby Euro-Americans justify, or avoid confronting, their oppression of third world peoples. Africa has been particularly insulted by this dynamic, as witness the pervasive "darkest Africa" image. This image, widespread in Western culture, evokes an Africa covered by jungles and inhabited by "uncivilized," "cannibalistic," "pagan," "savage" peoples. This "darkest Africa" image avoids the geographical reality. Less than 20 percent of the African continent is wooded savanna, for example. The image also ignores the history of African cultures and civilizations. Ample evidence suggests this distortion of reality was developed as a convenient rationale for the European and American slave trade. The Western powers, rather than exploiting, were civilizing and christianizing "uncivilized" and "pagan savages" (so the rationalization went). This dynamic also served to justify Western colonialism. From Tarzan movies to racist children's books like *Doctor Dolittle* and *Charlie and the Chocolate Factory*, the image of "savage" Africa and the myth of "the white man's burden" has been perpetuated in Western culture.

A 1972 *Time* magazine editorial lamenting the demise of *Life* magazine, stated that the "lavishness" of *Life's* enterprises included "organizing safaris into darkest Africa." The same year, the *New York Times'* C. L. Sulzberger wrote that "Africa has a history as dark as the skins of many of its people." Terms such as "darkest Africa," "primitive," "tribe" ("tribal") or "jungle," in reference to Africa, perpetuate myths and are especially inexcusable in such large circulation publications.

Ethnocentrism is similarly reflected in the term "pagan" to describe traditional religions. A February 1973 *Time* magazine article on Uganda stated, "Moslems account for only 500,000 of Uganda's 10 million people. Of the remainder, 5,000,000 are Christians and the rest pagan." *Pagan* is defined as "Heathen, a follower of a polytheistic religion; one that has little or no religion and that is marked by a frank delight in and uninhibited seeking after sensual pleasures and material goods." *Heathen* is defined as "Unenlightened; an unconverted member of a people or nation that does not acknowledge the God of the Bible. A person whose culture or enlightenment is of an inferior grade, especially an irreligious person." Now, the people of Uganda, like almost all Africans, have serious religious beliefs and practices. As used by Westerners, "pagan" connotes something wild, primitive and inferior—another term to watch out for.

The variety of traditional structures that African people live in are their "houses," not "huts." A *hut* is "an often small and temporary dwelling of simple construction." And to describe Africans as "natives" (noun) is derogatory terminology—as in, "the natives are restless." The dictionary definition of *native* includes: "one of a people inhabiting a territorial area at the time of its discovery or becoming familiar to a foreigner; one belonging to a people having a less complex civilization." Therefore, use of "native," like use of "pagan" often implies a value judgment of white superiority.

QUALIFYING ADJECTIVES

Words that would normally have positive connotations can have entirely different meanings when used in a racial context. For example, C. L. Sulzberger, the columnist of the *New York Times,* wrote in January 1975, about conversations he had with two people in Namibia. One was the white South African administrator of the country and the other a member of SWAPO, the Namibian liberation movement. The first is described as "Dirk Mudge, who as senior elected member of the administration is a kind of acting Prime Minister. . . ." But the second person is introduced as "Daniel Tijongarero, an intelligent Herero tribesman who is a member of SWAPO. . . ." What need was there for Sulzberger to state that Daniel Tijongarero is "intelligent"? Why not also state that Dirk Mudge was "intelligent"—or do we assume he wasn't?

A similar example from a 1968 *New York Times* article reporting on an address by Lyndon Johnson stated, "The President spoke to the well-dressed Negro officials and their wives." In what similar circumstances can one imagine a reporter finding it necessary to note that an audience of white government officials was "well-dressed"?

Still another word often used in a racist context is "qualified." In the 1960s white Americans often questioned whether Black people were "qualified" to hold public office, a question that was never raised (until too late) about white officials like Wallace, Maddox, Nixon, Agnew, Mitchell, et al. The question of qualifications has been raised even more frequently in recent years as white people question whether Black people are "qualified" to be hired for positions in industry and educational institutions. "We're looking for a qualified Black" has been heard again and again as institutions are confronted with affirmative action goals. Why stipulate that Blacks must be "qualified," when for others it is taken for granted that applicants must be "qualified"?

SPEAKING ENGLISH

Finally, the depiction in movies and children's books of third world people speaking English is often itself racist. Children's books about Puerto Ricans or Chicanos often connect poverty with a failure to speak English or to speak it well, thus blaming the victim and ignoring the racism which affects third world people regardless of their proficiency in English. Asian characters speak a stilted English ("Honorable so and so" or "Confucius say") or have a speech impediment ("rots or ruck," "very solly," "flied lice"). Native American characters speak another variation of stilted English ("Boy not hide. Indian take boy."), repeat certain Hollywood-Indian phrases ("Heap big" and "Many moons") or simply grunt out "Ugh" or "How." The repeated use of these language characterizations functions to make third world people seem less intelligent and less capable than the English-speaking white characters.

WRAP UP

A *Saturday Review* editorial[10] on "The Environment of Language" stated that language

> . . . has as much to do with the philosophical and political conditioning of a society as geography or climate . . . people in Western cultures do not realize the extent to which their racial attitudes have been conditioned since early childhood by the power of words to ennoble or condemn, augment or detract, glorify or demean. Negative language infects the subconscious of most Western people from the time they first learn to speak. Prejudice is not merely imparted or superimposed. It is metabolized in the bloodstream of society. What is needed is not so much a change in language as an awareness of the power of words to condition attitudes. If we can at least recognize the underpinnings of prejudice, we may be in a position to deal with the effects.

To recognize the racism in language is an important first step. Consciousness of the influence of language on our perceptions can help to negate much of that influence. But it is not enough to simply become aware of the affects of racism in conditioning attitudes. While we may not be able to change the language, we can definitely change our usage of the language. We can avoid using words that degrade people. We can make a conscious effort to use terminology that reflects a progressive perspective, as opposed to a distorting perspective. It is important for educators to provide students with opportunities to explore racism in language and to increase their awareness of it, as well as learning terminology that is positive and does not perpetuate negative human values.

NOTES

1. Simon Podair, "How Bigotry Builds Through Language," *Negro Digest,* March 1967.
2. Jose Armas, "Antonio and the Mayor: A Cultural Review of the Film," *The Journal of Ethnic Studies,* Fall 1975.
3. David R. Burgest, "The Racist Use of the English Language," *Black Scholar,* Sept. 1973.

4. Thomas Greenfield, "Race and Passive Voice at Monticello," *Crisis,* April 1975.

5. David R. Burgest, "Racism in Everyday Speech and Social Work Jargon," *Social Work,* July 1973.

6. William Ryan, *Blaming the Victim.* Pantheon Books, 1971.

7. Morton Fried, "The Myth of Tribe," *National History,* April 1975.

8. Evelyn Jones Rich, "Mind Your Language," *Africa Report,* Sept./Oct. 1974.

9. Steve Wolf, "Catalogers in Revolt Against LC's Racist, Sexist Headings," *Bulletin of Interracial Books for Children,* Vol. 6, Nos. 3 & 4, 1975.

10. "The Environment of Language," *Saturday Review,* April 8, 1967.

Also see:

Roger Bastide, "Color, Racism and Christianity," *Daedalus,* Spring 1967.

Kenneth J. Gergen, "The Significance of Skin Color in Human Relations," *Daedalus,* Spring 1967.

Lloyd Yabura, "Towards a Language of Humanism," *Rhythm,* Summer 1971.

UNESCO, "Recommendations Concerning Terminology in Education on Race Questions," June 1968.

38

SELF, IDENTITY, AND THE NAMING QUESTION
Reflections on the Language of Disability

IRVING KENNETH ZOLA

"When I use the word, it means just what I choose it to mean—neither more nor less"

—HUMPTY DUMPTY

1. THE POWER OF NAMING

Language . . . has as much to do with the philosophical and political conditioning of a society as geography or climate . . . people do not realize the extent to which their attitudes have been conditioned to ennoble or condemn, augment or detract, glorify or demean. Negative language inflicts the subconscious of most . . . people from

Zola, Irving Kenneth. "Self, Identity, and the Naming Question: Reflections on the Language of Disability." From Nagler, Mark (ed.) *Perspectives on Disability,* Second Edition, Palo Alto, California: Health Markets Research, 1993. pp. 15–23.

the time they first learn to speak. Prejudice is not merely imparted or superimposed. It is metabolized in the bloodstream of society. What is needed is not so much a change in language as an awareness of the power of words to condition attitudes. [1]

A step in this awareness is the recognition of how deep is the power of naming in Western culture. According to the Old Testament, God's first act after saying "Let there be light" was to call the light "Day" and the darkness "Night." Moreover, God's first act after the creation of Adam was to bring in every beast of the field so that Adam could give them names; and "whatsoever Adam called every living creature, that was the name thereof" (Genesis 2:20). Thus what one is called tends "to stick" and any unnaming process is not without its difficulties and consequences [2]. While a name has always connoted some aspect of one's status (e.g., job, location, gender, social class, ethnicity, kinship), the mid-twentieth century seems to be a time when the issue of naming has assumed a certain primacy [3,4]. In the post–World War II era Erik Erikson [5] and Alan Wheelis [6] noted that "Who am I" or the issue of identity had become a major psychological concern of the U.S. population. The writings of C. Wright Mills [7] as well as the Women's Movement [8], however, called attention to the danger of individualizing any issue as only a "personal problem."

The power of naming was thus recognized not only as a personal issue but a political one as well. While social scientists focused more on the general "labeling" process [9–13] and the measurement of attitudes toward people with various chronic diseases and disabilities [14, 15], a number of "liberation" or "rights" movements focused on the practical implications. They claimed that language was one of the mechanisms by which dominant groups kept others 'in place' [16,17]. Thus, as minority groups sought to gain more control over their lives, the issue of naming—what they are called—was one of the first battlegrounds. The resolution of this was not always clear-cut. For some, the original stigmas became the banner: Negroes and coloreds become Blacks. For others, only a completely new designation would suffice—a "Ms" has caught on as a form of address but "womyn," "wimmin" have not been so successful in severing the vocabulary connection to "men."

People with disabilities are in the midst of a similar struggle. The struggle is confounded by some special circumstances which mitigate against the easy development of either a disability pride or culture [18,19]. While most minority group members grow up in a recognized subculture and thus develop certain norms and expectations, people with chronic diseases and disabilities are not similarly prepared. The nature of their experience has been toward isolation. The vast majority of people who are born with or acquire such conditions do so within families who neither have these conditions nor associate with others who do. They are socialized into the world of the "normal" with all its values, prejudices, and vocabulary. As one generally attempts to rise out of one's status, there is always an attempt to put this status in some perspective. The statements that one is more than just a Black or a woman, etc., are commonplace. On the other hand, where chronic illness and disability are concerned, this negation is almost total and is tantamount to denial. Proof of successful integration is embodied in such statements as "I *never* think of myself as handicapped" or the supreme compliment, "I *never* think of you as handicapped."

What then of the institutions where too many spend too much of their time—the long-term hospitals, sanitoria, convalescent and nursing homes? These are aptly labeled "total institutions" [20], but "total" refers to their control over our lives, not to the potential fullness they offer. The subcultures formed within such places are largely defensive and designed to make life viable within the institution. Often this viability is achieved at such a cost that it cannot be transferred to the non-institutional world.

For most of their history, organizations of people with disabilities were not much more successful in their efforts to produce a viable subculture. Their memberships have been small in comparison to the potential disabled population, and they have been regarded more as social groups rather than serious places to gain technical knowledge or emotional support. And though there are some self-help groups which are becoming increasingly visible, militant and independent of medical influence, the movement is still in its infancy [21]. Long ago, Talcott Parsons articulated the basic dilemma facing such groups:

> The sick role is . . . a mechanism which . . . channels deviance so
> that the two most dangerous potentialities, namely group
> formation and successful establishment of the claim of legitimacy,
> are avoided. The sick are tied up, not with other deviants to form a
> "subculture" of the sick but each with a group of nonsick, his
> personal circle, and, above all, physicians. The sick thus become a
> statistical status and are deprived of the possibility of forming a
> solidary collectivity. Furthermore, to be sick is by definition to be in
> an undesirable state, so that it simply does not "make sense" to
> assert a claim that the way to deal with the frustrating aspects of
> the social system is for everyone to get sick [22, p. 477].

A mundane but dramatic way of characterizing this phenomenon can be seen in the rallying cries of current liberation movements. As the "melting pot" theory of America was finally buried, people could once again say, even though they were three generations removed from the immigrants, that they were proud to be Greek, Italian, Hungarian, or Polish. With the rise of black power, a derogatory label became a rallying cry, "Black is beautiful." And when women saw their strength in numbers, they shouted "Sisterhood is powerful." But what about those with a chronic illness or disability? Could they yell, "Long live cancer," "Up with multiple sclerosis," "I'm glad I had polio!"? "Don't you wish you were blind!" Thus, the tradition reversing of the stigma will not so easily provide a basis for a common positive identity.

2. SOME NEGATIVE FUNCTIONS OF LABELING

The struggle over labels often follows a pattern. It is far easier to agree on terms that should *not* be used than the designations that should replace them [23–25]. As with the racial, ethnic [26] and gender groups [27,28] before them, many had begun to note the negative qualities of certain "disability references" [29,30]. Others created quite useful glossaries [31].

Since, as Phillips [32] notes, the names one calls oneself reflect differing political strategies, we must go beyond a list of "do's" and "don'ts" to an analysis of the functions of such labeling [33–36]. As long ago as 1651, Thomas Hobbes—in setting his own social agenda—saw the importance of such clarifications, "seeing then that truth consists in the right ordering of names in our affirmations, a man that seeks precise truth has need to remember what every name he uses stands for; and to place it accordingly; or else he will find himself entangled in words as a bird in lime twigs; the more he struggles the more belimed" [37, p. 26].

There are at least two separate implications of such naming which have practical and political consequences. The first is connotational and associational. As Kenneth Burke [38, p. 4] wrote, "Call a man a villain and you have the choice of either attacking or avenging. Call him mistaken and you invite yourself to attempt to set him right." I would add, "Call a person sick or crazy and all their behavior becomes dismissable." Because someone has been labeled ill, all their activity and beliefs—past, present, and future—become related to and explainable in terms of their illness [20, 39]. Once this occurs, society can deny the validity of anything which they might say, do, or stand for. Being seen as the object of medical treatment evokes the image of many ascribed traits, such as weakness, helplessness, dependency, regressiveness, abnormality of appearance and depreciation of every mode of physical and mental functioning [17, 40, 41]. In the case of a person with a chronic illness and/or a permanent disability, these traits, once perceived to be temporary accompaniments of an illness, become indelible characteristics. "The individual is trapped in a state of suspended animation socially, is perpetually a patient, is chronically viewed as helpless and dependent, in need of cure but incurable" [17, p. 420].

A second function of labeling is its potential for spread, pervasiveness, generalization. An example of such inappropriate generalizing was provided in a study by Conant and Budoff [42]. They found that a group of sighted children and adults interpreted the labels "blind" and "legally blind" as meaning that the person was totally without vision—something which is true for only a small segment of people with that designation. What was problematic became a given. Another example of this process occurs when disability and person are equated. While it is commonplace to hear of doctors referring to people as "the appendicitis in Room 306" or "the amputee down the hall," such labeling is more common in popular culture than one might believe. My own analysis of the crime-mystery genre [43] noted that after an introductory description of characters with a disability, they are often referred to by their disability—e.g., "the dwarf," "the blind man," "the one armed," the "one-legged." This is usually done by some third person observer or where the person with the disability is the speaker. The disability is emphasized—e.g., "said the blind man." No other physical or social descriptor appears with such frequency.

Perhaps not unexpectedly, such stand-in appellations are most commonly applied to villains. They were commonplace during the heyday of the pulp magazines, where the disability was incorporated into their names—"One-Eyed Joe," "Scarface Kelly"—a tradition enshrined in the Dick Tracy comic strips. It is a tradition that continues, though with more subtlety. Today we may no longer have "Clubfoot the Avenger," a mad German master-criminal who crossed swords for 25 years with the British Secret Service [44–51], but we do have "The Deaf Man," the recurring thorn in the side of Ed McBain's long-running (over 30 years) 87th Precinct novels [52–54]. All such instances can reinforce an association between disability, evil, and abnormality [55].

A very old joke illustrates the pervasiveness of such labeling:

> A man is changing a flat tyre (sic) outside a mental hospital when the bolts from his wheel roll down a nearby sewer. Distraught, he is confronted by a patient watching him who suggests, "Why don't you take one bolt off each of the other wheels, and place it on the spare?" Surprised when it works, the driver says, "How come you of all people would think of that?" Replies the patient, "I may be crazy, but I'm not stupid."

This anecdote demonstrates the flaw in thinking that a person who is mad is therefore stupid or incapable of being insightful. As the social psychological literature has long noted, this is how stigma comes about—from a process of generalizing from a single experience, people are treated categorically rather than individually and are devalued in the process [56–58]. As Longmore so eloquently concludes, a "spoiling process" [59] results whereby "they obscure all other characteristics behind that one and swallow up the social identity of the individual within that restrictive category" [17, p. 419]. Peters puts it most concretely: "The label that's used to describe us is often far more important in shaping our view of ourselves—and the way others view us—than whether we sign, use a cane, sit in a wheelchair, or use a communication board" [23, p. 25].

While many have offered vocabulary suggestions to combat the above problems of connotation and pervasiveness, few have analytically delineated what is at stake in such name changes [17, 60, 61]. The most provocative and historically rooted analysis is an unpublished paper by Phillips [32] who delineates four distinct strategies which underlie the renaming. While she carefully notes that further investigation may change or expand her categorization, the very idea of her schema and the historical data describing the genesis of each "recoding" remain timely.

"Cripple" and "handicapped," as nouns or adjectives, she sees as primarily "names of acquiescence and accommodation," reflecting an acceptance of society's oppressive institutions. Terms such as "physically challenged" by so personalizing the disability run the risk of fostering a "blaming the victim" stance [62]. Such terms, as well as "physically different," "physically inconvenienced," not only may be so euphemistic that they confound the public as to who is being discussed but also contribute strongly to the denial of existing realities [33]. Two other strategies represent a more activist philosophy. "Handicapper" and "differently-abled" are "names of reaction and reflection" whose purpose is to emphasize "the can-do" aspects of having a disability. To the group of Michigan advocates who coined the term [63], a "Handicapper" determines the degree to which one's own physical or mental characteristics direct life's activities. Anger, says Phillips, is basic to "names of renegotiation and inversion" where the context sets the meaning. Perhaps the best examples occur when disability activists, in the privacy of their own circles, "talk dirty," referring to themselves as "blinks," "gimps," or telling "crip" jokes and expounding on the intricacies of "crip" time. More controversy arises, however, when people publicly proclaim such terms as a matter of pride. Recently, for example, many have written about the positive aspects of "being deaf" [64, 65] or, even more dramatically of being a "cripple" [66]. Kriegel [60, 61] says that "cripple" describes "an essential reality," a way of keeping what needs to be dealt with socially and politically in full view. Nancy Mairs [67], a prize-winning poet who has multiple sclerosis, clearly agrees; and in the opening remarks of her essay, "On Being a Cripple," states it most vividly:

> The other day I was thinking of writing an essay on being a cripple. I was thinking hard in one of the stalls of the women's room in my office building, as I was shoving my shirt into my jeans and tugging up my zipper. Preoccupied, I flushed, picked up my book bag, took my cane down from the hook, and unlatched the door. So many movements unbalanced me, and as I pulled the door open, I fell over backwards, landing fully clothed on the toilet seat with legs splayed in front of me: the old beetle-on-its-back routine. Saturday afternoon, the building deserted, I was free to laugh aloud as I wriggled back to my feet, my voice bouncing off the yellowish tiles from all directions. Had anyone been there with me, I'd have been still and faint and hot with chagrin.
>
> I decided that it was high time to write the essay. First, the matter of semantics. I am a cripple. I choose this word to name me. I choose from among several possibilities, the most common of which are handicapped and disabled. I made the choice a number of years ago, without thinking, unaware of my motives for doing so. Even now, I'm not sure what those motives are, but I recognize that they are complex and not entirely flattering. People—crippled

or not—wince at the word cripple, as they do not at handicapped or disabled. Perhaps I want them to wince. I want them to see me as a tough customer, one to whom the fates/gods/viruses have not been kind, but who can face the brutal truth of her existence squarely. As a cripple, I swagger [67, p. 9].

When Phillips' very titles may imply an evaluation of the particular strategies, it is clear from her own caveats that while many may try to impose their terminology as "the correct language," "None feel really right" [23, p. 25].

3. RECONTEXTUALIZING NAMES

The ultimate question, of course, is whether any of these renaming procedures, singly and alone, can deal with the connotational and generalization issues discussed previously. I would argue that the context of usage may be every bit as important (as Phillips implies) as the specific terminology. Thus one of the reasons for all the negative associations to many terms is a result of such contexts. Here social scientists, researchers and clinicians are particularly at fault in the medicalizing of disability [55, 68, 69]. In their writings and in the transmission of these writings by the popular press and media, people with varying diseases and disabilities are inevitably referred to as "patients," a term which describes a role, a relationship and a location (i.e., an institution or hospital) from which many connotations, as previously noted, flow. For the 43 million people now designated as having a physical, mental or biological disability, only a tiny proportion are continually resident in and under medical supervision and are thus truly patients. Similarly, the terms "suffering from," "afflicted with" are projections and evaluations of an outside world. No person with a disability is automatically "suffering" or "afflicted" except in specific situations where they do indeed "hurt," are "in pain," or "feel victimized."

I am not arguing, however, for the complete elimination of medical or physical terminology. As DeFerlice cautions, "The disabled movement has purchased political visibility at the price of physical invisibility. The crippled and lame had bodies, but the handicapped, or so the social workers say, are just a little late at the starting gate. I don't like that: it's banal. When we speak in metaphorical terms, we deny physical reality. The farther we get from our bodies, the more removed we are from the body politic . . ." [70].

One meaning I derive from his caution is that we must seek a change in the connotations and the pervasiveness of our names without denying the essential reality of our conditions. Thus biology may not determine our destiny, but, as with women, our physical, mental and biological differences are certainly part of that destiny [71, 72].

A way of contextualizing our relationship to our bodies and our disabilities may not be in changing terms but in changing grammars. Our continual use of nouns and adjectives can only perpetuate the equation of the individual equaling the disability. No matter what noun we use, it substitutes one categorical definition for another. An adjective colors and thus connotes the essential quality of the noun it modifies. Such adjectives as "misshapen," "deformed," "defective," "invalid"—far from connoting a specific quality of the individual—tend to taint the whole person.

The same is true with less charged terms. Thus "a disabled car" is one which has totally broken down. Could "a disabled person" be perceived as anything less? Prepositions, on the other hand, imply both "a relationship to" and "a separation from." At this historical juncture the awkwardness in phrasing that often results may be all to the good, for it makes both user and hearer stop and think about what is meant, as in the phrases "people *of* color" and "persons *with* disabilities."

Distance and relationship are also at the heart of some very common verb usages. The first is between the active and passive tense. Note the two dictionary meanings:

Active   asserting that the person or thing represented by the grammatical subjects performs the action represented by the verb [73, p. 12].

Passive   asserting that the grammatical subject to a verb is subjected to or affected by the action represented by that verb [73, p. 838].

Thus in describing an individual's relationship to an assistive device such as a wheelchair, the difference between "being confined to a wheelchair" and "using" one is a difference not only of terminology but of control. Medical language has long perpetuated this "disabled passivity" by its emphasis on what medicine continually *does* to its "patients" rather than *with* them [74, 75].

Similarly the issues of "connotation" and "pervasiveness" may be perpetuated by the differential use of the verbs "be" and "have." The French language makes careful distinctions between when to use "etre" (be) and when to use "avoir" (have). English daily usage is blurry, but another look at Webster's does show the possibilities:

be   to equal in meaning; to have same connotation as; to have identity with; to constitute the same class as [73, p. 96].

have   to hold in possession; to hold in one's use; to consist of; to stand in relationship to; to be marked or characterized by; to experience; SYN—to keep, control, retain, or experience [73, p. 526].

Like the issue of nouns versus prepositions, verbs can also code people in terms of categories (e.g., X is a redhead) instead of specific attributes (e.g., X has red hair), allowing people to feel that the stigmatized persons are fundamentally different and establishing greater psychological and social distance [76]. Thus, as between the active and passive tense, so it is between "I am . . ." Both specify a difference in distance and control in relation to whatever it is one "is" or "has." And since renaming relates to alternative images of distance and control, grammar, which tends to be normative, concise, shared and long-lasting, may serve us better than sheer name change. Though I personally may have a generic preference (e.g., for "disability" over "handicap"), I am not arguing for any "politically correct" usage but rather examining the political advantages and disadvantages of each [36].

For example, there may be stages in the coping with a particular condition or in the perceived efficacy of a particular "therapy" (e.g., the 12 steps in Alcoholics Anonymous) when "ownership" and thus the use of "I am" is deemed essential. Those old enough to remember President Kennedy's words at the Berlin Wall, "*Ich bin ein Berliner*" (I am a Berliner), will recall the power of its message of kinship. Similarly, when we politically strategize as a minority group [77] and seek a kinship across disease and disability groups [78], the political coming-out may require a personal ownership best conveyed in terms of "I am . . ."

On the other hand, there are times when the political goals involve groups for whom disease and disability is not a permanent or central issue. On my university campus, for a myriad of reasons, people with mobility impairments are virtually non-existent. Yet we are gradually retrofitting old buildings and guaranteeing accessibility in new ones. The alliance here is among women who are or may become pregnant, parents with small children, people with injuries or time-limited diseases, and others who perceive themselves at risk, such as aging staff or faculty. They rarely see themselves as disabled but often admit to having a temporary disability or sharing a part of "the disabled experience" (e.g., "Now I know what it's like to try to climb all those stairs"). Thus where coalition politics is needed, the concept of "having" versus "being" may be a more effective way of acknowledging multiple identities and kinship, as in our use of hyphenated personal and social lineages—e.g., Afro-American.

4. A FINAL CAVEAT

One of the sad findings in Phillips' study [32] is how divisive this struggle over names has become. People thus begin to chastise "non true-believers" and emphasize to others "politically correct" usage. In so doing, we may not only damage the unity so necessary to the cause of disability rights but also fail to see the forest for the trees. Our struggle is necessary because we live in a society which devalues, discriminates against and disparages people with disabilities [77, 79]. It is not our task to prove that we are worthy of the full resources and integration of our society. The fault is not in us, not in our diseases and disabilities [41, 62, 80, 81] but in mythical denials, social arrangement, political priorities and prejudices [82].

Here too, a renaming can be of service not of us but of our oppressors [83]. As Hughes and Hughes [84] note, when we turn the tables and create epithets for our oppressors, this may be a sign of a beginning cohesiveness. Thus the growing popularity of terms like TABs and MABs (temporarily or momentarily able-bodied) to describe the general population breaks down the separateness of "us" and "them" and emphasizes the continuity and inevitability of "the disability experience." Thus, too, those who have created the terms "handicappism" [85] and "healthism" [68, 86, 87] equate these with all the structural "-isms" in a society which operates to continue segregation and discrimination. To return finally to the issue of naming, the words of Philip Dunne reflect well the choices and consequences of language:

> If we hope to survive in this terrifying age, we must choose our words as we choose our actions. We should think how what we say might sound to other ears as well as to our own. Above all, we should strive for clarity . . . if clarity [is] the essence of style, it is also the heart and soul of truth, and it is for want of truth that human freedom could perish [88, p. 14].

REFERENCES

1. *Saturday Review,* Editorial, April 8, 1967.
2. LeGuin, U. K. She unnames them. *New Yorker,* January 21, p. 27, 1985.
3. Friedrich, O. What's in a name? *Time,* p. 16, August 18, 1986.
4. Vickery, H. Finding the right name for brand X. *Insight,* pp. 54–55, January 27, 1986.
5. Erikson, H. *Childhood and Society.* New York: Norton, 1950.
6. Wheelis, A. *The Quest for Identity.* New York: Norton, 1958.
7. Mills, D. W. *The Sociological Imagination.* Oxford: Oxford University Press, 1959.
8. Boston Women's Health Book Collective. *Women and Our Bodies* (In later revised versions, *Our Bodies Ourselves*). Boston: New England Free Press, 1970.
9. Becker, H. *Outsiders.* Glencoe, IL: The Free Press, 1963.
10. Becker, H. (Ed.) *The Other Side—Perspectives on Deviance.* Glencoe, IL: The Free Press, 1964.
11. Erikson, K., Notes on the sociology of deviance. *Social Problems* 9, 307–314, 1962.
12. Erikson, K. *Wayward Puritans: A Study in the Sociology of Deviance.* New York: Wiley, 1966.
13. Schur, E. *Crimes Without Victims.* Englewood Cliffs, N.J.: Prentice-Hall, 1965.
14. Siller, J. The measurement of attitudes toward physically disabled persons. In *Physical Appearance, Stigma, and Social Behavior: The Ontario Symposium* (Edited by Herman, P. D.; Zanna M. P.; and Higgins E. T.), Vol. 3, pp. 245–288. Lawrence Hillsdale, NJ: Enbaum Associates, 1986.
15. Yuker, H.; Block, J. Z., and Young, J. H. *The Measurement of Attitudes Toward Disabled Persons.* Albertson, NY: Human Resources Center, 1966.
16. Gumperz, J. J. (Ed.) *Language and Social Identity.* Cambridge: Cambridge University Press, 1982.
17. Longmore, P. K. A Note on language and the social identity of disabled people. *America Behavior Scientific* 28, (3), 419–423, 1985.
18. Johnson, M. Emotion and pride: the search for a disability culture. *Disability Rag,* January/February, pp. 1, 4–10, 1987.

19. Zola, I. K. Whose voice is this anyway? A commentary on recent collections about the experience of disability. *Medical Human Revision* 2 (1), 6–15, 1988.
20. Goffman, E. *Asylums*, New York: Anchor, 1961.
21. Crew, N., and Zola, I. K. et al. *Independent Living for Physically Disabled People*. San Francisco: Jossey-Bass, 1983.
22. Parsons, T. *The Social System*. Glencoe: The Free Press, 1951.
23. Peters, A. Developing a language. *Disability Rag*. March/April, 1986 p. 25.
24. Peters, A. The problem with 'Gimp'. *Disability Rag*. July/August, 1986 p. 22.
25. Peters, A. Do we have to be named? *Disability Rag*, November/December, 1986, p. 31, 35.
26. Moore, R. B. *Racism in the English Language—A Lesson Plan and Study Essay*. The Council of Interracial Books for Children, New York, 1976.
27. Shear, M. Equal writes. *Womens Revision Book 1* (11), 12–13, 1984.
28. Shear, M. Solving the great pronoun debate. *Ms*. pp. 106, 108–109, 1985.
29. Biklen, D., and Bogdan, R. Disabled—yes; handicapped—no: The language of disability, p. 5, insert in "Media Portrayals of Disabled People: A Study in Stereotypes." *Interracial Books Children Bull* 8 (3, 6, 7), 4–9, 1977.
30. Corcoran, P. J. Perjorative terms and attitudinal barriers—editorial. *Architectural Physics Medical Rehabilitation*, 58, 500, 1977.
31. Shear, M. No more supercrip. *New Directions for Women*, p. 10, November–December 1986.
32. Phillips, M. J. What we call ourselves: Self-referential naming among the disabled. *Seventh Annual Ethnography in Research Forum*. University of Pennsylvania. Philadelphia. 4–6, April 1986.
33. Chaffee, N. L. Disabled . . . handicapped . . . and in the image of God?—Our language reflects societal attitudes and influences theological perception. Unpublished paper, 1987.
34. Gill, C. J. The disability name game. *New World for Persons with Disabilities* 13 (8), 2, 1987.
35. Gillet, P. The power of words—can they make you feel better or worse? *Accent on Living*, pp. 38–39, 1987.
36. Lindsey, K. The pitfalls of politically correct language. *Sojourner*, p. 16, 1985.
37. Hobbes, T. *Leviathan*, New York: Dutton, 1950.
38. Burke, K. *Attitudes Toward History*, revised ed. Hermes, Oakland, CA, 1959.
39. Ling, B. G., Cullen, F. T., Frank, J. and Wozniak, J. F. The social rejection of former mental patients: Understanding why labels matter. *American Journal Sociology* 1987, 92 (6), 1,461–1,500, 1987.
40. Goodwin, D. Language: Perpetualizing the myths. *Impact, Inc.* (Newsletter of Center for Independent Living, Alton, IL.). Vol. 1, No. 2, pp. 1–2, 1986.
41. Zola, I. K. *Missing Pieces: A Chronicles of Living with a Disability*. Philadelphia: Temple University Press, 1982.
42. Conant, S. and Budoff, M. The development of sighted people's understanding of blindness. *Journal Visual Impairment Blindness* 76, 86–96, 1982.
43. Zola, I. K. Any distinguishing features: Portrayal of disability in the crime-mystery genre. *Policy Studying Journal* 15 (3), 485–513, 1987.
44. Williams, V. *The Man with the Clubfoot*. London: Jenkins, 1918.
45. Williams, V. *The Secret Hand*. London: Jenkins, 1918.
46. Williams, V. *Return of Clubfoot*. London: Jenkins, 1918.
47. Williams, V. *Clubfoot the Avenger*. London: Jenkins, 1924.

48. Williams, V. *The Crouching Beast.* London: Hodder & Stoughton, 1928.
49. Williams, V. *The Gold Comfit Box.* London: Hodder & Stoughton, 1932.
50. Williams, V. *The Spider's Touch.* London: Hodder and Stoughton, 1936.
51. Williams, V. *Courier to Marrakesh.* London: Hodder & Stoughton, 1944.
52. McBain, E. *Fuzz.* New York: Doubleday, 1968.
53. McBain, E. *Let's Hear It for the Deaf Man.* New York: Random House, 1973.
54. McBain, E. *Eight Black Horses.* New York: Avon, 1985.
55. Conrad, P. and Schneider, J. W. *Deviance and Medicalization: From Badness to Sickness.* C. V. St. Louis: Mosby, 1980.
56. Ainlay, S. C., Becker, G., and Coleman, L. M. (Eds) *The Dilemma of Difference: A Multidisciplinary View of Stigma,* New York: Plenum, 1986.
57. Jones, E. E.; Farina, A.; Hastorf, A. H.; Markus, H.; Miller, D.; and Scott R. *Social Stigma: The Psychology of Marked Relationships.* W. H. Freeman, New York, 1984.
58. Katz, I. *Stigma: A Social Psychological Analysis.* Lawrence Eribaum Associates, NJ: Hillsdale, 1981.
59. Goffman, E. *Stigma: Notes on the Management of Spoiled Identity.* Prentice-Hall, NJ: Englewood Cliffs, 1963.
60. Kriegel, L. Uncle Tom and Tiny Tim: Reflection on the cripple as Negro. *American Scholar* 38, 412–430, 1969.
61. Kriegel L. Coming through manhood, disease and the authentic self. In: *Rudely Stamp'd: Imaginal Disability and Prejudice* (edited by Bicklen, D. and Bailey, L.), pp. 49–63. University Press of America, Washington, D.C., 1981.
62. Ryan, W. *Blaming the Victim.* New York: Pantheon, 1970.
63. Gentile, E., and Taylor, J. K. Images, words and identity. Handicapper Programs. Michigan State University, East Lansing, MI, 1976.
64. *Disability Rag.* Cochlear implants: The final put-down. March/April, pp. 1, 4–8, 1987.
65. Innerst, C. A. Will to preserve deaf culture. *Insight.* November 24, pp. 50–51, 1986.
66. Milam, L. *The Crippled Liberation Front Marching Band Blues.* MHO and MHO Works, San Diego, CA, 1984.
67. Mairs, N. On being a cripple. In *Plaintest: Essays,* pp. 9–20. Tucson, AZ: University of Arizona Press, 1986.
68. Zola, I. K. Medicine as an institution of social control. *Social Revenue.* 20, 487–504, 1972.
69. Illich, I. *Medical Nemesis: The Expropriation of Health.* London: Calder & Boyars, 1975.
70. DeFelice, R. J. A crippled child grows up. *Newsweek,* November 3, p. 13, 1986.
71. Fine, M., and Asch, A. Disabled women: Sexism without the pedestal. *Journal Social Society Welfare* 8(2), 233–248, 1981.
72. Fine, M., and Asch, A. (Eds) *Women with Disabilities—Essays in Psychology, Culture, and Politics.* Philadelphia: Temple University Press, 1988.
73. *Webster's New Collegiate Dictionary.* Springfield, MA: Merriam, 1973.
74. Edelman, M. The political language of the helping professions. In *Political Language,* pp. 59–68. New York: Academic, 1977.
75. Szasz, T. S., and Hollender, M. H. A contribution to the philosophy of medicine: The basic models of the doctor-patient relationship. *AMA Arch. Internal Media* 97, 585–592, 1956.
76. Crocker, J. and Lutsky, N. Stigma and the dynamics of social cognition. In *The Dilemma of Difference: A Multidisciplinary View of Stigma* (Edited by Ainlay, S. C.), pp. 95–121. New York: Plenum, 1986.

77. Hahn, H. Disability policy and the problem of discrimination. *American Behaviour Scientist* 28, 293–318, 1985.

78. Harris, L. et al. *Disabled Americans' Self Perceptions: Bringing Disabled Americans into the Mainstream,* Study No. 854009, International Center for the Disabled, New York, 1986.

79. Scotch, R. K. *From Goodwill to Civil Rights: Transforming Federal Disability Policy,* Philadelphia: Temple University Press, 1984.

80. Crawford, R. You are dangerous to your health: the ideology of politics of victim blaming. *International Journal of Health Services* 7, 663–680, 1977.

81. Crawford, R. Individual responsibility and health politics. In *Health Care in America: Essays in Social History* (Edited by Reverby, S. and Rosner, D.), pp. 247–268. Temple University Press, Philadelphia, 1979.

82. Gleidman, J. and Roth, W. *The Unexpected Minority: Handicapped Children in America.* New York: Harcourt, Brace, Jovanovich, 1980.

83. Saxton, M. A. Peer counseling training program for disabled women. *Journal of Social Society Welfare* 8, 334–346, 1981.

84. Hughes, E. and Hughes, H. M. "What's in a name." In *Where People Meet—Racial and Ethnic Frontiers,* pp. 130–144. Glencoe, IL: The Free Press, 1952.

85. Bogdan, R. and Biklen, D. "Handicappism." *Social Policy,* pp. 14–19, March/April, 1977.

86. Crawford, R. Healthism and the medicalization of everyday life. *International Journal of Health Services,* 10, 365–388, 1980.

87. Zola, I. K. Healthism and disabling medicalization. In *Disabling Professions* (Edited by Illich, I.; Zola, I. K.; McKnight, J.; Caplan, J.; and Shaiken, H.), pp. 41–69. Marion Boyars, London, 1977.

88. Dunne, P. Faith, hope, and clarity. *Harvard Magazine* 88 (4), 10–14, 1986.

39

HOW TO TAME A WILD TONGUE

GLORIA ANZALDÚA

"We're going to have to control your tongue," the dentist says, pulling out all the metal from my mouth. Silver bits plop and tinkle into the basin. My mouth is a motherlode.

The dentist is cleaning out my roots. I get a whiff of the stench when I gasp. "I can't cap that tooth yet; you're still draining," he says.

From *Borderlands: the New Mestiza.* San Francisco: Spinsters/Aunt Lute 1987. pp. 53–64. © 1987 by Gloria Anzaldúa. With permission from the publisher.

"We're going to have to do something about your tongue," I hear the anger rising in his voice. My tongue keeps pushing out the wads of cotton, pushing back the drills, the long thin needles. "I've never seen anything as strong or as stubborn," he says. And I think, how do you tame a wild tongue, train it to be quiet, how do you bridle and saddle it? How do you make it lie down?

> *"Who is to say that robbing a people of its language is less violent than war?"*
> —RAY QWYN SMITH[1]

I remember being caught speaking Spanish at recess—that was good for three licks on the knuckles with a sharp ruler. I remember being sent to the corner of the classroom for "talking back" to the Anglo teacher when all I was trying to do was tell her how to pronounce my name. "If you want to be American, speak 'American.' If you don't like it, go back to Mexico where you belong."

"I want you to speak English. *Pa' hallar buen trabajo tienes que saber hablar el inglés bien. Qué vale toda in educación si todavía hablas inglés con un* 'accent,'" my mother would say, mortified that I spoke English like a Mexican. At Pan American University, I, and all Chicano students were required to take two speech classes. Their purpose: to get rid of our accents.

Attacks on one's form of expression with the intent to censor are a violation of the First Amendment. *El Anglo con cara de inocente nos arrancó la lengua.* Wild tongues can't be tamed; they can only be cut out.

OVERCOMING THE TRADITION OF SILENCE

> *Abogadas, escupimos el oscuro.*
> *Peleando con nuestra propia sombra*
> *el silencio nos sepulta.*

En boca cerrada no entran moscas. "Flies don't enter a closed mouth" is a saying I kept hearing when I was a child. *Ser habladora* was to be a gossip and a liar, to talk too much. *Muchachitas bien criadas,* well-bred girls don't answer back. *Es una falta de respeto* to talk back to one's mother or father. I remember one of the sins I'd recite to the priest in the confession box the few times I went to confession: talking back to my mother, *hablar pa' 'tras, repelar. Hocicona, repelona, chismosa,* having a big mouth, questioning, carrying tales are all signs of being *mal criada.* In my culture they are all words that are derogatory if applied to women—I've never heard them applied to men.

The first time I heard two women, a Puerto Rican and a Cuban, say the word "*nosotras,*" I was shocked. I had not known the word existed. Chicanas use *nosotros* whether we're male or female. We are robbed of our female being by the masculine plural. Language is a male discourse.

And our tongues have become
dry   the wilderness has
dried out our tongues   and
we have forgotten speech.

—Irena Klepfisz[2]

Even our own people, other Spanish speakers *nos quieren poner candados en la boca*. They would hold us back with their bag of *reglas de academia*.

OYÉ COMO LADRA: EL LENGUAJE DE LA FRONTERA

Quien tiene boca se equivoca.

—MEXICAN SAYING

"*Pocho*, cultural traitor, you're speaking the oppressor's language by speaking English; you're ruining the Spanish language," I have been accused by various Latinos and Latinas. Chicano Spanish is considered by the purist and by most Latinos deficient, a mutilation of Spanish.

But Chicano Spanish is a border tongue which developed naturally. Change, *evolución, enriquecimiento de palabras nuevas por invención o adopción* have created variants of Chicano Spanish, *un nuevo lenguaje. Un lenguaje que corresponde a un modo de vivir.* Chicano Spanish is not incorrect; it is a living language.

For a people who are neither Spanish nor live in a country in which Spanish is the first language; for a people who live in a country in which English is the reigning tongue but who are not Anglo; for a people who cannot entirely identify with either standard (formal, Castillian) Spanish nor standard English, what recourse is left to them but to create their own language? A language which they can connect their identity to, one capable of communicating the realities and values true to themselves—a language with terms that are neither *español ni inglés*, but both. We speak a patois, a forked tongue, a variation of two languages.

Chicano Spanish sprang out of the Chicanos' need to identify ourselves as a distinct people. We needed a language with which we could communicate with ourselves, a secret language. For some of us, language is a homeland closer than the Southwest—for many Chicanos today live in the Midwest and the East. And because we are a complex, heterogeneous people, we speak many languages. Some of the languages we speak are:

1. Standard English
2. Working class and slang English
3. Standard Spanish
4. Standard Mexican Spanish
5. North Mexican Spanish dialect

6. Chicano Spanish (Texas, New Mexico, Arizona and California have regional variations)
7. Tex-Mex
8. *Pachuco* (called *caló*)

My "home" tongues are the languages I speak with my sister and brothers, with my friends. They are the last five listed, with 6 and 7 being closest to my heart. From school, the media and job situations, I've picked up standard and working class English. From Mamagrande Locha and from reading Spanish and Mexican literature, I've picked up Standard Spanish and Standard Mexican Spanish. From *los recién llegados,* Mexican immigrants, and *braceros,* I learned the North Mexican dialect. With Mexicans I'll try to speak either Standard Mexican Spanish or the North Mexican dialect. From my parents and Chicanos living in the Valley, I picked up Chicano Texas Spanish, and I speak it with my mom, younger brother (who married a Mexican and who rarely mixes Spanish with English), aunts and older relatives.

With Chicanas from *Nuevo México* or *Arizona* I will speak Chicano Spanish a little, but often they don't understand what I'm saying. With most California Chicanas I speak entirely in English (unless I forget). When I first moved to San Francisco, I'd rattle off something in Spanish, unintentionally embarrassing them. Often it is only with another Chicana *tejana* that I can talk freely.

Words distorted by English are known as anglicisms or *pochismos.* The *pocho* is an anglicized Mexican or American of Mexican origin who speaks Spanish with an accent characteristic of North Americans and who distorts and reconstructs the language according to the influence of English.[3] Tex-Mex, or Spang-lish, comes most naturally to me. I may switch back and forth from English to Spanish in the same sentence or in the same word. With my sister and my brother Nune and with Chicano *tejano* contemporaries I speak in Tex-Mex.

From kids and people my own age I picked up *Pachuco.* *Pachuco* (the language of the zoot suiters) is a language of rebellion, both against Standard Spanish and Standard English. It is a secret language. Adults of the culture and outsiders cannot understand it. It is made up of slang words from both English and Spanish. *Ruca* means girl or woman, *vato* means guy or dude, *chale* means no, *simón* means yes, *churro* is sure, talk is *periquiar, pigionear* means petting, *que gacho* means how nerdy, *ponte águila* means watch out, death is called *la pelona.* Through lack of practice and not having others who can speak it, I've lost most of the *Pachuco* tongue.

CHICANO SPANISH

Chicanos, after 250 years of Spanish/Anglo colonization have developed significant differences in the Spanish we speak. We collapse two adjacent vowels into a single syllable and sometimes shift the stress in certain words such as *maíz/maiz, cohete/cuete.* We leave out certain consonants when they appear between vowels: *lado/lao, mojado/mojao.* Chicanos from South Texas pronounce *f* as *j* as in *jue (fue)*. Chicanos use "archaisms," words that are no longer in the Spanish language, words that have been evolved out. We say *semos, truje, haiga, ansina,* and *naiden*. We retain the "archaic" *j*, as in *jalar,* that derives from an earlier *h* (the French *halar* or the Germanic *halon* which was lost to standard Spanish in the 16th century), but which is still found in several regional dialects such as the one spoken in South Texas. (Due to geography, Chicanos from the Valley of South Texas were cut off linguistically from other Spanish speakers. We tend to use words that the Spaniards brought over from Medieval Spain. The majority of the Spanish colonizers in Mexico and the Southwest came from Extremadura—Hernán Cortés was one of them—and Andalucía. Andalucians pronounce *ll* like a *y*, and their *d*'s tend to be absorbed by adjacent vowels: *tirado* becomes *tirao*. They brought *et lenguaje popular, dialectos y regionalismos.*[4])

Chicanos and other Spanish speakers also shift *ll* to *y* and *z* to *s*.[5] We leave out initial syllables, saying *tar* for *estar, toy* for *estoy, hora* for *ahora (cubanos* and *puertorriqueños* also leave out initial letters of some words). We also leave out the final syllable such as *pa* for *para*. The intervocalic *y*, the *ll* as in *tortilla, ella, bottella,* gets replaced by *tortia* or *tortiya, ea, botea*. We add an additional syllable at the beginning of certain words: *atocar* for *tocar, agastar* for *gastar*. Sometimes we'll say *lavaste las vacijas,* other times *lavates* (substituting the *ates* verb endings for the *aste*).

We use anglicisms, words borrowed from English: *bola* from ball, *carpeta* from carpet, *máchina de lavar* (instead of *lavadora*) from washing machine. Tex-Mex argot, created by adding a Spanish sound at the beginning or end of an English word such as *cookiar* for cook, *watchar* for watch, *parkiar* for park, and *rapiar* for rape, is the result of the pressures on Spanish speakers to adapt to English.

We don't use the word *vosotros/as* or its accompanying verb form. We don't say *claro* (to mean yes), *imagínate,* or *me emociona,* unless we picked up Spanish from Latinas, out of a book, or in a classroom. Other Spanish-speaking groups are going through the same, or similar, development in their Spanish.

LINGUISTIC TERRORISM

> *Deslenguadas. Somos los del español deficiente.* We are your linguistic nightmare, your linguistic aberration, your linguistic *mestisaje,* the subject of your *burla*. Because we speak with tongues of fire we are culturally crucified. Racially, culturally and linguistically *somos huérfanos*—we speak an orphan tongue.

Chicanas who grew up speaking Chicano Spanish have internalized the belief that we speak poor Spanish. It is illegitimate, a bastard language. And because we internalize how our language has been used against us by the dominant culture, we use our language differences against each other.

Chicana feminists often skirt around each other with suspicion and hesitation. For the longest time I couldn't figure it out. Then it dawned on me. To be close to another Chicana is like looking into the mirror. We are afraid of what we'll see there. *Pena.* Shame. Low estimation of self. In childhood we are told that our language is wrong. Repeated attacks on our native tongue diminish our sense of self. The attacks continue throughout our lives.

Chicanas feel uncomfortable talking in Spanish to Latinas, afraid of their censure. Their language was not outlawed in their countries. They had a whole lifetime of being immersed in their native tongue; generations, centuries in which Spanish was a first language, taught in school, heard on radio and TV, and read in the newspaper.

If a person, Chicana or Latina, has a low estimation of my native tongue, she also has a low estimation of me. Often with *mexicanas y latinas* we'll speak English as a neutral language. Even among Chicanas we tend to speak English at parties or conferences. Yet, at the same time, we're afraid the other will think we're *agringadas* because we don't speak Chicano Spanish. We oppress each other trying to out-Chicano each other, vying to be the "real" Chicanas, to speak like Chicanos. There is no one Chicano language just as there is no one Chicano experience. A monolingual Chicana whose first language is English or Spanish is just as much a Chicana as one who speaks several variants of Spanish. A Chicana from Michigan or Chicago or Detroit is just as much a Chicana as one from the Southwest. Chicano Spanish is as diverse linguistically as it is regionally.

By the end of this century, Spanish speakers will comprise the biggest minority group in the U.S., a country where students in high schools and colleges are encouraged to take French classes because French is considered more "cultured." But for a language to remain alive it must be used.[6] By the end of this century English, and not Spanish, will be the mother tongue of most Chicanos and Latinos.

So, if you want to really hurt me, talk badly about my language. Ethnic identity is twin skin to linguistic identity—I am my language. Until I can take pride in my language, I cannot take pride in myself. Until I can accept as legitimate Chicano Texas Spanish, Tex-Mex and all the other languages I speak, I cannot accept the legitimacy of myself. Until I am free to write bilingually and to switch codes without having always to translate, while I still have to speak English or Spanish when I would rather speak Spanglish, and as long as I have to accommodate the English speakers rather than having them accommodate me, my tongue will be illegitimate.

I will no longer be made to feel ashamed of existing. I will have my voice: Indian, Spanish, white. I will have my serpent's tongue—my woman's voice, my sexual voice, my poet's voice. I will overcome the tradition of silence.

My fingers
Move sly against your palm
Like women everywhere, we speak in code . . .

—MELANIE KAYE/KANTROWITZ[7]

"VISTAS," CORRIDOS, Y COMIDA: MY NATIVE TONGUE

In the 1960s, I read my first Chicano novel. It was *City of Night* by John Rechy, a gay Texan, son of a Scottish father and a Mexican mother. For days I walked around in stunned amazement that a Chicano could write and could get published. When I read *I Am Joaquin*.[8] I was surprised to see a bilingual book by a Chicano in print. When I saw poetry written in Tex-Mex for the first time, a feeling of pure joy flashed through me. I felt like we really existed as a people. In 1971, when I started teaching High School English to Chicano students, I tried to supplement the required texts with works by Chicanos, only to be reprimanded and forbidden to do so by the principal. He claimed that I was supposed to teach "American" and English literature. At the risk of being fired, I swore my students to secrecy and slipped in Chicano short stories, poems, a play. In graduate school, while working toward a Ph.D., I had to "argue" with one advisor after the other, semester after semester, before I was allowed to make Chicano literature an area of focus.

Even before I read books by Chicanos or Mexicans, it was the Mexican movies I saw at the drive-in—the Thursday night special of $1.00 a carload—that gave me a sense of belonging. "*Vámonos a las vistas,*" my mother would call out and we'd all—grandmother, brothers, sister and cousins—squeeze into the car. We'd wolf down cheese and bologna white bread sandwiches while watching Pedro Infante in melodramatic tear-jerkers like *Nosotros los pobres,* the first "real" Mexican movie (that was not an imitation of European movies). I remember seeing *Cuando los hijos se van* and surmising that all Mexican movies played up the love a mother has for her children and what ungrateful sons and daughters suffer when they are not devoted to their mothers. I remember the singing-type "westerns" of Jorge Negrete and Miquel Aceves Mejía. When watching Mexican movies, I felt a sense of homecoming as well as alienation. People who were to amount to something didn't go to Mexican movies, or *bailes* or tune the radios to *bolero, rancherita,* and *corrído* music.

The whole time I was growing up, there was *norteño* music sometimes called North Mexican border music, or Tex-Mex music, or Chicano music, or *cantina* (bar) music. I grew up listening to *conjuntos,* three- or four-piece bands made up of folk musicians playing guitar, *bajo sexto,* drums and button accordion, which Chicanos had borrowed from the German immigrants who had come to Central Texas and Mexico to farm and build breweries. In the Rio Grande Valley, Steve Jordan and Little Joe Hernández were popular, and Flaco Jiménez was the accordion king. The rhythms of Tex-Mex music are those of the polka, also adapted from the Germans, who in turn had borrowed the polka from the Czechs and Bohemians.

I remember the hot, sultry evenings when *corridos*—songs of love and death on the Texas-Mexican borderlands—reverberated out of cheap amplifiers from the local *cantinas* and wafted in through my bedroom window.

Corridos first became widely used along the South Texas/Mexican border during the early conflict between Chicanos and Anglos. The *corridos* are usually about Mexican heroes who do valiant deeds against the Anglo oppressors. Pancho Villa's song, *"La cucaracha,"* is the most famous one. *Corridos* of John F. Kennedy and his death are still very popular in the Valley. Older Chicanos remember Lydia Mendoza, one of the great border *corrido* singers who was called *la Gloria de Tejas.* Her *"El tango negro,"* sung during the Great Depression, made her a singer of the people. The everpresent *corridos* narrated one hundred years of border history, bringing news of events as well as entertaining. These folk musicians and folk songs are our chief cultural mythmakers, and they made our hard lives seem bearable.

I grew up feeling ambivalent about our music. Country-western and rock-and-roll had more status. In the 50s and 60s, for the slightly educated and *agringado* Chicanos, there existed a sense of shame at being caught listening to our music. Yet I couldn't stop my feet from thumping to the music, could not stop humming the words, nor hide from myself the exhilaration I felt when I heard it.

There are more subtle ways that we internalize identification, especially in the forms of images and emotions. For me food and certain smells are tied to my identity, to my homeland. Wood smoke curling up to an immense blue sky; wood smoke perfuming my grandmother's clothes, her skin. The stench of cow manure and the yellow patches on the ground; the crack of a .22 rifle and the reek of cordite. Homemade white cheese sizzling in a pan, melting inside a folded *tortilla.* My sister Hilda's hot, spicy *menudo, chile colorado* making it deep red, pieces of *panza* and hominy floating on top. My brother Carito barbequing *fajitas* in the backyard. Even now and 3,000 miles away, I can see my mother spicing the ground beef, pork and venison with *chile.* My mouth salivates at the thought of the hot steaming *tamales* I would be eating if I were home.

SI LE PREGUNTAS A MI MAMÁ, "¿QUÉ ERES?"

> *"Identity is the essential core of who*
> *we are as individuals, the conscious*
> *experience of the self inside."*
>
> —Kaufman[9]

Nosotros los Chicanos straddle the borderlands. On one side of us, we are constantly exposed to the Spanish of the Mexicans, on the other side we hear the Anglos' incessant clamoring so that we forget our language. Among ourselves we don't say *nosotros los americanos, o nosotros los españoles, o nosotros los hispanos.* We say *nosotros los mexicanos* (by *mexicanos* we do not mean citizens of Mexico; we do not mean a national identity, but a racial one). We distinguish between *mexicanos del otro lado* and *mexicanos de este lado.* Deep in our hearts we believe that being Mexican has nothing to do with which country one lives in. Being Mexican is a state of soul—not one of mind, not one of citizenship. Neither eagle nor serpent, but both. And like the ocean, neither animal respects borders.

Dime con quien andas y te diré quien eres.
(Tell me who your friends are and I'll tell you who you are.)
—Mexican saying

Si le preguntas a mi mamá, "¿Qué eres?" te dirá, *"Soy mexicana,"* My brothers and sister say the same. I sometimes will answer *"soy mexicana"* and at others will say *"soy Chicana" o "soy tejana."* But I identified as *"Raza"* before I ever identified as *"mexicana"* or "Chicana."

As a culture, we call ourselves Spanish when referring to ourselves as a linguistic group and when copping out. It is then that we forget our predominant Indian genes. We are 70–80 percent Indian.[10] We call ourselves Hispanic[11] or Spanish-American or Latin American or Latin when linking ourselves to other Spanish-speaking peoples of the Western hemisphere and when copping out. We call ourselves Mexican-American[12] to signify we are neither Mexican nor American, but more the noun "American" than the adjective "Mexican" (and when copping out).

Chicanos and other people of color suffer economically for not acculturating. This voluntary (yet forced) alienation makes for psychological conflict, a kind of dual identity—we don't identify with the Anglo-American cultural values and we don't totally identify with the Mexican cultural values. We are a synergy of two cultures with various degrees of Mexicanness or Angloness. I have so internalized the borderland conflict that sometimes I feel like one cancels out the other and we are zero, nothing, no one. *A veces no soy nada ni nadis. Pero hasta cuando no lo soy, lo soy.*

When not copping out, when we know we are more than nothing, we call ourselves Mexican, referring to race and ancestry; *mestizo* when affirming both our Indian and Spanish (but we hardly ever own our Black ancestry); Chicano when referring to a politically aware people born and/or raised in the U.S.; *Raza* when referring to Chicanos; *tejanos* when we are Chicanos from Texas.

Chicanos did not know we were a people until 1965 when Cesar Chavez and the farmworkers united and *I Am Joaquín* was published and *la Raza Unida* party was formed in Texas. With that recognition, we became a distinct people. Something momentous happened to the Chicano soul—we became aware of our reality and acquired a name and a language (Chicano Spanish) that reflected that reality. Now that we had a name, some of the fragmented pieces began to fall together—who we were, what we were, how we had evolved. We began to get glimpses of what we might eventually become.

Yet the struggle of identities continues, the struggle of borders is our reality still. One day the inner struggle will cease and a true integration take place. In the meantime, *tenémos que hacer la lucha. ¿Quién está protegiendo los ranchos de mi gente? ¿Quién está tratando de cerrar la fisura entre la india y el blanco en nuestra sangre? El Chicano, si, el Chicano que anda como un ladrón en su propia casa.*

Los Chicanos, how patient we seem, how very patient. There is the quiet of the Indian about us.[13] We know how to survive. When other races have given up their tongue, we've kept ours. We know what it is to live under the hammer blow of the dominant *norteamericano* culture. But more than we count the blows, we count the days the weeks the years the centuries the eons until the white laws and commerce and customs will rot in the deserts they've created, lie bleached. *Humildes* yet proud, *quietos* yet wild, *nosotros los mexicanos-Chicanos* will walk by the crumbling ashes as we go about our business. Stubborn, persevering, impenetrable as stone, yet possessing a malleability that renders us unbreakable, we, the *mestizas* and *mestizos,* will remain.

NOTES

1. Ray Gwyn Smith, *Moorland is Cold Country,* unpublished book.
2. Irena Klepfisz, "Di rayze aheymi/The Journey Home," in *The Tribe of Dina: A Jewish Women's Anthology,* Melanie Kaye/Kantrowitz and Irena Klepfisz, eds. (Montpelier, VT. Sinister Wisdom Books, 1986), 49.
3. R. C. Ortega, *Dialectología Del Barrio,* trans. Horrencia S. Alwan (Los Angeles, CA: R. C. Ortega Publisher & Bookseller, 1977), 132.
4. Eduardo Hernandéz-Chávez, Andrew D. Cohen, and Anthony F. Beltramo, *El Lenguaje de los Chicanos: Regional and Social Characteristics of Language Used By Mexican Americans* (Arlington, VA: Center for Applied Linguistics, 1975), 39.
5. Hernandéz-Chávez, xvii.
6. Irena Klepfisz, "Secular Jewish Identity: Yidishkayt in America," in *The Tribe of Dina,* Kaye/Kantrowitz and Klepfisz, eds., 43.
7. Melanie Kaye/Kantrowitz, "Sign," in *We Speak In Code: Poems and Other Writings* (Pittsburgh, PA: Motherroot Publications, Inc., 1980), 85.
8. Rodolfo Gonzales, *I Am Joaquin/Yo Soy Joaquín* (New York, NY: Bantam Books, 1972). It was first published in 1967.
9. Kaufman, 68.
10. Chávez, 88–90.
11. "Hispanic" is derived from *Hispanis (España,* a name given to the Iberian Peninsula in ancient times when it was a part of the Roman Empire) and is a term designated by the U.S. government to make it easier to handle us on paper.
12. The Treaty of Guadalupe Hidalgo created the Mexican-American border in 1848.
13. Anglos, in order to alleviate their guilt for dispossessing the Chicano, stressed the Spanish part of us and perpetrated the myth of the Spanish Southwest. We have accepted the fiction that we are Hispanic, that is Spanish, in order to accommodate ourselves to the dominant culture and its abhorrence of Indians. Chávez, 88–91.

40

THE DARK SIDE OF SPORTS SYMBOLS

STANLEY D. EITZEN • MAXINE BACA ZINN

The teams that played in the 1995 World Series were the Atlanta Braves and Cleveland Indians. Inside Atlanta Fulton County Stadium and Jacobs Field, the Braves' fans did the "tomahawk chop" and enthusiastically shouted "Indian" chants. Similarly, the fans of the Indians, united behind their symbol, Chief Wahoo, waved fake tomahawks and wore "war paint" and other pseudo-Native American symbols. Outside these stadiums, Native American activists carried signs in protest of the inappropriate use of their symbols by Anglos. (In less politically correct times, there was no such uproar when these same teams met in the 1948 World Series.)

A group's symbols serve two fundamental purposes—they bind together the individual members and separate one group from another. Each of the thousands of street gangs in the U.S., for example, has a group identity that is displayed in its names, code words, gestures, distinctive clothing, and colors. The symbols of these gangs promote solidarity and set them apart from rivals.

Using symbols to achieve solidarity and community is common in American schools. Students, former students, faculty members, and others who identify with the institution adopt nicknames for its athletic teams, display the school colors, wave the school banner, wear special clothing and jewelry, and engage in ritual chants and songs.

A school's nickname is much more than a tag or a label. It conveys, symbolically, the characteristics and attributes that define the institution. In an important way, the symbols represent the institution's self-concept. Schools may have names that signify their ethnic heritage (e.g., the Bethany College Swedes), state history (University of Oklahoma Sooners), religion (Oklahoma Baptist College Prophets), or founder (Whittier College Poets). Most, though, utilize symbols of aggression and ferocity for their athletic teams—birds such as hawks, animals such as bulldogs, human categories such as pirates, and even the otherworldly such as devils.

Although school names and other symbols evoke strong emotions of solidarity among followers, there is also a potential dark side to their use. The names, mascots, logos, and flags chosen may be derogatory to some group.

USA Today (Magazine), Jan. 2001, v129 i2668, p. 48.

The symbols may dismiss, differentiate, demean, and trivialize marginalized groups such as African-Americans, Native Americans, and women. Thus, they serve to maintain the dominant status of powerful groups and subordinate those categorized as "others." That may not have been the intent of those who decided on the names and mascots for a particular school, but their use diminishes these "others," retaining the racial and gender inequities found in the large society. School symbols as used in sports, then, have power not only to maintain in-group solidarity, but to separate the in-group from the out-group and perpetuate the hierarchy between them.

SYMBOLS OF THE CONFEDERACY

At Nathan Bedford Forrest High School in Jacksonville, Fla., young African-American athletes wear the Confederate Army's colors on their uniforms and call themselves the Rebels. The school they play for is named after the slave-trading Confederate general who became the original grand wizard of the Ku Klux Klan.

Within the neo-Confederate culture found in parts of the South, certain symbols such as the Rebel battle flag and the singing of "Dixie" are zealously promoted. These symbols have two distinct meanings—one that promotes the South's heritage and another that symbolizes slavery, racial separation, and hate.

In 1948, the so-called Dixiecrats, rebelling against a strong civil rights plank in the Democratic platform, walked out of the party's convention. That year, the University of Mississippi adopted the Rebel flag, designated "Dixie" as the school's fight song, and introduced a mascot named Colonel Reb, a caricature of an Old South plantation owner. In 1962, James Meredith, despite the strong opposition of Gov. Ross Barnett and other white leaders in the state, became the first black student at the school. There were demonstrations at that time in support of segregation. Infused in these demonstrations was the showing of the Rebel flag and the singing of "Dixie" as symbols of defiance by the supporters of segregation.

Over the ensuing years, the use of these symbols at the University of Mississippi has caused considerable debate. On the one hand, they represented the state's heritage and as such were a source of pride, inspiration, and unity among its citizens. The opposing position was that these symbols represented a history of oppression against African-Americans, noting that the Rebel flag was also a prominent symbol of the Ku Klux Klan. Opponents argued further that, since almost one-third of Mississippians are African-Americans, the flagship university of that state should not use symbols that recall the degradation and demeaning of their ancestors. Is it proper, they ask, to use the key symbol of the Confederacy and African-American enslavement as a rallying symbol for the University of Mississippi's sports teams—teams composed of whites and blacks?

As a compromise, in 1983, 21 years after the University of Mississippi integrated, its chancellor ruled that the Rebel flag was no longer the official banner for the school. Chancellor Porter L. Fortune Jr. made it clear, however, that students would have the right to wave the flag at football games, and that they have done. Sports teams names such as the Rebels as well as mascots like Colonel Reb and songs such as "Dixie" have continued as official school symbols.

The debate still rages. Charles W. Eagles, a University of Mississippi history professor, sums up the ongoing controversy: "For some of us—those who believe in the University of Mississippi—the symbols prevent the university from being everything it can be. Others—those that are faithful to Ole Miss [the traditionalists]—think that if you took the symbols away, there wouldn't be anything there. The symbols are seen as a real burden for the university. But they're the backbone of Ole Miss." This debate demonstrates vividly the power of symbols, not only to unite or divide, but the hold they have on people, as seen in their resistance to change and in the organized efforts to remove those symbols interpreted as negative.

NATIVE AMERICAN SYMBOLS

The use of Native American names such as "Redmen," "Fighting Sioux," "Utes," and even "Savages" is common in high schools, community colleges, colleges, and universities. Many professional teams have also adopted Native American names—in baseball, the Atlanta Braves and Cleveland Indians; in football, the Washington Redskins and the Kansas City Chiefs; in basketball, the Golden State Warriors; and in hockey, the Chicago Blackhawks.

Defenders of Native American names, logos, and mascots argue that their use is a tribute to the indigenous peoples. Native Americans, the argument goes, are portrayed as brave, resourceful, and strong. Native American names were chosen for sports teams precisely because they represent these positive traits.

Other defenders claim that their use is no different from those names and mascots that represent other ethnic groups such as the "Irish," "Vikings," or "Norse." Because members of these ethnic groups accept the use of their names, Native Americans should also be proud of this recognition of their heritage, they maintain.

However, many Native Americans do object to their symbols being used by athletic teams. Since the early 1970s, individuals and organizations—such as the American Indian Movement (AIM)—have sought to eliminate the use of Native American names, mascots, and logos by sports teams. They use several key arguments, foremost among them being racial stereotyping. Names such as "Indian," "Brave," and "Chiefs" are not inherently offensive, but some names, logos, and mascots project a violent caricature of Native Americans ("scalpers," "savages"). Teams that use American Indian names commonly employ the "tomahawk chop," war paint, and mascots dressed as Native Americans. This depiction of Native Americans as bloodthirsty warriors distorts history, since whites invaded Indian lands, oppressed native peoples, and even employed and justified a policy of genocide toward them.

Some mascots are especially demeaning to Native Americans. Chief Wahoo of the Cleveland Indians is described by sportswriter Rick Telander as "the red-faced, big-nosed, grinning, drywall-toothed moron who graces the peak of every Cleveland Indians cap." Is such a caricature appropriate? Clyde Bellecourt, national director of AIM, summarizes the complaints: "If you look up the word 'redskin' in both the Webster's and Random House dictionaries, you'll find the word is defined as being offensive. Can you imagine if they called them the Washington Jews and the team mascot was a rabbi leading them in [the song] 'Hava Nagila,' fans in the stands wearing yarmulkes and waving little sponge torahs? The word "Indian" isn't offensive "Brave" isn't offensive, but it's the behavior that accompanies all of this that's offensive. The robber tomahawks. The chicken-feather headdresses. People wearing war paint and making these ridiculous war whoops with a tomahawk in one hand and a beer in the other. All of these things have significant meaning for us. And the psychological impact it has, especially on our youth, is devastating."

Another problem is the imitation or misuse of symbols that have religious significance to some Native American peoples. Utilizing dances, chants, drummings, and other rituals at sporting events clearly tends to trivialize their meaning.

Also problematic is the homogenization of American Indian cultures. Native Americans are portrayed uniformly, disregarding the sometimes enormous differences among the tribes. Thus, through the use of Indian names and mascots, society defines who Native Americans are instead of allowing them to determine how society thinks of them.

A few colleges and universities—such as Stanford, Siena, Miami of Ohio, Dartmouth, and St. John's—have taken these objections seriously and changed their names and mascots. Most high schools and colleges, though, resist such a change. Ironically, they insist on retaining the Native American symbols even though those schools do not have an American Indian heritage or significant Native American student representation. The members of these schools and their constituencies insist on retaining their Native American names because they are part of their collective identities. This allegiance to their school symbols seems to have higher priority than insensitivity to the negative consequences produced by inappropriate depictions of Native Americans.

SEXIST NAMES

Many studies have shown the varied slavery ways in which language acts in the defining, deprecation, and exclusion of women. Names do this, too. Naming a women's and men's athletic team is not a neutral process. The names chosen often are badges of femininity and masculinity, hence of inferiority and superiority. To the degree that this occurs, the names of women's and men's athletic teams reinforce a basic element of social structure: gender division and hierarchy. Team names reflect this division as well as the asymmetry that is associated with it. Despite advances made by women in sports since the implementation of Title IX in 1971, widespread naming practices continue to mark female athletes as unusual, aberrant, or invisible.

We examined the names and accompanying logos and mascots of sports teams for females and males at 1,185 coeducational four-year colleges and universities. We identified eight gender-linked practices associated with names and/or logos that diminished and trivialized women:

- *Physical markers.* One common naming practice emphasizes the physical appearance of women, such as the Angelo State Rambelles. As Casey Miller and Kate Swift argue in *The Handbook of Nonsexist Writing,* this practice is sexist because the "emphasis on the physical characteristics of women is offensive in contexts where men are described in terms of achievement."

- The use of "girl" or "gal" stresses the presumed immaturity and irresponsibility of women, such as the Elon College Golden Girls. As Miller and Swift note, "Just as "boy" can be blatantly offensive to minority men, so "girl" can have comparable patronizing and demeaning implications for women."

- *Feminine suffixes.* This is a popular form of sexual differentiation found in the names of athletic, social, and women's groups. The practice not only marks women, it denotes a feminine derivative by establishing a female negative trivial category. The devaluation is accomplished by tagging words with feminine suffixes like "ette." At Dillard University, for example, the men's team is the Blue Devils; the women's team, the Devilettes.

- *Lady.* This label has several meanings that demean women as athletes. "Lady," according to Miller and Swift, is used to "evoke a standard of propriety, correct behavior, and elegance," characteristics that are decidedly unathletic. Similarly, "lady" carries overtones recalling the age of chivalry. As Robin Lakoff maintains in *Language and Women's Place.* "This makes the term seem polite at first, but we must also remember that these implications are perilous: they suggest that a 'lady' is helpless, and cannot do things for herself." The use of "lady" for women's teams is common (e.g., the University of Florida Lady Gators). At Washington and Jefferson College, the men are Presidents and the women are First Ladies, which clearly marks the status of women's teams as inferior to that of the men.

- *Male as a false generic.* This practice assumes that the masculine in the language, word, or name choice is the norm, while ignoring the feminine altogether. Miller and Swift define this procedure as "terms used of a class or group that are not applicable to all members." The use of "mankind" to encompass both sexes has its parallel among men's and women's athletic teams that have the same name, for example, the Rams (Colorado State University) or the Hokies at Virginia Tech (a "Hokie" is a castrated turkey). In *Man Made Language,* Dale Spender has called the practice of treating the masculine as the norm as "one of the most pervasive and pernicious rules that has been encoded." Its consequence is to make women invisible as well as secondary to men, since they are robbed of a separate identity.

- *Male name with a female modifier.* This practice applies the feminine to a name that usually denotes a male, giving females lower status. Examples among sports teams are the Lady Friars of Providence College and the Lady Gamecocks of the University of South Carolina (a "gamecock" is a fighting rooster). As we note in *Fair and Foul: Beyond the Myths and Paradoxes of Sport,* using such oxymorons "reflects role conflict and contributes to the lack of acceptance of women's sport."

- *Double gender marking.* This occurs when the name for the women's team is a diminutive of the men's team name combined with "belle," "lady," or other feminine modifier. For example, at the University of Kentucky, the men's teams are the Wildcats and the women's teams are the Lady Kats. Compounding the feminine intensifies women's secondary status. In his book, *Grammar and Gender,* Dennis Baron argues that double gender marking occurs "perhaps to underline the inappropriateness or rarity of the feminine noun or to emphasize its negativity."

- *Male/female, paired polarity.* Women's and men's teams can be assigned names that represent a female/male opposition. When this occurs, the names of the men's teams embody competitiveness and other positive traits usually associated with sport, whereas the names for women's teams are lighthearted or cute. Successful athletes are believed to embody such traits as courage, bravura, boldness, self-confidence, and aggression. When the names given men's teams imply these traits, but those for women's teams suggest that females are playful and cuddly, women are trivialized and de-athleticized. For instance, the Mercer University men's teams are the Bears and the women are the Teddy Bears; at Fort Valley State College, the men's teams are the Wildcats and the women's teams are the Wildkittens.

Another grouping occurs when names which could be included in one of the above categories also incorporate race. This especially occurs with teams that adopt Native American symbols. The men's teams at Southeastern Oklahoma State University are the Savages and the women's teams are the Savagettes, utilizing the diminutive feminine suffix combined with a negative stereotype for the racial category. Similarly, at Montclair State College, the men are the Indians and the women are the Squaws. The word "squaw" also refers to a woman's pelvic area and means prostitute in some native languages. Vernon Bellecourt of the American Indian Movement says, "The issue itself is clear . . . The word 'squaw' has got to go in all its forms. It's demeaning and degrading to Indian women and all women."

Our survey found that slightly over half of U.S. colleges and universities have sexist names and/or logos for their athletic teams. Thus, the identity symbols for athletic teams at those schools contribute to the maintenance of male dominance within college sports. Since the traditional masculine gender role matches most athletic qualities better than the traditional feminine gender role, the images and symbols are male. Women do not fit into this scheme. They are "others," even when they do participate. Their team names and logos tend to perpetuate and strengthen the image of female inferiority by making them secondary, invisible, trivial, or unathletic.

RESISTANCE TO CHANGE

It is important to note that many schools do not have team names, mascots, and logos that are racist or sexist. They use race-and gender-neutral names such as Bears, Eagles, Seagulls, Saints, or Blue Streaks. Schools that currently employ racist or sexist names could change to neutral ones that embody the traits desired in athletic teams such as courage, strength, and aggressiveness. For some, such a change would be relatively easy—dropping the use of "lady" or "ette" as modifiers, for example. Teams with Native American or male names (stags, rams, hokies, centaurs) must adopt a new name or eliminate the racism or sexism that is inherent in their present names. A few schools have done so over the past 15 years or so. Most schools, however, resist changing names with passion because a name change negates the school's traditions.

Tradition, above all, is always a barrier to change. Students, alumni, faculty, and athletes become accustomed to a particular name for their university and its athletic teams, and it seems "natural." This is the argument made on behalf of the many teams that continue to use American Indian names and symbols for their teams despite the objections of Native Americans. So, too, with names that are sexist. Even if a school team name has the force of tradition, is it justified to continue using that name if it is racist or sexist? If a sexist team name reinforces and socializes sexist thinking, however subtly, it should be changed. If not, the institution is publicly sexist.

Many see the naming issue as trivial. It is not trivial, though, to the group being demeaned, degraded, and trivialized. Some progressives argue that there are more important issues to address than changing racist or sexist names of athletic teams. This illustrates the contradiction that the naming of teams is at once trivial and important. For African-Americans, whether the

University of Mississippi fans sing "Dixie" and wave the Confederate flag is not as important as ending discrimination and obtaining good jobs. Similarly, for Native Americans, the derogatory use of their heritage surrounding athletic contests is relatively unimportant compared to raising their standard of living. For women, the sexist naming of athletic teams is not as significant as pay equity, breaking the "glass ceiling," or achieving equity with men in athletic departments in resources, scholarships, and media attention.

Faced with a choice among these options, the naming issue would be secondary, but this sets up a false choice. We can work to remove all manifestations of racism and sexism on college campuses. Referring to language and relevant to the women's team names issue as well, the Association for Women in Psychology Ad Hoc Committee on Sexist Language has addressed and refuted the "trivial concern" argument: "The major objection, often even to discussing changing sexist language, is that it is a superficial matter compared with the real physical and economic oppression of women. And indeed, women's total oppression must end; we are not suggesting any diversion of energies from that struggle. We are, however, suggesting that this is an important part of it."

Symbols are extremely compelling in the messages they convey. Their importance is understood when rebellious groups demean or defame symbols of the powerful, such as the flag. Names and other symbols have the power to elevate or put down a group. If racist or sexist, they reinforce and, therefore, maintain the secondary status of African-Americans, Native Americans, or women through stereotyping, caricature, derogation, trivialization, diminution, or making them invisible. Most of us, however, fail to see the problem with symbols that demean or defame the powerless because these symbols support the existing power arrangements in society. Despite their apparent triviality, the symbols surrounding sports teams are important because they can—and often do—contribute to patterns of social dominance.

Colleges and universities, for the most part, are making major efforts to diversify their student bodies, faculties, and administrations by race, ethnicity, and sex. This laudable goal is clearly at odds with the existence of racist and sexist names and practices of their athletic teams. The leadership in these schools (boards of regents, chancellors, presidents, and faculty senates) must take a stand against racism and sexism in all its forms and take appropriate action. Removing all racist and sexist symbols such as names, mascots, flags, logos, and songs are an important beginning to this crucial project.

41

WHERE RACE AND GENDER MEET
Racism, Hate Crimes, and Pornography

HELEN ZIA

There is a specific area where racism, hate crimes, and pornography intersect, and where current civil rights law fails: racially motivated, gender-
based crimes against women of color. This area of bias-motivated sexual
assault has been called "ethnorape"; I refer to it as "hate rape."

I started looking into this issue after years of organizing against hate
killings of Asian Americans. After a while, I noticed that all the cases I could
name concerned male victims. I wondered why. Perhaps it was because Asian-
American men came into contact with perpetrator types more often or because
they are more hated and therefore more often attacked by racists. But the subordination and vulnerability of Asian-American women, who are thought to
be sexually exotic, subservient, and passive, argued against that interpretation. So where were the Asian-American women hate-crime victims?

Once I began looking, I found them, in random news clippings, in foot-
notes in books, through word of mouth. Let me share with you some examples I unearthed of bias-motivated attacks and sexual assaults:

- In February 1984, Ly Yung Cheung, a nineteen-year-old Chinese
  woman who was seven months pregnant, was pushed in front of a
  New York City subway train and decapitated. Her attacker, a white
  male high school teacher, claimed he suffered from "a phobia of
  Asian people" and was overcome with the urge to kill this woman.
  He successfully pleaded insanity. If this case had been investigated as
  a hate crime, there might have been more information about his so-
  called phobia and whether it was part of a pattern of racism. But it
  was not.

From Laura Lederer and Richard Delgado (eds.), *The Price We Pay The Case Against
Racist Speech, Hate Propaganda and Pornography.* New York: Hill & Wang, 1995.
Reprinted by permission of Dr. Laura J. Lederer.

- On December 7, 1984, fifty-two-year-old Japanese-American Helen Fukui disappeared in Denver, Colorado. Her decomposed body was found weeks later. Her disappearance on Pearl Harbor Day, when anti-Asian speech and incidents increase dramatically, was considered significant in the community. But the case was not investigated as a hate crime and no suspects were ever apprehended.

- In 1985 an eight-year-old Chinese girl named Jean Har-Kaw Fewel was found raped and lynched in Chapel Hill, North Carolina—two months after *Penthouse* featured pictures of Asian women in various poses of bondage and torture, including hanging bound from trees. Were epithets or pornography used during the attack? No one knows—her rape and killing were not investigated as a possible hate crime.

- Recently a serial rapist was convicted of kidnapping and raping a Japanese exchange student in Oregon. He had also assaulted a Japanese woman in Arizona, and another in San Francisco. He was sentenced to jail for these crimes, but they were never pursued as hate crimes, even though California has a hate statute. Was hate speech or race-specific pornography used? No one knows.

- At Ohio State University, two Asian women were gang raped by fraternity brothers in two separate incidents. One of the rapes was part of a racially targeted game called the "Ethnic Sex Challenge," in which the fraternity men followed an ethnic checklist indicating what kind of women to gang rape. Because the women feared humiliation and ostracism by their communities, neither reported the rapes. However, campus officials found out about the attacks, but did not take them up as hate crimes, or as anything else.

All of these incidents could have been investigated and prosecuted either as state hate crimes or as federal civil rights cases. But they were not. To have done so would have required one of two things: awareness and interest on the part of police investigators and prosecutors—who generally have a poor track record on race and gender issues—or awareness and support for civil rights charges by the Asian-American community—which is generally lacking on issues surrounding women, gender, sex, and sexual assault. The result is a double-silencing effect on the assaults and deaths of these women, who become invisible because of their gender and their race.

Although my research centers on hate crimes and Asian women, this silence and this failure to provide equal protection have parallels in all of the other classes protected by federal civil rights and hate statutes. That is, all other communities of color have a similar prosecution rate for hate crimes against the women in their communities—namely, zero. This dismal record is almost as bad in lesbian and gay antiviolence projects: the vast preponderance of hate crimes reported, tracked, and prosecuted concern gay men—very few concern lesbians. So where are all the women?

The answer to this question lies in the way our justice system was designed, and the way women are mere shadows in the existing civil rights framework. But in spite of this history, federal and state law do offer legal avenues for women to be heard. Federal civil rights prosecutions, for example, can be excellent platforms for high-visibility community education on the harmful impact of hate speech and behavior. When on June 19, 1982, two white auto workers in Detroit screamed racial epithets at Chinese-American Vincent Chin and said, "It's because of you motherfuckers that we're out of work," a public furor followed, raising the level of national discourse on what constitutes racism toward Asian Americans. Constitutional law professors, and members of the American Civil Liberties Union and the National Lawyers Guild had acted as if Asian Americans were not covered by civil rights law. Asian Americans emphatically corrected that misconception.

Hate crimes remedies can be used to force the criminal justice bureaucracy to adopt new attitudes. Patrick Purdy went to an elementary school in Stockton, California, in which 85 percent of the students came from Southeast Asia. When he selected that school as the place to open fire with his automatic weapon and killed five eight-year-olds and wounded thirty other children, the police and the media did not think it was a bias-motivated crime. Their denial reminds me of the response by the Montreal officials to the anti-feminist killings of fourteen women students there. But an outraged Asian-American community forced a state investigation into the Purdy incident and uncovered hate literature in the killer's effects. As a result, the community was validated, and, in addition, the criminal justice system and the media acquired a new level of understanding.

Imagine if a federal civil rights investigation had been launched in the case of the African-American student at St. John's University who was raped and sodomized by white members of the school lacrosse team, who were later acquitted. Investigators could have raised issues of those white men's attitudes toward the victim as a black woman, found out whether hate speech or race-specific pornography was present, investigated the overall racial climate on campus, and brought all of the silenced aspects of the incident to the public eye. Community discourse could have been raised to a high level.

Making these investigations happen will not be an easy road. Hate crimes efforts are generally expended on blatant cases, with high community consensus, not ones that bring up hard issues like gender-based violence. Yet these intersections of race and gender hatred are the very issues we must give voice to.

There is a serious difficulty with pushing for use of federal and state hate remedies. Some state statutes have been used against men of color: specifically, on behalf of white rape victims against African-American men. We know that the system, if left unchecked, will try to use antihate laws to enforce unequal justice. On the other hand, state hate statutes could be used to prosecute men of color who are believed to have assaulted women of color of another race—interminority assaults are increasing. Also, if violence against women generally were made into a hate crime, women of color could seek prosecutions against men in their own community for their gender-based violence—even if this would make it harder to win the support of men in communities of color, and of women in those communities who would not want to be accused of dividing the community.

But at least within the Asian-American antiviolence community, this discourse is taking place now. Asian-American feminists in San Francisco have prepared a critique of the Asian movement against hate crimes and the men of that movement are listening. Other communities of color should also examine the nexus between race and gender for women of color, and by extension, for all women.

The legal system must expand the boundaries of existing law to include the most invisible women. There are hundreds of cases involving women of color waiting to be filed. Activists in the violence-against-women movement must reexamine current views on gender-based violence. Not all sexual assaults are the same. Racism in a sexual assault adds another dimension to the pain and harm inflicted. By taking women of color out of the legal shadows, out of invisibility, all women make gains toward full human dignity and human rights.

42

FRATERNITIES AND COLLEGIATE RAPE CULTURE
Why Are Some Fraternities More Dangerous Places for Women?

A. AYRES BOSWELL • JOAN Z. SPADE

D ate rape and acquaintance rape on college campuses are topics of concern to both researchers and college administrators. Some estimate that 60 to 80 percent of rapes are date or acquaintance rape (Koss, Dinero, Seibel, and Cox 1988). Further, 1 out of 4 college women say they were raped or experienced an attempted rape, and 1 out of 12 college men say they forced a woman to have sexual intercourse against her will (Koss, Gidycz, and Wisniewski 1985).

From *Gender & Society,* Vol. 10, no. 2, 1996, pp. 133–147. Reprinted by permission from Sage Publications, Inc.

Although considerable attention focuses on the incidence of rape, we know relatively little about the context or the *rape culture* surrounding date and acquaintance rape. Rape culture is a set of values and beliefs that provide an environment conducive to rape (Buchwald, Fletcher, and Roth 1993; Herman 1984). The term applies to a generic culture surrounding and promoting rape, not the specific settings in which rape is likely to occur. We believe that the specific settings also are important in defining relationships between men and women.

Some have argued that fraternities are places where rape is likely to occur on college campuses (Martin and Hummer 1989; O'Sullivan 1993; Sanday 1990) and that the students most likely to accept rape myths and be more sexually aggressive are more likely to live in fraternities and sororities, consume higher doses of alcohol and drugs, and place a higher value on social life at college (Gwartney-Gibbs and Stockard 1989; Kalof and Cargill 1991). Others suggest that sexual aggression is learned in settings such as fraternities and is not part of predispositions or preexisting attitudes (Boeringer, Shehan, and Akers 1991). To prevent further incidences of rape on college campuses, we need to understand what it is about fraternities in particular and college life in general that may contribute to the maintenance of a rape culture on college campuses.

Our approach is to identify the social contexts that link fraternities to campus rape and promote a rape culture. Instead of assuming that all fraternities provide an environment conducive to rape, we compare the interactions of men and women at fraternities identified on campus as being especially *dangerous* places for women, where the likelihood of rape is high, to those seen as *safer* places, where the perceived probability of rape occurring is lower. Prior to collecting data for our study, we found that most women students identified some fraternities as having more sexually aggressive members and a higher probability of rape. These women also considered other fraternities as relatively safe houses, where a woman could go and get drunk if she wanted to and feel secure that the fraternity men would not take advantage of her. We compared parties at houses identified as high-risk and low-risk houses as well as at two local bars frequented by college students. Our analysis provides an opportunity to examine situations and contexts that hinder or facilitate positive social relations between undergraduate men and women.

The abusive attitudes toward women that some fraternities perpetuate exist within a general culture where rape is intertwined in traditional gender scripts. Men are viewed as initiators of sex and women as either passive partners or active resisters, preventing men from touching their bodies (LaPlante, McCormick, and Brannigan 1980). Rape culture is based on the assumptions that men are aggressive and dominant whereas women are passive and acquiescent (Buchwald et al. 1993; Herman 1984). What occurs on college campuses is an extension of the portrayal of domination and aggression of men over women that exemplifies the double standard of sexual behavior in U.S. society (Barthel 1988; Kimmel 1993).

Sexually active men are positively reinforced by being referred to as "studs," whereas women who are sexually active or report enjoying sex are derogatorily labeled as "sluts" (Herman 1984; O'Sullivan 1993). These gender scripts are embodied in rape myths and stereotypes such as "She really wanted it; she just said no because she didn't want me to think she was a bad girl" (Burke, Stets, and Pirog-Good 1989; Jenkins and Dambrot 1987; Lisak and Roth 1988; Malamuth 1986; Muehlenhard and Linton 1987; Peterson and Franzese 1987). Because men's sexuality is seen as more natural, acceptable, and uncontrollable than women's sexuality, many men and women excuse acquaintance rape by affirming that men cannot control their natural urges (Miller and Marshall 1987).

Whereas some researchers explain these attitudes toward sexuality and rape using an individual or a psychological interpretation, we argue that rape has a social basis, one in which both men and women create and recreate masculine and feminine identities and relations. Based on the assumption that rape is part of the social construction of gender, we examine how men and women "do gender" on a college campus (West and Zimmerman 1987). We focus on fraternities because they have been identified as settings that encourage rape (Sanday 1990). By comparing fraternities that are viewed by women as places where there is a high risk of rape to those where women believe there is a low risk of rape as well as two local commercial bars, we seek to identify characteristics that make some social settings more likely places for the occurrence of rape.

RESULTS

The Settings

Fraternity Parties   We observed several differences in the quality of the interaction of men and women at parties at high-risk fraternities compared to those at low-risk houses. A typical party at a low-risk house included an equal number of women and men. The social atmosphere was friendly, with considerable interaction between women and men. Men and women danced in groups and in couples, with many of the couples kissing and displaying affection toward each other. Brothers explained that, because many of the men in these houses had girlfriends, it was normal to see couples kissing on the dance floor. Coed groups engaged in conversations at many of these houses, with women and men engaging in friendly exchanges, giving the impression that they knew each other well. Almost no cursing and yelling was observed at parties in low-risk houses; when pushing occurred, the participants apologized. Respect for women extended to the women's bathrooms, which were clean and well supplied.

At high-risk houses, parties typically had skewed gender ratios, sometimes involving more men and other times involving more women. Gender segregation also was evident at these parties, with the men on one side of a room or in the bar drinking while women gathered in another area. Men treated women differently in the high-risk houses. The women's bathrooms in the high-risk houses were filthy, including clogged toilets and vomit in the sinks. When a brother was told of the mess in the bathroom at a high-risk house, he replied, "Good, maybe some of these beer wenches will leave so there will be more beer for us."

Men attending parties at high-risk houses treated women less respectfully, engaging in jokes, conversations, and behaviors that degraded women. Men made a display of assessing women's bodies and rated them with thumbs up or thumbs down for the other men in the sight of the women. One man attending a party at a high-risk fraternity said to another, "Did you know that this week is Women's Awareness Week? I guess that means we get to abuse them more this week." Men behaved more crudely at parties at high-risk houses. At one party, a brother dropped his pants, including his underwear, while dancing in front of several women. Another brother slid across the dance floor completely naked.

The atmosphere at parties in high-risk fraternities was less friendly overall. With the exception of greetings, men and women rarely smiled or laughed and spoke to each other less often than was the case at parties in low-risk houses. The few one-on-one conversations between women and men appeared to be strictly flirtatious (lots of eye contact, touching, and very close talking). It was rare to see a group of men and women together talking. Men were openly hostile, which made the high-risk parties seem almost threatening at times. For example, there was a lot of touching, pushing, profanity, and name calling, some done by women.

Students at parties at the high-risk houses seemed self-conscious and aware of the presence of members of the opposite sex, an awareness that was sexually charged. Dancing early in the evening was usually between women. Close to midnight, the sex ratio began to balance out with the arrival of more men or more women. Couples began to dance together but in a sexual way (close dancing with lots of pelvic thrusts). Men tried to pick up women using lines such as "Want to see my fish tank?" and "Let's go upstairs so that we can talk; I can't hear what you're saying in here."

Although many of the same people who attended high-risk parties also attended low-risk parties, their behavior changed as they moved from setting to setting. Group norms differed across contexts as well. At a party that was held jointly at a low-risk house with a high-risk fraternity, the ambience was that of a party at a high-risk fraternity with heavier drinking, less dancing, and fewer conversations between women and men. The men from both high- and low-risk fraternities were very aggressive; a fight broke out, and there was pushing and shoving on the dance floor and in general.

As others have found, fraternity brothers at high-risk houses on this campus told about routinely discussing their sexual exploits at breakfast the morning after parties and sometimes at house meetings (cf. Martin and Hummer 1989; O'Sullivan 1993; Sanday 1990). During these sessions, the brothers we interviewed said that men bragged about what they did the night before with stories of sexual conquests often told by the same men, usually sophomores. The women involved in these exploits were women they did not know or knew but did not respect, or *faceless victims*. Men usually treated girlfriends with respect and did not talk about them in these storytelling sessions. Men from low-risk houses, however, did not describe similar sessions in their houses.

The Bar Scene   The bar atmosphere and social context differed from those of fraternity parties. The music was not as loud, and both bars had places to sit and have conversations. At all fraternity parties, it was difficult to maintain conversations with loud music playing and no place to sit. The volume of music at parties at high-risk fraternities was even louder than it was at low-risk houses, making it virtually impossible to have conversations. In general, students in the local bars behaved in the same way that students did at parties in low-risk houses with conversations typical, most occurring between men and women.

The first bar, frequented by older students, had live entertainment every night of the week. Some nights were more crowded than others, and the atmosphere was friendly, relaxed, and conducive to conversation. People laughed and smiled and behaved politely toward each other. The ratio of men to women was fairly equal, with students congregating in mostly coed groups. Conversation flowed freely and people listened to each other.

Although the women and men at the first bar also were at parties at low- and high-risk fraternities, their behavior at the bar included none of the blatant sexual or intoxicated behaviors observed at some of these parties. As the evenings wore on, the number of one-on-one conversations between men and women increased and conversations shifted from small talk to topics such as war and AIDS. Conversations did not revolve around picking up another person, and most people left the bar with same-sex friends or in coed groups.

The second bar was less popular with older students. Younger students, often under the legal drinking age, went there to drink, sometimes after leaving campus parties. This bar was much smaller and usually not as crowded as the first bar. The atmosphere was more mellow and relaxed than it was at the fraternity parties. People went there to hang out and talk to each other.

On a couple of occasions, however, the atmosphere at the second bar became similar to that of a party at a high-risk fraternity. As the number of people in the bar increased, they removed chairs and tables, leaving no place to sit and talk. The music also was turned up louder, drowning out conversation. With no place to dance or sit, most people stood around but could not maintain conversations because of the noise and crowds. Interactions between women and men consisted mostly of flirting. Alcohol consumption also was greater than it was on the less crowded nights, and the number of visibly drunk people increased. The more people drank, the more conversation and socializing broke down. The only differences between this setting and that of a party at a high-risk house were that brothers no longer controlled the territory and bedrooms were not available upstairs.

Gender Relations

Relations between women and men are shaped by the contexts in which they meet and interact. As is the case on other college campuses, *hooking up* has replaced dating on this campus, and fraternities are places where many students hook up. Hooking up is a loosely applied term on college campuses that had different meanings for men and women on this campus.

Most men defined hooking up similarly. One man said it was something that happens

> when you are really drunk and meet up with a woman you sort of
> know, or possibly don't know at all and don't care about. You go
> home with her with the intention of getting as much sexual,
> physical pleasure as she'll give you, which can range anywhere
> from kissing to intercourse, without any strings attached.

The exception to this rule is when men hook up with women they admire. Men said they are less likely to press for sexual activity with someone they know and like because they want the relationship to continue and be based on respect.

Women's version of hooking up differed. Women said they hook up only with men they cared about and described hooking up as kissing and petting but not sexual intercourse. Many women said that hooking up was disappointing because they wanted longer-term relationships. First-year women students realized quickly that hook-ups were usually one-night stands with no strings attached, but many continued to hook up because they had few opportunities to develop relationships with men on campus. One first-year woman said that "70 percent of hook-ups never talk again and try to avoid one another; 26 percent may actually hear from them or talk to them again, and 4 percent may actually go on a date, which can lead to a relationship." Another first-year woman said, "It was fun in the beginning. You get a lot of attention and kiss a lot of boys and think this is what college is about, but it gets tiresome fast."

Whereas first-year women get tired of the hook-up scene early on, many men do not become bored with it until their junior or senior year. As one upperclassman said, "The whole game of hooking up became really meaningless and tiresome for me during my second semester of my sophomore year, but most of my friends didn't get bored with it until the following year."

In contrast to hooking up, students also described monogamous relationships with steady partners. Some type of commitment was expected, but most people did not anticipate marriage. The term *seeing each other* was applied when people were sexually involved but free to date other people. This type of relationship involved less commitment than did one of boyfriend/girlfriend but was not considered to be a hook-up.

The general consensus of women and men interviewed on this campus was that the Greek system, called "the hill," set the scene for gender relations. The predominance of Greek membership and subsequent living arrangements segregated men and women. During the week, little interaction occurred between women and men after their first year in college because students in fraternities or sororities live and dine in separate quarters. In addition, many non-Greek upper-class students move off campus into apartments. Therefore, students see each other in classes or in the library, but there is no place where students can just hang out together.

Both men and women said that fraternities dominate campus social life, a situation that everyone felt limited opportunities for meaningful interactions. One senior Greek man said,

> This environment is horrible and so unhealthy for good male and
> female relationships and interactions to occur. It is so segregated
> and male dominated. . . . It is our party, with our rules and our beer.
> We are allowing these women and other men to come to our party.
> Men can feel superior in their domain.

Comments from a senior woman reinforced his views: "Men are dominant; they are the kings of the campus. It is their environment that they allow us to enter; therefore, we have to abide by their rules." A junior woman described fraternity parties as

> good for meeting acquaintances but almost impossible to really get
> to know anyone. The environment is so superficial, probably
> because there are so many social cliques due to the Greek system.
> Also, the music is too loud and the people are too drunk to attempt
> to have a real conversation, anyway.

Some students claim that fraternities even control the dating relationships of their members. One senior woman said, "Guys dictate how dating occurs on this campus, whether it's cool, who it's with, how much time can be spent with the girlfriend and with the brothers." Couples either left campus for an evening or hung out separately with their own same-gender friends at fraternity parties, finally getting together with each other at about 2 A.M. Couples rarely went together to fraternity parties. Some men felt that a girlfriend was just a replacement for a hook-up. According to one junior man, "Basically a girlfriend is someone you go to at 2 A.M. after you've hung out with the guys. She is the sexual outlet that the guys can't provide you with."

Some fraternity brothers pressure each other to limit their time with and commitment to their girlfriends. One senior man said, "The hill [fraternities] and girlfriends don't mix." A brother described a constant battle between girlfriends and brothers over who the guy is going out with for the night, with the brothers usually winning. Brothers teased men with girlfriends with remarks such as "whipped" or "where's the ball and chain?" A brother from a high-risk house said that few brothers at his house had girlfriends; some did, but it was uncommon. One man said that from the minute he was a pledge he knew he would probably never have a girlfriend on this campus because "it was just not the norm in my house. No one has girlfriends; the guys have too much fun with [each other]."

The pressure on men to limit their commitment to girlfriends, however, was not true of all fraternities or of all men on campus. Couples attended low-risk fraternity parties together, and men in the low-risk houses went out on dates more often. A man in one low-risk house said that about 70 percent of the members of his house were involved in relationships with women, including the pledges (who were sophomores).

Treatment of Women

Not all men held negative attitudes toward women that are typical of a rape culture, and not all social contexts promoted the negative treatment of women. When men were asked whether they treated the women on campus with respect, the most common response was "On an individual basis, yes, but when you have a group of men together, no." Men said that, when together in groups with other men, they sensed a pressure to be disrespectful toward women. A first-year man's perception of the treatment of women was that "they are treated with more respect to their faces, but behind closed doors, with a group of men present, respect for women is not an issue." One senior man stated, "In general, college-aged men don't treat women their age with respect because 90 percent of them think of women as merely a means to sex." Women reinforced this perception. A first-year woman stated, "Men here are more interested in hooking up and drinking beer than they are in getting to know women as real people." Another woman said, "Men here use and abuse women."

Characteristic of rape culture, a double standard of sexual behavior for men versus women was prevalent on this campus. As one Greek senior man stated, "Women who sleep around are sluts and get bad reputations; men who do are champions and get a pat on the back from their brothers." Women also supported a double standard for sexual behavior by criticizing sexually active women. A first-year woman spoke out against women who are sexually active: "I think some girls here make it difficult for the men to respect women as a whole."

One concrete example of demeaning sexually active women on this campus is the "walk of shame." Fraternity brothers come out on the porches of their houses the night after parties and heckle women walking by. It is assumed that these women spent the night at fraternity houses and that the men they were with did not care enough about them to drive them home.

Although sororities now reside in former fraternity houses, this practice continues and sometimes the victims of hecklings are sorority women on their way to study in the library.

A junior man in a high-risk fraternity described another ritual of disrespect toward women called "chatter." When an unknown woman sleeps over at the house, the brothers yell degrading remarks out the window at her as she leaves the next morning such as "Fuck that bitch" and "Who is that slut?" He said that sometimes brothers harass the brothers whose girlfriends stay over instead of heckling those women.

Fraternity men most often mistreated women they did not know personally. Men and women alike reported incidents in which brothers observed other brothers having sex with unknown women or women they knew only casually. A sophomore woman's experience exemplifies this anonymous state: "I don't mind if 10 guys were watching or it was videotaped. That's expected on this campus. It's the fact that he didn't apologize or even offer to drive me home that really upset me." Descriptions of sexual encounters involved the satisfaction of men by nameless women. A brother in a high-risk fraternity described a similar occurrence:

> A brother of mine was hooking up upstairs with an unattractive woman who had been pursuing him all night. He told some brothers to go outside the window and watch. Well, one thing led to another and they were almost completely naked when the woman noticed the brothers outside. She was then unwilling to go any further, so the brother went outside and yelled at the other brothers and then closed the shades. I don't know if he scored or not, because the woman was pretty upset. But he did win the award for hooking up with the ugliest chick that weekend.

Attitudes toward Rape

> The sexually charged environment of college campuses raises many questions about cultures that facilitate the rape of women. How women and men define their sexual behavior is important legally as well as interpersonally. We asked students how they defined rape and had them compare it to the following legal definition: the perpetration of an act of sexual intercourse with a female against her will and consent, whether her will is overcome by force or fear resulting from the threat of force, or by drugs or intoxicants; or when, because of mental deficiency, she is incapable of exercising rational judgment.
> (Brownmiller 1975, 368)

When presented with this legal definition, most women interviewed recognized it as well as the complexities involved in applying it. A first-year woman said, "If a girl is drunk and the guy knows it and the girl says, 'Yes, I want to have sex,' and they do, that is still rape because the girl can't make a conscious, rational decision under the influence of alcohol." Some women disagreed. Another first-year woman stated, "I don't think it is fair that the guy gets blamed when both people involved are drunk."

The typical definition men gave for rape was "when a guy jumps out of the bushes and forces himself sexually onto a girl." When asked what date rape was, the most common answer was "when one person has sex with another person who did not consent." Many men said, however, that "date rape is when a woman wakes up the next morning and regrets having sex." Some men said that date rape was too gray an area to define. "Consent is a fine line," said a Greek senior man student. For the most part, the men we spoke with argued that rape did not occur on this campus. One Greek sophomore man said, "I think it is ridiculous that someone here would rape someone." A first-year man stated, "I have a problem with the word *rape*. It sounds so criminal, and we are not criminals; we are sane people."

Whether aware of the legal definitions of rape, most men resisted the idea that a woman who is intoxicated is unable to consent to sex. A Greek junior man said, "Men should not be responsible for women's drunkenness." One first-year man said, "If that is the legal definition of rape, then it happens all the time on this campus." A senior man said, "I don't care whether alcohol is involved or not; that is not rape. Rapists are people that have something seriously wrong with them." A first-year man even claimed that when women get drunk, they invite sex. He said, "Girls get so drunk here and then come on to us. What are we supposed to do? We are only human."

DISCUSSION AND CONCLUSION

These findings describe the physical and normative aspects of one college campus as they relate to attitudes about and relations between men and women. Our findings suggest that an explanation emphasizing rape culture also must focus on those characteristics of the social setting that play a role in defining heterosexual relationships on college campuses (Kalof and Cargill 1991). The degradation of women as portrayed in rape culture was not found in all fraternities on this campus. Both group norms and individual behavior changed as students went from one place to another. Although individual men are the ones who rape, we found that some settings are more likely places for rape than are others. Our findings suggest that rape cannot be seen only as an isolated act and blamed on individual behavior and proclivities, whether it be alcohol consumption or attitudes. We also must consider characteristics of the settings that promote the behaviors that reinforce a rape culture.

Relations between women and men at parties in low-risk fraternities varied considerably from those in high-risk houses. Peer pressure and situational norms influenced women as well as men. Although many men in high- and low-risk houses shared similar views and attitudes about the Greek system, women on this campus, and date rape, their behaviors at fraternity parties were quite different.

Women who are at highest risk of rape are women whom fraternity brothers did not know. These women are faceless victims, nameless acquaintances—not friends. Men said their responsibility to such persons and the level of guilt they feel later if the hook-ups end in sexual intercourse are much lower if they hook up with women they do not know. In high-risk houses, brothers treated women as subordinates and kept them at a distance. Men in high-risk houses actively discouraged ongoing heterosexual relationships, routinely degraded women, and participated more fully in the hook-up scene; thus, the probability that women would become faceless victims was higher in these houses. The flirtatious nature of the parties indicated that women go to these parties looking for available men, but finding boyfriends or relationships was difficult at parties in high-risk houses. However, in the low-risk houses, where more men had long-term relationships, the women were not strangers and were less likely to become faceless victims.

The social scene on this campus, and on most others, offers women and men few other options to socialize. Although there may be no such thing as a completely safe fraternity party for women, parties at low-risk houses and commercial bars encouraged men and women to get to know each other better and decreased the probability that women would become faceless victims. Although both men and women found the social scene on this campus demeaning, neither demanded different settings for socializing, and attendance at fraternity parties is a common form of entertainment.

These findings suggest that a more conducive environment for conversation can promote more positive interactions between men and women. Simple changes would provide the opportunity for men and women to interact in meaningful ways such as adding places to sit and lowering the volume of music at fraternity parties or having parties in neutral locations, where men are not in control. The typical party room in fraternity houses includes a place to dance but not to sit and talk. The music often is loud, making it difficult, if not impossible, to carry on conversations; however, there were more conversations at the low-risk parties, where there also was more respect shown toward women. Although the number of brothers who had steady girlfriends in the low-risk houses as compared to those in the high-risk houses may explain the differences, we found that commercial bars also provided a context for interaction between men and women. At the bars, students sat and talked and conversations between men and women flowed freely, resulting in deep discussions and fewer hook-ups.

Alcohol consumption was a major focus of social events here and intensified attitudes and orientations of a rape culture. Although pressure to drink was evident at all fraternity parties and at both bars, drinking dominated high-risk fraternity parties, at which nonalcoholic beverages usually were not available and people chugged beers and became visibly drunk. A rape culture is strengthened by rules that permit alcohol only at fraternity parties.

Under this system, men control the parties and dominate the men as well as the women who attend. As college administrators crack down on fraternities and alcohol on campus, however, the same behaviors and norms may transfer to other places such as parties in apartments or private homes where administrators have much less control. At commercial bars, interaction and socialization with others were as important as drinking, with the exception of the nights when the bar frequented by under-class students became crowded. Although one solution is to offer nonalcoholic social activities, such events receive little support on this campus. Either these alternative events lacked the prestige of the fraternity parties or the alcohol was seen as necessary to unwind, or both.

In many ways, the fraternities on this campus determined the settings in which men and women interacted. As others before us have found, pressures for conformity to the norms and values exist at both high-risk and low-risk houses (Kalof and Cargill 1991; Martin and Hummer 1989; Sanday 1990). The desire to be accepted is not unique to this campus or the Greek system (Holland and Eisenhart 1990; Horowitz 1988; Moffat 1989). The degree of conformity required by Greeks may be greater than that required in most social groups, with considerable pressure to adopt and maintain the image of their houses. The fraternity system intensifies the "groupthink syndrome" (Janis 1972) by solidifying the identity of the in-group and creating an us/them atmosphere. Within the fraternity culture, brothers are highly regarded and women are viewed as outsiders. For men in high-risk fraternities, women threatened their brotherhood; therefore, brothers discouraged relationships and harassed those who treated women as equals or with respect. The pressure to be one of the guys and hang out with the guys strengthens a rape culture on college campus by demeaning women and encouraging the segregation of men and women.

Students on this campus were aware of the contexts in which they operated and the choices available to them. They recognized that, in their interactions, they created differences between men and women that are not natural, essential, or biological (West and Zimmerman 1987). Not all men and women accepted the demeaning treatment of women, but they continued to participate in behaviors that supported aspects of a rape culture. Many women participated in the hook-up scene even after they had been humiliated and hurt because they had few other means of initiating contact with men on campus. Men and women alike played out this scene, recognizing its injustices in many cases but being unable to change the course of their behaviors.

Although this research provides some clues to gender relations on college campuses, it raises many questions. Why do men and women participate in activities that support a rape culture when they see its injustices? What would happen if alcohol were not controlled by groups of men who admit that they disrespect women when they get together? What can be done to give men and women on college campuses more opportunities to interact responsibly and get to know each other better? These questions should be studied on other campuses with a focus on the social settings in which the incidence of rape and the attitudes that support a rape culture exist. Fraternities are social contexts that may or may not foster a rape culture.

Our findings indicate that a rape culture exists in some fraternities, especially those we identified as high-risk houses. College administrators are responding to this situation by providing counseling and educational programs that increase awareness of date rape, including campaigns such as "No means no." These strategies are important in changing attitudes, values, and behaviors; however, changing individuals is not enough. The structure of campus life and the impact of that structure on gender relations on campus are highly determinative. To eliminate campus rape culture, student leaders and administrators must examine the situations in which women and men meet and restructure these settings to provide opportunities for respectful interaction. Change may not require abolishing fraternities; rather, it may require promoting settings that facilitate positive gender relations.

REFERENCES

Barthel, D. 1988. *Putting on appearances: Gender and advertising.* Philadelphia: Temple University Press.

Boeringer, S. B., C. L. Shehan, and R. L. Akers. 1991. Social contexts and social learning in sexual coercion and aggression: Assessing the contribution of fraternity membership. *Family Relations* 40: 58–64.

Brownmiller, S. 1975. *Against our will: Men, women and rape.* New York: Simon & Schuster.

Buchwald, E., P. R. Fletcher, and M. Roth, eds. 1993. *Transforming a rape culture.* Minneapolis. MN: Milkweed Editions.

Burke, P., J. E. Stets, and M. A. Pirog-Good. 1989. Gender identity, self-esteem, physical abuse and sexual abuse in dating relationships. In *Violence in dating relationships: Emerging social issues,* edited by M. A. Pirog-Good and J. E. Stets. New York: Praeger.

Gwartney-Gibbs, P., and J. Stockard. 1989. Courtship aggression and mixed-sex peer groups. In *Violence in dating relationships: Emerging social issues,* edited by M. A. Pirog-Good and J. E. Stets. New York: Praeger.

Herman. D. 1984. The rape culture. In *Women: A feminist perspective,* edited by J. Freeman. Mountain View, CA: Mayfield.

Holland. D. C., and M. A. Eisenhart. 1990. *Educated in romance: Women, achievement, and college culture.* Chicago: University of Chicago Press.

Horowitz, H. I. 1988. *Campus life: Undergraduate cultures from the end of the 18th century to the present.* Chicago: University of Chicago Press.

Hunter, F. 1953. *Community power structure.* Chapel Hill: University of North Carolina Press.

Jenkins, M. J., and F. H. Dambrot. 1987. The attribution of date rape: Observer's attitudes and sexual experiences and the dating situation. *Journal of Applied Social Psychology* 17:875–95.

Janis, I. L. 1972. *Victims of groupthink.* Boston: Houghton Mifflin.

Kalof, I., and T. Cargill. 1991. Fraternity and sorority membership and gender dominance attitudes. *Sex Roles* 25:417–23.

Kimmel, M. S. 1993. Clarence, William, Iron Mike, Tailhook, Senator Packwood, Spur Posse, Magic . . . and us. In *Transforming a rape culture,* edited by E. Buchwald, P. R. Fletcher, and M. Roth. Minneapolis, MN: Milkweed Editions.

Koss, M. P., T. E. Dinero, C. A. Seibel, and S. L. Cox. 1988. Stranger and acquaintance rape: Are there differences in the victim's experience? *Psychology of Women Quarterly* 12:1–24.

Koss, M. P., C. A. Gidycz, and N. Wisniewski. 1985. The scope of rape: Incidence and prevalence of sexual aggression and victimization in a national sample of higher education students. *Journal of Consulting and Clinical Psychology* 55:162–70.

LaPlante, M. N., N. McCormick, and G. G. Brannigan. 1980. Living the sexual script: College students' views of influence in sexual encounters. *Journal of Sex Research* 16:338–55.

Lisak, D., and S. Roth. 1988. Motivational factors in nonincarcerated sexually aggressive men. *Journal of Personality and Social Psychology* 55:795–802.

Malamuth, N. 1986. Predictors of naturalistic sexual aggression. *Journal of Personality, and Social Psychology.* 50:953–62.

Martin, P. Y., and R. Hummer. 1989. Fraternities and rape on campus. *Gender & Society* 3:457–73.

Miller, B., and J. C. Marshall. 1987. Coercive sex on the university campus. *Journal of College Student Personnel* 28:38–47.

Mollat, M. 1989. *Coming of age in New Jersey: College life in American culture.* New Brunswick, NJ: Rutgers University Press.

Muchlenhard, C. L., and M. A. Linton. 1987. Date rape and sexual aggression in dating situations: Incidence and risk factors. *Journal of Counseling Psychology* 34:186–96.

O'Sullivan, C. 1993. Fraternities and the rape culture. In *Transforming a rape culture,* edited by E. Buchwald, P. R. Fletcher, and M. Roth. Minneapolis, MN: Milkweed Editions.

Peterson, S. A., and B. Franzese. 1987. Correlates of college men's sexual abuse of women. *Journal of College Student Personnel* 28:223–28.

Sanday, P. R. 1990. *Fraternity gang rape: Sex, brotherhood, and privilege on campus.* New York: New York University Press.

West, C., and D. Zimmerman. 1987. Doing gender. *Gender & Society* 1:125–51.

43

THE CONSTRUCTION OF MASCULINITY
AND THE TRIAD OF MEN'S VIOLENCE

MICHAEL KAUFMAN

The all too familiar story: a woman raped, a wife battered, a lover abused. With a sense of immediacy and anger, the women's liberation movement has pushed the many forms of men's violence against women—from the most overt to the most subtle in form—into popular consciousness and public debate. These forms of violence are one aspect of our society's domination by men that, in outcome, if not always in design, reinforces that domination. The act of violence is many things at once. At the same instant it is the individual man acting out relations of sexual power; it is the violence of a society—a hierarchical, authoritarian, sexist, class-divided, militarist, racist, impersonal, crazy society—being focused through an individual man onto an individual woman. In the psyche of the individual man it might be his denial of social powerlessness through an act of aggression. In total these acts of violence are like a ritualized acting out of our social relations of power: the dominant and the weaker, the powerful and the powerless, the active and the passive . . . the masculine and the feminine.

For men, listening to the experience of women as the objects of men's violence is to shatter any complacency about the sex-based status quo. The power and anger of women's responses forces us to rethink the things we discovered when we were very young. When I was eleven or twelve years old a friend told me the difference between fucking and raping. It was simple: with rape you tied the woman to a tree. At the time the anatomical details were still a little vague, but in either case it was something "we" supposedly did. This knowledge was just one part of an education, started years before, about the relative power and privileges of men and women. I remember laughing when my friend explained all that to me. Now I shudder. The difference in my responses is partially that, at twelve, it was part of the posturing and pretense that accompanied my passage into adolescence. Now, of course, I have a different vantage point on the issue. It is the vantage point of an adult, but more importantly my view of the world is being reconstructed by the intervention of that majority whose voice has been suppressed: the women.

Reprinted from *Beyond Patriarchy: Essays on Pleasure, Power, and Change*, edited by Michael Kaufman. Toronto: Oxford University Press, 1987. Reprinted by permission.

484

This relearning of the reality of men's violence against women evokes many deep feelings and memories for men. As memories are recalled and recast, a new connection becomes clear: violence by men against women is only one corner of a triad of men's violence. The other two corners are violence against other men and violence against oneself.

On a psychological level the pervasiveness of violence is the result of what Herbert Marcuse called the "surplus repression" of our sexual and emotional desires.[1] The substitution of violence for desire (more precisely, the transmutation of violence into a form of emotionally gratifying activity) happens unequally in men and women. The construction of masculinity involves the construction of "surplus aggressiveness." The social context of this triad of violence is the institutionalization of violence in the operation of most aspects of social, economic, and political life.

The three corners of the triad reinforce one another. The first corner—violence against women—cannot be confronted successfully without simultaneously challenging the other two corners of the triad. And all this requires a dismantling of the social feeding ground of violence: patriarchal, heterosexist, authoritarian, class societies. These three corners and the societies in which they blossom feed on each other. And together, we surmise, they will fall.

THE SOCIAL CONTEXT

In spite of proclamations from the skewed research of sociobiologists, there is no good evidence that men's violence is the inevitable and natural result of male genes or hormones. To the contrary, anthropology tells us of many early societies with little or no violence against women, against children, or among men. However, given the complexity of the issues concerning the roots of violence, the essential question for us is not whether men are predisposed to violence but what society does with this violence. Why has the linchpin of so many societies been the manifold expression of violence perpetrated disproportionately by men? Why are so many forms of violence sanctioned or even encouraged? Exactly what is the nature of violence? And how are patterns of violence and the quest for domination built up and reinforced?

In other words, the key questions having to do with men's violence are not biological but are related to gender and society—which is why I speak not of "male violence" (a biological category) but rather of "men's violence" (the gender category).

For every apparently individual act of violence there is a social context. This is not to say there are no pathological acts of violence; but even in that case the "language" of the violent act, the way the violence manifests itself can only be understood within a certain social experience. We are interested here in the manifestations of violence that are accepted as more or less normal, even if reprehensible: fighting, war, rape, assault, psychological abuse, and so forth. What is the context of men's violence in the prevalent social orders of today?

Violence has long been institutionalized as an acceptable means of solving conflicts. But now the vast apparati of policing and war making maintained by countries the world over pose a threat to the future of life itself.

"Civilized" societies have been built and shaped through the decimation, containment, and exploitation of other peoples: extermination of native populations, colonialism, and slavery. Our relationship with the natural environment has often been described with the metaphor of rape. An attitude of conquering nature, of mastering an environment waiting to be exploited for profit, has great consequences when we possess a technology capable of permanently disrupting an ecological balance shaped over hundreds of millions of years.

The daily work life of industrial class societies is one of violence. Violence poses as economic rationality as some of us are turned into extensions of machines, while others become brains detached from bodies. Our industrial process becomes the modern-day rack of torture where we are stretched out of shape and ripped limb from limb. It is violence that exposes workers to the danger of chemicals, radiation, machinery, speedup, and muscle strain.

The racism, sexism, and heterosexism that have been institutionalized in our societies are socially regulated acts of violence. Our cities, our social structure, our work life, our relation with nature, our history are more than a backdrop to the prevalence of violence. They are violence; violence in an institutionalized form encoded into physical structures and socioeconomic relations. Much of the sociological analysis of violence in our societies implies simply that violence is learned by witnessing and experiencing social violence: man kicks boy, boy kicks dog.[2] Such experiences of transmitted violence are a reality, as the analysis of wife battering indicates, for many batterers were themselves abused as children. [T]hrough [the child's] psychological development he embraces and takes into himself a set of gender-based social relations: the person that is created through the process of maturation becomes the personal embodiment of those relations. By the time the child is five or six years old, the basis for lifelong masculinity has already been established.

The basis for the individual's acquisition of gender is that the prolonged period of human childhood results in powerful attachments to parental figures. (Through a very complex process, by the time a boy is five or six he claims for himself the power and activity society associates with masculinity.) He embraces the project of controlling himself and controlling the world. He comes to personify activity. Masculinity is a reaction against passivity and powerlessness, and with it comes a repression of a vast range of human desires and possibilities: those that are associated with femininity.

Masculinity is unconsciously rooted before the age of six, is reinforced as the child develops, and then positively explodes at adolescence, obtaining its definitive shape for the individual. The masculine norm has its own particular nuances and traits dependent on class, nation, race, religion, and ethnicity. And within each group it has its own personal expression. In adolescence the pain and fear involved in repressing "femininity" and passivity start to become evident. For most of us, the response to this inner pain is to reinforce the bulwarks of masculinity. The emotional pain created by obsessive masculinity is stifled by reinforcing masculinity itself.

THE FRAGILITY OF MASCULINITY

Masculinity is power. But masculinity is terrifyingly fragile because it does not really exist in the sense we are led to think it exists; that is, as a biological reality—something real that we have inside ourselves. It exists as ideology; it exists as scripted behavior; it exists within "gendered" relationships. But in the end it is just a social institution with a tenuous relationship to that with which it is supposed to be synonymous: our maleness, our biological sex. The young child does not know that sex does not equal gender. For him to be male is to be what he perceives as being masculine. The child is father to the man. Therefore, to be unmasculine is to be desexed—"castrated."

The tension between maleness and masculinity is intense because masculinity requires a suppression of a whole range of human needs, aims, feelings, and forms of expression. Masculinity is one-half of the narrow, surplus-repressive shape of the adult human psyche. Even when we are intellectually aware of the difference between biological maleness and masculinity, the masculine ideal is so embedded within ourselves that it is hard to untangle the person we might want to become (more "fully human," less sexist, less surplus-repressed, and so on) from the person we actually are.

But as children and adolescents (and often as adults), we are not aware of the difference between maleness and masculinity. With the exception of a tiny proportion of the population born as hermaphrodites, there can be no biological struggle to be male. The presence of a penis and testicles is all it takes. Yet boys and men harbor great insecurity about their male credentials. This insecurity exists because maleness is equated with masculinity; but the latter is a figment of our collective, patriarchal, surplus-repressive imaginations.

In a patriarchal society being male is highly valued, and men value their masculinity. But everywhere there are ambivalent feelings. That the initial internalization of masculinity is at the father's knee has lasting significance. Andrew Tolson states that "to the boy, masculinity is both mysterious and attractive (in its promise of a world of work and power), and yet, at the same time, threatening (in its strangeness, and emotional distance). . . . It works both ways; attracts and repels in dynamic contradiction. This simultaneous distance and attraction is internalized as a permanent emotional tension that the individual must, in some way, strive to overcome."[3]

Although maleness and masculinity are highly valued, men are everywhere unsure of their sexuality, our needs and fears, our strengths and weaknesses, our selves are created—not simply learned—through our lived reality. The violence of our social order nurtures a psychology of violence, which in turn reinforces the social, economic and political structures of violence. The ever-increasing demands of civilization and the constant building upon inherited structures of violence suggest that the development of civilization has been inseparable from a continuous increase in violence against humans and our natural environment.

It would be easy, yet ultimately not very useful, to slip into a use of the term "violence" as a metaphor for all our society's antagonisms, contradictions, and ills. For now, let us leave aside the social terrain and begin to unravel the nature of so-called individual violence.

THE TRIAD OF MEN'S VIOLENCE

The longevity of the oppression of women must be based on something more than conspiracy, something more complicated than biological handicap and more durable than economic exploitation (although in differing degrees all these may feature).

—JULIET MITCHELL[4]

It seems impossible to believe that mere greed could hold men to such a steadfastness of purpose.

—JOSEPH CONRAD[5]

The field in which the triad of men's violence is situated is a society, or societies, grounded in structures of domination and control. Although at times this control is symbolized and embodied in the individual father—patriarchy, by definition—it is more important to emphasize that patriarchal structures of authority, domination, and control are diffused throughout social, economic, political, and ideological activities and in our relations to the natural environment. Perhaps more than in any previous time during the long epoch of patriarchy, authority does *not* rest with the father, at least in much of the advanced capitalist and noncapitalist world. This has led more than one author to question the applicability of the term *patriarchy.*[6] But I think it still remains useful as a broad, descriptive category. In this sense Jessica Benjamin speaks of the current reign of patriarchy without the father. "The form of domination peculiar to this epoch expresses itself not directly as authority but indirectly as the transformation of all relationships and activity into objective, instrumental, depersonalized forms."[7]

The structures of domination and control form not simply the background to the triad of violence, but generate, and in turn are nurtured by, this violence. These structures refer both to our social relations and to our interaction with our natural environment. The relation between these two levels is obviously extremely complex. It appears that violence against nature—that is, the impossible and disastrous drive to dominate and conquer the natural world—is integrally connected with domination among humans. Some of these connections are quite obvious. One thinks of the bulldozing of the planet for profit in capitalist societies, societies characterized by the dominance of one class over others. But the link between the domination of nature and structures of domination of humans go beyond this.

THE INDIVIDUAL REPRODUCTION OF MALE DOMINATION

No man is born a butcher.

—BERTOLT BRECHT[8]

In a male-dominated society men have a number of privileges. Compared to women we are free to walk the streets at night, we have traditionally escaped domestic labor, and on average we have higher wages, better jobs, and more power. But these advantages in themselves cannot explain the individual reproduction of the relations of male domination, that is, why the individual male from a very early age embraces masculinity. The embracing of masculinity is not only a "socialization" into a certain gender role, as if there is a preformed human being who learns a role that he own masculinity and maleness, whether consciously or not. When men are encouraged to be open, as in men's support and counseling groups, it becomes apparent that there exists, often under the surface, an internal dialogue of doubt about one's male and masculine credentials.

MEN'S VIOLENCE AGAINST WOMEN

In spite of the inferior role which men assign to them, women are the privileged objects of their aggression.

—SIMONE DE BEAUVOIR[9]

Men's violence against women is the most common form of direct, personalized violence in the lives of most adults. From sexual harassment to rape, from incest to wife battering to the sight of violent pornographic images, few women escape some form of men's aggression.

My purpose here is not to list and evaluate the various forms of violence against women, nor to try to assess what can be classed as violence per se.[10] It is to understand this violence as an expression of the fragility of masculinity combined with men's power. I am interested in its place in the perpetuation of masculinity and male domination.

In the first place, men's violence against women is probably the clearest, most straightforward expression of relative male and female power. That the relative social, economic, and political power can be expressed in this manner is, to a large part, because of differences in physical strength and in a life-long training (or lack of training) in fighting. But it is also expressed this way because of the active/passive split. Activity as aggression is part of the masculine gender definition. That is not to say this definition always includes rape or battering, but it is one of the possibilities within a definition of activity that is ultimately grounded in the body.

Rape is a good example of the acting out of these relations of power and of the outcome of fragile masculinity in a surplus-repressive society. In the testimonies of rapists one hears over and over again expressions of inferiority, powerlessness, anger. But who can these men feel superior to? Rape is a crime that not only demonstrates physical power, but that does so in the language of male-female sex-gender relations. The testimonies of convicted rapists collected by Douglas Jackson in the late 1970s are chilling and revealing.[11] Hal: "I feel very inferior to others. . . . I felt rotten about myself and by committing rape I took this out on someone I thought was weaker than me, someone I could control." Len: "I feel a lot of what rape is isn't so much sexual desire as a person's feelings about themselves and how that relates to sex. My fear of relating to people turned to sex because . . . it just happens to be the fullest area to let your anger out on, to let your feelings out on."

Sometimes this anger and pain are experienced in relation to women but just as often not. In either case they are addressed to women who, as the Other in a phallocentric society, are objects of mystification to men, the objects to whom men from birth have learned to express and vent their feelings, or simply objects with less social power and weaker muscles. It is the crime against women par excellence because, through it, the full weight of a sexually based differentiation among humans is played out.

Within relationships, forms of men's violence such as rape, battering, and what Meg Luxton calls the "petty tyranny" of male domination in the household[12] must be understood both "in terms of violence directed against women as women and against women as wives."[13] The family provides an arena for the expression of needs and emotions not considered legitimate elsewhere.[14] It is the one of the only places where men feel safe enough to express emotions. As the dams break, the flood pours out on women and children.[15] The family also becomes the place where the violence suffered by individuals in their work lives is discharged. "At work men are powerless, so in their leisure time they want to have a feeling that they control their lives."[16]

While this violence can be discussed in terms of male aggression, it operates within the dualism of activity and passivity, masculinity and femininity. Neither can exist without the other. This is not to blame women for being beaten, nor to excuse men who beat. It is but an indication that the various forms of men's violence against women are a dynamic affirmation of a masculinity that can only exist as distinguished from femininity. It is my argument that masculinity needs constant nurturing and affirmation. This affirmation takes many different forms. The majority of men are not rapists or batterers, although it is probable that the majority of men have used superior physical strength or some sort of physical force or threat of force against a woman at least once as a teenager or an adult. But in those who harbor great personal doubts or strongly negative self-images, or who cannot cope with a daily feeling of powerlessness, violence against women can become a means of trying to affirm their personal power in the language of our sex-gender system. That these forms of violence only reconfirm the negative self-image and the feelings of powerlessness shows the fragility, artificiality, the precariousness of masculinity.

VIOLENCE AGAINST OTHER MEN

At a behavioral level, men's violence against other men is visible throughout society. Some forms, such as fighting, the ritualized display of violence of teenagers and some groups of adult men, institutionalized rape in prisons, and attacks on gays or racial minorities, are very direct expressions of this violence. In many sports, violence is incorporated into exercise and entertainment. More subtle forms are the verbal putdown or, combined with economic and other factors, the competition in the business, political, or academic world. In its most frightening form, violence has long been an acceptable and even preferred method of addressing differences and conflicts among different groups and states. In the case of war, as in many other manifestations of violence, violence against other men (and civilian women) combines with autonomous economic, ideological, and political factors.

But men's violence against other men is more than the sum of various activities and types of behavior. In this form of violence a number of things are happening at once, in addition to the autonomous factors involved. Sometimes mutual, sometimes one-sided, there is a discharge of aggression and hostility. But at the same time as discharging aggression, these acts of violence and the ever-present potential for men's violence against other men reinforce the reality that relations between men, whether at the individual or state level, are relations of power.[17]

Most men feel the presence of violence in their lives. Some of us had fathers who were domineering, rough, or even brutal. Some of us had fathers who simply were not there enough; most of us had fathers who either consciously or unconsciously were repelled by our need for touch and affection once we had passed a certain age. All of us had experiences of being beaten up or picked on when we were young. We learned to fight, or we learned to run; we learned to pick on others, or we learned how to talk or joke our way out of a confrontation. But either way these early experiences of violence caused an incredible amount of anxiety and required a huge expenditure of energy to resolve. That anxiety is crystallized in an unspoken fear (particularly among heterosexual men): all other men are my potential humiliators, my enemies, my competitors.

But this mutual hostility is not always expressed. Men have formed elaborate institutions of male bonding and buddying: clubs, gangs, teams, fishing trips, card games, bars, and gyms, not to mention that great fraternity of Man. Certainly, as many feminists have pointed out, straight male clubs are a subculture of male privilege. But they are also havens where men, by common consent, can find safety and security among other men. They are safe houses where our love and affection for other men can be expressed.

Freud suggested that great amounts of passivity are required for the establishment of social relations among men but also that this very passivity arouses a fear of losing one's power. (This fear takes the form, in a phallocentric, male-dominated society, of what Freud called "castration anxiety.") There is a constant tension of activity and passivity. Among their many functions and reasons for existence, male institutions mediate this tension between activity and passivity among men.

My thoughts take me back to grade six and the constant acting out of this drama. There was the challenge to fight and a punch in the stomach that knocked my wind out. There was our customary greeting with a slug in the shoulder. Before school, after school, during class change, at recess, whenever you saw another one of the boys whom you hadn't hit or been with in the past few minutes, you'd punch each other on the shoulder. I remember walking from class to class in terror of meeting Ed Skagle in the hall. Ed, a hefty young football player a grade ahead of me, would leave a big bruise with one of his friendly hellos. And this was the interesting thing about the whole business; most of the time it was friendly and affectionate. Long after the bruises have faded, I remember Ed's smile and the protective way he had of saying hello to me. But we couldn't express this affection without maintaining the active/passive equilibrium. More precisely, within the masculine psychology of surplus aggression, expressions of affection and of the need for other boys had to be balanced by an active assault.

But the traditional definition of masculinity is not only surplus aggression. It is also exclusive heterosexuality, for the maintenance of masculinity requires the repression of homosexuality.[18] Repression of homosexuality is one thing, but how do we explain the intense fear of homosexuality, the homophobia, that pervades so much male interaction? It isn't simply that many men may choose not to have sexual relations with other men; it is rather that they will find this possibility frightening or abhorrent.

Freud showed that the boy's renunciation of the father—and thus men—as an object of sexual love is a renunciation of what are felt to be passive sexual desires. For the boy to deviate from this norm is to experience severe anxiety, for what appears to be at stake is his ability to be active. Erotic attraction to other men is sacrificed because there is no model central to our society of active, erotic love for other males. The emotionally charged physical attachments of childhood with father and friends eventually breed feelings of passivity and danger and are sacrificed. The anxiety caused by the threat of losing power and activity is "the motive power behind the 'normal' boy's social learning of his sex and gender roles." Boys internalize "our culture's definition of 'normal' or 'real' man: the possessor of a penis, therefore loving only females and that actively; the possessor of a penis, therefore 'strong' and 'hard,' not 'soft,' 'weak,' 'yielding,' 'sentimental,' 'effeminate,' 'passive.' To deviate from this definition is not to be a real man. To deviate is to arouse [what Freud called] castration anxiety."[19]

Putting this in different terms, the young boy learns of the sexual hierarchy of society. This learning process is partly conscious and partly unconscious. For a boy, being a girl is a threat because it raises anxiety by representing a loss of power. Until real power is attained, the young boy courts power in the world of the imagination (with superheroes, guns, magic, and pretending to be grown-up). But the continued pull of passive aims, the attraction to girls and to mother, the fascination with the origin of babies ensure that a tension continues to exist. In this world, the only thing that is as bad as being a girl is being a sissy, that is, being like a girl.[20] Although the boy doesn't consciously equate being a girl or sissy with homosexual genital activity, at the time of puberty these feelings, thoughts, and anxieties are transferred onto homosexuality per se.

For the majority of men, the establishment of the masculine norm and the strong social prohibitions against homosexuality are enough to bury the erotic desire for other men. The repression of our bisexuality is not adequate, however, to keep this desire at bay. Some of the energy is transformed into derivative pleasures—muscle building, male comradeship, hero worship, religious rituals, war, sports—where our enjoyment of being with other men or admiring other men can be expressed. These forms of activity are not enough to neutralize our constitutional bisexuality, our organic fusion of passivity and activity, and our love for our fathers and our friends. The great majority of men, in addition to those men whose sexual preference is clearly homosexual, have, at some time in their childhood, adolescence, or adult life, had sexual or quasi-sexual relations with other males, or have fantasized or dreamed about such relationships. Those who don't (or don't recall that they have), invest a lot of energy in repressing and denying these thoughts and feelings. And to make things worse, all those highly charged male activities in the sports field, the meeting room, or the locker room do not dispel eroticized relations with other men. They can only reawaken those feelings. It is, as Freud would have said, the return of the repressed.

Nowhere has this been more stunningly captured than in the wrestling scene in the perhaps mistitled book, *Women in Love*, by D. H. Lawrence. It was late at night. Birkin had just come to Gerald's house after being put off following a marriage proposal. They talked of working, of loving, and fighting, and in the end stripped off their clothes and began to wrestle in front of the burning fire. As they wrestled, "they seemed to drive their white flesh deeper and deeper against each other, as if they would break into a oneness." They entwined, they wrestled, they pressed nearer and nearer. "A tense white knot of flesh [was] gripped in silence." The thin Birkin "seemed to penetrate into Gerald's more solid, more diffuse bulk, to interfuse his body through the body of the other, as if to bring it subtly into subjection, always seizing with some rapid necromantic foreknowledge every motion of the other flesh, converting and counteracting it, playing upon the limbs and trunk of Gerald like some hard wind. . . . Now and again came a sharp gasp of breath, or a sound like a sigh, then the rapid thudding of movement on the thickly-carpeted floor, then the strange sound of flesh escaping under flesh."[21]

The very institutions of male bonding and patriarchal power force men to constantly reexperience their closeness and attraction to other men, that is, the very thing so many men are afraid of. Our very attraction to ourselves, ambivalent as it may be, can only be generalized as an attraction to men in general.

A phobia is one means by which the ego tries to cope with anxiety. Homophobia is a means of trying to cope, not simply with our unsuccessfully repressed, eroticized attraction to other men, but with our whole anxiety over the unsuccessfully repressed passive sexual aims, whether directed toward males or females. Homophobia is not merely an individual phobia, although the strength of homophobia varies from individual to individual. It is a socially constructed phobia that is essential for the imposition and maintenance of masculinity. A key expression of homophobia is the obsessive denial of homosexual attraction; this denial is expressed as violence against other men. Or to put it differently, men's violence against other men is one of the chief means through which patriarchal society simultaneously expresses and discharges the attraction of men to other men.[22]

The specific ways that homophobia and men's violence toward other men are acted out varies from man to man, society to society, and class to class. The great amount of *directly expressed* violence and violent homophobia among some groups of working class youth would be well worth analyzing to give clues to the relation of class and gender.

This corner of the triad of men's violence interacts with and reinforces violence against women. This corner contains part of the logic of surplus aggression. Here we begin to explain the tendency of many men to use force as a means of simultaneously hiding and expressing their feelings. At the same time the fear of other men, in particular the fear of weakness and passivity in relation to other men, helps create our strong dependence on women for meeting our emotional needs and for emotional discharge. In a surplus-repressive patriarchal and class society, large amounts of anxiety and hostility are built up, ready to be discharged. But the fear of one's emotions and the fear of losing control mean that discharge only takes place in a safe situation. For many men that safety is provided by a relationship with a woman where the commitment of one's friend or lover creates the sense of security. What is more, because it is a relationship with a woman, it unconsciously resonates with that first great passive relation of the boy with his mother. But in this situation and in other acts of men's violence against women, there is also the security of interaction with someone who does not represent a psychic threat, who is less socially powerful, probably less physically powerful, and who is herself operating within a pattern of surplus passivity. And finally, given the fragility of masculine identity and the inner tension of what it means to be masculine, the ultimate acknowledgement of one's masculinity is in our power over women. This power can be expressed in many ways. Violence is one of them.

When I speak of a man's violence against himself, I am thinking of the very structure of the masculine ego. The formation of an ego on an edifice of what Herbert Marcuse called surplus repression and surplus aggression is the building of a precarious structure of internalized violence. The continual conscious and unconscious blocking and denial of passivity and all the emotions and feelings men associate with passivity—fear, pain, sadness, embarrassment—is a denial of part of what we are. The constant psychological and behavioral vigilance against passivity and its derivatives is a perpetual act of violence against oneself.

The denial and blocking of a whole range of human emotions and capacities are compounded by the blocking of avenues of discharge. The discharge of fear, hurt, and sadness, for example (through crying or trembling), is necessary because these painful emotions linger on even if they are not consciously felt. Men become pressure cookers. The failure to find safe avenues of emotional expression and discharge means that a whole range of emotions are transformed into anger and hostility. Part of the anger is directed at oneself in the form of guilt, self-hate, and various physiological and psychological symptoms. Part is directed at other men. Part of it is directed at women.

By the end of this process, our distance from ourselves is so great that the very symbol of maleness is turned into an object, a thing. Men's preoccupation with genital power and pleasure combines with a desensitization of the penis. As best he can, writes Emmanuel Reynaud, a man gives it "the coldness and the hardness of metal." It becomes his tool, his weapon, his thing. "What he loses in enjoyment he hopes to compensate for in power; but if he gains an undeniable power symbol, what pleasure can he really feel with a weapon between his legs?"[23]

BEYOND MEN'S VIOLENCE

Throughout Gabriel Garcia Márquez's *Autumn of the Patriarch,* the ageless dictator stalked his palace, his elephantine feet dragging forever on endless corridors that reeked of corruption. There was no escape from the world of terror, misery, and decay that he himself had created. His tragedy was that he was "condemned forever to live breathing the same air which asphyxiated him."[24] As men, are we similarly condemned; or is there a road of escape from the triad of men's violence and the precarious structures of masculinity that we ourselves recreate at our peril and that of women, children, and the world?

Prescribing a set of behavioral or legal changes to combat men's violence against women is obviously not enough. Even as more and more are convinced there is a problem, this realization does not touch the unconscious structures of masculinity. Any man who is sympathetic to feminism is aware of the painful contradiction between his conscious views and his deeper emotions and feelings.

The analysis in this article suggests that men and women must address each corner of the triad of men's violence and the socioeconomic, psychosexual orders on which they stand. Or to put it more strongly, it is impossible to deal successfully with any one corner of this triad in isolation from the others.

The social context that nurtures men's violence and the relation between socioeconomic transformation and the end of patriarchy have been major themes of socialist feminist thought. This framework, though it is not without controversy and unresolved problems, is one I accept. Patriarchy and systems of authoritarianism and class domination feed on each other. Radical socioeconomic and political change is a requirement for the end of men's violence. But organizing for macrosocial change is not enough to solve the problem of men's violence, not only because the problem is so pressing here and now, but because the continued existence of masculinity and surplus aggressiveness works against the fundamental macrosocial change we desire.

The many manifestations of violence against women have been an important focus of feminists. Women's campaigns and public education against rape, battering, sexual harassment, and more generally for control by women of their bodies are a key to challenging men's violence. Support by men, not only for the struggles waged by women, but in our own workplaces and among our friends is an important part of the struggle. There are many possible avenues for work by men among men. These include: forming counseling groups and support services for battering men (as is now happening in different cities in North America); championing the inclusion of clauses on sexual harassment in collective agreements and in the constitutions or bylaws of our trade unions, associations, schools, and political parties; raising money, campaigning for government funding, and finding other means of support for rape crisis centers and shelters for battered women; speaking out against violent and sexist pornography; building neighborhood campaigns against wife and child abuse; and personally refusing to collude with the sexism of our workmates, colleagues, and friends. The latter is perhaps the most difficult of all and requires patience, humor, and support from other men who are challenging sexism.

But because men's violence against women is inseparable from the other two corners of the triad of men's violence, solutions are very complex and difficult. Ideological changes and an awareness of problems are important but insufficient. While we can envisage changes in our child-rearing arrangements (which in turn would require radical economic changes) lasting solutions have to go far deeper. Only the development of non-surplus-repressive societies (whatever these might look like) will allow for the greater expression of human needs and, along with attacks on patriarchy per se, will reduce the split between active and passive psychological aims.[25]

The process of achieving these long-term goals contains many elements of economic, social, political, and psychological change, each of which requires a fundamental transformation of society. Such a transformation will not be created by an amalgam of changed individuals; but there *is* a relationship between personal change and our ability to construct organizational, political, and economic alternatives that will be able to mount a successful challenge to the status quo.

One avenue of personal struggle that is being engaged in by an increasing number of men has been the formation of men's support groups. Some groups focus on consciousness raising, but most groups stress the importance of men talking about their feelings, their relations with other men and with women, and any number of problems in their lives. At times these groups have been criticized by some antisexist men as yet another place for men to collude against women. The alternatives put forward are groups whose primary focus is either support for struggles led by women or the organization of direct, antisexist campaigns among men. These activities are very important, but so too is the development of new support structures among men. And these structures must go beyond the traditional form of consciousness raising.

Consciousness raising usually focuses on manifestations of the oppression of women and on the oppressive behavior of men. But as we have seen, masculinity is more than the sum total of oppressive forms of behavior. It is deeply and unconsciously embedded in the structure of our egos and superegos; it is what we have become. An awareness of oppressive behavior is important, but too often it only leads to guilt about being a man. Guilt is a profoundly conservative emotion and as such is not particularly useful for bringing about change. From a position of insecurity and guilt, people do not change or inspire others to change. After all, insecurity about one's male credentials played an important part in the individual acquisition of masculinity and men's violence in the first place.

There is a need to promote the personal strength and security necessary to allow men to make more fundamental personal changes and to confront sexism and heterosexism in our society at large. Support groups usually allow men to talk about our feelings, how we too have been hurt growing up in a surplus-repressive society, and how we, in turn, act at times in an oppressive manner. We begin to see the connections between painful and frustrating experiences in our own lives and related forms of oppressive behavior. As Sheila Rowbotham notes, "the exploration of the internal areas of consciousness is a political necessity for us."[26]

Talking among men is a major step, but it is still operating within the acceptable limits of what men like to think of as rational behavior. Deep barriers and fears remain even when we can begin to recognize them. As well as talking, men need to encourage direct expression of emotions—grief, anger, rage, hurt, love—within these groups and the physical closeness that has been blocked by the repression of passive aims, by social prohibition, and by our own superegos and sense of what is right. This discharge of emotions has many functions and outcomes: like all forms of emotional and physical discharge it lowers the tension within the human system and reduces the likelihood of a spontaneous discharge of emotions through outer- or inner-directed violence.

But the expression of emotions is not an end in itself; in this context it is a means to an end. Stifling the emotions connected with feelings of hurt and pain acts as a sort of glue that allows the original repression to remain. Emotional discharge, in a situation of support and encouragement, helps unglue the ego structures that require us to operate in patterned, phobic, oppressive, and surplus-aggressive forms. In a sense it loosens up the repressive structures and allows us fresh insight into ourselves and our past. But if this emotional discharge happens in isolation or against an unwitting victim, it only reinforces the feelings of being powerless, out of control, or a person who must obsessively control others. Only in situations that contradict these feelings—that is, with the support, affection, encouragement, and backing of other men who experience similar feelings—does the basis for change exist.[27]

The encouragement of emotional discharge and open dialogue among men also enhances the safety we begin to feel among each other and in turn helps us to tackle obsessive, even if unconscious, fear of other men. This unconscious fear and lack of safety are the experience of most heterosexual men throughout their lives. The pattern for homosexual men differs, but growing up and living in a heterosexist, patriarchal culture implants similar fears, even if one's adult reality is different.

Receiving emotional support and attention from a group of men is a major contradiction to experiences of distance, caution, fear, and neglect from other men. This contradiction is the mechanism that allows further discharge, emotional change, and more safety. Safety among even a small group of our brothers gives us greater safety and strength among men as a whole. This gives us the confidence and sense of personal power to confront sexism and homophobia in all its various manifestations. In a sense, this allows us each to be a model of a strong, powerful man who does not need to operate in an oppressive and violent fashion in relation to women, to other men, or to himself. And that, I hope, will play some small part in the challenge to the oppressive reality of patriarchal, authoritarian, and class societies. It will be changes in our own lives inseparably intertwined with changes in society as a whole that will sever the links in the triad of men's violence.

NOTES

My thanks to those who have given me comments on earlier drafts of this paper, in particular my father, Nathan Kaufman, and to Gad Horowitz. As well, I extend my appreciation to the men I have worked with in various counseling situations who have helped me develop insights into the individual acquisition of violence and masculinity.

1. Herbert Marcuse, *Eros and Civilization* (Boston: Beacon Press, 1975; New York: Vintage, 1962); Gad Horowitz, *Repression* (Toronto: University of Toronto Press, 1977).
2. This is the approach, for example, of Suzanne Steinmetz. She says that macrolevel social and economic conditions (such as poverty, unemployment, inadequate housing, and the glorification and acceptance of violence) lead to high crime rates and a tolerance of violence that in turn leads to family aggression. See her *Cycle of Violence* (New York: Praeger, 1977), 30.
3. Andrew Tolson, *The Limits of Masculinity* (London: Tavistock, 1977), 25.
4. Juliet Mitchell, *Psychoanalysis and Feminism* (New York: Vintage, 1975), 362.
5. Joseph Conrad, *Lord Jim* (New York: Bantam Books, 1981), 146; first published 1900.
6. See, for example, Michele Barrett's thought-provoking book *Women's Oppression Today* (London: Verso/New Left Books, 1980), 10–19, 250–1.
7. Jessica Benjamin, "Authority and the Family Revisited: or, A World Without Fathers?" *New German Critique* (Winter 1978), 35.
8. Bertolt Brecht, *Three Penny Novel*, trans. Desmond I. Vesey (Harmondsworth: Penguin, 1965), 282.
9. Simone de Beauvoir, in the *Nouvel Observateur*, Mar. 1, 1976. Quoted in Diana E. H. Russell and Nicole Van de Ven, eds., *Crimes Against Women* (Millbrae, Calif.: Les Femmes, 1976), xiv.
10. Among the sources on male violence that are useful, even if sometimes problematic, see Leonore E. Walker, *The Battered Woman* (New York: Harper Colophon, 1980); Russell and Van de Ven, *op. cit.*; Judith Lewis Herman, *Father-Daughter Incest.* (Cambridge, Mass.: Harvard University Press, 1981); Suzanne K. Steinmetz, *The Cycle of Violence* (New York: Praeger, 1977); Sylvia Levine and Joseph Koenig, *Why Men Rape* (Toronto: Macmillan, 1980); Susan Brownmiller, *op. cit.*; and Connie Guberman and Margie Wolfe, eds., *No Safe Place* (Toronto: Women's Press, 1985).
11. Levine and Koenig, *op. cit.*, pp. 28, 42, 56, 72.
12. Meg Luxton, *More Than a Labour of Love* (Toronto: Women's Press, 1980), 66.
13. Margaret M. Killoran, "The Sound of Silence Breaking: Toward a Metatheory of Wife Abuse" (M.A. thesis, McMaster University, 1981), 148.
14. Barrett and MacIntosh, *op. cit.*, 23.
15. Of course, household violence is not monopolized by men. In the United States roughly the same number of domestic homicides are committed by each sex. In 1975, 8.0% of homicides were committed by husbands against wives and 7.8% by wives against husbands. These figures, however, do not indicate the chain of violence, that is, the fact that most of these women were reacting to battering by their husbands. (See Steinmetz, *op. cit.*, p. 90.) Similarly, verbal and physical abuse of children appears to be committed by men and women equally. Only in the case of incest is there a near monopoly by men. Estimates vary greatly, but between one-fifth and one-third of all girls experience some sort of sexual contact with an adult male, in most cases with a father, stepfather, other relative, or teacher. (See Herman, *op. cit.*, 12 and *passim.*)
16. Luxton, *op. cit.*, p. 65.
17. This was pointed out by I. F. Stone in a 1972 article on the Vietnam war. At a briefing about the U.S. escalation of bombing in the North, the Pentagon official described U.S. strategy as two boys fighting: "If one boy gets the other in an arm lock, he can probably get his adversary to say 'uncle' if he increases the pressure

in sharp, painful jolts and gives every indication of willingness to break the boy's arm" ("Machismo in Washington," reprinted in Pleck and Sawyer, *op. cit.*, 131). Although women are also among the victims of war, I include war in the category of violence against men because I am here referring to the causality of war.

18. This is true both of masculinity as an institution and masculinity for the individual. Gay men keep certain parts of the self-oppressive masculine norm intact simply because they have grown up and live in a predominantly heterosexual, male-dominated society.

19. Horowitz, *op. cit.*, 99.

20. This formulation was first suggested to me by Charlie Kreiner at a men's counseling workshop in 1982.

21. D. H. Lawrence, *Women in Love* (Harmondsworth: Penguin, 1960), 304–5; first published 1921.

22. See Robin Wood's analysis of the film *Raging Bull*. M. Kaufman, ed. *Beyond Patriarchy* (Toronto: Oxford University Press, 1987).

23. Emmanuel Reynaud, *Holy Virility*, translated by Ros Schwartz (London: Plato Press, 1983), 41–2.

24. Gabriel Garcia Márquez, *Autumn of the Patriarch*, trans. Gregory Rabassa (Harmondsworth: Penguin, 1972), 111; first published 1967.

25. For a discussion on non-surplus-repressive societies, particularly in the sense of being complementary with Marx's notion of communism, see Horowitz, *op. cit.*, particularly chapter 7, and also Marcuse, *op. cit.*, especially chaps. 7, 10, and 11.

26. Rowbotham, *op. cit.*, 36.

27. As is apparent, although I have adopted a Freudian analysis of the unconscious and the mechanisms of repression, these observations on the therapeutic process—especially the importance of a supportive counseling environment, peer-counseling relations, emotional discharge, and the concept of contradiction—are those developed by forms of co-counseling, in particular, reevaluation counseling. But unlike the latter, I do not suppose that any of us can discharge all of our hurt, grief, and anger and uncover an essential self simply because our "self" is created.

44

HOMOPHOBIA AS A WEAPON OF SEXISM

SUZANNE PHARR

Patriarchy—an enforced belief in male dominance and control—is the ideology and sexism is the system that holds it in place. The catechism goes like this: Who do gender roles serve? Men and the women who seek power from them. Who suffers from gender roles? Women most completely and men in part. How are gender roles maintained? By the weapons of sexism: economics, violence, homophobia.

Why then don't we ardently pursue ways to eliminate gender roles and therefore sexism? It is my profound belief that all people have a spark in them that yearns for freedom, and the history of the world's atrocities—from the Nazi concentration camps to white dominance in South Africa to the battering of women—is the story of attempts to snuff out that spark. When that spark doesn't move forward to full flame, it is because the weapons designed to control and destroy have wrought such intense damage over time that the spark has been all but extinguished.

Sexism, that system by which women are kept subordinate to men, is kept in place by three powerful weapons designed to cause or threaten women with pain and loss. . . .

We have to look at economics not only as the root cause of sexism but also as the underlying, driving force that keeps all the oppressions in place. In the United States, our economic system is shaped like a pyramid, with a few people at the top, primarily white males, being supported by large numbers of unpaid or low-paid workers at the bottom. When we look at this pyramid, we begin to understand the major connection between sexism and racism because those groups at the bottom of the pyramid are women and people of color. We then begin to understand why there is such a fervent effort to keep those oppressive systems (racism and sexism and all the ways they are manifested) in place to maintain the unpaid and low-paid labor.

Susan DeMarco and Jim Hightower, writing for *Mother Jones,* report that *Forbes* magazine indicated that "the 400 richest families in America last year had an average net worth of $550 million each. These and less than a million other families—roughly 1 percent of our population—are at the prosperous

In *Homophobia: A Weapon of Sexism* by Suzanne Pharr, Chardon Press, new expanded edition 1997, distributed by the Women's Project, 2224 Main St., Little Rock, AR 72206. With permission from the publisher.

tip of our society. . . . In 1976, the wealthiest 1 percent of America's families owned 19.2 percent of the nation's total wealth. (This sum of wealth counts all of America's cash, real estate, stocks, bonds, factories, art, personal property, and anything else of financial value.) By 1983, those at this 1 percent tip of our economy owned 34.3 percent of our wealth. . . . *Today, the top 1 percent of Americans possesses more net wealth than the bottom 90 percent."* (My italics.) (May, 1988, pp. 32–33)

In order for this top-heavy system of economic inequity to maintain itself, the 90 percent on the bottom must keep supplying cheap labor. A very complex, intricate system of institutionalized oppressions is necessary to maintain the status quo so that the vast majority will not demand its fair share of wealth and resources and bring the system down. Every institution—schools, banks, churches, government, courts, media, etc.—as well as individuals must be enlisted in the campaign to maintain such a system of gross inequity.

What would happen if women gained the earning opportunities and power that men have? What would happen if these opportunities were distributed equitably, no matter what sex one was, no matter what race one was born into, and no matter where one lived? What if educational and training opportunities were equal? Would women spend most of our youth preparing for marriage? Would marriage be based on economic survival for women? What would happen to issues of power and control? Would women stay with our batterers? If a woman had economic independence in a society where women had equal opportunities, would she still be thought of as owned by her father or husband?

Economics is the great controller in both sexism and racism. If a person can't acquire food, shelter, and clothing and provide them for children, then that person can be forced to do many things in order to survive. The major tactic, worldwide, is to provide unrecompensed or inadequately recompensed labor for the benefit of those who control wealth. Hence, we see women performing unpaid labor in the home or filling low-paid jobs, and we see people of color in the lowest-paid jobs available.

The method is complex: limit educational and training opportunities for women and for people of color and then withhold adequate paying jobs with the excuse that people of color and women are incapable of filling them. Blame the economic victim and keep the victim's self-esteem low through invisibility and distortion within the media and education. Allow a few people of color and women to succeed among the profitmakers so that blaming those who don't "make it" can be intensified. Encourage those few who succeed in gaining power now to turn against those who remain behind rather than to use their resources to make change for all. Maintain the myth of scarcity—that there are not enough jobs, resources, etc., to go around—among the middle-class so that they will not unite with laborers, immigrants, and the unemployed. The method keeps in place a system of control and profit by a few and a constant source of cheap labor to maintain it.

If anyone steps out of line, take her/his job away. Let homelessness and hunger do their work. The economic weapon works. And we end up saying, "I would do this or that—be openly who I am, speak out against injustice, work for civil rights, join a labor union, go to a political march, etc.—if I didn't have this job. I can't afford to lose it." We stay in an abusive situation because we see no other way to survive. . . .

Violence against women is directly related to the condition of women in a society that refuses us equal pay, equal access to resources, and equal status with males. From this condition comes men's confirmation of their sense of ownership of women, power over women, and assumed right to control women for their own means. Men physically and emotionally abuse women because they *can*, because they live in a world that gives them permission. Male violence is fed by their sense of their *right* to dominate and control, and their sense of superiority over a group of people who, because of gender, they consider inferior to them.

It is not just the violence but the threat of violence that controls our lives. Because the burden of responsibility has been placed so often on the potential victim, as women we have curtailed our freedom in order to protect ourselves from violence. Because of the threat of rapists, we stay on alert, being careful not to walk in isolated places, being careful where we park our cars, adding incredible security measures to our homes—massive locks, lights, alarms, if we can afford them—and we avoid places where we will appear vulnerable or unprotected while the abuser walks with freedom. Fear, often now so commonplace that it is unacknowledged, shapes our lives, reducing our freedom. . . .

Part of the way sexism stays in place is the societal promise of survival, false and unfulfilled as it is, that women will not suffer violence if we attach ourselves to a man to protect us. A woman without a man is told she is vulnerable to external violence and, worse, that there is something wrong with her. When the male abuser calls a woman a lesbian, he is not so much labeling her a women who loves women as he is warning her that by resisting him, she is choosing to be outside society's protection from male institutions and therefore from wide-ranging, unspecified, ever-present violence. When she seeks assistance from woman friends or a battered women's shelter, he recognizes the power in woman bonding and fears loss of her servitude and loyalty: the potential loss of his control. The concern is not affectional/sexual identity: the concern is disloyalty and the threat is violence.

The threat of violence against women who step out of line or who are disloyal is made all the more powerful by the fact that women do not have to do anything—they may be paragons of virtue and subservience—to receive violence against our lives: the violence still comes. It comes because of the woman-hating that exists throughout society. Chance plays a larger part than virtue in keeping women safe. Hence, with violence always a threat to us, women can never feel completely secure and confident. Our sense of safety is always fragile and tenuous.

Many women say that verbal violence causes more harm than physical violence because it damages self-esteem so deeply. Women have not wanted to hear battered women say that the verbal abuse was as hurtful as the physical abuse: to acknowledge that truth would be tantamount to acknowledging that *virtually every woman is a battered woman.* It is difficult to keep strong against accusations of being a bitch, stupid, inferior, etc., etc. It is especially difficult when these individual assaults are backed up by a society that shows women in textbooks, advertising, TV programs, movies, etc. as debased, silly, inferior, and sexually objectified, and a society that gives tacit approval to pornography. When we internalize these messages, we call the result "low self-esteem," a therapeutic individualized term. It seems to me we should use the more political expression: when we internalize these messages, we experience *internalized sexism,* and we experience it in common with all women living in a sexist world. The violence against us is supported by a society in which woman-hating is deeply imbedded.

In "Eyes on the Prize," a 1987 Public Television documentary about the Civil Rights Movement, an older white woman says about her youth in the South that it was difficult to be anything different from what was around her when there was no vision for another way to be. Our society presents images of women that say it is appropriate to commit violence against us. Violence is committed against women because we are seen as inferior in status and in worth. It has been the work of the women's movement to present a vision of another way to be.

Every time a woman gains the strength to resist and leave her abuser, we are given a model of the importance of stepping out of line, of moving toward freedom. And we all gain strength when she says to violence, "Never again!" Thousands of women in the last fifteen years have resisted their abusers to come to this country's 1,100 battered women's shelters. There they have sat down with other women to share their stories, to discover that their stories again and again are the same, to develop an analysis that shows that violence is a statement about power and control, and to understand how sexism creates the climate for male violence. Those brave women are now a part of a movement that gives hope for another way to live in equality and peace.

Homophobia works effectively as a weapon of sexism because it is joined with a powerful arm, heterosexism. Heterosexism creates the climate for homophobia with its assumption that the world is and must be heterosexual and its display of power and privilege as the norm. Heterosexism is the systemic display of homophobia in the institutions of society. Heterosexism and homophobia work together to enforce compulsory heterosexuality and that bastion of patriarchal power, the nuclear family. The central focus of the right-wing attack against women's liberation is that women's equality, women's self-determination, women's control of our own bodies and lives will damage what they see as the crucial societal institution, the nuclear family. The attack has been led by fundamentalist ministers across the country. The two areas they have focused on most consistently are abortion and homosexuality, and their passion has led them to bomb women's clinics and to recommend de-programming for homosexuals and establishing camps to quarantine people with AIDS. To resist marriage and/or heterosexuality is to risk severe punishment and loss.

It is not by chance that when children approach puberty and increased sexual awareness they begin to taunt each other by calling these names: "queer," "faggot," "pervert." It is at puberty that the full force of society's pressure to conform to heterosexuality and prepare for marriage is brought to bear. Children know what we have taught them, and we have given clear messages that those who deviate from standard expectations are to be made to get back in line. The best controlling tactic at puberty is to be treated as an outsider, to be ostracized at a time when it feels most vital to be accepted. Those who are different must be made to suffer loss. It is also at puberty that misogyny begins to be more apparent, and girls are pressured to conform to societal norms that do not permit them to realize their full potential. It is at this time that their academic achievements begin to decrease as they are co-erced into compulsory heterosexuality and trained for dependency upon a man, that is, for economic survival.

There was a time when the two most condemning accusations against a woman meant to ostracize and disempower her were "whore" and "lesbian." The sexual revolution and changing attitudes about heterosexual behavior may have led to some lessening of the power of the word *whore,* though it still has strength as a threat to sexual property and prostitutes are stigmatized and abused. However, the word *lesbian* is still fully charged and carries with it the full threat of loss of power and privilege, the threat of being cut asunder, abandoned, and left outside society's protection.

To be a lesbian is to be *perceived* as someone who has stepped out of line, who has moved out of sexual/economic dependence on a male, who is woman-identified. A lesbian is perceived as someone who can live without a man, and who is therefore (however illogically) against men. A lesbian is per-ceived as being outside the acceptable, routinized order of things. She is seen as someone who has no societal institutions to protect her and who is not privileged to the protection of individual males. Many heterosexual women see her as someone who stands in contradiction to the sacrifices they have made to conform to compulsory heterosexuality. A lesbian is perceived as a threat to the nuclear family, to male dominance and control, to the very heart of sexism.

Gay men are perceived also as a threat to male dominance and control, and the homophobia expressed against them has the same roots in sexism as does homophobia against lesbians. Visible gay men are the objects of extreme hatred and fear by heterosexual men because their breaking ranks with male heterosexual solidarity is seen as a damaging rent in the very fabric of sexism. They are seen as betrayers, as traitors who must be punished and eliminated. In the beating and killing of gay men we see clear evidence of this hatred. When we see the fierce homophobia expressed toward gay men, we can begin to understand the ways sexism also affects males through imposing rigid, dehumanizing gender roles on them. The two circumstances in which it is legitimate for men to be openly physically affectionate with one another are in competitive sports and in the crisis of war. For many men, these two experiences are the highlights of their lives, and they think of them again and again with nostalgia. War and sports offer a cover of all-male safety and dominance to keep away the notion of affectionate openness being identified with homosexuality. When gay men break ranks with male roles through bonding and affection outside the arenas of war and sports, they are perceived as not being "real men," that is, as being identified with women, the weaker sex that must be dominated and that over the centuries has been the object of male hatred and abuse. Misogyny gets transferred to gay men with a vengeance and is increased by the fear that their sexual identity and behavior will bring down the entire system of male dominance and compulsory heterosexuality.

If lesbians are established as threats to the status quo, as outcasts who must be punished, homophobia can wield its power over all women through lesbian baiting. Lesbian baiting is an attempt to control women by labeling us as lesbians because our behavior is not acceptable, that is, when we are being independent, going our own way, living whole lives, fighting for our rights, demanding equal pay, saying no to violence, being self-assertive, bonding with and loving the company of women, assuming the right to our bodies, insisting upon our own authority, making changes that include us in society's decision-making; lesbian baiting occurs when women are called lesbians because we resist male dominance and control. And it has little or nothing to do with one's sexual identity.

To be named as lesbian threatens all women, not just lesbians, with great loss. And any woman who steps out of role risks being called a lesbian. To understand how this is a threat to all women, one must understand that any woman can be called a lesbian and there is no real way she can defend herself: there is no way to credential one's sexuality. ("The Children's Hour," a Lillian Hellman play, makes this point when a student asserts two teachers are lesbians and they have no way to disprove it.) She may be married or divorced, have children, dress in the most feminine manner, have sex with men, be celibate—but there are lesbians who do all those things. *Lesbians look like all women and all women look like lesbians.* There is no guaranteed method of identification, and as we all know, sexual identity can be kept hidden. (The same is true for men. There is no way to prove their sexual identity, though many go to extremes to prove heterosexuality.) Also, women are not necessarily born lesbian. Some seem to be, but others become lesbians later in life after having lived heterosexual lives. Lesbian baiting of heterosexual women would not work if there were a definitive way to identify lesbians (or heterosexuals).

We have yet to understand clearly how sexual identity develops. And this is disturbing to some people, especially those who are determined to discover how lesbian and gay identity is formed so that they will know where to start in eliminating it. (Isn't it odd that there is so little concern about discovering the causes of heterosexuality?) There are many theories: genetic makeup, hormones, socialization, environment, etc. But there is no conclusive evidence that indicates that heterosexuality comes from one process and homosexuality from another.

We do know, however, that sexual identity can be in flux, and we know that sexual identity means more than just the gender of people one is attracted to and has sex with. To be a lesbian has as many ramifications as for a woman to be heterosexual. It is more than sex, more than just the bedroom issue many would like to make it: it is a woman-centered life with all the social interconnections that entails. Some lesbians are in long-term relationships, some in short-term ones, some date, some are celibate, some are married to men, some remain as separate as possible from men, some have children by men, some by alternative insemination, some seem "feminine" by societal standards, some "masculine," some are doctors, lawyers and ministers, some laborers, housewives and writers: what all share in common is a sexual/affectional identity that focuses on women in its attractions and social relationships.

If lesbians are simply women with a particular sexual identity who look and act like all women, then the major difference in living out a lesbian sexual identity as opposed to a heterosexual identity is that as lesbians we live in a homophobic world that threatens and imposes damaging loss on us for *being who we are,* for choosing to live whole lives. Homophobic people often assert that homosexuals have the choice of not being homosexual; that is, we don't have to act out our sexual identity. In that case, I want to hear heterosexuals talk about their willingness not to act out their sexual identity, including not just sexual activity but heterosexual social interconnections and heterosexual privilege. It is a question of wholeness. It is very difficult for one to be denied the life of a sexual being, whether expressed in sex or in physical affection, and to feel complete, whole. For our loving relationships with humans feed the life of the spirit and enable us to overcome our basic isolation and to be interconnected with humankind.

If, then, any woman can be named a lesbian and be threatened with terrible losses, what is it she fears? Are these fears real? Being vulnerable to a homophobic world can lead to these losses:

- *Employment.* The loss of job leads us right back to the economic connection to sexism. This fear of job loss exists for almost every lesbian except perhaps those who are self-employed or in a business that does not require societal approval. Consider how many businesses or organizations you know that will hire and protect people who are openly gay or lesbian.

- *Family.* Their approval, acceptance, love.

- *Children.* Many lesbians and gay men have children, but very, very few gain custody in court challenges, even if the other parent is a known abuser. Other children may be kept away from us as though gays and lesbians are abusers. There are written and unwritten laws prohibiting lesbians and gays from being foster parents or from adopting children. There is an irrational fear that children in contact with lesbians and gays will become homosexual through influence or that they will be sexually abused. Despite our knowing that 95 percent of those who sexually abuse children are heterosexual men, there are no policies keeping heterosexual men from teaching or working with children, yet in almost every school system in America, visible gay men and lesbians are not hired through either written or unwritten law.

- *Heterosexual privilege and protection.* No institutions, other than those created by lesbians and gays—such as the Metropolitan Community Church, some counseling centers, political organizations such as the National Gay and Lesbian Task Force, the National Coalition of Black Lesbians and Gays, the Lambda Legal Defense and Education Fund, etc.—affirm homosexuality and offer protection. Affirmation and protection cannot be gained from the criminal justice system, mainline churches, educational institutions, the government.

- *Safety.* There is nowhere to turn for safety from physical and verbal attacks because the norm presently in this country is that it is acceptable to be overtly homophobic. Gay men are beaten on the streets; lesbians are kidnapped and "deprogrammed." The National Gay and Lesbian Task Force, in an extended study, has documented violence against lesbians and gay men and noted the inadequate response of the criminal justice system. One of the major differences between homophobia/heterosexism and racism and sexism is that because of the Civil Rights Movement and the women's movement racism and sexism are expressed more covertly (though with great harm); because there has not been a major, visible lesbian and gay movement, it is permissible to be overtly homophobic in any institution or public forum. Churches spew forth homophobia in the same way they did racism prior to the Civil Rights Movement. Few laws are in place to protect lesbians and gay men, and the criminal justice system is wracked with homophobia.

- *Mental health.* An overtly homophobic world in which there is full permission to treat lesbians and gay men with cruelty makes it difficult for lesbians and gay men to maintain a strong sense of well-being and self-esteem. Many lesbians and gay men are beaten, raped, killed, subjected to aversion therapy, or put in mental institutions. The impact of such hatred and negativity can lead one to depression and, in some cases, to suicide. The toll on the gay and lesbian community is devastating.

- *Community.* There is rejection by those who live in homophobic fear, those who are afraid of association with lesbians and gay men. For many in the gay and lesbian community, there is a loss of public acceptance, a loss of allies, a loss of place and belonging.

- *Credibility.* This fear is large for many people: the fear that they will no longer be respected, listened to, honored, believed. They fear they will be social outcasts.

The list goes on and on. But any one of these essential components of a full life is large enough to make one deeply fear its loss. A black woman once said to me in a workshop, "When I fought for Civil Rights, I always had my family and community to fall back on even when they didn't fully understand or accept what I was doing. I don't know if I could have borne losing them. And you people don't have either with you. It takes my breath away."

What does a woman have to do to get called a lesbian? Almost anything, sometimes nothing at all, but certainly anything that threatens the status quo, anything that steps out of role, anything that asserts the rights of women, anything that doesn't indicate submission and subordination. Assertiveness, standing up for oneself, asking for more pay, better working conditions, training for and accepting a non-traditional (you mean a man's?) job, enjoying the company of women, being financially independent, being in control of one's life, depending first and foremost upon oneself, thinking that one can do whatever needs to be done, but above all, working for the rights and equality of women.

In the backlash to the gains of the women's liberation movement, there has been an increased effort to keep definitions man-centered. Therefore, to work on behalf of women must mean to work against men. To love women must mean that one hates men. A very effective attack has been made against the word *feminist* to make it a derogatory word. In current backlash usage, *feminist* equals *man-hater* which equals *lesbian*. This formula is created in the hope that women will be frightened away from their work on behalf of women. Consequently, we now have women who believe in the rights of women and work for those rights while from fear deny that they are feminists, or refuse to use the word because it is so "abrasive."

So what does one do in an effort to keep from being called a lesbian? She steps back into line, into the role that is demanded of her, tries to behave in such a way that doesn't threaten the status of men, and if she works for women's rights, she begins modifying that work. When women's organizations begin doing significant social change work, they inevitably are lesbian-baited; that is, funders or institutions or community members tell us that they can't work with us because of our "man-hating attitudes" or the presence of lesbians. We are called too strident, told we are making enemies, not doing good. . . .

In my view, homophobia has been one of the major causes of the failure of the women's liberation movement to make deep and lasting change. (The other major block has been racism.) We were fierce when we set out but when threatened with the loss of heterosexual privilege, we began putting on brakes. Our best-known nationally distributed women's magazine was re-luctant to print articles about lesbians, began putting a man on the cover several times a year, and writing articles about women who succeeded in a man's world. We worried about our image, our being all right, our being "real women" despite our work. Instead of talking about the elimination of sexual gender roles, we stepped back and talked about "sex role stereotyping" as the issue. Change around the edges for middle-class white women began to be talked about as successes. We accepted tokenism and integration, forgetting that equality for all women, for all people—and not just equality of white middle-class women with white men—was the goal that we could never put behind us.

But despite backlash and retreats, change is growing from within. The women's liberation movement is beginning to gain strength again because there are women who are talking about liberation for all women. We are examining sexism, racism, homophobia, classism, anti-Semitism, ageism, ableism, and imperialism, and we see everything as connected. This change in point of view represents the third wave of the women's liberation movement, a new direction that does not get mass media coverage and recognition. It has been initiated by women of color and lesbians who were marginalized or rendered invisible by the white heterosexual leaders of earlier efforts. The first wave was the 19th and early 20th century campaign for the vote; the second, beginning in the 1960s, focused on the Equal Rights Amendment and abortion rights. Consisting of predominantly white middle-class women, both failed in recognizing issues of equality and empowerment for all women. The third wave of the movement, multi-racial and multi-issued, seeks the transformation of the world for us all. We know that we won't get there until everyone gets there; that we must move forward in a great strong line, hand in hand, not just a few at a time.

We know that the arguments about homophobia originating from mental health and Biblical/religious attitudes can be settled when we look at the sexism that permeates religious and psychiatric history. The women of the third wave of the women's liberation movement know that *without the existence of sexism, there would be no homophobia.*

Finally, we know that as long as the word *lesbian* can strike fear in any woman's heart, then work on behalf of women can be stopped; the only successful work against sexism must include work against homophobia.

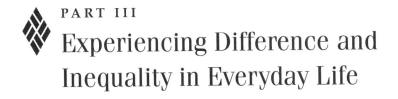

PART III

Experiencing Difference and Inequality in Everyday Life

INTRODUCTION

In Part I we examined the ways in which categories of difference are constructed and then transformed into systems of inequality. We continued this discussion in Part II with an exploration of how systems of inequality are maintained as oppression and privilege through the role of social institutions, language, and violence. In this section we will gain a more thorough understanding of the construction and maintenance of these systems by examining the experiences of difference and inequality in everyday life.

THE IMPORTANCE OF HEARING PERSONAL ACCOUNTS

The readings in this section help to put a face on what we have discussed thus far. Although theoretical explanations and statistical information can help us to understand the prevalence of inequality in our society, as well as the ways in which systems of oppression and privilege interconnect, the picture that they offer is far from complete. Through the examination of lived experiences we gain a more complete awareness of how categories of difference are constructed and how systems of oppression and privilege are manifested in everyday life.

Robert Jensen's discussion of the experience of being advantaged for being white in his article "White Privilege Shapes the U.S." (Reading 45) shows us the effect of **privilege** on one's **life chances.** By reading Annie Downey's experiences of receiving welfare in "I Am Your Welfare Reform" (Reading 52) and Sherri Muzher's encounters with negative stereotypes in "It's Not Easy Being an Arab-American" (Reading 46), we gain a greater understanding of how attitudes about oppressed groups become internalized and are manifested in feelings of shame and embarrassment. Furthermore, the stories of living life as a member of a marginalized group and its accompanying stereotypes allow us to more fully comprehend how such **internalized oppression** results in the desire to **pass**—to deny one's membership in an oppressed group and to attempt to portray oneself as a member of a less stigmatized group. Each of the readings in this section demonstrates the daily grind of oppression and the perks of privilege and deepens our understanding of these issues.

It is important to point out that although each of us experiences oppression and privilege each day, to examine the various factors of our own experiences while simultaneously living them is like a fish trying to examine the water in which it swims. To fully understand experiences of oppression and privilege we need to stand at a distance from these experiences. The accounts in this section provide us with the opportunity to stand "outside" and to look in on the experiences of others. By reading the stories in this section we will gain a greater understanding of the impact of oppression and privilege, not only on the lives of others but on our own lives as well.

PERSONAL ACCOUNTS AND "DECONSTRUCTING" STEREOTYPES

At the foundation of our prejudice regarding those whom we see as different from ourselves are **stereotypes**—rigid, oversimplified, and often exaggerated beliefs that are applied both to a category of people and to each individual in it. We learn these stereotypes through the process of socialization. They are fostered by the policies and practices of social institutions, as well as by our tendency to interact with people like ourselves, and we often have difficulty deconstructing or exposing the falsehoods in these stereotypes. Generally, it is not until we have frequent contact with those about whom we possess stereotypes that we are able to debunk them—and sometimes not even then. Through the sharing of personal experiences, the readings in this section provide a great deal of information that will serve to counter our stereotypes. As you read, be aware of the stereotypes that you possess and note your reactions when you encounter new information that challenges them.

THE LIVED EXPERIENCE OF THE MATRIX OF DOMINATION

Up to this point we have engaged in a primarily theoretical discussion of the matrix of domination. In examining the ways in which categories of difference are constructed and transformed into systems of inequality, we have noted some of the commonalities in the ways in which these categories are constructed. Further, our examination of the role of social institutions, language, and violence in maintaining systems of oppression and privilege has helped us to understand the similar foundations on which such systems rest. The readings in this section reveal the interrelationships of systems of oppression and privilege by providing us with an opportunity to witness the matrix of domination as lived experience. As you read the selections in this section, look closely to see how different systems of oppression and privilege interrelate in the stories the authors share. In addition, notice how some experience both oppression and privilege and how many experience more than one form of oppression simultaneously.

KEEP THIS IN MIND

Though reading personal accounts can serve to further our understanding of systems of oppression and privilege, it is important to not overgeneralize. The anecdotal evidence of a personal story doesn't in and of itself prove anything. Indeed, it is often anecdotal evidence that gets in the way of our fully seeing and accepting that systems of oppression and privilege exist. In addition, when we read the personal experiences of a member of a marginalized group, there is often a danger of expecting the writer to speak for the experiences of all members of that group. To avoid these pitfalls it is important to keep in mind the readings of the previous two sections. By understanding the experiences of the different groups examined in previous sections, we will better understand the experiences of the individuals discussed here. In addition, the readings here confirm the theoretical and statistical discussions elsewhere in this text.

A FINAL NOTE

As stated in Part I, a fundamental component to understanding the impact of systems of inequality is to employ our **empathy** skills—the ability to understand the experiences of others, even though you have not shared those experiences. The readings in this section are provided to aid you in honing your empathy skills. As you read these accounts, be mindful of how they increase your understanding of experiences with which you are not familiar. As you become more informed about the experiences of others, you will further your understanding of the construction, maintenance, and impact of systems of oppression and privilege.

45

WHITE PRIVILEGE SHAPES THE U.S.

ROBERT JENSEN

AFFIRMATIVE ACTION FOR WHITES IS A FACT OF LIFE

Here's what white privilege sounds like:

I'm sitting in my University of Texas office, talking to a very bright and very conservative white student about affirmative action in college admissions, which he opposes and I support.

The student says he wants a level playing field with no unearned advantages for anyone. I ask him whether he thinks that being white has advantages in the United States. Have either of us, I ask, ever benefited from being white in a world run mostly by white people? Yes, he concedes, there is something real and tangible we could call white privilege.

So, if we live in a world of white privilege—unearned white privilege—how does that affect your notion of a level playing field, I asked.

He paused for a moment and said, "That really doesn't matter."

That statement, I suggested to him, reveals the ultimate white privilege: the privilege to acknowledge that you have unearned privilege but to ignore what it means.

That exchange led me to rethink the way I talk about race and racism with students. It drove home the importance of confronting the dirty secret that we white people carry around with us every day in a world of white privilege, some of what we have is unearned. I think much of both the fear and anger that come up around discussions of affirmative action has its roots in that secret. So these days, my goal is to talk openly and honestly about white supremacy and white privilege.

White privilege, like any social phenomenon, is complex. In a white supremacist culture, all white people have privilege, whether or not they are overtly racist themselves.

There are general patterns, but such privilege plays out differently depending on context and other aspects of one's identity (in my case, being male gives me other kinds of privilege). Rather than try to tell others how white privilege has played out in their lives, I talk about how it has affected me.

"White Privilege Shapes the U.S." by Robert Jensen. *Baltimore Sun,* July 19, 1998. Contact Robert Jensen, Department of Journalism, University of Texas at Austin, Austin, TX 78712.

I am as white as white gets in this country. I am of northern European heritage and I was raised in North Dakota, one of the whitest states in the country. I grew up in a virtually all-white world surrounded by racism, both personal and institutional. Because I didn't live near a reservation, I didn't even have exposure to the state's only numerically significant nonwhite population, American Indians.

I have struggled to resist that racist training and the racism of my culture. I like to think I have changed, even though I routinely trip over the lingering effects of that internalized racism and the institutional racism around me. But no matter how much I "fix" myself, one thing never changes—I walk through the world with white privilege.

What does that mean? Perhaps most important, when I seek admission to a university, apply for a job, or hunt for an apartment, I don't look threatening. Almost all of the people evaluating me for those things look like me—they are white. They see in me a reflection of themselves—and in a racist world, that is an advantage. I smile. I am white. I am one of them. I am not dangerous. Even when I voice critical opinions, I am cut some slack. After all, I'm white.

My flaws also are more easily forgiven because I am white. Some complain that affirmative action has meant the university is saddled with mediocre minority professors. I have no doubt there are minority faculty who are mediocre, though I don't know very many. As Henry Louis Gates Jr. once pointed out, if affirmative action policies were in place for the next hundred years, it's possible that at the end of that time the university could have as many mediocre minority professors as it has mediocre white professors. That isn't meant as an insult to anyone, but it's a simple observation that white privilege has meant that scores of second-rate white professors have slid through the system because their flaws were overlooked out of solidarity based on race, as well as on gender, class and ideology.

Some people resist the assertions that the United States is still a bitterly racist society and that the racism has real effects on real people. But white folks have long cut other white folks a break. I know, because I am one of them. I am not a genius—as I like to say, I'm not the sharpest knife in the drawer. I have been teaching full time for six years and I've published a reasonable amount of scholarship. Some of it is the unexceptional stuff one churns out to get tenure, and some of it, I would argue, is worth reading. I worked hard, and I like to think that I'm a fairly decent teacher. Every once in a while, I leave my office at the end of the day feeling like I really accomplished something. When I cash my paycheck, I don't feel guilty.

But, all that said, I know I did not get where I am by merit alone, I benefited from, among other things, white privilege. That doesn't mean that I don't deserve my job, or that if I weren't white I would never have gotten the job. It means simply that all through my life, I have soaked up benefits for being white. I grew up in fertile farm country taken by force from nonwhite indigenous people. I was educated in a well-funded, virtually all-white public school system in which I learned that white people like me made this country great. There I also was taught a variety of skills, including how to take standardized tests written by and for white people.

All my life I have been hired for jobs by white people. I was accepted for graduate school by white people. And I was hired for a teaching position by the predominantly white University of Texas, headed by a white president, in a college headed by a white dean and in a department with a white chairman that at the time had one nonwhite tenured professor.

There certainly is individual variation in experience. Some white people have had it easier than I, probably because they came from wealthy families that gave them even more privilege. Some white people have had it tougher than I because they came from poorer families. White women face discrimination I will never know. But, in the end, white people all have drawn on white privilege somewhere in their lives.

Like anyone, I have overcome certain hardships in my life. I have worked hard to get where I am, and I work hard to stay there. But to feel good about myself and my work, I do not have to believe that "merit," as defined by white people in a white country, alone got me here. I can acknowledge that in addition to all that hard work, I got a significant boost from white privilege, which continues to protect me every day of my life from certain hardships.

At one time in my life, I would not have been able to say that, because I needed to believe that my success in life was due solely to my individual talent and effort. I saw myself as the heroic American, the rugged individualist. I was so deeply seduced by the culture's mythology that I couldn't see the fear that was binding me to those myths. Like all white Americans, I was living with the fear that maybe I didn't really deserve my success, that maybe luck and privilege had more to do with it than brains and hard work. I was afraid I wasn't heroic or rugged, that I wasn't special.

I let go of some of that fear when I realized that, indeed, I wasn't special, but that I was still me. What I do well, I still can take pride in, even when I know that the rules under which I work are stacked to my benefit. I believe that until we let go of the fiction that people have complete control over their fate—that we can will ourselves to be anything we choose—then we will live with that fear. Yes, we should all dream big and pursue our dreams and not let anyone or anything stop us. But we all are the product of both what we will ourselves to be and what the society in which we live lets us be.

White privilege is not something I get to decide whether I want to keep. Every time I walk into a store at the same time as a black man and the security guard follows him and leaves me alone to shop, I am benefiting from white privilege. There is not space here to list all the ways in which white privilege plays out in our daily lives, but it is clear that I will carry this privilege with me until the day white supremacy is erased from this society.

Frankly, I don't think I will live to see that day; I am realistic about the scope of the task. However, I continue to have hope, to believe in the creative power of human beings to engage the world honestly and act morally. A first step for white people, I think, is to not be afraid to admit that we have benefited from white privilege. It doesn't mean we are frauds who have no claim to our success. It means we face a choice about what we do with our success.

46

IT'S NOT EASY BEING AN ARAB-AMERICAN: ONE PERSON'S EXPERIENCE

SHERRI MUZHER

In an era where political correctness is the norm, there are few groups that are still legitimate targets for harassment and popular stereotyping—except for Arab-Americans.

With the recent abominable tragedies in New York, Pennsylvania and Washington, D.C., many in the Arab-American community are fearing retribution from fellow Americans, should the perpetrators be Arab. Already, violence has been reported on university campuses, and death threats have been called in to numerous Arab organizations.

When I was little, I remember being puzzled by all of the stereotypes of my culture. Whether it was watching "Bugs Bunny" or "Charlie's Angels," the Arabs were always the bad guys. In elementary and junior high school, there were the ignorant classmates who had an obsession with the words, "camel jockey."

"Why are we such bad people?" I once asked an Arab adult. He was horrified by my question, and yet saddened that the images perpetrated by the media and pop culture could make me question a proud heritage that was once the cradle of the world's civilization. Add to the recipe that I was of Palestinian descent.

I knew better, of course. I had heard enough personal testimonies from loved ones and Palestinian acquaintances to know that a huge injustice had been done to our people. Even now, every Palestinian group has condemned

Source: by courtesy and © 2001 Sherri Muzher, Media Monitors, http:www.mediamonitors. net/sherri22.html

this tragedy, and yet some analysts are determined to make some sort of link to the Palestinians.

While footage of a very small minority of Palestinians shown celebrating—most likely hardened by unconditional U.S. support for Israel—continues to be repeatedly shown, no footage was shown of the candlelight vigils held by Palestinian Jerusalemites. The propaganda continues.

The memories of anti-Arab discrimination during the Gulf War are still vivid. I was a senior at Michigan State University. There were reports that the MSU Department of Public Safety had submitted the names of all Arab-sounding names to the FBI. Comments such as "We should nuke all the Ay-rabs in Dearborn" and "Kill the sand n—s" were heard in the cafeteria at my residence hall. Fist fights were common. Uncomfortable stares followed us much of the time.

In 1995, the Oklahoma City bombing occurred. From Jerusalem, where I was then, I watched CNN and was dumbfounded to hear reporters' attempts to link the bombing to Arabs, even though American anti-government militias and Timothy McVeigh were already nailed as the perpetrators.

The usual racial profiling awaited us at the various airports. I don't think I have ever been on an international flight where I wasn't separated at the Detroit Metropolitan Airport without having my suitcase searched and asked a number of questions. Days later, the vandalism of Arab-owned property and death threats became known to us.

When TWA flight 800 exploded a few years ago, the same speculations arose. Radio disc jockeys aired skits and made derogatory comments about the "guilt" of Arabs in the explosion. Yet, the cause is still undetermined.

And now, it's starting all over again. There are good and bad in every culture, and every community has its radicals and extremists. Let's not forget our own Michigan militia.

It is so important that we not hold entire communities responsible for the acts of a few. Even if the perpetrators of the latest outrage turn out to be Arabs, that is hardly a reason to vilify a community. The Arab community has worked hard to be contributing and productive members of the great American tapestry. Whether they are doctors saving lives, small business owners, engineers or human rights activists, they make a difference as Americans. The horrors of the latest tragedy affect us as fellow Americans and human beings.

It has always been difficult being an Arab American, especially at a time when people are understandably angry and need to take it out on someone. The dehumanization of Arabs in pop culture has made it easier to place Arab Americans, as well as Muslim Americans, as targets.

We understand that there is nothing worse than feeling helpless. A lot of our relatives in the Middle East feel this helplessness every day.

As Americans, we are outraged that innocent people were taken in this barbaric and uncivilized manner. Let's be careful not to place our anger among those who are also innocent.

47

A DOZEN DEMONS

ELLIS COSE

In the workplace, the continuing relevance of race takes on a special force, partly because so much of life, at least for middle-class Americans, is defined by work, and partly because even people who accept that they will not be treated fairly in the world often hold out hope that their work will be treated fairly—that even a society that keeps neighborhoods racially separate and often makes after-hours social relations awkward will properly reward hard labor and competence. What most African Americans discover, however, is that the racial demons that have plagued them all their lives do not recognize business hours—that the stress of coping extends to a nonwork world that is chronically unwilling (or simply unable) to acknowledge the status their professions ought to confer.

The coping effort, in some cases, is relatively minor. It means accepting the fact, for instance, that it is folly to compete for a taxi on a street corner with whites. It means realizing that prudence dictates dressing up whenever you are likely to encounter strangers (including clerks, cops, and doormen) who can make your life miserable by mistaking you for a tramp, a slut, or a crook. And it means tolerating the unctuous boor whose only topic of party conversation is blacks he happens to know. But the price of this continual coping is not insignificant. In addition to creating an unhealthy level of stress, it puts many in such a wary state of mind that insults are seen where none were intended, often complicating communications even with sensitive, well-meaning whites who unwittingly stumble into the racial minefield.

What is it exactly that blacks spend so much time coping with? For lack of a better phrase, let's call them the dozen demons. This is not to say that they affect blacks only; as will become clear, members of other racial minority groups are often plagued by them as well. Nor is it to say that there are only twelve, or that all black Americans encounter every one. Still, if you're looking for a safe bet, you could not find one more certain than this: that any random gathering of black American professionals, asked what irks or troubles them, will eventually end up describing, in one guise or another, the following items.

1. *Inability to fit in.* During the mid 1980s, I had lunch in the Harvard Club in Manhattan with a newsroom recruiter from the *New York Times.* The lunch was primarily social, but my companion was also seeking help in identifying black, Hispanic, and Asian-American journalists he could lure to the *Times.* Though he had encountered plenty of people with good professional credentials, he was concerned about an attribute that was torturously difficult to gauge: the ability to fit into the often bewildering culture of the *Times.* He was desperate to hire good minority candidates, he said, yet hiring someone who could produce decent copy was not enough. He wanted people with class, people who could be "*Times* people."

As we talked, it became clear that he was focusing on such things as speech, manners, dress, and educational pedigree. He had in mind, apparently, a certain button-down sort, an intellectual, nonthreatening, quiet-spoken type—something of a cross between William F. Buckley and Bill Cosby. Someone who might be expected to have his own membership at the Harvard or Yale Club. Not surprisingly, he was not having much success. That most whites at the *Times* fit no such stereotype seemed not to have occurred to him. I suggested, rather gingerly, that perhaps he needed to expand his definition of a "*Times* person," that perhaps some of those he was eliminating for seemingly superficial reasons might have all the qualities the *Times* required.

Even as I made the argument, I knew that it was unpersuasive. Not because he disagreed—he did not offer much of a rebuttal—but because he and many similarly placed executives almost instinctively screened minority candidates according to criteria they did not apply to whites. The practice has nothing to do with malice. It stems more, I suspect, from an unexamined assumption that whites, purely because they are white, are likely to fit in, while blacks and other minority group members are not. Hence, he found it necessary to search for specific assurances that those he brought into the fold had qualities that would enable them, despite their color, to blend into the great white mass.

2. *Exclusion from the club.* Even the ability to fit in, however, does not necessarily guarantee acceptance. Many blacks who have made huge efforts to get the right education, master the right accent, and dress in the proper clothes still find that certain doors never seem to open, that there are private clubs—in both a real and a symbolic sense—they cannot join. . . .

In 1990, in testimony before the U.S. Senate Judiciary Committee, Darwin Davis, senior vice president of the Equitable Life Assurance Society, told of the frustrations he and some of his black friends had experienced in trying to join a country club. "I have openly approached fellow executives about memberships. Several times, they have said, 'My club has openings; it should be no problem. I'll get back to you.' Generally, one of two things happens. They are too embarrassed to talk to me or they come right out and tell me they were shocked when they made inquiries about bringing in a black. Some have even said they were told to get out of the club if they didn't like the situation as it is."

Davis, a white-haired, elegant, and genial raconteur who loves to play golf, told the Senate panel that his interest was not merely in the game but in the financial costs of exclusion. He was routinely reduced to entertaining golf-playing clients at a public course with poor facilities. "The best I can offer my client . . . where they have a great lunch and drinks, and use of the locker room and showers. Then, they get their shoes shined. I am out of the ball game with this client." Whenever he found out that a customer played golf, he became "anxious because I know I am on thin ice." It was "disheartening and demeaning," he added, "to know that it doesn't matter how hard I work, how proficient an executive I become, or how successful I become. I will be denied this one benefit that success is supposed to confer on those who have achieved."

Two years after his testimony, Davis told me his obsession with private clubs sprang in part from concerns about his children. Several years before, he had visited a club as a guest and happened to chance upon a white executive he knew. As they were talking, he noticed the man wave at someone on the practice range. It turned out that he had brought his son down to take a lesson from the club pro. Davis was suddenly struck by a depressing thought. "Damn!" he said to himself. "This is being perpetuated all over again. . . . I have a son the same age as his. And when my son grows up he's going to go through the same crap I'm going through if I don't do something about this. His son is learning how to . . . socialize, get lessons, and do business at a country club." His own son, Davis concluded, would "never ever be able to have the same advantages or even an equal footing."

3. *Low expectations.* Shortly after I arrived to take over the editorial pages of the New York *Daily News*, I was visited by a black employee who had worked at the paper for some time. More was on his mind than a simple desire to make my acquaintance. He had also come to talk about how his career was blocked, how the deck was stacked against him—how, in fact, it was stacked against any black person who worked there. His frustration and anger I easily understood. But what struck me as well was that his expectations left him absolutely no room to grow. He believed so strongly that the white men at the *Daily News* were out to stymie black achievement that he had no option but failure, whatever the reality of the situation.

Even those who refuse to internalize the expectation of failure are often left with nagging doubts, with a feeling, as journalist Joe Boyce puts it, "that no matter what you do in life, there are very few venues in which you can really be sure that you've exhausted your potential. Your achievement is defined by your color and its limitations. And even if in reality you've met your fullest potential, there's an aggravating, lingering doubt . . . because you're never sure. And that makes you angry."

During the late 1970s, I met a Harvard student, Mark Whitaker, who was interning for a summer in *Newsweek*'s Washington bureau. Whitaker made it clear that he intended to go far. He had it in mind to become editor of

Newsweek. I didn't know whether to be amused by his arrogance, awed by his ambition, or amazed by his naivete. I asked Whitaker—the product of a mixed (black/white) union—whether he had considered that his race might hold him back. He answered that maybe it would, but that he was not going to permit his color to smother his aspirations. He would not hold himself back. If he was to be stopped, it would be by someone else.

More than a decade later, when Whitaker had become a *Newsweek* assistant managing editor, I reminded him of our earlier conversation. He laughed his precocious comments off, attributing them to the ignorance and arrogance of youth. We both knew better, of course—just as we knew that many young blacks, for a variety of reasons, never even reach the point of believing that success was within their grasp.

Conrad Harper, former head of the Association of the Bar of the City of New York and a partner in Simpson Thacher & Barlett, said that throughout the years he had seen plenty of young associates "bitterly scarred by not being taken first as lawyers . . . but always first as African Americans." He had also seen affirmative action turned into a stigma and used as a club to beat capable people down. If someone's competency is consistently doubted, "the person begins to question his own abilities." The result, he added, is not only a terrible waste of talent, but in some cases psychological damage.

4. *Shattered hopes.* After two years toiling at an eminent law firm, the young associate walked away in disgust and became a public defender. For more than a year after leaving, he was "so filled with rage, I couldn't even talk about it much." A soft-spoken Mexican American, he bristles with emotion as he recalls those years.

He believes that he and other minority group hires simply never got a shot at the big assignments, which invariably went to white males. This sense of disappointment, he makes plain, was felt by all the nonwhites in his class. He remembers one in particular, a black woman who graduated with honors from Yale. All her peers thought she was headed for the stars. Yet when she was rated periodically, she was never included in the first tier but at the top of the second.

If he had been alone in his frustration, he says, one could reject his complaint as no more than a case of sour grapes. "But the fact that all of us were having the same kinds of feelings" means something more systemic was at work. He acknowledges that many whites had similar feelings, that in the intensely competitive environment of a top law firm, no one is guaranteed an easy time. But the sense of abandonment, he contends, was exacerbated for nonwhites. By his count, every minority group member who entered the firm with him ended up leaving, having concluded that nonwhites—barring the spectacularly odd exception—were not destined to make it in that world.

5. *Faint praise.* For a year and a half during the early 1980s, I was a resident fellow at the National Research Council–National Academy of Sciences, an august Washington institution that evaluates scientific research. One afternoon, I mentioned to a white colleague who was also a close friend that it

was a shame the NRC had so few blacks on staff. She replied, "Yes, it's too bad there aren't more blacks like you."

I was stunned enough by her comment to ask her what she meant. She answered, in effect, that there were so few really intelligent blacks around who could meet the standards of the NRC. I, of course, was a wonderful exception. Her words, I'm sure, were meant as a compliment, but they angered me, for I took her meaning to be that blacks (present company excluded) simply didn't have the intellect to hang out with the likes of her.

My colleague's attitude seemed to disallow the possibility of a better explanation for the scarcity of blacks than the supposedly low intellectual quality of the race. Perhaps there were so few blacks at the NRC—because they simply were not sought out, or because they were encouraged to believe, from childhood on, that they could never master the expertise that would land them in such a place. The ease with which she dismissed such possibilities in favor of a testimonial to my uniqueness disappointed and depressed me.

Blacks who have been singled out as exceptions often experience anger at the whites who commend them. One young woman, a Harvard-trained lawyer with a long list of "firsts" behind her name, had another reason for cringing whenever she was held up as a glistening departure from the norm for her race. "I don't like what it does to my relationships with other blacks," she said.

6. *Presumption of failure.* A year or so prior to my Harvard Club chat with the *Times* recruiter, I was visited at my office (then in Berkeley, California) by a *Times* assistant managing editor. I took him to lunch, and after a few drinks we fell into a discussion of people at the *Times,* among them a talented black editor whose career seemed to have stalled. Was he in line, I asked, for a high-level editorship that would soon be vacant? My companion agreed that the editor would probably do very well in the job, but then he pointed out that a black person had never held such a post at the *New York Times.* The *Times* would have to think hard, he indicated, before changing that, for they could not afford to have a black journalist fail in such a visible position. I didn't know whether the man even wanted the job (he later told me he might have preferred something else); I know that he didn't get it, that (at least in the eyes of one *Times* assistant managing editor in 1985) his prior work and credentials could not offset the questions raised by his color. Failure at the highest levels of the *Times* was a privilege apparently reserved for whites.

The *Times'* executive's reasoning reminded me of an encounter with a newspaper editor in Atlanta who had contacted me several years earlier. He had an editorial writer's position to fill and was interested in giving me a crack at it. I was intrigued enough to go to Atlanta and spend an evening with the man. We discovered we shared many interests and friends and hit it off famously. Still, I wondered: Why in the world was he recruiting me? Interesting though Atlanta might be, and as well as he and I got along, there had never been much chance that I would leap at the job. In no way did it represent a career advancement, and the editor's budget would barely permit him to pay the salary I was already making. As the evening wore on, I put the question to him bluntly. Why did he not offer the job to someone in his newsroom for whom it would be a real step up? His answer I found more than a little unsettling. One black person, he said, had already come on staff and not performed very well. He could not afford another black failure, so he had gone after someone overqualified in an attempt to buy himself insurance.

I'm sure he was not surprised that I turned the job down. . . . I don't doubt . . . that similar preconceptions still exist, that before many executives even ask whether a minority person can do a job, they ask whether they are prepared to take a flyer on a probable failure.

7. *Coping fatigue.* When Armetta Parker headed for Midland, Michigan, to take a job as a public relations professional at the Dow Chemical Company, she assumed that she was on her way to big-time corporate success. A bright, energetic black woman then in her early thirties, Parker had left a good position at a public utility in Detroit to get on the Fortune 100 fast track.

"Dow was everything I expected and more, and everything I expected and less," she says. The town of nearly forty thousand had only a few hundred black families, and virtually no single black people her own age. Though she expected a certain amount of social isolation, "I didn't expect to get the opportunity to take a really hard look at me, at what was important to me and what wasn't." She had to face that fact that success, in that kind of corporate environment, meant a great deal of work and no social life, and that it also required a great deal of faith in people who found it difficult to recognize competence in blacks. . . .

Nonetheless, Parker did extremely well, at least initially. Her first year at the company, she made it into "The Book"—the roster of those who had been identified as people on the fast track. But eventually she realized that "I was never going to be vice president of public affairs for Dow Chemical." She believed that her color, her gender, and her lack of a technical degree all were working against her. Moreover, "even if they gave it to me, I didn't want it. The price was too high." Part of that price would have been accepting the fact that her race was not seen as an asset but as something she had to overcome. And her positive traits were probably attributed to white genes, she surmised, even though she is no more "white" than most American blacks. Even her way of talking drew attention. Upon meeting her, one colleague remarked with evident pleasure and astonishment, "You don't speak ghettoese." She had an overwhelming sense that what he meant was "You're almost like us, but not enough like us to be acceptable." . . . She realized that "good corporate jobs can be corporate handcuffs. You have to decide how high of a price you're willing to pay."

8. *Pigeonholing.* Near the end of his brashly brilliant tenure as executive editor of the *Washington Post,* Ben Bradlee observed how much both Washington and the *Post* had changed. Once upon a time, he told me, one would not have thought of appointing a black city editor. Now one could not think of not seriously considering—and even favoring—a black person for the assignment.

Bradlee, I realized, was making several points. One was about himself and his fellow editors, about how they had matured to the extent that they valued all managerial talent—even in blacks. He was also acknowledging that blacks had become so central to Washington's political, economic, and social life that a black city editor had definite advantages, strictly as a function of race. His third point, I'm sure, was wholly unintended but clearly implied: that it was still possible, even for the most enlightened management, to classify jobs by color. And logic dictates that if certain managerial tasks are best handled by blacks, others are best left to whites.

What this logic has meant in terms of the larger corporate world is that black executives have landed, out of all proportion to their numbers, in community relations and public affairs, or in slots where their only relevant expertise concerns blacks and other minorities. The selfsame racial assumptions that make minorities seem perfect for certain initially desirable jobs can ultimately be responsible for trapping them there as others move on.

9. *Identity troubles.* The man was on the verge of retiring from his position as personnel vice president for one of America's largest companies. He had acquired the requisite symbols of success: a huge office, a generous compensation package, a summer home away from home. But he had paid a price. He had decided along the way, he said matter-of-factly, that he could no longer afford to be black.

I was so surprised by the man's statement that I sat silent for several seconds before asking him to explain. Clearly he had done nothing to alter his dark brown complexion. What he had altered, he told me, was the way he allowed himself to be perceived. Early in his career, he had been moderately outspoken about what he saw as racism within and outside his former corporation. He had learned, however, that his modest attempts at advocacy got him typecast as an undesirable. So when he changed jobs, he decided to disassociate himself from any hint of a racial agenda. The strategy had clearly furthered his career, even though other blacks in the company labeled him an Uncle Tom. He was aware of his reputation, and pained by what the others thought, but he had seen no other way to thrive. He noted as well, with evident pride, that he had not abandoned his race, that he had quietly made it his business to cultivate a few young blacks in the corporation and bring their careers along; and could point to some who were doing very well and would have been doing considerably worse without his intervention. His achievements brought him enough pleasure to balance out the distress of not being "black."

Putting aside for the moment what it means to be "black," the fear of being forced to shed one's identity in order to prosper is not at all uncommon. Georgetown University law professor Anita Allen tells of a worried student who asked whether her diction would have to be as precise as Allen's if she was to be successful as a lawyer. She feared, it seemed, not merely having to change her accent, but being required to discard an important part of herself.

10. *Self-censorship and silence.* . . . [M]any blacks find their voices stilled when sensitive racial issues are raised. A big-city police officer once shared

with me his frustration at waiting nineteen years to make detective. In those days before affirmative action, he had watched, one year after another, as less qualified whites were promoted over him. And each year he had swallowed his disappointment, twisted his face into a smile, and congratulated his white friends as he hid his rage—so determined was he to avoid being categorized as a race-obsessed troublemaker. And he had endured other affronts in silence, including a vicious beating by a group of white cops while carrying out a plainclothes assignment. As an undercover officer working within a militant black organization, he had been given a code word to whisper to a fellow officer if the need arose. When he was being brutalized, he had screamed out the word and discovered it to be worthless. His injuries had required surgery and more than thirty stitches. When he was asked by his superior to identify those who had beat him, he feigned ignorance; it seems a fellow officer had preceded his commander and bluntly passed along the message that it was safer to keep quiet.

Even though he made detective years ago, and even though, on the side, he managed to become a successful businessman and an exemplary member of the upwardly striving middle class, he says the anger still simmers within him. He worries that some day it will come pouring out, that some luckless white person will tick him off and he will explode, with tragic results. Knowing him, I don't believe he will ever reach that point. But I accept his fear that he could blow up as a measure of the intensity of his feelings, and of the terrible cost of having to hold them in.

11. *Mendacity.* Even more damaging than self-imposed silence are the lies that seem an integral part of America's approach to race. Many of the lies are simple self-deception, as when corporate executives claim their companies are utterly color-blind. Some stem from unwillingness to acknowledge racial bias, as when people who have no intention of voting for a candidate of another race tell pollsters that they will. And many are lies of business, social, or political convenience, as was the case with Massachusetts Senator Edward Brooke in the early 1970s.

At the time, Brooke was the highest-ranking black politician in America. His name was routinely trotted out as a vice presidential possibility, though everyone involved knew the exercise was a farce. According to received wisdom, America was not ready to accept a black on the ticket, but Brooke's name seemed to appear on virtually everyone's list. During one such period of vice-presidential hype, I interviewed Brooke for a newspaper profile. After asking the standard questions, I could no longer contain my curiosity. Wasn't he tired, I asked, of the charade of having his name bandied about when no one intended to select him? He nodded wearily and said yes, he was.

To me, his response spoke volumes, probably much more than he'd intended. But I took it as his agreement that lies of political convenience are not merely a nuisance for those interested in the truth but a source of profound disgust and cynicism for those on whose behalf the lies are supposedly told.

12. *Guilt by association.* In the mid 1980s, I was unceremoniously tossed out of Cafe Royale, a restaurant that catered to yuppies in San Francisco, on the orders of a maitre d'who apparently mistook me for someone who had caused trouble on a previous occasion. I sued the restaurant and eventually collected a few thousand dollars from its insurance company. But I will never forget the fury I experienced at being haughtily dismissed by an exalted waiter who would not suffer the inconvenience of having to distinguish one black person from another.

My first real understanding of how poisonous such an attitude could be came to me at the age of twelve or thirteen, when I went to Marshall Field's department store in downtown Chicago in search of a Mother's Day gift. While wandering from one section of the store to another, I gradually became aware that someone was shadowing me. That someone, I ascertained, was a plain-clothes security guard. Apparently I fit his profile of a shoplifter. For several minutes, I roamed through the store, trying to ignore him, but he was determined not to be ignored. Little by little, he made his surveillance more obvious, until we were practically walking in lock step. His tactics unsettled me so much that I could no longer concentrate on shopping. Finally, I whirled to face him.

He said nothing, merely glared as my outrage mounted. *How dare he treat me like a criminal,* I thought, *simply because I'm black.* I screamed something at him; I don't remember what. Whatever it was, it had no effect; he continued to stare at me with a look somewhere between amusement and disdain. I stalked out of the store, conceding him the victory, burning with anger and humiliation. . . .

[Many commentators argue] that America's cities have become so dangerous, largely as a result of young black thugs, that racial discrimination is justified—and is even a necessary tool of survival when directed at young black men. . . .

This rationalization strikes me, to put it mildly, as dangerous. For it inevitably takes one beyond the street, and beyond those black males who are certifiably dangerous. It quickly takes one into society at large, where blacks in no way connected with street crime find themselves victims of street-crime stereotypes. Members of the law-abiding black middle class also have sons, as do those countless African Americans without substantial financial resources who have tried to pound into their children, from birth, that virtue has its rewards, that there is value in following a moral path and shunning the temptations of the street. . . .

Countless members of the black middle class are in fact volunteering every spare moment in an attempt to do whatever they can (working in homeless shelters, volunteering in literacy programs, serving as formal mentors) to better the lives of those in the so-called underclass. At the same time, however, many who belong to America's black privileged class are struggling with problems of their own that are largely unseen or dismissed.

48

THE STORY OF MY BODY

JUDITH ORTIZ COFER

Migration is the story of my body.

—VICTOR HERNÁNDEZ CRUZ

SKIN

I was born a white girl in Puerto Rico but became a brown girl when I came to live in the United States. My Puerto Rican relatives call me tall; at the American school, some of my rougher classmates called me Skinny Bones, and the Shrimp because I was the smallest member of my classes all through grammar school until high school, when the midget Gladys was given the honorary post of front row center for class pictures and scorekeeper, bench warmer, in P.E. I reached my full stature of five feet in sixth grade.

I started out life as a pretty baby and learned to be a pretty girl from a pretty mother. Then at ten years of age I suffered one of the worst cases of chicken pox I have ever heard of. My entire body, including the inside of my ears and in between my toes, was covered with pustules which in a fit of panic at my appearance I scratched off my face, leaving permanent scars. A cruel school nurse told me I would always have them—tiny cuts that looked as if a mad cat had plunged its claws deep into my skin. I grew my hair long and hid behind it for the first years of my adolescence. This was when I learned to be invisible.

COLOR

In the animal world it indicates danger: the most colorful creatures are often the most poisonous. Color is also a way to attract and seduce a mate. In the human world color triggers many more complex and often deadly reactions. As a Puerto Rican girl born of "white" parents, I spent the first years of my life hearing people refer to me as *blanca*, white. My mother insisted that I protect myself from the intense island sun because I was more prone to sunburn than some of my darker, *trigueño*[1] playmates. People were always commenting within my hearing about how my black hair contrasted so nicely with my "pale" skin. I did not think of the color of my skin consciously except when I heard the adults talking about complexion. It seems to me that the subject is much more common in the conversation of mixed-race peoples than in mainstream United States society, where it is a touchy and sometimes even embarrassing topic to discuss, except in a political context. In Puerto Rico I heard many conversations about skin color. A pregnant woman could say, "I hope my baby doesn't turn out *prieto*" (slang for "dark" or "black") "like my husband's grandmother, although she was a good-looking *negra*[2] in her time." I am a combination of both, being olive-skinned—lighter than my mother yet darker than my fair-skinned father. In America, I am a person of color, obviously a Latina. On the Island I have been called everything from a *paloma blanca*,[3] after the song (by a black suitor), to *la gringa*.[4]

My first experience of color prejudice occurred in a supermarket in Paterson, New Jersey. It was Christmastime, and I was eight or nine years old. There was a display of toys in the store where I went two or three times a day to buy things for my mother, who never made lists but sent for milk, cigarettes, a can of this or that, as she remembered from hour to hour. I enjoyed being trusted with money and walking half a city block to the new, modern grocery store. It was owned by three good-looking Italian brothers. I liked the younger one with the crew-cut blond hair. The two older ones watched me and the other Puerto Rican kids as if they thought we were going to steal something. The oldest one would sometimes even try to hurry me with my purchases, although part of my pleasure in these expeditions came from looking at everything in the well-stocked aisles. I was also teaching myself to read English by sounding out the labels in packages: L&M cigarettes, Borden's homogenized milk, Red Devil potted ham, Nestle's chocolate mix, Quaker oats, Bustelo coffee, Wonder bread, Colgate toothpaste, Ivory soap, and Goya (makers of products used in Puerto Rican dishes) everything—these are some of the brand names that taught me nouns. Several times this man had come up to me, wearing his blood-stained butcher's apron, and towering over me had asked in a harsh voice whether there was something he could help me find. On the way out I would glance at the younger brother who ran one of the registers and he would often smile and wink at me.

It was the mean brother who first referred to me as "colored." It was a few days before Christmas, and my parents had already told my brother and me that since we were in Los Estados[5] now, we would get our presents on December 25

---

[1]*trigueño:* Brown-skinned.
[2]*negra:* Black.
[3]*paloma blanca:* White dove.
[4]*la gringa:* A white, non-Latina woman.
[5]*Los Estados:* "The States"—that is, the United States.

instead of Los Reyes, Three Kings Day, when gifts are exchanged in Puerto Rico. We were to give them a wish list that they would take to Santa Claus, who apparently lived in the Macy's store downtown—at least that's where we had caught a glimpse of him when we went shopping. Since my parents were timid about entering the fancy store, we did not approach the huge man in the red suit. I was not interested in sitting on a stranger's lap anyway. But I did covet Susie, the talking schoolteacher doll that was displayed in the center aisle of the Italian brothers' supermarket. She talked when you pulled a string on her back. Susie had a limited repertoire of three sentences: I think she could say: "Hello, I'm Susie Schoolteacher," "Two plus two is four," and one other thing I cannot remember. The day the older brother chased me away, I was reaching to touch Susie's blond curls. I had been told many times, as most children have, not to touch anything in the store that I was not buying. But I had been looking at Susie for weeks. In my mind, she was my doll. After all, I had put her on my Christmas wish list. The moment is frozen in my mind as if there were a photograph of it on file. It was not a turning point, a disaster, or an earth-shaking revelation. It was simply the first time I considered—if naively—the meaning of skin color in human relations.

I reached to touch Susie's hair. It seems to me that I had to get on tip-toe, since the toys were stacked on a table and she sat like a princess on top of the fancy box she came in. Then I heard the booming "Hey, kid, what do you think you're doing!" spoken very loudly from the meat counter. I felt caught, although I knew I was not doing anything criminal. I remember not looking at the man, but standing there, feeling humiliated because I knew everyone in the store must have heard him yell at me. I felt him approach, and when I knew he was behind me, I turned around to face the bloody butcher's apron. His large chest was at my eye level. He blocked my way. I started to run out of the place, but even as I reached the door I heard him shout after me: "Don't come in here unless you gonna buy something. You PR kids put your dirty hands on stuff. You always look dirty. But maybe dirty brown is your natural color." I heard him laugh and someone else too in the back. Outside in the sunlight I looked at my hands. My nails needed a little cleaning as they always did, since I liked to paint with watercolors, but I took a bath every night. I thought the man was dirtier than I was in his stained apron. He was also always sweaty—it showed in big yellow circles under his shirt-sleeves. I sat on the front steps of the apartment building where we lived and looked closely at my hands, which showed the only skin I could see, since it was bitter cold and I was wearing my quilted play coat, dungarees, and a knitted navy cap of my father's. I was not light pink like my friend Charlene and her sister Kathy, who had blue eyes and light brown hair. My skin is the color of the coffee my grandmother made, which was half milk, *leche con café* rather than *café*

---

[6]*leche con café . . . café con leche:* Milk with coffee (light brown) . . . coffee with milk (dark brown).

con leche.[6] My mother is the opposite mix. She has a lot of café in her color. I could not understand how my skin looked like dirt to the supermarket man.

I went in and washed my hands thoroughly with soap and hot water, and borrowing my mother's nail file, I cleaned the crusted watercolors from underneath my nails. I was pleased with the results. My skin was the same color as before, but I knew I was clean. Clean enough to run my fingers through Susie's fine gold hair when she came home to me.

SIZE

My mother is barely four feet eleven inches in height, which is average for women in her family. When I grew to five feet by age twelve, she was amazed and began to use the word tall to describe me, as in "Since you are tall, this dress will look good on you." As with the color of my skin, I didn't consciously think about my height or size until other people made an issue of it. It is around the preadolescent years that in America the games children play for fun become fierce competitions where everyone is out to "prove" they are better than others. It was in the playground and sports fields that my size-related problems began. No matter how familiar the story is, every child who is the last chosen for a team knows the torment of waiting to be called up. At the Paterson, New Jersey, public schools that I attended, the volleyball or softball game was the metaphor for the battlefield of life to the inner city kids—the black kids versus the Puerto Rican kids, the whites versus the blacks versus the Puerto Rican kids; and I was 4F,[7] skinny, short, bespectacled, and apparently impervious to the blood thirst that drove many of my classmates to play ball as if their lives depended on it. Perhaps they did. I would rather be reading a book than sweating, grunting, and running the risk of pain and injury. I simply did not see the point in competitive sports. My main form of exercise then was walking to the library, many city blocks away from my barrio.

Still, I wanted to be wanted. I wanted to be chosen for the team. Physical education was compulsory, a class where you were actually given a grade. On my mainly all A report card, the C for compassion I always received from the P.E. teachers shamed me the same as a bad grade in a real class. Invariably, my father would say: "How can you make a low grade for *playing games?*" He did not understand. Even if I had managed to make a hit (it never happened) or get the ball over that ridiculously high net, I already had a reputation as a "shrimp," a hopeless nonathlete. It was an area where the girls who didn't like me for one reason or another—mainly because I did better than they on academic subjects—could lord it over me; the playing field was the place where even the smallest girl could make me feel powerless and

---

[7]4F: Draft-board classification meaning "unfit for military service"; hence, not physically fit.

inferior. I instinctively understood the politics even then; how the not choosing me until the teacher forced one of the team captains to call my name was a coup of sorts—there, you little show-off, tomorrow you can beat us in spelling and geography, but this afternoon you are the loser. Or perhaps those were only my own bitter thoughts as I sat or stood in the sidelines while the big girls were grabbed like fish and I, the little brown tadpole, was ignored until Teacher looked over in my general direction and shouted, "Call Ortiz," or, worse, "Somebody's *got* to take her."

No wonder I read Wonder Woman comics and had Legion of Super Heroes daydreams. Although I wanted to think of myself as "intellectual," my body was demanding that I notice it. I saw the little swelling around my once-flat nipples, the fine hairs growing in secret places; but my knees were still bigger than my thighs, and I always wore long- or half-sleeve blouses to hide my bony upper arms. I wanted flesh on my bones—a thick layer of it. I saw a new product advertised on TV. Wate-On. They showed skinny men and women before and after taking the stuff, and it was a transformation like the ninety-seven-pound-weakling-turned-into-Charles-Atlas ads that I saw on the back covers of my comic books. The Wate-On was very expensive. I tried to explain my need for it in Spanish to my mother, but it didn't translate very well, even to my ears—and she said with a tone of finality, eat more of my good food and you'll get fat—anybody can get fat. Right. Except me. I was going to have to join a circus someday as Skinny Bones, the woman without flesh.

Wonder Woman was stacked. She had a cleavage framed by the spread wings of a golden eagle and a muscular body that has become fashionable with women only recently. But since I wanted a body that would serve me in P.E., hers was my ideal. The breasts were an indulgence I allowed myself. Perhaps the daydreams of bigger girls were more glamorous, since our ambitions are filtered through our needs, but I wanted first a powerful body. I daydreamed of leaping up above the gray landscape of the city to where the sky was clear and blue, and in anger and self-pity, I fantasized about scooping my enemies up by their hair from the playing fields and dumping them on a barren asteroid. I would put the P.E. teachers each on their own rock in space too, where they would be the loneliest people in the universe, since I knew they had no "inner resources," no imagination, and in outer space, there would be no air for them to fill their deflated volleyballs with. In my mind all P.E. teachers have blended into one large spiky-haired woman with a whistle on a string around her neck and a volleyball under one arm. My Wonder Woman fantasies of revenge were a source of comfort to me in my early career as a shrimp.

I was saved from more years of P.E. torment by the fact that in my sophomore year of high school I transferred to a school where the midget, Gladys, was the focal point of interest for the people who must rank according to size. Because her height was considered a handicap, there was an unspoken rule about mentioning size around Gladys, but of course, there was no need to say anything. Gladys knew her place: front row center in class photographs. I gladly moved to the left or to the right of her, as far as I could without leaving the picture completely.

LOOKS

Many photographs were taken of me as a baby by my mother to send to my father, who was stationed overseas during the first two years of my life. With the Army in Panama when I was born, he later traveled often on tours of duty with the Navy. I was a healthy, pretty baby. Recently, I read that people are drawn to big-eyed round-faced creatures, like puppies, kittens, and certain other mammals and marsupials, koalas, for example, and, of course, infants. I was all eyes, since my head and body, even as I grew older, remained thin and small-boned. As a young child I got a lot of attention from my relatives and many other people we met in our barrio. My mother's beauty may have had something to do with how much attention we got from strangers in stores and on the street. I can imagine it. In the pictures I have seen of us together, she is a stunning young woman by Latino standards: long, curly black hair, and round curves in a compact frame. From her I learned how to move, smile, and talk like an attractive woman. I remember going into a bodega[8] for our groceries and being given candy by the proprietor as a reward for being *bonita*, pretty.

I can see in the photographs, and I also remember, that I was dressed in the pretty clothes, the stiff, frilly dresses, with layers of crinolines underneath, the glossy patent leather shoes, and, on special occasions, the skull-hugging little hats and the white gloves that were popular in the late fifties and early sixties. My mother was proud of my looks, although I was a bit too thin. She could dress me up like a doll and take me by the hand to visit relatives, or go to the Spanish mass at the Catholic church and show me off. How was I to know that she and the others who called me "pretty" were representatives of an aesthetic that would not apply when I went out into the mainstream world of school?

In my Paterson, New Jersey, public schools there were still quite a few white children, although the demographics of the city were changing rapidly. The original waves of Italian and Irish immigrants, silk-mill workers, and laborers in the cloth industries had been "assimilated." Their children were now the middle-class parents of my peers. Many of them moved their children to the Catholic schools that proliferated enough to have leagues of basketball teams. The names I recall hearing still ring in my ears: Don Bosco High versus St. Mary's High, St. Joseph's versus St. John's. Later I too would be transferred to the safer environment of a Catholic school. But I started school at Public School Number 11. I came there from Puerto Rico, thinking

---

[8]*bodega:* Market.

myself a pretty girl, and found that the hierarchy for popularity was as follows: pretty white girl, pretty Jewish girl, pretty Puerto Rican girl, pretty black girl. Drop the last two categories; teachers were too busy to have more than one favorite per class, and it was simply understood that if there was a big part in the school play, or any competition where the main qualification was "presentability" (such as escorting a school visitor to or from the principal's office), the classroom's public address speaker would be requesting the pretty and/or nice-looking white boy or girl. By the time I was in sixth grade, I was sometimes called by the principal to represent my class because I dressed neatly (I knew this from a progress report sent to my mother, which I translated for her) and because all the "presentable" white girls had moved to the Catholic schools (I later surmised this part). But I was still not one of the popular girls with the boys. I remember one incident where I stepped out into the playground in my baggy gym shorts and one Puerto Rican boy said to the other: "What do you think?" The other one answered: "Her face is OK, but look at the toothpick legs." The next best thing to a compliment I got was when my favorite male teacher, while handing out the class pictures, commented that with my long neck and delicate features I resembled the movie star Audrey Hepburn. But the Puerto Rican boys had learned to respond to a fuller figure: long necks and a perfect little nose were not what they looked for in a girl. That is when I decided I was a "brain." I did not settle into the role easily. I was nearly devastated by what the chicken pox episode had done to my self-image. But I looked into the mirror less often after I was told that I would always have scars on my face, and I hid behind my long black hair and my books.

After the problems at the public school got to the point where even non-confrontational little me got beaten up several times, my parents enrolled me at St. Joseph's High School. I was then a minority of one among the Italian and Irish kids. But I found several good friends there—other girls who took their studies seriously. We did our homework together and talked about the Jackies. The Jackies were two popular girls, one blonde and the other red-haired, who had women's bodies. Their curves showed even in the blue jumper uniforms with straps that we all wore. The blonde Jackie would often let one of the straps fall off her shoulder, and although she, like all of us, wore a white blouse underneath, all the boys stared at her arm. My friends and I talked about this and practiced letting our straps fall off our shoulders. But it wasn't the same without breasts or hips.

My final two and a half years of high school were spent in Augusta, Georgia, where my parents moved our family in search of a more peaceful environment. Then we became part of a little community of our Army-connected relatives and friends. School was yet another matter. I was enrolled in a huge school of nearly two thousand students that had just that year been forced to integrate. There were two black girls and there was me. I did extremely well academically. As to my social life, it was, for the most part, uneventful—yet it is in my memory blighted by one incident. In my junior year, I became wildly infatuated with a pretty white boy. I'll call him Ted. Oh, he was pretty: yellow hair that fell over his forehead, a smile to die for—and he was a great dancer. I watched him at Teen Town, the youth center at the base where all the military brats gathered on Saturday nights. My father had retired from the Navy, and we had all our base privileges—one other reason we moved to Augusta. Ted looked like an angel to me. I worked on him for a year before he asked me out. This meant maneuvering to be within the periphery of his vision at every possible occasion. I took the long way to my classes in school just to pass by his locker, I went to football games, which I detested, and I danced (I too was a good dancer) in front of him at Teen Town—this took some fancy footwork, since it involved subtly moving my partner toward the right spot on the dance floor. When Ted finally approached me, "A Million to One" was playing on the jukebox, and when he took me in his arms, the odds suddenly turned in my favor. He asked me to go to a school dance the following Saturday. I said yes, breathlessly. I said yes, but there were obstacles to surmount at home. My father did not allow me to date casually. I was allowed to go to major events like a prom or a concert with a boy who had been properly screened. There was such a boy in my life, a neighbor who wanted to be a Baptist missionary and was practicing his anthropological skills on my family. If I was desperate to go somewhere and needed a date, I'd resort to Gary. This is the type of religious nut that Gary was: when the school bus did not show up one day, he put his hands over his face and prayed to Christ to get us a way to get to school. Within minutes a mother in a station wagon, on her way to town, stopped to ask why we weren't in school. Gary informed her that the Lord had sent her just in time to find us a way to get there in time for roll call. He assumed that I was impressed. Gary was even good-looking in a bland sort of way, but he kissed me with his lips tightly pressed together. I think Gary probably ended up marrying a native woman from wherever he may have gone to preach the Gospel according to Paul. She probably believes that all white men pray to God for transportation and kiss with their mouths closed. But it was Ted's mouth, his whole beautiful self, that concerned me in those days. I knew my father would say no to our date, but planned to run away from home if necessary. I told my mother how important this date was. I cajoled and pleaded with her from Sunday to Wednesday. She listened to my arguments and must have heard the note of desperation in my voice. She said very gently to me: "You better be ready for disappointment." I did not ask what she meant. I did not want her fears for me to taint my happiness. I asked her to tell my father about my date. Thursday at breakfast my father looked at me across the table with his eyebrows together. My mother looked at him with her mouth set in a straight line. I looked down at my bowl of cereal. Nobody said anything. Friday I tried on every dress in my closet. Ted would be picking me up at six on Saturday: dinner and then the sock hop at school. Friday night I was in my room doing my nails or something else in preparation for Saturday (I know I groomed myself nonstop all week) when the telephone rang. I ran to get it. It was Ted. His voice sounded funny when he said my name, so funny that I felt compelled to ask: "Is something wrong?" Ted blurted it all out without a preamble. His father had asked who he was going out with. Ted had told him my name. "Ortiz? That's Spanish, isn't it?" the father had asked. Ted had told him yes, then shown him my picture in the yearbook. Ted's father had shaken his head. No. Ted would not be taking me out. Ted's father had known Puerto Ricans in the Army. He had lived in New York City while studying architecture and had seen how the spics lived. Like rats. Ted repeated his father's words to me as if I should understand *his* predicament when I heard why he was breaking our date. I don't remember what I said before hanging up. I do recall the darkness of my room that sleepless night and the heaviness of my blanket in which I wrapped myself like a shroud. And I remember my parents' respect for my pain and their gentleness toward me that weekend. My mother did not say "I warned you," and I was grateful for her understanding silence.

In college, I suddenly became an "exotic" woman to the men who had survived the popularity wars in high school, who were not practicing to be worldly: they had to act liberal in their politics, in their lifestyles, and in the women they went out with. I dated heavily for a while, then married young. I had discovered that I needed stability more than social life. I had brains for sure and some talent in writing. These facts were a constant in my life. My skin color, my size, and my appearance were variables—things that were judged according to my current self-image, the aesthetic values of the time, the places I was in, and the people I met. My studies, later my writing, the respect of people who saw me as an individual person they cared about, these were the criteria for my sense of self-worth that I would concentrate on in my adult life.

49

"GEE, YOU DON'T SEEM LIKE AN INDIAN FROM THE RESERVATION"

BARBARA CAMERON

One of the very first words I learned in my Lakota language was *wasicu*, which designates white people. At that early age, my comprehension of wasicu was gained from observing and listening to my family discussing the wasicu. My grandmother always referred to white people as the "wasicu sica" with emphasis on *sica*, our word for terrible or bad. By the age of five I had seen one Indian man gunned down in the back by the police and was a silent witness to a gang of white teenage boys beating up an elderly Indian man. I'd hear stories of Indian ranch hands being "accidentally" shot by white ranchers. I quickly began to understand the wasicu menace my family spoke of.

My hatred for the wasicu was solidly implanted by the time I entered first grade. Unfortunately in first grade I became teacher's pet so my teacher had a fondness for hugging me, which always repulsed me. I couldn't stand the idea of a white person touching me. Eventually I realized that it wasn't the white skin that I hated, but it was their culture of deceit, greed, racism, and violence.

During my first memorable visit to a white town, I was appalled that they thought of themselves as superior to my people. Their manner of living appeared devoid of life and bordered on hostility even for one another. They were separated from each other by their perfectly, politely fenced square plots of green lawn. The only lawns on my reservation were the lawns of the BIA* officials or white Christians. The white people always seemed so loud, obnoxious, and vulgar. And the white parents were either screaming at their kids, threatening them with some form of punishment or hitting them. After spending a day around white people, I was always happy to go back to the reservation where people followed a relaxed yet respectful code of relating with each other. The easy teasing and joking that were inherent with the Lakota were a welcome relief after a day with the plastic faces.

Cameron, Barbara. " 'Gee, You Don't Seem Like an Indian from the Reservation.' " In Moraga, Cherríe, and Anzaldúa, Gloria (eds.). *This Bridge Called My Back: Writings By Radical Women of Color.* New York: Kitchen Table: Women of Color Press. 1983. p. 46–52.
*Bureau of Indian Affairs.

I vividly remember two occasions during my childhood in which I was cognizant of being an Indian. The first time was at about three years of age when my family took me to my first pow-wow. I kept asking my grandmother, "Where are the Indians? Where are the Indians? Are they going to have bows and arrows?" I was very curious and strangely excited about the prospect of seeing real live Indians even though I myself was one. It's a memory that has remained with me through all these years because it's so full of the subtleties of my culture. There was a sweet wonderful aroma in the air from the dancers and from the traditional food booths. There were lots of grandmothers and grandfathers with young children running about. Pow-wows in the Plains usually last for three days, sometimes longer, with Indian people traveling from all parts of our country to dance, to share food and laughter, and to be with each other. I could sense the importance of our gathering times and it was the beginning of my awareness that my people are a great and different nation.

The second time in my childhood when I knew very clearly that I am Indian occurred when I was attending an all-white (except for me) elementary school. During Halloween my friends and I went trick or treating. At one of the last stops, the mother knew all of the children except for me. She asked me to remove my mask so she could see who I was. After I removed my mask, she realized I was an Indian and quite cruelly told me so, refusing to give me the treats my friends had received. It was a stingingly painful experience.

I told my mother about it the next evening after I tried to understand it. My mother was outraged and explained the realities of being an Indian in South Dakota. My mother paid a visit to the woman, which resulted in their expressing a barrage of equal hatred for one another. I remember sitting in our pick-up hearing the intensity of the anger and feeling very sad that my mother had to defend her child to someone who wasn't worthy of her presence.

I spent a part of my childhood feeling great sadness and helplessness about how it seemed that Indians were open game for the white people, to kill, maim, beat up, insult, rape, cheat, or whatever atrocity the white people wanted to play with. There was also a rage and frustration that has not died. When I look back on reservation life, it seems that I spent a great deal of time attending the funerals of my relatives or friends of my family. During one year I went to funerals of four murder victims. Most of my non-Indian friends have not seen a dead body or have not been to a funeral. Death was so common on the reservation that I did not understand the implications of the high death rate until after I moved away and was surprised to learn that I've seen more dead bodies than my friends will probably ever see in their lifetime.

Because of experiencing racial violence, I sometimes panic when I'm the only non-white in a roomful of whites, even if they are my closest friends; I wonder if I'll leave the room alive. The seemingly copacetic gay world of San Francisco becomes a mere dream after the panic leaves. I think to myself that it's truly insane for me to feel the panic. I want to scream out my anger and disgust with myself for feeling distrustful of my white friends and I want to banish the society that has fostered those feelings of alienation. I wonder at the amount of assimilation which has affected me and how long my "Indianness" will allow me to remain in a city that is far removed from the lives of many Native Americans.

"Alienation" and "assimilation" are two common words used to describe contemporary Indian people. I've come to despise those two words because what leads to "alienation" and "assimilation" should not be so concisely defined. And I generally mistrust words that are used to define Native Americans and Brown People. I don't like being put under a magnifying glass and having cute liberal terms describe who I am. The "alienation" or "assimilation" that I manifest is often in how I speak. There isn't necessarily a third world language but there is an Indian way of talking that is an essential part of me. I like it, I love it, yet I deny it. I "save" it for when I'm around other Indians. It is a way of talking that involves "Indian humor" which I know for sure non-Indian people would not necessarily understand.

Articulate. Articulate. I've heard that word used many times to describe third world people. White people seem so surprised to find brown people who can speak fluent English and are even perhaps educated. We then become "articulate." I think I spend a lot of time being articulate with white people. Or as one person said to me a few years ago, "Gee, you don't seem like an Indian from the reservation."

I often read about the dilemmas of contemporary Indians caught between the white and Indian worlds. For most of us, it is an uneasy balance to maintain. Sometimes some of us are not so successful with it. Native Americans have a very high suicide rate.

> When I was about 20, I dreamt of myself at the age of 25–26, standing at a place on my reservation, looking to the North, watching a glorious, many-colored horse galloping toward me from the sky. My eyes were riveted and attracted to the beauty and overwhelming strength of the horse. The horse's eyes were staring directly into mine, hypnotizing me and holding my attention. Slowly from the East, an eagle was gliding toward the horse. My attention began to be drawn toward the calm of the eagle but I still did not want to lose sight of the horse. Finally the two met with the eagle sailing into the horse causing it to disintegrate. The eagle flew gently on.

I take this prophetic dream as an analogy of my balance between the white [horse] and Indian [eagle] worlds. Now that I am 26, I find that I've gone as far into my exploration of the white world as I want. It doesn't mean that I'm going to run off to live in a tipi. It simply means that I'm not interested in pursuing a society that uses analysis, research, and experimentation to concretize their vision of cruel destinies for those who are not bastards of the Pilgrims; a society with arrogance rising, moon in oppression, and sun in destruction.

Racism is not easy for me to write about because of my own racism toward other people of color, and because of a complex set of "racisms" within the Indian community. At times animosity exists between half-breed, full-blood, light-skinned Indians, dark-skinned Indians, and non-Indians who attempt to pass as Indians. The U.S. government has practiced for many years its divisiveness in the Indian community by instilling and perpetuating these Indian versus Indian tactics. Native Americans are the foremost group of people who continuously fight against premeditated cultural genocide.

I've grown up with misconceptions about Blacks, Chicanos, and Asians. I'm still in the process of trying to eliminate my racist pictures of other people of color. I know most of *my* images of other races come from television, books, movies, newspapers, and magazines. Who can pinpoint exactly where racism comes from? There are certain political dogmas that are excellent in their "analysis" of racism and how it feeds the capitalist system. To intellectually understand that it is wrong or politically incorrect to be racist leaves me cold. A lot of poor or working class white and brown people are just as racist as the "capitalist pig." We are *all* continually pumped with gross and inaccurate images of everyone else and we *all* pump it out. I don't think there are easy answers or formulas. My personal attempts at eliminating my racism have to start at the base level of those mindsets that inhibit my relationships with people.

Racism among third world people is an area that needs to be discussed and dealt with honestly. We form alliances loosely based on the fact that we have a common oppressor, yet we do not have a commitment to talk about our own fears and misconceptions about each other. I've noticed that liberal, consciousness-raised white people tend to be incredibly polite to third world people at parties or other social situations. It's almost as if they make a point to SHAKE YOUR HAND or to introduce themselves and then run down all the latest right-on third world or Native American books they've just read. On the other hand it's been my experience that if there are several third world gay people at a party, we make a point of avoiding each other, and spend our time talking to the whites to show how sophisticated and intelligent we are. I've always wanted to introduce myself to other third world people but wondered how I would introduce myself or what would I say. There are so many things I would want to say, except sometimes I don't want to remember I'm Third World or Native American. I don't want to remember sometimes because it means recognizing that we're outlaws.

At the Third World Gay Conference in October 1979, the Asian and Native American people in attendance felt the issues affecting us were not adequately included in the workshops. Our representation and leadership had minimal input, which resulted in a skimpy educational process about our struggles. The conference glaringly pointed out to us the narrow definition held by some people that third world means black people only. It was a depressing experience to sit in the lobby of Harambee House with other Native Americans and Asians, feeling removed from other third world groups with whom there is supposed to be this automatic solidarity and empathy. The Indian group sat in my motel room discussing and exchanging our experiences within the third world context. We didn't spend much time in workshops conducted by other third world people because of feeling unwelcomed at the conference and demoralized by having an invisible presence. What's worse than being invisible among your own kind?

It is of particular importance to us as third world gay people to begin a serious interchange of sharing and educating ourselves about each other. We not only must struggle with the racism and homophobia of straight white America, but must often struggle with the homophobia that exists within our third world communities. Being third world doesn't always connote a political awareness or activism. I've met a number of third world and Native American lesbians who've said they're just into "being themselves," and that politics has no meaning in their lives. I agree that everyone is entitled to "be themselves" but in a society that denies respect and basic rights to people because of their ethnic background, I feel that individuals cannot idly sit by and allow themselves to be co-opted by the dominant society. I don't know what moves a person to be politically active or to attempt to raise the quality of life in our world. I only know what motivates my political responsibility . . . the death of Anna Mae Aquash—Native American freedom fighter—"mysteriously" murdered by a bullet in the head; Raymond Yellow Thunder—forced to dance naked in front of a white VFW club in Nebraska—murdered; Rita Silk-Nauni—imprisoned for life for defending her child; my dear friend Mani Lucas-Papago—shot in the back of the head outside of a gay bar in Phoenix. The list could go on and on. My Native American History, recent and past, moves me to continue as a political activist.

And in the white gay community there is rampant racism which is never adequately addressed or acknowledged. My friend Chrystos from the Menominee Nation gave a poetry reading in May 1980, at a Bay Area feminist bookstore. Her reading consisted of poems and journal entries in which she wrote honestly from her heart about the many "isms" and contradictions in most of our lives. Chrystos' bluntly revealing observations on her experiences with the white-lesbian-feminist community are similar to mine and are probably echoed by other lesbians of color.

Her honesty was courageous and should be representative of the kind of forum our community needs to openly discuss mutual racism. A few days following Chrystos' reading, a friend who was in the same bookstore overheard a white lesbian denounce Chrystos' reading as anti-lesbian and racist.

A few years ago, a white lesbian telephoned me requesting an interview, explaining that she was taking Native American courses at a local university, and that she needed data for her paper on gay Native Americans. I agreed to the interview with the idea that I would be helping a "sister" and would also be able to educate her about Native American struggles. After we completed the interview, she began a diatribe on how sexist Native Americans are, followed by a questioning session in which I was to enlighten her mind about why Native Americans are so sexist. I attempted to rationally answer her inanely racist and insulting questions, although my inner response was to tell her to remove herself from my house. Later it became very clear how I had been manipulated as a sounding board for her ugly and distorted views about Native Americans. Her arrogance and disrespect were characteristic of the racist white people in South Dakota. If I tried to point it out, I'm sure she would have vehemently denied her racism.

During the Brigg's Initiative scare, I was invited to speak at a rally to represent Native American solidarity against the initiative. The person who spoke prior to me expressed a pro-Bakke sentiment which the audience booed and hissed. His comments left the predominantly white audience angry and in disruption. A white lesbian stood up demanding that a third world person address the racist comments he had made. The MC, rather than taking responsibility for restoring order at the rally, realized that I was the next speaker and I was also T-H-I-R-D-W-O-R-L-D!! I refused to address the remarks of the previous speaker because of the attitudes of the MC and the white lesbian that only third world people are responsible for speaking out against racism. *It is inappropriate for progressive or liberal white people to expect warriors in brown armor to eradicate racism.* There must be co-responsibility from people of color and white people to equally work on this issue. It is not just MY responsibility to point out and educate about racist activities and beliefs.

Redman, redskin, savage, heathen, injun, american indian, first americans, indigenous peoples, natives, amerindian, native american, nigger, negro, black, wet back, greaser, mexican, spanish, latin, hispanic, chicano, chink, oriental, asian, disadvantaged, special interest group, minority, third world, fourth world, people of color, illegal aliens—oh, yes, about them, will the U.S. government recognize that the Founding Fathers (you know George Washington and all those guys) are this country's first illegal aliens.

We are named by others and we are named by ourselves.

Epilogue . . .

Following writing most of this, I went to visit my home in South Dakota. It was my first visit in eight years. I kept putting off my visit year after year because I could not tolerate the white people there and the ruralness and poverty of the reservation. And because in the eight years since I left home, I came out as a lesbian. My visit home was overwhelming. Floods and floods of locked memories broke. I rediscovered myself there in the hills, on the prairies, in the sky, on the road, in the quiet nights, among the stars, listening to the distant yelps of coyotes, walking on Lakota earth, seeing Bear Butte, looking at my grandparents' cragged faces, standing under wakiyan, smelling the Paha Sapa [Black Hills], and being with my precious circle of relatives.

My sense of time changed, my manner of speaking changed, and a certain freedom with myself returned.

I was sad to leave but recognized that a significant part of myself has never left and never will. And that part is what gives me strength—the strength of my people's enduring history and continuing belief in the sovereignty of our lives.

50

ON BEING BLACKANESE

MITZI UEHARA-CARTER

"Umm . . . excuse me. Where are you from?"
"I'm from Houston, Texas."
"Oh . . . but your parents, where are they from?"
(Hmm. Should I continue to play stupid or just tell them.) "My dad is from Houston, and my mom is from Okinawa, Japan."
"And your dad is black then?"
"Yup."
"So do you speak Japanese?"
"Some."
"Wow. Say something."

This is not a rare conversation. I cannot count the number of times I've pulled this script out to rehearse with random people who have accosted me in the past. "That's so exotic, so cool that you're mixed." It's not that these questions or comments bother me or that I am offended by their bluntness. I think it's more of the attitudes of bewilderment and the exoticism of my being and even the slight bossiness to do something "exotic" that annoy me. I think I am also annoyed because I am still exploring what it means to be both Japanese and Black and still have difficulty trying to express what that means to others.

In many ways and for many years I have grappled with the idea of being a product of two cultures brought together by an unwanted colonization of American military bases on my mother's homeland of Okinawa. Author of "In the Realm of a Dying Emperor," Norma Field expressed these sentiments more clearly than I ever could. "Many years into my growing up, I thought I had understood the awkward piquancy of biracial children with the formulation, they are nothing if not the embodiment of sex itself; now, I modify it to, the biracial offspring of war are at once more offensive and intriguing because they bear the imprint of sex as domination." Of course this is not how I feel about myself all the time, but rather it is the invisible bug that itches under my skin every now and then. It itches when I read about Okinawan girls being raped by U.S. Servicemen, when I see mail order bride ads, when I notice the high divorce or separation rate among Asian women and GI's who were married a few years after WWII, when I see the half-way hidden looks

From *Interracial Voice*, Vol. 5, 1996, p. 56–58. Reprinted by permission of the publisher.

of disgust at my mother by other Japanese women when I walk by her side as a daughter. Our bodies, our presence, our reality is a nuisance to some because we defy a definite and demarcated set of boundaries. We confuse those who are trying to organize ethnic groups by highlighting these boundaries because they don't know how to include us or exclude us. We are blackanese, hapas, eurasians, multiracial. . . .

My mother has been the center of jokes and derogatory comments since my older sister was born. She was the one who took my sister by the hand and led her through the streets of Bangkok and Okinawa as eyes stared and people gathered to talk about the sambo baby. She was the one who took all my siblings to the grocery stores, the malls, the park, school, Burger King, hospitals, church. In each of these public arenas we were stared at either in fascination because we were a new "sight" or stared at with a look of disgust or both. Nigga-chink, Black-Jap, Black-Japanese mutt. The neighborhood kids, friends, and adults labeled my siblings and me with these terms especially after they recognized that my mother was completely intent on making us learn about Okinawan culture. On New Year's Day, we had black-eyed peas and mochi. We cleaned the house to start the year fresh and clean. "Don't laugh with your mouth too wide and show yo teeth too much," my mom would always tell us. "Be like a woman." I had not realized that I covered my mouth each time I laughed until someone pointed it out in my freshman year in college. When we disobeyed my mother's rule or screamed, we were being too "American." If I ever left the house with rollers in my hair, my mom would say I shouldn't do American things. "Agijibiyo . . . Where you learn this from? You are Okinawan too. Dame desuyo. Don't talk so much like Americans; listen first." There were several other cultural traits and values that I had inevitably inherited (and cherish) being raised by a Japanese mother.

Growing up in an all-Black neighborhood and attending predominately Black and Latino schools until college influenced my identity also. I was definitely not accepted in the Japanese circles as Japanese for several reasons, but that introduces another subject on acceptance into Japanese communities. Now this is not to say that the Black community I associated with embraced me as Blackanese, even though I think it is more accepting of multiracial people than probably any other group (because of the one-drop rule, etc.). There is still an exclusion for those who wish to encompass all parts of their heritage with equal weight, and there is also a subtle push to identify more with one's black heritage than the other part because "society won't see you as mixed or Japanese but BLACK." I can't count the number of times I have heard this argument. What I do know is that no society can tell me that I am more of one culture than another because of the way someone else defines me. I am Blackanese—a mixture of the two in ways that cannot be divided. My body and mentality is not split down the middle where half is black and the other half is Japanese. I have taken the aspects of both worlds to create my own worldview and identity. Like Anna Vale said in Itabari Njeri's article "Sushi and

Grits," my mother raised me the best way she knew how, "to be a good Japanese daughter."

My father, on the other hand, never constantly sat down to "teach" us about being Black. We were surrounded by Blackness and lived it. He was always tired when he came home from work. He'd sit back in his sofa and blast his jazz. My mom would be in the kitchen with her little tape player listening to her Japanese and Okinawan tapes my aunt sent every other month from California. My siblings and I would stay at my grandmother's house once in a while (she cooked the best collard greens), and when my mom came to pick us up she'd teach her how to cook a southern meal for my father. Our meals were somewhat of an indicator of how much my mom held onto her traditions. My father would make his requests for chicken, steak or okra and my mom had learned to cook these things, but we always had Japanese rice on the side with nori and tofu and fishcake with these really noisome beans that are supposed to be good for you (according to my mom. I swear she knows what every Japanese magazine has to say about food and health). It was my mother who told us that we would be discriminated against because of our color, and it was my Japanese mother to whom we ran when we were called niggers at the public swimming pool in Houston. To say to this woman, "Mom, we are just Black" would be a disrespectful slap in the face. The woman who raised us and cried for years from her family's coldness and rejection because of her decision to marry interracially, cried when my father's sister wouldn't let her be a part of the family picture because she was a "Jap." This woman who happens to be my mother will never hear, "Mom, I'm just Black" from my mouth because I'm not and no person—society or government—will force me to do that and deny my reality and my being, no matter how offensive I am to their country or how much of a nuisance I am to their cause. I am Blackanese.

51

NICKEL-AND-DIMED ON (NOT) GETTING BY IN AMERICA

BARBARA EHRENREICH

At the beginning of June 1998 I leave behind everything that normally soothes the ego and sustains the body—home, career, companion, reputation, ATM card—for a plunge into the low-wage workforce. There, I become another, occupationally much diminished "Barbara Ehrenreich"—depicted on job-application forms as a divorced homemaker whose sole work experience consists of housekeeping in a few private homes. I am terrified, at the beginning, of being unmasked for what I am: a middle-class journalist setting out to explore the world that welfare mothers are entering, at the rate of approximately 50,000 a month, as welfare reform kicks in. Happily, though, my fears turn out to be entirely unwarranted: during a month of poverty and toil, my name goes unnoticed and for the most part unuttered. In this parallel universe where my father never got out of the mines and I never got through college, I am "baby," "honey," "blondie," and, most commonly, "girl."

My first task is to find a place to live. I figure that if I can earn $7 an hour—which, from the want ads, seems doable—I can afford to spend $500 on rent, or maybe, with severe economies, $600. In the Key West area, where I live, this pretty much confines me to flophouses and trailer homes—like the one, a pleasing fifteen-minute drive from town, that has no air-conditioning, no screens, no fans, no television, and, by way of diversion, only the challenge of evading the landlord's Doberman pinscher. The big problem with this place, though, is the rent, which at $675 a month is well beyond my reach. All right, Key West is expensive. But so is New York City, or the Bay Area, or Jackson Hole, or Telluride, or Boston, or any other place where tourists and the wealthy compete for living space with the people who clean their toilets and fry their hash browns.[1] Still, it is a shock to realize that "trailer trash" has become, for me, a demographic category to aspire to.

So I decide to make the common trade-off between affordability and convenience, and go for a $500-a-month efficiency thirty miles up a two-lane highway from the employment opportunities of Key West, meaning forty-five minutes if there's no road construction and I don't get caught behind some sun-dazed Canadian tourists. I hate the drive, along a roadside studded with white crosses commemorating the more effective head-on collisions, but

Harper's Magazine, January 1999, volume 298, p. 37(1).

it's a sweet little place—a cabin, more or less, set in the swampy back yard of the converted mobile home where my landlord, an affable TV repairman, lives with his bartender girlfriend. Anthropologically speaking, a bustling trailer park would be preferable, but here I have a gleaming white floor and a firm mattress, and the few resident bugs are easily vanquished.

Besides, I am not doing this for the anthropology. My aim is nothing so mistily subjective as to "experience poverty" or find out how it "really feels" to be a long-term low-wage worker. I've had enough unchosen encounters with poverty and the world of low-wage work to know it's not a place you want to visit for touristic purposes; it just smells too much like fear. And with all my real-life assets—bank account, IRA, health insurance, multiroom home—waiting indulgently in the background, I am, of course, thoroughly insulated from the terrors that afflict the genuinely poor.

No, this is a purely objective, scientific sort of mission. The humanitarian rationale for welfare reform—as opposed to the more punitive and stingy impulses that may actually have motivated it—is that work will lift poor women out of poverty while simultaneously inflating their self-esteem and hence their future value in the labor market. Thus, whatever the hassles involved in finding child care, transportation, etc., the transition from welfare to work will end happily, in greater prosperity for all. Now there are many problems with this comforting prediction, such as the fact that the economy will inevitably undergo a downturn, eliminating many jobs. Even without a downturn, the influx of a million former welfare recipients into the low-wage labor market could depress wages by as much as 11.9 percent, according to the Economic Policy Institute (EPI) in Washington, D.C.

But is it really possible to make a living on the kinds of jobs currently available to unskilled people? Mathematically, the answer is no, as can be shown by taking $6 to $7 an hour, perhaps subtracting a dollar or two an hour for child care, multiplying by 160 hours a month, and comparing the result to the prevailing rents. According to the National Coalition for the Homeless, for example, in 1998 it took, on average nationwide, an hourly wage of $8.89 to afford a one-bedroom apartment, and the Preamble Center for Public Policy estimates that the odds against a typical welfare recipient's landing a job at such a "living wage" are about 97 to 1. If these numbers are right, low-wage work is not a solution to poverty and possibly not even to homelessness.

It may seem excessive to put this proposition to an experimental test. As certain family members keep unhelpfully reminding me, the viability of low-wage work could be tested, after a fashion, without ever leaving my study. I could just pay myself $7 an hour for eight hours a day, charge myself for room and board, and total up the numbers after a month. Why leave the people and work that I love? But I am an experimental scientist by training. In that business, you don't just sit at a desk and theorize; you plunge into the everyday chaos of nature, where surprises lurk in the most mundane measurements. Maybe, when I got into it, I would discover some hidden economies in the world of the low-wage worker. After all, if 30 percent of the workforce toils for less than $8 an hour, according to the EPI, they may have found some tricks as yet unknown to me. Maybe—who knows?—I would even be able to detect in myself the bracing psychological effects of getting out of the house, as promised by the welfare wonks at places like the Heritage Foundation. Or, on the other hand, maybe there would be unexpected costs—physical, mental, or financial—to throw off all my calculations. Ideally, I should do this with two small children in tow, that being the welfare average, but mine are grown and no one is willing to lend me theirs for a month-long vacation in penury. So this is not the perfect experiment, just a test of the best possible case: an unencumbered woman, smart and even strong, attempting to live more or less off the land.

On the morning of my first full day of job searching, I take a red pen to the want ads, which are auspiciously numerous. Everyone in Key West's booming "hospitality industry" seems to be looking for someone like me—trainable, flexible, and with suitably humble expectations as to pay. . . .

Most of the big hotels run ads almost continually, just to build a supply of applicants to replace the current workers as they drift away or are fired, so finding a job is just a matter of being at the right place at the right time and flexible enough to take whatever is being offered that day. This finally happens to me at a one of the big discount hotel chains, where I go, as usual, for housekeeping and am sent, instead, to try out as a waitress at the attached "family restaurant," a dismal spot with a counter and about thirty tables that looks out on a parking garage and features such tempting fare as "Polish [sic] sausage and BBQ sauce" on 95-degree days. Phillip, the dapper young West Indian who introduces himself as the manager, interviews me with about as much enthusiasm as if he were a clerk processing me for Medicare, the principal questions being what shifts can I work and when can I start. I mutter something about being woefully out of practice as a waitress, but he's already on to the uniform: I'm to show up tomorrow wearing black slacks and black shoes; he'll provide the rust-colored polo shirt with HEARTHSIDE embroidered on it, though I might want to wear my own shirt to get to work, ha ha. At the word "tomorrow," something between fear and indignation rises in my chest. I want to say, "Thank you for your time, sir, but this is just an experiment, you know, not my actual life."

So begins my career at the Hearthside, I shall call it, one small profit center within a global discount hotel chain, where for two weeks I work from 2:00 till 10:00 P.M. for $2.43 an hour plus tips.[2] In some futile bid for gentility, the management has barred employees from using the front door, so my first day I enter through the kitchen, where a red-faced man with shoulder-length blond hair is throwing frozen steaks against the wall and yelling, "Fuck this shit!" "That's just Jack," explains Gail, the wiry middle-aged waitress who is assigned to train me. "He's on the rag again"—a condition occasioned, in this instance, by the fact that the cook on the morning shift had forgotten to thaw out the steaks. For the next eight hours, I run after the agile Gail, absorbing bits of instruction along with fragments of personal tragedy. All food must be trayed, and the reason she's so tired today is that she woke up in a cold sweat thinking of her boyfriend, who killed himself recently in an upstate prison. No refills on lemonade. And the reason he was in prison is that a few DUIs caught up with him, that's all, could have happened to anyone. Carry the creamers to the table in a monkey bowl, never in your hand. And after he was gone she spent several months living in her truck, peeing in a plastic pee bottle and reading by candlelight at night, but you can't live in a truck in the summer, since you need to have the windows down, which means anything can get in, from mosquitoes on up.

At least Gail puts to rest any fears I had of appearing overqualified. From the first day on, I find that of all the things I have left behind, such as home and identity, what I miss the most is competence. Not that I have ever felt utterly competent in the writing business, in which one day's success augurs nothing at all for the next. But in my writing life, I at least have some notion of procedure: do the research, make the outline, rough out a draft, etc. As a server, though I am beset by requests like bees: more iced tea here, ketchup over there, a to-go box for table fourteen, and where are the high chairs, anyway? Of the twenty-seven tables, up to six are usually mine at any time, though on slow afternoons or if Gail is off, I sometimes have the whole place to myself. There is the touch-screen computer-ordering system to master, which is, I suppose, meant to minimize server-cook contact, but in practice requires constant verbal fine-tuning: "That's gravy on the mashed, okay? None on the meatloaf," and so forth—while the cook scowls as if I were inventing these refinements just to torment him. Plus, something I had forgotten in the years since I was eighteen: about a third of a server's job is "side work" that's invisible to customers—sweeping, scrubbing, slicing, refilling, and restocking. If it isn't all done, every little bit of it, you're going to face the 6:00 P.M. dinner rush defenseless and probably go down in flames. I screw up dozens of times at the beginning, sustained in my shame entirely by Gail's support—"It's okay, baby, everyone does that sometime"—because, to my total surprise and despite the scientific detachment I am doing my best to maintain, I care. . . .

On my first Friday at the Hearthside there is a "mandatory meeting for all restaurant employees," which I attend, eager for insight into our overall marketing strategy and the niche (your basic Ohio cuisine with a tropical twist?) we aim to inhabit. But there is no "we" at this meeting. Phillip, our top manager except for an occasional "consultant" sent out by corporate headquarters, opens it with a sneer: "The break room—it's disgusting. Butts in the ashtrays, newspapers lying around, crumbs." This windowless little room, which also houses the time clock for the entire hotel, is where we stash our bags and civilian clothes and take our half-hour meal breaks. But a break room is not a right, he tells us. It can be taken away. We should also know that the lockers in the break room and whatever is in them can be searched at any time. Then comes gossip; there has been gossip; gossip (which seems to mean employees talking among themselves) must stop. Off-duty employees are henceforth barred from eating at the restaurant, because "other servers gather around them and gossip." When Phillip has exhausted his agenda of rebukes, Joan complains about the condition of the ladies' room and I throw in my two bits about the vacuum cleaner. But I don't see any backup coming from my fellow servers, each of whom has subsided into her own personal funk; Gail, my role model, stares sorrowfully at a point six inches from her nose. The meeting ends when Andy, one of the cooks, gets up, muttering about breaking up his day off for this almighty bullshit.

Just four days later we are suddenly summoned into the kitchen at 3:30 P.M., even though there are live tables on the floor. We all—about ten of us—stand around Phillip, who announces grimly that there has been a report of some "drug activity" on the night shift and that, as a result, we are now to be a "drug-free" workplace, meaning that all new hires will be tested, as will possibly current employees on a random basis. I am glad that this part of the kitchen is so dark, because I find myself blushing as hard as if I had been caught toking up in the ladies' room myself: I haven't been treated this way—lined up in the corridor, threatened with locker searches, peppered with care-lessly aimed accusations—since junior high school. Back on the floor, Joan cracks, "Next they'll be telling us we can't have sex on the job." When I ask Stu what happened to inspire the crackdown, he just mutters about "man-agement decisions" and takes the opportunity to upbraid Gail and me for be-ing too generous, with the rolls. From now on there's to be only one per customer, and it goes out with the dinner, not with the salad. He's also been riding the cooks, prompting Andy to come out of the kitchen and observe—with the serenity of a man whose customary implement is a butcher knife—that "Stu has a death wish today."

The other problem, in addition to the less-than-nurturing management style, is that this job shows no sign of being financially viable. You might imag-ine, from a comfortable distance, that people who live, year in and year out, on $6 to $10 an hour have discovered some survival stratagems unknown to the middle class. But no. It's not hard to get my co-workers to talk about their liv-ing situations, because housing, in almost every case, is the principal source of disruption in their lives, the first thing they fill you in on when they arrive for their shifts. After a week, I have compiled the following survey:

- Gail is sharing a room in a well-known down-town flophouse for which she and a roommate pay about $250 a week. Her roommate, a male friend, has begun hitting on her, driving her nuts, but the rent would be impossible alone.

- Claude, the Haitian cook, is desperate to get out of the two-room apartment he shares with his girlfriend and two other, unrelated, people. As far as I can determine, the other Haitian men (most of whom only speak Creole) live in similarly crowded situations.

- Annette, a twenty-year-old server who is six months pregnant and has been abandoned by her boyfriend, lives with her mother, a postal clerk.

- Marianne and her boyfriend are paying $170 a week for a one-person trailer.
- Jack, who is, at $10 an hour, the wealthiest of us, lives in the trailer he owns, paying only the $400-a-month lot fee.
- The other white cook, Andy, lives on his dry-docked boat, which, as far as I can tell from his loving descriptions, can't be more than twenty feet long. He offers to take me out on it, once it's repaired, but the offer comes with inquiries as to my marital status, so I do not follow up on it.
- Tina and her husband are paying $60 a night for a double room in a Days Inn. This is because they have no car and the Days Inn is within walking distance of the Hearthside. When Marianne, one of the breakfast servers, is tossed out of her trailer for subletting (which is against the trailer-park rules), she leaves her boyfriend and moves in with Tina and her husband.
- Joan, who had fooled me with her numerous and tasteful outfits (hostesses wear their own clothes), lives in a van she parks behind a shopping center at night and showers in Tina's motel room. The clothes are from thrift shops.[3]

It strikes me, in my middle-class solipsism, that there is gross improvidence in some of these arrangements. When Gail and I are wrapping silverware in napkins—the only task for which we are permitted to sit—she tells me she is thinking of escaping from her roommate by moving into the Days Inn herself. I am astounded: How can she even think of paying between $40 and $60 a day? But if I was afraid of sounding like a social worker, I come out just sounding like a fool. She squints at me in disbelief, "And where am I supposed to get a month's rent and a month's deposit for an apartment?" I'd been feeling pretty smug about my $500 efficiency, but of course it was made possible only by the $1,300 I had allotted myself for start-up costs when I began my low-wage life: $1,000 for the first month's rent and deposit, $100 for initial groceries and cash in my pocket, $200 stuffed away for emergencies. In poverty, as in certain propositions in physics, starting conditions are everything.

There are no secret economies that nourish the poor; on the contrary, there are a host of special costs. If you can't put up the two months' rent you need to secure an apartment, you end up paying through the nose for a room by the week. If you have only a room, with a hot plate at best, you can't save by cooking up huge lentil stews that can be frozen for the week ahead. You eat fast food, or the hot dogs and styrofoam cups of soup that can be microwaved in a convenience store. If you have no money for health insurance—and the Hearthside's niggardly plan kicks in only after three months—you go without routine care or prescription drugs and end up paying the price. Gail, for example, was fine until she ran out of money for estrogen pills. She is supposed to be on the company plan by now, but they claim to have lost her application form and need to begin the paperwork all over again. So she spends $9 per migraine pill to control the headaches she wouldn't have, she insists, if her estrogen supplements were covered. Similarly, Marianne's boyfriend lost his job as a roofer because he missed so much time after getting a cut on his foot for which he couldn't afford the prescribed antibiotic.

My own situation, when I sit down to assess it after two weeks of work, would not be much better if this were my actual life. The seductive thing about waitressing is that you don't have to wait for payday to feel a few bills in your pocket, and my tips usually cover meals and gas, plus something left over to stuff into the kitchen drawer I use as a bank. But as the tourist business slows in the summer heat, I sometimes leave work with only $20 in tips (the gross is higher, but servers share about 15 percent of their tips with the busboys and bartenders). With wages included, this amounts to about the minimum wage of $5.15 an hour. Although the sum in the drawer is piling up, at the present rate of accumulation it will be more than a hundred dollars short of my rent when the end of the month comes around. Nor can I see any expenses to cut. True, I haven't gone the lentil-stew route yet, but that's because I don't have a large cooking pot, pot holders, or a ladle to stir with (which cost about $30 at Kmart, less at thrift stores), not to mention onions, carrots, and the indispensable bay leaf. I do make my lunch almost every day—usually some slow-burning, high-protein combo like frozen chicken patties with melted cheese on top and canned pinto beans on the side. Dinner is at the Hearthside, which offers its employees a choice of BLT, fish sandwich, or hamburger for only $2. The burger lasts longest, especially if it's heaped with gut-puckering jalapenos, but by midnight my stomach is growling again.

So unless I want to start using my car as a residence, I have to find a second, or alternative, job. I call all the hotels where I filled out housekeeping applications weeks ago—the Hyatt, Holiday Inn, Econo Lodge, Hojo's, Best Western, plus a half dozen or so locally run guesthouses. Nothing. Then I start making the rounds again, wasting whole mornings waiting for some assistant manager to show up, even dipping into places so creepy that the front-desk clerk greets you from behind bulletproof glass and sells pints of liquor over the counter. But either someone has exposed my real-life housekeeping habits—which are, shall we say, mellow—or I am at the wrong end of some infallible ethnic equation: most, but by no means all, of the working housekeepers I see on my job searches are African Americans, Spanish-speaking, or immigrants from the Central European post-Communist world, whereas servers are almost invariably white and monolingually English-speaking. When I finally get a positive response, I have been identified once again as server material. Jerry's, which is part of a well-known national family restaurant chain and physically attached here to another budget hotel chain, is ready to use me at once. The prospect is both exciting and terrifying, because, with about the same number of tables and counter seats, Jerry's attracts three or four times the volume of customers as the gloomy old Hearthside. . . .

I start out with the beautiful, heroic idea of handling the two jobs at once, and for two days I almost do it: the breakfast/lunch shift at Jerry's, which goes till 2:00, arriving at the Hearthside at 2:10, and attempting to hold out until 10:00. In the ten minutes between jobs, I pick up a spicy chicken sandwich at the Wendy's drive-through window, gobble it down in the car, and change from khaki slacks to black, from Hawaiian to rust polo. There is a problem, though. When during the 3:00 to 4:00 P.M. dead time I finally sit down to wrap silver, my flesh seems to bond to the seat. I try to refuel with a purloined cup of soup, as I've seen Gail and Joan do dozens of times, but a manager catches me and hisses "No eating!" though there's not a customer around to be offended by the sight of food making contact with a server's lips. So I tell Gail I'm going to quit, and she hugs me and says she might just follow me to Jerry's herself.

But the chances of this are minuscule. She has left the flophouse and her annoying roommate and is back to living in her beat-up old truck. But guess what? she reports to me excitedly later that evening: Phillip has given her permission to park overnight in the hotel parking lot, as long as she keeps out of sight, and the parking lot should be totally safe, since it's patrolled by a hotel security guard! With the Hearthside offering benefits like that, how could anyone think of leaving? . . .

Management at Jerry's is generally calmer and more "professional" than at the Hearthside, with two exceptions. One is Joy, a plump, blowsy woman in her early thirties, who once kindly devoted several minutes to instructing me in the correct one-handed method of carrying trays but whose moods change disconcertingly from shift to shift and even within one. Then there's B.J., a.k.a. B.J.-the-bitch, whose contribution is to stand by the kitchen counter and yell, "Nita, your order's up, move it!" or, "Barbara, didn't you see you've got another table out there? Come on, girl!" Among other things, she is hated for having replaced the whipped-cream squirt cans with big plastic whipped-cream-filled baggies that have to be squeezed with both hands—because, reportedly, she saw or thought she saw employees trying to inhale the propellant gas from the squirt cans, in the hope that it might be nitrous oxide. On my third night, she pulls me aside abruptly and brings her face so close that it looks as if she's planning to butt me with her forehead. But instead of saying, "You're fired," she says, "You're doing fine." The only trouble is I'm spending time chatting with customers: "That's how they're getting you." Furthermore I am letting them "run me," which means harassment by sequential demands: you bring the ketchup and they decide they want extra Thousand Island; you bring that and they announce they now need a side of fries; and so on into distraction. Finally she tells me not to take her wrong. She tries to say things in a nice way, but you get into a mode, you know, because everything has to move so fast. . . .[4]

I make the decision to move closer to Key West. First, because of the drive. Second and third, also because of the drive: gas is eating up $4 to $5 a day, and although Jerry's is as high-volume as you can get, the tips average only 10 percent, and not just for a newbie like me. Between the base pay of $2.15 an hour and the obligation to share tips with the busboys and dishwashers, we're averaging only about $7.50 an hour. Then there is the $30 I had to spend on the regulation tan slacks worn by Jerry's servers—a setback it could take weeks to absorb. (I had combed the town's two downscale department stores hoping for something cheaper but decided in the end that these marked-down Dockers, originally $49, were more likely to survive a daily washing.) Of my fellow servers, everyone who lacks a working husband or boyfriend seems to have a second job: Nita does something at a computer eight hours a day; another welds. Without the forty-five-minute commute, I can picture myself working two jobs and having the time to shower between them.

So I take the $500 deposit I have coming from my landlord, the $400 I have earned toward the next month's rent; plus the $200 reserved for emergencies, and use the $1,100 to pay the rent and deposit on trailer number 46 in the Overseas Trailer Park, a mile from the cluster of budget hotels that constitute Key West's version of an industrial park. Number 46 is about eight feet in width and shaped like a barbell inside, with a narrow region—because of the sink and the stove—separating the bedroom from what might optimistically be called the "living" area, with its two-person table and half-sized couch. The bathroom is so small my knees rub against the shower stall when I sit on the toilet, and you can't just leap out of the bed; you have to climb down to the foot of it in order to find a patch of floor space to stand on. Outside, I am within a few yards of a liquor store, a bar that advertises "free beer tomorrow," a convenience store, and a Burger King—but no supermarket or, alas, laundromat. By reputation, the Overseas park is a nest of crime and crack, and I am hoping at least for some vibrant, multicultural street life. But desolation rules night and day, except for a thin stream of pedestrian traffic heading for their jobs at the Sheraton or 7-Eleven. There are not exactly people here but what amounts to canned labor, being preserved from the heat between shifts.

In line with my reduced living conditions, a new form of ugliness arises at Jerry's. First we are confronted—via an announcement on the computers through which we input orders—with the new rule that the hotel bar is henceforth off-limits to restaurant employees. The culprit, I learn through the grapevine, is the ultra-efficient gal who trained me—another trailer-home dweller and a mother of three. Something had set her off one morning, so she slipped out for a nip and returned to the floor impaired. This mostly hurts Ellen, whose habit it is to free her hair from its rubber band and drop by the bar for a couple of Zins before heading home at the end of the shift, but all of us feel the chill. Then the next day, when I go for straws, for the first time I find the dry-storage room locked. Ted, the portly assistant manager who opens it for me, explains that he caught one of the dishwashers attempting to steal something, and, unfortunately, the miscreant will be with us until a replacement can be found—hence the locked door. I neglect to ask what he had been trying to steal, but Ted tells me who he is—the kid with the buzz cut and the earring. You know, he's back there right now.

I wish I could say I rushed back and confronted George to get his side of the story. I wish I could say I stood up to Ted and insisted that George be given a translator and allowed to defend himself, or announced that I'd find a lawyer who'd handle the case pro bono. The mystery to me is that there's not much worth stealing in the dry-storage room, at least not in any fenceable quantity: "Is Gyorgi here, and am having 200—maybe 250—ketchup packets. What do you say?" My guess is that he had taken—if he had taken anything at all—some Saltines or a can of cherry-pie mix, and that the motive for taking it was hunger.

So why didn't I intervene? Certainly not because I was held back by the kind of moral paralysis that can pass as journalistic objectivity. On the contrary, something new—something loathsome and servile—had infected me, along with the kitchen odors that I could still sniff on my bra when I finally undressed at night. In real life I am moderately brave, but plenty of brave people shed their courage in concentration camps, and maybe something similar goes on in the infinitely more congenial milieu of the low-wage American workplace. Maybe, in a month or two more at Jerry's, I might have regained my crusading spirit. Then again, in a month or two I might have turned into a different person altogether—say, the kind of person who would have turned George in.

But this is not something I am slated to find out. When my month-long plunge into poverty is almost over, I finally land my dream job—housekeeping. I do this by walking into the personnel office of the only place I figure I might have some credibility, the hotel attached to Jerry's, and confiding urgently that I have to have a second job if I am to pay my rent and, no, it couldn't be front-desk clerk. "All right," the personnel lady fairly spits, "so it's housekeeping," and she marches me back to meet Maria, the housekeeping manager, a tiny, frenetic Hispanic woman who greets me as "babe" and hands me a pamphlet emphasizing the need for a positive attitude. The hours are nine in the morning till whenever, the pay is $6.10 an hour, and there's one week of vacation a year. I don't have to ask about health insurance once I meet Carlotta, the middle-aged African-American woman who will be training me. Carla, as she tells me to call her, is missing all of her top front teeth.

On that first day of housekeeping and last day of my entire project—although I don't yet know it's the last—Carla is in a foul mood. We have been given nineteen rooms to clean, most of them "checkouts," as opposed to "stay-overs," that require the whole enchilada of bed-stripping, vacuuming, and bathroom-scrubbing. When one of the rooms that had been listed as a stay-over turns out to be a checkout, Carla calls Maria to complain, but of course to no avail. "So make up the motherfucker," Carla orders me, and I do the beds while she sloshes around the bathroom. For four hours without a break I strip and remake beds, taking about four and a half minutes per queen-sized bed, which I could get down to three if there were any reason to.

We try to avoid vacuuming by picking up the larger specks by hand, but often there is nothing to do but drag the monstrous vacuum cleaner—it weighs about thirty pounds—off our cart and try to wrestle it around the floor. Sometimes Carla hands me the squirt bottle of "BAM" (an acronym for something that begins, ominously, with "butyric"; the rest has been worn off the label) and lets me do the bathrooms. No service ethic challenges me here to new heights of performance. I just concentrate on removing the pubic hairs from the bathtubs, or at least the dark ones that I can see. . . .

When I request permission to leave at about 3:30, another housekeeper warns me that no one has so far succeeded in combining housekeeping at the hotel with serving at Jerry's: "Some kid did it once for five days, and you're no kid." With that helpful information in mind, I rush back to number 46, down four Advils (the name brand this time), shower, stooping to fit into the stall, and attempt to compose myself for the oncoming shift. So much for what Marx termed the "reproduction of labor power," meaning the things a worker has to do just so she'll be ready to work again. The only unforeseen obstacle to the smooth transition from job to job is that my tan Jerry's slacks, which had looked reasonably clean by 40-watt bulb last night when I hand-washed my Hawaiian shirt, prove by daylight to be mottled with ketchup and ranch-dressing stains. I spend most of my hour-long break between jobs attempting to remove the edible portions with a sponge and then drying the slacks over the hood of my car in the sun.

I can do this two-job thing, is my theory, if I can drink enough caffeine and avoid getting distracted by George's ever more obvious suffering.[5] The first few days after being caught he seemed not to understand the trouble he was in, and our chirpy little conversations had continued. But the last couple of shifts he's been listless and unshaven, and tonight he looks like the ghost we all know him to be, with dark half-moons hanging from his eyes. At one point, when I am briefly immobilized by the task of filling little paper cups with sour cream for baked potatoes, he comes over and looks as if he'd like to explore the limits of our shared vocabulary, but I am called to the floor for a table. I resolve to give him all my tips that night and to hell with the experiment in low-wage money management. At eight, Ellen and I grab a snack together standing at the mephitic end of the kitchen counter, but I can only manage two or three mozzarella sticks and lunch had been a mere handful of McNuggets. I am not tired at all, I assure myself, though it may be that there is simply no more "I" left to do the tiredness monitoring. What I would see, if I were more alert to the situation, is that the forces of destruction are already massing against me. There is only one cook on duty, a young man named Jesus ("Hay-Sue," that is) and he is new to the job. And there is Joy, who shows up to take over in the middle of the shift, wearing high heels and a long, clingy white dress and fuming as if she'd just been stood up in some cocktail bar.

Then it comes, the perfect storm. Four of my tables fill up at once. Four tables is nothing for me now, but only so long as they are obligingly staggered.

As I bev table 27, tables 25, 28, and 24 are watching enviously. As I bev 25, 24 glowers because their bevs haven't even been ordered. Twenty-eight is four yuppyish types, meaning everything on the side and agonizing instructions as to the chicken Caesars. Twenty-five is a middle-aged black couple, who complain, with some justice, that the iced tea isn't fresh and the tabletop is sticky. But table 24 is the meteorological event of the century: ten British tourists who seem to have made the decision to absorb the American experience entirely by mouth. Here everyone has at least two drinks—iced tea and milk shake, Michelob and water (with lemon slice, please)—and a huge promiscuous orgy of breakfast specials, mozz sticks, chicken strips, quesadillas, burgers with cheese and without, sides of hash browns with cheddar, with onions, with gravy, seasoned fries, plain fries, banana splits. Poor Jesus! Poor me! Because when I arrive with their first tray of food—after three prior trips just to refill bevs—Princess Di refuses to eat her chicken strips with her pancake-and-sausage special, since, as she now reveals, the strips were meant to be an appetizer. Maybe the others would have accepted their meals, but Di, who is deep into her third Michelob, insists that everything else go back while they work on their "starters." Meanwhile, the yuppies are waving me down for more decaf and the black couple looks ready to summon the NAACP.

Much of what happened next is lost in the fog of war. Jesus starts going under. The little printer on the counter in front of him is spewing out orders faster than he can rip them off, much less produce the meals. Even the invincible Ellen is ashen from stress. I bring table 24 their reheated main courses, which they immediately reject as either too cold or fossilized by the microwave. When I return to the kitchen with their trays (three trays in three trips), Joy confronts me with arms akimbo: "What is this?" She means the food—the plates of rejected pancakes, hash browns in assorted flavors, toasts, burgers, sausages, eggs. "Uh, scrambled with cheddar," I try, "and that's . . ." "NO," she screams in my face. "Is it a traditional, a super-scramble, an eye-opener?" I pretend to study my check for a clue, but entropy has been up to its tricks, not only on the plates but in my head, and I have to admit that the original order is beyond reconstruction. "You don't know an eye-opener from a traditional?" she demands in outrage. All I know, in fact, is that my legs have lost interest in the current venture and have announced their intention to fold. I am saved by a yuppie (mercifully not one of mine) who chooses this moment to charge into the kitchen to bellow that his food is twenty-five minutes late. Joy screams at him to get the hell out of her kitchen, please, and then turns on Jesus in a fury, hurling an empty tray across the room for emphasis.

I leave. I don't walk out; I just leave. I don't finish my side work or pick up my credit-card tips, if any, at the cash register or, of course, ask Joy's permission to go. And the surprising thing is that you can walk out without permission, that the door opens, that the thick tropical night air parts to let me pass, that my car is still parked where I left it. There is no vindication in this exit, no fuck-you surge of relief, just an overwhelming, dank sense of failure pressing down on me and the entire parking lot. I had gone into this venture in the spirit of science, to test a mathematical proposition, but somewhere along the line, in the tunnel vision imposed by long shifts and relentless concentration, it became a test of myself, and clearly I have failed. Not only had I flamed out as a housekeeper/server, I had even forgotten to give George my tips, and, for reasons perhaps best known to hardworking, generous people like Gail and Ellen, this hurts. I don't cry, but I am in a position to realize, for the first time in many years, that the tear ducts are still there, and still capable of doing their job.

When I moved out of the trailer park, I gave the key to number 46 to Gail and arranged for my deposit to be transferred to her. She told me that Joan is still living in her van and that Stu had been fired from the Hearthside. I never found out what happened to George.

In one month, I had earned approximately $1,040 and spent $517 on food, gas, toiletries, laundry, phone, and utilities. If I had remained in my $500 efficiency, I would have been able to pay the rent and have $22 left over (which is $78 less than the cash I had in my pocket at the start of the month). During this time I bought no clothing except for the required slacks and no prescription drugs or medical care (I did finally buy some vitamin B to compensate for the lack of vegetables in my diet). Perhaps I could have saved a little on food if I had gotten to a supermarket more often, instead of convenience stores, but it should be noted that I lost almost four pounds in four weeks, on a diet weighted heavily toward burgers and fries.

How former welfare recipients and single mothers will (and do) survive in the low-wage workforce, I cannot imagine. Maybe they will figure out how to condense their lives—including child-raising, laundry, romance, and meals—into the couple of hours between full-time jobs. Maybe they will take up residence in their vehicles, if they have one. All I know is that I couldn't hold two jobs and I couldn't make enough money to live on with one. And I had advantages unthinkable to many of the long-term poor—health, stamina, a working car, and no children to care for and support. Certainly nothing in my experience contradicts the conclusion of Kathryn Edin and Laura Lein, in their recent book *Making Ends Meet: How Single Mothers Survive Welfare and Low-Wage Work,* that low-wage work actually involves more hardship and deprivation than life at the mercy of the welfare state. In the coming months and years, economic conditions for the working poor are bound to worsen, even without the almost inevitable recession. As mentioned earlier, the influx of former welfare recipients into the low-skilled workforce will have a depressing effect on both wages and the number of jobs available. A general economic downturn will only enhance these effects, and the working poor will of course be facing it without the slight, but nonetheless often saving, protection of welfare as a backup.

The thinking behind welfare reform was that even the humblest jobs are morally uplifting and psychologically buoying. In reality they are likely to be fraught with insult and stress. But I did discover one redeeming feature of the most abject low-wage work—the camaraderie of people who are, in almost all cases, far too smart and funny and caring for the work they do and the wages they're paid. The hope, of course, is that someday these people will come to know what they're worth, and take appropriate action.

NOTES

1. According to the Department of Housing and Urban Development, the "fair-market rent" for an efficiency is $551 here in Monroe County, Florida. A comparable rent in the five boroughs of New York City is $704; in San Francisco, $713; and in the heart of Silicon Valley, $808. The fair-market rent for an area is defined as the amount that would be needed to pay rent plus utilities for "privately owned, decent, safe, and sanitary rental housing of a modest (non-luxury) nature with suitable amenities."
2. According to the Fair Labor Standards Act, employers are not required to pay "tipped employees," such as restaurant servers, more than $2.13 an hour in direct wages. However, if the sum of tips plus $2.13 an hour falls below the minimum wage, or $5.15 an hour, the employer is required to make up the difference. This fact was not mentioned by managers or otherwise publicized at either of the restaurants where I worked.
3. I could find no statistics on the number of employed people living in cars or vans, but according to the National Coalition for the Homeless's 1997 report "Myths and Facts about Homelessness," nearly one in five homeless people (in twenty-nine cities across the nation) is employed in a full- or part-time job.
4. In *Workers in a Lean World: Unions in the International Economy* (Verso, 1997), Kim Moody cites studies finding an increase in stress-related workplace injuries and illness between the mid-1980s and the early 1990s. He argues that rising stress levels reflect a new system of "management by stress," in which workers in a variety of industries are being squeezed to extract maximum productivity, to the detriment of their health.
5. In 1996, the number of persons holding two or more jobs averaged 7.8 million, or 6.2 percent of the workforce. It was about the same rate for men and for women (6.1 versus 6.2), though the kinds of jobs differ by gender. About two thirds of multiple jobholders work one job full-time and the other part-time. Only a heroic minority— 4 percent of men and 2 percent of women—work two full-time jobs simultaneously. (From John F. Stinson Jr., "New Data on Multiple Jobholding Available from the CPS," in the *Monthly Labor Review,* March 1997.)

52

I AM YOUR WELFARE REFORM

ANNIE DOWNEY

I am a single mother of two children, each with a different father. I am a hussy, a welfare rider—burden to everyone and everything. I am anything you want me to be—a faceless number who has no story.

My daughter's father has a job and makes over two grand a month; my son's father owns blue-chip stock in AT&T, Disney, and Campbell's. I call the welfare office, gather old bills, look for day care, write for my degree project, graduate with my son slung on my hip, breastfeeding.

At the welfare office they tell me to follow one of the caseworkers into a small room without windows. The caseworker hands me a packet and a pencil. There is an older woman with graying hair and polyester pants and the same pencil and packet. I glance at her; she looks at me; we are both ashamed. I try hard to fill out the packet correctly, answering all the questions. I am nervous. There are so many questions that near the end I start to get careless. I just want to leave. I hand the case worker the packet in an envelope; she asks for my pencil and does not look at me. I exit unnoticed. For five years I've exited unnoticed. I can't imagine how to get a job. I ride the bus home.

After a few weeks a letter arrives assigning me to "Group 3." I don't even finish reading it. When my grandmother calls later to tell me that I confuse sex with love, I tell her that I am getting a job. She asks what kind. I say, "Any job."

It is 5:00 A.M. My alarm wakes up my kids. I try nursing my son back to sleep, but my daughter keeps him up with her questions: "What time is it? Who's going to take care of us when you leave?" I want to cry. It is still dark and I am exhausted. I've had three hours of sleep. I get ready for work, put some laundry in the washer, make breakfast, set out clothes for the kids, make lunches. I carry my son; my daughter follows. They cling to me. They cry when I leave. I see their faces pressed against the porch window and the sitter trying to get them inside.

I slice meat for $5.50 an hour for nine hours a day, five days a week. I barely feed my kids; I barely pay the bills.

• I struggle against welfare. But I know that without welfare I would have nothing. On welfare I went from teen mom to woman with an education. I

In *Harper's Magazine,* May 1998. Reprinted by permission of the author.

published two magazines, became an editor, a teacher. Welfare, along with Section 8 housing grants and Reach Up, gave my children a life. My daughter loves school and does well there. My son is round and at twenty months speaks wondrous sentences about the moon and stars. Welfare gave me what was necessary to be a mother.

Still, I cannot claim it. There is too much shame in me: the disgusted looks in the grocery lines, the angry voices of *Oprah* panelists, the unmitigated rage of the blue and white collars. I'm not what those voices say I am. I never buy expensive ice cream in pints. I don't do drugs. I don't own a hot tub.

I am one of 12 million people who account for less than 1 percent of the federal budget. I am one of the 26 percent of AFDC recipients who are mothers and the 36.6 percent who are white. I am one of the 68 percent of teen mothers who were sexually abused. I am $600 a month below the poverty level for a family of three. I am a hot political issue. I am 145-65-8563. Group 3.

I have brown hair and eyes. I write prose. My mother has been married and divorced twice. I have never been married. I love Pablo Neruda's poetry, Louise Gluck's essays. I love my stepfather but not my real father. My favorite book is *Love in the Time of Cholera* by Gabriel García Márquez; my favorite movie, *The Color Purple*. I miss my son's father. I love jazz. I've always wanted to learn how to ballroom dance. I have a story, and a life, and a face.

53

LEARNING TO FIGHT

GEOFFREY CANADA

On union Avenue, failure to fight would mean that you would be set upon over and over again. Sometimes for years. Later I would see what the older boys did to Butchie.

Butchie was a "manchild," very big for his age. At thirteen he was the size of a fully grown man. Butchie was a gentle giant. He loved to play with the younger boys and was not particularly athletic. Butchie had one flaw: he would not fight. Everyone picked on him. The older teenagers (fifteen and sixteen) were really hard on him. He was forever being punched in the midsection and

From *Fist Stick Knife Gun: A Personal History of Violence in America.* © 1995 Geoffrey Canada. Reprinted by permission of Beacon Press, Boston.

chest by the older boys for no reason. (It was against the rules to punch in the face unless it was a "fair fight.")

I don't know what set the older boys off, or why they picked that Saturday morning, but it was decided that Butchie had to be taught a lesson. The older boys felt that Butchie was giving the block a bad reputation. Everyone had to be taught that we didn't tolerate cowards. Suddenly two of them grabbed Butchie. Knowing that something was wrong, that this was not the rough and tumble play we sometimes engaged in, Butchie broke away. Six of the older boys took off after him. Butchie zigzagged between the parked cars, trying desperately to make it to his building and the safety of his apartment. One of the boys cut him off and, kicking and yelling, Butchie was snagged.

By the time the other five boys caught up, Butchie was screaming for his mother. We knew that his mother often drank heavily on the weekends and were not surprised when her window did not open and no one came to his aid. One of the rules of the block was that you were not allowed to cry for your mother. Whatever happened you had to "take it like a man." A vicious punch to the stomach and a snarled command, "Shut the fuck up," and Butchie became quiet and stopped struggling. The boys marched him up the block, away from his apartment. Butchie, head bowed, hands held behind his back, looked like a captured prisoner.

There are about twelve of us younger boys out that morning playing football in the street. When the action started we stopped playing and prepared to escape to our individual apartment buildings. We didn't know if the older boys were after us, too—they were sometimes unpredictable—and we nervously kept one eye on them and one on a clear avenue of escape. As they marched Butchie down the block it became apparent that we were meant to learn from what was going to happen to Butchie, that they were really doing this for us.

The older boys took Butchie and "stretched" him. This was accomplished by four boys grabbing Butchie, one on each arm, one on each leg. Then they placed him on the trunk of a car (in the early 1960s the cars were all large) and pulled with all their might until Butchie was stretched out over the back of the car. When Butchie was completely, helplessly exposed, two of the boys began to punch him in his stomach and chest. The beating was savage. Butchie's cries for help seemed only to infuriate them more. I couldn't believe that a human body could take that amount of punishment. When they finished with him, Butchie just collapsed in the fetal position and cried. The older boys walked away talking, as if nothing had happened.

To those of us who watched, the lesson was brutal and unmistakable. No matter who you fought, he could never beat you *that* bad. So it was better to fight even if you couldn't win than to end up being "stretched" for being a coward. We all fought, some with more skill and determination than others, but we all fought.

The day my brother John went out to play on the block and had to fight Paul Henry there was plenty of wild swinging and a couple of blows landed, but they did no real damage. When no one got the better of the other after six or seven minutes, the fight was broken up. John and Paul Henry were made to shake hands and became best of friends in no time.

John was free. He could go outside without fear. I was still trapped. I needed help figuring out what would happen when I went outside. John was not much help to me about how the block worked. He was proud that he could go out and play while we were still stuck in the house. I mentioned something about going downstairs and having Ma come down to watch over me and John laughed at me, called me a baby. He had changed, he had accepted the rules—no getting mothers to fight your battles. His only instructions to me were to fight back, don't let the boys your age hit you without hitting back. Within a week I decided I just couldn't take it, and I went downstairs.

The moment I went outside I began to learn about the structure of the block and its codes of conduct. Each excursion taught me more. The first thing I learned was that John, even though he was just a year older than me, was in a different category than I was. John's peers had some status on the block; my peers were considered too young to have any.

At the top of the pecking order were the young adults in their late teens (seventeen, eighteen, and nineteen). They owned the block; they were the strongest and the toughest. Many of them belonged to a gang called the Disciples. Quite a few had been arrested as part of a police crackdown on gangs in the late fifties and early sixties. Several came out of jail during my first few years on Union Avenue. They often spent large amounts of time in other areas of the Bronx, so they were really absentee rulers.

At this time there were some girls involved in gang activities as well; many of the larger male gangs had female counterparts whose members fought and intimidated other girls. On Union Avenue there was a group of older girls who demanded respect, and received it, from even the toughest boys on the block. Some of these girls were skilled fighters, and boys would say "she can fight like a boy" to indicate that a girl had mastered the more sophisticated techniques of fistfighting. Girls on Union Avenue sometimes found themselves facing the same kind of violence as did boys, but this happened less often. All in all there was less pressure on girls to fight for status, although some did; for girls to fight there usually had to be a major triggering incident.

But status was a major issue for boys on the block. The next category in the pecking order was the one we all referred to as the "older boys," fifteen and sixteen years old. They belonged to a group we sometimes called the Young Disciples, and they were the real rulers of Union Avenue. This was the group that set the rules of conduct on the block and enforced law and order. They were the ones who had stretched Butchie.

Next were boys nine, ten, and eleven, just learning the rules. While they were allowed to go into the street and play, most of them were not allowed off the block without their mother's permission. My brother John belonged to this group.

The lowest group was those children who could not leave the sidewalk, children too young to have any status at all. I belonged to this group and I hated it. The sidewalk, while it provided plenty of opportunity to play with other children, seemed to me to be the sidelines. The real action happened in the street.

There were few expectations placed on us in terms of fighting, but we were not exempt. There was very little natural animosity among us. We played punchball, tag, and "red light, green light, one-two-three." It was the older boys who caused the problems. Invariably, when the older boys were sitting on the stoop and one of them had a brother, or cousin amongst us, it would be he who began the prelude to violence.

I'd been outside for more than a week and thought that I had escaped having to fight anyone because all the boys were my friends. But sure enough, Billy started in on me.

"David, can you beat Geoff?"

David looked at me, then back at Billy. "I don't know."

"What! You can't beat Geoff? I thought you was tough. You scared? I know you ain't scared. You betta not be scared."

I didn't like where this conversation was heading. David was my friend and I didn't know Billy; he was just an older boy who lived in my building. David looked at me again and this time his face changed; he looked threatening; he seemed angry.

"I ain't scared of him."

I was lost. Just ten minutes before David and I were playing, having a good time. Now he looked like I was his worst enemy. I became scared, scared of David, scared of Billy, scared of Union Avenue. I looked for help to the other boys sitting casually on the stoop. Their faces scared me more. Most of them barely noticed what was going on, the rest were looking half interested. I was most disheartened by the reaction of my brother John. Almost in a state of panic, I looked to him for help. He looked me directly in the eye, shook his head no, then barely perceptibly pointed his chin toward David as if to say, Quit stalling; you know what you have to do. Then he looked away as if this didn't concern him at all.

The other sidewalk boys were the only ones totally caught up in the drama. They knew that their day would also come, and they were trying to learn what they could about me in case they had to fight me tomorrow, or next week, or whenever.

During the time I was sizing up my situation I made a serious error. I showed on my face what was going on in my head. My fear and my confusion were obvious to anyone paying attention. This, I would later learn, was a rookie mistake and could have deadly consequences on the streets.

Billy saw my panic and called to alert the others. "Look at Geoff; he's scared. He's scared of you, David. Go kick his ass."

It was not lost on me that the questioning part of this drama was over. Billy had given David a direct command. I thought I was saved, however, because Billy had cursed. My rationale was that no big boy could use curses at a little boy. My brother would surely step in now and say, "C'mon, Billy, you can't curse at my little brother. After all, he's only seven." Then he would take me upstairs and tell Ma.

When I looked at John again I saw only that his eyes urged me to act, implored me to act. There would be no rescue coming from him. What was worse, the other older boys had become interested when Billy yelled, "Kick his ass," and were now looking toward David and me. In their eyes this was just a little sport, not a real fight, but a momentary distraction that could prove to be slightly more interesting than talking about the Yankees, or the Giants, or their girlfriends. They smiled at my terror. Their smiles seemed to say, "I remember when I was like that. You'll see, it's not so bad."

Thinking on your feet is critical in the ghetto. There was so much to learn and so much of it was so important. It was my brother's reaction that clued me in. I knew John. He was a vicious tease at times, but he loved me. He would never allow me to be harmed and not help or at least go for help. He was telling me I had to go through this alone. I knew I could run upstairs, but what about tomorrow? Was I willing to become a prisoner in my apartment again? And what about how everyone was smiling at me? How was I ever going to play in the street with them if they thought I was such a baby? So I made the decision not to run but to fight.

I decided to maximize the benefits the situation afforded. I said, not quite with the conviction that I'd hoped for, "I'm not afraid of David. He can't beat me. C'mon, David, you wanna fight?"

There was only one problem—I didn't know how to fight. I hadn't seen Dan taking back John's coat, or John's fight with Paul Henry. But a funny thing happened after I challenged David. When I looked back at him, he didn't look quite so confident. He didn't look like he wanted to fight anymore. This gave me courage.

Billy taunted David, "You gonna let him talk to you like that? Go on, kick his ass."

Then Paul Henry chimed in, "Don't be scared, little Geoff. Go git him."

I was surprised. I didn't expect anyone to support me, especially not Paul Henry. But as I would learn later, most of these fights were viewed as sport by the bystanders. You rooted for the favorite or the underdog. Almost everyone had someone to root for them when they fought.

David put up his balled-up fists and said, "Come on." I didn't know how to fight, but I knew how to pretend fight. So I "put up my dukes" and stood like a boxer. We circled one another.

"Come on."

"No, *you* come on."

Luckily for me, David didn't know how to fight either. The older boys called out encouragement to us, but we didn't really know how to throw a punch. At one point we came close enough to one another for me to grab David, and we began to wrestle. I was good at this, having spent many an hour wrestling with my three brothers.

Wrestling wasn't allowed in a "real" fight, but they let us go at it a few moments before they broke us up. The older boys pronounced the fight a tie and made us shake hands and "be friends." They rubbed our heads and said, "You're all right," and then gave us some pointers on how to really fight. We both basked in the glory of their attention. The other sidewalk boys looked at us with envy. We had passed the first test. We were on our way to becoming respected members of Union Avenue.

David and I became good friends. Since we'd had a tie we didn't have to worry about any other older boys making us fight again. The rule was that if you fought an opponent, and could prove it by having witnesses, you didn't have to fight that person again at the command of the older boys. This was important, because everyone, and I mean everyone, had to prove he could beat other boys his age. Union Avenue, like most other inner-city neighborhoods, had a clear pecking order within the groups as well as between them when it came to violence. The order changed some as boys won or lost fights, but by and large the same boys remained at the top. New boys who came on the block had to be placed in the pecking order. If they had no credentials, no one to vouch for their ability, they had to fight different people on the block until it could be ascertained exactly where they fit in. If you refused to fight, you moved to the bottom of the order. If you fought and lost, your status still remained unclear until you'd won a fight. Then you'd be placed somewhere between the person you lost to and the person you beat.

The pecking order was important because it was used to resolve disputes that arose over games, or girls, or money, and also to maintain order and discipline on the block. Although we were not a gang, there were clear rules of conduct, and if you broke those rules there were clear consequences. The ranking system also prevented violence because it gave a way for boys to back down; if everybody knew you couldn't beat someone and you backed down, it was no big deal most of the time.

My "fight" with David placed me on top of the pecking order for boys on the sidewalk. I managed to get through the rest of the summer without having to fight anyone else. I had learned so much about how Union Avenue functioned that I figured I would soon know all I needed about how to survive on the block.

54

APPEARANCES

CARMEN VÁZQUEZ

North of Market Street and east of Twin Peaks, where you can see the white fog mushroom above San Francisco's hills, is a place called the Castro. Gay men, lesbians, and bisexuals stroll leisurely up and down the bustling streets. They jaywalk with abandon. Night and day they fill the cafés and bars, and on weekends they line up for a double feature of vintage classics at their ornate and beloved Castro theater.

The 24 bus line brings people into and out of the Castro. People from all walks of life ride the electric-powered coaches. They come from the opulence of San Francisco's Marina and the squalor of Bayview projects. The very gay Castro is in the middle of its route. Every day, boys in pairs or gangs from either end of the city board the bus for a ride through the Castro and a bit of fun. Sometimes their fun is fulfilled with passionately obscene derision: "Fucking cocksucking faggots." "Dyke cunts." "Diseased butt fuckers." Sometimes, their fun is brutal.

Brian boarded the 24 Divisadero and handed his transfer to the driver one late June night. Epithets were fired at him the moment he turned for a seat. He slid his slight frame into an empty seat next to an old woman with silver blue hair who clutched her handbag and stared straight ahead. Brian stuffed his hands into the pockets of his worn brown bomber jacket and stared with her. He heard the flip of a skateboard in the back. The taunting shouts grew louder. "Faggot!" From the corner of his eye, he saw a beer bottle hurtling past the window and crash on the street. A man in his forties, wearing a Giants baseball cap and warmup jacket, yelled at the driver to stop the bus and get the hoodlums off. The bus driver ignored him and pulled out.

Brian dug his hands deeper into his pockets and clenched his jaw. It was just five stops to the top of the hill. When he got up to move toward the exit, the skateboard slammed into his gut and one kick followed another until every boy had got his kick in. Despite the plea of the passengers, the driver never called the police.

Brian spent a week in a hospital bed, afraid that he would never walk again. A lawsuit filed by Brian against the city states, "As claimant lay crum-

From *Homophobia: How We All Pay the Price*, Warren J. Blumenfeld, ed. © 1992 Warren J. Blumenfeld. Reprinted by permission of Beacon Press, Boston.

pled and bleeding on the floor of the bus, the bus driver tried to force claimant off the bus so that the driver could get off work and go home. Claimant was severely beaten by a gang of young men on the #24 Divisadero Bus who perceived that he was gay."

On the south side of Market Street, night brings a chill wind and rough trade. On a brisk November night, men with sculptured torsos and thighs wrapped in leather walked with precision. The clamor of steel on the heels of their boots echoed in the darkness. Young men and women walked by the men in leather, who smiled in silence. They admired the studded bracelets on Mickey's wrists, the shine of his flowing hair, and the rise of his laughter. They were, each of them, eager to be among the safety of like company where they could dance with abandon to the pulse of hard rock, the hypnotism of disco, or the measured steps of country soul. They looked forward to a few drinks, flirting with strangers, finding Mr. or Ms. Right or, maybe, someone to spend the night with.

At the end of the street, a lone black street lamp shone through the mist. The men in leather walked under the light and disappeared into the next street. As they reached the corner, Mickey and his friends could hear the raucous sounds of the Garden spill onto the street. They shimmied and rocked down the block and through the doors.

The Garden was packed with men and women in sweat-stained shirts. Blue smoke stung the eyes. The sour and sweet smell of beer hung in the air. Strobe lights pulsed over the dancers. Mickey pulled off his wash-faded black denim jacket and wrapped it around his waist. An iridescent blue tank top hung easy on his shoulders. Impatient with the wait for a drink, Mickey steered his girlfriend onto the crowded dance floor.

Reeling to the music and immersed in the pleasure of his rhythms, Mickey never saw the ice pick plunge into his neck. It was just a bump with a drunk yelling, "Lame-assed faggot." "Faggot. Faggot. Faggot. Punk faggot." Mickey thought it was a punch to the neck. He ran after the roaring drunk man for seven steps, then lurched and fell on the dance floor, blood gushing everywhere. His girlfriend screamed. The dance floor spun black.

Mickey was rushed to San Francisco General Hospital, where thirty-six stitches were used by trauma staff to close the wound on his neck. Doctors said the pick used in the attack against him was millimeters away from his spinal cord. His assailant, charged with attempted murder, pleaded innocent.

Mickey and Brian were unfortunate stand-ins for any gay man. Mickey was thin and wiry, a great dancer clad in black denim, earrings dangling from his ear. Brian was slight of build, wore a leather jacket, and boarded a bus in the Castro. Dress like a homo, dance like a homo, must be a homo. The homophobic fury directed at lesbians, gay men, and bisexuals in America most often finds its target. Ironclad evidence of sexual orientation, however, is not necessary for someone to qualify as a potential victim of deadly fury. Appearances will do.

The incidents described above are based on actual events reported to the San Francisco Police and Community United Against Violence (CUAV), an agency serving victims of antilesbian and antigay violence where I worked for four years. The names of the victims have been changed. Both men assaulted were straight.

Incidents of antilesbian and antigay violence are not uncommon or limited to San Francisco. A *San Francisco Examiner* survey estimates that over one million hate-motivated physical assaults take place each year against lesbians, gays, and bisexuals. The National Gay and Lesbian Task Force conducted a survey in 1984 that found that 94 percent of all lesbians and gay men surveyed reported being physically assaulted, threatened, or harassed in an antigay incident at one time or another. The great majority of these incidents go unreported.

To my knowledge, no agency other than CUAV keeps track of incidents of antigay violence involving heterosexuals as victims. An average of 3 percent of the over three hundred victims seen by CUAV each year identify as heterosexuals. This may or may not be an accurate gauge of the actual prevalence of antigay violence directed at heterosexuals. Most law enforcement agencies, including those in San Francisco, have no way of documenting this form of assault other than under a generic "harassment" code. The actual incidence of violence directed at heterosexuals that is motivated by homophobia is probably much higher than CUAV's six to nine victims a year. Despite the official paucity of data, however, it is a fact that incidents of antigay and antilesbian violence in which straight men and women are victimized do occur. Shelters for battered women are filled with stories of lesbian baiting of staff and of women whose husbands and boyfriends repeatedly called them "dykes" or "whores" as they beat them.[1] I have personally experienced verbal abuse while in the company of a straight friend, who was assumed to be my lover.

Why does it happen? I have no definitive answers to that question. Understanding homophobic violence is no less complex than understanding racial violence. The institutional and ideological reinforcements of homophobia are myriad and deeply woven into our culture. I offer one perspective that I hope will contribute to a better understanding of how homophobia works and why it threatens all that we value as humane.

At the simplest level, looking or behaving like the stereotypical gay man or lesbian is reason enough to provoke a homophobic assault. Beneath the veneer of the effeminate gay male or the butch dyke, however, is a more basic trigger for homophobic violence. I call it *gender betrayal.*

---

[1]See Suzanne Pharr, *Homophobia: A Weapon of Sexism* (Inverness, Calif.: Chardon, 1988). [Author's note]

The clearest expression I have heard of this sense of gender betrayal comes from Doug Barr, who was acquitted of murder in an incident of gay bashing in San Francisco that resulted in the death of John O'Connell, a gay man. Barr is currently serving a prison sentence for related assaults on the same night that O'Connell was killed. He was interviewed for a special report on homophobia produced by ABC's *20/20* (10 April 1986). When asked what he and his friends thought of gay men, he said, "We hate homosexuals. They degrade our manhood. We was brought up in a high school where guys are football players, mean and macho. Homosexuals are sissies who wear dresses. I'd rather be seen as a football player."

Doug Barr's perspective is one shared by many young men. I have made about three hundred presentations to high school students in San Francisco, to boards of directors and staffs of nonprofit organizations, and at conferences and workshops on the topic of homophobia or "being lesbian or gay." Over and over again, I have asked, "Why do gay men and lesbians bother you?" The most popular response to the question is, "Because they act like girls," or, "Because they think they're men." I have even been told, quite explicitly, "I don't care what they do in bed, but they shouldn't act like that."

They shouldn't act like that. Women who are not identified by their relationship to a man, who value their female friendships, who like and are knowledgeable about sports, or work as blue-collar laborers and wear what they wish are very likely to be "lesbian baited" at some point in their lives. Men who are not pursuing sexual conquests of women at every available opportunity, who disdain sports, who choose to stay at home and be a househusband, who are employed as hairdressers, designers, or housecleaners, or who dress in any way remotely resembling traditional female attire (an earring will do) are very likely to experience the taunts and sometimes the brutality of "fag bashing."

The straitjacket of gender roles suffocates many lesbians, gay men, and bisexuals, forcing them into closets without an exit and threatening our very existence when we tear the closet open. It also, however, threatens all heterosexuals unwilling to be bound by their assigned gender identity. Why, then, does it persist?

Suzanne Pharr's examination of homophobia as a phenomenon based in sexism and misogyny offers a succinct and logical explanation for the virulence of homophobia in Western civilization:

> It is not by chance that when children approach puberty and
> increased sexual awareness they begin to taunt each other by
> calling these names: "queer," "faggot," "pervert." It is at puberty
> that the full force of society's pressure to conform to heterosexuality
> and prepare for marriage is brought to bear. Children know what
> we have taught them, and we have given clear messages that those
> who deviate from standard expectations are to be made to get back
> in line. . . .

To be named as lesbian threatens all women, not just lesbians, with great loss. And any woman who steps out of role risks being called a lesbian. To understand how this is a threat to all women, one must understand that any woman can be called a lesbian and there is no real way she can defend herself: there is no real way to credential one's sexuality. (*The Children's Hour,* a Lillian Hellman play, makes this point when a student asserts two teachers are lesbians and they have no way to disprove it.) She may be married or divorced, have children, dress in the most feminine manner, have sex with men, be celibate—but there are lesbians who do all these things. *Lesbians look like all women and all women look like lesbians.*[2]

I would add that gay men look like all men and all men look like gay men. There is no guaranteed method for identifying sexual orientation. Those small or outrageous deviations we sometimes take from the idealized mystique of "real men" and "real women" place all of us—lesbians, gay men, bisexuals, and heterosexuals alike—at risk of violence, derision, isolation, and hatred.

It is a frightening reality. Dorothy Ehrlich, executive director of the Northern California American Civil Liberties Union (ACLU), was the victim of a verbal assault in the Castro several years ago. Dorothy lives with her husband, Gary, and her two children, Jill and Paul, in one of those worn and comfortable Victorian homes that grace so many San Francisco neighborhoods. Their home is several blocks from the Castro, but Dorothy recalls the many times she and Gary could hear, from the safety of their bedroom, shouts of "faggot" and men running in the streets.

When Jill was an infant, Gary and Dorothy had occasion to experience for themselves how frightening even the threat of homophobic violence can be. One foggy, chilly night they decided to go for a walk in the Castro. Dorothy is a small woman whom some might call petite; she wore her hair short at the time and delights in the comfort of jeans and oversized wool jackets. Gary is very tall and lean, a bespectacled and bearded cross between a professor and a basketball player who wears jean jackets and tweed jackets with the exact same slouch. On this night they were crossing Castro Street, huddled close together with Jill in Dorothy's arms. As they reached the corner, their backs to the street, they heard a truck rev its engine and roar up Castro, the dreaded "faggot" spewing from young men they could not see in the fog. They looked around them for the intended victims, but there was no one else on the corner with them. They were the target that night: Dorothy and Gary and Jill. They were walking on "gay turf," and it was reason enough to make them a target. "It was so frightening," Dorothy said. "So frightening and unreal."

---

[2]Ibid., 17–19. [Author's note]

But it is real. The *20/20* report on homophobia ends with the story of Tom and Jan Matarrase who are married, have a child, and lived in Brooklyn, New York, at the time of their encounter with homophobic violence. On camera, Tom and Jan are walking down a street in Brooklyn lined with brown town-houses and black wrought-iron gates. It is snowing, and, with hands en-twined, they walk slowly down the street where they were assaulted. Tom is wearing a khaki trenchcoat, slacks, and loafers. Snowflakes melt into the tight dark curls on his head. Jan is almost his height, her short bobbed hair mov-ing softly as she walks. She is wearing a black leather jacket, a red scarf, and burnt orange cords. The broadness of her hips and softness of her face belie the tomboy flavor of her carriage and clothes, and it is hard to believe that she was mistaken for a gay man. But she was.

They were walking home, holding hands and engrossed with each other. On the other side of the street, Jan saw a group of boys moving toward them. As the gang approached, Jan heard a distinct taunt meant for her and Tom: "Aw, look at the cute gay couple." Tom and Jan quickened their step, but it was too late. Before they could say anything, Tom was being punched in the face and slammed against a car. Jan ran toward Tom and the car, screaming desperately that Tom was her husband. Fists pummeled her face as well. Out-numbered and in fear for their lives, Tom yelled at Jan to please open her jacket and show their assailants that she was a woman. The beating subsided only when Jan was able to show her breasts.

For the *20/20* interview, Jan and Tom sat in the warmth of their living room, their infant son in Jan's lap. The interviewer asked them how they felt when people said they looked like a gay couple. "We used to laugh," they said. "But now we realize how heavy the implications are. Now we know what the gay community goes through. We had no idea how widespread it was. It's on every level."

Sadly, it *is* on every level. Enforced heterosexism and the pressure to con-form to aggressive masculine and passive feminine roles place fag bashers and lesbian baiters in the same psychic prison with their victims, gay or straight. Until all children are free to realize their full potential, until all women and men are free from the stigma, threats, alienation, or violence that come from stepping outside their roles, we are all at risk.

The economic and ideological underpinnings of enforced heterosexism and sexism or any other form of systematic oppression are formidable foes and far too complex for the scope of this essay. It is important to remember, however, that bigots are natural allies and that poverty or the fear of it has the power to seduce us all into conformity. In Castro graffiti, *faggot* appears right next to *nigger* and *kike*. Race betrayal or any threat to the sanctimony of light-skinned privilege engenders no less a rage than gender betrayal, most especially when we have a great stake in the elusive privilege of proper gen-der roles or the right skin color. *Queer lover* and *fag hag* are cut from the same mold that gave us *nigger lover,* a mold forged by fears of change and a loss of privilege.

Unfortunately, our sacrifices to conformity rarely guarantee the privilege or protection we were promised. Lesbians, gay men, and bisexuals who have tried to pass know that. Heterosexuals who have been perceived to be gay know that. Those of us with a vision of tomorrow that goes beyond tolerance to a genuine celebration of humanity's diversity have innumerable fronts to fight on. Homophobia is one of them.

But how will this front be won? With a lot of help, and not easily. Challenges to homophobia and the rigidity of gender roles must go beyond the visible lesbian and gay movement. Lesbians, gay men, and bisexuals alone cannot defuse the power of stigmatization and the license it gives to frighten, wound, or kill. Literally millions of us are needed on this front, straight and gay alike. We invite any heterosexual unwilling to live with the damage that "real men" or "real women" messages wreck on them, on their children, and on lesbians, gay men, and bisexuals to join us. We ask that you not let queer jokes go unchallenged at work, at home, in the media, or anywhere. We ask that you foster in your children a genuine respect for themselves and their right to be who and what they wish to be, regardless of their gender. We ask that you embrace your daughter's desire to swing a bat or be a carpenter, that you nurture your son's efforts to express affection and sentiment. We ask that you teach your children how painful and destructive words like *faggot* or *bulldyke* are. We ask that you invite your lesbian, gay, and bisexual friends and relatives into the routine of your lives without demanding silence or discretion from them. We invite you to study our history, read the literature written by our people, patronize our businesses, come into our homes and neighborhoods. We ask that you give us your vote when we need it to protect our privacy or to elect open lesbians, gay men, and bisexuals to office. We ask that you stand with us in public demonstrations to demand our right to live as free people, without fear. We ask that you respect our dignity by acting to end the poison of homophobia.

Until individuals are free to choose their roles and be bound only by the limits of their own imagination, *faggot, dyke,* and *pervert* will continue to be playground words and adult weapons that hurt and limit far many more people than their intended victims. Whether we like it or not, the romance of virile men and dainty women, of Mother, Father, Dick, Jane, Sally, and Spot is doomed to extinction and dangerous in a world that can no longer meet the expectations conjured by history. There is much to be won and so little to lose in the realization of a world where the dignity of each person is worthy of celebration and protection. The struggle to end homophobia can and must be won, for all our sakes. Personhood is imminent.

55

BISEXUALITY, FEMINISM, MEN AND ME

ROBYN OCHS

Where does feminist consciousness come from? Why do some women begin to question what has been presented to us as given and, as a result of that questioning, come to understand the ways in which women have been systematically limited? Each of us takes a different road to feminism. Many of our journeys begin with a pivotal event or transition that forces us to question our assumed reality.

My own route to feminism was long, convoluted and closely connected with my developing bisexual consciousness. In my early twenties I realized that my emotional and sexual attractions toward women as well as men were not going to go away, and I began to address those feelings. Forced off-balance by the turbulence of these emotions and their implications for my future, I began for the first time to consciously question the assumptions I had made about my life. I began to understand that many of my choices had not been freely made, but rather had been made within the context of a system that Adrienne Rich calls "compulsory heterosexuality," a system that posits heterosexuality as the only way to be.[1] In this essay I describe my own journey: what I learned and what I unlearned, and how these changes in my thinking have fundamentally changed my relationships with men.

I grew up believing that women deserved equal pay for equal work and that we had the right not to be raped or battered and the right to control our own reproduction. These beliefs were firmly held by my mother and grandmothers. In the kitchen of the house I grew up in, a cartoon showing two toddlers looking into their diapers was tacked to the bulletin board next to the telephone. One of the toddlers was saying to the other, "So *that* explains the difference in our salaries." Had I been asked as a young person whether I was a feminist I would have answered in the affirmative. To me, these issues were the essence of feminism.

But despite adopting the feminist label for external causes, I did not escape female socialization. I learned some "basic truths": that as a woman my value was in my body, and that mine was not "good enough"; that sooner or later every woman needs a man; and that I would have to behave in certain

From Weise, Elizabeth (ed.), *Closer to Home: Bisexuality and Feminism*. Seattle, WA: Seal Press, 1992. © 1992 by Robyn Ochs. With permission from the publisher.

ways in order to get myself one. These truths, which very much shaped my behavior for many years, I'll describe in greater detail below.

MY BODY AND ME

Like many women, I grew up hating my body. I remember wearing shorts over my bathing suit as a preteen to hide my "ugly" fat thighs. As a teenager, I spent a lot of time worrying whether I was attractive enough. Of course, I was never quite up to standard. I wanted very much to have the kind of exterior that would cause scouting agents from pinup magazines or from modeling agencies to approach me on the street to recruit me. Needless to say, this never happened, reinforcing my belief that physically I was a total failure as a woman. I fantasized about being a dancer but I knew I did not have the requisite "dancer's body." I thought my size 7 1/2 feet enormous. For the record, I have always been more or less average in weight. But average was not good enough. As long as I didn't look like one of those women in *Playboy,* I wasn't pretty enough.

> Too big too short too stocky too busty too round too many zits
> blackheads disgusting pinch an inch fail the pencil test cellulite
> don't go out without makeup don't let them see what you *really*
> look like they'll run away in terror but if you are really lucky and
> have a few beers and do it in the dark he might not notice so make
> sure to turn off the light before . . .

I never questioned my standards of measurement, never realized that these standards are determined by a male-dominated culture and reinforced by a multibillion-dollar "feminity" industry that sells women cosmetics, diet aids, plastic surgery, fashion magazines, liposuction, creams and girdles. I took my inability to live up to these standards as personal failure and never drew any connections between my experience and that of other women.

MEN AND ME

Men, you can't live without 'em. Sooner or later I would end up with one. My grandfather used to tell me that it was good that I was short, as that way I would have the option of marrying either a tall man or a short one. There aren't enough men to go around and it gets harder and harder to find one as you get older. Men aren't comfortable with women who are more educated/smarter/earn more than they. My fifty-year-old aunt never married. She waited *too long,* and by then it was *too late* because she was *too old, poor dear.* It's just as easy to fall in love with a rich man as a poor man. Men lead.

I always had a boyfriend. From age thirteen until after college, I don't remember going for more than a month without being in a relationship or at least having a crush. Having a boyfriend was a measure of my worth. I would select the boy and flirt with him until he asked me out. Most times, like the Mounties, I got my man. In dance, this is called backleading, directing the action from the follower's position. It allows the man to look like he is in control.

I learned that there's a man shortage. There are more women than men. And "good men" are extremely rare. Therefore, if you manage to get hold of a good one, you'd better hang on to him. This message got louder as I moved into my twenties. I saw older women in their thirties and beyond searching frantically for a suitable partner with whom to reproduce the human species and make their lives meaningful. I learned that you'd better pay attention to your "biological clock."

THE UNLEARNING

These messages had a powerful grip on me. How did I begin to unlearn them? The women studies class I took in college helped a bit. However, I continued to consider feminism only in terms of situations outside of myself. I looked at my environment and catalogued the injustices, but did not look inside.

It wasn't until I was considering a relationship with a woman that I began to see the relevance of the feminist theory I had read as a first-year college student to my own life. My perspective changed dramatically. For example, in my first relationship with a woman, it became quickly apparent that in many ways I fit quite neatly into the passive "femme" role of the butch/femme stereotype. I was behaving as I had always behaved in relationships, but for the first time, now that my lover was a woman, my "normal" behavior appeared to me (and probably to her as well) strange and unbalanced. Why were my lover and I behaving so differently? Suddenly our roles appeared constructed rather than natural. I won't pretend that I woke up one day and found myself suddenly freed of my conditioning. Rather, I spent several years unfolding and unraveling the layers of misinformation I had internalized, learning more with each subsequent relationship or incident.

My body image began to change. Through the firsthand experience of my own attractions, I learned that women, and their bodies, are beautiful, though I did not immediately apply this knowledge to my opinion of my own body. There was one woman friend on whom I had a crush for more than two years. I thought she was beautiful, with her solid, powerful angles and healthy fullness. One day, with a sense of shock, I realized that her body was not so very different from mine and that I had been holding myself to a different, unattainable standard than I had been holding her and other women to. It was this experience of seeing my image reflected in another woman that finally allowed me to begin developing a positive relationship with my own body.

I learned from firsthand experience about the privilege differential that results when the gender of your partner changes. Before I had experienced some of society's disapproval and disregard, I had no sense of the privileges I had experienced in heterosexual relationships. In subsequent years, each time I changed partners I was painfully aware of this absurd double standard and began to strategize ways to live in such a way that I could challenge rather than collaborate with these injustices. I have made a personal commitment to be "out" as bisexual at every possible opportunity and to avoid taking privileges with a male lover that I would not have with my female lover. For these reasons, I have chosen not to marry, though I hope someday to establish a "domestic partnership" and have a "commitment ceremony." If I feel someone would be unwilling to hear me talk about a same-sex lover, I disclose nothing about *any* of my relationships, even if my current partner is of the opposite sex. This is not very easy, and occasionally I backslide, but I am rewarded with the knowledge that I am not contributing to the oppression of lesbian, gay, and bisexual people when I am in an opposite-sex relationship.

It was empowering to realize that men as romantic partners were optional, not required. I no longer felt pressured to lower my relationship standards in light of the shortage of good men. Yes, I might get involved with and spend the rest of my life with one, but then again I might choose to spend my life with a woman. Or perhaps simply with myself. This was to be my choice.

I realized how I had been performing my designated gender role. It's amazing how being in a same-sex relationship can make you realize just how much of most heterosexual relationships is scripted from the first date to the bedroom to the dishes. In relationships with women, I learned how to lead and learned that I like to lead sometimes. As sometimes I like to follow. And as sometimes I prefer to negotiate every step with my partner, or to dance alone.

Finally, I made a personal commitment to hold men and women to the same standards in relationships. I realized that in our society women are grateful when a man behaves in a sensitive manner, but expect sensitivity of a woman as a matter of course. I decided that I would not settle for less from men, realizing that it means that I may be categorically eliminating most men as potential partners. So be it.

My experience with being in relationships with women has been in a way like a trip abroad. I learned that many of the things I had accepted as natural truths were socially constructed, and the first time I returned to a heterosexual relationship things felt different. I hadn't yet learned how to construct a relationship on my own terms, but I was aware that things were not quite right. As time passed, my self awareness and self-confidence increased. I gathered more experience in lesbian relationships and began to apply my knowledge to subsequent heterosexual relationships.

It is not possible to know who or where I would be today had I remained heterosexual in my attractions and in my self-identity. Perhaps other events in my life would have triggered a feminist consciousness. At any rate, it is entirely clear to me that it was loving a woman that made me realize I had fallen outside my "script," which in turn forced me to realize there *was* a script. From there, I moved toward a critical self-awareness and the realization that I could shape and write my own life.

NOTES

Thanks to Marti Hohmann, Rebecca Kaplan and Annie Senghas for their feedback and support while I was writing this essay.

1. Adrienne Rich, "Compulsory Heterosexuality and Lesbian Existence," *Signs: Journal of Women in Culture and Society* 5, no. 4, (1980), pp. 631–60.

PART IV

◆ Resistance and Social Change

INTRODUCTION

Throughout this text we have explored how elements of the social structure construct categories of difference with regard to race, class, gender, and sexuality and transform them into systems of oppression and privilege. In Part I we examined why such categories are constructed as well as the social factors involved in the process of transforming them into systems of inequality. In Part II we explored the significance of social institutions in maintaining these systems of inequality as systems of oppression and privilege. The readings in Part III provided us with personal representations illustrating how such systems impact daily lives. The readings in each of the preceding sections have prepared us for the task of this one—to understand the ways in which we can work toward the transformation of systems of oppression and privilege into a system of equal access to opportunity.

Beginning the work of transforming systems of oppression and privilege is often difficult. When we first become aware of systems of inequality, many of us are overwhelmed and do not have a clear idea of where to begin to bring about positive social change. Furthermore, as we discuss later in this section, many of us are motivated to work for social change because of the pain that we or someone close to us experienced as a result of systems of oppression. Because of our proximity to the injustice we may not feel physically or emotionally capable of challenging "the system."

Starting to transform systems of oppression and privilege is also hindered by the role of social institutions in maintaining these systems. As discussed in Part II, social institutions work to maintain systems of inequality based on ideologies that endorse and justify the interests of the dominant group. As a result, they are not likely to be open to challenges. Actions to bring about positive social change are therefore met with resistance on the parts of these institutions and discredited, if not omitted from history altogether. For example, in April 1989 in Beijing, China, a massive demonstration of Chinese students for democratic reform began on Tiananmen Square. Joined by workers, intellectuals, and civil servants until over one million people filled the square, the protestors demanded that the leadership of the country resign. The government responded on June 3 and 4 with troops and tanks, killing thousands to quell a "counter-revolutionary rebellion." Government reaction to these protests has been followed by silence. There is no public discussion of the incident in China, except for occasional government accounts defending the actions of the military. Editors of newspapers in China delete even vague references to the protests. Groups and individuals protesting injustice in the United States have been met with similar acts of

resistance (e.g., the WTO protests in Seattle[1]) and attempts to render their political activism invisible (e.g., the lack of media coverage of peace rallies and antiwar protests since September 11[2]). Faced with the possibility of opposition and, moreover, lacking an awareness of previous efforts to transform systems of oppression and privilege, those who would begin work toward positive social change face major difficulty.

Finally, beginning the work of transforming systems of oppression and privilege into systems of equal access to opportunity is often difficult because we underestimate our ability to impact these systems. In essence, we doubt that we will be able to bring about change. However, as Margaret Mead said, "Never doubt that a small group of thoughtful, committed citizens can change the world; indeed, it's the only thing that ever has." Efforts to create social equality are often begun by everyday individuals.

The readings in this section examine the various ways individuals and groups have worked to create positive social change. Those who bring about social change come from all walks of life. As you read these selections, consider the systems of oppression and privilege that you would like to see change—and the ways in which you would like to go about working for this change. Create your own image of what a system of equal access to opportunity would look like.

Before beginning this process it is important to remember that difference isn't always negative. On the contrary, the preservation of a distinct identity is often central to working toward positive social change. Differences are not problematic; rather, as stated in Part I of this text, it is when the meanings and values applied to these *differences* transform them into systems of *inequality* that such constructs become problematic. As we work to find solutions to inequality, it is important that we seek not to eliminate difference but rather to transform the ways in which difference has been established into a system where each individual is seen as valuable.

WHAT IS SOCIAL CHANGE?

In order to transform systems of oppression and privilege into systems of equality, it is important that we understand the concept of social change. **Social change**—fundamental alterations in the patterns of culture, structure, and social behavior over time—is always occurring. It can result from a variety of actions and can be inspired from a number of motivations. From individual actions to collective behavior, efforts and movements to transform systems of oppression and privilege work toward **positive social change**—

---

[1]For a discussion of the WTO protests, see Cockburn, Alexander, and Jeffrey St. Clair. 2000. *Five Days That Shook the World: Seattle and Beyond.* New York: Verso.
[2]*The Nation,* Volume 33(22), December 31, 2001, p. 8.

changing patterns of the social structure and social behavior in an effort to reduce oppression and increase inclusion for all members of society.

Such efforts often involve conflicts in **ideology.** As we discussed in Part
II, the maintenance of systems of oppression depends on the presence of ideologies that provide the basis of inequality. The clash in ideology that results
from challenging beliefs, values, and attitudes that see members of certain
groups as inferior or superior is generally seen as disruptive to the social order and may result in strong reactions on the part of those interested in maintaining the power of the dominant group. For example, on November 14,
1960, Ruby Bridges became the first black child to enter an all-white school in
the history of the U.S. South. Although only in first grade and six years old,
she was an agent for social change—and also represented a clash in ideology
with the racially segregated South. As a result, she needed to be escorted by
U.S. marshals on the first day of school and spent her first year in that school
in a class of one because all the parents pulled their children out of school to
protest the integration. Although clashes in ideology such as this may act as
deterrents for those wanting to transform systems of oppression, the reality
that dominant ideologies don't always win out in the end can also serve as
encouragement.

WHAT ARE THE GOALS OF SOCIAL CHANGE?

When seeking positive social change, we must have a clear idea of the goals
we are working toward. Just as there are divergent approaches to positive social change, there are also many goals. The general goal in seeking to transform systems of oppression is to develop systems in which all have access to
important resources and none are advantaged at the expense of others, but
specific goals of positive social change are defined by those who seek it. As
you read this section, consider the injustices that have come to matter to you
and imagine how you would like to see these transformed.

For some, discussions of social change are centered around a goal of creating a society based on a system of **social justice**—a system in which each
member of society has the opportunity and power to fully participate in the
social system. As mentioned in Part I, in the United States we have a system
based on a **civil rights** framework. Such a framework is based on the concept
of "majority rule," where the will of the "majority" becomes the will for all,
with some people inevitably losing. A *social justice* framework stands in contrast to such a system and provides the opportunity for each member of society to benefit. It relies on three principles:

The first principle is that *people have options.* These options relate to having
access to resources and can include opportunity for work, adequate healthcare, access to housing, freedom from harassment or discrimination, and so
on. In some ways, the United States can be seen as meeting this principle in
that with our vast resources it appears that we all have the *option* of access to

these resources. For example, with regard to opportunity for work and career choice, many of us who grew up in the United States were presented with the notion that anyone has the option to be president. You do not need to be of any particular race, class, gender, or sexuality in order to have this option.

The second principle of a social justice framework is that *people are aware of their options.* In such a framework we need to be made aware of our opportunities to access important resources such as attending college, applying for jobs, purchasing property, and receiving adequate healthcare. Considering again the opportunity to become president, many of us who grew up in the United States heard that this was a possibility and thus we were aware of this option. Indeed, we often heard such messages along with Horatio Alger stories and notions of achieving the "American dream." Many of these messages were rooted in the assumption that the United States is a **meritocracy**—a system in which people's success is a result of their talents, abilities, and efforts. However, as Robert Jensen illustrated in Part III (Reading 45), the notion of a meritocracy ignores the advantages that are given to some and denied to others. In a socially just system, people are aware of their options and their opportunities and are not hindered by unfair disadvantages.

The third and final principle of a socially just system is that *people have the power to act on their options.* This is where the system of civil rights—and thus the system of the United States—departs from that of a social justice framework. As noted above, the assumption of a meritocracy sits at the core of the American dream. A system of oppression and privilege that derives from the social construction of difference results in an unequal distribution of power. Because of this unequal distribution, it is not our individual talents, abilities and efforts that lead to our ability to succeed but our access to power. Power, typically viewed as an ability to control people or things, can be defined in many ways. In the case of running for president, one's power directly relates to the amount of money one is able to raise to run a successful campaign. For example, according to the *United States Federal Elections Commission Annual Report,* in 2000 the four major presidential candidates for president (Buchanan, Bush, Gore, and Nader) spent in excess of $150 million. From our discussion in Part II of the distribution of income and wealth in the United States, it is obvious that there are very few people who possess or have access to the power to be able to act on their option to become president. Considering this, it is clear that a civil rights system departs from one based on social justice.

A social justice framework is one of many possibilities in framing our efforts to transform systems of oppression and privilege. Another possible framework relies on **empowerment**—a process of defining ourselves rather than being defined by others. In a system based on empowerment, those who have experienced oppression are given the opportunity to create their own power in improving their own circumstances. Whatever the specific goal each of us sets our sights on, we need to establish our own strategies for working toward that goal. Many of the readings in this section offer insights that may be useful in establishing these strategies.

WHAT MOTIVATES WORK FOR SOCIAL CHANGE?

Much work has been done in a variety of contexts to bring about positive social change to transform systems of oppression and privilege. The factors that precipitate such work come from a variety of sources. Work for positive social change can be motivated by personal experiences; at other times it is motivated by dissatisfaction with social systems on the part of large groups of people. In order to understand how to create positive social change, it is important to understand what has motivated others to become involved in such efforts.

Motivation for working toward positive social change can come from factors related to the social system. For example, according to Neil Smelser (1962), when important aspects of a social system appear to be "out of joint," such as when standards of living are not what people expect them to be, people may experience **structural strain.** As an illustration, consider the notion that the United States is thought to be an affluent society. Whether our economy is in a state of recession or boom, poverty rates continue to be quite high. Further, as illustrated in Part I, such poverty rates are arbitrarily determined and don't necessarily reflect the experience of poverty accurately. According to Smelser, as the strain from this situation accumulates over time, individuals become motivated to use courses of action not defined by existing institutional arrangements. As people begin to see the strain as a problem in need of a solution, they develop shared ideas about how they should respond to it.

At other times, motivation for working toward positive social change requires precipitating factors, such as the recent mobilization on many campuses and in numerous cities to work for peace in response to the events of September 11, 2001. Other precipitating factors can be hearing stories of social injustice experienced on the part of individuals. For example, there has recently been increasing dialogue and organization around the need for the enactment of hate crimes legislation in the United States. Much of the motivation for working on such legislation arose from the brutal killings of James Byrd,[3]

---

[3]James Byrd, 49, was beaten unconscious, then dragged by a chain from the back of a pickup truck to his death after accepting a ride from three white men in Jasper, Texas, in June, 1998. One of the men, John William King, was found guilty and given the death penalty for his role in the killing. Another man, Lawrence Brewer, was also found guilty and sentenced to death. The third suspect, Shawn Berry, was sentenced to life in prison. Byrd's body was dismembered in the assault and many of his body parts were found about a mile from his torso. When he was found, his body was so badly disfigured that Byrd had to be identified by fingerprints.

Matthew Shepard,[4] Billy Jack Gaither,[5] and Juana Vega.[6] Acts of brutality such as these, motivated by hatred for someone seen as different or "other," have motivated individuals, organizations, and government officials to work to enact legislation to reduce the likelihood that hate crimes will continue to occur.

Whether the motivation for working toward positive social change comes from witnessing inconsistencies between structural values, hearing stories of violence committed by those who hate, our own personal experiences with inequality, or some other source, taking on the challenge of working to improve our social environment does not occur unless we can imagine a reality that differs from what already exists. Returning to Part I, one of the fundamental aspects of critical thinking is the ability to imagine alternative ways of thinking. For example, if children experienced an inclusive representation of history, how might that positively impact their perceptions of their own race as well as those of others? What lasting impact might that have on constructions of race and the interactions of those who identify as belonging to different race categories? Critical thinking is a fundamental tool for those desiring to create positive social change. Imagining alternatives to the current social order can provide us not only with the motivation to work for positive social change, but also with a goal and some strategies for achieving that goal.

WHO CREATES POSITIVE SOCIAL CHANGE?

When we think of positive social change, we often think of large **social movements**—sustained, organized collective effort. In addition, we tend to think of those who work toward such change as being charismatic leaders with large groups of followers. Thus, if asked who were great makers of so-

---

[4]Matthew Shepard, a University of Wyoming student, was lured from a bar and attacked by two men, allegedly because they presumed he was gay. He was struck 18 times in the head with a pistol and left to die on a fence outside Laramie in October, 1998. He was found unconscious 18 hours after he was kidnapped and died five days later. One of his attackers, Russell Henderson, was sentenced to two consecutive life sentences after pleading guilty. The other man accused in the murder, Aaron McKinney, was sentenced to life without parole.

[5]The body of Billy Jack Gaither, a 39-year-old textile worker, was found in rural Sylacauga, Alabama, some 40 miles southeast of Birmingham on February 20, 1999. Two men, Steven Eric Mullins and Charles Monroe Butler, Jr., confessed to the killing in early March after waiving their right to counsel. After bludgeoning Gaither with an axe handle, the men burned the victim's remains. They then drove his car to a deserted location and burned it as well.

[6]Juana Vega was murdered in November 2001 by Pablo Parilla, the brother of her partner. Upset about his sister's relationship with a woman, he shot Vega five times and then repeatedly hit her with the gun and kicked her motionless body. Parilla confessed to the killing and, at the time of this writing, is currently awaiting trial.

cial justice, we may mention names such as Martin Luther King, Malcolm X, Emma Goldman, Ghandi, Cesar Chavez, and Jane Addams. Moreover, many of us may imagine activists as fitting a "radical" image that we don't see ourselves fitting into. In any event, we rarely identify ourselves when describing agents of change.

Although it is true that a great deal of the positive social change that has occurred in our society has involved the organization of movements and the participation of great leaders, the earlier example of Ruby Bridges illustrates that such social transformation has also involved the actions of a wide array of individuals coming from all walks of life. Thus, there is no "model" activist. An activist can be anyone with the motivation and ideas of how to transform a situation of inequality.

For example, in 1996 Kelli Peterson, a Salt Lake City East High School student, created a group that provided safe space for support and dialogue for lesbian, gay, and bisexual students and their allies at her school. Many studies and reports have indicated the need for such a group. For example, the Massachusetts Governor's Commission on Gay and Lesbian Youth recently found that 97 percent of high school students reported regularly hearing words like "faggot" and "dyke" at their schools, with 53 percent hearing their teachers use such language. When Kelli attempted to establish a gay/straight alliance, the School Board voted to ban all noncurricular clubs rather than allow the alliance to be formed. Through her commitment and motivation, however, she worked to organize students, faculty, and community members to overturn this decision. The gay/straight alliance now meets regularly at Salt Lake City East High School, offering a safer environment for lesbian, gay, bisexual, and transgender students and their allies.

Just as each of us participates in constructing categories of difference and systems of oppression and privilege, we can also participate in transforming them into systems of equality. Once we locate our source of motivation and establish a new vision of what is possible, we are well on our way toward creating this change.

WHERE DOES POSITIVE SOCIAL CHANGE OCCUR?

Just as a vast array of social activists and endless contributing factors transform categories of difference, there are also a large number of contexts within which we can enact positive social change. Further, as categories of difference are constructed and transformed into systems of inequality in a variety of contexts—institutional, interpersonal, and internal—so too can we work to transform systems of oppression in all contexts.

The first site of working toward positive social change is often the internal context—within ourselves. We are able to begin this work once we are able to transform how we view ourselves and our memberships within a system of oppression. To be effective agents for social change, we often must transform the negative perceptions we have of ourselves before we are able to effectively work at transforming systems of oppression in other contexts. This often involves a transformation of identity through the restoration of dignity and overcoming a previously stigmatized status.

Transforming systems of oppression within ourselves requires that we examine not only our own internalized oppression but also how we have internalized oppressive attitudes about others. One of the reasons systems of oppression persist is that individuals in those systems, regardless of their location in them, internalize the ideas of the dominant group. As Collins notes in "Toward a New Vision" (Reading 56), we often fail to see how our own ideas and behaviors perpetuate someone else's subjugation. She quotes Audre Lorde as saying:

> The true focus of revolutionary change is never merely the oppressive situations which we seek to escape but that piece of the oppressor which is planted deep within each of us (1984, p. 123).

As this quote illustrates, if we desire to engender positive social change, we need first to examine not only the ideas we have internalized that oppress ourselves but also those notions that perpetuate the oppression of others.

Transformations of systems of oppression and privilege can also occur in interpersonal contexts. Indeed, it is at this level that a great deal of positive social change begins. Here we can often use the dynamics of our interpersonal relationships as a source of leverage in seeking to transform inequality. Love between family members, commitment between spouses/partners, philosophical or religious alliances between members of communities, political coalitions between members of an organization, and so on, can all provide a foundation that makes challenges regarding oppressive or discriminatory behavior more likely to be heard and seen as valid.

We can also seek to transform systems of oppression and privilege within institutional contexts. This can involve seeking to transform the institution from within, with members of the institution using their power to create change in individuals and policies. For example, a teacher can use her or his position within the institution to change her or his students through using a curriculum that is inclusive and focuses on transformation rather than perpetuation of systems of oppression. Additionally, a social scientist can use her or his knowledge and skills as a researcher and status as a member of an academic institution to demonstrate the importance of transforming difference within other institutions. Further, institutions can establish policies and procedures that set precedents for the more inclusive treatment of marginalized groups. For example, when President Harry S. Truman officially desegregated the military in 1948, he helped to establish a precedent for future inclusion of blacks and African Americans in the United States.

Transforming systems of oppression and privilege within institutional contexts also involves individuals outside the institutions who use a variety of means to pressure it to change. The use of methods such as protests, boycotts (withdrawal of support, usually through money), and informing the public of the institution's discriminatory policies and practices have been very effective in bringing about change within these contexts.

It is important to note here, however, that institutions in the United States are generally organized around systems of oppression and privilege, as the readings in this text have made clear. As a result, we are often limited in the amount of change that we can occur within these structures. For example, a woman who works in a large corporation that is dominated by males may risk loss of advancement, if not job security, if she challenges sexist hiring and operating practices of the institution. In addition, we should not expect that positive change will result merely because members of marginalized groups are present in powerful positions within these organizations. The success of marginalized *individuals* within an organization should not be assumed to reflect a positive change in institutional policies toward that *group.* As Lorber discusses in "Dismantling Noah's Ark" (Reading 60), we assume that gender inequality will cease to exist in the workplace as more women get positions of prestige and authority. She argues, however, that social policies that ignore the patriarchal structure on which they are built and assume that institutional changes will occur on the individual level will inevitably fail. These failures, in turn, will be blamed on the subordinated individual rather than on the social structure itself.

Regardless of the context within which we focus our efforts to generate positive social change, such change is possible from a variety of starting points. As you read this section, take note of the strategies and tools used and think critically about the possibilities that they reveal for you to transform systems of oppression and privilege in your own social world.

STRATEGIES: THE IMPORTANCE OF COALITION

As the previous discussion indicates, there are a variety of ways in which we can work to transform systems of oppression and privilege. However, it is difficult, and perhaps dangerous, to try to discern which is the *best* strategy. Indeed, such debates over strategies for generating positive social change have often stood in the way of creating any change at all and have generally only served to perpetuate inequality. However, it is important to note here that, regardless of the strategies we choose to use in the formation of positive social change, it is important to build coalitions and work across categories of difference.

Throughout this text the connections between forms of oppression have been made clear. Systems of oppression share similarities in how they are established and maintained as well as in their effect. Thus, if we seek to transform such systems we need to examine their foundations and the underlying aspects of the social structure that serve to perpetuate them. Such a *system-* rather than *issue*-based focus not only enables us to build coalitions but *requires* us to do so.

As Collins notes in "Toward a New Vision" (Reading 56), we often get caught up in asserting that there is one type of oppression that is most important and all others, as a result, become less important. As mentioned earlier, such a debate is not only endless, but is also likely to defeat all efforts to transform systems of oppression and privilege. Rather than focusing on ranking oppressions, Collins argues, we need to focus on how systems of stratification interconnect. As we discussed in Parts I and II, Collins sees these systems as operating within a matrix of domination. Significant problems occur when we miss these parallels and interconnections. Understanding the interconnections among various forms of oppression will help us to forge stronger alliances and coalitions. In addition, it is important that we understand the ideological foundations shared by various forms of stratification. We cannot hope to eradicate one form of inequality if others remain intact. While these alliances and coalitions may be difficult to develop and maintain, they are necessary if we are to eradicate all forms of domination.

FURTHER BARRIERS TO CREATING POSITIVE SOCIAL CHANGE

While coalition building presents an effective strategy for transforming categories of difference, it also can present a variety of barriers, institutional as well as personal, to bringing about positive social change. In addition to these barriers, we may face other obstacles in both interpersonal and institutional contexts.

Social control mechanisms, which reward conformity and punish or discourage nonconformity, are effective means of regulating the behavior of societal members. These mechanisms also create barriers to transforming systems of oppression by thwarting efforts to bring about positive social change. Anne Wilson Schaef (1981) offers an example of one such mechanism. Focusing on the social control of women, she uses the term *stoppers* to refer to anything that keeps women where the dominant group wants them to be. People seeking to create positive social change often face such stoppers regardless of the form of oppression that they may be seeking to transform. For example, heterosexual men who challenge other men on their sexism may experience challenges to their masculinity or have their heterosexuality called into question by other men. Women who speak out against sexism risk being called lesbians or facing physical violence. People of color who speak out about racism in their workplace face accusations of being "too angry" or "having an agenda." People who speak out against the war risk being called "un-Amercian" or having their civil liberties curtailed.[7]

---

[7]Armed government agents detained Nancy Oden, Green Party USA coordinating committee member, on November 1, 2001, at Bangor International Airport in Bangor Maine as she attempted to board an American Airlines flight to Chicago. Her name had been flagged by airport computers due to the Green Party's opposition to the war in Afghanistan.

Stoppers also exist within institutional contexts and can have a more severe impact than those that occur on an individual level. As mentioned at the beginning of this essay, efforts to transform systems of oppression and privilege are often met with resistance on the part of institutions. For example, the social institution of the state may enact policies seeking to repress the efforts of those working to transform systems of oppression and privilege. The experiences of political prisoners, including Angela Davis[8] and Leonard Peltier,[9] offer clear examples of the ways in which institutions may work to prevent the transformation of systems of oppression.

Again, to effectively transform systems of oppression and privilege it is important to be aware of individual as well as institutional barriers. Having this awareness will enable us to create effective strategies for moving beyond them.

CONCLUSION

Despite the barriers that we face when seeking to transform systems of oppression and privilege, opportunities for bringing about such change continually present themselves. As mentioned earlier, there is no single cause for inequality, and thus there is no single solution. Thinking critically about categories of difference and structures of inequality can present us with endless options for generating positive social change. By challenging our assumptions and being aware of our own standpoint, we can become more aware of how our own ideas perpetuate someone else's subjugation. By imagining alternative ways of constructing our social world, we are able to establish goals for our social action. Finally, by employing a reflexive analysis we are able to challenge dominant ideas and question rigid belief systems. Such questions and challenges will provide a good foundation for creating a structure where each individual is seen as valuable. As you read the selections in the final chapters of this text, take note of how your process of critical thinking helps

---

[8]Currently a professor of history at the University of California–Santa Cruz, Davis was placed on the FBI's Ten Most Wanted list in 1970, after she was accused of planning the kidnapping of three imprisoned African American activists in San Quentin and supplying the gun that killed four people during the incident. She was incarcerated on charges of murder, kidnapping, and conspiracy, and her case was taken up by supporters across the country. In 1972, after 18 months in jail, she was tried and acquitted of all crimes.

[9]On June 26, 1975, two FBI agents and one Native American were killed in a shootout on the Pine Ridge Indian Reservation. This firefight led to what many see as the false incarceration of American Indian Movement member Leonard Peltier. Now 54 years old, Peltier is serving his 24th year of incarceration in Leavenworth Penitentiary in Kansas. He stands accused of the murders of the two FBI agents. To date, no credible evidence has been presented to suggest that he is guilty. All others who have been brought to trial regarding this incident were acquitted on the basis of self-defense.

you to become aware of your own goals for transforming systems of oppression and privilege.

REFERENCES

Lorde, Audre. 1984. *Sister Outsider.* Trumansberg, NY: The Crossing Press.

Schaef, Anne Wilson. 1981. *Women's Reality: An Emerging Female System in the White Male Society.* Minneapolis, MN: Winston Press.

Smelser, Neil J. 1962. *Theory of Collective Behavior.* New York: Free Press.

56

TOWARD A NEW VISION
Race, Class, and Gender as Categories of Analysis and Connection

PATRICIA HILL COLLINS

The true focus of revolutionary change is never merely the oppressive situations which we seek to escape, but that piece of the oppressor which is planted deep within each of us.

—AUDRE LORDE, *SISTER OUTSIDER,* 123

Audre Lorde's statement raises a troublesome issue for scholars and activists working for social change. While many of us have little difficulty assessing our own victimization within some major system of oppression, whether it be by race, social class, religion, sexual orientation, ethnicity, age or gender, we typically fail to see how our thoughts and actions uphold someone else's subordination. Thus, white feminists routinely point with confidence to their oppression as women but resist seeing how much their white skin privileges them. African-Americans who possess eloquent analyses of racism often persist in viewing poor White women as symbols of white power. The radical left fares little better. "If only people of color and women could see their true class interests," they argue, "class solidarity would eliminate racism and sexism." In essence, each group identifies the type of oppression with which it feels most comfortable as being fundamental and classifies all other types as being of lesser importance.

Oppression is full of such contradictions. Errors in political judgment that we make concerning how we teach our courses, what we tell our children, and which organizations are worthy of our time, talents and financial support flow smoothly from errors in theoretical analysis about the nature of oppression and activism. Once we realize that there are few pure victims or oppressors, and that each one of us derives varying amounts of penalty and privilege from the multiple systems of oppression that frame our lives, then we will be in a position to see the need for new ways of thought and action.

In *Race, Sex, & Class,* 1, no. 1, Fall 1993. Reprinted by permission of the author.

To get at that "piece of the oppressor which is planted deep within each of us," we need at least two things. First, we need new visions of what oppression is, new categories of analysis that are inclusive of race, class, and gender as distinctive yet interlocking structures of oppression. Adhering to a stance of comparing and ranking oppressions—the proverbial, "I'm more oppressed than you"—locks us all into a dangerous dance of competing for attention, resources, and theoretical supremacy. Instead, I suggest that we examine our different experiences within the more fundamental relationship of damnation and subordination. To focus on the particular arrangements that race or class or gender takes in our time and place without seeing these structures as sometimes parallel and sometimes interlocking dimensions of the more fundamental relationship of domination and subordination may temporarily ease our consciences. But while such thinking may lead to short-term social reforms, it is simply inadequate for the task of bringing about long-term social transformation.

While race, class and gender as categories of analysis are essential in helping us understand the structural bases of domination and subordination, new ways of thinking that are not accompanied by new ways of acting offer incomplete prospects for change. To get at that "piece of the oppressor which is planted deep within each of us," we also need to change our daily behavior. Currently, we are all enmeshed in a complex web of problematic relationships that grant our mirror images full human subjectivity while stereotyping and objectifying those most different than ourselves. We often assume that the people we work with, teach, send our children to school with, and sit next to . . . will act and feel in prescribed ways because they belong to given race, social class or gender categories. These judgments by category must be replaced with fully human relationships that transcend the legitimate differences created by race, class and gender as categories of analysis. We require new categories of connection, new visions of what our relationships with one another can be. . . .

[This discussion] addresses this need for new patterns of thought and action. I focus on two basic questions. First, how can we reconceptualize race, class and gender as categories of analysis? Second, how can we transcend the barriers created by our experiences with race, class and gender oppression in order to build the types of coalitions essential for social exchange? To address these questions I contend that we must acquire both new theories of how race, class and gender have shaped the experiences not just of women of color, but of all groups. Moreover, we must see the connections between the categories of analysis and the personal issues in our everyday lives, particularly our scholarship, our teaching and our relationships with our colleagues and students. As Audre Lorde points out, change starts with self, and relationships that we have with those around us must always be the primary site for social change.

HOW CAN WE RECONCEPTUALIZE RACE, CLASS AND GENDER AS CATEGORIES OF *ANALYSIS?*

To me, we must shift our discourse away from additive analyses of oppression (Spelman, 1982; Collins, 1989). Such approaches are typically based on two key premises. First, they depend on either/or, dichotomous thinking. Persons, things and ideas are conceptualized in terms of their opposites. For example, Black/White, man/woman, thought/feeling, and fact/opinion are defined in oppositional terms. Thought and feeling are not seen as two different and interconnected ways of approaching truth that can coexist in scholarship and teaching. Instead, feeling is defined as antithetical to reason, as its opposite. In spite of the fact that we all have "both/and" identities, (I am both a college professor and a mother—I don't stop being a mother when I drop my child off at school, or forget everything I learned while scrubbing the toilet), we persist in trying to classify each other in either/or categories. I live each day as an African-American woman—a race/gender specific experience. And I am not alone. Everyone has a race/gender/class specific identity. Either/or, dichotomous thinking is especially troublesome when applied to theories of oppression because every individual must be classified as being either oppressed or not oppressed. The both/and position of simultaneously being oppressed and oppressor becomes conceptually impossible.

A second premise of additive analyses of oppression is that these dichotomous differences must be ranked. One side of the dichotomy is typically labeled dominant and the other subordinate. Thus, Whites rule Blacks, men are deemed superior to women, and reason is seen as being preferable to emotion. Applying this premise to discussions of oppression leads to the assumption that oppression can be quantified, and that some groups are oppressed more than others. I am frequently asked, "Which has been most oppressive to you, your status as a Black person or your status as a woman?" What I am really being asked to do is divide myself into little boxes and rank my various statuses. If I experience oppression as a both/and phenomenon, why should I analyze it any differently?

Additive analyses of oppression rest squarely on the twin pillars of either/or thinking and the necessity to quantify and rank all relationships in order to know where one stands. Such approaches typically see African-American women as being more oppressed than everyone else because the majority of Black women experience the negative effects of race, class and gender oppression simultaneously. In essence, if you add together separate oppressions, you are left with a grand oppression greater than the sum of its parts.

I am not denying that specific groups experience oppression more harshly than others—lynching is certainly objectively worse than being held up as a sex object. But we must be careful not to confuse this issue of the saliency of one type of oppression in people's lives with a theoretical stance positing the interlocking nature of oppression. Race, class and gender may all structure a situation but may not be equally visible and/or important in people's self-definitions. In certain contexts, such as the antebellum American South and contemporary South America, racial oppression is more visibly salient, while in other contexts, such as Haiti, El Salvador and Nicaragua, social class oppression may be more apparent. For middle-class White women, gender may assume experiential primacy unavailable to poor Hispanic women struggling with the ongoing issues of low-paid jobs and the frustrations of the welfare bureaucracy. This recognition that one category may have salience over another for a given time and place does not minimize the theoretical importance of assuming that race, class and gender as categories of analysis structure all relationships.

In order to move toward new visions of what oppression is, I think that we need to ask new questions. How are relationships of domination and subordination structured and maintained in the American political economy? How do race, class and gender function as parallel and interlocking systems that shape this basic relationship of domination and subordination? Questions such as these promise to move us away from futile theoretical struggles concerned with ranking oppressions and towards analyses that assume race, class and gender are all present in any given setting, even if one appears more visible and salient than the others. Our task becomes redefined as one of reconceptualizing oppression by uncovering the connections among race, class and gender as categories of analysis.

1. The Institutional Dimension of Oppression

Sandra Harding's contention that gender oppression is structured along three main dimensions—the institutional, the symbolic and the individual—offers a useful model for a more comprehensive analysis encompassing race, class and gender oppression (Harding 1989). Systemic relationships of domination and subordination structured through social institutions such as schools, businesses, hospitals, the workplace and government agencies represent the institutional dimension of oppression. Racism, sexism and elitism all have concrete institutional locations. Even though the workings of the institutional dimension of oppression are often obscured with ideologies claiming equality of opportunity, in actuality, race, class and gender place Asian-American women, Native American men, White men, African-American women and other groups in distinct institutional niches with varying degrees of penalty and privilege.

Even though I realize that many . . . would not share this assumption, let us assume that the institutions of American society discriminate, whether by design or by accident. While many of us are familiar with how race, gender and class operate separately to structure inequality, I want to focus on how these three systems interlock in structuring the institutional dimension of oppression. To get at the interlocking nature of race, class and gender, I want you to think about the antebellum plantation as a guiding metaphor for a variety of American social institutions. Even though slavery is typically analyzed as a racist institution, and occasionally as a class institution, I suggest that slavery was a race, class, gender specific institution. Removing any one piece from our analysis diminishes our understanding of the true nature of relations of domination and subordination under slavery.

Slavery was a profoundly patriarchal institution. It rested on the dual tenets of White male authority and White male property, a joining of the political and the economic within the institution of the family. Heterosexism was assumed and all Whites were expected to marry. Control over affluent White women's sexuality remained key to slavery's survival because property was to be passed on to the legitimate heirs of the slave owner. Ensuring affluent White women's virginity and chastity was deeply intertwined with maintenance of property relations.

Under slavery, we see varying levels of institutional protection given to affluent White women, working class and poor White women and enslaved African women. Poor White women enjoyed few of the protections held out to their upper class sisters. Moreover, the devalued status of Black women was key in keeping all White women in their assigned places. Controlling Black women's fertility was also key to the continuation of slavery, for children born to slave mothers themselves were slaves.

African-American women shared the devalued status of chattel with their husbands, fathers and sons. Racism stripped Blacks as a group of legal rights, education and control over their own persons. African-Americans could be whipped, branded, sold, or killed, not because they were poor, or because they were women, but because they were Black. Racism ensured that Blacks would continue to serve Whites and suffer economic exploitation at the hands of all Whites.

So we have a very interesting chain of command on the plantation—the affluent White master as the reigning patriarch, his White wife helpmate to serve him, help him manage his property and bring up his heirs, his faithful servants whose production and reproduction were tied to the requirements of the capitalist political economy and largely propertyless, working class White men and women watching from afar. In essence, the foundations for the contemporary roles of elite White women, poor Black women, working class White men and a series of other groups can be seen in stark relief in this fundamental American social institution. While Blacks experienced the most harsh treatment under slavery, and thus made slavery clearly visible as a racist institution, race, class and gender interlocked in structuring slavery's systemic organization of domination and subordination.

Even today, the plantation remains a compelling metaphor for institutional oppression. Certainly the actual conditions of oppression are not as severe now as they were then. To argue, as some do, that things have not changed all that much denigrates the achievements of those who struggled for social change before us. But the basic relationships among Black men, Black women, elite White women, elite White men, working class White men and working class White women as groups remain essentially intact.

A brief analysis of key American social institutions most controlled by elite White men should convince us of the interlocking nature of race, class and gender in structuring the institutional dimension of oppression. For example, if you are from an American college or university, is your campus a modern plantation? Who controls your university's political economy? Are elite White men overrepresented among the upper administrators and trustees controlling your university's finances and policies? Are elite White men being joined by growing numbers of elite White women helpmates? What kinds of people are in your classrooms grooming the next generation who will occupy these and other decision-making positions? Who are the support staff that produce the mass mailings, order the supplies, fix the leaky pipes? Do African-Americans, Hispanics or other people of color form the majority of the invisible workers who feed you, wash your dishes, and clean up your offices and libraries after everyone else has gone home?

If your college is anything like mine, you know the answers to these questions. You may be affiliated with an institution that has Hispanic women as vice-presidents for finance, or substantial numbers of Black men among the faculty. If so, you are fortunate. Much more typical are colleges where a modified version of the plantation as a metaphor for the institutional dimension of oppression survives.

2. The Symbolic Dimension of Oppression

Widespread, societally sanctioned ideologies used to justify relations of domination and subordination comprise the symbolic dimension of oppression. Central to this process is the use of stereotypical or controlling images of diverse race, class and gender groups. In order to assess the power of this dimension of oppression, I want you to make a list, either on paper or in your head, of "masculine" and "feminine" characteristics. If your list is anything like that compiled by most people, it reflects some variation of the following:

Masculine	*Feminine*
aggressive	passive
leader	follower
rational	emotional
strong	weak
intellectual	physical

Not only does this list reflect either/or dichotomous thinking and the need to rank both sides of the dichotomy, but ask yourself exactly which men and women you had in mind when compiling these characteristics. This list applies almost exclusively to middle class White men and women. The allegedly "masculine" qualities that you probably listed are only acceptable when exhibited by elite White men, or when used by Black and Hispanic men against each other or against women of color. Aggressive Black and Hispanic men are seen as dangerous, not powerful, and are often penalized when they exhibit any of the allegedly "masculine" characteristics. Working class and poor White men fare slightly better and are also denied the allegedly "masculine" symbols of leadership, intellectual competence, and human rationality. Women of color and working class and poor White women are also not represented on this list, for they have never had the luxury of being "ladies." What appear to be universal categories representing all men and women instead are unmasked as being applicable to only a small group.

It is important to see how the symbolic images applied to different race, class and gender groups interact in maintaining systems of domination and subordination. If I were to ask you to repeat the same assignment, only this time, by making separate lists for Black men, Black women, Hispanic women and Hispanic men, I suspect that your gender symbolism would be quite different. In comparing all of the lists, you might begin to see the interdependence of symbols applied to all groups. For example, the elevated images of White womanhood need devalued images of Black womanhood in order to maintain credibility.

While the above exercise reveals the interlocking nature of race, class and gender in structuring the symbolic dimension of oppression, part of its importance lies in demonstrating how race, class and gender pervade a wide range of what appears to be universal language. Attending to diversity in our scholarship, in our teaching, and in our daily lives provides a new angle of vision on interpretations of reality thought to be natural, normal and "true." Moreover, viewing images of masculinity and femininity as universal gender symbolism, rather than as symbolic images that are race, class and gender specific, renders the experiences of people of color and of nonprivileged White women and men invisible. One way to dehumanize an individual or group is to deny the reality of their experiences. So when we refuse to deal with race or class because they do not appear to be directly relevant to gender, we are actually becoming part of some one else's problem.

Assuming that everyone is affected differently by the same interlocking set of symbolic images allows us to move forward toward new analyses. Women of color and White women have different relations to White male authority and this difference explains the distinct gender symbolism applied to both groups. Black women encounter controlling images such as the mammy, the matriarch, the mule and the whore, that encourage others to reject us as fully human people. Ironically, the negative nature of these images simultaneously encourages us to reject them. In contrast, White women are offered seductive images, those that promise to reward them for supporting the status quo. And yet seductive images can be equally controlling. Consider, for example, the views of Nancy White, a 73-year-old Black woman, concerning images of rejection and seduction:

> My mother used to say that the black woman is the white man's
> mule and the white woman is his dog. Now, she said that to say
> this: we do the heavy work and get beat whether we do it well or
> not. But the white woman is closer to the master and he pats them
> on the head and lets them sleep in the house, but he ain't gon' treat
> neither one like he was dealing with a person. (Gwaltney, 148)

Both sets of images stimulate particular political stances. By broadening the
analysis beyond the confines of race, we can see the varying levels of rejection and seduction available to each of us due to our race, class and gender
identity. Each of us lives with an allotted portion of institutional privilege and
penalty, and with varying levels of rejection and seduction inherent in the
symbolic images applied to us. This is the context in which we make our
choices. Taken together, the institutional and symbolic dimensions of oppression create a structural backdrop against which all of us live our lives.

3. The Individual Dimension of Oppression

Whether we benefit or not, we all live within institutions that reproduce race,
class and gender oppression. Even if we never have any contact with members of other race, class and gender groups, we all encounter images of these
groups and are exposed to the symbolic meanings attached to those images.
On this dimension of oppression, our individual biographies vary tremendously. As a result of our institutional and symbolic statuses, all of our
choices become political acts.

Each of us must come to terms with the multiple ways in which race,
class and gender as categories of analysis frame our individual biographies.
I have lived my entire life as an African-American woman from a working
class family and this basic fact has had a profound impact on my personal biography. Imagine how different your life might be if you had been born
Black, or White, or poor, or of a different race/class/gender group than the
one with which you are most familiar. The institutional treatment you would
have received and the symbolic meanings attached to your very existence
might differ dramatically from that you now consider to be natural, normal
and part of everyday life. You might be the same, but your personal biography might have been quite different.

I believe that each of us carries around the cumulative effect of our lives
within multiple structures of oppression. If you want to see how much you
have been affected by this whole thing, I ask you one simple question—who
are your close friends? Who are the people with whom you can share your
hopes, dreams, vulnerabilities, fears and victories? Do they look like you? If
they are all the same, circumstance may be the cause. For the first seven years
of my life I saw only low income Black people. My friends from those years
reflected the composition of my community. But now that I am an adult, can
the defense of circumstance explain the patterns of people that I trust as my
friends and colleagues? When given other alternatives, if my friends and col-

leagues reflect the homogeneity of one race, class and gender group, then these categories of analysis have indeed become barriers to connection.

I am not suggesting that people are doomed to follow the paths laid out for them by race, class and gender as categories of analysis. While these three structures certainly frame my opportunity structure, I as an individual always have the choice of accepting things as they are, or trying to change them. As Nikki Giovanni points out, "we've got to live in the real world. If we don't like the world we're living in, change it. And if we can't change it, we change ourselves. We can do something" (Tate 1983, 68). While a piece of the oppressor may be planted deep within each of us, we each have the choice of accepting that piece or challenging it as part of the "true focus of revolutionary change."

HOW CAN WE TRANSCEND THE BARRIERS CREATED BY OUR EXPERIENCES WITH RACE, CLASS AND GENDER OPPRESSION IN ORDER TO BUILD THE TYPES OF COALITIONS ESSENTIAL FOR SOCIAL CHANGE?

Reconceptualizing oppression and seeing the barriers created by race, class and gender as interlocking categories of analysis is a vital first step. But we must transcend these barriers by moving toward race, class and gender as categories of connection, by building relationships and coalitions that will bring about social change. What are some of the issues involved in doing this?

1. Differences in Power and Privilege

First, we must recognize that our differing experiences with oppression create problems in the relationships among us. Each of us lives within a system that vests us with varying levels of power and privilege. These differences in power, whether structured along axes of race, class, gender, age or sexual orientation, frame our relationships. African-American writer June Jordan describes her discomfort on a Caribbean vacation with Olive, the Black woman who cleaned her room:

> . . . even though both "Olive" and "I" live inside a conflict neither one of us created, and even though both of us therefore hurt inside that conflict, I may be one of the monsters she needs to eliminate from her universe and, in a sense, she may be one of the monsters in mine (1985, 47).

Differences in power constrain our ability to connect with one another even when we think we are engaged in dialogue across differences. Let me give you an example. One year, the students in my course "Sociology of the Black Community" got into a heated discussion about the reasons for the upsurge of racial incidents on college campuses. Black students complained vehemently about the apathy and resistance they felt most White students expressed about examining their own racism. Mark, a White male student, found their comments particularly unsettling. After claiming that all the Black people he had ever known had expressed no such beliefs to him, he questioned how representative the viewpoints of his fellow students actually were. When pushed further, Mark revealed that he had participated in conversations over the years with the Black domestic worker employed by his family. Since she had never expressed such strong feelings about White racism, Mark was genuinely shocked by class discussions. Ask yourselves whether that domestic worker was in a position to speak freely. Would it have been wise for her to do so in a situation where the power between the two parties was so unequal?

In extreme cases, members of privileged groups can erase the very presence of the less privileged. When I first moved to Cincinnati, my family and I went on a picnic at a local park. Picnicking next to us was a family of White Appalachians. When I went to push my daughter on the swings, several of the children came over. They had missing, yellowed and broken teeth, they wore old clothing and their poverty was evident. I was shocked. Growing up in a large eastern city, I had never seen such awful poverty among Whites. The segregated neighborhoods in which I grew up made White poverty all but invisible. More importantly, the privileges attached to my newly acquired social class position allowed me to ignore and minimize the poverty among Whites that I did encounter. My reactions to those children made me realize how confining phrases such as "well, at least they're not Black," had become for me. In learning to grant human subjectivity to the Black victims of poverty, I had simultaneously learned to demand White victims of poverty. By applying categories of race to the objective conditions confronting me, I was quantifying and ranking oppressions and missing the very real suffering which, in fact, is the real issue.

One common pattern of relationships across differences in power is one that I label "voyeurism." From the perspective of the privileged, the lives of people of color, of the poor, and of women are interesting for their entertainment value. The privileged become voyeurs, passive onlookers who do not relate to the less powerful, but who are interested in seeing how the "different" live. Over the years, I have heard numerous African-American students complain about professors who never call on them except when a so-called Black issue is being discussed. The students' interest in discussing race or qualifications for doing so appear unimportant to the professor's efforts to use Black students' experiences as stories to make the material come alive for the White student audience. Asking Black students to perform on cue and provide a Black experience for their White classmates can be seen as voyeurism at its worst.

Members of subordinate groups do not willingly participate in such exchanges but often do so because members of dominant groups control the institutional and symbolic apparatuses of oppression. Racial/ethnic groups, women, and the poor have never had the luxury of being voyeurs of the lives of the privileged. Our ability to survive in hostile settings has hinged on our ability to learn intricate details about the behavior and world view of the powerful and adjust our behavior accordingly. I need only point to the difference in perception of those men and women in abusive relationships. Where men can view their girlfriends and wives as sex objects, helpmates and a collection of stereotypes categories of voyeurism—women must be attuned to every nuance of their partners' behavior. Are women "naturally" better in relating to people with more power than themselves, or have circumstances mandated that men and women develop different skills? . . .

Coming from a tradition where most relationships across difference are squarely rooted in relations of domination and subordination, we have much less experience relating to people as different but equal. The classroom is potentially one powerful and safe space where dialogues among individuals of unequal power relationships can occur. The relationship between Mark, the student in my class, and the domestic worker is typical of a whole series of relationships that people have when they relate across differences in power and privilege. The relationship among Mark and his classmates represents the power of the classroom to minimize those differences so that people of different levels of power can use race, class and gender as categories of analysis in order to generate meaningful dialogues. In this case, the classroom equalized racial difference so that Black students who normally felt silenced spoke out. White students like Mark, generally unaware of how they had been privileged by their whiteness, lost that privilege in the classroom and thus became open to genuine dialogue. . . .

2. Coalitions around Common Causes

A second issue in building relationships and coalitions essential for social change concerns knowing the real reasons for coalition. Just what brings people together? One powerful catalyst fostering group solidarity is the presence of a common enemy. African-American, Hispanic, Asian-American, and women's studies all share the common intellectual heritage of challenging what passes for certified knowledge in the academy. But politically expedient relationships and coalitions like these are fragile because, as June Jordan points out:

> It occurs to me that much organizational grief could be avoided if people understood that partnership in misery does not necessarily provide for partnership for change. When we get the monsters off our backs all of us may want to run in very different directions (1985, 47).

Sharing a common cause assists individuals and groups in maintaining relationships that transcend their differences. Building effective coalitions involves struggling to hear one another and developing empathy for each other's points of view. The coalitions that I have been involved in that lasted and that worked have been those where commitment to a specific issue mandated collaboration as the best strategy for addressing the issue at hand.

Several years ago, masters degree in hand, I chose to teach in an inner-city parochial school in danger of closing. The money was awful, the conditions were poor, but the need was great. In my job, I had to work with a range of individuals who, on the surface, had very little in common. We had White nuns, Black middle class graduate students, Blacks from the "community," some of whom had been incarcerated and/or were affiliated with a range of federal anti-poverty programs. Parents formed another part of this community, Harvard faculty another, and a few well-meaning White liberals from Colorado were sprinkled in for good measure.

As you might imagine, tension was high. Initially, our differences seemed insurmountable. But as time passed, we found a common bond that we each brought to the school. In spite of profound differences in our personal biographies, differences that in other settings would have hampered our ability to relate to one another, we found that we were all deeply committed to the education of Black children. By learning to value each other's commitment and by recognizing that we each had different skills that were essential to actualizing that commitment, we built an effective coalition around a common cause. Our school was successful, and the children we taught benefited from the diversity we offered them.

. . . None of us alone has a comprehensive vision of how race, class and gender operate as categories of analysis or how they might be used as categories of connection. Our personal biographies offer us partial views. Few of us can manage to study race, class and gender simultaneously. Instead, we each know more about some dimensions of this larger story and less about others. . . . Just as the members of the school had special skills to offer to the task of building the school, we have areas of specialization and expertise, whether scholarly, theoretical, pedagogical or within areas of race, class or gender. We do not all have to do the same thing in the same way. Instead, we must support each other's efforts, realizing that they are all part of the larger enterprise of bringing about social change.

3. Building Empathy

A third issue involved in building the types of relationships and coalitions essential for social change concerns the issue of individual accountability. Race, class and gender oppression form the structural backdrop against which we frame our relationship—these are the forces that encourage us to substitute voyeurism . . . for fully human relationships. But while we may not have created this situation, we are each responsible for making individual, personal choices concerning which elements of race, class and gender oppression we will accept and which we will work to change.

One essential component of this accountability involves developing empathy for the experiences of individuals and groups different than ourselves. Empathy begins with taking an interest in the facts of other people's lives, both as individuals and as groups. If you care about me, you should want to know not only the details of my personal biography but a sense of how race, class and gender as categories of analysis created the institutional and symbolic backdrop for my personal biography. How can you hope to assess my character without knowing the details of the circumstances I face?

Moreover, by taking a theoretical stance that we have all been affected by race, class and gender as categories of analysis that have structured our treatment, we open up possibilities for using those same constructs as categories of connection in building empathy. For example, I have a good White woman friend with whom I share common interests and beliefs. But we know that our racial differences have provided us with different experiences. So we talk about them. We do not assume that because I am Black, race has only affected me and not her or that because I am a Black woman, race neutralizes the effect of gender in my life while accenting it in hers. We take those same categories of analysis that have created cleavages in our lives, in this case, categories of race and gender, and use them as categories of connection in building empathy for each other's experiences.

Finding common causes and building empathy is difficult, no matter which side of privilege we inhabit. Building empathy from the dominant side of privilege is difficult, simply because individuals from privileged backgrounds are not encouraged to do so. For example, in order for those of you who are White to develop empathy for the experiences of people of color, you must grapple with how your white skin has privileged you. This is difficult to do, because it not only entails the intellectual process of seeing how whiteness is elevated in institutions and symbols, but it also involves the often painful process of seeing how your whiteness has shaped your personal biography. Intellectual stances against the institutional and symbolic dimensions of racism are generally easier to maintain than sustained self-reflection about how racism has shaped all of our individual biographies. Were and are your fathers, uncles, and grandfathers really more capable than mine, or can their accomplishments be explained in part by the racism members of my family experienced? Did your mothers stand silently by and watch all this happen? More importantly, how have they passed on the benefits of their whiteness to you?

These are difficult questions, and I have tremendous respect for my colleagues and students who are trying to answer them. Since there is no compelling reason to examine the source and meaning of one's own privilege, I know that those who do so have freely chosen this stance. They are making conscious efforts to root out the piece of the oppressor planted within them. To me, they are entitled to the support of people of color in their efforts. Men who declare themselves feminists, members of the middle class who ally themselves with anti-poverty struggles, heterosexuals who support gays and lesbians, are all trying to grow, and their efforts place them far ahead of the majority who never think of engaging in such important struggles.

Building empathy from the subordinate side of privilege is also difficult, but for different reasons. Members of subordinate groups are understandably reluctant to abandon a basic mistrust of members of powerful groups because this basic mistrust has traditionally been central to their survival. As a Black woman, it would be foolish for me to assume that White women, or Black men, or White men or any other group with a history of exploiting African-American women have my best interests at heart. These groups enjoy varying amounts of privilege over me and therefore I must carefully watch them and be prepared for a relation of domination and subordination.

Like the privileged, members of subordinate groups must also work toward replacing judgments by category with new ways of thinking and acting. Refusing to do so stifles prospects for effective coalition and social change. Let me use another example from my own experiences. When I was an undergraduate, I had little time or patience for the theorizing of the privileged. My initial years at a private, elite institution were difficult, not because the coursework was challenging (it was, but that wasn't what distracted me) or because I had to work while my classmates lived on family allowances (I was used to work). The adjustment was difficult because I was surrounded by so many people who took their privilege for granted. Most of them felt entitled to their wealth. That astounded me.

I remember one incident of watching a White woman down the hall in my dormitory try to pick out which sweater to wear. The sweaters were piled up on her bed in all the colors of the rainbow, sweater after sweater. She asked my advice in a way that let me know that choosing a sweater was one of the most important decisions she had to make on a daily basis. Standing knee-deep in her sweaters, I realized how different our lives were. She did not have to worry about maintaining a solid academic average so that she could receive financial aid. Because she was in the majority, she was not treated as a representative of her race. She did not have to consider how her classroom comments or basic existence on campus contributed to the treatment her group would receive. Her allowance protected her from having to work, so she was free to spend her time studying, partying, or in her case, worrying about which sweater to wear. The degree of inequality in our lives and her unquestioned sense of entitlement concerning that inequality offended me. For a while, I categorized all affluent White women as being superficial, arrogant, overly concerned with material possessions, and part of my problem. But had I continued to classify people in this way, I would have missed out on making some very good friends whose discomfort with their inherited or acquired social class privileges pushed them to examine their position.

Since I opened with the words of Audre Lorde, it seems appropriate to close with another of her ideas. . . .

> Each of us is called upon to take a stand. So in these days ahead, as we examine ourselves and each other, our works, our fears, our differences, our sisterhood and survivals, I urge you to tackle what is most difficult for us all, self-scrutiny of our complacencies, the

idea that since each of us believes she is on the side of right, she need not examine her position (1985).

I urge you to examine your position.

REFERENCES

Butler, Johnella. 1989. "Difficult Dialogues." *The Women's Review of Books* 6, no. 5.

Collins, Patricia Hill. 1989. "The Social Construction of Black Feminist Thought." *Signs.* Summer 1989.

Gwaltney, John Langston. 1980. *Drylongso: A Self-Portrait of Black America.* New York: Vintage.

Harding, Sandra. 1986. *The Science Question in Feminism.* Ithaca, New York: Cornell University Press.

Jordan, June. 1985. *On Call: Political Essays.* Boston: South End Press.

Lorde, Audre. 1984. *Sister Outsider.* Trumansberg, New York: The Crossing Press.

———. 1985. "Sisterhood and Survival." Keynote address, conference on the Black Woman Writer and the Diaspora, Michigan State University.

Spelman, Elizabeth. 1982. "Theories of Race and Gender: The Erasure of Black Women." *Quest* 5: 36–32.

Tate, Claudia, ed. 1983. *Black Women Writers at Work.* New York: Continuum.

57

CULTURAL RESISTANCE
Reconstructing Our Own Images

YEN LE ESPIRITU

O ne day/I going to write/about you," wrote Lois-Ann Yamanaka (1993) in "Empty Heart" (p. 548). And Asian Americans did write— "to inscribe our faces on the blank pages and screens of America's hegemonic culture" (Kim, 1993, p. xii). As a result, Asian Americans' objectification as the exotic aliens who are different from, and other than, Euro-Americans has never been absolute. Within the confines of race, class, and gender oppression, Asian Americans have maintained independent self-definitions, challenging controlling images and replacing them with Asian American standpoints. The civil rights and ethnic studies movements of the late 1960s were training grounds for Asian American cultural workers and the development of oppositional projects. Grounded in the U.S. black power movement and in anticolonial struggles of Third World countries, Asian American antihegemonic projects have been unified by a common goal of articulating cultural resistance. Given the historical distortions and misrepresentations of Asian Americans in mainstream media, most cultural projects produced by Asian American men and women perform the important tasks of correcting histories, shaping legacies, creating new cultures, constructing a politics of resistance, and opening spaces for the forcibly excluded (Kim, 1993, p. xiii; Fung, 1994, p. 165).

Fighting the exoticization of Asian Americans has been central in the ongoing work of cultural resistance. As discussed above, Asian Americans, however rooted in this country, are represented as recent transplants from Asia or as bearers of an exotic culture. The Chinese American playwright Frank Chin noted that New York critics of his play *Chickencoop Chinaman* complained in the early 1970s that his characters did not speak, dress, or act "like Orientals" (Kim, 1982, p. xv). Similarly, a reviewer described Maxine Hong Kingston's *The Woman Warrior* as a tale of "East meets West" and praised the book for its "myths rich and varied as Chinese brocade"—even though *The Woman Warrior* is deliberately anti-exotic and anti-nostalgic

Espiritu, Yen Le. "Cultural Resistance: Reconstructing Our Own Images." From *Asian American Women and Men: Labor, Laws, and Love*. Thousand Oaks, CA: Sage Publications, 1997, pp. 98–107. Reprinted by permission of the publisher.

(quoted in Kim, 1982, p. xvi). In both of these examples, the qualifier *American* has been blithely excised from the term *Asian American*.

Asian American cultural workers simply do not accept the exotic, one-dimensional caricatures of themselves in U.S. mass media. In the preface of *Aiiieeeee!*, a landmark collection of Asian American writers (in this case, Chinese, Japanese, and Filipinos), published in the mid-1970s, the editors announced that the anthology, and the title *Aiiieeeee!* itself, challenged the exoticization of Asian Americans.

> The pushers of white American culture . . . pictured the yellow man
> as something that when wounded, sad, angry, or swearing, or
> wondering whined, shouted, or screamed "aiiieeeee!" Asian
> America, so long ignored and forcibly excluded from creative
> participation in American culture, is wounded, sad, angry,
> swearing, and wondering, and this is his AIIIEEEEE!!! It is more
> than a whine, shout, or scream. It is fifty years of our whole voice.
> (Chan et al., 1974, p. xii)

The publication of *Aiiieeeee!* gave Asian American writers visibility and credibility and sparked other oppositional projects. Jessica Hagedorn, a Filipina American writer, described the legacy of *Aiiieeeee!*: "We could not be ignored; suddenly, we were no longer silent. Like other writers of color in America, we were beginning to challenge the long-cherished concepts of a xenophobic literary canon dominated by white heterosexual males" (Hagedorn, 1993, p. xviii). Inspired by *Aiiieeeee!* and by other "irreverent and blasphemous" American writers, Hagedorn created an anthology of contemporary Asian American fiction in 1993—"a book I wanted to read but had never been available to me" (Hagedorn, 1993, p. xxx). In the tradition of *Aiiieeeee!*, the title of Hagedorn's anthology, *Charlie Chan Is Dead*, is vigorously political, defying and stamping out the vestiges of a "fake 'Asian' pop icon" (Hagedorn, 1993, p. xxi). In the anthology's preface, Elaine Kim (1993) contested the homogenization of Asian Americans by juxtaposing the one-dimensional Charlie Chan to the many ways of being Asian American in contemporary United States:

> Charlie Chan is dead, never to be revived. Gone for good his
> yellowface asexual bulk, his fortune-cookie English, his stereotyp-
> ical Orientalist version of "the [Confucian] Chinese family," chal-
> lenged by an array of characters, some hip and articulate, some
> brooding and sexy, some insolent and others innocent, but all as
> unexpected as a Korean American who writes in French, a Chinese-
> Panamanian-German who longs too late to know her father, a mean
> Japanese American grandmother, a Chinese American flam-dive, or
> a teenaged Filipino American male prostitute. Instead of "model
> minorities," we find human beings with rich and complex pasts
> and brave, often flamboyant dreams of the future. (p. xiii)

Taking up this theme, Wayne Chang's commercial film *Chan Is Missing* (1981) offers a range of Chinatown characters who indirectly convey the message that Chinese Americans, like other Americans, are heterogeneous (Chan, 1994, p. 530). Portraying Asian Americans in all our contradictions and complexities—as exiled, assimilated, rebellious, noble—Asian American cultural projects reveal heterogeneity rather than "producing regulating ideas of cultural unity or integration" (Lowe, 1994, p. 53). In so doing, these projects destabilize the dominant racist discourse that constructs Asians as a homogeneous group who are "all alike" and readily conform to "types" such as the Yellow Peril, the Oriental mastermind, and the sexy Suzie Wong (Lowe, 1991).

Asian American cultural projects also deconstruct the myth of the benevolent United States promised to women and men from Asia. Carlos Bulosan's *America Is in the Heart* (1943/1973), one of the core works of Asian American literature, challenges the narrative of the United States as the land of opportunity. Seduced by the promise of individual freedom through education, the protagonist Carlos discovers that as a Filipino immigrant in the United States, he is denied access to formal schooling. This disjunction between the promise of education and the unequal access of different racial and economic groups to that education—reinforced by Carlos's observations of the exploitation, marginality, and violence suffered by his compatriots in the United States—challenges his faith in the promise of U.S. democracy and abundance (Lowe, 1994, p. 56). John Okada's *No-No Boy* (1957) is another searing indictment of U.S. racist hysteria. In this portrayal of the aftermath of the internment of Japanese Americans during World War II, the protagonist, Ichiro, angrily refuses to adjust to his postinternment and postimprisonment circumstances, thus dramatizing the Asian American subject's refusal to accept the subordinating terms of assimilation (Lowe, 1994, p. 59). In the following excerpt from the poem by Cao Tan, "Tomorrow I Will Be Home," a Vietnamese refugee describes the emasculating effect of U.S. society:

> Tomorrow I will be home and someone will ask
> What have you learned in the States?
> If you want to give me a broom
> I'll tell you, I am a first class janitor.
> I wash dishes much faster than the best housewife
> And do a vacuum job better than any child
> Every day I run like a madman in my brand new car
> Every night I bury my head in my pillow and cry. . . .
>
> Bich (1989)

To reject the myth of a benevolent United States is also to refute ideological racism: the justification of inequalities through a set of controlling images that attribute physical and intellectual traits to racially defined groups (Hamamoto, 1994, p. 3). In the 1980 autobiographical fiction *China Men*, Maxine Hong Kingston smashed the controlling image of the emasculated Asian man by foregrounding the legalized racism that turned immigrant Chinese "men" into "women" at the turn of the century. In his search for the Gold Mountain, the novel's male protagonist Tan Ao finds instead the Land of Women, where he is caught and transformed into an Oriental courtesan. Because Kingston reveals at the end of the legend that the Land of Women was in North America, readers familiar with Chinese American history will readily see that "the ignominy suffered by Tan Ao in a foreign land symbolizes the emasculation of Chinamen by the dominant culture" (Cheung, 1990, p. 240). Later in the novel, the father's failure as a provider—his emasculation—inverts the sexual roles in the family. His silence and impotent rage deepen as his wife takes on active power in the family and assumes the "masculine" traits of aggressiveness and authority. As a means of releasing his sense of frustration and powerlessness in racist America, the father lapses into silence, screams "wordless male screams in his sleep," and spouts furious misogynistic curses that frighten his daughter (Sledge, 1980, p. 10). The author/narrator Maxine traces her father's abusive behavior back to his feeling of emasculation in America: "We knew that it was to feed us you had to endure demons and physical labor" (cited in Goellnicht, 1992, p. 201). Similarly, in Louis Chu's 1961 novel *Eat a Bowl of Tea,* the protagonist's sexual impotence represents the social powerlessness of generations of Chinatown bachelors prevented by discriminatory laws and policies from establishing a traditional family life (Kim, 1982, p. xviii).

More recently, Steven Okazaki's film *American Sons* (1995)[1] tells the stories of four Asian American men who reveal how incidents of prejudice and bigotry shaped their identity and affected the way they perceived themselves and society. About his film, Okazaki (1995) explained, "Prejudice, bigotry, and violence twist and demean individual lives. *American Sons* looks at difficult issues, such as hate violence, in order to show this intimate and disturbing examination of the deep psychological damage that racism causes over generations" (n.p.). Asian American men's increasing involvement in hip-hop—a highly masculinized cultural form and a distinctly American phenomenon—is yet another contemporary denouncement of this stereotype of themselves as "effeminate, nerdy, asocial foreigners" (Choe, 1996). By exposing the role of the large society in the emasculation and oppression of Asian men, Kingston, Chu, and Okazaki invalidated the naturalization and normalization of Asian men's asexuality in U.S. popular culture.

Finally, Asian American cultural workers reject the narrative of salvation: the myth that Asian women (and a feminized Asia) are saved, through sexual relations with white men (and a masculinized United States), from the excesses of their own culture. Instead, they underscore the considerable potential for abuse in these inherently unequal relationships. Writing in Vietnamese, transplanted Vietnamese writer Tran Dieu Hang described the gloomy existence of Vietnamese women in sexist and racist U.S. society—an accursed land that singles out women, especially immigrant women, for oppression and violence. Her short story "Roi Ngay Van Moi" ("There Will Come New Days"; 1986) depicts the brutal rape of a young refugee woman by her American sponsor despite her tearful pleas in limited English (Tran, 1993, pp. 72–73). Marianne Villanueva's short story "Opportunity" (1991) also calls attention to the sexualization and racialization of Asian women. As the protagonist Nina, a "mail-order bride" from the Philippines, enters the hotel lobby to meet her American fiance, the bellboys snicker and whisper *puta,* whore: a reminder that U.S. economic and cultural colonization of the Philippines always forms the backdrop to any relations between Filipinos and Americans (Wong, 1993, p. 53). Characterizing Filipino American literature as "literature of exile," Oscar Campomanes (1992) underscored the legacy of U.S. colonization of the Philippines: "The signifiers 'Filipinos' and 'Philippines' evoke colonialist meanings and cultural redactions which possess inordinate power to shape the fates of the writers and of Filipino peoples everywhere" (p. 52). Theresa Hak Kyung Cha's *Dictee* (1982), a Korean American text, likewise challenges the myth of U.S. benevolence in Asia by tracing the impact of colonial and imperial damage and dislocation on the Korean subject (Lowe, 1994, p. 61). As Sau-Ling Cynthia Wong (1993) suggested, "To the extent that most typical cases of Asian immigration to the United States stem from an imbalance of resources writ large in the world economy, it holds in itself the seed of exploitation" (p. 53).

CONTROLLING IMAGES, GENDER, AND CULTURAL NATIONALISM

Cultural nationalism has been crucial in Asian Americans' struggles for self-determination. Emerging in the early 1970s, this unitary Asian American identity was primarily racial, male, and heterosexual. Asian American literature produced in those years highlighted Chinese and Japanese American male perspectives, obscuring gender and other intercommunity differences (Kim, 1993). Asian American male writers, concerned with recuperating their identities as men and as Americans, objectified both white and Asian women in their writings (Kim, 1990, p. 70). In a controversial essay entitled "Racist Love," Frank Chin and Jeffrey Paul Chan (1972) pointed to the stereotype of the emasculated Asian American man:

> The white stereotype of Asian is unique in that it is the only racial stereotype completely devoid of manhood. Our nobility is that of an efficient housewife. At our worst we are contemptible because we are womanly, effeminate, devoid of all the traditionally masculine qualities of originality, daring, physical courage, creativity. (p. 68)

In taking whites to task for their racist debasement of Asian American men, however, Chin and Chan succumbed to the influence of Eurocentric gender ideology, particularly its emphasis on oppositional dichotomous sex roles (Collins, 1991, p. 184). In a critique of "Racist Love," King-Kok Cheung

(1990) contended that Chin and Chan buttressed patriarchy "by invoking gender stereotypes, by disparaging domestic efficiency as 'feminine,' and by slotting desirable traits such as originality, daring, physical courage, and creativity under the rubric of masculinity" (p. 237). Similarly, Wong (1993) argued that in their influential "Introduction" to *Aiiieeeee! An Anthology of Asian American Writers* (1974), Chan, Chin, Inada, and Wong operated on the premise that a true Asian American sensibility is "non-Christian, nonfeminine, and nonimmigrant" (p. 8).

Though limited and limiting, a masculine cultural nationalist agenda appealed to Asian American activists because of its potential to oppose and disrupt the logic of racial domination. In the following excerpt, Elaine Kim (1993), a pioneer in the field of Asian American literature, explained the appeal of cultural nationalism:

> Certainly it was possible for me as a Korean American female to accept the fixed masculinist Asian American identity posited in Asian American cultural nationalism, even when it rendered invisible or at least muted women's oppression, anger, and ways of loving and interpreted Korean Americans as imperfect imitations of Chinese Americans; because I could see in everyday life that not all material and psychic violence to women of color comes from men, and because, as my friends use to say, "No Chinese [American] ever called me a 'Gook.' " (p. x)

Kim's statement suggests that for Asian American women, and for other women of color, gender is only a part of a larger pattern of unequal social relations. Despite the constraints of patriarchy, racism inscribes these women's lives and binds them to Asian American men in what Collins (1991) called a "love and trouble" tradition (p. 184).

Because the racial oppression of Asian Americans involves the "feminization" of Asian men (Said, 1979), Asian American women are caught between the need to expose the problems of male privilege and the desire to unite with men to contest the overarching racial ideology that confines them both. As Cheung (1990) suggested, Asian American women may be simultaneously sympathetic and angry toward the men in their ethnic community: sensitive to the men's marginality but resentful of their sexism (p. 239). Maxine Hong Kingston's writings seem to reflect these conflicting emotions. As discussed above, in the opening legend of *China Men*, the male protagonist Tan Ao is captured in the Land of Women (North America), where he is forced to become a woman—to have his feet bound, his ears pierced, his eyebrows plucked, his cheeks and lips painted. Cheung (1990) argued that this legend is double-edged, pointing not only to the racist debasement of Chinese Americans in their adopted country but also to the subjugation of Chinese women both in China and in the United States (p. 240). Although the effeminization suffered by Tan Ao is brutal, it is the same mutilation that many Chinese women were for centuries forced to bear. According to Goellnicht's (1992) reading of Kingston's work, this opening myth suggests that the author both deplores the emasculation of her forefathers by mainstream America and critiques the Confucian patriarchal practices of her ancestral homeland (p. 194). In *China Men,* Kingston also showed no acceptance of sexist practices by immigrant men. The father in this novel/autobiography is depicted as a broken man who attempts to reassert male authority by denigrating those who are even more powerless—the women and children in his family (Cheung, 1990, p. 241; Goellnicht, 1992, p. 200).

Along the same lines, Maxine Hong Kingston's *The Woman Warrior* (1977) reveals the narrator's contradictory attitudes toward her childhood "home," which is simultaneously a site of "woman hatred" and an area of resistance against the racism of the dominant culture. The community that nourishes her imagination and suffuses her with warmth is the same community that relegates women to an inferior position, limiting them to the role of serving men (Rabine, 1987, pp. 477–478). In the following passage, the narrator voices her mixed feelings toward the Chinese American community:

> I looked at their ink drawings of poor people snagging their neighbors' flotage with long flood hooks and pushing the girl babies on down the river. And I had to get out of hating range. . . . I refuse to shy my way anymore through our Chinatown, which tasks me with the old sayings and the stories. The swordswoman and I are not so dissimilar. May my people understand the resemblance so that I can return to them. (Kingston, 1977, p. 62)

Similarly, in a critique of Asian American sexual politics, Kayo Hatta's short video *Otemba* (1988) depicts a girl's-eye view of the final days of her mother's pregnancy as her father hopes and prays for the birth of a boy (see Tajima, 1991, p. 26).

Stripped of the privileges of masculinity, some Asian American men have attempted to reassert male authority by subordinating feminism to nationalist concerns. Lisa Lowe (1991) argued that this identity politics displaces gender differences into a false opposition of "nationalism" and "assimilation." From this limited perspective, Asian American feminists who expose Asian American sexism are cast as "assimilationist," as betraying Asian American "nationalism." Maxine Hong Kingston's *The Woman Warrior* (1977) and Amy Tan's *The Joy Luck Club* (1989) are the targets of such nationalist criticisms. Frank Chin, Ben Tong, and others have accused these and other women novelists of feminizing Asian American literature by exaggerating the community's patriarchal structure, thus undermining the power of Asian American men to combat the racist stereotypes of the dominant white culture. For example, when Kingston's *The Woman Warrior* received favorable reviews, Chin accused her of attempting to "cash in on the feminist fad" (Chan, 1994, p. 528). Another Asian American male had this to say about the movie *The Joy Luck Club:*

> The movie was powerful. But it could have been powerful *and inclusive,* if at least one of the Asian male characters was portrayed

as something other than monstrously evil or simply wimpy. We are used to this message coming out of Hollywood, but it disturbed me deeply to hear the same message coming from Amy Tan and Wayne Wang—people of my own color. (Yoon, 1993)

Whereas Chin and others cast this tension in terms of nationalism and assimilationism, Lisa Lowe (1991) argued that it is more a debate between nationalist and feminist concerns in Asian American discourse. This insistence on a fixed masculinist identity, according to Lowe (1991), "can be itself a colonial figure used to displace the challenges of heterogeneity, or subalternity, by casting them as assimilationist or anti-ethnic" (pp. 33–34).

But cultural nationalism need not be patriarchal. Rejecting the ideology of oppositional dichotomous sex roles, Asian American cultural workers have also engaged in cross-gender projects. In a recent review of Asian American independent filmmaking, Renee Tajima (1991) reported that some of the best feminist films have been made by Asian American men. For example, Arthur Dong's *Lotus* (1987) exposes women's exploitation through the practice of footbinding (Tajima, 1991, p. 24). Asian American men have also made use of personal documentary, in both diary and autobiographical form—an approach known to be the realm of women filmmakers. Finally, there is no particular gender affiliation in subject matters: Just as Arthur Dong profiles his mother in *Sewing Woman,* Lori Tsang portrays her father's life in *Chinaman's Choice* (Tajima, 1991, p. 24).

CONCLUSION

Ideological representations of gender and sexuality are central in the exercise and maintenance of racial, patriarchal, and class domination. In the Asian American case, this ideological racism has taken seemingly contrasting forms: Asian men have been cast as both hypersexual and asexual, and Asian women have been rendered both superfeminine and masculine. Although in apparent disjunction, both forms exit to define, maintain, and justify white male supremacy. The racialization of Asian American manhood and womanhood underscores the interconnections of race, gender, and class. As categories of difference, race and gender relations do not parallel but intersect and confirm each other, and it is the complicity among these categories of difference that enables U.S. elites to justify and maintain their cultural, social, and economic power. Responding to the ideological assaults on their gender identities, Asian American cultural workers have engaged in a wide range of oppositional projects to defend Asian American manhood and womanhood. In the process, some have embraced a masculinist cultural nationalism, a stance that marginalizes Asian American women and their needs. Though sensitive to the emasculation of Asian American men, Asian American feminists have pointed out that Asian American nationalism insists on a fixed masculinist identity, thus obscuring gender differences. Though divergent, both the nationalist and feminist positions advance the dichotomous stance of man or woman, gender or race or class, without recognizing the complex relationality of these categories of oppression. It is only when Asian Americans recognize the intersections of race, gender, and class that we can transform the existing hierarchical structure.

NOTE

1. I thank Takeo Wong for calling my attention to this film.

REFERENCES

Bich, N. N. (Ed.). (1989). *War and Exile: A Vietnamese Anthology.* Springfield, VA: Vietnam PEN Abroad.

Bulosan, C. (1973). *America Is in the Heart: A Personal History.* Seattle: Washington University Press. (Original work published 1946.)

Campomanes, O. (1992). Filipinos in the United States and Their Literature of Exile. In S. G. Lim & A. Ling (Eds.), *Reading the Literatures of Asian America* (pp. 49–78). Philadelphia: Temple University Press.

Cha, T. H. K. (1982). *Dictee.* New York: Tanam.

Chan, J. P., Chin, F., Inada, L. F., & Wong, S. (1974). *Aiiieeeee! An Anthology of Asian American Writers.* Washington, DC: Howard University Press.

Chan, S. (1994). The Asian American Movement, 1960s–1980s. In S. Chan, D. H. Daniels, M. T. Garcia, & T. P. Wilson (Eds.), *Peoples of Color in the American West* (pp. 525–533). Lexington, MA: D. C. Heath.

Cheung, K. K. (1990) The Woman Warrior versus the Chinaman Pacific: Must a Chinese American Critic Choose Between Feminism and Heroism? In M. Hirsch & E. F. Keller (Eds.), *Conflicts in Feminism* (pp. 234–251). New York: Routledge.

Chin, F., & Chan, J. P. (1972). Racist Love. In R. Kostelanetz (Ed.), *Seeing through Shuck* (pp. 65–79). New York: Ballantine.

Choe, Laura. (1996, February 10). "Versions": Asian Americans in Hip Hop. Paper presented at the California Studies Conference, Long Beach, CA.

Chu, L. (1961). *Eat a Bowl of Tea.* Seattle: University of Washington Press.

Collins, P. H. (1990). *Black Feminist Thought: Knowledge, Consciousness, and the Politics of Empowerment.* New York: Routledge.

Dong, A. (Director). (1982). *Sewing Woman* [Film]. San Francisco: Deep Focus Productions.

Fung, R. (1994). Seeing Yellow: Asian Identities in Film and Video. In K. Aguilar–San Juan (Ed.), *The State of Asian America* (pp. 161–171). Boston: South End.

Goellnicht, D. C. (1992). Tang Ao in America: Male Subject Positions in *China Men.* In S. G. Lim and A. Ling (Eds.), *Reading the Literature of Asian America* (pp. 191–212). Philadelphia: Temple University Press.

Hagedorn, J. (1993). Introduction: "Role of Dead Man Requires Very Little Acting." In J. Hagedorn (Ed.), *Charlie Chan Is Dead: An Anthology of Contemporary Asian American Fiction* (pp. xxi–xxx). New York: Penguin.

Hamamoto, D. Y. (1994). *Monitored Peril: Asian Americans and the Politics of Representation*. Minneapolis: University of Minnesota Press.

Kim, E. (1982). *Asian American Literature: An Introduction to the Writings and Their Social Context*. Philadelphia: Temple University Press.

———. (1990). "Such Opposite Creatures" Men and Women in Asian American Literature. *Michigan Quarterly Review, 29*, 68–93.

———. (1993). Preface. In J. Hagedorn (Ed.), *Charlie Chan Is Dead: An Anthology of Contemporary Asian American Fiction* (pp. vii–xiv). New York: Penguin.

Kingston, M. H. (1977). *The Woman Warrior.* New York: Vintage.

———. (1980). *China Men.* New York: Knopf.

Lowe, L. (1991). Heterogeneity, Hybridity, Multiplicity: Marking Asian American Difference. *Diaspora, 1*, 24–44.

———. (1994). Canon, Institutionalization, Identity: Contradictions for Asian American Studies. In D. Palumbo-Liu (Ed.), *The Ethnic Canon: Histories, Institutions, and Interventions* (pp. 48–68). Minneapolis: University of Minnesota Press.

Okada, J. (1957). *No-No Boy.* Rutland, VT: Charles E. Tuttle.

Okazaki, S. (1995). *American Sons.* Promotional brochure for the film of that name.

Rabine, L. W. (1987). No Lost Paradise: Social Gender and Symbolic Gender in the Writings of Maxine Hong Kingston. *Signs: Journal of Women in Culture and Society, 12*, 471–511.

Said, E. (1979). *Orientalism.* New York: Random House.

Sledge, L. C. (1980). Maxine Kingston's *China Men:* The Family Historian as Epic Poet. *Melus,* 7-3-22.

Tajima, R. (1991). Moving the Image: Asian American Independent Filmmaking 1970–1990. In R. Leong (Ed.), *Moving the Image: Independent Asian Pacific American Media Arts* (pp. 10–33). Los Angeles: University of California at Los Angeles, Asian American Studies Center, and Visual Communications, Southern California Asian American Studies Central.

Tran, Q. P. (1993). Exile and Home in Contemporary Vietnamese American Feminine Writing. *Amerasia Journal, 19*, 71–83.

Villanueva, M. (1991). *Ginseng and Other Tales from Manila.* Corvallis, OR: Calyx.

Wong, S. L. C. (1993). *Reading Asian American Literature: From Necessity to Extravagance.* Princeton, NJ: Princeton University Press.

Yamanaka, L. A. (1993). Empty Heart. In J. Hagedorn (Ed.), *Charlie Chan Is Dead: An Anthology of Contemporary Asian American Fiction* (pp. 544–550). New York: Penguin.

Yoon, D. D. (1993, November 26). Asian American Male: Wimp or What? *Asian Week,* p. 16.

58

"NO EVICTIONS. WE WON'T MOVE!"
The Struggle to Save the I-Hotel

LARRY SOLOMON

"This land is too valuable to permit poor people to park on it."
—JUSTIN HERMAN, FORMER EXECUTIVE DIRECTOR OF THE
SAN FRANCISCO REDEVELOPMENT AGENCY, 1970[1]

The land Herman was referring to in the quote above was a city block in the heart of downtown San Francisco's growing Financial District. One of the most famous skylines in the world was being reshaped. The "Wall Street of the West" had been expanding for years and the 800 block of Kearny Street was prime real estate. It was also the block where the International Hotel stood.

And it became the block where the rights of people of color who were low-income and elderly tenants were fought over for nearly a decade. The movement to save the "I-Hotel," as it was called, is one of the most important chapters in the history of Asian American struggle and of housing conflicts. It was a protracted campaign that eventually drew hundreds of people into the ranks of activism. It was, as the *San Francisco Chronicle* put it, "a cause celebre for the politically engaged."[2]

In the late 1970s, the I-Hotel was just about all that was left of Manilatown, once a thriving community of mostly male Filipino immigrants that covered 10 blocks between San Francisco's Chinatown and Financial districts. During the 1920s and 1930s, the I-Hotel (built the year after the devastating 1906 earthquake) became home to thousands of seasonal Asian laborers. Many young Filipino and Chinese men who worked as day laborers, dishwashers, messengers and at any other profession that was deemed "appropriate for Orientals" lived there. So did old-timers, who settled in San Francisco following years of working in seasonal harvests, on merchant ships, in canneries in Alaska and Washington, and so on, up and down the Pacific Coast. Many of the old-timers, though not citizens, had served in both World Wars, but the U.S. government denied some of them promised benefits after the fighting stopped.

From *Roots of Justice: Stories of Organizing in Communities of Color.* Oakland, CA: Chardon Press, pp. 98–107.

Asian women were, for the most part, excluded from entering the U.S. until 1965, thereby preventing most of the men who lived in Chinatown and Manilatown from establishing families. Further, California's antimiscegenation laws prevented Filipinos and other Asians from marrying outside the race. Nevertheless, "race preservation" was the concern of white elite California in the 1930s; testimony before the House Committee on Immigration and Naturalization warned that "the Filipinos are . . . a social menace as they will not leave our white girls alone and frequently intermarry."[3]

Yet a different kind of family life persisted, as the bachelor society of Filipino men preserved their culture in the pool halls, barber shops and other Manilatown meeting places. As one of the Filipino elders who lived in the I-Hotel remarked in 1987, "Have here a good neighborhood, and good and very kind country men, old and new friends. . . . I have stayed here so long that I call this hotel my home."[4]

"It was a good place for brown people—Filipinos—specifically coming for jobs in Alaska or on the farms—a unique place where you met friends to guide you and maybe recommend you for jobs," said longtime resident Nick Napeek.[5]

Fellow resident Peter Yamamoto echoed the sentiment:

> Living in the I-Hotel and Manilatown-Chinatown, you realize the
> need of Filipinos and Chinese to live within their community,
> where they could find the day-to-day things that they could not
> find living in, say, the Tenderloin—a cheap hotel, their food, their
> friends. [It] was a beautiful place, with camaraderie.[6]

URBAN RENEWAL = FILIPINO REMOVAL

After World War II, San Francisco made plans to expand its downtown business sector, particularly the area around the Financial District. Redevelopment was the buzzword of the time and more and more corporate headquarters moved into the area. As the high-rises went up during the building boom of the late 1950s and 1960s, many small businesses and residential hotels were torn down.

The city's spreading "urban renewal" project had already torn through the heart of the Fillmore District, west of downtown, decimating hundreds of homes and displacing thousands of residents in the city's largest Black community. But it was the Financial District redevelopment that became top priority for the city's expansion, as the opening of the Bay Area Rapid Transit system in the mid-1970s made it easier for white-collar workers to commute from the outlying areas into downtown to work in the major banks, trading companies and other corporate entities moving into the area.

The effect, of course, was to change the landscape of the community. Manilatown was devastated. Ten full blocks of low-cost housing, restaurants, barber shops, markets, clubs and other businesses that benefited a Filipino community that numbered around 10,000 people were destroyed.

By the end of the expansion, thousands of people had been displaced. More than 4,000 low-income units were torn down in favor of high-rise buildings (including the famous Transamerica Pyramid and the Bank of America's world headquarters) and parking lots. Four out of every five low-cost residential hotels in the area were gone by the end of the 1970s.

One of the hotels slated for demolition was the International Hotel, where tenants could rent rooms for only 50 dollars a month. In the late 1960s, most of the hotel's tenants were poor, and almost all were elderly—in the community they were referred to as manongs, an Ilocano term of respect for the "old-timers." One of the manongs, Felix Ayson, remarked in 1986, "Most of my time and my years in America I spend in this hotel, so it is my home. Whenever no work in the country, I come here and find a job in the city, and I live here." Ayson had lived in the I-Hotel since 1928.[7]

More than three million elderly people in America's cities depended on low-cost residential hotels in the 1950s and 1960s, but by the close of the 1960s, the hotels had become synonymous with urban decay and blight as politicians and investors sought to justify redevelopment.

In March 1968, Milton Meyer and Company, headed by San Francisco business magnate Walter Shorenstein, bought the I-Hotel and made plans to construct a multilevel parking lot on the site. Shorenstein secured a demolition permit in September, and in October he ordered the evictions of the 196 tenants, giving them until the first of the year to be out. "We deeply regret having to disrupt the lives of these good people," Shorenstein said as the eviction notices went out.[8]

In the dizzying pace of downtown redevelopment, the sale of the I-Hotel and the eviction notices to its tenants were barely noticed, except by a few, including Joaquin Legaspi, director of the Manilatown Information Center, a multiservice provider for the community. San Francisco State College professor Jovina Navarro, who had been active in the Filipino community, also learned of the evictions and put out the first word on the college campus, leading to a series of highly publicized protests, led by newly politicized Asian American students at San Francisco State and UC Berkeley. At the time, students at both campuses were beginning to press for ethnic studies programs and were also in the midst of protests over the war in Vietnam.

Many students involved in the campus-based Third World Liberation Front sought to practice the principles espoused in their new ethnic studies and consciousness movements; the idea, a novel one on college campuses, was to go back into the community and work for justice. The early I-Hotel demonstrations became a political introduction for large numbers of Asian American students in search of their cultural roots.

"It was a generation of a lot of activism," recalled Terry Bautista, who was active in the defense of the manongs. "We were looking for our own voice. The I-Hotel struggle was a good application of what ethnic studies was all about— go study your community and look for justice where there isn't any. There was just so much going on at the time. You couldn't help but be political."[9]

"Fight to Save the I-Hotel" became a battle cry among young activists and organizers.

The sudden interest in the hotel and publicity from the community soon led to a change in direction; a lease agreement between Milton Meyer and Company and the United Filipino Association (UFA), led by Ness Aquino, was drawn up and plans to make the land into a parking lot were shelved. But before the agreement could be signed, a fire broke out in the building, killing three tenants and giving Shorenstein justification to cancel the agreement and go ahead with demolition.

RETURNING RESOURCES TO THE COMMUNITY

The community continued to resist demolition by staging increasingly loud demonstrations, and most of the elderly tenants, including some who had been at the hotel for more than 20 years, refused to leave. Eventually, the UFA secured a three-year lease agreement, promising to bring the building up to housing code standards within a year. Volunteers, mostly from UC Berkeley's Asian American Studies program, worked to refurbish the hotel. Floyd Huen, who headed the UC program, later recalled using student fees in the project and justifying it as "returning resources to the community."[10]

Over the next several years, the fight over who controlled the hotel was tied up in the courts. The UFA dissolved and in its place the International Hotel Tenants Association (IHTA) was organized, led by Emil de Guzman.

Bill Sorro, in his 20s at the time of the demonstrations but not a student, was the only young person living in the I-Hotel at the time. Between 1970 and 1974, he called the three-story building his home:

> I was just another tenant; I paid my $45 a month in rent, I mean, I had responsibilities there—I painted, cleaned bathrooms, really whatever needed to be done. I wanted to get involved in the Filipino community, so I knew the issues, but I really saw myself as another tenant. . . . I related to the old-timers. I was part of them. They were like the relatives in my family. They were like my uncles, you know.
>
> People just focus on the big events and the evictions, but you have to understand that there were nine years of hard work that we put into that hotel. It was day-to-day, outside of the media spotlight, by a whole spectrum of people, across race and class lines. We really made good connections with the old-timers and were there for more than just demonstrations. We did all the related work that isn't very glamorous. We helped them understand their rights to Social Security and Medicare. I mean, these were immigrants and many of them just didn't know.
>
> Also, as part of our work as budding revolutionaries, we tried to figure out how to change the environment of the community of

people in the hotel to see themselves as being part of more than just their locked-in building. We provided social activities, we got a bus from UC Berkeley and took them out for day trips to the beach to have a barbecue and that kind of thing. I think we really succeeded in developing a trust between the young people and the tenants. Now they may not have agreed with all of our revolutionary rhetoric, but they were like your grandparents. They understood your heart and showed a lot of patience with you. It was a special thing.[11]

The International Hotel had become a symbol of more than just a housing struggle. For the many people who became intimately involved with the residents and their community, the hotel became a matter of the heart. The folks who worked to bring the hotel back from the brink of destruction were also able to use the media to communicate that, after all, these were elders who were being threatened. Hotel organizers were able to sway public opinion and, as a result, make the city's political leaders feel the heat. It appeared as though the hotel was going to survive its most direct challenge.

Tired of the bad press and the extensive community support of the hotel at any mention of demolition, Shorenstein secretly sold it in 1973 to a Thai businessman named Supasit Mahaguna and his Four Seas Investment Corporation for just over $850,000. Four Seas applied for a demolition permit but was immediately met with more protests and litigation. Finally, in 1976, Superior Court Judge Ira Brown, a former San Francisco landlord himself, ruled in favor of Four Seas and ordered the evictions. San Francisco Mayor George Moscone attempted to broker a deal that would have the city buy the hotel and sell it back to the tenants, but at $1.3 million, the price was impossible.

Eventually, the eviction order stuck and the San Francisco Sheriff's Office and Police Department were ordered to re-post eviction notices.

NO EVICTIONS! WE WON'T MOVE!

Word spread among people who had initially defended the hotel and who had promised support if another attempt was ever made to kick the tenants out. For Asian American activists and organizers, who had been politicized in the heat of the first battle and were presently working in the community, word that eviction notices were going up was a beacon call.

On January 7, 1977, more than 350 supporters from the IHTA, Asian Community Center, Kearny Street Workshop and other community groups and organizations in solidarity with the tenants formed a human barricade to prevent the police from posting the notices. Chanting "No eviction! We won't move!" the demonstrators forced the city and the police into retreat. The next week, after notices were finally posted, some 5,000 people linked arms around the entire block to prevent the forced eviction of tenants. The show of resistance and "threat of violence" forced Judge Brown to grant an immediate stay of eviction. Brown cited unconfirmed reports that tenant supporters had been stockpiling automatic weapons and gasoline.

In May, however, a court ruling strengthened Four Seas' claim of ownership and eviction notices again appeared. Again they were met by massive demonstrations, including a night when another human fence grew eight people deep in front of the hotel. "We have been terrorized by insecurity and fear," tenant Felix Ayson shouted to supporters during the eighth eviction attempt in the now nine-year-long struggle. "We are here to fight for our right to stay!" Again, the tenants won a stay of eviction.[12]

On August 2, I-Hotel tenants Wahat Tampao, Nita Radar, Benny Gallo, Ayson and others conducted a sit-in at City Hall to pressure the mayor and Board of Supervisors to support the struggle. The next day, however, the conservative California Supreme Court lifted the stay and reordered the evictions. This time sheriff's deputies and city police came with a show of force stronger than before. Again they were met with resistance.

Terry Bautista remembers the duties of the young organizers leading up to the evictions:

> We all took on any assignments that were needed. Some were needed to work the phones. Some were lookouts on the roof. I remember 20 or more people sleeping on a stage inside the building, while large numbers of other people were helping the tenants. Some would stay with them in their rooms to make sure that nothing happened to them. My job was to be a lookout [for police] at the front door. It was basically sentry duty. The cops could come at any time and we had to be ready. It was like we were getting ready for war.[13]

The plan of action for the inevitable day when the police would come with full force was to form the largest human barricade possible, seven to eight rows deep around the block with even more people layered inside the building, up every step, outside every room. Even the Reverend Jim Jones (yes, *that* Jim Jones) of the People's Temple had mobilized more than 300 of his followers and arrived on the scene in seven busloads. "Just imagine, it was wall-to-wall people around the whole block," Bautista says. "It was a constant mass of protest. It really was incredible."

The police had cordoned off a two-square-mile perimeter to stop what probably would have been thousands more who intended to come to the hotel in support of the tenants.

Tenant Nick Napeek remembers getting home around 4 P.M. on the night of August 3. He had heard that the police were coming that night. Around 10 P.M. he started telling the other, older tenants on his side of the building to go inside their rooms and lock up.

The riot police could be seen blocks away practicing maneuvers in full riot gear; a battalion of mounted police had their horses ready for action.

Finally at 3 A.M. on August 4, the cry from somewhere in the crowd came: "They're coming!" Some 400 police in full riot gear rushed the 3,000-person-strong barricade to evict the 50 or so tenants barricaded inside the hotel.

The resulting scene, captured on film in Curtis Choy's moving documentary *The Fall of the I-Hotel,* was of demonstrators, who had been linked arm-in-arm, being forcibly moved out of the way, of police moving in and breaking down doors and of their brutality to some tenants who didn't move quickly enough for them. Tenant Tony Goolsby told *East-West,* "They threw us up against a wall in the middle of the building. . . . One told me, 'If you don't move, I'll break your fucking neck!' "[14]

San Francisco Sheriff Richard Hongisto, who had earlier spent five days in jail for contempt of court when he refused to carry out an eviction order, apparently had a change of heart by the time he was leading the line of cops into the hotel. In a dramatic moment, with cameras flashing all around him, Hongisto used a sledge hammer to break down doors to tenants' rooms.

The pictures of old immigrant tenants being forced out into the street were shown on newscasts across the country and in many places outside of the U.S. The entire spectacle, according to most observers, including those who had never supported the tenants' stand, was disgraceful.

Tenant Florentino Ragadeo, who had lived in the same room for more than 20 years after serving in the U.S. Army and surviving the Bataan Death March in World War II, reserved blame for the real culprits. "I do not blame policeman, not blame sheriff," he told *East-West* days after the evictions. "The judge! The mayor! I know that they are the ones who have the right to stop the eviction. Especially the owner of the hotel. Before you evict, you should find a place for the tenants . . . I'm crying all the time . . . It's not right."[15]

"It was like the Roman Legions coming after the Christians," recalled de Guzman. "It was incredible humiliation. We had these elderly men who had to drag themselves to the street, and they were suddenly homeless. A lot of the manongs didn't really live much longer. It's like their hearts were broken."[16]

PRESERVING HERITAGE AND HISTORY

On the 10th anniversary of the eviction, de Guzman explained the importance of fighting back against the powerful interests who wanted the hotel gone from sight. "For me and many of us who were born and raised in San Francisco, who have a lot of memories of what Manilatown was like as a community where our own fathers, relatives and friends hung out, the real issue was not the eviction but the attempt to destroy our heritage. The hotel was part of that historical foundation which we wanted to preserve."[17]

For more than a decade, the struggle to preserve the I-Hotel and all that it represented often occupied center stage in San Francisco politics. The issues of low-income housing, the rights of the elderly and people of color and the fight against "urban renewal" ("people rights over property rights," was a slogan from the demonstrations) were all ingredients in a struggle that eventually captured international attention.

Though the battle against eviction was lost and the hotel destroyed two years later—its fine bricks, ironically, used in the construction of million-dollar homes in other parts of the Bay Area—the struggle lives on in spirit. Many of the young Asian Americans, who became activists during that effort, found an important issue they could truly identify with. Politicized by the movement, many have stayed to work in the communities they rediscovered in 1968. A real pan-Asian American political identity was formed and from the subsequent work of these and other activists came a plethora of community services designed to meet the needs of Chinese, Japanese, Filipino, Korean, Cambodian, Vietnamese and other Asian immigrant populations.

"These were old people," said Bautista who, 20 years later, is still active, serving on the national council of Filipino Civil Rights Advocates. "You had to have a certain level of sympathy for them. We knew that we had to be accountable to our community. The system wanted control and wasn't willing to just give it up. Even though the manongs were evicted, the system really didn't win. We weren't defeated in one important sense: We learned the lesson of fighting back."[18]

Bill Sorro continues to work as a committed organizer, these days for low-income tenants in San Francisco's Mission District. "We can look back at the I-Hotel," he said, "and say that 20 years later, the same principles apply. Back then we called it self-determination. Today it's community empowerment. Whatever you want to call it, it's the same idea. People have rights; tenants have rights. We have to recognize those rights and fight back when we get pushed around. For the tenants in Manilatown we said, we're going to organize, fight back. That we should never let go of. If we ever stop fighting, then we've really lost."[19]

Today, 20 years since the 50 elderly tenants were forced out of their homes to make room for a parking garage, the lot at Kearny and Jackson streets remains empty. Ironically enough, it was never made into a parking structure, as developers and the city could never decide on a suitable project. Called "the Hole" now by locals, it is a strange sight in an area where giant skyscrapers dominate the terrain. To many, though, the lot is not just wasted land, but a monument to protest and to organized community struggle.

NOTES

1. Choy, *The Fall of the I-Hotel,* film.
2. *San Francisco Chronicle,* May 25, 1986.
3. Takaki, *Strangers from a Different Shore,* pp. 328–330.
4. *Asian Week,* August 7, 1987.
5. Ibid.
6. *San Francisco Chronicle,* May 25, 1986.
7. Ibid.
8. *San Francisco Chronicle,* March 17, 1968.

9. Terry Bautista, interview with author, August 3, 1997.
10. Wei, *Asian American Movement*, p. 106.
11. Bill Sorro, interview with author, August 4, 1997.
11. *Asian Week*, August 7, 1987.
12. *East-West*, August 6, 1977.
13. See note 9.
14. *East-West*, August 6, 1977.
15. Ibid.
16. *San Francisco Chronicle*, August 1, 1997.
17. Ibid.
18. See note 9.
19. See note 11.

59

SEEING MORE THAN BLACK AND WHITE
Latinos, Racism, and the Cultural Divides

ELIZABETH MARTINEZ

A certain relish seems irresistible to this Latina as the mass media have been compelled to sit up, look south of the border, and take notice. Probably the Chiapas uprising and Mexico's recent political turmoil have won us no more than a brief day in the sun. Or even less: liberal Ted Koppel still hadn't noticed the historic assassination of presidential candidate Colosio three days afterward. But it's been sweet, anyway.

When Kissinger said years ago "nothing important ever happens in the south," he articulated a contemptuous indifference toward Latin America, its people, and their culture which has long dominated U.S. institutions and attitudes. Mexico may be great for a vacation, and some people like burritos, but the usual image of Latin America combines incompetence with absurdity in loud colors. My parents, both Spanish teachers, endured decades of being told kids were better off learning French.

U.S. political culture is not only Anglo-dominated but also embraces an exceptionally stubborn national self-centeredness, with no global vision other than relations of domination. The U.S. refuses to see itself as one nation

From Z *Magazine* 7 (May 1994): 56–60. Reprinted by permission from Z Magazine, 18 Millfield St., Woods Hole, MA 02543, (508) 548–9063.

sitting on a continent with 20 others all speaking languages other than English and having the right not to be dominated.

Such arrogant indifference extends to Latinos within the U.S. The mass media complain, "people can't relate to Hispanics"—or Asians, they say. Such arrogant indifference has played an important role in invisibilizing La Raza (except where we become a serious nuisance or a handy scapegoat). It is one reason the U.S. harbors an exclusively white-on-Black concept of racism. It is one barrier to new thinking about racism which is crucial today. There are others.

GOOD-BYE WHITE MAJORITY

In a society as thoroughly and violently racialized as the United States, white-Black relations have defined racism for centuries. Today the composition and culture of the U.S. are changing rapidly. We need to consider seriously whether we can afford to maintain an exclusively white/Black model of racism when the population will be 32 percent Latin/Asian/Pacific American and Native American—in short, neither Black nor white—by the year 2050. We are challenged to recognize that multi-colored racism is mushrooming, and then strategize how to resist it. We are challenged to move beyond a dualism comprised of two white supremacist inventions: Blackness and Whiteness.

At stake in those challenges is building a united anti-racist force strong enough to resist contemporary racist strategies of divide-and-conquer. Strong enough in the long run, to help defeat racism itself. Doesn't an exclusively Black/white model of racism discourage the perception of common interests among people of color and thus impede a solidarity that can challenge white supremacy? Doesn't it encourage the isolation of African Americans from potential allies? Doesn't it advise all people of color to spend too much energy understanding our lives in relation to Whiteness, and thus freeze us in a defensive, often self-destructive mode?

NO "OPPRESSION OLYMPICS"

For a Latina to talk about recognizing the multi-colored varieties of racism is not, and should not be, yet another round in the Oppression Olympics. We don't need more competition among different social groupings for that "Most Oppressed" gold. We don't need more comparisons of suffering between women and Blacks, the disabled and the gay, Latino teenagers and white seniors, or whatever. We don't need more surveys like the recent much publicized Harris Poll showing that different peoples of color are prejudiced toward each other—a poll patently designed to demonstrate that us coloreds are no better than white folk. (The survey never asked people about positive attitudes.)

Rather, we need greater knowledge, understanding, and openness to learning about each other's histories and present needs as a basis for working together. Nothing could seem more urgent in an era when increasing impoverishment encourages a self-imposed separatism among people of color as a desperate attempt at community survival. Nothing could seem more important as we search for new social change strategies in a time of ideological confusion.

My call to rethink concepts of racism in the U.S. today is being sounded elsewhere. Among academics, liberal foundation administrators, and activist-intellectuals, you can hear talk of the need for a new "racial paradigm" or model. But new thinking seems to proceed in fits and starts, as if dogged by a fear of stepping on toes, of feeling threatened, or of losing one's base. With a few notable exceptions, even our progressive scholars of color do not make the leap from perfunctorily saluting a vague multi-culturalism to serious analysis. We seem to have made little progress, if any, since Bob Blauner's 1972 book *Racial Oppression in America.* Recognizing the limits of the white-Black axis, Blauner critiqued White America's ignorance of and indifference to the Chicano/a experience with racism.

Real opposition to new paradigms also exists. There are academics scrambling for one flavor of ethnic studies funds versus another. There are politicians who cultivate distrust of others to keep their own communities loyal. When we hear, for example, of Black/Latino friction, dismay should be quickly followed by investigation. In cities like Los Angeles and New York, it may turn out that political figures scrapping for patronage and payola have played a narrow nationalist game, whipping up economic anxiety and generating resentment that sets communities against each other.

So the goal here, in speaking about moving beyond a bipolar concept of racism is to build stronger unity against white supremacy. The goal is to see our similarities of experience and needs. If that goal sounds naive, think about the hundreds of organizations formed by grassroots women of different colors coming together in recent years. Their growth is one of today's most energetic motions and it spans all ages. Think about the multicultural environmental justice movement. Think about the coalitions to save schools. Small rainbows of our own making are there, to brighten a long road through hellish times.

It is in such practice, through daily struggle together, that we are most likely to find the road to greater solidarity against a common enemy. But we also need a will to find it and ideas about where, including some new theory.

THE WEST GOES EAST

Until very recently, Latino invisibility—like that of Native Americans and Asian/Pacific Americans—has been close to absolute in U.S. seats of power, major institutions, and the non-Latino public mind. Having lived on both the East and West Coasts for long periods, I feel qualified to pronounce: an especially myopic view of Latinos prevails in the East. This, despite such data as a 24.4 percent Latino population of New York City alone in 1991, or the fact that in 1990 more Puerto Ricans were killed by New York police under suspicious circumstances than any other ethnic group. Latino populations are growing rapidly in many eastern cities and the rural South, yet remain invisible or stigmatized—usually both.

Eastern blinders persist. I've even heard that the need for a new racial paradigm is dismissed in New York as a California hangup. A black Puerto Rican friend in New York, when we talked about experiences of racism common to Black and brown, said "People here don't see Border Patrol brutality against Mexicans as a form of police repression," despite the fact that the Border Patrol is the largest and most uncontrolled police force in the U.S. It would seem that an old ignorance has combined with new immigrant bashing to sustain divisions today.

While the East (and most of the Midwest) usually remains myopic, the West Coast has barely begun to move away from its own denial. Less than two years ago in San Francisco, a city almost half Latino or Asian/Pacific American, a leading daily newspaper could publish a major series on contemporary racial issues and follow the exclusively Black-white paradigm. Although millions of TV viewers saw massive Latino participation in the April 1992 Los Angeles uprising, which included 18 out of 50 deaths and the majority of arrests, the mass media and most people labeled that event "a Black riot."

If the West Coast has more recognition of those who are neither Black nor white, it is mostly out of fear about the proximate demise of its white majority. A second, closely related reason is the relentless campaign by California Gov. Pete Wilson to scapegoat immigrants for economic problems and pass racist, unconstitutional laws attacking their health, education, and children's future. Wilson has almost single-handedly made the word "immigrant" mean Mexican or other Latino (and sometimes Asian). Who thinks of all the people coming from the former Soviet Union and other countries? The absolute racism of this has too often been successfully masked by reactionary anti-immigrant groups like FAIR blaming immigrants for the staggering African-American unemployment rate.

Wilson's immigrant bashing is likely to provide a model for other parts of the country. The five states with the highest immigration rates—California, Florida, New York, Illinois and Texas—all have a governor up for re-election in 1994. Wilson's tactics won't appear in every campaign but some of the five states will surely see intensified awareness and stigmatization of Latinos as well as Asian/Pacific Islanders. *Editor's Note:* While the specific references are dated, the larger reality is still true: immigration remains a controversial issue in local and regional elections.

As this suggests, what has been a regional issue mostly limited to western states is becoming a national issue. If you thought Latinos were just "Messicans" down at the border, wake up—they are all over North Carolina, Pennsylvania and 8th Avenue Manhattan now. A qualitative change is taking place. With the broader geographic spread of Latinos and Asian/Pacific Islanders has come a nationalization of racist practices and attitudes that were once regional. The west goes east, we could say.

Like the monster Hydra, racism is growing some ugly new heads. We will have to look at them closely.

THE ROOTS OF RACISM AND LATINOS

A bipolar model of racism—racism as white on Black—has never really been accurate. Looking for the roots of racism in the U.S. we can begin with the genocide against American Indians which made possible the U.S. land base, crucial to white settlement and early capitalist growth. Soon came the massive enslavement of African people which facilitated that growth. As slave labor became economically critical, "blackness" became ideologically critical; it provided the very source of "whiteness" and the heart of racism. Franz Fanon would write, "colour is the most outward manifestation of race."

If Native Americans had been a crucial labor force during those same centuries, living and working in the white man's sphere, our racist ideology might have evolved differently. "The tawny," as Ben Franklin dubbed them, might have defined the opposite of what he called "the lovely white." But with Indians decimated and survivors moved to distant concentration camps, they became unlikely candidates for this function. Similarly, Mexicans were concentrated in the distant West; elsewhere Anglo fear of them or need to control was rare. They also did not provide the foundation for a definition of whiteness.

Some anti-racist left activists have put forth the idea that only African Americans experience racism as such and that the suffering of other people of color results from national minority rather than racial oppression. From this viewpoint, the exclusively white/Black model for racism is correct. Latinos, then, experience exploitation and repression for reasons of culture and nationality—not for their "race." (It should go without saying that while racism is an all-too-real social fact, race has no scientific basis.)

Does the distinction hold? This and other theoretical questions call for more analysis and more expertise than one article can offer. In the meantime, let's try on the idea that Latinos do suffer for their nationality and culture, especially language. They became part of the U.S. through the 1846–48 war on Mexico and thus a foreign population to be colonized. But as they were reduced to cheap or semi-slave labor, they quickly came to suffer for their "race"—meaning, as non-whites. In the Southwest of a super-racialized nation the broad parallelism of race and class embrace Mexicans ferociously.

The bridge here might be a definition of racism as "the reduction of the cultural to the biological," in the words of French scholar Christian Delacampagne now working in Egypt. Or: "racism exists wherever it is claimed that a given social status is explained by a given natural characteristic." We know that line: Mexicans are just naturally lazy and have too many children, so they're poor and exploited.

The discrimination, oppression and hatred experienced by Native Americans, Mexicans, Asian/Pacific Islanders, and Arab Americans are forms of racism. Speaking only of Latinos, we have seen in California and the Southwest, especially along the border, almost 150 years of relentless repression which today includes Central Americans among its targets. That history reveals hundreds of lynchings between 1847 and 1935, the use of counterinsurgency armed forces beginning with the Texas Rangers, random torture and murder by Anglo ranchers, forced labor, rape by border lawmen, and the prevailing Anglo belief that a Mexican life doesn't equal a dog's in value.

But wait. If color is so key to racial definition, as Fanon and others say, perhaps people of Mexican background experience racism less than national minority oppression because they are not dark enough as a group. For White America, shades of skin color are crucial to defining worth. The influence of those shades has also been internalized by communities of color. Many Latinos can and often want to pass for whites; therefore, White America may see them as less threatening than darker sisters and brothers.

Here we confront more of the complexity around us today, with questions like: What about the usually poor, very dark Mexican or Central American of strong Indian or African heritage? (Yes, folks, 200,000–300,000 Africans were brought to Mexico as slaves, which is far, far more than the Spaniards who came.) And what about the effects of accented speech or foreign name, characteristics that may instantly subvert "passing"?

What about those cases where a Mexican-American is never accepted, no matter how light-skinned, well-dressed or well-spoken? A Chicano lawyer friend coming home from a professional conference in suit, tie and briefcase found himself on a bus near San Diego that was suddenly stopped by the Border Patrol. An agent came on board and made a beeline through the all-white rows of passengers direct to my friend. "Your papers." The agent didn't believe Jose was coming from a U.S. conference and took him off the bus to await proof. Jose was lucky; too many Chicanos and Mexicans end up killed.

In a land where the national identity is white, having the "wrong" nationality becomes grounds for racist abuse. Who would draw a sharp line between today's national minority oppression in the form of immigrant-bashing, and racism?

None of this aims to equate the African American and Latino experiences; that isn't necessary even if it were accurate. Many reasons exist for the persistence of the white/Black paradigm of racism; they include numbers, history, and the psychology of whiteness. In particular they include centuries of slave revolts, a Civil War, and an ongoing resistance to racism that cracked this society wide open while the world watched. Nor has the misery imposed on Black people lessened in recent years. New thinking about racism can and should keep this experience at the center.

A DEADLY DUALISM

The exclusively white/Black concept of race and racism in the U.S. rests on a western, Protestant form of dualism woven into both race and gender relations from earliest times. In the dualist universe there is only black and white. A disdain, indeed fear, of mixture haunts the Yankee soul; there is no room for any kind of multi-faceted identity, any hybridism.

As a people, La Raza combines three sets of roots—indigenous, European, and African—all in widely varying degrees. In short we represent a profoundly un-American concept: *mestizaje* (pronounced mess-tee-zah-hey), the mixing of peoples and emergence of new peoples. A highly racialized society like this one cannot deal with or allow room for *mestizaje*. It has never learned to do much more than hiss "miscegenation!" Or, like that Alabama high school principal who recently denied the right of a mixed-blood pupil to attend the prom, to say: "your parents made a mistake." Apparently we, all the millions of La Raza, are just that—a mistake.

Mexicans in the U.S. also defy the either-or, dualistic mind in that, on the one hand, we are a colonized people displaced from the ancestral homeland with roots in the present-day U.S. that go back centuries. Those ancestors didn't cross the border; the border crossed them. At the same time many of us have come to the U.S. more recently as "immigrants" seeking work. The complexity of Raza baffles and frustrates most Anglos; they want to put one neat label on us. It baffles many Latinos too, who often end up categorizing themselves racially as "Other" for lack of anything better. For that matter, the term "Latino" which I use here is a monumental simplification; it refers to 20-plus nationalities and a wide range of classes.

But we need to grapple with the complexity, for there is more to come. If anything, this nation will see more *mestizaje* in the future, embracing innumerable ethnic combinations. What will be its effects? Only one thing seems certain: "white" shall cease to be the national identity.

A glimpse at the next century tells us how much we need to look beyond the white/Black model of race relations and racism. White/Black are real poles, central to the history of U.S. racism. We can neither ignore them nor stop there. But our effectiveness in fighting racism depends on seeing the changes taking place, trying to perceive the contours of the future. From the time of the Greeks to the present, racism around the world has had certain commonalties but no permanently fixed character. It is evolving again today, and we'd best labor to read the new faces of this Hydra-headed monster. Remember, for every head that Hydra lost it grew two more.

Sometimes the problem seems so clear. Last year I showed slides of Chicano history to an Oakland high school class with 47 African Americans and three Latino students. The images included lynchings and police beatings of Mexicans and other Latinos, and many years of resistance. At the end one Black student asked, "Seems like we have had a lot of experiences in common—so why can't Blacks and Mexicans get along better?" No answers, but there was the first step: asking the question.

60

DISMANTLING NOAH'S ARK
Gender and Equality

JUDITH LORBER

The defeated Equal Rights Amendment to the United States Constitution read simply, "Equality of rights under the law shall not be denied or abridged by the United States or any state on account of sex." Equal rights for women is a goal that resonates with individualism and freedom of choice. Yet that goal failed because, legally, in order to be treated alike, people have to *be* alike, and the prevailing belief in Western societies is that women and men are intrinsically different. Biological rationales for gender inequality not only are still part of the taken-for-granted assumptions of everyday reality in Western countries; they are built into public policy and law. As a result, the liberal feminist goal of equality for women in Western societies will probably, as Robert Connell sardonically points out, have as little effect in countering men's domination of women as the rallying cries of liberal philosophers that all *men* were equal had in countering rich men's domination of poor men: "Liberal feminism took the doctrine of 'rights' seriously and turned it against the patriarchal model of citizenship. 'Equal rights' is more than a slogan; it is a wholly logical doctrine that is as effective against the 'aristocracy of sex' as the doctrine of the 'rights of man' was against the aristocracy of property" (Connell 1990, 512).

If women and men are alike, unlike treatment is inequality, but if they are not alike, dissimilar treatment is appropriate. As Catherine MacKinnon says:

> Gender is socially constructed *as difference* epistemologically, and sex discrimination law bounds gender equality *by difference* doctrinally. Socially one tells a woman from a man by their difference from each other, but a woman is discriminated against on the basis of sex only when she can first be said to be the same as man. A built-in tension exists between this concept of equality, which presupposes sameness, and this concept of sex, which presupposes difference. Sex equality becomes a contradiction in terms, something of an oxymoron. (1990, 215)

Lorber, Judith, "Dismantling Noah's Ark," from *Paradoxes of Gender*. New Haven: Yale University Press, 1994. p. 282–302. Reprinted by permission of the publisher.

Less emphasis on masculinity and femininity in bringing up children, depiction of diverse behavior by women and men in the mass media, and encouraging men's access to jobs traditionally filled by women and women's access to jobs traditionally filled by men are familiar ways feminists have recommended to avoid creating *unnecessary* differences—that is, differences that go beyond the biological. The alternative goal—equity—recognizes differences but tries to compensate for them by giving women benefits or protections, such as maternity leave or assignment to nonhazardous work. The goals of equality and of equity are actually the same: "for women to be in some way the same as men, whether this sameness be interpreted as identical treatment or as access to the same opportunities" (Jaggar 1990, 250).

Much of the debate over gender equality revolves around procreation and sexuality (Kay 1985). The subjects of the debate seem to be females and males, not women and men. Females and males are physiologically different, so if they are treated differently, it is supposedly not an equal-rights problem. But a closer look at the way women are treated in Western societies clearly indicates that although the rationale is biological, the differential treatment is political. In bureaucratic organizations, the workers and, more crucially, the people in the top positions, are expected to be *male:*

> It is the man's body, its sexuality, minimal responsibility in procreation, and conventional control of emotions that pervades work and organizational processes. Women's bodies—female sexuality, their ability to procreate and their pregnancy, breast-feeding, and child care, menstruation, and mythic "emotionality"—are suspect, stigmatized, and used as grounds for control and exclusion. . . . To function at the top of male hierarchies requires that women render irrelevant everything that makes them women. (Acker 1990, 152, 153)

In order for female workers to be treated the same as male workers, their biological differences are considered disabilities that are not their fault. For example, in order to give females time off while pregnant and immediately after childbirth without discriminating against males, pregnancy in the United States is treated the way a male disability like a prostate infection would be, as an illness. The problem is that *women* are still discriminated against because their time off for pregnancy and childbirth is held against them as workers, whereas men's time off from work because of illness is not. Responsible women workers (especially the career-oriented) are supposed to use efficient contraception to time their pregnancies and childbirths, just as they are supposed to work out efficient child-care arrangements. But their ability to do so is heavily influenced by government policies on access to contraception and abortion, by employers' policies on maternity leave, and by the availability of affordable child care in their community.

The status of women and men is as much an issue of power and privilege as is the status of people of different races and social classes. To *not* ask why a social category called "men" has power over a social category called "women" is to accept the assumption that men's domination is natural and to seek for natural causes. In theories of race, it is the very categories themselves that are problematic, that are questions for theoretical analysis: Are they cultural divisions, structural divisions, or deliberate social constructions by the dominant group whose purpose is to justify the continuation of its dominance? Either way, "as myth and as a global sign, . . . it superimposes a 'natural' unity over a plethora of . . . differences" (E. B. Higginbotham 1992, 270). Once pulled apart, the discourse of race reveals the social structural underpinnings that maintain racial inequality.

In *Capital*, Karl Marx provided the theory of class as relations to the means of production—that is, classes are social groupings with a material base, personal consequences, and ideological justification. The two classes (capitalists, or owners of the means of production, and the proletariat, or exploited workers) are inherently unequal not because of some intrinsic characteristics, although that was long the prevailing belief, but because of the different relations of each to the means of production and their conflictual interdependence. For race and class, then, the relational and political aspects of the categories are clear. The dominant groups define themselves and the subordinate groups as they construct and justify the boundaries of exclusion and power.

The concept of gender, however, has been theoretically grounded in sexuality and procreation. This conceptualization undermines the feminist focus on the relational aspects of women's and men's social status and the political aspects of gender inequality. I am arguing that gender inequality is located solely in the structure of gendered social practices and institutions. Procreation and sexuality are constructed as conditions of subordination within the social institution of gender; the social institution of gender is not built on procreation and sexuality. Human sexual reproduction is universal, but gender inequality is not. The gender status of women affects the social construction of sexuality, fertility, pregnancy, childbirth, and parenting, not the other way around. Responsibility for the work in the domestic sphere is an outcome of women's gender status, not its cause.

EXPLOITING WOMEN

As a group, men own most of the private property, monopolize the better jobs, and make the laws. The outcome of this inequality is men's double exploitation of women in the job market and in the home. Even if they have no other privileges, men reap the advantages of women's domestic labor. Procreative differences are not the cause of women's exploitation but its justification. Women are subordinated in all industrial societies not because they are child bearers or child minders but because owners, managers, and governments depend on them as low-paid, accessible, responsible workers. They are the primary child carers not because of their procreative capabilities but because they are economically disadvantaged and have little choice but to do the unwaged work of social reproduction. Each form of exploitation of women's labor reinforces the other. Women's economic value as waged and unwaged workers is the *main* reason for their subordination in modern societies; they are the "last colony" (Mies, Bennholdt-Thomsen, and von Werlhof 1988).

An often-cited United Nations report (1980) claims that women do two-thirds of the world's work, receive 10 percent of the income, and own 1 percent of the property. Underlying that statement is the world economic system that exploits working-class women and, in particular, women of color by paying them barely subsistence-level wages so that they must expand their non-waged work in order to maintain their families. Working-class women's labor as unpaid housewives and poorly paid domestic servants, child carers, sex workers, subsistence farmers, sellers and traders of petty commodities, and pieceworkers in the home and in sweatshop factories, combined with middle-class women's work as low-paid office workers, service workers, teachers, nurses, librarians, and social workers, adds up to two-thirds of the world's work at one-tenth of the world's income. The exploitation of women as waged and unwaged workers swells the profits of a small number of capitalists, the men who own 99 percent of the world's private property. It also increases the accumulation of surplus in state-owned economies. The ideology of women's intrinsic sex differences and propensity for love and service mystifies what is in reality simple exploitation—exploitation that is compounded for economically disadvantaged women and women of color (Attwood 1990; Sokoloff 1980).

Men's emotional and sexual exploitation of women, their objectification of women in culture and devaluation in the world's main religions, their rendering women invisible in standard histories, and their ideological justification of legal controls over women's bodies—the patriarchal component of gender inequality—are the *means* of subordination. The psychological investment of women in their children and the stigmatization of men's and women's homosexual love and women's sexuality inscribe the gender order in men's and women's personalities and identities. Tying women to children *and* men emotionally meets men's needs for biological inheritance, emotional sustenance, and heterosexual relationships. Whether it is direct, by restricting access to contraception and abortion, or indirect, by invoking women's purported nurturant and caretaking qualities and claiming they are therefore indispensable as mothers of small children, the effect is to coopt women into a structure of gender inequality through "bonds of love" (Benjamin 1988).

More intimate parenting by men might break the cycle of the reproduction of mothering and gendered personality structures that alienate men emotionally and bond women to their children so intensely. It might also diminish the level of violence and sexual exploitation. But alone, it will not produce gender equality. Gendered parenting, personality structures, sexual exploitation, and physical violence help maintain men's control over women, but they are not the cause of institutionalized gender inequality. The basic cause is women's deprivation of rights of access to property and well-paid jobs, which makes them economically dependent and emotionally and sexually vulnerable. This deprivation has been systematic and state-supported, and it persists because it advantages men both as property owners and as workers. Married women with children whose husbands have good jobs collude in this exploitation because their material well-being and social status and that of their children are higher when they live with a man than if they try to make a life on their own. Women with children who have neither the resources of a man's economic support nor a secure position of their own in the workplace are unlikely, because of their need to rely on government assistance, to protest the system as a system. But they, of all women, experience its oppression firsthand.

Most families cannot survive economically without women's paid work. If choices have to be made between child care and paid work, women neglect, abandon, or board out their children (Boswell 1988; Fuchs 1984). As "bad mothers," they then bear the brunt of these decisions emotionally and socially (Gordon 1989). Men invest time and energy in the care and teaching of children (sometimes only sons) when it is to their advantage. The intense battles over child custody indicate that many men today want children they can claim through biological connection or through investment in time and energy (Smart and Sevenhuijsen 1989). Some men may be more willing than some women to organize their work lives around parenting, but in most countries, the structure of work denies them the opportunity, just as the lack of good child care outside the home penalizes women for their work commitments. But even where work schedules are flexible and the state provides child-care leave to either parent, as in Sweden, few men take on substantial amounts of child care and housework. As service to others, this work has emotional rewards, not the tangible monetary payoff men in industrial and postindustrial societies have been taught to seek as a mark of masculinity. The love and respect that are the rewards of family work attest to a woman's, not a man's, worth.

STRUCTURED EQUALITY

How can we restructure the institutionalized arrangements that subordinate and exploit women and build a society that is potentially egalitarian for women and men? Since race and class are intertwined with gender in the social arrangements that reproduce inequality, it is highly unlikely that gender inequality alone could (or should) be redressed without considering racial and economic exploitation. For example, capitalism currently exploits women as a reserve army of cheap labor, but it also exploits disadvantaged men. Socialism accumulates more surplus if some workers are paid less than others, but these lesser-paid workers are not necessarily women. These systems do not need gendered job segregation or gendered occupational stratification to survive in their current forms; they need only low-cost workers and hierarchies of management. If the low-paid and high-paid workers were a random mix of women and men, and the owners and managers were also mixed on gender, equality of women and men in each stratum could be accomplished without altering income inequalities or managerial hierarchies.

In order to make all workers equal, everyone who does any kind of socially useful work, including the caretakers of dependents, must receive a wage that sustains a comfortable standard of living. Job segregation on the basis of gender and race would then be superfluous. Shared or rotated management would flatten hierarchies, and so there would be no point for the members of any group to monopolize positions of authority. But if some people, or some groups of people, disproportionately continued to be the caretakers of dependents, and production work continued to be more highly valued than social reproduction, inequality would persist. As Cynthia Cockburn says: "Until the symbolic man-as-citizen has his mind on the cooker, his eye on a toddler and a hand on granddad's wheelchair, no constitution will guarantee social equality" (1991, 97). For true equality, care of children and the elderly would have to be made every able-bodied adult's responsibility equally, perhaps in a vertical kinship system, with each competent adult responsible for a child and an elderly parent or grandparent (Lorber 1975).

Pregnancy and childbirth are not insurmountable barriers to structures of equality. Childbearing is not most modern women's main role in life. As Connell suggests, in postindustrial societies,

> childbearing can be made a fairly short episode in any woman's life, and can be made socially equivalent to conception, pregnancy-support and infant care in men's lives. We have the knowledge and resources to share childcare and domestic work among adults to any extent desired in a balance between efficiency and privacy. Large numbers of men and women can choose to be childless without any danger of depopulation; a free choice of forms of cathexis becomes a general possibility. (1987, 280)

That is, if parenting is seen as many adults' responsibility, then social, emotional, and economic support during pregnancy and childbirth could certainly be given by the nonpregnant and the nonbirthers to the woman who gestates and delivers a child for the household. Structuring for equality would do away not with procreative differences but with social roles and patterns of behavior that assign responsibilities that have nothing to do with pregnancy and childbirth to all females, many of whom are not and never will be birth mothers. Egalitarian child care and child support are already structured into some dual-career and two-income families, joint custody arrangements, and gay and lesbian households.

If every adult in a household is to be equal, household income has to be shared equally; otherwise the one with more economic resources has greater bargaining power. Even a household of unequal earners can be structured for equality. All household income could be pooled and allocated first to food, clothing, shelter, transportation, medical care, school fees, and other household expenses (perhaps including paid child care, house cleaning, laundry), donations, gifts, entertainment, vacations, retirement, and savings for emergencies. After that, to ensure equal resources, the remainder could be split evenly among the adult members of the household for their individual use (cf. Hertz 1986, 84–113). Each adult in a household should be able to claim the same amount of discretionary income, regardless of earnings, since that surplus buys the freedom to travel, donate, entertain, give gifts, save, work on private projects, and so on. Any earnings from this discretionary income should belong to the investor who is risking her or his own money. Individuals should also be able to leave what they have accumulated to whomever they want.

Any family work not done through paid services, as well as responsibility for hiring, overseeing, and transportation, would have to be evenly split or allocated by desirability, competence, convenience, and time. If all adults shared responsibility for domestic work, each would have equivalent time for educational and occupational advancement and political work. Any grouping of adults could share both the income from paid work and their domestic labor and thus provide economic support and nurturing care for the children, elderly, and sick in a household. If the economic system and the political system were also structured for equality (by equitable income distribution and rotated positions of authority), the egalitarian structure of domestic life would support and be supported by the egalitarian structure of work and government.

Freed of exploitive economic, kinship, and procreative relationships, sexuality could indeed be the result of individual desires. But all kinds of sexual behavior would not be acceptable in an egalitarian society. Relations between adults and children and those imbued with acts of violence would erase the structural conditions of equality—that no one be exploited or subordinated in any way or by any means by anyone or any social institution. Children's equality depends on the protection of adults, protection that is violated by sexual exploitation. Violence creates the ultimate condition of inequality—unequal power—and so any use or threat of physical harm of one person by another must be absolutely forbidden legally and tabooed culturally as well. But for socially competent adults, all consenting sexual relationships, including those with *fantasies* of violence, would have equal value in a society structured for equality.

A structure of cultural equality would mean that all symbolic and ideological representations would have equal worth. The forms and content of culture might not even be that different from much that is produced throughout the world today, but the meanings would be different: "In a world in which the power structure was such that both men and women equally could be represented clothed or unclothed in a variety of poses and positions without any implications of dominance or submission—in a world of total and, so to speak, unconscious equality, the female nude would not be problematic" (Nochlin 1988, 30). What about pornography? In a utopian social order, such as true communism, says Alan Soble, "the making of pornography . . . will surely be libidinally satisfying, but that is not why it or any other work is meaningful and satisfying. It is nonalienated labor because it would be freely chosen, the project would be collectively planned without a hierarchy of authority, its completion would involve a playful creativity, and the product would be appreciated and admired by others" (1986, 127).

Currently, the subordination, exploitation, and even extermination of some social groups by others as well as the inequality of individuals within all social groups is part of the laws, governments, and criminal justice systems of most countries, even those supposedly organized for equality. If societies are to reverse this pattern and build on their traditional or constitutional structures of equality, at a minimum every proposed law, court order, or state policy must be examined first for its effect on all the structural conditions of equality—the distribution of economic resources; production of knowledge and culture; shares of political power; help for children, the elderly, the sick, the less physically and mentally competent; valuation of ethnic traditions and religious beliefs; and acceptance of consenting adults' sexual practices.

Does a social world structured for equality mean people will be a varied, motley crew, or a version of middle-class, white, Anglo-Saxon Protestant men? It would probably take as deliberate an effort to counteract hegemonic masculine values in workplaces and other organizations as it would be to structure them for equality. That is, conscious reorganization along the lines suggested by Patricia Yancey Martin would be necessary to construct a social order based on qualities of "inclusion, participation and diversity" (1993, 290). These are the necessary conditions for gender equality.

INTO AND OUT OF NOAH'S ARK

Human beings have constructed and used gender—human beings can deconstruct and stop using gender. The most obvious way would be to deliberately and self-consciously *not* use gender to organize social life. Gender-neutrality resonates with Western concepts of achievement, in which individual talents, ambitions, strengths, and weaknesses constitute the only basis for work roles and leadership positions. Gender-neutrality assumes that women and men who are similarly educated and trained are interchangeable and that gender equality will come when more women get the equivalent of prestigious men's jobs and positions of authority and more men participate in housework and child care.

Women and men at present are rarely interchangeable because the social order is structured to advantage men and disadvantage women. In the micropolitics of everyday life and the macropolitics of laws and state policies, dominant men are so privileged that they continue to dominate without much conscious effort. Women and subordinate men have to show that they are as good as dominant men to succeed economically, politically, or artistically—the burden of proof is on them. Social policies that ignore this structure of the gender inequality and assume that remedies can take place on the individual level are doomed to failure, and the failure will be attributed to the attitudes, competencies, and motivations of the individuals concerned, both dominant and subordinate, not to the social structure.

Whether without a revolution it is possible to structure gender equality in social orders that are organized to guarantee the privileges of dominant men is questionable. To see how deeply gender inequality organizes work, parenting, leadership, politics, and culture in modern societies, consider what a world would be like where women and men equally worked in every occupation and profession, equally took care of children, governed equally, equally produced culture.

In a world of scrupulous gender equality, equal numbers of girls and boys would be educated and trained for the liberal arts and for the sciences, for clerical and manual labor, and for all the professions. Among those with equal credentials, women and men would be hired in an alternating fashion for the same type of job—or only men would be hired to do women's types of jobs and only women would be hired to do the men's types of jobs until half of every work force was made up of men and half, women.

If men did women's work, would the pay increase, autonomy be encouraged, and the work gain in prestige? If women were not seen as taking over men's work, but performing it interchangeably with men, would the work be devalued, deskilled, and paid less? Would upward mobility be restricted in order to encourage rapid turnover and low wages if half of all lower-level workers were men? If a work process was degraded, all workers would suffer, and they might resist employers as a group, instead of men competing against women for the best jobs or for any jobs at all.

If men as well as women cared for children, many ways might be found to equalize responsibility for parenting: crèches at work for breast-feeding and bottle-feeding parents, men taking as much time off as women to care for sick children, "daddy tracks" if "mommy tracks" persisted (in which case, there would probably be no separate tracks for parents). Please note that in no way am I suggesting that *females* and *males* could be interchanged, only women and men. Males do not get pregnant, but they can take care of infants; females gestate and lactate, but that does not mean that only they must take parental leave. Equal child care would involve staffing community child-care centers and schools with equal numbers of men and women doing every kind of task. How would primary parents who were interchangeably women and men alter children's gendered psychological development? How would children be socialized if their caretakers and teachers were equally women and men?

What would happen if positions of responsibility were alternated between women and men? In elected positions, two women then two men
could run against each other alternately to ensure that neither men nor
women predominated. In appointed positions, women and men of equal
qualifications would be alternated. What would be the effect on concepts of
authority and leadership? On training and grooming for advancement? On
gendered patterns of deference? On sexual harassment?

Although some modern countries have a high percentage of doctors and
lawyers who are women, professional work has been stratified by gender,
with men in the more prestigious sectors and in the policy-making positions.
The same is true of education; women mostly occupy the lower grades of
teaching and the lower levels of administration. Scientific research in all modern countries is dominated by men. These are the arenas where knowledge is
produced in response to theoretical questions and pragmatic problems. If
half of all medical specialists, medical school faculties, and researchers were
women; if half the police and lawyers and judges at all levels were women; if
half the university professors, deans, provosts, presidents, and chancellors
were women; if half the scientists in the world were women, what changes
are predictable in medical practice and research priorities, in the criminal justice system and the interpretation of laws, in the knowledge produced and
the knowledge taught, in the scientific problems considered important
enough to command enormous resources?

Suppose women had equal time with men in all cultural productions. In
art museums, an equal number of acquisitions by women and men would be
the rule. In concerts, an equal number of pieces composed by women and by
men would be played by an equal number of women and men musicians. An
equal number of books by women and by men would appear on every publisher's list. An equal number of movies produced, directed, and written by
women and by men would feature, in any year, an equal number of women
and men heroes. The same principles would be used for every television
channel's programming. How would canons of taste be affected? How would
prestigious prizes be awarded? Would symbolic language change if women's
experiences were as privileged as men's experiences?

In sports, every competition would have an equal number of women's
and men's teams and players, the rules of competition would be the same for
women and for men, and women's and men's events would receive equal
time, pay, and prize money. The featured main event would alternate between women and men. The media would cover women's and men's sports
and sports heroes equally. Would men begin to identify with women's sports
stars? Would women turn out to be physiologically similar to men in ways
that are now hidden by the rules of the games? Would some sports competitions become unisex?

Perhaps the most drastic upset of current ways of thinking would occur
if all the armed forces were half women and half men, including combat
units. In many wars and revolutions, women have fought side by side with

men, both openly and disguised as men. Frenchwomen played such an important part in the resistance to Nazism, running escape lines, sabotaging, spying, and printing clandestine newspapers, that they finally could no longer be denied the right to vote (M. L. Rossiter 1986, 223). According to the *New York Times* of May 2, 1993, during World War II, Russian women were machine gunners and snipers, served on artillery and tank crews, and flew in three all-woman air force fighter and bomber units. In Israel, women fought in the underground for nationhood and in the War of Independence, reaching levels as high as 20 percent of all soldiers. On April 30, 1993, the *Jerusalem Post* published the following fifty-year-old news story:

> Malka Epstein, a 22-year-old girl, is now a legendary figure in
> Central Poland where she leads a guerrilla unit with headquarters
> in old quarry caves in the Kielce district. From these headquarters
> this girl has been conducting sabotage raids on Nazi units in the
> last 18 months. She is credited with having destroyed many
> German munition stores and with derailing trains carrying German
> soldiers to the Russian front.

As long as battles and wars are fought, women must be able to fight if they are to be equal with men. Otherwise, men will continue to feel that since they put their lives on the line and women do not, they are entitled to privileges and powers unavailable to women (W. Brown 1992, 25–26). Moreover, the idea of aggressive masculinity as protective of women lets men define which women are deserving of their protection. In World War II, women civilians were tortured, executed, bombed, and gassed; in all wars, they have been raped and murdered. Women should compose half of the peacemakers, but as long as there are wars, to be equal, they should be half of the fighters, too.

The other side of this exchange of expectations of men and women is that the nurturance and service to others that defines the "good woman" in Western cultures should apply to the "good man" as well. As Kay Ann Johnson points out, the Maoist utopian vision of the complete person (*tomien-shou*) broke down the distinction between the intellectual and the manual laborer, the philosopher and the peasant, the artist and the artisan, but was never applied to women and men: "Never was it suggested, even in the most utopian movements, that men should learn from women . . . the value of, and how to perform, the nurturant human services" (1983, 167).

Other radical changes in concepts of femininity and masculinity would occur in a scrupulously equal world. All forms of sexuality would have to be recognized as equally valid. There would, therefore, have to be equal numbers of pornographic magazines, movies, strip shows, erotic dancers, and any other sexual productions for heterosexual, homosexual, bisexual, transvestite, and sadomasochistic women as for the same groups of men. Movies, television, books, and popular songs can be expected to show women as sexual pursuers equally with men, and homosexuality and heterosexuality as producing equally happy and tragic relationships. You might see plots revolving around heterosexual women sexually harassing and abusing heterosexual men, and gay men and lesbians sexually harassing each other and heterosexuals.

Suppose all the major religions allowed women to become priests, to rise in the religious hierarchy, and to interpret the Old and New Testaments, the Qur'an, the Bhaghavad Gita. Since the practices of the world's major religions were originally based on social orders that separated women and men and assigned them different roles in life, fundamentalists could not allow women and men the same religious roles. But what would happen if religions that now profess gender equality really gave women and men an equal chance to be leaders? If liturgies were completely gender-neutral? If "God" were not "the Lord," "our Father," or "King of the universe" but "the Leader," "our Parent," "Creator of the universe"?

The very radicalness of the effect of the scrupulous gender equality throughout a whole social society, the cries of outrage you would predict if absolutely equal numbers of women and men had to be constantly maintained in all areas of life, the sense of unreality about a completely gender-balanced world, all make clear how very far the most progressive, most industrialized, most postmodern, most egalitarian society today would have to go to become truly gender-neutral. What government would organize a system of complete gender balance? Not only do we still want to know immediately whether an infant is a boy or girl, that information, that categorization, combined with race and other social characteristics, tells us and the infants just where in their social order they are going to be placed, and whether they are going to be encouraged to live their lives as dominant, self-confident, and central to society or as subordinate, subverted, and peripheral to the main action. When we no longer ask "boy or girl?" in order to start gendering an infant, when the information about genitalia is as irrelevant as the color of the child's eyes (but not yet the color of skin), then and only then will women and men be socially interchangeable and really equal. And when that happens, there will no longer be any need for gender at all.

Does all this equality mean that no one will criticize, satirize, parody, oppose, challenge, resist, rebel, start new groups, or live alone? I doubt it. Free of gender, race, and class inequality, what might we all be? Perhaps culturally identified women, men, heterosexuals, homosexuals, citizens of different countries, adherents of different religions, members of different occupations and professions, of different birth and social parents, and so on. Perhaps people free to experience *jouissance*—the erotic passions expressed in human bodies, human identities, deeply held beliefs, work, love, spirituality. Perhaps what Donna Haraway predicts—cyborgs who understand and can control the interface of humans and technology, who belong now to one group, now to another, identified with many or with none at all:

> The cyborg is a creature in a post-gender world; it has no truck with
> bisexuality, pre-Oedipal symbiosis, unalienated labor, or other
> seductions to organic wholeness through a final appropriation of all

the powers of the parts into a higher unity. . . . The cyborg is resolutely committed to partiality, irony, intimacy, and perversity. It is oppositional, utopian, and completely without innocence. . . . I would rather be a cyborg than a goddess. (1985, 67, 101)

So would I.

REFERENCES

Acker, Joan. 1990. Hierarchies, jobs, and bodies: A theory of gendered organizations. *Gender & Society* 4:139–58.

Attwood, Lynne. 1990. *The new Soviet man and woman: Sex-role socialization in the USSR.* Bloomington: Indiana University Press.

Benjamin, Jessica. 1988. *The bonds of love: Psychoanalysis, feminism, and the problem of domination.* New York: Pantheon.

Boswell, John. 1988. *The kindness of strangers: The abandonment of children in Western Europe from late antiquity to the Renaissance.* New York: Pantheon.

Brown, Wendy. 1992. Finding the man in the state. *Feminist Studies* 18:7–34.

Cockburn, Cynthia. 1991. *In the way of women: Men's resistance to sex equality in organizations.* Ithaca, N.Y.: ILR Press.

Connell, Robert W. 1987. *Gender and power: Society, the person, and sexual politics.* Stanford, Calif.: Stanford University Press.

―――. 1990. The state, gender, and sexual politics: Theory and appraisal. *Theory and Society* 19:507–44.

Fuchs, Rachel Ginnes. 1984. *Abandoned children: Foundlings and child welfare in nineteenth-century France.* Albany: State University of New York Press.

Gordon, Linda. 1989. *Heroes of their own lives: The politics and history of family violence, Boston, 1880–1960.* New York: Penguin.

Haraway, Donna. 1985. A manifesto for cyborgs. *Socialist Review* 15(2):65–107.

Hertz, Rosanna. 1986. *More equal than others: Women and men in dual-career marriages.* Berkeley: University of California Press.

Higginbotham, Evelyn Brooks. 1992. African-American women's history and the metalanguage of race. *Signs* 17:251–74.

Jaggar, Alison M. 1990. Sexual difference and sexual equality. In Rhode, Deborah L. (ed.). *Theoretical perspectives on cultural difference.* New Haven: Yale University Press.

Johnson, Kay Ann. 1983. *Women, the family and peasant revolution in China.* Chicago: University of Chicago Press.

Kay, Herma Hill. 1985. Models of equality. *University of Illinois Law Review,* 1985 (1):39–88.

Lorber, Judith. 1975. Beyond equality of the sexes: The question of the children. *Family Coordinator* 24:465–72.

MacKinnon, Catharine A. 1989. *Toward a feminist theory of the state.* Cambridge, Mass.: Harvard University Press.

―――. 1990. Legal perspectives on sexual difference. In Rhode, Deborah L. (ed.). *Theoretical perspectives on cultural difference.* New Haven: Yale University Press.

Martin, Patricia Yancey. 1993. Feminist practice in organizations: Implications for management. In Fagenson, Ellen A. (ed.). *Women in management: Trends, issues and challenges in managerial diversity.* Newbury Park, Calif.: Sage.

Mies, Maria, Veronika Bennholdt-Thomsen, and Claudia von Werlhof. 1988. *Women: The last colony.* London: Zed Books.

Nochlin, Linda. 1988. *Women, art, and power and other essays.* New York: Harper & Row.

Rossiter, Margaret L. 1986. *Women in the resistance.* New York: Praeger.

Smart, Carol, and Selma Sevenhuijsen (eds.). 1989. *Child custody and the politics of gender.* New York and London: Routledge.

Soble, Alan. 1986. *Pornography: Marxism, feminism and the future of sexuality.* New Haven: Yale University Press.

Sokoloff, Natalie J. 1980. *Between money and love.* New York: Praeger.

United Nations. 1980. *Program of action for the second half of the United Nations decade for women: Equality, development and peace.* New York: United Nations.

61

THE NEW STUDENT MOVEMENT
LIZA FEATHERSTONE

"We have the university by the balls," said Nati Passow, a University of Pennsylvania junior, in a meeting with his fellow antisweatshop protesters. "Whatever way we twist them is going to hurt." Passow was one of thirteen Penn students—the group later grew to include forty—occupying the university president's office around the clock in early February to protest the sweatshop conditions under which clothing bearing the U-Penn logo is made. The Penn students, along with hundreds of other members of United Students Against Sweatshops nationwide, were demanding that their university withdraw from the Fair Labor Association (FLA), an industry-backed monitoring group, and instead join the Worker Rights Consortium (WRC), an organization independent of industry influence, founded by students in close cooperation with scholars, activists and workers' rights organizations in the global South.

At first the administration met the students with barely polite condescension. In one meeting, President Judith Rodin was accompanied by

From the May 15, 2000, issue of *The Nation*.

U-Penn professor Larry Gross, an earring-wearing baby boomer well-known on campus for his left-wing views, who urged the protesters to have more faith in the administration and mocked the sit-in strategy, claiming he'd "been there, done that." President Rodin assured them that a task force would review the problem by February 29, and there was no way she could speed up its decision. She admonished them to "respect the process."

Watching the Penn students negotiate with their university's president, it was clear they didn't believe any of her assurances. They knew there was no reason to trust that the administration would meet one more arbitrary deadline after missing so many others—so they stayed in the office. After eight days of torture by folk-singing, acoustic guitar, recorders, tambourines and ringing cell phones, as well as a flurry of international news coverage, Judith Rodin met the protesters halfway by withdrawing from the FLA. (To students' frustration, the task force decided in early April to postpone a decision about WRC membership until later this spring.)

The most remarkable thing about the Penn students' action was that it wasn't an isolated or spontaneous burst of idealism. Penn's was just the first antisweatshop sit-in of the year; by mid-April students at the universities of Michigan, Wisconsin, Oregon, Iowa and Kentucky, as well as SUNY–Albany, Tulane, Purdue and Macalester, had followed suit. And the sit-in wasn't the protesters' only tactic: Purdue students held an eleven-day hunger strike. Other students chose less somber gestures of dissent. In late February the University of North Carolina's antisweatshop group, Students for Economic Justice, held a nude-optional party titled "I'd Rather Go Naked Than Wear Sweatshop Clothes." In late March, in an exuberant expression of the same principle, twelve Syracuse students biked across campus nude. The protests were a coordinated effort; members of United Students Against Sweatshops (USAS), which was founded three years ago and now has chapters at more than 200 schools, work closely with one another, a process made easier by the many listservs and websites that the students use to publicize actions, distribute information and help fuel turnout.

Though the largest, most successful—and before Seattle, the most visible— thread of the movement has focused on improving work conditions in the $2.5 billion collegiate apparel industry, university licensing policies have not been the only targets of recent anticorporate agitation on campus. This year, from UC–Davis to the University of Vermont, students have held globalization teach-ins, planned civil disobedience for the April IMF/World Bank meetings, protested labor policies at the Gap and launched vigorous campaigns to drive Starbucks out of university dining services. In snowy January, at the conservative Virginia Commonwealth University, twenty students slept outside the vice president's office for two nights to protest the university's contract with McDonald's (the school promised the fast-food behemoth a twenty-year monopoly over the Student Commons). Students at Johns Hopkins and at Wesleyan held sit-ins demanding better wages for university workers. And at the end of March hundreds of students, many bearing hideously deformed papier-mache puppets to illustrate the potential horrors of biotechnology, joined Boston's carnivalesque protest against genetic engineering.

With a joie de vivre that the American economic left has probably lacked since before WWI, college students are increasingly engaged in well-organized, thoughtful and morally outraged resistance to corporate power. These activists, more than any student radicals in years, passionately denounce the wealth gap, globally and in the United States, as well as the lack of democratic accountability in a world dominated by corporations. While some attend traditionally political schools like Evergreen, Michigan and Wisconsin, this movement does not revolve around usual suspects; some of this winter's most dramatic actions took place at campuses that have always been conservative, like the University of Pennsylvania, Virginia Commonwealth and Johns Hopkins. At this article's writing in late April, students were staging several significant anticorporate protests every week. It is neither too soon, nor too naively optimistic, to call it a movement.

Few of these students resemble—either in appearance or tactics—the hooded anarchist kids who famously threw rocks through Starbucks windows in Seattle last November. They look as if they shop at the Gap (and most of them do). Yet the movement does have an antihierarchical spirit; the Penn antisweat group, for example, made all decisions by consensus. Unlike their anarchist cohort, however, the student anticorporatists have leaders and spokespeople—and most of them agree that if the movement is to maintain momentum, they will need many more. Fortunately, each major action seems to draw more people in, and new leaders are emerging fast—some students who were on the periphery of the Penn group when I visited the sit-in in early February, for example, have already assumed official leadership positions within the organization.

Much of the struggle concerns the corporatization of higher education. Universities are run increasingly like private firms, and have ever-more intimate relations with private industry [see David L. Kirp, "The New U," April 17]. During one antisweat occupation in mid-April, for example, student activists at the University of Oregon led a campus tour of sites that illustrated the institution's numerous ties to corporations (one stop was the Phil Knight Library, named after Nike's president and CEO). A nationwide student group called 180/Movement for Democracy and Education, based at the University of Wisconsin, articulates this problem, and its connection to other issues, more consistently than any other group, even leading teach-ins on how World Trade Organization policies affect higher education. But almost all of the current student struggles—whether over tuition increases, apparel licenses, socially responsible investing, McDonald's in the student union, the rights of university laundry workers, a dining-hall contractor's investment in private prisons or solidarity with the striking students in Mexico—focus on the reality of the university as corporate actor.

Battle lines are now being drawn on a number of campuses, including Penn and Wisconsin, over whether universities will give in to student demands and agree to join the Worker Rights Consortium. WRC members require their apparel licensees to comply with a strict code of conduct—guaranteeing workers a living wage and the right to organize unions—and mandate full public disclosure of wages, factory locations and working conditions. By denying industry any role in its governance and giving power instead to a board composed of administrators, students and human rights scholars and activists, the WRC provides a nascent model for the kind of university decision making the students would like to see: a process free of corporate influence. It is also a model in which, so far, student activists have set the terms of discussion. No wonder so many university administrators, many of whom now like to be called "CEOs," have resisted it so savagely, even, in several cases, permitting quite forceful police treatment of peaceful protesters.

Yet many universities that once rebuffed the students' entreaties have since backed down, a testament to the skill and energy of the student organizers. The wave of sit-ins this spring was deliberately timed to precede the WRC's early April founding conference. Before the Penn sit-in, only a handful of institutions, none of which had substantial apparel-licensing contracts, belonged to the new organization; now forty-seven institutions belong, and the WRC founding meeting was attended by students or administrators from forty schools. The night before the meeting, the entire ten-school University of California system joined the organization and sent a representative to New York for the event. Some institutions joined without any building takeovers, choosing to avert bad publicity through graceful capitulation. "A lot of them joined without a sit-in because they thought there would be a sit-in the next day," says Maria Roeper, an antisweat activist taking a semester off from Haverford to coordinate the WRC.

Indeed, student activists have managed to put administrators on the defensive. On April 7 student antisweat protesters wearing duct tape over their mouths—to protest the fact that students have no say in campus decisions—met the University of Oregon president at the airport, frightening him so badly he left the baggage claim and hid in the bathroom. Even more striking, that same day, was the sight of dozens of suited university administrators at the WRC conference scurrying to "organize" among themselves. Many were pressured into WRC membership and worry that they won't have as much influence as they want over the new monitoring organization. Administrators were supposed to elect their representatives to the governing board at the founding meeting, but instead they asked for more time; they are now expected to do so later this spring, after holding their own meeting in Chicago. "It's only natural that they should want to do that," says Roeper. "The student group [USAS] did have a lot of power."

Industry, too, is getting nervous. Top officials of the Fair Labor Association, founded in 1996 by the Clinton Administration along with business representatives and some human rights groups, have been touring campuses, trying to convince students of their organization's good intentions. (Unlike the WRC, the FLA allows industry to choose its own monitors and doesn't include provisions for a living wage.) A week before the consortium's founding conference, Nike, which supports the FLA, canceled its contract with Brown University, objecting to the university's WRC membership. Nike has repeatedly denounced the WRC, calling it a "gotcha" monitoring system. "Nike is using Brown to threaten other schools," said Brown antisweat activist Nicholas Reville at the conference. More recently, Nike's Phil Knight, who had pledged $30 million to the University of Oregon for its sports stadium, indignantly withdrew the offer after the school announced its membership in the WRC.

In the recent history of student activism, the new emphasis on economics represents quite a shift. Ten years ago, there was plenty of student organizing, but it was fragmentary and sporadic, and most of it focused on what some, mostly its detractors, liked to call "identity politics," fighting the oppression of racial and sexual minorities, and of women. Admirable as they were—and effective in improving social relations on many campuses—there was little sense of solidarity among these groups, and they often seemed insular, bearing little relation to life outside the university.

That political moment is over, partly because in the larger world, organized feminism is in a lull and the mainstream gay movement now focuses on issues like inclusion in the military, gay marriage and hate-crimes legislation—moderate goals that don't speak to student idealism. By contrast, the economic left—especially the labor movement, and the burgeoning resistance to global capital—is enjoying a resurgence, both in numbers and in vision. The new student anticorporatists are building strong relationships with unions, which are, in turn, showing remarkable dedication to the new generation. During February's Penn sit-in, a different union local brought the students dinner almost every night. "Seattle helped the unions see that the students were serious," explains Simon Greer, Jobs With Justice's Workers' Rights board director. When the University of Wisconsin sent in the cops to drag away fifty-four peaceful antisweat protesters, George Becker, president of the United Steelworkers, issued a statement denouncing the administration's "oppressive actions."

The early-nineties struggles haven't vanished without a trace; indeed, it sometimes seems as if, through the anticorporate movement, they have returned to their early-seventies roots as movements for radical liberation. Many of the leaders are women, and feminist analysis informs the movement's focus; the antisweat activists, for instance, frequently point out that most sweatshop workers are women. And although the struggle against homophobia has largely disappeared from the student progressive agenda, the tactics—militant, theatrical and often campy direct action—of early-nineties groups like ACT UP and Queer Nation have clearly influenced the new crew of student activists.

Anticorporatism also has the potential to be a movement for racial justice. Farah Mongeau, a University of Michigan law student and member of U-M's Students of Color Coalition (SCC), points out, "[Sweatshop labor] obviously affects people of color. People of color are the ones who work in the sweatshops." Yet, although many core organizers are South Asian, the anti-sweatshop movement is mostly white. Organizing by students of color is on the upswing, but its relationship to the anticorporate groups can be uneasy. Some students of color say this is partly because white activists receive better treatment from those in power. At Michigan in February, SCC members protesting a racist secret society held a sit-in at the same time as the antisweat organization and resented the fact that while they were ignored for weeks, the predominantly white group got a meeting with the president immediately. Likewise, Justin Higgins, sophomore class president at North Carolina Central University, a historically black and working-class college, who in February had just joined the regional student anti-WTO/IMF coalition, said he wasn't planning to go to Washington, DC, and wasn't sorry to have missed Seattle. "If there had been black students [in Seattle]," Higgins said, "there would have been real bullets, not rubber bullets."

On the other hand, some less visible economic-justice campaigns on campus have been more racially mixed: those fighting university tuition hikes, for instance. And the student movement's relationship with labor may help break down its whiteness. In its early stages, very few black students were involved in the Johns Hopkins action demanding higher wages for university workers, for example, though the low-wage workers at the school are predominantly people of color. But when local unions got involved in the sit-in, they were able to recruit members of the black student group. On other campuses, multiracial alliances between anticorporate and prison activists are beginning to emerge. In early April students at ten campuses launched a boycott campaign against Sodexho-Marriott, which operates more than 500 campus dining halls, is the largest investor in US private prisons and is also currently facing censure from the National Labor Relations Board. In an April sit-in at SUNY–Albany, activists, in addition to sweatshop-related demands, insisted that the university drop Sodexho-Marriott if the company did not divest from private prisons and improve its labor practices.

Part of the problem with early-to-mid-nineties student "identity politics" was an obsession with representation—only queers could talk about homophobia; only people of color could talk about racism—which seriously limited its constituency. Such first-person politics also restricted diverse activists' ability to work together and find common ground. Yet its premise— drawn from seventies feminism—that the personal is political laid the foundation for one of the core assumptions of the current anticorporate movement, which is that because we are consumers, we are personally implicated in the depredations of capital. In the antisweat movement, students initially got involved because they were horrified to find out about the exploitation behind products that were a part of their everyday lives. Says Penn sophomore and USAS member Roopa Gona, "We're talking about our clothes." Student public-education campaigns about Starbucks—which, in mid-April, was pressured into buying Fair Trade Coffee—and genetically modified food also focus on buying power. The consumer experience is one that everyone has in common, rather than one that emphasizes power differences among students.

Exposing the sweatshop horror behind ubiquitous logos is subversive, especially in a culture completely hypnotized by them. The whole purpose of logos and brands is commodity fetishism; we are supposed to crave them but not question the conditions under which they were made. But, as Naomi Klein observes in her new book, *No Logo: Taking Aim at the Brand Bullies,* companies trafficking in image are particularly vulnerable when those images are tarnished. Obscure information-technology companies can quietly outsource their data-entry work to Mexican sweatshops, but companies like Disney, Starbucks and the Gap are different: Their prominence in consumers' hearts and minds makes it far easier for activists to publicize their wrongdoings. Like other contemporary anticorporatists—those vandalizing and protesting under Golden Arches worldwide, for instance—students have expertly used big capital's catchy logos against it. And just like the Nike swoosh, "we can think of the university itself as a brand, a logo, that students consume," says veteran antisweat activist and University of North Carolina junior Todd Pugatch. Universities, especially prestigious ones or those with high-profile sports teams, depend on image, too. The recognizability of the University of Michigan's big yellow M, like that of McDonald's, can backfire if the logo comes to symbolize exploitation and corporate greed.

Still, brand targeting has limits. One of the ways in which contemporary capitalism maintains its hold on us is by defining everyone as consumers— rather than, say, citizens, workers or activists. A crucial problem for the anticorporate movement is how to appeal to a wider public without reducing politics to shopping. And students are realizing that simply as indignant shoppers, they can't be very effective. Boycotts in the apparel industry are futile because all major clothing companies use sweatshop labor, explains Laurie Eichenbaum, a Penn senior and USAS organizer who was wearing a red Old Navy fleece when I met her: "There is no good alternative." Saurav Sarkar, of Yale Students Against Sweatshops, says, "That's the most common misperception about us. People say, 'Oh, I don't want to stop buying clothes at the Gap.' " Crucial to the anticorporate movement's gradual evolution beyond consumer consciousness and toward labor solidarity and broad structural change, as UNC's Pugatch observes, will be its relationship with workers, in the US labor movement as well as in the global South. If the WRC develops as the students hope, it will help give workers and unions a stronger voice in the apparel industry, rather than simply conferring a Good Housekeeping-style seal of approval on "sweat-free" brands.

Despite this emerging vision, not all students come to anticorporate activism with a radical outlook. "People are drawn in by the horror stories," says Maria Roeper, but then they start seeing how the whole system works. Students are also radicalized by their university's intransigence and by the realization that institutions only change when they're forced to do so. David

Corson-Knowles, a Yale freshman and spokesperson for the Student Alliance to Reform Corporations (STARC), a national group founded at Yale, says he thinks his group will eventually convince the Yale Corporation—which has the CEO of Procter & Gamble on its board—to invest responsibly "because we're right." But in a group discussion in a coffee shop near campus, it's clear that students from the Student/Labor Action Coalition (SLAC) and the Yale chapter of United Students Against Sweatshops—older groups that have been struggling with the administration for longer and use more confrontational tactics—beg to differ. Yale SLAC activist Laurie Kimmington, a senior, says of the university's administrators, "They want to do nothing, as much as possible." Danielle Linzer, a Penn sophomore and STARC leader, admitted this might be the case. STARC, she acknowledged, had a "more conservative approach to reform" than United Students Against Sweatshops, but, she said, "we're a newer group, so we haven't yet been stalled the way they have."

All in all, it's impossible not to feel at least cautiously optimistic about this new movement. "We are training an entire generation to think differently about—pause—"captialism," says Kimmington. She glances at my notebook and at the STARC activists across the cafe table and giggles cheerfully. "Oops, maybe I shouldn't say that."